FOOD & WINE
annual cookbook 2012

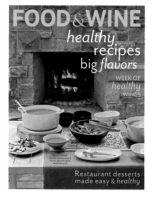

FOOD & WINE
ANNUAL COOKBOOK 2012

EDITOR **Kate Heddings**

ART DIRECTOR **Courtney Waddell Eckersley**

DESIGNER **Michelle Leong**

FEATURES EDITOR **Michael Endelman**

SENIOR EDITOR **Susan Choung**

COPY EDITOR **Lisa Leventer**

EDITORIAL ASSISTANTS **Cristina Sciarra, Maren Ellingboe**

ASSOCIATE WINE EDITOR **Megan Krigbaum**

PRODUCTION MANAGER **Matt Carson**

DEPUTY PHOTO EDITOR **Anthony LaSala**

FRONT COVER

PHOTOGRAPHER **David Malosh**

FOOD STYLIST **Cyd Raftus McDowell**

STYLE EDITOR **Paige Hicks**

BACK COVER

PHOTOGRAPHER (SALAD) **Michael Turek**

PHOTOGRAPHER (RIBS) **Cedric Angeles**

PHOTOGRAPHER (CAKES) **Kate Mathis**

FLAP PHOTOGRAPHS

DANA COWIN **Mat Szwajkos** (Swig Productions/Fordcast.com/ Ford Motor Company Summer Food Tour)

KATE HEDDINGS **Andrew French**

ISBN 978-1-932624-41-0

ISSN 1097-1564

Published by
American Express Publishing Corporation
1120 Avenue of the Americas
New York, New York 10036

Manufactured in
the United States of America

FOOD & WINE MAGAZINE

SVP / EDITOR IN CHIEF **Dana Cowin**

CREATIVE DIRECTOR **Stephen Scoble**

MANAGING EDITOR **Mary Ellen Ward**

EXECUTIVE EDITOR **Pamela Kaufman**

EXECUTIVE FOOD EDITOR **Tina Ujlaki**

EXECUTIVE WINE EDITOR **Ray Isle**

EXECUTIVE DIGITAL EDITOR **Rebecca Bauer**

DEPUTY EDITOR **Christine Quinlan**

FEATURES

FEATURES EDITOR **Michael Endelman**

RESTAURANT EDITOR **Kate Krader**

TRAVEL EDITOR **Gina Hamadey**

STYLE EDITOR **Jessica Romm**

ASSOCIATE WINE EDITOR **Megan Krigbaum**

EDITORIAL ASSISTANTS **Maren Ellingboe, Chelsea Morse, M. Elizabeth Sheldon**

FOOD

DEPUTY EDITOR **Kate Heddings**

SENIOR EDITOR **Kristin Donnelly**

ASSOCIATE EDITOR **Daniel Gritzer**

TEST KITCHEN SUPERVISOR **Marcia Kiesel**

SENIOR RECIPE DEVELOPER **Grace Parisi**

ASSISTANT RECIPE TESTER **Justin Chapple**

EDITORIAL ASSISTANT **Maggie Mariolis**

TEST KITCHEN ASSISTANT **Gina Mungiovi**

ART

ART DIRECTOR **Courtney Waddell Eckersley**

SENIOR DESIGNERS **James Maikowski, Michael Patti**

BOOK DESIGNER **Michelle Leong**

DIGITAL DESIGNER **Jon Moran**

PHOTO

DIRECTOR OF PHOTOGRAPHY **Fredrika Stjärne**

DEPUTY PHOTO EDITOR **Anthony LaSala**

ASSOCIATE PHOTO EDITOR **Sara Parks**

PHOTO ASSISTANT **Tomi Omololu-Lange**

PRODUCTION

PRODUCTION DIRECTOR **M. Cristina Martinez**

PRODUCTION MANAGER **Matt Carson**

PRODUCTION ASSISTANT **Amelia Grohman**

COPY & RESEARCH

COPY DIRECTOR **Michele Berkover Petry**

SENIOR COPY EDITOR **Ann Lien**

ASSISTANT RESEARCH EDITORS **Erin Laverty, John Mantia**

DIGITAL MEDIA

DESIGN DIRECTOR **Patricia Sanchez**

SENIOR EDITOR **Alex Vallis**

ASSOCIATE EDITORS **Alessandra Bulow, Lawrence Marcus**

ASSOCIATE ART DIRECTOR **Jooyoung Hsu**

EDITORIAL PROJECT COORDINATOR **Kerianne Hansen**

AMERICAN EXPRESS PUBLISHING CORPORATION

PRESIDENT / CHIEF EXECUTIVE OFFICER **Ed Kelly**

CHIEF MARKETING OFFICER & PRESIDENT, DIGITAL MEDIA **Mark V. Stanich**

SVP / CHIEF FINANCIAL OFFICER **Paul B. Francis**

VPs / GENERAL MANAGERS **Frank Bland, Keith Strohmeier**

VP, BOOKS & PRODUCTS / PUBLISHER **Marshall Corey**

DIRECTOR, BOOK PROGRAMS **Bruce Spanier**

SENIOR MARKETING MANAGER, BRANDED BOOKS **Eric Lucie**

ASSISTANT MARKETING MANAGER **Stacy Mallis**

DIRECTOR OF FULFILLMENT & PREMIUM VALUE **Philip Black**

MANAGER OF CUSTOMER EXPERIENCE & PRODUCT DEVELOPMENT **Charles Graver**

DIRECTOR OF FINANCE **Thomas Noonan**

ASSOCIATE BUSINESS MANAGER **Uma Mahabir**

OPERATIONS DIRECTOR (PREPRESS) **Rosalie Abatemarco Samat**

OPERATIONS DIRECTOR (MANUFACTURING) **Anthony White**

SENIOR MANAGER, CONTRACTS & RIGHTS **Jeniqua Moore**

FOOD & WINE

annual
cookbook 2012

AN ENTIRE YEAR OF RECIPES

FOOD&WINE
BOOKS

American Express Publishing Corporation, New York

grilled lamb chops with garlic, chiles and anchovies, PAGE 162

contents

sun-dried tomato and arugula pizza, PAGE 293

foreword

The 700 recipes in this collection reveal a substantial shift in how America cooks and eats. For instance, the vegetable chapter is nearly twice as large as the one in last year's edition, with brilliant dishes like Kimchi-Creamed Collard Greens (page 250). Clearly, we've become as obsessed with vegetables as we are with pork.

You'll also notice a *lot* of pies, both classic (Old-Fashioned Apple Pie, page 334) and creative (Pear and Fig Pie-in-a-Jar, page 340). While cupcakes and doughnuts go in and out of style, pies have quietly become the darling of the sweets world.

Plus, you'll see many of the recipes in this edition paired with craft beer instead of wine, a reflection of our growing fascination with artisanal everything. One of our favorite match-ups is pitmaster Chris Lilly's Chicken with White Barbecue Sauce (page 122) and a hoppy Samuel Adams IPA. We hope this book inspires some substantial shifts in your own cooking.

Editor in Chief
FOOD & WINE Magazine

Editor
FOOD & WINE Cookbooks

Chefs Eduard Frauneder, top, and Wolfgang Ban, below right, at their New York restaurant Edi & the Wolf, where they serve foods inspired by their homeland, like Austrian cheese spread, OPPOSITE; recipe, page 12.

starters

Bacon and Romaine Skewers with Blue Cheese Dressing

⏱ TOTAL: 25 MIN • MAKES 24 SKEWERS

Wedge salad (iceberg lettuce with blue cheese dressing and bacon) is a classic American dish. Here the steak-house staple is speared on a skewer and reconfigured as a playful cocktail snack.

- 4 ounces crumbled Maytag blue cheese
- ¾ cup mayonnaise
- ½ cup sour cream
- 1 tablespoon fresh lemon juice
- 1 teaspoon Worcestershire sauce
- ½ teaspoon garlic powder

Salt and freshly ground pepper

- 4 ounces slab bacon, cut into large dice
- ½ pound romaine hearts, small leaves whole, large leaves cut into pieces

1. In a food processor, pulse the blue cheese, mayonnaise, sour cream, lemon juice, Worcestershire sauce and garlic powder until smooth. Season with salt and pepper.

2. In a large skillet, cook the bacon over moderate heat until crisp, about 5 minutes. Drain the bacon on paper towels.

3. Thread a few romaine leaves and bacon cubes onto each of 24 long bamboo skewers. Arrange the skewers on a platter and serve with the blue cheese dressing on the side. —*James Holmes*

quick skewer tips

soak Before grilling, submerge wooden skewers in water for 20 minutes to prevent burning.

flavor Thread ingredients onto sugarcane or rosemary sprigs instead of bamboo or metal.

double up Use two skewers when grilling smaller items to avoid losing food in between the grates.

Tequila-Mustard-Glazed Chicken Skewers

ACTIVE: 35 MIN; TOTAL: 1 HR 35 MIN
MAKES 24 SKEWERS ●

James Holmes, the chef at Olivia in Austin, developed the sweet and tangy glaze for these grilled chicken thighs while experimenting with homemade mustards.

MARINATED CHICKEN

- ½ cup tequila
- ½ cup light brown sugar
- 3 tablespoons extra-virgin olive oil
- 4 garlic cloves, chopped
- 1 tablespoon chopped oregano
- 1 tablespoon kosher salt
- 3 pounds skinless, boneless chicken thighs, cut into ½-inch-wide strips

TEQUILA MUSTARD

- 4 large egg yolks
- ¼ cup water
- ¼ cup malt vinegar
- ¼ cup honey
- ¼ cup tequila
- 2 tablespoons freshly squeezed lime juice
- 1 tablespoon dry mustard
- 1 tablespoon ground coriander
- 1 tablespoon ground cumin
- 1 tablespoon chile powder
- 1 teaspoon finely grated lime zest

Salt

1. MARINATE THE CHICKEN In a large bowl, combine the tequila, brown sugar, olive oil, garlic, oregano and salt. Add the chicken and toss to coat. Cover the bowl and refrigerate the chicken for 1 hour.

2. MEANWHILE, MAKE THE MUSTARD In a saucepan, whisk together the egg yolks, water, malt vinegar, honey, tequila, lime juice, dry mustard, coriander, cumin and chile powder. Cook over low heat, whisking, until thickened, 5 minutes; do not boil. Transfer to a heatproof bowl. Stir in the lime zest; season with salt. Let cool to room temperature, then refrigerate.

3. Soak 24 bamboo skewers in water for 30 minutes. Light a grill or preheat a grill pan. Transfer ½ cup of the mustard to a small

bowl. Thread the chicken onto the top third of the skewers; grill over moderate heat, turning, until browned and almost cooked, about 8 minutes. Brush the chicken with the reserved ½ cup of mustard and grill until glazed and cooked through. Serve the skewers with the remaining mustard.

—*James Holmes*

WINE Ripe, full-bodied California Roussanne: 2008 Stolpman L'Avion.

Roasted Beet, Carrot and Scallion Skewers with Tarragon

ACTIVE: 30 MIN; TOTAL: 1 HR 35 MIN
MAKES 12 SKEWERS ● ●

"It may not be widely known, but we have olive growers in South Texas, and they're making some great olive oil," says Austin chef James Holmes. He drizzles that local oil on this simple mix of grilled beets, carrots and scallions.

- 6 medium beets (about 2 inches in diameter), stems trimmed
- 4 medium carrots, cut into twenty-four 1½-by-½-inch sticks

Extra-virgin olive oil, for drizzling

- 12 scallions, white and tender green parts, cut into twenty-four 1½-inch lengths

Salt and freshly ground pepper

- 2 tablespoons chopped tarragon

1. Preheat the oven to 350°. Put the beets and carrots in 2 separate baking dishes and lightly drizzle both with olive oil. Cover with aluminum foil and bake until tender, about 45 minutes for the carrots and 1 hour for the beets. When cool enough to handle, peel the beets and cut into twenty-four 1½-inch-by-½-inch sticks.

2. Light a grill or preheat a grill pan. Alternately thread 2 each of the beet, carrot and scallion pieces onto 12 bamboo skewers. Drizzle lightly with olive oil and grill until lightly browned, about 2 minutes per side. Transfer the skewers to a platter and drizzle with a little more olive oil. Season with salt and pepper, sprinkle with the tarragon and serve. —*James Holmes*

● HEALTHY ● MAKE AHEAD ● VEGETARIAN ● STAFF FAVORITE

bacon and romaine skewers with blue cheese dressing

Austrian Cheese Spread with Pumpkin Seed Oil

📷 PAGE 9

⏱ TOTAL: 5 MIN • MAKES 1½ CUPS ● ●

8 ounces cream cheese, softened
¼ cup toasted pumpkin seeds,
2 tablespoons finely chopped
1 tablespoon pumpkin seed oil
1½ teaspoons Dijon mustard
Salt and freshly ground pepper

Blend the cream cheese with the chopped pumpkin seeds, the pumpkin seed oil and mustard and season with salt and pepper. Top with the whole pumpkin seeds and serve. —*Wolfgang Ban and Eduard Frauneder*
SERVE WITH Dark bread.

Gouda, Pancetta and Onion Fondue with Pretzels

⏱ TOTAL: 40 MIN • 8 SERVINGS ●

Author Laura Werlin created this cumin-spiced Gouda fondue after tasting Leyden, a Dutch cheese flecked with cumin seeds.

4 ounces thickly sliced pancetta, chopped
1 red onion, thinly sliced
1 teaspoon ground cumin
Salt and freshly ground pepper
1 pound Gouda, coarsely shredded
2 tablespoons all-purpose flour
¾ cup dry Riesling
8 soft pretzels, warmed
Cubed seeded rye bread, cornichons and other pickled vegetables, for serving

1. In a medium skillet, cook the chopped pancetta over moderately high heat, stirring occasionally, until crisp, about 8 minutes. Using a slotted spoon, transfer the pancetta to a plate. Pour off all but 1 tablespoon of the fat in the skillet. Add the sliced onion, cover and cook over moderate heat until softened, about 5 minutes. Add 2 tablespoons of water to the skillet and cook, stirring occasionally, until the onion is lightly browned, about 5 minutes longer. Stir in the cumin and season the onion with salt and pepper.

2. In a bowl, toss the cheese with the flour. In a medium saucepan, bring the wine to a simmer over moderate heat. Add the cheese in handfuls and stir constantly until each batch is completely melted before adding more. Cook, stirring vigorously, until creamy, about 2 minutes longer. Stir in the pancetta and half of the onion and season generously with pepper. Float the remaining onion on top of the fondue and serve with warm pretzels, rye bread cubes, cornichons and pickled vegetables. —*Laura Werlin*
WINE Bright, focused Pinot Noir: 2009 J. Hofstätter Meczan Pinot Nero.

Italian Fontina Fonduta

⏱ TOTAL: 30 MIN • 8 SERVINGS ●

1 loaf of ciabatta, cut into 1-inch cubes or sticks
Extra-virgin olive oil, for brushing
1 pound Italian Fontina cheese, cut into ½-inch pieces
½ cup milk
½ cup heavy cream
6 tablespoons unsalted butter, cut into tablespoons
4 large egg yolks
Salt and freshly ground white pepper
Truffle salt (optional)
Assorted crudites, for dipping

1. Preheat the oven to 375°. Spread the ciabatta cubes on 2 baking sheets and brush with oil. Bake for about 10 minutes, until crisp.
2. In a large saucepan, combine the Fontina, milk and cream and cook over moderate heat, stirring, until the cheese starts to melt, about 4 minutes. Whisk in the butter and egg yolks and cook over low heat, stirring, until the fondue is very smooth, about 3 minutes longer. Remove from the heat and season lightly with salt and pepper.
3. Transfer the Fontina fondue to a warmed serving bowl or fondue pot and sprinkle with truffle salt, if using. Serve right away, with the toasted ciabatta and crudités. —*Linda Meyers*
WINE White peach–scented sparkling wine: NV Zardetto Prosecco Brut.

Flatbreads with Cucumber Raita

⏱ TOTAL: 25 MIN • 4 SERVINGS ●

1 cup plain Greek-style yogurt
1 cup peeled, diced seedless cucumber, plus ½ cup diced unpeeled cucumber for garnish
2 tablespoons chopped mint
1 tablespoon chopped cilantro
1 garlic clove, minced
½ teaspoon finely grated lemon zest
½ teaspoon ground cumin
Salt and freshly ground black pepper
Extra-virgin olive oil, for drizzling
Cayenne pepper, for sprinkling
Lavash or pocketless pita bread, warmed

In a large, shallow bowl, mix the yogurt, peeled cucumber, mint, cilantro, garlic, lemon zest and cumin and season with salt and black pepper. Scatter the unpeeled cucumber on top. Drizzle the raita with olive oil and sprinkle with cayenne. Serve with flatbreads. —*Marcie Turney*

Spring Garlic and Fennel Puree

ACTIVE: 30 MIN; TOTAL: 1 HR
MAKES ABOUT 2 CUPS ● ●

This wonderful dip from *Top Chef: All-Stars* winner Richard Blais combines simmered sweet garlic and fennel with cream and a little milk to lighten it. It's fantastic served with grilled bread or as a sauce for grilled chicken or fish.

1 cup heavy cream
4 large heads of garlic, cloves peeled
1 small fennel bulb—trimmed, cored and thinly sliced crosswise
3 tablespoons milk
Salt and freshly ground white pepper

In a medium saucepan, bring the cream, garlic and fennel to a simmer. Cover and cook over low heat for 15 minutes. Uncover and simmer until the garlic and fennel are very tender, 15 minutes. Let cool slightly, then transfer to a blender. Add the milk and puree until smooth. Season with salt and pepper and serve warm. —*Richard Blais*

● HEALTHY ● MAKE AHEAD ● VEGETARIAN ● STAFF FAVORITE

gouda, pancetta and onion fondue with pretzels

Roasted Beet Toasts with Horseradish Cream
ACTIVE: 30 MIN; TOTAL: 1 HR 30 MIN
MAKES 16 TOASTS ● ● ●

- 1 pound medium red and yellow beets, about 1½ inches wide
- Olive oil, for rubbing
- Salt and freshly ground black pepper
- 16 slices of cocktail rye bread or sixteen 3-inch squares or rounds of thinly sliced dense rye bread
- 2 tablespoons unsalted butter, melted
- ½ cup crème fraîche
- 3 tablespoons heavy cream
- 2 tablespoons prepared horseradish, drained
- 2 teaspoons chopped parsley
- ¼ cup red wine vinegar
- 8 red pearl onions, peeled and thinly sliced
- Chervil sprigs and minced chives, for garnish

1. Preheat the oven to 350°. Put the beets in a small roasting pan and add ½ cup of water. Cover the pan with foil and bake the beets for 1 hour, until tender. Let cool slightly, then peel and slice them ⅛ inch thick. Drizzle with a little oil and season with salt and pepper.
2. Meanwhile, brush the rye bread with the melted butter and arrange on a baking sheet. Bake for about 8 minutes, until crisp.
3. In a small bowl, whisk the crème fraîche and cream until thick. Fold in the horseradish and parsley; season with salt and pepper.
4. In a small saucepan, bring the vinegar and ¼ cup of water to a boil. Add the pearl onions and simmer over moderate heat for 1 minute. Season the onions with salt and let cool in the brine. Drain the onions on paper towels.
5. Arrange the beet slices on the toasts, overlapping them slightly. Scatter the pickled onions over the beets. Top the toasts with small dollops of the horseradish cream, garnish with chervil sprigs and chives and serve.
—*Traci Des Jardins*

WINE Juicy, berry-scented sparkling rosé: NV Conde de Subirats Cava Rosé.

Cabbage and Mushroom Toasts
ACTIVE: 35 MIN; TOTAL: 1 HR
8 SERVINGS ● ●

- ¼ cup dried porcini mushrooms
- 4 tablespoons unsalted butter
- ½ pound fresh shiitake mushrooms, stemmed and caps thinly sliced
- Salt and freshly ground pepper
- 1 shallot, minced
- 1 garlic clove, minced
- 4 cups finely shredded green cabbage
- ¼ cup heavy cream
- 2 tablespoons chopped tarragon leaves
- Eight ½-inch-thick slices of peasant bread
- Extra-virgin olive oil, for brushing

1. In a small heatproof bowl, cover the dried porcini with 1 cup of boiling water and let stand until softened, about 15 minutes. Drain the porcini and reserve the soaking liquid. Finely chop the porcini.
2. In a large skillet, melt 2 tablespoons of the butter. Add the porcini and shiitake and season with salt and pepper. Cook over high heat, stirring occasionally, until the shiitake are softened and lightly browned, about 8 minutes. Add the shallot and garlic and cook until fragrant, about 2 minutes. Add the porcini soaking liquid, stopping before you reach the grit at the bottom. Boil until the liquid is evaporated, about 5 minutes. Scrape the mixture into a bowl.
3. Add the remaining 2 tablespoons of butter to the skillet. Add the cabbage, season with salt and pepper and cook over moderately low heat, stirring frequently, until the cabbage is very tender, about 15 minutes. Add a few tablespoons of water to the skillet if it looks dry. Return the mushroom mixture to the skillet. Add the cream and tarragon and simmer until the cream is nearly evaporated, about 5 minutes.
4. Heat a cast-iron grill pan. Brush the bread with oil and grill over high heat, turning once, until toasted. Spread the cabbage-mushroom mixture on the toasts and serve.
—*Steven Satterfield*

Squash and Kale Toasts
ACTIVE: 30 MIN; TOTAL: 1 HR
8 SERVINGS ● ● ●

At Miller Union in Atlanta, chef Steven Satterfield often serves local cheeses and seasonal vegetables on bite-size toasts like these, which are topped with wilted kale, Delicata squash and Parmigiano-Reggiano. Satterfield is a huge fan of kale, particularly when it's paired with sweet roasted squash. Look for Tuscan kale (also called *cavolo nero*, Lacinato or Dinosaur kale) when possible; it's especially tender and tasty.

- 2 small Delicata squash (2 pounds)—peeled, halved lengthwise, seeded and sliced crosswise ½ inch thick
- ½ cup extra-virgin olive oil, plus more for brushing
- Salt and freshly ground pepper
- 1 pound kale—thick stems and ribs discarded, leaves coarsely chopped
- 4 garlic cloves, thinly sliced
- Eight ½-inch-thick slices of peasant bread
- 4 ounces shaved Parmigiano-Reggiano cheese (1½ loose cups)

1. Preheat the oven to 350°. In a medium bowl, toss the squash with 2 tablespoons of the olive oil and season with salt and pepper. Spread the squash on a baking sheet and roast for about 30 minutes, turning once, until tender and lightly browned.
2. In a large skillet, heat the remaining ¼ cup plus 2 tablespoons of olive oil. Add the kale and cook until it is wilted, about 8 minutes. Add the garlic slices and cook until the kale is tender, about 3 minutes longer. Season the kale with salt and pepper. Add the squash and toss gently to combine.
3. Heat a cast-iron grill pan. Brush the bread with olive oil and grill over high heat, turning once, until toasted. Mound the squash and kale on the toasts, top with the shaved cheese and serve.
—*Steven Satterfield*

MAKE AHEAD The recipe can be prepared through Step 2 and refrigerated overnight. Rewarm in a skillet before serving.

● HEALTHY ● MAKE AHEAD ● VEGETARIAN ● STAFF FAVORITE

Feta and Radish Toasts

⏱ TOTAL: 20 MIN • 8 SERVINGS ● ○

Chef Steven Satterfield serves some combination of feta and radishes almost every day at his Atlanta restaurant. He says you can use any assortment of radishes for these toasts, like Watermelon, Cherry Belle or Pink Beauty. If you slice the radishes ahead of time, keep them in a bowl of ice water, which makes them extra-cold and crispy.

Eight ½-inch-thick slices of
 peasant bread
¼ cup extra-virgin olive oil, plus more
 for drizzling
6 ounces feta cheese
 (preferably goat), crumbled
8 to 10 radishes, thinly sliced
1 bunch of watercress, thick stems
 discarded
Salt and freshly ground pepper

Heat a cast-iron grill pan. Brush the bread with the ¼ cup of olive oil and grill over high heat, turning once, until toasted. Top the toasts with the feta, radishes and watercress. Drizzle with olive oil, sprinkle with salt and freshly ground pepper and serve. —*Steven Satterfield*

Bruschetta with Mozzarella and Smashed Fresh Favas

⏱ TOTAL: 30 MIN • 4 SERVINGS ● ○

Philadephia chef Marcie Turney drew inspiration from her trips to Italy to create these toasts topped with a vibrant green fava-bean puree and buffalo mozzarella.

1 pound fresh fava beans, shelled
 (about 2 cups)
2 tablespoons extra-virgin olive oil
1 teaspoon fresh lemon juice
½ teaspoon finely grated lemon zest
Salt and freshly ground pepper
16 grilled baguette slices
¼ pound buffalo mozzarella,
 torn into thin strips
Aged balsamic vinegar, for drizzling
2 tablespoons thinly sliced
 mint leaves

1. In a saucepan of boiling water, cook the fava beans until the skins start to loosen, 1½ minutes. Drain and squeeze out the favas. Transfer the favas to a food processor and add the oil, lemon juice and zest and pulse to a coarse puree. Season with salt and pepper.
2. Spread the fava-bean puree on the toasts and top with the mozzarella strips. Drizzle the toasts with the balsamic vinegar, scatter the mint on top and serve. —*Marcie Turney*

Wild Mushroom and Burrata Bruschetta

ACTIVE: 25 MIN; TOTAL: 1 HR 25 MIN
8 SERVINGS ●

Seattle chef Ethan Stowell's menus often include burrata (cream-filled mozzarella). Here, he places cool slices of the cheese on toasts piled with grilled mushrooms.

1 pound shiitake mushrooms, stems
 discarded and caps quartered
1 pound cremini mushrooms,
 quartered
2 garlic cloves, minced
1½ teaspoons chopped rosemary
1 teaspoon finely grated lemon zest
½ cup extra-virgin olive oil, plus
 more for brushing
Salt and freshly ground pepper
16 slices of peasant bread (from
 a long loaf), about ⅓ inch thick
1 pound burrata cheese,
 cut into 16 slices

1. In a large bowl, toss the mushrooms with the garlic, rosemary, lemon zest and the ½ cup of olive oil and let stand for 1 hour.
2. Light a grill or preheat a grill pan. Spread the mushrooms on a lightly oiled perforated grill tray and season with salt and pepper. Grill over moderately high heat, stirring occasionally, until browned, about 8 minutes. Brush the bread with oil and grill, turning once, until toasted, 1 minute.
3. Top the toasts with the mushrooms, then top each with a slice of burrata and serve. —*Ethan Stowell*

WINE Earthy, cranberry-scented Sonoma Coast Pinot Noir: 2009 Pali Riviera.

Whipped Feta with Cucumbers

ACTIVE: 20 MIN; TOTAL: 1 HR 50 MIN
4 TO 6 SERVINGS ● ● ○

At his Chicago restaurant, the Purple Pig, Jimmy Bannos, Jr., looks to the Mediterranean, serving mostly Italian- and Greek-inflected dishes, like this whipped feta with olive oil–marinated cucumbers.

1 pound feta cheese, cut into
 2 pieces, at room temperature
¼ pound cream cheese, softened
2 tablespoons heavy cream
¼ cup extra-virgin olive oil
2 tablespoons fresh lemon juice
2 cucumbers (1½ pounds)—halved,
 seeded and cut into ½-inch dice
1 tablespoon chopped oregano
Salt and freshly ground pepper
Toasted pita or baguette slices, for serving

1. In a bowl, cover the feta with water and let stand for 30 minutes. Drain and crumble the feta. Transfer to a food processor and puree. Add the cream cheese, heavy cream, 2 tablespoons of the olive oil and 1 tablespoon of the lemon juice and process until smooth. Refrigerate for 1 hour.
2. Meanwhile, in a bowl, toss the diced cucumbers with the remaining 2 tablespoons of olive oil, 1 tablespoon of lemon juice and the oregano; season with salt and pepper. Cover and chill for 1 hour.
3. Serve the feta lightly chilled, with the cucumbers and toasts. —*Jimmy Bannos, Jr.*

feta lexicon

greek feta Salty and tangy, Greek feta has at least 70 percent sheep milk; goat milk makes it drier.

bulgarian feta Creamy and less salty, this type—made from sheep milk—has a grassy flavor.

american feta Tangy and crumbly, this feta can be made from sheep, goat or cow milk.

Parmesan Tuiles with Heirloom Tomato Salad

⏱ TOTAL: 45 MIN • 4 SERVINGS ●

Chopped red, green and orange tomatoes are tossed with olive oil and fresh herbs, then served on crisp Parmesan tuiles. The result: a supremely colorful, incredibly easy hors d'oeuvre.

  6 tablespoons freshly grated
     Parmigiano-Reggiano cheese
1½ tablespoons unsalted butter,
     softened
  1 tablespoon plus 2 teaspoons
     all-purpose flour, plus more
     for pressing
Freshly ground pepper
1½ cups finely diced heirloom
     tomatoes, preferably a mix of colors
  1 tablespoon snipped chives
  1 teaspoon coarsely chopped
     tarragon
  2 teaspoons extra-virgin olive oil
Salt

1. Preheat the oven to 400° and line a large baking sheet with parchment paper. In a medium bowl, combine the Parmigiano-Reggiano cheese with the butter, flour and a generous pinch of pepper and mash the ingredients until a dough forms. Form the dough into a 4-inch log. Cut the log into 12 equal slices and arrange the slices on the baking sheet. Using your fingers, press the slices into 1½-inch rounds.
2. Bake the tuiles on the lowest rack in the oven for about 7 minutes, rotating the pan halfway through baking, until the tuiles are golden brown and sizzling. Let the tuiles cool completely, then transfer them to a paper towel–lined plate and blot the excess fat.
3. In a small bowl, toss the tomatoes with the chives, tarragon and olive oil and season with salt and pepper. Spoon the salad over the tuiles and serve right away.
—*Grace Parisi*
MAKE AHEAD The Parmesan tuiles can be stored in an airtight container for up to 1 week. Recrisp in a warm oven before topping with the tomato salad.

Smoked Trout and Caper Cream Cheese Toasts

⏱ TOTAL: 20 MIN • 10 SERVINGS ●

Wisconsin chef Tory Miller devised this variation on the classic combination of bagels, lox and cream cheese using smoked trout and English muffins. The spread would be equally good on other breads, such as a baguette, or the bagel that inspired it.

  4 ounces cream cheese, softened
  1 small shallot, minced
  1 tablespoon chopped chives, plus
     1-inch lengths for garnish
  1 tablespoon chopped drained capers
  1 tablespoon fresh lemon juice
Salt and freshly ground pepper
  5 English muffins—split, toasted
     and buttered
½ pound skinless smoked trout fillet,
     coarsely chopped

1. In a bowl, combine the cream cheese, shallot, chopped chives, capers and lemon juice. Season with salt and pepper.
2. Spread the English muffins with the caper cream cheese. Top with the smoked trout, garnish with the chive pieces and serve.
—*Tory Miller*
WINE Rich California sparkling wine: 2006 Iron Horse Wedding Cuvée.

Pumpernickel with Avocado, Charred Corn and Tomato

⏱ TOTAL: 30 MIN • 4 SERVINGS ● ● ●

  1 ear of corn, shucked
Extra-virgin olive oil
  2 teaspoons sherry vinegar
  8 yellow cherry tomatoes, halved
  8 red cherry tomatoes, halved
  1 medium Green Zebra or other
     sweet heirloom tomato, diced
  1 serrano chile, seeded and minced
  1 tablespoon chopped cilantro
Salt and freshly ground pepper
  4 grilled slices of pumpernickel
  1 Hass avocado, halved and pitted,
     each half cut into 8 slices
¼ cup sliced jarred pickled onions

1. Light a grill or preheat a grill pan. Brush the corn with oil and grill over moderate heat until lightly charred, 8 minutes. Cut the kernels from the cob.
2. In a bowl, mix 2 tablespoons of oil with the vinegar. Fold in the corn, tomatoes, chile and cilantro and season with salt and pepper. Top the bread with the sliced avocado, tomato salad and pickled onions and serve.
—*Marcie Turney*

Salami-Egg Canapés

⏱ ACTIVE: 20 MIN; TOTAL: 40 MIN
MAKES ABOUT 5 DOZEN CANAPÉS ●

Gustav Klimt and strudel are two icons in *Neue Cuisine: The Elegant Tastes of Vienna* by New York City chef Kurt Gutenbrunner and food writer Jane Sigal. The book celebrates Austrian art and recipes like these hearty, fun salami-and-egg canapés.

  5 large eggs
  6 ounces sliced spicy salami
¼ cup mayonnaise
  2 tablespoons Dijon mustard
  5 cornichons, plus thinly sliced
     cornichons for garnish
  8 thin slices of German dark
     wheat bread—crusts removed,
     bread toasted and cut into
     1½-inch squares
Capers and chopped fresh herbs,
     for garnish

1. In a saucepan, cover the eggs with cold water and bring to a boil; cook over moderate heat for 10 minutes. Drain the eggs and immediately fill the pan with cold water. Add ice to the pan; let the eggs stand until chilled. Drain the eggs, peel and coarsely chop.
2. In a food processor, combine the hard-boiled eggs, salami, mayonnaise, mustard and whole cornichons; pulse the ingredients until a smooth mixture forms.
3. Spread the mixture on the toast squares. Garnish with the sliced cornichons, capers and chopped herbs and serve.
—*Kurt Gutenbrunner*
MAKE AHEAD The salami-egg spread can be refrigerated overnight.

● HEALTHY ● MAKE AHEAD ● VEGETARIAN ● STAFF FAVORITE

parmesan tuiles with heirloom tomato salad

Bacon, Cheddar and Onion Quiche

ACTIVE: 40 MIN; TOTAL: 4 HR

6 SERVINGS ●

"To make a proper *tarte flambé,* you need a wood-burning oven with a stone floor," explains chef Jean-Georges Vongerichten of the thin-crusted Alsatian pizza topped with bacon, onions and *fromage blanc.* Here, he folds those same basic ingredients (replacing the *fromage blanc* with cheddar cheese) into a light custard and bakes it in a buttery pastry crust. "Not everyone has a pizza oven at home, so I decided to make it in the form of a quiche."

PASTRY

2 cups all-purpose flour, plus more for dusting

½ teaspoon salt

¼ teaspoon freshly ground black pepper

1½ sticks cold unsalted butter, cut into small pieces

½ cup ice water

FILLING

¼ pound thickly sliced bacon

1 tablespoon vegetable oil

1 large onion, sliced ¼ inch thick

Kosher salt and freshly ground black pepper

3 large eggs

¾ cup milk

½ cup crème fraîche

3½ ounces aged white cheddar cheese, shredded (1¼ cups)

2 tablespoons chopped dill

1. PREPARE THE PASTRY In a medium bowl, whisk together the 2 cups of flour with the salt and freshly ground pepper. Using a pastry cutter or 2 knives, cut in the cold butter pieces until they resemble small peas. Sprinkle the ice water on top and mix until the dough begins to come together. Turn the pastry out onto a lightly floured work surface and gently knead 2 or 3 times, just until it comes together. Pat the pastry into a disk, wrap in plastic and refrigerate until thoroughly chilled, 1 hour.

2. On a lightly floured work surface, roll out the chilled pastry to a 12-inch round, about ⅛ inch thick. Carefully ease the pastry into an 11-inch fluted tart pan with a removable bottom. Trim the overhang so that it is flush with the rim of the tart pan. Refrigerate the tart shell for 20 minutes.

3. Preheat the oven to 375°. Line the tart shell with aluminum foil and fill to the top with pie weights or dried beans. Bake until the pastry is golden, about 50 minutes. Remove the aluminum foil and weights and bake the shell until richly browned and crisp, about 25 minutes longer. Transfer the tart shell to a rack to cool, about 10 minutes. Turn the oven temperature down to 325°.

4. MEANWHILE, PREPARE THE FILLING In a large skillet, cook the sliced bacon over moderate heat, turning, until browned and crisp, about 6 minutes. Transfer the bacon to paper towels to drain, then coarsely chop. Wipe out the skillet and add the vegetable oil. When the oil is hot, add the sliced onion and season with salt and freshly ground pepper. Cover and cook over moderately low heat, stirring occasionally, until the onion is lightly caramelized and very soft, about 8 minutes. Let the onion cool.

5. In a medium bowl, whisk the eggs. Whisk in the milk, crème fraîche, 1 teaspoon of salt and ¼ teaspoon of freshly ground pepper. Spread the caramelized onion in the tart shell followed by the bacon and cheese. Pour the custard on top.

6. Bake the quiche for about 35 minutes, until the custard is just set. Transfer the quiche to a rack and let cool for 15 minutes. Sprinkle the chopped dill on the top. Unmold the quiche and serve in wedges.
—*Jean-Georges Vongerichten*

SERVE WITH Watercress salad lightly dressed with extra-virgin olive oil and freshly squeezed lemon juice.

MAKE AHEAD The unbaked pastry dough can be refrigerated for up to 3 days. The baked pastry shell can be cooled, wrapped in plastic and stored overnight at room temperature before proceeding.

WINE Affordable sparkling wine: Pierre Sparr NV Brut Réserve Crémant d'Alsace.

Lemongrass Shrimp on Toast

TOTAL: 45 MIN PLUS 4 HR MARINATING

6 SERVINGS

For his elegant hors d'oeuvre, fashion designer and avid cook Zang Toi adds a bit of Asian flair from his native Malaysia. He marinates shrimp in a spicy coconut-milk mixture, then serves them on toast squares moistened with a little crème fraîche.

8 macadamia nuts, chopped

3 medium shallots, chopped

3 garlic cloves, chopped

2 small dried red chiles, crushed

2 tablespoons minced fresh lemongrass bulb

1 tablespoon minced fresh ginger

1 tablespoon freshly squeezed lime juice

1 tablespoon sugar

½ cup unsweetened coconut milk

1 teaspoon freshly ground pepper

Kosher salt

1 pound medium shrimp, shelled and deveined

2 tablespoons vegetable oil

6 thin slices of white sandwich bread—crusts removed, toasted and cut into 4 squares each

½ cup crème fraîche

Cilantro leaves, for garnish

1. In a mini food processor, puree the macadamia nuts, shallots, garlic, dried chiles, lemongrass, ginger, fresh lime juice and sugar. Transfer the paste to a large bowl and stir in the coconut milk, freshly ground pepper and ½ teaspoon of salt. Add the shrimp and turn to coat with the marinade. Cover and refrigerate the shrimp for at least 4 hours or overnight.

2. In a nonstick skillet, heat the oil. Add the shrimp and season with salt. Cook over moderately high heat until the shrimp are golden and just cooked through, 3 minutes. Spread each toast with crème fraîche and top with a shrimp. Garnish with cilantro and serve. —*Zang Toiw*

WINE Lively, lime-inflected Australian Riesling: 2009 Penfolds Thomas Hyland.

● HEALTHY ● MAKE AHEAD ● VEGETARIAN ● STAFF FAVORITE

Brandade de Morue au Gratin (Whipped Salt Cod Gratin)

TOTAL: 1 HR PLUS 24 HR SOAKING
8 TO 10 SERVINGS ● ●

- 1 pound skinless salt cod fillet
- 1 pound large red-skinned potatoes
- 1½ cups whole milk
- 8 large garlic cloves, peeled
- 1 teaspoon finely grated lemon zest
- 2 tablespoons fresh lemon juice
- ⅛ teaspoon cayenne pepper
- ¾ cup extra-virgin olive oil, plus more for the baking dish
- Freshly ground black pepper
- 2 tablespoons freshly grated Parmigiano-Reggiano cheese
- 2 baguettes, cut into rounds and toasted, for serving

1. Put the salt cod in a bowl and cover with 1 inch of cold water. Refrigerate for 24 hours, changing the water 4 times.
2. Put the potatoes in a large saucepan, cover with water and boil over moderately high heat until tender, about 30 minutes. Drain and let the potatoes cool to warm.
3. Meanwhile, drain the cod and transfer to a saucepan. Add 2 quarts of water; bring just to a boil. Drain the cod and rinse out the pan. Return the cod to the pan, add 4 cups of water and bring to a boil. Simmer over low heat for 5 minutes. Drain the cod and return it to the pan, add the milk and garlic and bring to a boil. Cover and simmer for 10 minutes.
4. Peel the potatoes and break into chunks, then transfer to a food processor. Add the cod, milk, garlic cloves, lemon zest, lemon juice and cayenne and process until smooth. With the machine on, slowly pour in the ¾ cup of olive oil until incorporated. Season the brandade with black pepper.
5. Preheat the oven to 400°. Lightly oil a 9-by-13-inch baking dish and spread the *brandade* in the dish. Sprinkle the cheese on top. Bake on the top shelf of the oven for 20 minutes, until golden brown. Serve with toasts.
—*Jacques Pépin*
WINE Bright, dry Alsace Riesling: 2010 Lucien Albrecht Réserve Riesling.

Rustic Vegetable Tart

ACTIVE: 1 HR 15 MIN; TOTAL: 2 HR 15 MIN
8 SERVINGS ● ● ●

PASTRY
- 1½ cups all-purpose flour, plus more for dusting
- ½ cup fine cornmeal or polenta
- 1 teaspoon salt
- 2 tablespoons chopped chives
- 4 tablespoons cold unsalted butter, cut into small pieces
- 4 tablespoons cold vegetable shortening
- ¼ cup plus 2 tablespoons ice water
FILLING
- 4 pounds fava beans in the shell
- ¾ pound thin asparagus, trimmed
- 3 tablespoons extra-virgin olive oil, plus more for brushing
- 10 large garlic cloves, thinly sliced
- 2 bunches of scallions, thinly sliced
- Salt and freshly ground pepper
- 1 cup shredded Gruyère cheese

1. MAKE THE PASTRY In a food processor, combine the 1½ cups of flour with the cornmeal, salt and chives and process to blend. Add the butter and pulse a few times until the pieces are the size of small peas. Add the shortening and pulse a few times. Sprinkle the ice water over the mixture and pulse until the dough barely comes together. Scrape the dough onto a lightly floured work surface and knead to form a ball. Flatten the ball into a disk, wrap in plastic and refrigerate for 1 hour, or until firm.
2. MAKE THE FILLING Remove the favas from the pods. Fill a large skillet halfway with salted water and bring to a boil. Add the favas and blanch. Using a slotted spoon, transfer the favas to a baking sheet. Let cool slightly, then peel. Add the asparagus to the boiling water; cook until just tender, about 3 minutes. Drain and transfer to the baking sheet to cool, then cut into 1-inch pieces.
3. Wipe out the skillet and heat the 3 tablespoons of olive oil. Add the garlic and cook over low heat, stirring, until golden, 1½ minutes. Add the scallions and cook them over moderate heat until softened, 2 minutes. Add the favas and asparagus and cook until heated through, about 2 minutes. Season with salt and pepper. Let cool.
4. Preheat the oven to 400°. On a floured work surface, roll out the pastry to a 14-inch round, about ⅛ inch thick. Roll the pastry around the rolling pin and carefully transfer to a parchment paper–lined baking sheet. Scrape the vegetable mixture into the center of the pastry, leaving a 1½-inch border all around. Fold the edges up over the filling and scatter the Gruyère on top. Brush the edges with olive oil. Bake the tart on the bottom rack of the oven for about 30 minutes, until the crust is crisp on the bottom and golden brown. Let the tart cool to warm. Cut into wedges and serve. —*Kenny Rochford*
WINE Bright, citrusy California Sauvignon Blanc: 2010 Medlock Ames.

Sardine Toasts

⟳ TOTAL: 25 MIN • 6 SERVINGS ●
Bar du Square, a hangout for winemakers in Beaune, France, doesn't serve a lot of food. But it does offer an outstanding snack that comes to the table as components to be assembled DIY-style: a can of good-quality sardines, a basket of toasts and little bowls of sweet balsamic glaze and flaky salt.

- 24 baguette slices, cut on the diagonal ⅓ inch thick
- Extra-virgin olive oil, for brushing
- ¾ cup balsamic vinegar
- 2 cans (3.75 ounces each) olive oil–packed sardines, drained
- Flaky salt, such as Maldon

1. Preheat the oven to 400°. Arrange the baguette slices on a baking sheet and brush generously with oil. Toast for about 10 minutes, until the bread is golden brown; let cool.
2. Meanwhile, in a small saucepan, boil the vinegar over moderately high heat until it is reduced to ¼ cup, about 12 minutes; let cool.
3. Arrange the toasts on a platter and top with the sardines. Drizzle with a little of the reduced balsamic. Serve with flaky salt for sprinkling. —*Bar du Square*

Eggplant, Plantain and Goat Cheese Napoleons
ACTIVE: 1 HR; TOTAL: 1 HR 40 MIN
4 SERVINGS ●

This refined, layered dish uses the same basic ingredients as *boronia,* a dip of mashed roasted plantains, eggplant, onions and garlic from the Colombian Andes.

One 12-ounce eggplant, peeled and sliced crosswise into twelve ½-inch-thick rounds
Salt
1 very ripe sweet plantain (about ½ pound), unpeeled
1 tablespoon extra-virgin olive oil, plus more for frying
1 small onion, thinly sliced
1 garlic clove, thinly sliced
Freshly ground pepper
2 tablespoons pine nuts
4 kalamata olives, pitted and cut into ¼-inch dice
2 plum tomatoes—peeled, seeded and cut into ¼-inch dice
2 tablespoons golden raisins, chopped
2 tablespoons thinly sliced basil leaves
1 large egg beaten with 1 tablespoon of water
2 cups fine fresh bread crumbs
All-purpose flour, for dredging
¼ cup fresh goat cheese, softened

ingredient tip

fromage blanc This soft cream cheese used in chef Ludo Lefebvre's savory custard at far right has the consistency of sour cream and a mild, nutty flavor. Substitute: plain whole-milk yogurt.

quark A soft unripened cheese, quark is richer and milder than low-fat yogurt. Substitute: crème fraîche (a tangy, slightly sweet thickened cream).

1. Preheat the oven to 350°. Put the eggplant slices on a large baking sheet and sprinkle all over with salt. Let stand until the eggplant releases its water and is starting to soften, about 1 hour.
2. Meanwhile, put the plantain in a small baking dish and pierce the skin with a fork. Bake the plantain until very soft, 40 minutes.
3. In a small skillet, heat the 1 tablespoon of olive oil. Add the onion and garlic, cover and cook over moderate heat, stirring occasionally, until very soft and browned, about 7 minutes. Peel the baked plantain and add it to the skillet. Using a fork, mash the plantain until smooth and incorporated with the onion and garlic. Season with salt and freshly ground pepper. Cover the mashed plantain mixture and keep warm.
4. Put the pine nuts in a pie plate and bake until golden brown, about 3 minutes. Transfer the nuts to a bowl and let cool. Stir in the olives, diced tomatoes, golden raisins and sliced basil leaves. Season the tomato salsa with salt and pepper.
5. Put the egg wash, bread crumbs and flour in 3 separate shallow bowls. Pat the eggplant slices dry, then dredge them in flour. Dip the slices in the egg, allowing any excess to drip off, then coat the slices in bread crumbs.
6. In a large skillet, heat ⅛ inch of olive oil until shimmering. Add half of the eggplant slices and fry over moderate heat until they are golden brown outside and tender within, 3 minutes per side. Transfer the eggplant to paper towels to drain. Repeat with the remaining eggplant slices.
7. Arrange the fried eggplant slices on a baking sheet and reheat them in the oven. Place an eggplant slice on each of 4 plates. Spread about 1½ tablespoons of the plantain puree over each eggplant slice, followed by ½ tablespoon of goat cheese. Repeat to form 1 more layer, then top with the remaining slices of fried eggplant. Spoon the tomato salsa over and around the napoleons and serve.
—*Pedro Miguel Schiaffino*
MAKE AHEAD The plantain puree can be refrigerated overnight.
WINE Crisp Spanish sparkling wine: NV Anna de Codorníu Cava.

Fromage Blanc Custards with Radish Salad
ACTIVE: 20 MIN; TOTAL: 2 HR 30 MIN
6 SERVINGS ●
L.A. chef Ludo Lefebvre turns radishes into a colorful salad served on top of a divine custard that's really a savory panna cotta.

½ cup milk
1 garlic clove, smashed
Two ⅛-inch-thick slices of fresh ginger, smashed
1¼ teaspoons unflavored powdered gelatin
⅔ cup *fromage blanc* or plain whole-milk yogurt
½ cup crème fraîche
Salt and freshly ground white pepper
1 small black radish, cut into thin matchsticks (½ cup)
1 small Watermelon radish, cut into thin matchsticks (½ cup)
6 French or red radishes, cut into thin matchsticks
1 tablespoon coarsely chopped chives
2 tablespoons extra-virgin olive oil
1 chive flower, separated into blossoms, for garnish (optional)

1. In a small saucepan, bring the milk, garlic and ginger to a simmer over moderate heat. Cover and let stand for 10 minutes.
2. Strain the milk into another small saucepan. Lightly sprinkle the powdered gelatin over the warm milk and let stand until softened, about 5 minutes.
3. Rewarm the milk over low heat, gently whisking a few times, until the gelatin dissolves, about 1 minute. Remove from the heat and gently whisk in the *fromage blanc* and crème fraîche until smooth. Season with salt and white pepper. Pour into six 4-ounce ramekins. Cover and refrigerate until chilled and set, about 2 hours.
4. In a medium bowl, combine all the radishes with the chives. Drizzle with the olive oil, season with salt and white pepper and toss well. Top each custard with the radish salad, garnish with chive blossoms and serve.
—*Ludo Lefebvre*

● HEALTHY ● MAKE AHEAD ● VEGETARIAN ● STAFF FAVORITE

fromage blanc custard with radish salad

Salty Black-and-White Sesame Cocktail Cookies

ACTIVE: 30 MIN; TOTAL: 2 HR
MAKES ABOUT 4 DOZEN COOKIES ● ● ●

"In these cookies, you start with a sweet dough and the sesame seeds push it over on the sweet-savory continuum," says cookbook author Dorie Greenspan.

  1 cup all-purpose flour
  ¾ cup almond meal or ground almonds (see Note)
  ⅓ cup sugar
  1 teaspoon fine sea salt
  1 stick cold unsalted butter, cut into ½-inch dice
  1 large egg, beaten
Black and white sesame seeds, for sprinkling

1. In a food processor, pulse the flour, almond meal, sugar and sea salt until the mixture is combined. Add the butter and pulse until the mixture forms large clumps.
2. Turn the dough out onto a work surface and knead gently until it comes together. Divide the dough in half and press each half into a disk. Roll out each disk between 2 sheets of wax paper to ¼ inch thick. Slide the wax paper–covered disks onto a baking sheet and freeze for at least 1 hour, until firm.
3. Preheat the oven to 350° and line 2 large baking sheets with parchment paper. Working with one piece of dough at a time, peel off the top sheet of wax paper. Using a 1½-inch round cookie cutter, stamp out the cookies as close together as possible. Arrange the cookies 1 inch apart on the prepared baking sheets. Lightly brush the cookies with the beaten egg and sprinkle with the black and white sesame seeds.
4. Bake the sesame cookies for 17 to 20 minutes, until they are lightly browned; shift the baking sheets from top to bottom and front to back halfway through. Let the cookies cool on the baking sheets for 3 minutes, then transfer them to a wire rack and let them cool completely. —*Dorie Greenspan*
NOTE Almond meal is available at health-food stores and many grocery stores. To make your own, simply process 4½ ounces blanched almonds until finely ground.
MAKE AHEAD The rolled-out frozen cookie dough can be wrapped in plastic and kept frozen for up to 2 weeks; thaw the dough slightly before using. The baked cookies can be kept in an airtight container at room temperature for up to 2 days.
WINE Green-appley California sparkling wine: NV Scharffenberger Brut.

Spicy Cheddar Witch Fingers

ACTIVE: 15 MIN; TOTAL: 1 HR
MAKES 3 DOZEN CRACKERS ● ●

On Halloween, F&W's Grace Parisi shapes these cheesy crackers into creepy witch fingers, pressing a sliced almond onto the end of each one to make the nail. During the rest of the year, she rolls the dough into logs and cuts them into coins before baking.

  ½ pound extra-sharp white cheddar cheese
  6 tablespoons unsalted butter, softened
  1 teaspoon kosher salt
  ½ teaspoon cayenne pepper
  1 cup all-purpose flour
  1 large egg yolk mixed with 1 tablespoon of water
  36 sliced almonds (about ⅓ cup)

1. In a food processor, grate the cheddar cheese. Add the butter, salt and cayenne and process until smooth. Add the flour and pulse until incorporated. Turn the dough out onto a work surface and knead until smooth.
2. Divide the dough into 36 pieces and roll each piece into a 4-inch finger. Arrange the fingers on 2 parchment paper–lined baking sheets and brush with the egg wash. Press an almond slice onto the end of each finger to resemble a fingernail. Refrigerate the cheese fingers until firm, about 15 minutes.
3. Preheat the oven to 350°. Bake the cheese fingers in the upper and lower thirds of the oven until puffed and golden, 25 minutes, shifting the pans halfway through baking. Let the cheese fingers cool completely, then arrange on a platter and serve. —*Grace Parisi*

Cheddar Gougères

ACTIVE: 15 MIN; TOTAL: 1 HR
MAKES 40 GOUGÈRES ● ●

Some artisans are assisting bigger, more established companies that want to create something handcrafted. Vermont's tiny Jasper Hill Farm, for instance, is helping big Cabot age its incredible Cabot Clothbound Cheddar, a cheese that's perfect for making these cheesy puffs called gougères.

  1 stick unsalted butter, plus more for the baking sheets
  1 cup water
  ½ teaspoon kosher salt
  1 cup all-purpose flour
  4 large eggs
  1 cup shredded Cabot Clothbound Cheddar

1. Preheat the oven to 425° and position racks in the upper and middle thirds. Lightly butter 2 large baking sheets. In a large saucepan, combine the 1 stick of butter with the water and kosher salt and bring to a boil. Remove from the heat. Add the flour and whisk until smooth. Let cool slightly, then, using an electric mixer at medium speed, beat in the eggs 1 at a time, beating thoroughly between additions. Beat in all but 2 tablespoons of the cheese.
2. Using a 1-tablespoon ice cream scoop, scoop level mounds of the dough onto the baking sheets, 1½ inches apart. Sprinkle with the remaining 2 tablespoons of cheese and bake for 28 minutes, until golden and risen; shift the pans from top to bottom and front to back halfway through baking.
3. Lower the oven temperature to 400°. Pierce each gougère near the bottom with a skewer and return the pans to the oven. Bake for about 8 minutes longer, until crisp and deeply golden. Transfer the gougères to racks to cool. Serve the gougères warm or at room temperature. —*Veronica Pedraza*
MAKE AHEAD The gougères can be refrigerated for 3 days or frozen for up to 3 weeks. Recrisp in a 325° oven before serving.
WINE Light, citrusy Spanish cava: NV Castillo Perelada Brut Reserva.

● HEALTHY ● MAKE AHEAD ● VEGETARIAN ● STAFF FAVORITE

salty black-and-white sesame cocktail cookies

Apricot-Tarragon Cocktail Cookies

ACTIVE: 30 MIN; TOTAL: 2 HR

MAKES ABOUT 5 DOZEN COOKIES ● ●

"I don't know where I got the idea to add tarragon to these apricot cookies," says cookbook author and CookieBar founder Dorie Greenspan. "But when I tried it, I thought, That's the way it's supposed to be." To prevent the apricots from burning or drying out too quickly, use the freshest, plumpest dried fruit you can find.

- ½ cup dried Turkish apricots, finely chopped
- 2 tablespoons minced tarragon
- ½ cup sugar
- 1 stick unsalted butter, softened
- 1 large egg yolk
- ⅓ cup extra-virgin olive oil
- ¾ teaspoon sea salt
- 2 cups all-purpose flour

wine pairing tips

Sparkling wines pair well with a range of starters. Here, four popular types and their best matches.

champagne Produced only in the Champagne region of France, this bright, lively wine is excellent with everything from caviar to popcorn.

prosecco Its frothiness and hint of sweetness make this bubbly Italian wine terrific with sweet-and-savory starters like the Rosemary, Almond and Parmesan Cocktail Cookies, at right.

lambrusco The dry, juicy elements of this red Italian sparkling wine pairs well with rich, cured meats.

cava This Spanish sparkler has a fruity character that's fabulous with cheesy hors d'oeuvres like the Cheddar Gougères on page 22.

1. In a small bowl, cover the apricots with hot water; let stand for 10 minutes, until plump. Transfer to paper towels to drain.

2. In another small bowl, rub the tarragon leaves into the sugar until they are moist and aromatic. In a standing mixer fitted with the paddle, beat the butter with the tarragon sugar at low speed until creamy. Beat in the egg yolk until just combined, about 1 minute. Slowly drizzle in the olive oil and beat until smooth. Add the salt and flour and beat until just incorporated. Using a large spatula, fold in the apricots.

3. Turn the cookie dough out onto a work surface and knead until it just comes together. Divide the dough in half and press each half into a disk. Roll out each disk between 2 sheets of wax paper to about ¼ inch thick. Slide the wax paper–covered disks onto a baking sheet and freeze for at least 1 hour, until very firm.

4. Preheat the oven to 350° and line 2 large baking sheets with parchment paper. Working with one piece of cookie dough at a time, peel off the top sheet of wax paper. Using a 1½-inch round cookie cutter, stamp out the cookies as close together as possible. Arrange the cookies 1 inch apart on the prepared baking sheets.

5. Bake the cookies for about 20 minutes, until they are lightly golden; shift the baking sheets from top to bottom and front to back halfway through. Let the cookies cool on the baking sheets for 3 minutes, then transfer them to a wire rack to cool completely.
—*Dorie Greenspan*

MAKE AHEAD The rolled-out frozen cookie dough can be kept in the freezer for 2 weeks.

WINE Bright, fruity white wine: 2010 Left Foot Charley Pinot Blanc.

Rosemary, Almond and Parmesan Cocktail Cookies

ACTIVE: 30 MIN; TOTAL: 2 HR

MAKES ABOUT 5 DOZEN COOKIES ● ●

To bring out the flavor of the rosemary in these barely sweet cookies, author Dorie Greenspan first rubs the leaves with granulated sugar, a technique she learned from renowned French pastry chef Pierre Hermé.

- ½ cup slivered almonds
- 3 tablespoons sugar
- 2 tablespoons finely chopped rosemary
- 2 cups all-purpose flour
- ⅓ cup freshly grated Parmigiano-Reggiano cheese (1 ounce)
- ½ teaspoon salt
- 2 sticks cold unsalted butter, cut into small dice
- 2 large egg yolks, beaten

1. Preheat the oven to 350°. Spread the almonds in a pie plate and toast for about 10 minutes, until golden. Turn off the oven and let the almonds cool.

2. In a bowl, rub the sugar with the rosemary until moist and aromatic. In a food processor, combine the rosemary sugar with the almonds, flour, cheese and salt and pulse until the almonds are coarsely chopped. Add the butter and pulse until the mixture resembles a coarse meal. Add the egg yolks and pulse until large clumps of dough form.

3. Transfer the dough to a work surface and knead gently until it just comes together. Divide the dough in half and press each piece into a disk. Roll out each disk between 2 sheets of wax paper to about ¼ inch thick. Slide the wax paper–covered disks onto a baking sheet and keep in the freezer for at least 1 hour, until very firm.

4. Preheat the oven to 350° and line 2 large baking sheets with parchment paper. Working with one piece of dough at a time, peel off the top sheet of wax paper. Using a 1½-inch round cookie cutter, stamp out cookies as close together as possible. Arrange the cookies about 1 inch apart on the prepared baking sheets.

5. Bake the cookies for about 20 minutes, until lightly golden; shift the baking sheets from top to bottom and front to back halfway through. Let the cookies cool on the baking sheets for 3 minutes, then transfer them to a wire rack to cool completely.
—*Dorie Greenspan*

MAKE AHEAD The rolled-out frozen cookie dough can be kept in the freezer for 2 weeks.

WINE Crisp, citrusy Prosecco: NV Nino Franco Rustico Prosecco di Valdobbiadene.

● HEALTHY ● MAKE AHEAD ○ VEGETARIAN ● STAFF FAVORITE

Chocolate-Cayenne Cocktail Cookies

ACTIVE: 30 MIN; TOTAL: 2 HR
MAKES ABOUT 6 DOZEN COOKIES ● ●

Rich, dark Valrhona cocoa is used to make these spicy, unexpectedly tender cookies, flecked with flaky Maldon salt.

1½ cups all-purpose flour
½ cup unsweetened cocoa powder
½ teaspoon cayenne pepper
½ teaspoon fine sea salt
2 sticks unsalted butter, softened
⅓ cup confectioners' sugar
2 tablespoons granulated sugar
1 large egg yolk

Maldon salt, for sprinkling

1. Sift the flour, cocoa powder, cayenne pepper and sea salt into a large bowl and whisk to combine. In a standing mixer fitted with the paddle attachment, beat the softened butter with both sugars at low speed until creamy. Add the egg yolk and beat until smooth, then add the dry ingredients and beat until incorporated.
2. Turn the dough out onto a work surface and knead gently until it comes together. Divide the dough in half and press each half into a disk. Roll out each disk between 2 sheets of wax paper to about ¼ inch thick. Slide the wax paper–covered disks onto a baking sheet and keep in the freezer for at least 1 hour, until very firm.
3. Preheat the oven to 350° and line 2 large baking sheets with parchment paper. Working with one piece of dough at a time, peel off the top sheet of wax paper. Using a 1½-inch round cookie cutter, stamp out the cookies as close together as possible. Arrange the cookies about 1 inch apart on the parchment paper–lined baking sheets and sprinkle with some Maldon salt.
4. Bake the cookies for about 15 minutes, until they are just firm; shift the baking sheets from top to bottom and front to back halfway through. Let the cookies cool on the baking sheets for 3 minutes, then transfer them to a wire rack to cool completely.
—Dorie Greenspan

MAKE AHEAD The rolled-out frozen cookie dough can be wrapped in plastic and kept frozen for up to 2 weeks. The baked cookies can be kept in an airtight container at room temperature for up to 2 days.

WINE Frothy, fruity sparkling red: NV Medici Ermete Solo Lambrusco.

Spinach and Green Pea Empanadas

ACTIVE: 1 HR; TOTAL: 2 HR 30 MIN
MAKES 32 EMPANADAS ● ●

"In Argentina, we eat so much beef. When I talked to [local chef] Mauricio Couly about making empanadas, I said, 'It would be great to fill them with something that is not meat,'" winemaker Piero Incisa della Rocchetta recalls. Couly uses a mix of spinach, fava beans, green beans and a good amount of mint. He makes his own paprika-spiced empanada dough; store-bought empanada wrappers (available in the freezer section of many supermarkets and specialty food stores) work well, too.

DOUGH
1½ cups water
1 tablespoon kosher salt
3 tablespoons unsalted butter or lard
2 teaspoons sweet smoked paprika (pimentón de la Vera)
3¾ cups all-purpose flour, plus more for dusting

FILLING
10 ounces spinach, stemmed
½ cup shelled fava beans or thawed frozen lima beans
¼ pound green beans
2 tablespoons unsalted butter
3 tablespoons extra-virgin olive oil
1 medium onion, thinly sliced
2 garlic cloves, minced
1 cup frozen peas, thawed
2 tablespoons chopped fresh mint leaves
1 tablespoon chopped fresh thyme

Salt and freshly ground pepper

1. MAKE THE DOUGH In a small saucepan, combine the water, salt, butter and sweet smoked paprika and bring to a boil. Pour the mixture into a large bowl and let cool to room temperature. Stir in the 3¾ cups of flour until the dough comes together. On a lightly floured work surface, gently knead the dough until smooth. Wrap the dough in plastic and refrigerate until firm, about 1 hour.
2. PREPARE THE FILLING In a saucepan of boiling salted water, cook the spinach for 1 minute. Using a slotted spoon, transfer the spinach to a colander. Add the fava beans to the boiling water and cook until bright green, 1 minute. Using a slotted spoon, transfer the fava beans to a plate. Add the green beans to the boiling water and cook until tender, 4 minutes. Drain and finely chop the green beans. Peel the tough outer skins from the fava beans. Squeeze the excess water from the spinach, then coarsely chop it.
3. In a large skillet, melt the butter in the olive oil. Add the onion and cook over moderate heat, stirring occasionally, until softened, about 10 minutes. Add the garlic and cook until fragrant, about 3 minutes. Stir in the spinach, fava beans, green beans and peas and cook, stirring, until heated through, about 2 minutes. Stir in the mint and thyme and season with salt and pepper.
4. Preheat the oven to 350°. Lightly oil 2 large baking sheets. On a floured work surface, roll out the dough ⅛ inch thick. Using a 3½-inch round biscuit cutter, cut out 32 rounds from the dough. Moisten the edge of 1 dough round with water. Mound 1 tablespoon of the vegetable filling on half of the round and fold the other side over. Press to seal the dough and pinch at intervals to make pleats. Repeat with the remaining dough rounds and vegetable filling.
5. Arrange the empanadas on the prepared baking sheets and bake in the upper and lower thirds of the oven for about 30 minutes, until browned. Serve warm or at room temperature. —Mauricio Couly

MAKE AHEAD The empanadas can be frozen for up to 1 month before baking.

WINE Silky, aromatic Pinot Noir: 2009 Bodega Chacra Cincuenta y Cinco.

Natchitoches-Style Meat Pies

ACTIVE: 45 MIN; TOTAL: 1 HR 30 MIN
MAKES 16 MEAT PIES ●

At Besh Steak in New Orleans, John Besh prepares mini meat pies with house-made dough and a rich, spiced filling of beef, pork and chicken liver sautéed in duck fat. A meat-pie shortcut for the home cook: Use store-bought empanada dough instead of making your own. The cooks at Besh Steak use duck fat to sauté the meat filling. At home, butter is a perfectly fine substitute.

- 4 tablespoons unsalted butter
- ½ pound lean ground beef
- ½ pound ground pork
- ¼ pound chicken livers, trimmed and finely chopped
- 1 onion, finely chopped
- 1 small green bell pepper, finely chopped
- 4 large garlic cloves, minced
- 1 teaspoon cayenne pepper
- ½ teaspoon ground cloves
- ½ teaspoon chopped thyme

Salt and freshly ground black pepper
- ¼ cup low-sodium chicken broth
- 16 empanada wrappers, thawed (see Note)

Vegetable oil, for frying
Ranch dressing mixed with chopped cilantro, for serving

1. In a large skillet, melt the butter. Add the beef, pork and chicken livers and cook over moderate heat, stirring, until lightly browned, about 8 minutes. Add the onion, bell pepper, garlic, cayenne, cloves and thyme; season with salt and black pepper. Cook until the vegetables are tender, about 6 minutes. Tilt the pan and spoon off the fat. Add the chicken broth and scrape up any browned bits stuck to the bottom of the skillet. Scrape the filling into a bowl, cover and refrigerate for about 30 minutes, until chilled.

2. Arrange 8 empanada wrappers on a work surface. Lightly brush the edges with water and spoon half of the meat filling into the centers. Fold in half, pressing out any air, and seal; crimp the edges with a fork. Transfer the meat pies to a wax paper–lined baking sheet. Repeat with the remaining empanada wrappers and meat filling.

3. Line a baking sheet with paper towels and place a rack on top. In a large, deep skillet, heat 1½ inches of oil to 375°. Fry the meat pies in batches, turning once, until golden brown, about 5 minutes. Drain on the rack and serve with the ranch dressing.
—*John Besh*

VARIATION To bake the meat pies, arrange them on 2 parchment paper–lined baking sheets. Prick each pie with a fork, brush the tops with beaten egg and bake at 425° for about 20 minutes, until golden.

NOTE Empanada wrappers are available in the freezer section at most supermarkets; look for the Goya brand.

MAKE AHEAD The meat filling can be refrigerated for up to 5 days.

WINE Rich, spicy Washington state Merlot: 2007 Chateau Ste. Michelle Columbia Valley.

Yucca Empanadas

ACTIVE: 1 HR; TOTAL: 1 HR 35 MIN
MAKES 18 EMPANADAS ● ●

"We try to make a different menu every day, often using the same ingredients," says consulting chef Pedro Miguel Schiaffino about the challenges of creating recipes for Aqua Expeditions' cruise line on the Peruvian Amazon. Yucca, one of the most ubiquitous root vegetables in the area, appears in many of his dishes. Here he turns pure yucca into a dough for fried empanadas, a typical street food in Iquitos, the largest city in the Peruvian rain forest.

- 1 pound frozen peeled yucca pieces, or 3 pounds fresh yucca—peeled, cored and cut into 1-inch pieces
Salt
- 2 tablespoons extra-virgin olive oil
- 1 small red onion, minced
- 1 red bell pepper, finely diced
- 2 garlic cloves, minced
- ¼ teaspoon ground turmeric
- ½ teaspoon smoked sweet paprika
- ½ teaspoon ground cumin
- 1 teaspoon crushed red pepper
- 2 tablespoons chopped golden raisins
- 2 scallions, minced
- 2 tablespoons red wine vinegar
- ⅓ cup Brazil nuts
- 4 ounces fresh mozzarella, cut into ½-inch dice

Vegetable oil, for deep-frying

1. In a medium saucepan, cover the yucca pieces with water and boil over moderately high heat until very tender, about 25 minutes for fresh or frozen. Drain well and return the yucca to the pan; shake over moderate heat for 10 seconds to dry the yucca out. Pass it through a ricer and add a large pinch of salt. Gently knead the yucca to form a firm dough. Cover the dough with plastic wrap and let cool to room temperature.

2. Preheat the oven to 350°. In a large skillet, heat the olive oil. Add the onion, bell pepper and garlic and cook over moderate heat until softened, about 7 minutes. Add the turmeric, paprika, cumin and crushed red pepper and cook, stirring, until fragrant, about 1 minute. Add the raisins, scallions and red wine vinegar and cook until the vinegar has been absorbed, about 1 minute. Transfer the mixture to a bowl and let cool.

3. Spread the Brazil nuts in a pie plate and toast in the oven until lightly browned, about 5 minutes; let them cool, then chop. Stir the chopped nuts and mozzarella into the onion mixture; season with salt.

4. Using lightly oiled hands, pinch off 1 tablespoon of yucca dough and form into a 2½-inch round, about ⅛ inch thick. Add 1 rounded teaspoon of the vegetable-cheese filling and enclose it in the dough, pinching it shut and lightly rolling it into a ball. Repeat with the remaining dough and filling. You should have about 18 balls.

5. In a medium saucepan, heat 1 inch of vegetable oil to 375°. Working in batches, fry the empanadas, turning, until golden brown and crisp, about 2 minutes per side. Drain on paper towels and serve right away.
—*Pedro Miguel Schiaffino*

MAKE AHEAD The vegetable-cheese filling can be refrigerated overnight. Bring to room temperature before proceeding.

● HEALTHY ● MAKE AHEAD ● VEGETARIAN ● STAFF FAVORITE

natchitoches-style meat pies

Cocktail Meatballs

ACTIVE: 25 MIN; TOTAL: 1 HR
MAKES ABOUT 4 DOZEN MINI-MEATBALLS

- 5 slices of packaged white sandwich bread
- 1 cup milk
- 3 large eggs, beaten
- 1 small white onion, minced
- 1 tablespoon salt
- 2 teaspoons sweet paprika
- 1 teaspoon dry mustard
- ½ teaspoon freshly ground black pepper
- ½ teaspoon ground mace
- 2 pounds lean ground beef

Vegetable oil, for brushing

- 1 cup ketchup
- ½ cup currant jelly
- ½ cup dry sherry
- 1 tablespoon Worcestershire sauce

1. Preheat the broiler. In a large bowl, soak the bread in the milk for 1 minute, until softened, then squeeze out the excess milk and return the bread to the bowl. Add the eggs, onion, salt, paprika, dry mustard, pepper and mace and mix until smooth. Add the ground beef and mix until evenly combined.

2. Brush a large rimmed baking sheet with oil. Using a 2-tablespoon-size ice cream scoop, form the meat into 1½-inch balls; roll until smooth. Transfer the meatballs to the baking sheet and brush the tops with oil. Broil 10 inches from the heat for about 10 minutes, shifting the sheet occasionally, until the meatballs are sizzling and browned.

3. Meanwhile, in a large, deep skillet, combine the ketchup with the currant jelly, dry sherry and Worcestershire sauce. Add ½ cup of water and bring to a simmer, whisking until the jelly is melted.

4. Using a slotted spoon, add the meatballs to the sauce and simmer over low heat until thickly glazed, about 15 minutes. Transfer the meatballs to a bowl and serve with picks.
—*Debra Shaw*

MAKE AHEAD The recipe can be prepared through Step 2 and refrigerated for 3 days.
COCKTAIL Dry, clean gin martini.

Shrimp and Pork Spring Rolls

ACTIVE: 1 HR; TOTAL: 1 HR 30 MIN
6 SERVINGS ●

These supremely crispy spring rolls are filled with shrimp, pork and colorful julienned vegetables. The fried shallots add extra crunch to the spring rolls, but they're optional.

- ½ pound medium shrimp—shelled, deveined and cut into ½-inch pieces
- 2 teaspoons soy sauce

Salt and freshly ground white pepper

- ¼ pound ground pork
- ¾ teaspoon Asian sesame oil
- 3 medium dried shiitake mushrooms
- ½ cup boiling-hot water
- 2 tablespoons vegetable oil, plus 1 quart for frying
- 2 large eggs, lightly beaten
- 1 garlic clove, minced
- 1 small carrot, cut into julienne strips
- ½ cup julienned jicama
- ½ cup julienned green beans
- 3 large shallots, thinly sliced and separated into rings
- 1 small Kirby cucumber—halved, seeded and cut into julienne strips
- 12 spring roll wrappers, thawed if frozen (see Note)

Asian chile sauce, for serving

1. In a bowl, toss the shrimp with 1 teaspoon of the soy sauce and ¼ teaspoon each of salt and pepper. In another bowl, toss the pork with the remaining 1 teaspoon of soy sauce and ¼ teaspoon each of the sesame oil, salt and pepper. Cover and refrigerate the shrimp and pork for 30 minutes.

2. Meanwhile, in a small bowl, cover the dried shiitake with the hot water. Let the mushrooms stand until softened, about 20 minutes. Discard the mushroom stems and thinly slice the shiitake caps.

3. In a small nonstick skillet, heat 1 teaspoon of the vegetable oil. Add half of the beaten eggs, spreading them over the bottom of the pan. Cook over low heat until almost set, 30 seconds. Carefully turn the egg and cook until set, about 10 seconds. Transfer to a plate and cut into thin strips.

4. In a large nonstick skillet, heat 1 tablespoon of the vegetable oil. Add the shrimp and cook over moderately high heat, stirring, until just cooked through, about 1 minute. Using a slotted spoon, transfer the shrimp to a bowl. Add the garlic to the skillet and cook until fragrant, about 20 seconds. Add the pork and cook, breaking up the meat, until no pink remains, 2 minutes. Add the pork to the shrimp.

5. Heat the remaining 2 teaspoons of vegetable oil in the skillet. Add the carrot, jicama, green beans and shiitake and cook over moderate heat, tossing, until the vegetables are softened, about 2 minutes. Add to the shrimp and pork.

6. In a large saucepan, heat the remaining 1 quart of vegetable oil to 375°. Add the shallot rings and cook, stirring a few times, until browned and crisp, about 2 minutes. Using a slotted spoon, transfer the fried shallots to paper towels to drain, then add them to the spring-roll filling along with the egg strips, cucumber and remaining ½ teaspoon of sesame oil. Toss well and season the filling with salt and white pepper.

7. On a work surface, brush the edge of 1 spring roll wrapper with a little of the remaining beaten egg. Spread ⅓ cup of the shrimp-and-pork filling on the wrapper. Bring the bottom end of the wrapper over the filling and roll up the wrapper like a cigar, folding in the edges as you roll. Repeat with the remaining wrappers, filling and beaten egg.

8. Reheat the vegetable oil to 375°. Working in batches, fry the spring rolls, turning once or twice, until golden brown and crisp, about 2 minutes. Drain on paper towels. Keep the cooked spring rolls warm in a preheated oven. Cut each spring roll in half, arrange on a platter and serve with chile sauce.
—*Zang Toi*

NOTE Look for thin spring-roll wrappers, also known as *lumpia* wrappers, made with wheat flour; they're available at Asian markets, usually in the freezer section. Don't use egg roll wrappers; they're too thick.

MAKE AHEAD The spring rolls can be assembled and then refrigerated for up to 3 hours before frying them.

● HEALTHY ● MAKE AHEAD ● VEGETARIAN ● STAFF FAVORITE

Pork-Scallion Pot Stickers

TOTAL: 1 HR • MAKES ABOUT 3½ DOZEN POT STICKERS ●

Ayako Yoshikawa Gordon of Pure Concepts, a purveyor of sustainable prepared foods, makes these gingery dumplings using pork from Rain Shadow Meats, a butcher in Seattle's Melrose Market. Rain Shadow sells the pot stickers one day a week.

- ½ pound ground pork
- 2 cups finely chopped green cabbage
- 1 cup thinly sliced scallions (about 5 large)
- 1½ tablespoons minced fresh ginger
- 3 garlic cloves, minced
- 2 shiitake mushrooms, stems discarded and caps finely chopped
- 1 tablespoon toasted sesame oil
- 1 tablespoon soy sauce, plus more for dipping
- 1 teaspoon kosher salt
- ½ teaspoon freshly ground white pepper
- 1 package round gyoza wrappers (48)
- ¼ cup vegetable oil
- 1 cup water

1. In a bowl, mix the pork with the cabbage, scallions, ginger, garlic, shiitake, sesame oil, soy sauce, salt and white pepper.

2. Line a baking sheet with wax paper. On a work surface, brush the edges of 4 gyoza wrappers with water. Place a scant tablespoon of the pork-scallion filling in the center of each wrapper. Bring the edges of each gyoza wrapper together over the filling; press and pleat to seal. Lift each pot sticker by the pleated edge, transfer to the baking sheet and press down lightly to flatten the bottom. Repeat with the remaining gyoza wrappers and pork-scallion filling.

3. In a large nonstick skillet, heat 2 tablespoons of the vegetable oil until shimmering. Arrange half of the pot stickers in the skillet, pleated rims facing up, and cook over high heat until the bottoms are lightly browned, about 2 minutes. Add ½ cup of the water to the skillet, then cover and simmer until the pork filling is cooked through,

about 5 minutes. Uncover and cook until the water has evaporated and the pot stickers are well browned on the bottom, about 1 minute; transfer to a plate. Repeat with the remaining oil, pot stickers and water. Serve the pot stickers with soy sauce.
—*Ayako Yoshikawa Gordon*

MAKE AHEAD Freeze the uncooked pot stickers on a floured baking sheet, then transfer them to a plastic bag and freeze for up to 1 month. Cook from frozen.

WINE Lightly fruity California sparkling wine: NV J Brut Rosé.

Korean Sushi Rolls with Walnut-Edamame Crumble

ACTIVE: 1 HR; TOTAL: 2 HR
MAKES 10 LARGE ROLLS ● ● ○ ○

David Chang, the chef-owner of New York City's Momofuku restaurants, got the idea for these playful rolls after visiting a temple in South Korea; the nuns served him a snack of edamame mixed with walnuts and molasses. Unlike other sushi rolls, they can be served warm.

- 2 cups sushi rice, rinsed well
- 2 cups water
- 1 tablespoon canola oil
- 2 cups coarsely chopped walnuts
- 1 cup shelled edamame (4 ounces)
- 3 tablespoons molasses
- 1½ tablespoons soy sauce, plus more for serving
- 1 tablespoon toasted sesame seeds
- 10 sheets of nori (see Note)
- 20 shiso leaves (see Note)
- 10 nori-length pieces of pickled daikon or other Asian pickled radish (see Note)
- 2 large carrots, cut into thin 2-inch-long matchsticks

1. In a saucepan, bring the rice and the water to a boil. Cover and cook over low heat for 15 minutes, until the water is absorbed. Remove from the heat and let stand, covered, for 10 minutes. Scrape the rice into a bowl. Cover with a kitchen towel; let stand until cool enough to handle, 30 minutes.

2. Meanwhile, heat the oil in a medium nonstick skillet. Add the chopped walnuts and cook over high heat, stirring, until lightly toasted, about 3 minutes. Add the edamame, molasses and the 1½ tablespoons of soy sauce and cook over moderately high heat, stirring, until sticky, about 5 minutes. Stir in the sesame seeds. Transfer the walnut-edamame mixture to a bowl and let cool.

3. Set 1 nori sheet on a bamboo sushi mat. With lightly moistened hands, pat ⅔ cup of the sushi rice onto the nori in a rectangle that covers the lower two-thirds of the sheet, about ⅓ inch thick. Crush 2 rice grains in the empty corners to act as glue. Arrange 2 shiso leaves over the rice. In the center of the shiso leaf, arrange a piece of pickled daikon, 2 tablespoons of carrots and 2 tablespoons of the walnut-edamame mixture. Lift the end of the bamboo mat nearest you up and over, pressing to tuck the filling into a cylinder. Tightly roll up the fillings. Repeat to form the remaining 9 rolls. Using a sharp knife, cut each roll into 6 pieces and transfer to a platter. Serve with soy sauce.
—*David Chang*

NOTE Nori, shiso and pickled daikon are available at many Asian markets.

MAKE AHEAD The rolls can be kept at room temperature for up to 4 hours.

WINE Vibrant, creamy Champagne: NV Pierre Moncuit Blanc de Blancs Grand Cru Brut.

ingredient tip

Common in Asian cooking, these pantry items are also gluten-free.

tamari Wheat-free versions of tamari can fill in for soy sauce.

rice paper These rice-flour-based wrappers are a great substitute for spring roll or *lumpia* (a Filipino version of egg roll) wrappers.

kombu This dried kelp can stand in for dashi powder (which has wheat protein) to make savory broths.

do-it-yourself sushi

Making maki (sushi rolls) requires just three things: high-quality ingredients, a bamboo mat and practice. *Iron Chef* star **Masaharu Morimoto** raises the sushi bar for home cooks.

first: make the sushi rice *Morimoto recommends using a rice cooker. Season the rice to taste: Start with ½ cup of sweetened vinegar for every 5 cups of cooked rice, adding more by the tablespoon if desired.*

1. Rinse 2 cups of short-grain Japanese rice 5 times, then drain in a colander and let dry for 15 minutes.

2. Cook the rice in a rice cooker according to the manufacturer's instructions. Alternatively, in a medium saucepan, combine the rice with 2 cups of cold water and bring to a boil over high heat. Cover and cook over moderate heat for 10 minutes. Reduce the heat to low and cook for 10 minutes longer. Remove from the heat and let stand, covered, for 15 minutes.

3. Meanwhile, in a small saucepan, combine ¼ cup of sake-mash vinegar (or white wine vinegar), ¼ cup of rice vinegar, ¼ cup of sugar and 2 tablespoons of salt and warm over moderate heat, stirring to dissolve the sugar.

4. Transfer the rice to a very large bowl. Sprinkle ½ cup of the seasoned vinegar all over the rice: Drizzle onto a spatula while waving it back and forth. Using a slicing motion with the spatula, gently separate the rice grains while mixing in the seasoning. Fan the rice while mixing it to help it dry. Wipe down any stray grains from the side of the bowl. Cover the rice with a damp towel to keep warm.

fish prep tips

To be eaten safely, sushi-grade fish must be handled correctly: It should be frozen for at least one day to kill any parasites. For the best flavor and texture in oily, strong-smelling fresh fish, such as salmon and mackerel, rub the fillets with fine sea salt and let them stand for about 30 minutes; rinse the fish well, pat dry and sprinkle all over with rice vinegar.

second: prepare the fillings

crab
Meat from Dungeness, blue or king crabs is best. Pick over the meat to remove bits of shell.

tuna
If a piece of tuna is sinewy, simply scrape the meat off the sinews with a sharp knife.

salmon
Slice salmon across the grain into strips about 4 inches long and ¼ inch thick.

cucumber
Seed a cucumber, then slice it—including some of the skin— into a thin julienne.

avocado
Cut a ripe Hass avocado in half. Carefully strike the pit with the blade of a heavy chef's knife, then twist the knife to remove the pit. Peel the halves, then cut them into ¼-inch-thick slices.

third: form the maki *"Use your fingertips to delicately spread the rice," says Morimoto, who has 38 years of sushi-making experience. "You want a little space between the rice grains so that they remain fluffy." Then add desired fillings and wasabi, considering the size and color of the ingredients and taking care not to overstuff the roll: "Rice, wasabi and fish should be in harmony." The process may seem imposing, but Morimoto says anyone can make a well-balanced maki at home. "Don't be afraid," he advises. "It's like a taco of seaweed and rice."*

1. SPREAD THE RICE Carefully wave a 4-by-7½-inch sheet of nori (dried seaweed) over an open flame until crisp and fragrant, then transfer to a clean bamboo mat. Wet your hands in water that's seasoned with rice vinegar, then scoop up ½ cup of sushi rice. Gently form the rice into a loosely packed, palm-width log. Place the log at one edge of the nori and begin spreading it across to the other side. (Nori and bamboo mats can be purchased at Asian markets or online at *amazon.com*.)

2. ADD THE WASABI AND FILLING Continue to spread the rice all over the nori, rewetting your hands as necessary in the vinegar water, until an even layer covers all but a ¼-inch border at the top edge of the sheet of nori. Spread about ¼ teaspoon of wasabi lengthwise along the middle of the rice. (Morimoto recommends more wasabi with fatty fish like salmon and mackerel, less with lean fish like fluke and halibut.) Lay about 2 ounces of the filling (either a single ingredient or a combination) along the center of the rice.

3. ROLL THE MAKI Roll the bamboo mat up and away from you, curling the nori and sushi rice around the filling; use your fingers to hold the filling in place as you roll, applying a firm grip but making sure not to squeeze the roll too tightly. Secure the roll with the ¼-inch flap of nori. Once the roll is sealed along the edge, gently squeeze it, pressing lightly on the top and sides, to compress the roll slightly and form a rough square shape. Press on each end of the roll to make a neat surface.

4. CUT THE MAKI Lift the roll off the bamboo mat and transfer it to a clean work surface. Dip the tip of a long, sharp knife into water that's been seasoned with rice vinegar; let the vinegar water run down the length of the blade. Using a long slicing motion, cut the roll in half, then cut each half into thirds to form six even pieces, rewetting the blade of the knife as needed. Serve the maki right away, cut side down, with *gari* (thin slices of young ginger pickled in sugar and vinegar) and good-quality soy sauce for dipping.

Mini Blini Napoleons

ACTIVE: 30 MIN; TOTAL: 1 HR
MAKES 42 PIECES ● ●

This stacked architectural take on blini and caviar makes more blini than you'll need; extras are great with smoked salmon.

¼ cup warm water
1½ teaspoons active dry yeast
1½ teaspoons sugar
1½ cups milk, plus more as needed
1 large egg, beaten
1 cup all-purpose flour
¾ cup buckwheat flour
½ teaspoon salt
4 tablespoons unsalted butter, melted, plus more for brushing
1½ cups crème fraîche
1 bunch chives, finely chopped
1½ ounces caviar

1. In a bowl, combine the water, yeast and sugar and let stand for 5 minutes. Whisk in the 1½ cups of milk and the egg. Add both flours and the salt and whisk until smooth, then whisk in the 4 tablespoons of melted butter. Cover and let stand for 30 minutes.
2. Set a 10-inch nonstick skillet over moderate heat and brush with butter. Pour in a scant ⅓ cup of the batter and swirl to coat the pan. Cook the blini until tiny bubbles form on the surface and the bottom is browned, 2 minutes. Carefully flip the blini and cook until the bottom is lightly browned in spots, 30 seconds. Transfer to a baking sheet. Repeat with the remaining batter, buttering the pan and whisking in 1 or 2 tablespoons of milk to thin the batter as needed. You should have about 13 blini. Let cool slightly.
3. In a bowl, using a handheld electric mixer, beat the crème fraîche until stiff. Spread a thin layer on 8 or 9 blini and stack them; top with a plain blini. Trim off the rounded edges of the stack and cut into 1-inch squares. Dip a layered side of each square into the chives and set them on a platter. Dollop caviar on top and serve. —*Bob Spiegel*
WINE Light, lemony sparkling wine: NV Adami Garbèl Prosecco.

Buckwheat-Potato Knishes with Caviar

ACTIVE: 1 HR; TOTAL: 3 HR 30 MIN
MAKES 8 KNISHES ●

DOUGH
1 teaspoon active dry yeast
1 tablespoon plus ½ teaspoon sugar
6 tablespoons milk, warmed
1½ cups all-purpose flour, plus more for dusting
¼ cup buckwheat flour
1 teaspoon kosher salt
1 large egg, beaten
1 tablespoon unsalted butter, melted
FILLING
1 medium russet potato (½ pound), peeled and cut into 1-inch chunks
Salt
2 tablespoons vegetable oil, plus more for frying
1 medium leek, white and tender green parts, cut into ½-inch dice
1 tablespoon unsalted butter
¼ cup cream cheese, at room temperature
2 tablespoons heavy cream
Freshly ground pepper
1 large egg, lightly beaten
Sour cream, chopped dill, thinly sliced red onion and trout or paddlefish caviar, for garnish

1. PREPARE THE DOUGH In a small bowl, stir the yeast and ½ teaspoon of the sugar into the warm milk. Let stand until foamy, about 5 minutes.
2. In a large bowl, whisk the 1½ cups of all-purpose flour with the buckwheat flour, salt and the remaining 1 tablespoon of sugar. Stir in the yeast mixture, beaten egg and melted butter and knead until a smooth dough forms. Transfer the dough to a lightly oiled bowl, cover with plastic wrap and let stand in a warm place until doubled in volume, about 1¼ hours. Punch down the dough, cover and let rise again until doubled, about 1¼ hours longer.

3. MEANWHILE, PREPARE THE FILLING In a medium saucepan, cover the potato chunks with water and bring to a boil. Add a large pinch of salt and cook over moderately high heat until tender, about 8 minutes. Drain the potato and return the chunks to the pan, shaking over the heat to dry them out, about 10 seconds. Pass the warm potatoes through a ricer into a large bowl or mash them with a potato masher.
4. In a medium skillet, heat the 2 tablespoons of oil. Add the leek and a pinch of salt and cook over moderate heat, stirring occasionally, until softened, about 6 minutes. Remove from the heat and stir in the butter. Add the leek to the potatoes along with the cream cheese and heavy cream. Stir well and season with salt and pepper.
5. Punch down the dough again. Transfer to a lightly floured work surface and shape it into a rectangle. Roll the dough out into a 8-by-20-inch rectangle, about ⅛ inch thick. Cut the dough into eight 4-by-5-inch rectangles. Set 1 rectangle with a long side toward you and spoon ¼ cup of the potato filling on the top third; leave a ⅓-inch border on the top and sides. Bring the bottom of the dough up and over the filling, fold all the sides over themselves and press to seal. Repeat to form the remaining knishes. Brush with the beaten egg, coating the seams well. Place on a parchment paper–lined baking sheet and freeze for 10 minutes.
6. Preheat the oven to 350°. In a medium saucepan, heat 1½ inches of vegetable oil to 375°. Set a wire rack over a rimmed baking sheet near the stove. Fry 2 knishes at a time, turning them a few times, until richly browned, about 2 minutes. Using a slotted spoon, transfer the knishes to the rack to drain. Keep the fried knishes hot in the oven.
7. Cut the knishes on the diagonal into 2½-inch pieces. Top them with sour cream, dill, red onion and caviar and serve right away. —*Mario Carbone and Rich Torrisi*
MAKE AHEAD The knish filling can be refrigerated overnight. Bring to room temperature before proceeding.
WINE Lively California sparkling wine: NV Roederer Estate Brut.

● HEALTHY ● MAKE AHEAD ○ VEGETARIAN ● STAFF FAVORITE

buckwheat-potato knishes with caviar

Mixed-Bean Crudités with Olive-Anchovy Aioli

ACTIVE: 20 MIN; TOTAL: 1 HR
4 TO 6 SERVINGS ●

  1 large garlic clove, smashed
Pinch of salt
  6 plump oil-packed anchovies, chopped
  ½ cup mayonnaise
  ⅓ cup finely chopped pitted green olives
  ½ teaspoon finely grated lemon zest
  1 tablespoon fresh lemon juice
  ¼ cup extra-virgin olive oil
 1½ pounds mixed beans, such as string beans, haricots verts, romano beans, Dragon Tongues, yellow wax beans and purple beans

1. On a cutting board, mash the garlic with the salt to a paste. Add the anchovies and mash to a paste. Scrape the paste into a bowl and stir in the mayonnaise, olives, lemon zest and lemon juice. Gradually whisk in the olive oil. Cover the aioli with plastic wrap and refrigerate until chilled.

2. Meanwhile, fill a large bowl with ice water. Bring a large pot filled with 1 inch of salted water to a rolling boil. Spread the beans in a steamer basket and steam just until they are crisp-tender and the color is still vibrant, especially the purple beans (which turn green when fully cooked), about 1 to 2 minutes. Immediately plunge the beans into the ice water to stop them from cooking further; let cool completely. Drain the beans and pat them dry. Transfer the beans to a platter and serve with the aioli. —*Grace Parisi*

quick dips

anchoïade Puree anchovy, garlic and olive oil. Serve with black radish, fennel wedges and broccoli.

pistachio dip Grind pistachios, then mix with mayonnaise, lemon juice, vinegar, minced shallot and garlic, crème fraîche and fresh herbs. Serve with Belgian endive.

herbed crème fraîche Blend minced parsley, tarragon and chives with crème fraîche and fresh lemon juice; season with salt. Serve with blanched asparagus.

Mozzarella with Summer Squash and Olive Puree

⟳ TOTAL: 15 MIN • 4 SERVINGS ●

This dish, from chef Mathieu Perez of Paris's Aux Deux Amis, is a take on the classic Italian mozzarella-tomato-basil Caprese salad. It depends on young, very fresh zucchini and summer squash. To prepare the recipe like Perez does at the restaurant, grate the olives finely with a Microplane grater instead of pureeing them.

  ½ cup pitted kalamata olives, chopped
  1 pound fresh buffalo mozzarella, cut into wedges
  1 small zucchini, very thinly sliced
  1 small yellow squash, very thinly sliced
Extra-virgin olive oil, for drizzling
Flaky sea salt, freshly ground white pepper and piment d'Espelette or hot paprika, for sprinkling

In a mini processor, puree the olives. Strain the puree through a fine sieve; you should have about ¼ cup. Spread the olive puree on plates and arrange the mozzarella wedges and zucchini and squash slices on top. Drizzle olive oil over the cheese and sprinkle with salt, white pepper and piment d'Espelette. —*Mathieu Perez*

Zucchini-Tomato Verrines

TOTAL: 45 MIN PLUS 4 HR CHILLING
6 SERVINGS ●

Most Paris bistros serve at least one *verrine*: a multitextured salad or dessert layered in a glass. This one comes from French-born food stylist Béatrice Peltre of the blog La Tartine Gourmande.

  2 tablespoons pine nuts
  4 medium tomatoes—peeled, seeded and finely diced
  ½ cup finely diced zucchini
  1 garlic clove, minced
  3 tablespoons extra-virgin olive oil
  1 tablespoon fresh lemon juice
Pinch of ground cumin
  1 tablespoon each of finely chopped basil, dill and chives, plus small basil leaves for garnish
Salt and freshly ground pepper
  ½ cup mascarpone cheese, at room temperature
  2 large eggs, separated
  ⅓ cup finely grated Parmigiano-Reggiano cheese (about 1 ounce)
  3 very thin slices of prosciutto, cut in half

1. In a small skillet, toast the pine nuts over moderately low heat, tossing, until golden, about 4 minutes.

2. In a large bowl, toss the tomatoes with the zucchini, garlic, olive oil, lemon juice, cumin and chopped herbs. Season with salt and pepper. Spoon the zucchini-tomato salad into 6 small glasses or jars.

3. In a medium bowl, mix the mascarpone cheese with the 2 egg yolks and grated Parmigiano cheese. In another bowl, beat the egg whites with a pinch of salt until soft peaks form. Using a rubber spatula, fold the beaten whites into the mascarpone until no streaks remain. Season with salt and freshly ground pepper. Spoon the mascarpone cream into each glass over the zucchini-tomato salad. Cover each glass with plastic wrap and refrigerate for at least 4 hours.

4. Meanwhile, in a large nonstick skillet, cook the prosciutto slices over moderately low heat, turning once, until browned and just crisp, about 5 minutes. Transfer the prosciutto to a paper towel–lined plate.

5. Sprinkle the pine nuts over the mascarpone cream, top each *verrine* with a prosciutto crisp and a few basil leaves and serve. —*Béatrice Peltre*

MAKE AHEAD The *verrines* can be prepared through Step 2 and refrigerated overnight.

● HEALTHY ● MAKE AHEAD ● VEGETARIAN ● STAFF FAVORITE

mixed-bean crudités with olive-anchovy aioli

Pressure-Cooker-Braised Pine Nuts with Butternut Squash

TOTAL: 1 HR 15 MIN • 4 SERVINGS

- 1   small butternut squash (2¼ pounds)
- 1   tablespoon extra-virgin olive oil, plus more for drizzling

Salt and freshly ground pepper

- 1   cup Italian pine nuts (3½ ounces)
- 1   large shallot, minced
- 1   teaspoon tomato paste
- ½   cup dry white wine
- 1   cup low-sodium chicken broth

Pinch of saffron threads

Finely grated orange zest

- ½   cup Parmigiano-Reggiano shavings

1. Preheat the oven to 350°. Peel and slice the butternut squash ½ inch thick; spread on a baking sheet, drizzle with olive oil and season with salt and pepper. Cover with foil and roast until the squash is tender but not browned, about 45 minutes. Meanwhile, spread the pine nuts on a baking sheet and toast until golden, about 4 minutes.

2. Let the squash cool slightly, then transfer to a food processor and puree until smooth. Set aside 1 cup of the puree and reserve the rest for another use.

3. Heat the 1 tablespoon of olive oil in a pressure cooker. Add the shallot and cook over moderate heat, stirring, until softened, about 4 minutes. Add the pine nuts and tomato paste and cook, stirring, for 2 minutes. Add the wine and boil until reduced to 2 tablespoons, about 5 minutes. Add the chicken broth. Cover and cook at 15 PSI (see Note) for 7 minutes. Place the pressure cooker in the sink and run cold water over the lid to depressurize it rapidly; remove the lid once it can be released without force.

4. Return the pressure cooker to medium heat, uncovered, and bring the contents to a boil. Allow the liquid to reduce until the pine nuts are suspended in a thick sauce, about 4 minutes. Stir in the reserved squash puree and saffron and cook until heated through. Stir in a tablespoon of water if the puree is too thick. Season with salt and freshly ground pepper. Spoon the mixture into bowls, garnish with orange zest and the cheese shavings and serve right away.
—*Maxime Bilet and Nathan Myhrvold*

NOTE Fifteen pounds per square inch (PSI) is the most common setting for pressure cookers. Products vary, however, so be sure to consult the owner's manual.

Grilled Shrimp with Oregano and Lemon

ACTIVE: 30 MIN; TOTAL: 1 HR 30 MIN

8 SERVINGS ●

- ½   cup salted capers—rinsed, soaked for 1 hour and drained
- ½   cup oregano leaves
- 1   garlic clove, minced
- ¾   cup extra-virgin olive oil
- 1   teaspoon finely grated lemon zest
- 3   tablespoons freshly squeezed lemon juice

Freshly ground pepper

- 2½ pounds large shrimp, shelled and deveined

Salt

1. On a cutting board, finely chop the drained capers with the oregano leaves and garlic. Transfer the mixture to a bowl and stir in ½ cup plus 2 tablespoons of the olive oil along with the lemon zest and lemon juice. Season the sauce with pepper.

2. Light a grill or preheat a grill pan. In a large bowl, toss the shrimp with the remaining 2 tablespoons of olive oil and season lightly with salt and freshly ground pepper. Thread the shrimp onto metal skewers and grill over high heat, turning once, until the shrimp are lightly charred and cooked through, about 3 minutes per side. Remove the shrimp from the skewers and transfer them to a platter. Spoon the sauce on top and serve.
—*Ethan Stowell*

SERVE WITH Crusty bread.

MAKE AHEAD The sauce can be kept in the refrigerator overnight. Bring it to room temperature before serving.

WINE Crisp, zesty California Sauvignon Blanc: 2010 Geyser Peak Winery.

Pickled Shrimp with Creamy Spinach Dip

TOTAL: 30 MIN PLUS 8 HR MARINATING

8 SERVINGS ●

SHRIMP

- 3   cups water
- 2   cups white wine vinegar
- 1   cup sugar
- 4   garlic cloves, finely chopped
- 2   jalapeños, thinly sliced
- 2   bay leaves
- 1   tablespoon crushed red pepper
- 2   teaspoons kosher salt
- 1   teaspoon black peppercorns
- 1   teaspoon allspice berries
- 2   pounds large shrimp (16 to 20 per pound)—shelled and deveined, tails left on

DIP

- 1   cup heavy cream
- 1   pound spinach—stemmed, washed, dried and leaves coarsely chopped
- 1   cup crème fraîche
- 1   tablespoon fresh lemon juice

Salt

Cilantro leaves, for garnish

1. PREPARE THE SHRIMP In a large saucepan, combine the water with the vinegar, sugar, garlic, jalapeños, bay leaves, crushed red pepper, salt, peppercorns and allspice berries and bring to a boil to dissolve the sugar. Add the shrimp and cook, stirring, for 1 minute. Transfer the shrimp and liquid to a large bowl and let cool to room temperature. Cover and refrigerate for 8 to 10 hours.

2. MAKE THE DIP In a large saucepan, boil the cream over high heat until reduced by half, about 3 minutes. Add the spinach and cook, stirring, until wilted, about 1 minute. Transfer the spinach mixture to a bowl and let cool. Stir in the crème fraîche and lemon juice and season with salt.

3. Using a slotted spoon, lift the shrimp and jalapeños from the marinade and arrange on a platter. Garnish with cilantro leaves and serve the spinach dip in a bowl alongside.
—*James Holmes*

BEER Tangy hefeweizen: Harpoon UFO.

● HEALTHY ● MAKE AHEAD ○ VEGETARIAN ● STAFF FAVORITE

Tartare Delmonico with Béarnaise Sauce

ACTIVE: 30 MIN; TOTAL: 1 HR 30 MIN
4 SERVINGS ●

For their unconventional tartare, chefs Rich Torrisi and Mario Carbone of New York's Torrisi Italian Specialties quickly sear beef before finely chopping it. As an homage to Delmonico's, they use the Delmonico steak cut—the eye of the rib eye. "If you get a good steak at a place like Delmonico's, chances are you're having béarnaise with it," says Torrisi. "And if you get beef tartare, it should have an egg yolk. We mixed up those two ideas."

¾ pound boneless beef rib eye steak (about 1 inch thick)
Salt and freshly ground pepper
¼ cup white wine vinegar
2 small shallots, minced
2 large egg yolks
4 tablespoons unsalted butter, melted and hot
2 teaspoons chopped tarragon
¼ cup chopped parsley
¼ cup minced chives
1 tablespoon extra-virgin olive oil
Thick kettle-style potato chips, for serving

1. Light a grill or preheat a grill pan. Season the steak with salt and pepper and grill over high heat just until nicely charred outside and raw within, about 1½ minutes per side. Let the steak cool, then refrigerate until thoroughly chilled, about 1 hour.
2. Meanwhile, in a small saucepan, combine the wine vinegar with half of the minced shallots and boil over high heat until the vinegar is reduced to 1 tablespoon, about 3 minutes. Transfer the reduction to a small stainless steel bowl.
3. In a small saucepan, bring ½ inch of water to a boil; keep the water simmering over low heat. Add the egg yolks to the vinegar reduction and whisk over the simmering water until the mixture is thick, about 1 minute; if the egg sticks to the sides, remove the bowl from the simmering water to prevent overcooking the yolks.

4. Remove the bowl from the simmering water; gradually whisk in the butter. Stir in the tarragon; season with salt and pepper.
5. Trim the fat and silver skin from the steak. Chop the meat very finely and transfer to a bowl; alternatively, pass the meat through a meat grinder. Stir in the parsley, chives, olive oil and the remaining shallots; season lightly with salt and pepper.
6. Mound the tartare in the center of each plate. Carefully reheat the béarnaise sauce over the pan of simmering water, whisking constantly. Spoon the sauce over the steak tartare and serve right away, with potato chips. —*Mario Carbone and Rich Torrisi*
WINE Full-bodied, high-acid white: 2009 Bergström Riesling.

Crab and Celery Root Remoulade

TOTAL: 45 MIN PLUS 2 HR CHILLING
4 SERVINGS ● ●

2 tablespoons mayonnaise
2 tablespoons minced scallion
2 dashes Tabasco
1½ teaspoons whole-grain mustard
2 teaspoons dry white wine
1½ tablespoons fresh lemon juice
Pinch of celery seeds
½ pound celery root, peeled and halved
1 medium carrot
¼ cup very thinly sliced red onion
1 celery rib, very thinly sliced on a diagonal
½ pound cooked Dungeness crab (1¼ pounds in the shell) or other crab
Kosher salt and freshly ground pepper

1. In a medium bowl, whisk the mayonnaise, scallion, Tabasco, mustard, wine, lemon juice and celery seeds.
2. Using a mandoline, slice the celery root and carrot paper-thin. Finely julienne the celery root and carrot slices. Add the celery root, carrot, onion, celery and crab to the dressing and toss. Season with salt and pepper. Cover and refrigerate for at least 2 hours, then serve. —*Gabriel Rucker*

Tuna Ceviche with Avocado and Cilantro

ACTIVE: 30 MIN; TOTAL: 1 HR 30 MIN
6 SERVINGS ● ● ●

With only a few ingredients, this *salpimentado* (salt-and-pepper) ceviche from Chicago chef Rick Bayless is typical of what's served at stands around the southern tip of the Baja peninsula. Cooks often make it with *sierra,* a large and meaty Mexican fish, but tuna works just as well. Bayless, the host of PBS's *Mexico—One Plate at a Time,* got the idea for this recipe from Don Emiliano restaurant in San José del Cabo.

1 pound sushi-grade tuna, sliced ¼ inch thick
1 small red onion, halved and thinly sliced
¾ cup fresh lime juice (from about 5 limes)
1 teaspoon freshly ground black pepper
1 large Hass avocado, cut into ⅓-inch dice
¼ cup coarsely chopped cilantro, plus cilantro leaves for garnish
Salt
Tortilla chips, for serving

1. Line a baking sheet with plastic wrap. Arrange the tuna slices in a single layer on the baking sheet and freeze until fairly firm, about 15 minutes.
2. Stack the slices of tuna. Using a very sharp chef's knife, cut the tuna into neat ¼-inch cubes. Transfer the cubed tuna to a medium glass or ceramic bowl and stir in the red onion, lime juice and black pepper. Cover the tuna with plastic wrap and refrigerate for 1 hour, stirring gently with a plastic spatula every 15 to 20 minutes (the diced tuna will change color slightly).
3. Just before serving, gently fold in the diced avocado and chopped cilantro and season with salt. Transfer the ceviche to a bowl or individual glasses. Garnish with cilantro leaves and serve with tortilla chips. —*Rick Bayless*
BEER Light, lively Mexican lager: Pacifico.

As part of a dinner menu for members of R.E.M., Georgia chef Hugh Acheson assembles his grilled fall vegetable salad with boiled dressing, OPPOSITE; recipe, page 60.

salads

salads

Little Gem Salad with Lemon Vinaigrette

⏱ TOTAL: 30 MIN • 4 SERVINGS ●

This lovely salad from L.A. chef Nancy Silverton features Little Gem lettuce, a smaller, sweeter variety of romaine. If you can't find it, use hearts of romaine instead.

1 cup walnut halves
1 tablespoon walnut oil
Kosher salt
1 small shallot, minced
¼ cup fresh lemon juice
1 tablespoon Champagne vinegar
½ cup extra-virgin olive oil
Freshly ground pepper
4 ounces yellow squash, thinly sliced
3 thin red onion slices, separated into rings
4 heads of Little Gem lettuce
¼ cup freshly grated Pecorino Romano cheese, plus more for serving

1. Preheat the oven to 350°. Toast the walnuts on a pie plate until golden, 12 minutes. Let cool, then coarsely chop the nuts. Transfer to a bowl and toss with the walnut oil and a pinch of salt. In a small bowl, combine the shallot, lemon juice and vinegar and season with salt. Let stand for 10 minutes. Slowly whisk in the olive oil and season with pepper.
2. In a large bowl, toss the squash with the onion, lettuce, walnuts, ¼ cup of Pecorino Romano and half of the dressing. Serve with additional cheese. Reserve the remaining dressing for another use.
—Nancy Silverton (Adapted from The Mozza Cookbook: Recipes from Los Angeles's Favorite Italian Restaurant and Pizzeria by Nancy Silverton with Matt Molina and Carolynn Carreño, published by Alfred A. Knopf/A Division of Random House, Inc.)

Boston Lettuce and Radish Salad

⏱ TOTAL: 25 MIN • 8 SERVINGS ● ●

Katherine Anderson, the owner of Marigold and Mint flower and herb shop in Seattle, also adds sugar snap peas to this salad when they're in season, for a sweet crunch.

¼ cup extra-virgin olive oil
2 tablespoons sherry vinegar
½ teaspoon Dijon mustard
Salt and freshly ground black pepper
2 bunches of radishes (about 20)— tops reserved for another use, radishes very thinly sliced
3 heads of Boston lettuce, outer leaves discarded and tender inner leaves torn

In a large bowl, whisk the extra-virgin olive oil with the sherry vinegar and Dijon mustard and season with salt and freshly ground black pepper. Add the sliced radishes and Boston lettuce to the bowl, toss well, then serve the salad right away.
—Katherine Anderson

Caesar On the Light Side

⏱ TOTAL: 15 MIN • 4 SERVINGS ● ●

Star chef and healthy-eating advocate Jamie Oliver makes his Caesar salad dressing with thick Greek-style yogurt, which he often uses as a lighter alternative to heavy cream and sour cream. Oliver turns this salad into a more substantial dish by adding broiled, flaked salmon or grilled chicken breast.

⅓ cup low-fat or nonfat Greek-style yogurt
2 anchovy fillets, mashed
1 garlic clove, minced
2 tablespoons fresh lemon juice
2 teaspoons Worcestershire sauce
2 tablespoons extra-virgin olive oil
¼ cup freshly grated Parmigiano-Reggiano cheese
Salt and freshly ground pepper
1 large head of romaine lettuce, torn into bite-size pieces

1. In a small bowl, whisk the yogurt with the anchovies, garlic, lemon juice and Worcestershire sauce. Whisk in the oil and half of the cheese and season with salt and pepper.
2. In a large bowl, toss the romaine with half of the dressing and the remaining cheese. Serve, passing the remaining dressing at the table. —Jamie Oliver

Goddess Salad with Haricots Verts and Feta

⏱ TOTAL: 30 MIN • 6 SERVINGS ●

This bright-flavored salad from chef-owner Robert Moore of Moore's Delicatessen in Burbank, California, combines Bibb lettuce, haricots verts, feta cheese and hard-boiled eggs in a fresh thyme dressing. "It's the perfect salad for lunch or dinner," says Moore. It's also one of the few salads that's great almost any time of year.

Salt
½ pound haricots verts
1 tablespoon minced shallot
1 small garlic clove, minced
1 teaspoon Dijon mustard
3 tablespoons cider vinegar
3 tablespoons fresh lemon juice
¾ cup canola oil
1½ teaspoons thyme leaves
Freshly ground pepper
2 heads of Bibb or butter lettuce, torn into large pieces
½ pound feta cheese, crumbled
1 large seedless cucumber, thinly sliced
3 large hard-boiled eggs, quartered

1. In a medium saucepan of salted boiling water, cook the haricots verts until they are crisp-tender, about 4 minutes. Drain and cool under running water, then pat dry.
2. In a mini food processor, combine the shallot, garlic, mustard, cider vinegar and lemon juice and process until smooth. With the machine running, add the canola oil in a thin stream. Add the thyme and pulse until minced. Season the dressing with salt and freshly ground pepper.
3. In a large bowl, combine the lettuce with the crumbled feta, cucumber, hard-boiled eggs and haricots verts. Add three-fourths of the dressing and toss to coat. Drizzle with the remaining dressing and serve.
—Robert Moore

MAKE AHEAD The blanched haricots verts from Step 1 and the dressing from Step 2 can be refrigerated in separate containers for up to 3 days.

● HEALTHY ● MAKE AHEAD ● VEGETARIAN ● STAFF FAVORITE

boston lettuce and radish salad

Mixed Greens and Herb Salad with Figs and Walnuts

⏱ TOTAL: 20 MIN • 4 SERVINGS ● ●

Using whole herb leaves adds bursts of flavor to this salad. If you can find good fresh figs, use them here in place of dried.

½ cup walnuts
1 tablespoon sherry vinegar
¼ cup extra-virgin olive oil
Salt and freshly ground pepper
4 ounces dried Black Mission figs, thinly sliced (⅔ cup)
8 cups mixed greens
½ cup flat-leaf parsley leaves
2 tablespoons torn mint leaves
2 tablespoons chopped dill
2 tablespoons snipped chives
1 ounce fresh pecorino, shaved

1. Preheat the oven to 350°. Spread the walnuts in a pie plate and toast until golden, about 10 minutes; let cool, then coarsely chop.
2. In a large bowl, whisk the vinegar with the oil and season with salt and pepper. Add the figs, greens, parsley, mint, dill, chives, pecorino and walnuts and toss gently. Serve right away. —*Jessica Theroux*

Boston Lettuce with Cilantro and Walnuts

⏱ TOTAL: 10 MIN • 8 SERVINGS ● ●

Star Moscow restaurateur Katya Drozdova serves simple salads like this one from chef Dmitry Leonov. The combination of cilantro and walnuts is a distinctly Georgian touch.

2 tablespoons vegetable oil
2 tablespoons white wine vinegar
1 tablespoon freshly squeezed lemon juice
Salt and freshly ground black pepper
10 medium radishes, very thinly sliced on a mandoline
5 scallions, thinly sliced
1 head of Boston lettuce, small leaves left whole and large leaves torn
2 tablespoons chopped cilantro
3 tablespoons chopped walnuts

In a large bowl, whisk the oil with the vinegar and lemon juice and season with salt and pepper. Add the radishes, scallions, lettuce and cilantro and toss well. Garnish with the walnuts and serve right away.
—*Dmitry Leonov*

Chopped Salad with Blue Cheese Dressing

⏱ TOTAL: 25 MIN • 6 SERVINGS ●

This is the perfect salad for people who love blue cheese: Cookbook author Laura Werlin whisks some into the vinaigrette, then sprinkles more on top of the salad.

½ cup walnuts
1 tablespoon minced shallot
1½ teaspoons Dijon mustard
3 tablespoons sherry vinegar
Kosher salt and freshly ground black pepper
¼ cup extra-virgin olive oil
4 ounces blue cheese, crumbled
2 romaine hearts, quartered lengthwise and thinly sliced crosswise
½ fennel bulb, cored and finely chopped
2 carrots, finely chopped
½ seedless cucumber, seeded and cut into ½-inch dice
1 Fuji apple, cut into ½-inch dice
1 Hass avocado, cut into ½-inch dice
2 tablespoons thinly shredded basil leaves

1. Preheat the oven to 350°. Spread the walnuts in a pie plate and toast them for about 10 minutes, until they are golden. Let cool, then coarsely chop.
2. In a large bowl, whisk the shallot with the Dijon mustard and sherry vinegar and season generously with salt and pepper. Add the olive oil and whisk until smooth. Add half of the blue cheese and whisk until the dressing is creamy. Add the lettuce, fennel, carrots, cucumber, apple, avocado, basil and walnuts and season with salt and pepper. Toss the salad well to coat with the dressing. Top with the remaining blue cheese and serve right away. —*Laura Werlin*

Crunchy Cabbage Icebox Salad

TOTAL: 45 MIN PLUS 4 HR CHILLING
10 SERVINGS ● ● ●

"This is a salad you can keep in your refrigerator until you're ready to serve; just like your summer slaw, but for winter," says Jenn Louis, the chef at Lincoln restaurant and Sunshine Tavern in Portland, Oregon. The crisp vegetables in the salad mixed with the creamy cilantro-mint-yogurt dressing would also be excellent as a filling in Louis's Chicken Tinga Tacos (page 115).

3 cups fat-free plain Greek yogurt
½ cup skim milk
1 small garlic clove, minced
1 teaspoon cayenne pepper
½ cup thinly sliced chives
2 tablespoons chopped cilantro
1 tablespoon chopped mint
4 tablespoons freshly squeezed lime juice
Salt and freshly ground black pepper
1 Hass avocado, thinly sliced
8 cups finely shredded green cabbage (from a 2-pound head)
8 radishes, halved and thinly sliced
2 cups finely julienned peeled jicama (8 ounces)
3 scallions, thinly sliced
1 cup thinly sliced celery (3 ribs)
4 ounces crumbled Cotija cheese
¼ cup toasted pumpkin seeds

1. In a medium bowl, whisk the yogurt, milk, garlic, cayenne pepper, chives, cilantro, mint and 3 tablespoons of the lime juice. Season with salt and freshly ground black pepper.
2. In a small bowl, toss the avocado with the remaining 1 tablespoon of lime juice.
3. In a large baking dish or shallow casserole, spread the shredded cabbage in a thin layer. Top with the sliced radishes, jicama, scallions, celery and avocado. Spread the yogurt dressing on top, then sprinkle with the Cotija cheese. Cover the dish with plastic wrap and refrigerate for at least 4 hours or overnight. Just before serving, sprinkle the toasted pumpkin seeds on top.
—*Jenn Louis*

● HEALTHY ● MAKE AHEAD ● VEGETARIAN ● STAFF FAVORITE

mixed greens and herb salad with figs and walnuts

Spinach Salad with Citrus and Roasted Beets

**ACTIVE: 30 MIN; TOTAL: 1 HR 45 MIN
8 SERVINGS** ● ●

Curly leaf spinach has great texture and flavor and holds this mustardy dressing well.

- 12 small beets
- ¼ cup extra-virgin olive oil, plus more for drizzling
- ½ small red onion, very thinly sliced
- ¼ cup red wine vinegar
- Salt
- 3 tangerines
- 1 large red grapefruit
- 1½ tablespoons Dijon mustard
- Freshly ground black pepper
- ¾ pound curly leaf spinach (12 cups), stemmed and torn into bite-size pieces

1. Preheat the oven to 350°. Put the beets in a medium baking dish. Drizzle lightly with olive oil and rub to coat the beets. Cover with foil and bake for about 1 hour and 15 minutes, until the beets are tender. When the beets are cool enough to handle, peel and quarter them.
2. Meanwhile, in a small bowl, cover the onion slices with the vinegar. Add a large pinch of salt and mix well. Let stand for about 1 hour.
3. Using a sharp knife, peel the tangerines and grapefruit, removing all of the bitter white pith. Working over a bowl, cut in between the membranes to release the sections.
4. In a small bowl, whisk the mustard with 3 tablespoons of the vinegar from the onion slices. Whisk in the ¼ cup of olive oil and season with salt and pepper.
5. Put the spinach in a large bowl. Drain the onion slices and add to the spinach along with the tangerine, grapefruit and beets. Drizzle the mustard dressing over the salad and toss well. Serve right away.
—*Steven Satterfield*

MAKE AHEAD The roasted beets, pickled onion, tangerine and grapefruit sections and the mustard dressing can be refrigerated separately overnight. Bring to room temperature before making the salad.

Green Salad with Italian Vinaigrette

TOTAL: 15 MIN • 8 SERVINGS ● ●

With lots of vinegar, fresh parsley and garlic, this bold vinaigrette is a nostalgic upgrade of a pizza-parlor staple. "We never used creamy dressing when I was growing up; Italian vinaigrette was what we always had," says designer and home cook Linda Meyers.

- ¼ cup extra-virgin olive oil
- 3 tablespoons red wine vinegar
- 1 garlic clove, minced
- 1 tablespoon chopped parsley
- 1 teaspoon dried oregano
- 1 teaspoon Italian seasoning
- Salt and freshly ground pepper
- 1 head of Boston lettuce, torn
- 4 cups mesclun (4 ounces)
- 1 cucumber—peeled, seeded and cut into thin half-moons
- 1 pint cherry tomatoes, halved

1. In a small bowl, blend the olive oil, red wine vinegar, garlic, parsley, oregano and Italian seasoning. Season the Italian vinaigrette with salt and pepper.
2. In a large bowl, toss the remaining ingredients with the vinaigrette and serve.
—*Linda Meyers*

Boston Lettuce Salad with Herbs

TOTAL: 10 MIN • 2 SERVINGS ● ●

The herbed vinaigrette here would be lovely on any summer lettuces.

- ½ cup flat-leaf parsley leaves
- 1 large scallion, white and pale green parts only, chopped
- 2 teaspoons coarsely chopped tarragon
- 3 tablespoons vegetable oil
- 2 teaspoons white wine vinegar
- 1 tablespoon water
- Salt and freshly ground pepper
- 1 head of Boston lettuce, separated into leaves
- Chervil or tiny tarragon sprigs, for garnish

1. In a blender, combine the parsley, scallion, tarragon, vegetable oil, white wine vinegar and water and puree. Season the vinaigrette with salt and pepper.
2. On 2 plates, decoratively stack the Boston lettuce leaves to form a flower shape, using the largest leaves on the bottom and working up to the smallest leaves. Drizzle the salads with the vinaigrette, garnish with the herb sprigs and serve right away.
—*Marcia Kiesel*

Grilled Apricots with Burrata, Country Ham and Arugula

TOTAL: 30 MIN • 8 SERVINGS ●

Los Angeles chef Travis Lett uses burrata, a cream-filled mozzarella, to give his salad a bit of richness. "We've got this awesome burrata-maker in L.A., Gioia Cheese—one of the best producers of burrata outside of Italy," he says. Depending on the season, Lett also likes to make the salad with plums, peaches and pears.

- 1¼ pounds apricots, halved and pitted
- ¼ cup extra-virgin olive oil, plus more for brushing
- Sea salt and freshly ground pepper
- 1½ tablespoons freshly squeezed lemon juice
- 1 small head of radicchio, cored and thinly sliced
- 5 ounces baby arugula
- ½ pound burrata cheese, shredded
- 4 ounces shaved country ham
- 1 tablespoon aged balsamic vinegar

1. Light a grill or preheat a grill pan. Brush the apricots with olive oil and season with salt and pepper. Grill over high heat, cut side down, just until lightly charred, about 5 minutes. Let cool.
2. In a large bowl, whisk the lemon juice with the ¼ cup of olive oil and season with salt and pepper. Add the apricots, radicchio and arugula and toss gently. Transfer the salad to a platter and top with the burrata, ham and balsamic vinegar. Serve right away.
—*Travis Lett*

● HEALTHY ● MAKE AHEAD ○ VEGETARIAN ● STAFF FAVORITE

grilled apricots with burrata, country ham and arugula

Peach and Pistachio Salad

⏲ **TOTAL: 30 MIN • 6 SERVINGS** ● ●

Firm, underripe peaches are fantastic in this jicama-arugula salad because they're super-crunchy and not overly sweet.

- 1 large shallot, thinly sliced
- 1 large hot red chile, thinly sliced
- ½ teaspoon sugar
- 2½ tablespoons white wine vinegar
- 6 tablespoons extra-virgin
  olive oil
- Salt and freshly ground pepper
- 3 underripe medium peaches,
  very thinly sliced
- 1 small jicama (about 8 ounces),
  peeled and cut into
  ⅛-inch-thick matchsticks
- ¾ cup shelled, salted pistachios,
  coarsely chopped
- 2 cups baby arugula

In a large bowl, combine the shallot, red chile, sugar and white wine vinegar and let stand for 5 minutes. Whisk in the olive oil and season with salt and pepper. Add the peaches, jicama and pistachios and toss well. Fold in the arugula and season the salad with salt and pepper. Serve right away.
—*Grace Parisi*

autumn salad

In a bowl, whisk 2 tablespoons red wine vinegar, 1 tablespoon each of cranberry juice and finely chopped dried cranberries and ½ teaspoon Cranberry-Anise Bitters (page 391) or Peychaud's bitters. Gradually add 2 tablespoons olive oil in a thin stream, whisking constantly. Season the cranberry vinaigrette with salt and freshly ground pepper. Toss with arugula, endives, diced apples, crumbled farmer cheese and toasted pumpkin seeds.
—*Brad Thomas Parsons*

Hotel Russel Erskine Watercress Salad

⏲ **TOTAL: 20 MIN • 6 TO 8 SERVINGS** ● ●

This salad is Alabama chef James Boyce's homage to one served at a historic Huntsville hotel. The blend of horseradish, Worcestershire sauce and dry mustard makes for an unusually zesty vinaigrette.

- 2½ tablespoons cider vinegar
- 1½ teaspoons sugar
- 1½ teaspoons prepared horseradish
- ½ teaspoon Worcestershire sauce
- ½ teaspoon sweet paprika
- Pinch of dry mustard
- ½ cup extra-virgin olive oil
- Four 6-ounce bunches of watercress,
  thick stems discarded
- Salt and freshly ground white pepper

1. In a blender, combine the cider vinegar, sugar, horseradish, Worcestershire sauce, paprika and mustard. Gradually add the olive oil in a thin stream and blend until the dressing is emulsified.
2. In a large bowl, toss the watercress with the dressing. Season with salt and white pepper and serve right away.
—*James Boyce*

Endive Salad with Persimmons and Hazelnuts

⏲ **TOTAL: 30 MIN • 10 SERVINGS** ● ●

- ½ cup hazelnuts
- 1 pound Belgian endives, cut
  crosswise into 1-inch pieces
- 1 pound radicchio or Treviso, torn
- 1 Bosc pear—quartered, cored and
  cut into ½-inch cubes
- 1 fuyu persimmon, cut into
  ½-inch cubes
- 4 ounces baby arugula
- 2 tablespoons Dijon mustard
- 2 tablespoons fresh lemon juice
- 2 tablespoons white wine vinegar
- ¼ cup extra-virgin olive oil
- ¼ cup canola oil
- ¼ cup hazelnut oil
- Salt and freshly ground pepper

1. Preheat the oven to 375°. Spread the hazelnuts in a pie plate and toast for about 14 minutes, until fragrant and the skins blister. Transfer the nuts to a kitchen towel and let cool slightly. Rub the nuts together to remove the skins, then transfer to a work surface and coarsely chop. Let cool completely.
2. In a large bowl, toss the endives, radicchio, pear, persimmon and arugula. In a small bowl, whisk the mustard, lemon juice and vinegar. Whisk in the olive, canola and hazelnut oils and season with salt and pepper. Just before serving, pour the dressing over the salad, toss well and garnish with the toasted hazelnuts. —*Jeff Cerciello*
WINE Nutty oxidized white: 2007 Domaine Berthet-Bondet Côtes du Jura Tradition.

Jicama, Citrus and Watercress Salad

⏲ **TOTAL: 30 MIN • 6 SERVINGS** ● ●

- ¼ cup pomegranate juice
- 1 tablespoon seasoned rice vinegar
- 1½ teaspoons agave nectar
- 1½ teaspoons Dijon mustard
- ½ teaspoon finely grated
  lime zest
- ½ cup canola oil
- Salt and freshly ground pepper
- 1 red grapefruit
- 2 navel oranges
- 1 pound jicama, peeled and cut into
  2-by-¼-inch matchsticks
- 2 bunches of watercress,
  thick stems discarded
- ⅓ cup pomegranate seeds

1. In a blender, combine the pomegranate juice, vinegar, agave nectar, mustard and lime zest. With the machine on, add the oil in a thin stream and blend until emulsified. Season the dressing with salt and pepper.
2. Using a sharp knife, peel the grapefruit and oranges, removing all of the bitter white pith. Working over a bowl, cut in between the membranes to release the sections. Add the jicama, watercress and pomegranate seeds to the bowl. Add the dressing, toss gently and serve right away. —*Steve Sicinski*

● HEALTHY ● MAKE AHEAD ● VEGETARIAN ● STAFF FAVORITE

endive salad with persimmons and hazelnuts

Lao Mixed Salad with Peanuts and Fried Shallots

⏱ **TOTAL: 35 MIN • 4 SERVINGS** ● ●

A specialty of Luang Prabang, a small city in Laos, this salad includes an array of hearty ingredients: greens, fried shallot and garlic, hard-boiled egg, salted peanuts, tomatoes and cucumber.

- 1 **large hard-boiled egg,** peeled and halved
- 1 **tablespoon plus 1 teaspoon** white vinegar
- 1 **teaspoon honey**
- 2 **tablespoons plus 2 teaspoons** vegetable oil, plus more for frying

Salt and freshly ground black pepper

- 1 **large shallot, thinly sliced and** separated into rings
- 2 **large garlic cloves, thinly sliced**
- 2 **medium tomatoes, sliced**
- 1 **medium cucumber, peeled and sliced**
- 4 **cups packed mesclun salad**
- 1 **bunch of watercress (6 ounces),** thick stems discarded
- 2 **tablespoons chopped salted peanuts**

1. Separate the egg yolk from the white. Thinly slice the white. Put the egg yolk in a blender, add the vinegar and honey and blend until smooth. With the blender on, slowly pour in the 2 tablespoons plus 2 teaspoons of oil. Season the dressing with salt and pepper.
2. In a medium skillet, heat ¼ inch of oil. Add the shallot rings and fry over moderate heat, stirring a few times, until golden brown and crisp, about 3 minutes. With a slotted spoon, transfer the shallot rings to paper towels to drain. Add the garlic to the hot oil and fry, stirring a few times, until golden, about 1 minute. Transfer the garlic to the paper towels.
3. In a large bowl, drizzle the tomato and cucumber slices with 1 tablespoon of the dressing and toss gently. Arrange the slices around a platter. Add the mesclun, watercress and sliced egg white to the bowl, top with the remaining dressing and toss well. Mound the salad on the platter, garnish with the peanuts and the fried shallot and garlic and serve. —*Sebastien Rubis*

Celery, Grilled Grape and Mushroom Salad

⏱ **TOTAL: 45 MIN • 6 SERVINGS** ● ●

"Celery is a vegetable people either love or hate, and we try to get people to love all their vegetables," says chef Amanda Cohen of New York City's Dirt Candy. She sets off celery's bitterness and crunch with meaty oyster mushrooms and grapes that have been grilled until almost bursting.

- 2 **tablespoons white wine vinegar**
- 2 **teaspoons fresh lemon juice**
- ½ **teaspoon celery seeds**
- ¼ **teaspoon Dijon mustard**
- 2 **small garlic cloves, minced**
- ½ **cup plus 1 tablespoon extra-virgin** olive oil, plus more for brushing
- ¼ **cup roasted almond oil**

Salt and freshly ground pepper

- ½ **cup flat-leaf parsley leaves**
- ½ **cup tender celery leaves** (from 1 head)
- ¼ **cup salted roasted almonds,** chopped
- 1 **pound king oyster mushrooms,** sliced lengthwise ¼ inch thick
- 2 **cups green grapes (12 ounces)**
- 2 **heads of butter lettuce,** leaves separated
- 2 **cups very thinly sliced celery**

1. In a small bowl, whisk the vinegar with the lemon juice, celery seeds, mustard and half of the garlic. Gradually whisk in ¼ cup of the olive oil and the almond oil until emulsified. Season the dressing with salt and pepper.
2. In a mini food processor, combine the remaining garlic with the parsley, celery leaves and almonds and pulse until finely chopped. Add another ¼ cup of the olive oil and puree to a chunky paste. Season the pesto with salt and pepper.
3. Light a grill or preheat a grill pan. Brush the mushrooms with oil and season with salt and pepper. Grill over high heat, turning once, until tender and browned, 5 minutes. In a bowl, toss the grapes with the remaining 1 tablespoon of olive oil and season with salt and pepper. Grill over high heat until the

skins begin to blacken in spots, 3 minutes; line the grill with perforated foil if the grapes will fall through. Transfer the grapes and mushrooms to a bowl; toss with the pesto.
4. Arrange the lettuce leaves on a platter and drizzle with half of the dressing. Spoon the mushroom-and-grape salad onto the lettuce. Toss the celery with the remaining dressing, spoon it on top and serve.
—*Amanda Cohen*

Cabbage, Cucumber and Fennel Salad with Dill

ACTIVE: 30 MIN; TOTAL: 1 HR
10 SERVINGS ●

To keep the vegetables in this salad crisp, chef Jeff Cerciello of L.A.'s Farmshop restaurant soaks them in ice water and then dries them in a salad spinner.

- 1¼ **pounds Savoy cabbage, very thinly** sliced on a mandoline (6 cups)
- 1 **medium sweet onion, very thinly** sliced on a mandoline
- 1½ **pounds fennel bulbs—halved,** cored and very thinly shaved on a mandoline

Ice water

- 1 **seedless cucumber, halved** lengthwise and sliced crosswise ⅛ inch thick

Kosher salt

- 1 **cup crème fraîche**
- 2 **tablespoons white wine vinegar**
- ½ **cup chopped dill**
- 3 **tablespoons poppy seeds**

1. Put the cabbage, onion and fennel in 3 separate bowls and cover with ice water; let stand for 30 minutes. Drain the vegetables and spin dry in a salad spinner. In another bowl, toss the cucumbers with 2 teaspoons of salt and cover with ice water. Let stand for 30 minutes, then drain and pat dry.
2. In a large bowl, whisk the crème fraîche with the vinegar until stiff. Add the dill and poppy seeds and season generously with salt. Fold in the cabbage, onion, fennel and cucumber and serve right away.
—*Jeff Cerciello*

● HEALTHY ● MAKE AHEAD ○ VEGETARIAN ○ STAFF FAVORITE

cabbage, cucumber and fennel salad with dill

Roasted Brussels Sprouts with Cabbage and Pine Nuts

⏱ TOTAL: 40 MIN • 4 SERVINGS ●●○○

If you're worried about pesticides on your produce, simplify your choices by eating more cabbage and brussels sprouts, which have very little pesticide residue (even when not organic). Nicolas Jammet of the Sweetgreen chain in Washington, DC, unites them in this fantastic fruit-and-nut-studded salad.

- ½ cup pine nuts
- 1 pound brussels sprouts, quartered
- 6 tablespoons extra-virgin olive oil
- Salt and freshly ground black pepper
- 3 tablespoons fresh lemon juice
- 2 tablespoons honey
- 2 teaspoons Dijon mustard
- ⅛ teaspoon cayenne pepper
- ½ teaspoon pure chile powder, such as ancho
- 1½ pounds red cabbage, very thinly sliced on a mandoline (6 cups)
- ½ cup dried cranberries
- 4 garlic cloves, thinly sliced
- 1 ounce Parmigiano-Reggiano cheese, thinly shaved

1. Preheat the oven to 450°. Spread the pine nuts in a pie plate and toast for about 3 minutes, until golden brown. On a large rimmed baking sheet, toss the brussels sprouts with 1 tablespoon of the olive oil and season with salt and freshly ground black pepper. Roast for about 15 minutes, until the brussels sprouts are lightly caramelized and tender.
2. Meanwhile, in a small bowl, whisk the lemon juice with the honey, mustard, cayenne and chile powder. Slowly whisk in ¼ cup of the olive oil; season the dressing with salt and freshly ground black pepper.
3. In a large bowl, toss the cabbage with the toasted pine nuts and cranberries. In a small skillet, heat the remaining olive oil. Add the garlic and cook over moderate heat until golden, about 1 minute. Scrape the garlic and hot oil over the cabbage. Add the brussels sprouts and toss, then add the dressing and toss again. Scatter the cheese shavings over the top and serve. —*Nicolas Jammet*

Greek-Style Tomato Salad with Mint and Feta

⏱ TOTAL: 20 MIN • 6 SERVINGS ●○

A classic Greek salad has tomatoes and feta; this version by chef André Natera of Dallas's Fairmont Hotel also takes advantage of the mint and arugula that grow so well in his roof garden.

- 1½ pounds tomatoes, cored and diced (4 cups)
- 2 tablespoons torn mint leaves
- 2 radishes, thinly sliced (¼ cup)
- ¼ cup extra-virgin olive oil
- Salt and freshly ground pepper
- 2 cups baby arugula (2 ounces)
- ½ cup crumbled feta (3 ounces)

In a large bowl, toss the tomatoes with the mint, radishes and olive oil and season with salt and freshly ground pepper. Add the arugula and half of the feta and toss gently. Transfer the salad to a platter and sprinkle the remaining feta on top. Serve right away. —*André Natera*

Tomato Salad with Pickled Walnuts and Blue Cheese

⏱ TOTAL: 15 MIN • 4 SERVINGS ○

Top Chef: All-Stars winner Richard Blais garnishes his take on a Caprese salad with pickled walnuts, made by tossing candied walnuts with vinegar. (Alternatively, use British pickled walnuts, available at some specialty food stores.) "The blue cheese and celery add a little 'adultness,'" he says.

- ½ cup candied walnuts, coarsely chopped
- 1 tablespoon plus 1 teaspoon sherry vinegar
- 2 teaspoons Dijon mustard
- 3 tablespoons extra-virgin olive oil
- Salt and freshly ground pepper
- 2 pounds assorted heirloom tomatoes—thickly sliced, quartered or halved if small
- 2 small celery ribs with leaves, ribs thinly sliced crosswise
- ¼ cup crumbled blue cheese

1. In a small bowl, toss the candied walnuts with 2 teaspoons of the sherry vinegar and let stand for 10 minutes.
2. In another bowl, whisk the mustard with the remaining 2 teaspoons of vinegar and the olive oil and season with salt and pepper.
3. Arrange the tomatoes on a platter; season with salt. Add the celery and leaves, nuts and cheese. Drizzle with the dressing and serve. —*Richard Blais*

Fresh Tomato and Caper Salad

⏱ ACTIVE: 15 MIN; TOTAL: 45 MIN
4 SERVINGS ●○

When guests sit down to the dinner table, Moroccan hosts often set out small salads to eat with bread or on their own. Paula Wolfert, author of *The Food of Morocco*, found this salad in Essaouira, along the country's Atlantic coast. She says that it's rare to see capers in Moroccan salads, even though the country is one of the world's leading suppliers.

- 2 pounds red tomatoes—peeled, halved, seeded and finely diced (about 3 cups)
- 2 small celery ribs, finely diced (¼ cup)
- 1 small red onion, finely diced (½ cup)
- 1 small green bell pepper— peeled, cored, seeded and diced
- 1 tablespoon finely chopped preserved lemon peel (see Note)
- 2 tablespoons capers
- 3 tablespoons extra-virgin olive oil or argan oil (see Note)
- 2 tablespoons freshly squeezed lemon juice
- Salt and freshly ground black pepper

In a large bowl, toss the tomatoes with the celery, onion, green bell pepper, preserved lemon peel and capers. Add the olive oil and lemon juice and toss again. Season with salt and pepper. Refrigerate the salad for at least 30 minutes before serving. —*Paula Wolfert*
NOTE Preserved lemons are cured in salt and lemon juice. Argan oil has an intense, nutty flavor. Both ingredients are available from *chefshop.com* and at Middle Eastern and specialty food markets.

● HEALTHY ● MAKE AHEAD ○ VEGETARIAN ● STAFF FAVORITE

tomato salad with pickled walnuts and blue cheese

Israeli Couscous and Tomato Salad with Arugula Pesto

⏱ TOTAL: 30 MIN • 8 SERVINGS ● ● ○ ○

The trick to making this bright, peppery arugula pesto is to blanch the arugula and squeeze it dry. That way, when you blend it with the pine nuts, garlic, olive oil and cheese, the resulting mixture isn't too watery.

  6 cups packed arugula (6 ounces), plus whole leaves for garnish
  2 cups Israeli couscous (12 ounces)
  ½ cup extra-virgin olive oil, plus more for drizzling
  ¼ cup pine nuts
  4 garlic cloves, chopped
  ¼ cup freshly grated Parmigiano-Reggiano cheese
Salt and freshly ground black pepper
1½ pints red cherry tomatoes, halved
  4 yellow or orange tomatoes, cut into 1-inch dice

1. Bring a large saucepan of salted water to a boil. Add the 6 cups of arugula; blanch for about 10 seconds. Using a slotted spoon, transfer the arugula to a colander. Rinse under cold water to stop the cooking, then drain thoroughly.
2. Add the Israeli couscous to the boiling water and cook over moderately high heat, stirring occasionally, until it is al dente, about 10 minutes. Drain the couscous and spread it out on a large baking sheet. Drizzle lightly with olive oil and toss to prevent it from clumping. Let the couscous cool to room temperature.
3. In a small skillet, toast the pine nuts over moderate heat, tossing them, until they are golden brown and fragrant, about 2 minutes. Let the pine nuts cool.
4. Carefully squeeze the excess water from the blanched arugula and coarsely chop it. Transfer the arugula to a food processor. Add the toasted pine nuts, garlic, grated Parmigiano-Reggiano cheese and the ½ cup of olive oil and process until the pine nuts are finely chopped. Season the arugula pesto with salt and black pepper.

5. Transfer the couscous to a large serving bowl and stir in the arugula pesto. Gently fold in the tomatoes. Garnish with the arugula leaves and serve. —*Jeremy Sewall*
MAKE AHEAD The couscous salad can be refrigerated for up to 2 hours.

Grilled Bread and Marinated Tomato Salad

ACTIVE: 30 MIN; TOTAL: 1 HR 30 MIN
8 SERVINGS ○

Grilling the bread for this *panzanella* (bread salad) adds a slight smokiness and crunch. The dish is great for entertaining—the tomatoes marinate ahead of time, so to serve the dish all you have to do is grill the bread and assemble the salad.

  1 garlic clove, smashed
Salt
  2 pounds heirloom tomatoes, cut into 1-inch pieces
  1 small red onion, thinly sliced
  ¼ cup red wine vinegar
  ¾ cup extra-virgin olive oil, plus more for brushing
Freshly ground pepper
  1 loaf of country bread (12 ounces), sliced ½ inch thick
  2 bunches of arugula (6 ounces each), stems discarded
  5 ounces *ricotta salata*, crumbled (1¼ cups)

1. On a cutting board, using the flat side of a chef's knife, mash the garlic clove to a paste with a pinch of salt; transfer to a large bowl. Add the tomatoes, onion, vinegar and the ¾ cup of olive oil and season with salt and pepper. Let the mixture stand at room temperature, stirring a few times, for at least 1 hour or up to 2 hours.
2. Light a grill or preheat a grill pan. Brush the bread with olive oil and grill over high heat until toasted and lightly charred in spots, 1 minute per side. Let cool slightly, then cut into ½-inch cubes.
3. Add the bread and arugula to the tomatoes along with the *ricotta salata* and toss to combine. Serve right away. —*Ethan Stowell*

Tomato Aspic

ACTIVE: 30 MIN; TOTAL: 3 HR 30 MIN
8 SERVINGS ● ●

Chilled jellied salads were popular on hot days in '60s-era Mississippi, and they were often a centerpiece at ladies' luncheons. This tomato aspic, which acclaimed Southern cookbook author Martha Hall Foose created for the 2011 movie *The Help*, is like a wobbly take on a Virgin Mary.

 24 ounces canned tomato juice
  2 envelopes unflavored powdered gelatin (1½ tablespoons)
  ½ tablespoon dark brown sugar
  ½ tablespoon kosher salt
  ½ tablespoon pickling spices, ground
  ½ teaspoon hot sauce
  ½ teaspoon finely grated lemon zest
1½ tablespoons fresh lemon juice
Vegetable oil, for brushing
  ½ small onion, minced
  ½ small green bell pepper, finely chopped
  2 small celery ribs, finely chopped
Sliced hard-boiled eggs and steamed asparagus, for serving

1. In a large bowl, combine ½ cup of the tomato juice with the gelatin; let stand for about 5 minutes.
2. In a large saucepan, combine the remaining tomato juice with the dark brown sugar, salt, pickling spices, hot sauce, lemon zest and lemon juice and heat just until warm. Add the gelatin mixture and stir until it dissolves completely. Return the mixture to the large bowl and refrigerate until cold but not set, about 1 hour.
3. Lightly oil eight ½-cup ramekins. Stir the onion, bell pepper and celery into the tomato aspic and spoon it into the prepared ramekins. Refrigerate for at least 2 hours, until chilled and set.
4. Carefully unmold the aspics onto plates and serve with sliced hard-boiled eggs and steamed asparagus spears. —*Martha Hall Foose*
MAKE AHEAD The aspics can be refrigerated in their ramekins for up to up to 3 days.

● HEALTHY ● MAKE AHEAD ○ VEGETARIAN ○ STAFF FAVORITE

israeli couscous and tomato salad with arugula pesto

salads

Green Bean Slaw

⏱ TOTAL: 30 MIN • 10 SERVINGS ● ●

1¼ pounds haricots verts
     (thin green beans)
2 tablespoons extra-virgin olive oil
1 garlic clove, minced
¼ cup plus 1 tablespoon cider vinegar
2½ tablespoons water
1½ teaspoons Dijon mustard
1½ teaspoons honey
¼ teaspoon celery seeds
1 medium carrot, cut into fine julienne
1 medium parsnip, cut into
     fine julienne
1 red bell pepper, cut into fine julienne
½ small red onion, thinly sliced
Worcestershire sauce
Hot sauce
Salt and freshly ground black pepper
1 hard-boiled egg, chopped,
     for garnish (optional)

1. In a large pot of boiling salted water, cook the beans until they are crisp-tender, about 2 minutes. Drain, rinse and pat dry.
2. In a large skillet, heat the olive oil. Add the garlic and cook over moderate heat until fragrant, about 30 seconds. Stir in the vinegar, water, mustard, honey and celery seeds. Add the carrot, parsnip, red pepper and onion and toss until warmed through, about 1 minute. Transfer to a large bowl. Add the beans and toss well. Add a few dashes of Worcestershire sauce and hot sauce and season with salt and pepper. Garnish the slaw with the chopped egg and serve warm or at room temperature. —Lee Woolver

vegan tip

Hijiki, wakame and other seaweeds have a brininess that tastes of the ocean. A good substitute for fish, they add richness and savory umami notes to vegetable dishes, as in the Hijiki Salad and Wakame and Cucumber Salad on this page.

Asian Cucumber Salad

⏱ TOTAL: 10 MIN • 4 SERVINGS ● ● ●

½ pound Japanese or English
     cucumbers, peeled and thinly sliced
     lengthwise on a mandoline
1 medium carrot, very thinly sliced
     on a mandoline
3 scallion greens, cut into thin strips
2 tablespoons extra-virgin olive oil
Juice of 1 lime
Salt and freshly ground pepper

In a large bowl, toss all of the ingredients together and serve. —Santos Majano

Worms in Dirt (Hijiki Salad)

ACTIVE: 30 MIN; TOTAL: 2 HR 30 MIN
8 SERVINGS ● ●

Black Japanese seaweed (hijiki) mixed with squiggly fried tofu strips makes a tasty Halloween salad that just happens to look like worms in a freshly dug grave.

1 cup dried hijiki (2 ounces), see Note
¼ cup soy sauce
¼ cup mirin
2 teaspoons sugar
½ teaspoon dashi powder (see Note),
     dissolved in ½ cup of hot water
2 tablespoons vegetable oil
4 carrots, cut into 3-inch matchsticks
1 cup thinly sliced fried tofu,
     about 1 ounce (see Note)
2 tablespoons seasoned
     rice vinegar
2 teaspoons toasted sesame oil
Black sesame seeds, for garnish

1. In a bowl, cover the hijiki with warm water and let stand for 1 hour. Drain, pressing out any excess water. In a small bowl, combine the soy, mirin, sugar and dissolved dashi.
2. Heat the vegetable oil in a saucepan. Add the carrots and fried tofu and cook over high heat for 1 minute. Stir in the hijiki. Add the soy mixture and simmer over moderately low heat, stirring occasionally, until the carrots are tender and the liquid is absorbed, about 15 minutes.

3. Transfer the hijiki salad to a large bowl and refrigerate until chilled, 1 hour.
4. In a small bowl, whisk the vinegar with the sesame oil. Add the dressing to the salad and toss to coat. Sprinkle with sesame seeds and serve. —Grace Parisi

NOTE Dried hijiki, dashi powder and fried tofu (aburaage) are sold at Japanese markets.
MAKE AHEAD The hijiki salad can be refrigerated overnight.

Wakame and Cucumber Salad

⏱ ACTIVE: 20 MIN; TOTAL: 40 MIN
4 SERVINGS ● ● ●

Kacie Loparto harvests seaweed along the coast of Maine and sells it at farmers' markets and on her website, shesellsseaweed.com. She especially loves wakame mixed with miso, ginger and cucumber.

2 ounces wakame (see Note)
¼ cup rice vinegar
1 tablespoon fresh lime juice
1 tablespoon yellow miso paste
1 tablespoon finely grated
     fresh ginger
1 teaspoon honey
½ cup vegetable oil
1 teaspoon toasted sesame oil
Salt
6 small Persian cucumbers (or 1 large
     seedless cucumber), thinly sliced
2 scallions, thinly sliced
Toasted sesame seeds, for garnish

1. Bring a medium saucepan of water to a boil. Add the wakame and remove the saucepan from the heat; let stand until softened, 20 minutes. Drain the wakame, rinse under cold water and pat dry. Remove any tough ribs from the wakame and thinly slice.
2. In a medium bowl, whisk the rice vinegar with the lime juice, miso paste, ginger, and honey. Whisk in the vegetable oil and sesame oil and season the dressing with salt. Add the wakame along with the cucumbers and scallions and toss well. Garnish the salad with toasted sesame seeds and serve right away. —Kacie Loparto

NOTE Wakame is available at Asian markets.

54

● HEALTHY ● MAKE AHEAD ● VEGETARIAN ● STAFF FAVORITE

green bean slaw

Kohlrabi, Fennel and Blueberry Salad

⏲ **TOTAL: 30 MIN • 6 SERVINGS** ● ●

Kohlrabi tastes a lot like a broccoli stem, but it's milder and sweeter and the texture is crisper. F&W Best New Chef 2011 Stephanie Izard of Girl & the Goat in Chicago thinks it's an underappreciated vegetable, so she makes it the star of this excellent salad. She likes the dish so much that she takes some home to eat a few times a week.

½ cup sliced almonds

2 tablespoons minced peeled fresh ginger

2 tablespoons minced shallot

1 tablespoon white balsamic vinegar

1 tablespoon mayonnaise

1½ teaspoons Dijon mustard

1 teaspoon soy sauce

1 teaspoon pure maple syrup

¼ cup grapeseed oil

Salt and freshly ground pepper

1¼ pounds kohlrabi, peeled and very thinly sliced on a mandoline

1 fennel bulb, trimmed and thinly sliced on a mandoline

2 ounces semifirm goat cheese, such as Evalon, Garrotxa or Manchester, shaved (½ cup)

1 cup blueberries or pitted, halved sweet cherries

2 tablespoons torn mint leaves

1. Preheat the oven to 350° and spread the almonds in a pie plate. Toast for about 7 minutes, until golden. Let cool.

2. In a mini food processor or a blender, combine the ginger, shallot, vinegar, mayonnaise, mustard, soy sauce and maple syrup and puree. With the blender on, add the grapeseed oil in a thin stream and blend until creamy. Season the dressing with salt and pepper.

3. In a large bowl, toss the kohlrabi with the fennel, cheese, toasted almonds and dressing. Season with salt and pepper and toss to coat. Add the blueberries and mint, toss gently and serve. —*Stephanie Izard*

WINE Lively, substantial white: 2010 Pine Ridge Chenin Blanc–Viognier.

Grilled Eggplant Salad with Walnuts

⏲ **TOTAL: 35 MIN • 8 SERVINGS** ● ● ●

Terrific as a salad or a spread for flatbread, *adzhapsandali* is like the country of Georgia's version of ratatouille. Grilling the eggplant gives the dish a luscious, smoky flavor.

Two 1-pound eggplants, sliced lengthwise ½ inch thick

1 large jalapeño

Vegetable oil, for brushing

Salt

¼ cup chopped cilantro

3 tablespoons white wine vinegar

1 garlic clove, minced

5 medium tomatoes, cut into ½-inch dice

1 small red onion, thinly sliced into rings

2 tablespoons chopped walnuts

Grilled flatbread, for serving

1. Light a grill or preheat a grill pan. Brush the eggplant slices and the jalapeño all over with vegetable oil and season with salt. Grill the eggplant over moderate heat until nicely charred and tender, about 4 minutes per side. Transfer the eggplant to a work surface and let cool. Grill the jalapeño, turning it occasionally, until charred and almost tender, about 4 minutes. Peel and seed the jalapeño, then finely chop it. Cut the eggplant into ½-inch dice.

2. In a large bowl, combine the cilantro, vinegar and garlic. Add the eggplant, jalapeño, tomatoes and onion, season with salt and toss. Garnish with the walnuts and serve the salad with grilled flatbread. —*Dmitry Leonov*

MAKE AHEAD The salad can stand at room temperature for up to 1 hour.

Cucumber and Baby Pea Salad

⏲ **TOTAL: 20 MIN • 8 SERVINGS** ● ● ●

This untraditional green salad from Seattle chef Ethan Stowell contains no lettuce and no vinaigrette—just sliced cucumbers, baby peas, parsley leaves and fresh basil in a tangy yogurt dressing.

1 cup plain whole-milk Greek yogurt

3 tablespoons fresh lemon juice

¼ cup extra-virgin olive oil

1 cup flat-leaf parsley leaves

¼ cup finely shredded basil leaves

Salt and freshly ground pepper

1 pound frozen baby peas, thawed

3 large seedless cucumbers (about 1 pound each)—peeled, halved lengthwise, seeded and sliced crosswise ½ inch thick

In a large bowl, whisk the yogurt with the lemon juice and olive oil. Add the parsley and basil and season with salt and pepper. Stir in the peas and cucumbers and serve. —*Ethan Stowell*

MAKE AHEAD The salad can be refrigerated for up to 4 hours. Serve lightly chilled.

Shaved Zucchini Salad with Parmigiano and Pistachios

⏲ **TOTAL: 15 MIN • 6 SERVINGS** ● ●

One of the great things about this lemony salad from Burgundy winemaker Louis-Michel Liger-Belair is that it's so quick to make. Since the zucchini is served raw, be sure to use the smallest, freshest ones you can find. The salad can be garnished with roasted pistachios, which add a little sweetness, or Italian pine nuts.

3 tablespoons extra-virgin olive oil

1 teaspoon finely grated lemon zest

1½ tablespoons fresh lemon juice

Salt and freshly ground pepper

2 pounds small, firm zucchini, very thinly sliced lengthwise on a mandoline

⅓ cup shaved Parmigiano-Reggiano cheese (about 1½ ounces)

3 tablespoons lightly salted roasted pistachios

In a small bowl, whisk the oil with the lemon zest and juice. Season with salt and pepper. In a large bowl, toss the sliced zucchini with the lemon dressing. Add the Parmigiano-Reggiano cheese and pistachios, toss again and serve. —*Louis-Michel Liger-Belair*

● HEALTHY ● MAKE AHEAD ● VEGETARIAN ● STAFF FAVORITE

Grilled Carrot Salad with Brown Butter Vinaigrette

ACTIVE: 30 MIN; TOTAL: 2 HR 15 MIN
6 SERVINGS ●

Grilling concentrates the sweetness of fresh baby carrots. (Bagged "baby" carrots will never taste the same.) F&W Best New Chef 2011 Bryce Gilmore of Barley Swine in Austin marinates them, then tosses them with a wonderful and unusual dressing of browned butter pureed with marcona almonds and sherry vinegar.

- ½ cup extra-virgin olive oil
- 2 tablespoons sweet smoked paprika
- 1 tablespoon ground fennel
- 1 tablespoon ground coriander
- 2 garlic cloves, thinly sliced
- 4 thyme sprigs
- 1 pound baby carrots, halved lengthwise and tops trimmed to 1 inch

Salt and freshly ground pepper
- 4 tablespoons unsalted butter
- 2 tablespoons sherry vinegar
- 1 tablespoon water
- 2 tablespoons marcona almonds, plus chopped almonds for garnish
- 5 ounces baby arugula

1. In a large bowl, combine the olive oil with the paprika, fennel, coriander, garlic and thyme sprigs. Add the baby carrots and let stand for 2 hours.

2. Preheat a grill pan. Remove the carrots from the marinade and season with salt and freshly ground pepper. Grill over moderate heat, turning, until crisp-tender, about 6 minutes. Transfer to a bowl.

3. Meanwhile, in a small skillet, cook the butter over moderate heat until lightly browned and nutty-smelling, shaking the pan gently, about 5 minutes. Scrape the butter and solids into a blender. Add the vinegar, water and the 2 tablespoons of almonds; puree until smooth. Season the vinaigrette with salt and pepper.

4. Add the vinaigrette and arugula to the carrots; toss to coat. Transfer the salad to plates, sprinkle with chopped almonds and serve.
—*Bryce Gilmore*

Grilled Broccoli and Bread Salad with Pickled Shallots

⏱ **TOTAL: 45 MIN • 4 SERVINGS** ● ●

"Grilling over an open flame is my favorite way of cooking," says chef Charlie Parker of Plum restaurant in Oakland, California. "It gives food so much flavor without the need for butter." Here, he serves lightly charred broccoli and ciabatta cubes in a twist on an Italian bread-and-tomato salad.

- 2 large shallots, thinly sliced
- ¼ cup golden raisins
- ½ cup dry sherry
- ¼ cup sherry vinegar
- ¼ cup agave nectar
- 1 teaspoon chopped thyme

Kosher salt
Grated zest and juice of 1 Meyer lemon
- ½ cup extra-virgin olive oil

Freshly ground pepper
- 4 garlic cloves, minced
- 2 teaspoons crushed red pepper
- 2 teaspoons chopped rosemary
- 1 pound broccoli, cut into long spears, stems peeled
- ½ pound vegan ciabatta, sliced ½ inch thick
- 2 tablespoons toasted pine nuts

1. Put the shallots and the raisins in 2 separate small, heatproof bowls. In a small saucepan, combine the sherry, vinegar and agave nectar and bring to a boil. Pour 2 tablespoons of the hot mixture over the raisins; pour the rest over the shallots and add the thyme and 1 teaspoon of salt. Cover both bowls.

2. Light a grill. In a small bowl, combine the lemon zest and lemon juice with the olive oil and season with salt and freshly ground pepper. Set aside 3 tablespoons of the dressing. Add the minced garlic, crushed red pepper and chopped rosemary to the remaining dressing in the bowl.

3. On a rimmed baking sheet, drizzle the broccoli with half of the dressing from the bowl and toss well. Season with salt and pepper. Brush the remaining dressing from the bowl on the ciabatta slices. Grill the broccoli over moderate heat, turning, until lightly charred and barely tender, about 8 minutes. Transfer the broccoli to a bowl, cover with foil and let steam for about 5 minutes. Grill the ciabatta over moderate heat until crisp, about 1 minute.

4. Cut the ciabatta into 1-inch cubes. Transfer to a platter and top with the grilled broccoli. Drain the raisins and shallots and scatter them over the broccoli. Garnish the salad with the toasted pine nuts, drizzle with the reserved 3 tablespoons of dressing and serve right away. —*Charlie Parker*

WINE Minerally Loire Valley white: 2008 Marc Pesnot La Bohème.

Avocado, Orange and Jicama Salad

⏱ **TOTAL: 30 MIN • 6 SERVINGS** ● ● ●

Feta is a fun, briny addition to this Mexican mix of jicama, avocado and cilantro from California visual artist MB Boissonnault. She created this salad for Dig Gardens in Santa Cruz, which hosts a weekly pop-up restaurant in its greenhouse.

- 3 navel oranges
- 2 tablespoons fresh lime juice
- 1 tablespoon cider vinegar
- 2 tablespoons extra-virgin olive oil

Pinch of cayenne pepper
Salt and freshly ground black pepper
- 1 small jicama (1 pound)— peeled, quartered and thinly sliced
- 2 Hass avocados, quartered lengthwise and thinly sliced
- 1 cup crumbled feta cheese
- ¼ cup chopped cilantro

1. Using a sharp knife, peel the oranges, removing all of the bitter white pith. Working over a small bowl, cut in between the membranes to release the sections.

2. Squeeze the membranes over a bowl to extract the juice. Whisk in the lime juice, vinegar, olive oil and cayenne; season with salt and freshly ground pepper. Add the jicama and let stand for 15 minutes. Fold in the orange sections, avocados, feta and cilantro. Serve right away.
—*MB Boissonnault*

Beet and Apple Salad

ACTIVE: 30 MIN; TOTAL: 2 HR 15 MIN
8 SERVINGS ● ● ●

New York chef George Mendes uses fresh horseradish and a rare Austrian vinegar for his salad. This version calls for jarred horse-radish and supermarket cider vinegar.

- 4 large beets (2½ pounds)
- 5 thyme sprigs
- ½ cup extra-virgin olive oil, plus more for drizzling
- Salt and freshly ground pepper
- ¼ cup apple-cider vinegar
- 1 teaspoon Dijon mustard
- 3 tablespoons prepared horseradish
- ⅓ cup salted pistachios, chopped
- 1 green apple, thinly sliced

1. Preheat the oven to 375°. In a baking dish, lightly drizzle the beets and thyme with olive oil. Season with salt and pepper. Cover with foil and roast until the beets are tender, about 1 hour and 45 minutes. Let cool, then peel the beets and cut them into ¾-inch dice.

2. In a bowl, whisk the vinegar with the mustard. Whisk in the ½ cup of oil until emulsi-fied. Add the horseradish and season with salt and pepper; toss with the beets and pistachios. Transfer to a platter, top with the apple and serve. —*George Mendes*

bitter greens with ale vinaigrette

In a small bowl, whisk 3 ounces India Pale Ale with 1 tablespoon minced shallot, 1 teaspoon grated orange zest, 1 tablespoon honey and 1 teaspoon Dijon mustard. Gradually add 4 tablespoons extra-virgin olive oil in a stream, whisking constantly. Season the vinaigrette with salt and pepper and toss with bitter greens, pecans and orange segments. —*Sean Paxton*

Pickled Beet Salad

⊙ TOTAL: 15 MIN • 8 SERVINGS ● ● ●

- 1 quart pickled beets, drained and cut into wedges
- 3 tablespoons extra-virgin olive oil
- Finely grated zest of 1 lemon
- Salt and freshly ground pepper
- ¼ cup chopped fennel fronds
- ¼ cup chopped parsley

Arrange the beets on a platter. In a small bowl, combine the olive oil and lemon zest and season with salt and pepper. Drizzle the beets with the olive oil dressing, scatter the fennel fronds and parsley on top and serve. —*Kenny Rochford*

Beet and Red Cabbage Salad with Lentils and Blue Cheese

⊙ TOTAL: 45 MIN • 8 TO 10 SERVINGS

- ½ cup French green lentils
- Salt
- 4 ounces thickly sliced bacon, cut crosswise ¼ inch thick
- ½ cup extra-virgin olive oil
- 3 tablespoons freshly squeezed lemon juice
- Freshly ground black pepper
- 1½ pounds vacuum-packed beets, cut into wedges
- ¼ cup coarsely chopped parsley
- ½ pound red cabbage, cut into ½-by-2-inch pieces
- ¼ pound green-leaf lettuce, torn into large pieces
- ¼ pound blue cheese, such as Roquefort, crumbled (about 1 cup)

1. In a small pot, cover the lentils with 2 inches of water and bring to a boil. Add ¼ teaspoon of salt and simmer the lentils over moderate heat until they are tender, 25 to 30 minutes. Drain the lentils, rinse with cold water and then drain again.

2. Meanwhile, in a large skillet, cook the bacon over moderate heat, stirring occa-sionally, until crispy. Using a slotted spoon, transfer to a paper towel–lined plate.

3. In a bowl, whisk the olive oil with the lemon juice, then season the dressing with salt and freshly ground black pepper.

4. In a large bowl, toss the beets, parsley and lentils with one-third of the dressing. Add the red cabbage, lettuce and the remaining dressing to the bowl and toss gently. Season the salad with salt and pepper, top with the bacon and blue cheese and serve. —*Emma Jessen Krut*

Beet Salad with Watercress and Fresh Pecorino

ACTIVE: 20 MIN; TOTAL: 1 HR 45 MIN
8 SERVINGS ●

Seattle chef Ethan Stowell uses beets two different ways in this recipe. He slowly roasts some of them, giving the salad a bit of sweet-ness, and thinly shaves the rest for a fresh, earthy crispness.

- 2 pounds small beets (preferably Chioggia), ¼ pound peeled and very thinly sliced on a mandoline
- ¾ cup extra-virgin olive oil, plus more for rubbing
- Salt and freshly ground black pepper
- ¼ cup fresh orange juice
- ¼ cup white balsamic vinegar
- 3 bunches of watercress (6 ounces each), thick stems discarded
- 6 ounces young pecorino cheese, such as Toscano or Sardo, shaved

1. Preheat the oven to 350°. In a small bak-ing dish, rub the whole beets with olive oil and season with salt and pepper. Cover the baking dish tightly with aluminum foil and roast the beets for about 1 hour and 15 min-utes, until they are tender when pierced with a knife. Let cool, then peel the beets and cut them into wedges.

2. In a large bowl, whisk the ¾ cup of olive oil with the orange juice and balsamic vin-egar; season the dressing with salt and pep-per. Add the roasted beet wedges, shaved beets, watercress and shaved pecorino and toss well to coat. Transfer the salad to a large platter and serve right away. —*Ethan Stowell*

● HEALTHY ● MAKE AHEAD ● VEGETARIAN ● STAFF FAVORITE

beet salad with watercress and fresh pecorino

Shaved Vegetable Salad

⏱ TOTAL: 30 MIN • 10 SERVINGS ● ● ●

Cleveland chef Michael Symon tosses his tangle of multicolored vegetables with a lemon-dill dressing. Because they're served raw, the vegetables should be sliced very thin, in a food processor or preferably on a mandoline. Symon likes using a salty Greek feta for the salad's cheese garnish.

- ½ cup sliced almonds
- 1 small celery root, peeled and very thinly sliced crosswise
- 1 small golden beet, peeled and very thinly sliced crosswise
- 1 small red onion, very thinly sliced crosswise
- 2 medium carrots, very thinly sliced crosswise
- 6 radishes, very thinly sliced crosswise
- 1 garlic clove, minced
- ¼ cup fresh lemon juice
- ¼ cup plus 2 tablespoons extra-virgin olive oil
- 2 tablespoons chopped dill

Salt and freshly ground pepper

- 6 ounces feta cheese, sliced

superfast salads

pepper and pine nut Mix roasted red, yellow and orange bell peppers with fresh basil leaves and toasted pine nuts. Dress with red wine vinegar and olive oil.

zucchini and mint Thinly shave zucchini and toss with toasted sliced almonds, torn mint leaves and crumbled *ricotta salata* cheese. Dress with freshly squeezed lemon juice and olive oil.

watercress and orange Toss watercress with seeded orange sections and pitted green olives. Top with shaved pecorino cheese and dress with olive oil.

1. Preheat the oven to 350° and spread the almonds in a pie plate. Toast until golden, about 7 minutes. Let cool.

2. In a large bowl, combine the celery root, beet, onion, carrots and radishes. In a small bowl, whisk the garlic with the lemon juice, oil and dill and season with salt and pepper. Add the dressing and feta to the sliced vegetables and toss well. Transfer to a platter, garnish with the almonds and serve.
—*Michael Symon*

Grilled Fall Vegetable Salad with Boiled Dressing

📷 PAGE 39

ACTIVE: 40 MIN; TOTAL: 1 HR 20 MIN
8 SERVINGS ● ● ●

Boiled dressings—which aren't actually boiled but heated gently in a double boiler—are butter-based vinaigrettes that became popular in the South because of the one-time lack of good-quality vegetable oils. In this version for a grilled vegetable salad, Georgia chef Hugh Acheson gently cooks egg yolks, spices and vinegar until silky and light, then whips in the luxuriously rich combination of butter, cream and crème fraîche.

- 12 baby beets, trimmed
- 12 baby carrots, peeled and trimmed
- 12 baby turnips, peeled and trimmed
- 16 thin asparagus spears, trimmed
- 8 baby leeks or large scallions, trimmed
- 2 teaspoons extra-virgin olive oil, plus more for drizzling

Salt and freshly ground black pepper

- 2 large egg yolks
- ¼ cup sherry vinegar
- 1 teaspoon all-purpose flour
- ½ teaspoon dry mustard
- ¼ teaspoon sugar

Pinch of cayenne pepper

- 1 teaspoon unsalted butter
- ¼ cup heavy cream
- 1 tablespoon crème fraîche
- 1 tablespoon plus 2 teaspoons fresh lemon juice
- ½ teaspoon finely grated lemon zest
- 8 cups arugula (4 ounces)

1. Preheat the oven to 400°. Put the beets in a small baking dish, cover with foil and roast for about 40 minutes, until tender. When cool enough to handle, peel and halve the beets and transfer them to a large rimmed baking sheet.

2. Meanwhile, bring a large saucepan of salted water to a boil. Add the carrots and boil over moderately high heat until crisp-tender, about 4 minutes. With a slotted spoon, transfer the carrots to the baking sheet with the beets. Add the turnips to the boiling water and cook until just tender, about 3 minutes; transfer to the baking sheet with the other vegetables. Repeat with the asparagus, cooking until bright green, about 2 minutes; transfer the asparagus to the baking sheet. Add the leeks and cook until just tender, about 2 minutes; transfer them to the baking sheet. Halve the carrots, turnips and leeks lengthwise. Drizzle all of the vegetables with olive oil and season with salt and freshly ground black pepper.

3. In a medium stainless steel bowl, whisk the egg yolks with the sherry vinegar, flour, dry mustard, sugar and cayenne pepper until smooth. Set the bowl over a saucepan of simmering water and whisk over moderately low heat until hot and thick, about 2 minutes. Remove the bowl from the heat. Whisk in the butter, then the cream, crème fraîche, 1 tablespoon of the lemon juice and the lemon zest. Season the boiled dressing with salt and freshly ground black pepper.

4. Light a grill or preheat a grill pan. Grill the vegetables over medium heat, turning them once or twice, until they are lightly charred, about 5 minutes.

5. On a large platter, toss the arugula with the 2 teaspoons of oil and the remaining 2 teaspoons of fresh lemon juice, then season the greens with salt and freshly ground black pepper. Arrange the grilled vegetables over the arugula and serve right away, with the boiled dressing on the side.
—*Hugh Acheson*

MAKE AHEAD The blanched vegetables and roasted beets can be refrigerated overnight. The boiled dressing can be refrigerated for up to 1 week.

● HEALTHY ● MAKE AHEAD ● VEGETARIAN ● STAFF FAVORITE

Warm Mushroom Salad with Bacon Vinaigrette

TOTAL: 1 HR • 6 SERVINGS ●

- ½ cup extra-virgin olive oil
- ½ cup vegetable oil
- 1 head of garlic, cloves crushed but not peeled
- 1 pound mixed wild mushrooms, such as oyster, enoki and shiitake—thick stems discarded, caps thickly sliced
- Salt and freshly ground pepper
- ¾ cup pecans
- ½ pound thickly sliced bacon, cut crosswise into ¼-inch strips
- 1 leek, white and tender green parts only, thinly sliced
- ½ cup cider vinegar
- 1 teaspoon sorghum or molasses
- 1 teaspoon fresh lemon juice
- 6 ounces sturdy baby greens, such as arugula, *tatsoi*, mustard or spinach
- 3 ounces cold fresh goat cheese, crumbled

1. Preheat the oven to 425°. In a saucepan, bring both oils to a simmer with the garlic. Cook over low heat until fragrant, 15 minutes. Strain the oil and discard the garlic.

2. In a large bowl, toss the mushrooms with 6 tablespoons of the garlic oil and season with salt and pepper. (Reserve the remaining garlic oil for later use.) Spread the mushrooms in a baking pan and roast for 35 minutes, stirring once or twice, until crisp and golden. Spread the pecans in a pie plate and toast for 7 minutes, until fragrant. Let cool.

3. In a large skillet, cook the bacon over moderately low heat, stirring frequently, until crisp, about 8 minutes. Using a slotted spoon, transfer the bacon to a paper towel–lined plate. Strain the bacon fat into a heatproof bowl and return half of it to the skillet. Add the sliced leek to the skillet and cook over moderately low heat until softened, about 6 minutes. Add the cider vinegar and simmer until reduced to 3 tablespoons, about 5 minutes. Remove from the heat and whisk in the sorghum, lemon juice and the remaining bacon fat.

4. In a large bowl, toss the greens with the vinaigrette, mushrooms and pecans. Season with salt and pepper and toss again. Sprinkle with the bacon and goat cheese and serve. —*Kevin Willmann*

Warm Corn Chowder Salad with Bacon and Cider Vinegar

ACTIVE: 25 MIN; TOTAL: 45 MIN 10 SERVINGS ● ●

In this riff on corn chowder, TV's Fabulous Beekman Boys toss fresh corn, potatoes and bacon with cider vinegar. They grow at least five varieties of sweet corn on their New York farm each summer, and they're always coming up with new ways to use it. Because the corn for this salad is barely cooked, it's best to use the juiciest kernels available.

- 4 thick slices of bacon (4 ounces), cut crosswise ½ inch thick
- 1 pound Yukon gold potatoes, peeled and cut into ½-inch dice
- 2 red bell peppers, cut into ½-inch dice
- 8 ears of corn, kernels removed
- 1 medium red onion, thinly sliced
- ¼ cup cider vinegar
- ¼ teaspoon crushed red pepper
- Salt

1. In a large skillet, cook the bacon over moderately low heat, stirring a few times, until it is crisp, about 5 minutes. Using a slotted spoon, transfer the bacon to paper towels and let drain.

2. Pour off all but 3 tablespoons of the bacon fat in the skillet. Add the potatoes and cook over moderate heat until they start to brown, about 3 minutes. Stir and cook for about 2 minutes longer, until almost tender. Add the diced red peppers and cook, stirring occasionally, until the potatoes and peppers are tender, about 5 minutes. Add the corn kernels and cook, stirring, until heated through, about 3 minutes.

3. Transfer the vegetables to a large bowl and stir in the onion, cider vinegar, crushed red pepper and bacon. Season the salad with salt and serve right away. —*Josh Kilmer-Purcell and Brent Ridge*

Radishes with Sour Cream Dressing and Nigella Seeds

TOTAL: 15 MIN • 4 SERVINGS ● ●

Crunchy nigella seeds (available online at *kalustyans.com*) have a nutty, peppery flavor that's fabulous in this pretty radish salad.

- 1½ teaspoons nigella seeds
- 1½ teaspoons yellow mustard seeds
- ½ cup sour cream
- 2 teaspoons sherry vinegar
- ½ teaspoon ground cumin
- Salt and freshly ground pepper
- 3 bunches assorted radishes, such as black, breakfast, daikon, icicle and watermelon (about 30), thinly sliced

1. In a small skillet, toast the nigella and mustard seeds over moderate heat until fragrant, about 1 minute. Transfer the seeds to a plate to cool completely.

2. In a small bowl, combine the sour cream with the sherry vinegar and cumin and season with salt and pepper.

3. Arrange the radishes on a large plate or platter. Drizzle with the dressing, garnish with the toasted seeds and serve. —*Marcia Kiesel*

VARIATION To turn this into a radish slaw, use a julienne peeler or a mandoline to cut the radishes into matchsticks, then toss with the sour cream dressing and the toasted nigella and mustard seeds.

fast radish snacks

asian Place thinly sliced radishes in unseasoned rice vinegar and low-sodium soy sauce, marinate for 30 minutes and drain.

mediterranean Toss radishes with olive oil and sea salt; roast at 500° until crisp-tender.

danish Arrange radish slices on buttered brown bread and sprinkle with sea salt and freshly ground black pepper.

TV's Fabulous Beekman Boys host a potluck on their grand lawn. The first course: chilled tomato soup with goat-milk yogurt, OPPOSITE; *recipe, page 84.*

soups

Nordic Winter Vegetable Soup

ACTIVE: 20 MIN; TOTAL: 1 HR

8 SERVINGS ● ● ●

In her new book, *The Nordic Diet,* chef Trina Hahnemann recalls growing up in Denmark eating a wide range of intensely seasonal, often vegetarian meals like this simple soup. She calls the root vegetables in it the "gold of Nordic soil" because they're high in nutrients and grow well in cold climates.

- 2 tablespoons extra-virgin olive oil
- 1 large onion, thinly sliced
- 2 leeks, white and tender green parts only, thinly sliced
- 2 garlic cloves, minced
- 1 cup pearled barley
- 2 quarts low-sodium vegetable broth
- 1 quart water
- 10 thyme sprigs
- 2 bay leaves
- 1½ pounds celery root, peeled and cut into ½-inch cubes
- 1 pound parsnips, peeled and cut into ½-inch pieces
- Salt and freshly ground pepper
- 1 pound baby spinach
- 1 teaspoon freshly grated nutmeg
- Hearty whole-grain rye bread, for serving

1. In a large pot, heat the olive oil. Add the onion, leeks and garlic and cook over moderate heat, stirring occasionally, until tender, about 5 minutes. Stir in the barley. Add the vegetable broth, water, thyme and bay leaves and bring to a boil. Add the celery root and parsnips and season with salt and freshly ground pepper. Simmer the soup over moderately low heat until the barley and root vegetables are tender, about 40 minutes. Discard the thyme sprigs and bay leaves.

2. Stir in the baby spinach and nutmeg and simmer for about 5 minutes. Season the soup with salt and pepper and serve in deep bowls with whole-grain rye bread.

—Trina Hahnemann

WINE Green apple–scented, balanced Chardonnay: 2009 Calera Central Coast.

French (Canadian) Onion Soup

ACTIVE: 40 MIN; TOTAL: 5 HR

10 SERVINGS ●

Hugue Dufour, an alum of Montreal's Au Pied de Cochon who was also the chef at M. Wells in Long Island City, New York, makes a pork broth for his French onion soup instead of a beef stock. He uses bacon for smokiness and a pig's foot for richness. Omit the pig's foot for a lighter broth.

- 2 pounds lean slab bacon, in 1 piece
- 1 whole pig's foot or 2 halves
- 8 large yellow onions— 1 whole, 7 sliced ¼ inch thick
- 2 gallons water
- ¼ cup rendered pork fat or vegetable oil
- Salt
- ½ cup all-purpose flour
- Two 12-ounce bottles brown ale
- 6 rosemary sprigs
- Freshly ground pepper
- 12 ounces rustic bread, cubed
- 6 tablespoons unsalted butter, melted
- 6 garlic cloves, peeled
- 4 cups shredded Gruyère cheese (about ½ pound)

1. In a pot, cover the bacon, pig's foot and whole onion with the water and boil. Simmer over moderately low heat until the foot is tender, 3½ hours. Strain the broth and return to the pot, reserving the bacon and pig's foot.

2. Boil the broth until reduced to 2 quarts, 25 minutes; skim off the fat or refrigerate overnight and then skim off the fat. Remove all the lean meat from the bacon and pig's foot, cut into bite-size pieces and reserve.

3. Meanwhile, in a large pot, heat the rendered fat. Add the sliced onions and season with salt. Cover and cook over high heat, stirring, until the onions are wilted, 15 minutes. Reduce the heat to moderate and cook until the onions are very soft, 30 minutes. Uncover and cook over moderately high heat, stirring, until the onions are lightly browned, 10 minutes. Remove from the heat and stir in the flour until smooth.

4. Return the pot to the burner, then add the strained broth, ale and 4 of the rosemary sprigs and cook over moderately low heat, stirring, until the soup thickens. Simmer the soup for about 15 minutes, until no floury taste remains. Add the reserved meat and season the soup with salt and pepper. Discard the rosemary.

5. Preheat the oven to 350°. On a rimmed baking sheet, toss the bread cubes, melted butter, garlic and the remaining 2 rosemary sprigs; season with salt and pepper. Bake for 30 minutes, until the croutons are crisp. Discard the rosemary and garlic.

6. Preheat the broiler. Ladle the soup into heatproof bowls on a baking sheet and top with the croutons and cheese. Broil for about 2 minutes, until bubbling, and serve.

—Hugue Dufour

WINE Robust, fruit-forward Merlot: 2007 Château de Bellevue Les Griottes.

Stracciatella with Spinach

⟳ **TOTAL: 15 MIN • 8 SERVINGS** ●

This classic Italian soup with spinach and delicate bits of egg is ready in 15 minutes.

- 3 large eggs
- 1 tablespoon chopped parsley
- ¼ teaspoon freshly grated nutmeg
- Salt and freshly ground pepper
- ½ cup freshly grated Parmigiano-Reggiano cheese, plus more for serving
- 2 quarts chicken stock
- 1½ cups baby spinach leaves

1. In a small bowl, whisk the eggs, parsley, nutmeg and a large pinch each of salt and pepper. Stir in the ½ cup of grated cheese.

2. In a large saucepan, bring the stock to a boil over moderately high heat. Vigorously whisk in the eggs, then stir in the spinach. Cook over low heat, stirring a few times, until the egg and spinach are cooked, 2 minutes. Remove from the heat and season with salt and pepper. Ladle the soup into small bowls and serve with more cheese. *—Linda Meyers*

WINE Citrusy, minerally Sauvignon Blanc: 2010 Simonnet-Febvre Saint-Bris.

● HEALTHY ● MAKE AHEAD ● VEGETARIAN ● STAFF FAVORITE

french (canadian) onion soup

Sweet Onion and Corn Soup

ACTIVE: 30 MIN; TOTAL: 1 HR 30 MIN
8 SERVINGS ● ●

- 3 quarts water
- 9 ears of corn, shucked
- 3 tablespoons unsalted butter
- 2 large sweet onions (1 pound), thinly sliced
- 2 teaspoons sugar
- 1 medium Yukon Gold potato, peeled and cut into ½-inch dice
- ½ cup dry white wine
- 1 thyme sprig
- ½ cup heavy cream

Salt and freshly ground pepper
Chive flowers, pulled apart, for garnish

1. In a large pot, bring the water to a boil. Add the corn, cover and cook over moderately high heat until barely tender, about 5 minutes. Transfer the corn to a bowl to cool.
2. Cut the kernels from the cobs. Return the cobs to the pot, cover and simmer for 30 minutes. Discard the cobs and reserve the corn broth; you should have about 4 cups.
3. In another large pot, melt 2 tablespoons of the butter. Add the onions, cover and cook over moderate heat, stirring occasionally, until they are softened, about 8 minutes. Add the sugar and cook over moderate heat until the onions are caramelized, about 4 minutes.
4. Reserve 1 cup of the corn kernels. Add the remaining corn kernels and the potato to the onions in the pot. Add the wine and simmer over moderately high heat until almost evaporated, about 2 minutes. Add the corn broth, thyme and heavy cream, cover and simmer until the potato is tender, about 10 minutes.
5. Discard the thyme. Working in batches, puree the soup in a blender. Return the soup to the pot and season with salt and pepper.
6. In a medium skillet, melt the remaining 1 tablespoon of butter. Add the reserved 1 cup of corn, cover and cook over moderately high heat until richly browned, about 3 minutes. Season with salt. Ladle the soup into bowls, garnish with the sautéed corn and chive flowers and serve. —*Joe Wolfson*

Asparagus Soup with Parmesan Shortbread Coins

ACTIVE: 50 MIN; TOTAL: 1 HR 30 MIN
6 SERVINGS ● ●

SHORTBREAD
- 1½ cups all-purpose flour
- 1½ cups freshly grated Parmigiano-Reggiano cheese (6 ounces)
- 1 teaspoon dried thyme
- 1 teaspoon finely grated lemon zest
- 1 teaspoon kosher salt
- 1½ sticks unsalted butter, softened
- 2 large egg yolks

SOUP
- 2 tablespoons unsalted butter
- 1 medium onion, thinly sliced
- 1½ pounds asparagus, cut into 1-inch pieces
- 1 quart low-sodium chicken broth
- ¼ cup tarragon leaves, plus more for garnish
- 1 tablespoon flat-leaf parsley leaves
- ¾ cup heavy cream
- ½ cup frozen baby peas, thawed

Salt and freshly ground white pepper
Finely grated lemon zest, for garnish

1. MAKE THE SHORTBREAD In a standing electric mixer fitted with the paddle, combine the flour, cheese, thyme, lemon zest and salt. Add the butter and egg yolks and beat at medium speed until lightly moistened crumbs form. Gather the crumbs and knead to form a 2-inch-thick log. Wrap in plastic and refrigerate until chilled, about 30 minutes.
2. Preheat the oven to 325° and line 2 baking sheets with parchment. Slice the log ¼ inch thick and arrange on the baking sheets. Bake for about 20 minutes, until golden around the edges; let cool on the sheets.
3. MAKE THE SOUP In a large pot, melt the butter. Add the onion, cover and cook over moderate heat, stirring, until softened, about 6 minutes. Add the asparagus and cook for 1 minute. Add the broth and simmer until the asparagus is tender, about 10 minutes.
4. Add the ¼ cup of tarragon and the parsley. Working in batches, puree the soup in a blender. Return the soup to the pot, add the cream and peas and rewarm. Season with salt and white pepper and garnish with tarragon and lemon zest. Serve with the Parmesan coins. —*Carla Hall*

WINE Grassy, vibrant Grüner Veltliner: 2009 Huber Obere Steigen.

Tuscan Kale and Squash Minestra

⏲ TOTAL: 45 MIN • MAKES 2 QUARTS ● ● ●

- ¼ cup extra-virgin olive oil
- 1 large onion, finely chopped

One 2-pound butternut squash, neck only, peeled and cut into ½-inch cubes (2½ cups)
- 2 garlic cloves, minced
- 1 teaspoon finely chopped rosemary
- 1 pound Tuscan kale, stemmed and leaves coarsely chopped
- 4 cups chicken stock

Salt and freshly ground pepper
- ½ cup ditalini or tubettini pasta
- 1 cup drained canned navy beans

Shaved Parmigiano-Reggiano cheese and garlic toasts, for serving

1. In a large pot, heat 2 tablespoons of the oil. Add the onion, cover and cook over moderate heat, stirring, until softened, 4 minutes. Add the squash, cover and cook, stirring, until lightly browned in spots but not tender, 5 minutes. Stir in the garlic and rosemary and cook until fragrant, 1 minute. Add the kale and cook, stirring, until wilted, 5 minutes. Add the stock, cover and simmer until the kale and squash are just tender, 8 minutes. Season with salt and pepper.
2. Meanwhile, bring a medium saucepan of salted water to a boil. Add the pasta and cook until al dente. Drain the pasta.
3. Add the pasta and navy beans to the soup and simmer until the soup is slightly thickened, about 5 minutes. Stir in the remaining 2 tablespoons of olive oil. Ladle the soup into deep bowls and garnish with shaved Parmigiano-Reggiano cheese. Serve with garlic toasts. —*Grace Parisi*

WINE Creamy, spicy Pinot Blanc from Oregon: 2010 Ponzi Vineyards.

● HEALTHY ● MAKE AHEAD ○ VEGETARIAN ● STAFF FAVORITE

asparagus soup with parmesan shortbread coins

Pressure-Cooker Caramelized Carrot Soup

⏱ **TOTAL: 35 MIN • 4 SERVINGS** ● ●

To caramelize carrots in a pressure cooker, *Modernist Cuisine* co-author Nathan Myhrvold adds a bit of baking soda: It increases the pH, which speeds up the Maillard (browning) reaction.

- 1 stick unsalted butter
- 1 pound carrots, peeled and cut into ½-inch pieces
- ½ teaspoon salt
- ¼ teaspoon baking soda
- 2 cups fresh carrot juice
- Freshly ground pepper
- 1 tablespoon minced fresh ginger
- 1 teaspoon chopped tarragon
- ¼ teaspoon caraway seeds, chopped

appliance guide

The latest pressure cookers are safer, quieter and easier to handle than the ones your grandmother used. Here, F&W's top picks:

fagor chef This 6-quart stovetop cooker (below) has an easy-to-read pressure gauge and built-in timer. *$160; williams-sonoma.com.*

kuhn rikon duromatic Sturdy handles on this 7-quart stovetop model make sautéing and lifting feel natural. *$270; kuhnrikon.com.*

cuisinart This affordable 6-quart electric model has a modern design and simple controls. *$100; cuisinart.com.*

1. In a pressure cooker, combine 6 tablespoons of the butter with the carrots and cook uncovered until the butter is melted. Stir in the salt and baking soda, cover and cook at 15 PSI (see Note) for 10 minutes. Place the pressure cooker in the sink and run cold water over the lid to depressurize it rapidly; remove the lid once it can be released without force.

2. Add the carrot juice to the cooker and stir to release any caramelized bits stuck to the pot. Return the cooker to medium heat, uncovered, and rewarm the contents. Transfer the contents of the cooker and the remaining 2 tablespoons of butter to a blender and puree until smooth. Season the soup with pepper and pour into bowls. Garnish with the ginger, tarragon and caraway seeds and serve.
—*Maxime Bilet and Nathan Myhrvold*

NOTE Fifteen pounds per square inch (PSI) is the most common setting for pressure cookers. Products vary, however, so be sure to consult the owner's manual.

Chunky Tomato Soup

ACTIVE: 15 MIN; TOTAL: 50 MIN

8 SERVINGS ● ● ●

- 6 tablespoons extra-virgin olive oil
- 1 onion, finely chopped
- 1 fennel bulb, trimmed and finely chopped
- 4 thyme sprigs
- 3 tablespoons tomato paste
- Salt and freshly ground pepper
- 1 quart water
- Two 28-ounce cans peeled Italian tomatoes—drained and finely chopped, juices reserved
- Pan-Fried Potato Croutons, Fennel-Orange Gremolata (recipes follow) and diced Fontina cheese, for serving

1. In a large soup pot, heat the olive oil. Add the onion, fennel and thyme and cook the vegetables over moderately high heat, stirring occasionally, until the onion and fennel are softened, about 8 minutes. Stir in the tomato paste and season with salt and ground pepper. Cook, stirring, for 5 minutes.

Add the water and the tomatoes and their juices and bring to a boil. Simmer the soup over moderate heat, stirring occasionally, until the liquid is reduced by one-third, about 30 minutes. Discard the thyme.

2. Transfer half of the soup to a blender and puree until smooth. Return the puree to the soup pot. Serve the tomato soup with Pan-Fried Potato Croutons, Fennel-Orange Gremolata and diced Fontina cheese.
—*Steven Satterfield*

PAN-FRIED POTATO CROUTONS

⏱ **TOTAL: 25 MIN**

8 GARNISH SERVINGS ● ●

- 1 pound Yukon Gold potatoes, peeled and cut into ½-inch cubes
- Salt
- 1 tablespoon unsalted butter
- 2 tablespoons extra-virgin olive oil
- Freshly ground pepper

1. Put the potatoes in a medium saucepan and cover with 1 inch of water. Season with salt and bring to a boil. Drain the potatoes in a colander and let stand for 5 minutes.

2. In a medium nonstick skillet, melt the butter in the olive oil. Add the potatoes and cook over high heat, stirring occasionally, until golden and crispy, about 5 minutes. Season with salt and pepper and serve. —*SS*

MAKE AHEAD The croutons can be kept at room temperature for up to 3 hours. Reheat before serving.

FENNEL-ORANGE GREMOLATA

⏱ **TOTAL: 10 MIN • MAKES ½ CUP** ● ●

- ¼ cup chopped fennel fronds
- ¼ cup finely chopped flat-leaf parsley leaves
- 1 teaspoon finely grated orange zest
- 1 tablespoon extra-virgin olive oil
- Salt

Mix all of the ingredients in a small bowl. —*SS*

MAKE AHEAD The gremolata can be refrigerated for up to 3 hours.

● HEALTHY ● MAKE AHEAD ● VEGETARIAN ● STAFF FAVORITE

do-it-yourself stock

Classic and innovative versions of this kitchen essential: two from master chef André Soltner, and another from FOOD & WINE's Marcia Kiesel that takes less than an hour.

Classic Chicken Stock

ACTIVE: 20 MIN; TOTAL: 2 HR 20 MIN • MAKES 3 QUARTS ● ●

This stock from André Soltner is perfect for making sauces, gravies, braises and soups. "If you use enough bones, it will be a little thick when cold, which means you have a good stock," Soltner says.

- 1 gallon cold water
- One 4-pound chicken
- 2 leeks, coarsely chopped
- 2 carrots, coarsely chopped
- 2 celery ribs, coarsely chopped
- 2 unpeeled garlic cloves
- 1 medium onion, coarsely chopped
- 4 parsley sprigs
- 2 thyme sprigs
- 1 bay leaf

Combine all of the ingredients in a large pot and bring to a boil. Reduce the heat, partially cover and simmer for 1 hour, skimming as necessary. Transfer the chicken to a rimmed baking sheet and let cool slightly. Remove all of the meat from the chicken and return the bones and skin to the pot; reserve the meat for another use. Partially cover and simmer the stock for 1 hour longer. Strain the stock and let cool. Skim off the fat before using.
—André Soltner

MAKE AHEAD The stock can be refrigerated for up to 3 days or frozen for up to 1 month.

Pressure-Cooker Stock

ACTIVE: 10 MIN; TOTAL: 50 MIN • MAKES 3 QUARTS ● ●

F&W's Marcia Kiesel developed this time-saving recipe using a pressure cooker to extract deep chicken flavor in less than half the time of the conventional method.

- 3½ quarts cold water
- 3½ pounds chicken wings
- 2 leeks, coarsely chopped
- 2 carrots, coarsely chopped
- 2 celery ribs, coarsely chopped
- 2 garlic cloves, peeled
- 1 medium onion, coarsely chopped
- 2 parsley sprigs
- 2 thyme sprigs
- 1 bay leaf

Combine all of the ingredients in a pressure cooker. (For product recommendations, see the Appliance Guide on the opposite page.)

> **stock tip**
> *"If you have a good chicken stock, you can use it to make any kind of sauce, even a sauce for fish and other seafood,"*
> *says Soltner.*

Close and seal the pressure cooker and bring it to full pressure according to the manufacturer's instructions. Cook for 25 minutes, then strain the stock and let cool. Skim off the fat before using.
—Marcia Kiesel

MAKE AHEAD The stock can be refrigerated for up to 3 days or frozen for up to 1 month.

small-batch chicken stock

When cooking for only a few people, Soltner prefers to make small amounts of stock using this shortcut method.

Before roasting a chicken, cut off any trimmings (wings, feet, tail, neck), cut them into pieces and add to the pan with the bird. When the bird is fully cooked, remove it from the pan and let it rest. Discard any excess fat or oil in the pan, then add chopped carrot, celery, onion and garlic to the roasted trimmings; continue to cook until the vegetables are browned, about 10 minutes. Add a splash of white or red wine and enough water to just cover the vegetables and meat trimmings. Bring to a boil, then simmer until the stock is slightly reduced and flavorful, about 15 minutes. Strain. The stock can then be used to make a quick sauce for the chicken by stirring in a small amount of butter and herbs. —André Soltner

Spiced Butternut Squash Soup

ACTIVE: 30 MIN; TOTAL: 1 HR 15 MIN
6 TO 8 SERVINGS ● ●

Aged goat cheese is a key ingredient in this creamy soup from Morocco.

LA KAMA SPICE BLEND

- 1 teaspoon ground ginger
- 1 teaspoon ground turmeric
- 1 teaspoon ground white pepper
- ½ teaspoon ground cinnamon
- ½ teaspoon ground cubeb pepper (optional, see Note)
- ¼ teaspoon freshly grated nutmeg

SOUP

- 1 medium onion, coarsely chopped
- 1½ tablespoons extra-virgin olive oil

Coarse salt

- 2 pounds butternut, kabocha or calabaza squash—peeled, seeded and cut into 1½-inch cubes
- 2 tablespoons tomato paste
- 1 quart water
- ½ cup crème fraîche or heavy cream
- ¼ pound aged goat cheese, shredded

Harissa

Freshly ground black pepper

1. MAKE THE SPICE BLEND In a small bowl, combine all of the ingredients. Sift through a fine sieve and store in an airtight container.
2. MAKE THE SOUP In a large, heavy pot, toss the onion with the olive oil and 1 teaspoon of salt. Cover and cook over moderately low heat, stirring occasionally, until the onion is very soft, about 10 minutes. Stir in the squash, cover with a round of parchment paper and the lid and cook for 20 minutes.
3. Add the tomato paste, 1 teaspoon of the spice blend and the water to the pot and bring to a boil. Reduce the heat and simmer until the squash is tender, about 20 minutes. Let the squash cool.
4. Working in batches, puree the soup in a blender; add the crème fraîche, three-fourths of the cheese and 1 teaspoon of harissa to the last batch. Return all of the soup to the pot and season with salt and black pepper. Serve, passing the remaining cheese and more harissa at the table. —*Paula Wolfert*

NOTE Cubeb pepper (also known as tailed pepper) has an aromatic and bitter flavor that works well in the spice mix. It's available as dried berries at *kalustyans.com*. Crush the berries to a powder in a mortar.

Beet and Tomato Soup with Cumin

ACTIVE: 30 MIN; TOTAL: 1 HR 45 MIN
6 SERVINGS ● ● ●

- 1 pound medium beets
- 3 tablespoons extra-virgin olive oil
- 4 medium shallots, thinly sliced
- 3 medium tomatoes, chopped

Salt and freshly ground pepper

- 1 teaspoon ground cumin, plus more for garnish
- 1 quart vegetable stock or chicken stock
- 1 tablespoon tomato paste
- ¼ cup plus 2 tablespoons crème fraîche
- 2 tablespoons chopped flat-leaf parsley

1. In a large saucepan, cover the beets with water. Bring to a boil and cook over moderately high heat until tender, about 1 hour; if necessary, add more water to keep the beets covered. Drain the beets and let cool slightly, then peel and coarsely chop.
2. Wipe out the saucepan and heat the olive oil in it. Add the shallots and cook over moderate heat until softened, about 4 minutes. Add the tomatoes and chopped beets, season with salt and pepper and cook, stirring occasionally, until the tomatoes release their juices, about 5 minutes. Add the 1 teaspoon of cumin and cook, stirring, until fragrant, about 1 minute. Stir in the vegetable stock and tomato paste and bring to a boil. Cover and simmer over low heat for 10 minutes.
3. Puree the soup in batches in a food processor. Rewarm the soup in the saucepan and season with salt and pepper.
4. Ladle the soup into bowls. Top with crème fraîche, sprinkle with a little cumin and the chopped parsley and serve right away. —*Benjamin Leroux*

Barley Soup with Scotch

⏱ **TOTAL: 40 MIN • 4 SERVINGS** ●

Chefs David McMillan and Frédéric Morin serve this hearty, Scotch-spiked soup at Joe Beef in Montreal. The idea for the recipe came to Morin while he was in his uncle's barley field. He could smell the peat from the neighboring farm, which reminded him of Scotch whisky.

- 1½ quarts vegetable broth
- 1 cup barley grits (see Note)
- 2 tablespoons plus 1 teaspoon vegetable oil
- 1 large onion, finely diced
- 1 tablespoon Scotch whisky
- 2 tablespoons unsalted butter

Salt and freshly ground pepper

- ¼ cup celery leaves
- 1 ounce dry salami, sliced paper-thin

Crème fraîche, for serving

1. In a medium saucepan, bring the broth to a boil. Cover and keep hot over low heat. In a large skillet, cook the barley over moderately high heat, tossing, until lightly browned, about 2 minutes. Transfer to a plate to cool.
2. Add the 2 tablespoons of oil to the skillet and add the onion. Cook over moderate heat, stirring a few times, until softened, about 10 minutes. Add the barley and stir well. Add 1 cup of the hot broth and cook over moderate heat, stirring often, until most of the broth has been absorbed. Continue adding more broth, 1 cup at a time, and stirring often between additions. The soup is finished when all of the broth has been added and the barley is just tender, about 25 minutes. Add the whisky, then stir in the butter. Season with salt and pepper.
3. In a small skillet, heat the remaining 1 teaspoon of oil. Add the celery and cook over moderately high heat, tossing, until just wilted, 10 seconds. Ladle the soup into shallow bowls. Top with the salami and crème fraîche. Garnish with the celery leaves and serve. —*David McMillan and Frédéric Morin*
NOTE Barley grits are either pearled barley or whole-grain barley that has been cut into small pieces. They're available at health-food stores or specialty markets.

● HEALTHY ● MAKE AHEAD ● VEGETARIAN ● STAFF FAVORITE

Pea Porridge with Fresh Cheese and Ham

⏱ **TOTAL: 20 MIN • 4 SERVINGS**

Sweet peas and yogurt make this porridge creamy and tangy.

2 paper-thin slices of serrano ham
3½ cups fresh or frozen peas, thawed
¼ cup plain whole-milk Greek yogurt
1 teaspoon chopped tarragon
1 teaspoon sherry vinegar
½ cup heavy cream, warmed
Salt and freshly ground black pepper
Cayenne pepper
¼ cup fresh ricotta
Pea shoots, for garnish

1. Preheat the oven to 400°. Lay the ham on a rack set over a baking sheet and bake until crisp. Let cool, then break into shards.
2. In a saucepan of boiling salted water, cook 3 cups of the peas until tender, 3 minutes. Drain and transfer to a food processor. Add the yogurt, tarragon and vinegar and process to a chunky puree. Add the cream and pulse to blend; transfer to a saucepan and reheat. Season with salt, pepper and cayenne. Spoon the porridge into bowls. Top with the ricotta, ham, pea shoots and remaining peas; serve.
—*Bowman Brown and Viet Pham*
WINE Albariño from Spain's Rías Baixas region: 2009 Condes de Albarei.

Red Lentil Soup

ACTIVE: 20 MIN; TOTAL: 1 HR
6 TO 8 SERVINGS ● ● ● ●

1½ tablespoons extra-virgin olive oil
1 onion, cut into ¼-inch dice
2 garlic cloves, minced
1 large celery rib, cut into ¼-inch dice
1 large carrot, cut into ¼-inch dice
1 baking potato (6 ounces), peeled and cut into 1-inch dice
1 rounded cup red lentils (8 ounces)
1½ quarts vegetable stock or broth
½ teaspoon ground cumin
¼ teaspoon cayenne pepper
2 tablespoons fresh lemon juice
Salt and freshly ground pepper

1. In a large saucepan, heat the olive oil. Add the onion and garlic and cook over moderately high heat until fragrant, about 2 minutes. Add the celery and carrot and cook over moderate heat for 5 minutes. Add the potato, lentils and vegetable stock; bring to a boil. Cover and simmer until the vegetables are very tender, about 40 minutes.
2. Puree the soup in batches and return it to the saucepan. Add the cumin, cayenne and lemon juice and season with salt and pepper. Ladle the soup into bowls and serve.
—*Soup Cycle, Portland, OR*
WINE Chenin Blanc from the Loire Valley: 2007 Château La Tour Grise Les Amandiers Saumur Blanc.

Two-Mushroom Velouté

⏱ **TOTAL: 40 MIN • 6 SERVINGS** ● ●

1¼ pounds white mushrooms—1 pound finely chopped, ¼ pound thinly sliced
1 tablespoon fresh lemon juice
4½ cups chicken stock or low-sodium broth
1 pound shiitake mushrooms, stems discarded and caps finely chopped
2 large garlic cloves, minced
2 teaspoons vegetable oil
Salt and freshly ground pepper
¼ cup crème fraîche
1½ teaspoons ground coriander
Chopped chervil or parsley, for garnish

1. In a bowl, toss the chopped white mushrooms with the lemon juice. In a large saucepan, combine the chicken stock with the chopped white and shiitake mushrooms and the garlic and bring to a boil; simmer over moderately low heat until the mushrooms are tender, about 10 minutes.
2. Meanwhile, in a medium nonstick skillet, heat the oil. Add the sliced white mushrooms and cook over moderately high heat, stirring, until golden brown and tender, about 4 minutes. Season with salt and pepper.
3. Working in batches, puree the soup in a blender until very smooth; return it to the saucepan and whisk in the crème fraîche. Simmer for 2 minutes. Add the coriander and season with salt and pepper. Ladle the soup into bowls, garnish with the sautéed mushrooms and chervil and serve.
—*Joël Robuchon*
MAKE AHEAD The soup and sautéed mushrooms can be refrigerated separately overnight. Reheat gently.

Zucchini Soup with Crème Fraîche

⏱ **TOTAL: 30 MIN • 6 SERVINGS** ● ● ●

Winemaker Jeremy Seysses has developed a wide repertoire of dishes to use up the zucchini from his half-acre garden: ratatouille, sautéed zucchini, zucchini fritters, stuffed zucchini, zucchini cake. But this ultra-simple soup is the family favorite. "We have nothing from the garden for an eternity, then all of a sudden we have to eat zucchini every day for two months just to keep up," he says. His soup can be served warm, or chilled for a sunny evening. ("Yes, we actually do get occasional sunny evenings in Burgundy," he reports.)

2 tablespoons extra-virgin olive oil
2 medium onions, coarsely chopped
1¾ pounds medium zucchini, quartered lengthwise and cut crosswise ½ inch thick
3 cups vegetable stock
Salt and freshly ground pepper
3 tablespoons crème fraîche
Sherry vinegar, for drizzling

1. In a saucepan, heat the olive oil. Add the chopped onions and cook over moderate heat, stirring, until softened, about 5 minutes. Add the zucchini and cook, stirring, until sizzling, about 2 minutes. Add the vegetable stock and bring to a boil. Simmer the soup over moderate heat until the zucchini is tender, about 10 minutes.
2. Working in batches, puree the soup in a blender. Rewarm the soup in the saucepan, season with salt and pepper and whisk in the crème fraîche. Ladle the soup into bowls and garnish with a little sherry vinegar.
—*Jeremy Seysses*
WINE Concentrated, minerally white Burgundy: 2007 Morey Saint-Denis.

White Bean and Ham Stew

ACTIVE: 40 MIN; TOTAL: 3 HR
8 SERVINGS ● ●

This hearty stew called *garbure,* from south-western France, is loaded with vegetables, beans and meat. Master chef Jacques Pépin's version includes ham hocks and cabbage and is topped with toasted bread and melted Gruyère. It's traditional to add some red wine to the last few spoonfuls of broth and sip it straight from the bowl.

- 4 meaty smoked ham hocks (about 3½ pounds)
- ½ pound dried cannellini or borlotti beans (1¼ cups), picked over and rinsed
- 3 quarts water
- 2 medium red-skinned potatoes, peeled and cut into 1-inch pieces
- 1 large leek, white and pale green parts only, cut into 1-inch pieces
- 1 large celery rib, cut into ½-inch pieces
- 1 large carrot, cut into ½-inch pieces
- 1 large parsnip, cut into ½-inch pieces
- ½ pound Savoy cabbage, cut into 2-inch pieces

Salt and freshly ground black pepper
Eight ¼-inch-thick slices of peasant bread, lightly toasted
- 2 cups shredded Gruyère or Comté cheese

1. In a large pot, combine the smoked ham hocks with the cannellini beans and water and bring to a boil. Cover and simmer over low heat for 1 hour. Add the potatoes, leek, celery, carrot, parsnip, cabbage and ½ tea-spoon of salt. Cover the stew and simmer over low heat for 1 hour.

2. Transfer the ham hocks to a plate. Simmer the stew uncovered over moderate heat until thickened and the beans and vegetables are very tender, about 45 minutes.

3. Meanwhile, discard the skin and bones from the hocks and cut the meat into bite-size pieces. Add the meat to the stew as it simmers. Season the stew with pepper.

4. Preheat the broiler. Ladle the hot stew into 8 heatproof soup bowls and place the bowls on a large cookie sheet. Cover each bowl with a toast and spread the cheese on top. Broil 4 inches from the heat, rotating the bowls as necessary, until the cheese is lightly browned, about 3 minutes. Serve right away. *—Jacques Pépin*

MAKE AHEAD The stew can be refrigerated for up to 3 days. Reheat thoroughly, adding a little stock or water if necessary, before topping and broiling.

WINE Bright, juicy Beaujolais: 2009 Michel Tête Domaine du Clos du Fief Juliénas.

Classic Split Pea Soup

ACTIVE: 15 MIN; TOTAL: 3 HR
MAKES ABOUT 8 CUPS ● ● ●

Steven Satterfield, chef and co-owner of Miller Union restaurant in Atlanta, soaks split peas for an hour before simmering them in the soup, so they're more tender and the soup is smoother. Meat eaters can add bacon bits; vegetarians can top it with fried onion rings and parsley *pistou.*

- 1 pound green split peas
- 3 quarts water
- 2 tablespoons vegetable oil
- 2 celery ribs, cut into ½-inch dice
- 2 carrots, cut into ½-inch dice
- 1 onion, cut into ½-inch dice
- 1 teaspoon marjoram leaves
- 1 teaspoon thyme leaves

Salt and freshly ground pepper
Parsley Pistou, Onion Rings (recipes follow) and crispy bacon (optional), for serving

1. In a large pot, combine the split peas and water and bring to a boil. Simmer for 2 min-utes, cover and let stand for 1 hour.

2. In a medium skillet, heat the oil. Add the celery, carrots, onion, marjoram and thyme and cook over moderate heat, stirring occa-sionally, until the vegetables are softened, about 8 minutes. Scrape the mixture into the split peas and simmer over moderately low heat, stirring occasionally, until the peas have dissolved and the soup is thickened,

about 2 hours. Season with salt and pepper. Serve with Parsley Pistou, Onion Rings and crispy bacon. *—Steven Satterfield*

PARSLEY PISTOU
TOTAL: 10 MIN • MAKES 1 CUP ● ●

- 1 cup packed flat-leaf parsley leaves
- 1 garlic clove, minced
- ⅔ cup extra-virgin olive oil
- 1 tablespoon freshly grated Parmigiano-Reggiano cheese
- ½ teaspoon finely grated orange zest

Salt

In a blender, puree the parsley leaves with the garlic and olive oil. Stir in the Parmigiano-Reggiano and grated orange zest and season the *pistou* with salt. *—SS*

ONION RINGS
TOTAL: 15 MIN
8 GARNISH SERVINGS ● ●

Vegetable oil, for frying
- ⅓ cup all-purpose flour
- ⅓ cup fine cornmeal
- 1½ tablespoons cornstarch
- 1 teaspoon fine salt, plus more for seasoning
- 1 cup buttermilk
- 1 large egg
- 1 large sweet onion, cut into ¼-inch-thick rings

1. In a medium saucepan, heat 1 inch of veg-etable oil to 350°. In a shallow bowl, whisk together the flour, fine cornmeal, cornstarch and the 1 teaspoon of salt. In another shallow bowl, whisk the buttermilk with the egg until thoroughly combined.

2. Working in batches, dredge the onion rings in the flour mixture. Dip the rings in the buttermilk mixture, allowing the excess to drip off. Fry the rings until golden brown and crisp, about 1 minute per batch. Drain on paper towels and season with salt. Serve the onion rings hot. *—SS*

MAKE AHEAD The recipe can be made up to 3 hours ahead. Recrisp before serving.

● HEALTHY ● MAKE AHEAD ● VEGETARIAN ● STAFF FAVORITE

white bean and ham stew

Beer and Cheddar Soup

⏱ **TOTAL: 45 MIN • 6 SERVINGS** ●

When Jonathon Erdeljac opened Jonathon's Oak Cliff in Dallas, he knew he wanted to serve this rich soup made with two kinds of cheddar, jalapeño and bacon. The soup is on his menu all day every Friday.

½ pound piece of slab bacon, sliced ⅓ inch thick and cut into ⅓-inch dice
1 celery rib, finely chopped
1 small onion, finely chopped
1 large jalapeño, seeded and chopped
2 large garlic cloves, minced
1 tablespoon chopped thyme
One 12-ounce bottle lager or pilsner
About 2¼ cups low-sodium chicken broth
4 tablespoons unsalted butter
¼ cup all-purpose flour
1 cup heavy cream
½ pound sharp yellow cheddar cheese, coarsely shredded
4 ounces smoked cheddar cheese, coarsely shredded
Salt and freshly ground pepper
Garlic-rubbed toasts, for serving

1. In a large saucepan, cook the bacon over moderate heat until the fat is rendered and the bacon is crisp, about 7 minutes. Using a slotted spoon, transfer the bacon to a bowl. Add the chopped celery, onion, jalapeño, garlic and thyme to the saucepan and cook over moderate heat, stirring, until softened, about 8 minutes. Add half of the beer and cook until the liquid is reduced by half, about 5 minutes. Add 2¼ cups of chicken broth and bring to a simmer.

2. In a small skillet, melt the butter. Add the flour and cook over moderate heat, stirring, until lightly browned, about 2 minutes. Whisk this roux into the soup until incorporated and bring to a simmer. Cook until thickened, about 8 minutes. Add the heavy cream, both cheddar cheeses and the remaining beer and simmer, stirring occasionally, until thick and creamy, about 5 minutes. Stir in the bacon and season the soup with salt and pepper. Add a few tablespoons of broth if the soup is too thick. Serve the soup with garlic toasts.
—*Jonathon Erdeljac*

MAKE AHEAD The cheddar soup can be refrigerated overnight.

Silky Cauliflower Soup

ACTIVE: 20 MIN; TOTAL: 50 MIN
8 SERVINGS ●

Chef Steven Satterfield of Miller Union in Atlanta created this pureed cauliflower soup with mix-and-match options. Guests can customize their bowls with seared scallops, herb salad, Dijon-roasted cauliflower or any combination of the three.

1 stick unsalted butter
1 onion, coarsely chopped
1 shallot, coarsely chopped
2 garlic cloves, sliced
One 2-pound head of cauliflower, cut into medium-size florets
4 thyme sprigs
1 bay leaf
1 quart low-sodium chicken broth
1 quart water
Salt and freshly ground pepper
Pinch of freshly grated nutmeg
Dijon-Roasted Cauliflower, Seared Scallops and Herb Salad (recipes follow), for serving

1. In a soup pot, melt the butter. Add the onion, shallot and garlic and cook over moderately low heat, stirring occasionally, until softened, about 5 minutes. Add the cauliflower, thyme and bay leaf and cook, stirring occasionally, until the cauliflower is barely softened, about 5 minutes. Add the broth and water and season with salt and pepper. Simmer over moderately low heat until the cauliflower is softened, about 30 minutes. Discard the thyme sprigs and bay leaf.

2. Puree the soup in batches until it is very smooth. Season with the nutmeg. Serve with Dijon-Roasted Cauliflower, Seared Scallops and Herb Salad. —*Steven Satterfield*

MAKE AHEAD The soup can be refrigerated for up to 2 days.

DIJON-ROASTED CAULIFLOWER

⏱ **TOTAL: 35 MIN**
8 GARNISH SERVINGS ● ● ●

3 tablespoons Dijon mustard
2 tablespoons extra-virgin olive oil
1 garlic clove, minced
Salt and freshly ground pepper
One 2-pound head of cauliflower, cut into 1-inch florets

Preheat the oven to 400°. In a small bowl, whisk the Dijon mustard with the olive oil and minced garlic, then season with salt and pepper. Toss in the cauliflower florets and spread on a baking sheet. Roast for 30 minutes, then serve. —*SS*

MAKE AHEAD The cauliflower can be made up to 6 hours ahead.

SEARED SCALLOPS

⏱ **TOTAL: 5 MIN**
8 GARNISH SERVINGS ●

1 tablespoon extra-virgin olive oil
16 sea scallops, trimmed
Salt and freshly ground pepper

In a large skillet, heat the olive oil. Season the scallops with salt and ground pepper and add to the pan. Cook over high heat, turning once, until cooked through, about 5 minutes. Serve the scallops hot. —*SS*

HERB SALAD

⏱ **TOTAL: 10 MIN • MAKES ¾ CUP** ●

¼ cup snipped chives
¼ cup tarragon leaves
¼ cup flat-leaf parsley leaves
1½ teaspoons extra-virgin olive oil
½ teaspoon white wine vinegar
Salt and freshly ground pepper

In a bowl, toss the herbs with the olive oil and white wine vinegar. Season with salt and pepper and serve right away. —*SS*

● HEALTHY ● MAKE AHEAD ● VEGETARIAN ● STAFF FAVORITE

Shrimp Bisque with Crab and Tapioca

ACTIVE: 1 HR; TOTAL: 2 HR

6 SERVINGS ● ●

At La Provence in New Orleans, John Besh, an F&W Best New Chef 1999, simmers the broth for his bisque with crushed blue crab shells. F&W's Grace Parisi flavors the broth instead with chopped shrimp boiled in their shells for a home version of Besh's tapioca-studded soup.

- ¼ cup vegetable oil
- ½ pound medium shrimp, coarsely chopped, with shells and tails
- 2 tablespoons all-purpose flour
- 2 onions, finely chopped
- 4 garlic cloves, chopped
- 1 celery rib, chopped
- ¼ cup raw white rice, coarsely ground in a spice grinder
- 1 thyme sprig
- 1 bay leaf
- 1 teaspoon crushed red pepper
- 1 tablespoon tomato paste
- ¼ cup brandy
- 2 cups bottled clam juice (16 ounces)
- 1½ cups heavy cream
- ½ teaspoon Worcestershire sauce
- ½ teaspoon hot sauce

Salt

- 2 cups whole milk
- ½ cup small pearl tapioca (not instant), rinsed
- 1 pound jumbo lump crab

Snipped chives, for garnish

1. In a large pot, heat the oil. Add the shrimp and cook over high heat, stirring occasionally, until pink, about 6 minutes. Stir in the flour and cook for 1 minute. Add the onions, garlic and celery and cook over moderate heat until softened, about 10 minutes. Add the rice powder, thyme, bay leaf, crushed red pepper and tomato paste and cook, stirring, for 3 minutes. Add the brandy and simmer until nearly evaporated. Add the clam juice, cream and 2 cups of water and bring to a boil. Simmer over moderately low heat until slightly reduced, about 20 minutes.

2. Transfer the mixture to a blender or food processor and pulse until the solids are finely chopped. Wipe out the pot. Strain the bisque into the pot; press hard to extract as much liquid as possible. Stir in the Worcestershire sauce and hot sauce; season with salt.

3. In a large saucepan, combine the milk with 1 cup of water and bring to a simmer. Add the tapioca and cook, stirring constantly, until the pearls are translucent all the way through, about 15 minutes.

4. Stir the pearl tapioca and its milk into the bisque and add the crab. Spoon the bisque into shallow bowls, garnish with the snipped chives and serve. —*John Besh*

MAKE AHEAD The bisque can be prepared through Step 3 and refrigerated overnight.

WINE Brisk northern Italian white: 2009 Abbazia di Novacella Kerner.

Creamy Oyster Stew with Fennel and Brown Bread Toasts

ACTIVE: 30 MIN; TOTAL: 1 HR

8 SERVINGS ●

Rather than serving this luxurious stew with oyster crackers, Jeremy Sewall, chef at Boston's Island Creek Oyster Bar, brushes brown bread with rosemary butter, toasts it until crisp and dunks a piece in each bowl.

- 3 tablespoons unsalted butter
- 1 large rosemary sprig
- 1 fennel bulb—cored and finely diced, stems finely chopped
- 1 quart heavy cream
- 2 small leeks, white and pale green parts only, thinly sliced

Eight 1-inch-thick slices of brown bread

- 1 cup frozen baby peas, thawed
- 1 teaspoon finely grated lemon zest
- 2 tablespoons fresh lemon juice
- 2½ dozen shucked oysters, with their liquor

Salt and freshly ground pepper

- 2 tablespoons minced chives

1. In a small saucepan, melt the butter with the rosemary over low heat. Remove from the heat and let the rosemary butter cool to room temperature; discard the rosemary.

2. In a large saucepan, combine the chopped fennel stems with the cream and bring to a boil. Simmer over low heat for 20 minutes. Strain the cream and discard the chopped fennel stems. Return the cream to the saucepan. Add the diced fennel and simmer over moderate heat until tender, about 8 minutes. Add the leeks and simmer for 2 minutes. Remove the pan from the heat and let stand for 10 minutes.

3. Preheat the oven to 350°. Brush the bread with the rosemary butter and arrange on a baking sheet. Bake the bread for about 8 minutes, until lightly toasted.

4. Bring the cream back to a boil. Stir in the peas, lemon zest and lemon juice. Remove from the heat and stir in the oysters and their liquor. Let the stew stand for 1 minute. Season with salt and pepper.

5. Ladle the stew into bowls and stand a piece of toast in each bowl. Garnish with the chives and serve. —*Jeremy Sewall*

MAKE AHEAD The recipe can be prepared through Step 2 and refrigerated overnight.

WINE Ripe California Chardonnay: 2009 St. Francis Sonoma County.

three easy superfast soups

caribbean tomato Simmer good-quality creamy tomato soup with sautéed onion and garlic and jerk paste. Add shrimp and heat for 2 minutes. Stir in cooked rice.

black bean Sauté diced onion with cumin. Simmer with canned black beans, their liquid and water until slightly thickened. Add salt and pepper; stir in cilantro.

green grape gazpacho In a blender, puree cucumber, green grapes, almonds, scallions, vinegar, yogurt, buttermilk and olive oil. Season with salt and white pepper. Refrigerate until chilled.

soups

Momma Rochelle's Gumbo

ACTIVE: 30 MIN; TOTAL: 2 HR 45 MIN
8 SERVINGS ●

There's one item that never changes on the menu at La Provence in New Orleans: John Besh's gumbo, based on the classic dish he grew up with. Here, inspired by Besh's new cookbook, *My Family Table*, F&W's Grace Parisi streamlines the chef's recipe so that it's practical for the home cook.

- ½ cup canola oil
- ½ cup all-purpose flour
- 1 large onion, finely chopped
- 1 celery rib, finely chopped
- 2 green bell peppers, finely chopped
- 6 garlic cloves, minced
- ¼ cup tomato paste
- 2½ quarts chicken stock or low-sodium broth
- ¼ cup Worcestershire sauce
- 1 teaspoon dried oregano
- 1 teaspoon dried thyme
- 1 bay leaf
- 1½ pounds andouille sausage or spicy kielbasa, sliced ½ inch thick
- ½ pound okra, thinly sliced
Salt and freshly ground pepper
- 8 skinless, boneless chicken breasts (about 6 ounces each), lightly pounded
- 2 tablespoons extra-virgin olive oil
- 2 scallions, thinly sliced
Steamed white rice and hot sauce, for serving

1. In a large pot, combine the oil and flour and cook over moderately high heat, stirring constantly, until golden, about 5 minutes. Add the onion, celery, bell peppers and garlic and cook over moderate heat, stirring frequently, until the vegetables are tender, about 10 minutes. Stir in the tomato paste and cook for 1 minute. Add the chicken stock, Worcestershire sauce, oregano, thyme and bay leaf and bring to a simmer. Add the andouille and okra and simmer over low heat until the okra is broken down and the gumbo is thickened, about 2 hours. Season with salt and pepper. Discard the bay leaf.

2. Preheat a grill pan or light a grill. Brush the chicken with the olive oil and season with salt and pepper. Grill over moderate heat, turning once, until lightly charred and cooked through, about 10 minutes. Let the chicken rest for 5 minutes, then thinly slice it crosswise.

3. Spoon the gumbo into shallow bowls. Top with the chicken and scallions and serve with rice and hot sauce.
—*John Besh*

MAKE AHEAD The gumbo can be refrigerated overnight without the chicken.
WINE Minerally, peach-scented Grenache Blanc: 2009 Topanga Vineyards Celadon.

Southwest Seafood Chowder

TOTAL: 1 HR 30 MIN • 8 SERVINGS ● ●

As a native New Englander, chef Steve Sicinski loves traditional clam chowder. But when he was cooking at a spa in Sedona, Arizona, he preferred making this healthier tomato-based version with Southwestern flavors.

- ¼ cup canola oil
- 1 yellow onion, coarsely chopped
- 5 garlic cloves, smashed
- 2 large ancho chiles, seeded and torn into large pieces
- 1 teaspoon fennel seeds
- 1 cup dry white wine
One 28-ounce can crushed tomatoes
- 1 cup 2-percent milk
- 2 dozen cherrystone clams, scrubbed
Salt and freshly ground pepper
- 1 pound Yukon Gold potatoes, peeled and cut into ½-inch pieces
- 1 small red onion, finely chopped
- 1 celery rib, finely chopped
- 1 fennel bulb, finely chopped
One 10-ounce package frozen corn kernels, thawed
- 1½ teaspoons smoked sweet paprika
- 1 pound skinless halibut fillet, cut into 1½-inch cubes
- 1 pound shelled and deveined medium shrimp
Oyster crackers or crusty bread, for serving

1. In a large pot, heat 2 tablespoons of the canola oil. Add the yellow onion, garlic, ancho chiles and fennel seeds and cook over moderate heat, stirring frequently, until the onion is lightly browned, about 8 minutes. Add the white wine and cook until the mixture is reduced by half, about 5 minutes. Add the crushed tomatoes and 4 cups of water and bring to a boil. Cook over moderate heat until the vegetables and ancho chiles are very tender and the broth is slightly reduced, about 15 minutes. Stir in the milk.

2. Working in batches, puree the soup in a blender. Strain the soup into a heatproof bowl and rinse out the pot.

3. Add 1 cup of water to the pot along with the clams. Cover and cook over high heat until the clams open, about 8 minutes. Discard any clams that do not open. Transfer the clams to a bowl and remove them from their shells; rinse to remove any grit. Chop the clams. Pour the clam cooking broth into a bowl and let the grit settle, then add the broth to the soup, stopping before you reach the grit at the bottom. Season the soup lightly with salt and pepper.

4. Rinse out the pot and wipe it dry. Add the remaining 2 tablespoons of canola oil to the pot and heat until shimmering. Add the potatoes and cook over moderately high heat, stirring occasionally, until they are lightly browned in spots, about 5 minutes. Stir in the red onion, the chopped celery and fennel and the corn kernels. Add the paprika and cook over moderate heat, stirring, until the celery is crisp-tender, about 7 minutes. Add the soup and bring to a boil.

5. Add the halibut, shrimp and clams to the soup and simmer until the halibut is white and the shrimp are pink, about 5 minutes. Season with salt and pepper. Ladle the soup into shallow bowls and serve right away, with oyster crackers or crusty bread.
—*Steve Sicinski*

MAKE AHEAD The recipe can be prepared through Step 4 and refrigerated overnight in an airtight container. Bring the soup to a boil before proceeding.
WINE Round, full-bodied white: 2009 Copain Tous Ensemble Viognier.

● HEALTHY ● MAKE AHEAD ● VEGETARIAN ● STAFF FAVORITE

Miso Clam Chowder with Parsley Oil

ACTIVE: 45 MIN; TOTAL: 1 HR
6 TO 8 SERVINGS ● ●

½ cup dry white wine
4 dozen littleneck clams, scrubbed
3 tablespoons unsalted butter
6 ounces thick-cut bacon, cut crosswise into ¼-inch matchsticks
1 onion, finely chopped
3 garlic cloves, minced
2 celery ribs, finely diced
1 teaspoon chopped thyme
2 bay leaves
1½ tablespoons white miso paste
1 cup heavy cream or half-and-half
3 Yukon Gold potatoes (1½ pounds), peeled and cut into ¾-inch cubes
Salt and freshly ground pepper
1 cup flat-leaf parsley leaves
½ cup canola oil

1. In a soup pot, bring the wine and 1½ cups of water to a boil. Add the clams, cover and cook over high heat until the clams open, 8 to 10 minutes. Using a slotted spoon, transfer the clams to a bowl; discard any that do not open. Remove the clams from their shells and rinse to remove any sand, then coarsely chop them. Strain the broth into a heatproof bowl, stopping before you reach the sand at the bottom; you should have 3 cups.
2. Rinse out the pot and dry it. Add the butter and bacon and cook over moderately high heat, stirring occasionally, until the bacon is crisp and golden, about 6 minutes. Add the chopped onion, garlic, celery, thyme and bay leaves and cook until the vegetables are tender, about 5 minutes. Stir in the miso. Gradually add the clam broth. Add the cream and 1 cup of water to the pot and bring to a simmer. Add the potato cubes and season lightly with salt and pepper. Simmer over low heat for about 8 minutes, until the potatoes are tender.
3. Meanwhile, in a blender, combine the parsley with ¼ cup of water and puree until finely chopped. Add the oil and puree until smooth. Season with salt.

4. Using the back of a spoon, crush a few of the potatoes against the side of the pot to thicken the soup slightly. Add the reserved clams and simmer just until heated through. Discard the bay leaves. Serve in bowls, drizzled with the parsley oil. —*David Myers*
WINE Minerally, juicy Italian white: 2010 DonnaChiara Greco di Tufo.

Thai Shrimp and Coconut Soup

🕒 ACTIVE: 20 MIN; TOTAL: 45 MIN
4 SERVINGS ●

5 Thai chiles, seeded and chopped
4 stalks of fresh lemongrass, tender inner bulb only, finely chopped
4 garlic cloves, coarsely chopped
⅓ cup coarsely chopped peeled fresh ginger
1 large shallot, coarsely chopped
1 tablespoon coconut or vegetable oil
3½ cups unsweetened coconut milk
¼ cup plus 2 tablespoons dark brown sugar
¼ cup Asian fish sauce
¼ cup tamarind concentrate
6 fresh kaffir lime leaves
3 tablespoons fresh lime juice
Salt and freshly ground pepper
¾ pound medium shrimp, shelled and deveined
Cooked rice vermicelli or steamed rice, for serving (optional)

1. In a blender, combine the chiles, lemongrass, garlic, ginger, shallot and ¼ cup of water and puree until smooth.
2. In a saucepan, heat the oil. Add the lemongrass puree and cook over moderately high heat, stirring, until fragrant, 2 minutes. Whisk in the coconut milk, brown sugar, fish sauce, tamarind, lime leaves and 1½ cups of water; bring to a gentle boil. Simmer over low heat, stirring occasionally, until the soup is flavorful and slightly reduced, 15 minutes.
3. Stir the lime juice into the soup; season with salt and pepper. Add the shrimp; simmer until slightly curled and just cooked through, 1 minute. Ladle the soup into bowls, add the noodles and serve. —*Harold Dieterle*

Lobster, Clam and Kimchi Stew

TOTAL: 50 MIN • 8 SERVINGS ● ● ●

3 tablespoons vegetable oil
4 scallions, cut into 1-inch lengths
1 large onion, cut into ½-inch dice
4 garlic cloves, minced
1 pound daikon, peeled and cut into ¾-inch dice (2½ cups)
2 cups kimchi, chopped
6 cups water
One 2-pound lobster—halved lengthwise, claws detached and cracked
1 tablespoon Asian fish sauce
1 tablespoon soy sauce
1 tablespoon *gochujang* (Korean red chile paste, available at Asian markets)
2 dozen littleneck clams, scrubbed
1 bunch of watercress—thick stems discarded, the rest chopped

1. In a large pot, heat the oil. Add the scallions and cook over moderate heat until softened, 2 minutes. With a slotted spoon, transfer the scallions to a plate. Add the onion and garlic to the pot and cook, stirring occasionally, until softened, 7 minutes. Add the daikon and kimchi and cook for 1 minute. Add the water and bring to a boil.
2. Add the lobster to the pot and simmer over moderate heat, turning, until the shells are bright red, 6 minutes. Transfer the lobster to a large rimmed baking sheet. When cool enough to handle, remove the tail and claw meat; discard the dark intestinal vein that runs down the tail. Cut the meat into bite-size pieces. Discard the tail and claw shells. Return the lobster body to the pot. Cover and simmer over low heat for 10 minutes. Discard the lobster body shells.
3. Stir the fish sauce, soy sauce and red pepper paste into the broth and bring to a boil over moderately high heat. Add the clams, cover and cook until they are all open. Add the lobster meat, scallions and watercress to the soup and remove from the heat. Ladle into bowls and serve. —*Marja Vongerichten*
WINE Bright, citrusy Sonoma Sauvignon Blanc: 2010 Simi.

● HEALTHY ● MAKE AHEAD ● VEGETARIAN ● STAFF FAVORITE

miso clam chowder with parsley oil

Quick Vietnamese Noodle Soup with Beef

⏱ **TOTAL: 20 MIN • 4 SERVINGS** ● ●

Star chef and cookbook author Rocco DiSpirito created this leaner take on the Vietnamese beef soup called pho. In place of the traditional rice sticks, he likes to heat *shirataki* noodles (a low-calorie noodle made from tofu or sweet potato) in store-bought chicken broth seasoned with lime juice.

- 3 cups chicken stock or low-sodium broth
- 2 cups water
- 1 tablespoon agave nectar
- 1 tablespoon finely grated fresh ginger
- 1 tablespoon soy sauce
- Two 8-ounce packages *shirataki* noodles, rinsed and drained (see Note)
- 2 tablespoons fresh lime juice, plus lime wedges for serving
- Salt and freshly ground pepper
- ½ pound trimmed beef tenderloin, very thinly sliced across the grain
- 1 teaspoon toasted sesame oil
- ½ cup chopped basil
- ¼ cup chopped cilantro
- ¼ cup chopped scallions
- 1 cup mung bean sprouts
- Sriracha or other garlic-chile sauce, for serving

1. In a large saucepan, combine the chicken stock with the water, agave nectar, grated ginger and soy sauce and bring to a boil. Add the noodles and simmer over low heat for 2 minutes. Add the lime juice and season with salt and pepper.

2. Using tongs, transfer the noodles to bowls. Add the beef slices to the noodles and ladle the hot broth on top. Drizzle the soup with the sesame oil and top with the basil, cilantro, scallions and bean sprouts. Serve with lime wedges and chile sauce.
—*Rocco DiSpirito*

NOTE *Shirataki* noodles are sold refrigerated at health-food stores or online at *miraclenoodle.com.*

WINE Smooth, berry-rich Malbec: 2008 Reunión.

Shiitake and Swiss Chard Soup with Hand-Cut Noodles

📷 **PAGE 394**

ACTIVE: 30 MIN; TOTAL: 1 HR 30 MIN
8 SERVINGS ● ● ●

David Chang, the guru behind New York's Momofuku restaurants, flavors this fabulous soup with both dried and fresh shiitake.

- One 1-ounce sheet of dried kombu (see Note)
- 3½ quarts plus ¾ cup water
- 3 ounces dried shiitake mushrooms, finely ground in a food processor
- 2 cups all-purpose flour
- ½ cup soy sauce
- ¼ cup mirin
- 6 ounces fresh shiitake mushrooms, stemmed and caps thinly sliced
- 1 pound Swiss chard—stems finely chopped, leaves coarsely chopped
- Kimchi and honey, for serving

1. In a large pot, combine the kombu with 3½ quarts of water; bring to a simmer. Cook over low heat, without boiling, for 30 minutes. Discard the kombu and bring the cooking broth to a boil. Add the ground mushrooms and return to a boil. Remove from the heat, cover and let steep for 30 minutes.

2. Meanwhile, in a standing electric mixer fitted with the dough hook, mix the flour with ¾ cup of water at medium speed just until the flour is moistened. Increase the speed to medium-high and beat until a smooth, firm, elastic dough forms, 8 to 10 minutes. Wrap the dough in plastic and let it stand for 30 minutes.

3. Strain the broth into a heatproof bowl. Wipe out the pot and return the broth to it. Add the soy sauce and mirin and bring to a boil. Add the sliced shiitake and Swiss chard and cook just until tender, 2 minutes; keep warm.

4. On a lightly floured surface, roll the dough out ⅛ inch thick. Using a pastry wheel, slice the dough into uneven strips. Bring the broth back to a boil; add the noodles. Cook, stirring, until tender and the soup is slightly thickened, 5 minutes. Ladle into bowls; garnish with kimchi and honey. —*David Chang*

NOTE Kombu, a type of kelp often used to flavor Japanese soups, is available at Japanese markets and at some supermarkets and health-food stores.

Soothing Tofu and Zucchini Soup with Bean Sprouts

⏱ **TOTAL: 30 MIN • 8 SERVINGS** ● ●

In Korea, almost every restaurant has a version of this comforting dish, usually made with meat. For his vegetarian alternative, David Chang, an F&W Best New Chef 2006, prepares a broth with *doenjang* (Korean miso paste) and a little sugar, then spices it with red pepper powder and fresh chile.

- 1 tablespoon canola oil
- 1 large onion, coarsely chopped
- 2 large garlic cloves, minced
- 2 quarts water
- ¼ cup plus 2 tablespoons *doenjang* (Korean soybean paste, see Note) or dark miso
- 2 tablespoons soy sauce
- 1 tablespoon light brown sugar
- ½ teaspoon *gochugaru* (Korean red pepper powder, see Note) or Aleppo chiles
- ½ pound mung bean sprouts
- 1 medium zucchini, very thinly sliced
- 14 to 16 ounces soft tofu, cut into ½-inch cubes
- 1 spicy green long chile, preferably Korean, thinly sliced

Heat the canola oil in a large pot. Add the onion and garlic and cook over moderate heat, stirring occasionally, until softened, about 5 minutes. Add the water and *doenjang* and whisk until dissolved. Add the soy sauce, brown sugar and *gochugaru* and bring to a boil. Add the bean sprouts and zucchini and cook until the zucchini is just tender, about 2 minutes. Add the tofu cubes and cook until heated through, about 2 minutes. Ladle into bowls, garnish with the sliced chile and serve. —*David Chang*

SERVE WITH Steamed white rice.

NOTE *Doenjang* and *gochugaru* are available at Korean and Asian markets.

● HEALTHY ● MAKE AHEAD ● VEGETARIAN ● STAFF FAVORITE

quick vietnamese noodle soup with beef

Chilled Peach Soup with Fresh Goat Cheese

ACTIVE: 30 MIN; TOTAL: 1 HR 30 MIN
PLUS OVERNIGHT MARINATING
4 SERVINGS ● ●

F&W Best New Chef 2011 Jason Franey of Canlis in Seattle makes this sweet and tangy summer soup by marinating fresh peaches overnight with dried apricots, honey, white balsamic vinegar and olive oil and then pureeing the mixture. Since peaches can vary in flavor, Franey suggests seasoning with vinegar to taste as you puree.

- 3 cups sliced peeled peaches (about 4 peaches)
- ¼ cup finely diced peeled seedless cucumber, plus thin slices for garnish
- ¼ cup finely diced yellow bell pepper, plus thin slices for garnish
- ¼ cup diced dried apricots
- 2 tablespoons honey
- 3 tablespoons crumbled fresh goat cheese, plus more for garnish
- ¼ cup white balsamic vinegar, plus more for seasoning
- ¼ cup plus 2 tablespoons extra-virgin olive oil, plus more for drizzling
- Kosher salt
- 1 large garlic clove
- 2 cups diced baguette (½ inch)
- Basil leaves, for garnish
- Freshly ground black pepper

1. In a bowl, toss the peaches with the diced cucumber, yellow pepper and apricots. Add the honey, 3 tablespoons of goat cheese, ¼ cup of vinegar and 2 tablespoons of the olive oil. Stir in 1½ teaspoons of salt. Add the garlic. Cover and refrigerate overnight.
2. Remove the garlic from the bowl and discard. Transfer the contents of the bowl to a blender and puree. Add ¼ cup of water and puree until very smooth and creamy; add more water if the soup seems too thick. Season with salt and vinegar. Refrigerate the soup until very cold, about 1 hour.
3. Meanwhile, in a medium skillet, heat the remaining ¼ cup of oil. Add the diced bread and cook over moderate heat, stirring, until golden and crisp, about 2 minutes. Using a slotted spoon, transfer the croutons to paper towels and season with salt.
4. Pour the peach soup into shallow bowls and garnish with the sliced cucumber, sliced bell pepper, goat cheese, croutons and basil. Drizzle lightly with olive oil, season with black pepper and serve. —*Jason Franey*

WINE Lively, refreshing Champagne: NV Gosset Brut Excellence.

Chilled Fennel-Grapefruit Velouté with Lemon Olive Oil

ACTIVE: 15 MIN; TOTAL: 1 HR 40 MIN
4 SERVINGS ● ● ● ●

At Sola restaurant in Paris, chef Hiroki Yoshitake cleverly uses grapefruit oil to boost the flavor in his chilled four-ingredient soup. Lemon olive oil, easier to find in the US, is a terrific alternative. The citrus oil is used in two different ways: for sautéing fennel before pureeing it with grapefruit juice, and for garnishing the soup just before serving.

- 2 tablespoons lemon olive oil (see Note), plus more for garnish
- One 1-pound fennel bulb, cored and thinly sliced, plus chopped fennel fronds for garnish
- Salt
- 3 cups water
- ¼ cup plus 2 tablespoons fresh grapefruit juice, strained
- Pinch of sugar

1. In a medium saucepan, heat the 2 tablespoons of lemon olive oil. Add the sliced fennel and a pinch of salt, cover and cook over moderately low heat, stirring a few times, until the fennel is softened, about 10 minutes. Add the water and bring to a boil. Simmer over low heat until the fennel is very tender, about 20 minutes.
2. In a blender, puree the fennel soup in batches until smooth. Transfer the soup to a medium bowl and refrigerate until chilled, about 1 hour.
3. Stir the fresh grapefruit juice into the chilled fennel soup, then add the sugar and season the soup with salt.
4. Ladle the soup into bowls, garnish with a little lemon olive oil and chopped fennel fronds and serve. —*Hiroki Yoshitake*

NOTE Olive oil pressed or infused with lemon is available at most supermarkets and specialty food stores.

MAKE AHEAD The fennel-grapefruit soup can be refrigerated overnight.

Chilled Cucumber Soup

⏱ ACTIVE: 15 MIN; TOTAL: 45 MIN
4 SERVINGS ● ● ●

Chef Eric Skokan of Black Cat restaurant in Boulder, Colorado, grows hundreds of vegetables at his farm, analyzing each variety for its best use. For this tangy chilled soup he prefers the Zagross Persian cucumber, but any Persian cucumber will work well here. The variety's sweet scent and thin skin makes it ideal for pureeing.

- Four 4-ounce Persian cucumbers— 3 coarsely chopped, 1 peeled and diced
- ½ cup ice cubes
- ¼ cup cold water
- ¼ cup grapeseed oil
- 1 teaspoon fresh lemon juice
- 1 small jalapeño, seeded and minced
- 2 tablespoons shredded mint leaves
- Salt
- ½ cup borage leaves or celery leaves
- ¼ cup plain Greek yogurt
- Extra-virgin olive oil, for drizzling

1. In a blender, combine the chopped cucumbers, ice, water, grapeseed oil, lemon juice and half each of the jalapeño and mint and puree. Season with salt and refrigerate until cold, about 30 minutes.
2. Meanwhile, blanch the borage in boiling salted water for 5 seconds. Drain, rinse and squeeze dry. Finely chop the borage.
3. Pour the cucumber soup into bowls and garnish with the diced cucumber, borage, yogurt and the remaining jalapeño and mint. Drizzle the soup with olive oil and serve. —*Eric Skokan*

MAKE AHEAD The Chilled Cucumber Soup can be refrigerated overnight.

● HEALTHY ● MAKE AHEAD ○ VEGETARIAN ● STAFF FAVORITE

chilled peach soup with fresh goat cheese

Chilled Tomato Soup with Goat-Milk Yogurt

📷 PAGE 63

ACTIVE: 25 MIN; TOTAL: 1 HOUR 40 MIN

10 SERVINGS ● ● ○

Josh Kilmer-Purcell and Brent Ridge, TV's Fabulous Beekman Boys, make yogurt from the goat milk produced on the Beekman Farm in upstate New York. They blend the tangy yogurt into this herb-flecked soup.

- 5 pounds yellow or orange tomatoes, cored
- 6 medium scallions, coarsely chopped
- ½ cup parsley leaves, plus a small handful for garnish
- ½ cup celery or lovage leaves, plus a small handful for garnish
- 2 tablespoons tarragon leaves
- ¼ cup fresh lime juice
- 2 teaspoons honey
- 2 cups goat-milk yogurt
- ½ cup cold water
- ¼ cup extra-virgin olive oil

Salt and freshly ground white pepper

Cherry or grape tomatoes, halved, for garnish

1. Set a coarse sieve over a bowl. Halve the tomatoes crosswise and squeeze the seeds and juice into the sieve. Let the liquid drain into the bowl and discard the seeds.

2. Coarsely chop the yellow or orange tomatoes and transfer them to a blender. Add the strained tomato liquid, the scallions, the ½ cup each of parsley and celery (or lovage) leaves, the tarragon, lime juice, honey, yogurt and cold water and puree, working in batches if necessary. With the machine on, gradually pour in the olive oil and blend until all of the ingredients are completely incorporated.

3. Season the soup with salt and freshly ground white pepper and refrigerate until completely chilled, about 1 hour.

4. Ladle the soup into small bowls, garnish with cherry tomatoes and parsley and celery leaves and serve.

—Josh Kilmer-Purcell and Brent Ridge

Icy Tomato Soup

ACTIVE: 20 MIN; TOTAL: 1 HR 30 MIN

6 SERVINGS ● ○

Plum tomatoes, cherry tomatoes and tomato paste make this soup from chef Alexandra Guarnaschelli ultra-tomatoey. At The Darby restaurant in New York City, Guarnaschelli presents the chilled soup over a bowl of cracked ice.

- 2½ pounds plum tomatoes, coarsely chopped
- 3 cups water
- 1 tablespoon tomato paste
- 1 onion, minced
- 2 garlic cloves, minced
- 1 teaspoon dried oregano
- ¼ teaspoon crushed red pepper

Pinch of granulated sugar

- ½ cup heavy cream

Salt and freshly ground black pepper

- 1 pint cherry tomatoes
- 1 tablespoon extra-virgin olive oil
- 1 teaspoon confectioners' sugar
- 2 tablespoons chopped dill

1. In a medium saucepan, combine the plum tomatoes with the water, tomato paste, onion, garlic, oregano, crushed red pepper and granulated sugar. Simmer over moderate heat, stirring a few times, until the tomatoes are very tender, about 20 minutes. Add the cream and simmer for 1 minute.

2. Puree the soup in a blender and pass it through a coarse strainer into a medium bowl. Season with salt and black pepper. Refrigerate the soup until cold, about 1 hour.

3. Meanwhile, preheat the oven to 375°. Spread the cherry tomatoes on a rimmed baking sheet and toss with the olive oil, confectioners' sugar and a large pinch of salt. Bake for about 10 minutes, until the skins start to wrinkle. Transfer the tomatoes to a bowl and toss with the dill.

4. Ladle the soup into bowls, garnish with the roasted cherry tomatoes and serve.

—Alexandra Guarnaschelli

MAKE AHEAD The tomato soup can be prepared through Step 2 and refrigerated overnight in an airtight container.

Chilled Persian Yogurt Soup

ACTIVE: 30 MIN; TOTAL: 1 HR 30 MIN

6 SERVINGS ● ● ● ○

"Ask anyone on my staff their favorite summer dish, and they'll tell you it's this one," says chef Hoss Zaré of Zaré at Fly Trap in San Francisco. Filled with herbs, nuts and raisins, the soup is scented with dried rose petals. "Rose petals are one of those Persian ingredients I'm very careful with," Zaré says. "Dried petals have a more delicate flavor than rose water."

- ½ cup walnuts
- ¼ cup dried rose petals, crushed (optional, see Note)
- 2 cups 2 percent plain Greek yogurt
- 1½ cups ice water
- ½ cup golden raisins
- ½ seedless cucumber, peeled and finely diced (1 cup)
- ¼ cup finely chopped mint
- ¼ cup finely chopped dill
- ¼ cup finely chopped chives

Salt and freshly ground pepper

Ground sumac, for garnish (optional, see Note)

1. Preheat the oven to 350°. Spread the walnuts in a pie plate and toast for about 10 minutes. Let cool, then finely chop.

2. Meanwhile, in a small bowl, cover the rose petals with cold water and let stand until softened, about 20 minutes. Drain the petals and squeeze dry.

3. In a large bowl, whisk the yogurt with the ice water. Stir in the raisins, diced cucumber, chopped mint, dill and chives, toasted walnuts and rose petals and season with salt and pepper. Refrigerate the soup until very cold, about 1 hour.

4. Ladle the chilled soup into shallow bowls, sprinkle with ground sumac and serve.

—Hoss Zaré

SERVE WITH Grilled bread.

NOTE Find dried rose petals and sumac at specialty food stores or *kalustyans.com*.

MAKE AHEAD The yogurt soup can be prepared through Step 3 and refrigerated overnight in an airtight container.

● HEALTHY ● MAKE AHEAD ○ VEGETARIAN ● STAFF FAVORITE

chilled persian yogurt soup

Winemaker Piero Incisa della Rocchetta entertains at his winery in Patagonia, where he serves dishes like spaghetti with bottarga and almond bread crumbs, OPPOSITE; *recipe, page 89.*

pasta

Spinach Fettuccine with Tangy Grilled Summer Squash

ACTIVE: 45 MIN; TOTAL: 1 HR 45 MIN PLUS
OVERNIGHT MARINATING • 4 SERVINGS

● ● ●

Six 4-ounce summer squash—
  4 sliced lengthwise ⅓ inch thick,
  2 sliced lengthwise ⅛ inch thick
    on a mandoline
  2 tablespoons kosher salt, plus more
    for seasoning
  1 tablespoon cider vinegar
1½ teaspoons sugar
  ½ cup plus 1 tablespoon
    extra-virgin olive oil
  5 garlic cloves
  3 large tarragon sprigs, plus
    2 tablespoons chopped tarragon
  ½ cup mint leaves, plus ¼ cup
    chopped mint
  ⅛ teaspoon saffron threads, crumbled
  2 tablespoons rice vinegar
  1 pound vegan fresh spinach fettuccine
Freshly ground pepper

1. Toss the ⅓-inch-thick squash slices with the 2 tablespoons of kosher salt and let them stand for 45 minutes.

2. In a large bowl, combine the cider vinegar with the sugar and stir to dissolve the sugar. Rinse and dry the salted squash and add it to the bowl; toss to coat with the vinegar.

3. In a blender, puree the ½ cup of olive oil with the garlic and transfer to a small saucepan. Bring to a simmer, then pour the garlic oil over the squash. Add the tarragon sprigs and mint leaves and press to compact. Cover and refrigerate overnight.

4. Light a grill or preheat a grill pan. Lift the squash out of the marinade; scrape any excess marinade back into the bowl and reserve. Grill the marinated squash over high heat until nicely charred, about 1 minute per side. Cut the squash into 1-inch pieces.

5. Bring a large pot of salted water to a boil. Meanwhile, in a large, deep skillet, heat ¼ cup of the reserved marinade and add the saffron. Add the ⅛-inch-thick squash slices and cook over high heat, tossing, until al

dente, about 1 minute. Add the rice vinegar, season lightly with salt and toss well. Add the grilled squash and toss to heat through. Remove from the heat.

6. Cook the fettuccine until al dente. Reserve ¾ cup of the pasta cooking water. Drain the pasta and add it to the skillet. Toss well over moderate heat, gradually adding the reserved pasta cooking water to make a sauce. Season with salt and pepper and transfer to a large bowl. Drizzle the remaining 1 tablespoon of olive oil all over, sprinkle with the chopped tarragon and mint and serve right away.
—*Amanda Cohen*

WINE Vibrant Sauvignon Blanc: 2009 Robert Mondavi Fumé Blanc.

Spaghetti with Sun-Dried-Tomato-Almond Pesto

TOTAL: 45 MIN • 4 SERVINGS ●

  ½ cup drained oil-packed sun-dried
    tomatoes (3 ounces)
  ⅓ cup salted roasted almonds
  1 large garlic clove, sliced
  ½ cup extra-virgin olive oil, plus more
    for drizzling
Salt and freshly ground pepper
  ½ cup fresh bread crumbs
  ¾ pound spaghetti
  2 tablespoons chopped parsley

1. In a food processor, pulse the tomatoes, almonds and garlic. Add ¼ cup of the oil and puree. Season with salt and pepper.

2. In a skillet, toast the bread crumbs in 2 tablespoons of the oil, stirring, until golden. Transfer the crumbs to a plate; season with salt and pepper.

3. In a large pot of boiling salted water, cook the spaghetti until al dente. Drain the pasta, reserving ½ cup of the cooking liquid. In the pot, toss the spaghetti with the sun-dried-tomato-almond pesto, reserved cooking water and remaining 2 tablespoons of olive oil until the sauce clings to the pasta. Transfer the pasta to bowls, sprinkle with the bread crumbs and parsley and drizzle with olive oil. Serve. —*Marcie Turney*
WINE Fresh Sicilian white: 2010 Regaleali.

Angel Hair with Green-and-Yellow-Tomato Sauce

TOTAL: 20 MIN
4 FIRST-COURSE SERVINGS ● ●

  2 tablespoons pure olive oil
  4 garlic cloves, minced
  2 large shallots, minced
  1 pound yellow tomatoes, diced
  1 pound ripe green heirloom tomatoes,
    such as Green Zebra, diced
  ¼ cup chopped basil
  2 sage leaves, finely chopped
Salt
  ½ pound angel hair pasta
  2 tablespoons unsalted butter, at
    room temperature, or 2 tablespoons
    extra-virgin olive oil

1. In a skillet, heat the oil. Add the garlic and cook over low heat until fragrant, 2 minutes. Add the shallots and cook over moderate heat, stirring, until softened, 4 minutes.

2. In a bowl, toss the tomatoes with the garlic, shallots, basil and sage. Season with salt.

3. In a pot of boiling salted water, cook the pasta until al dente; drain and transfer to the bowl. Toss well with the butter and serve.
—*Emilee and Jere Gettle*

Fried-Zucchini Spaghetti

TOTAL: 45 MIN • 4 SERVINGS ● ● ●

  1 pound small zucchini,
    very thinly sliced crosswise
  ¼ cup all-purpose flour
Salt
  6 tablespoons extra-virgin olive oil
  ¾ pound spaghetti
  1 cup shredded Parmigiano-Reggiano
    cheese, plus more for serving
  ½ cup torn basil leaves
Freshly ground pepper
Lemon wedges, for serving

1. In a medium bowl, toss the zucchini with the flour and a pinch of salt. In a very large skillet, heat half of the oil until shimmering. Add half of the zucchini and fry over high heat, turning once or twice, until browned

● HEALTHY ● MAKE AHEAD ● VEGETARIAN ● STAFF FAVORITE

and crisp, about 3 to 4 minutes. Using a slotted spoon, transfer the zucchini to a paper towel–lined wire rack and season with salt. Repeat with the remaining oil and zucchini.

2. Meanwhile, cook the spaghetti in a large pot of boiling salted water until al dente. Drain, reserving ½ cup of the pasta cooking liquid. Return the pasta to the pot and toss with the 1 cup of cheese, the basil and a generous pinch of pepper. Add the reserved pasta water a little at a time, tossing well to coat. Transfer the pasta to a bowl and top with the zucchini. Serve with lemon wedges and additional cheese. —*Gwyneth Paltrow*

WINE Fresh, zippy California Sauvignon Blanc: 2010 Quivira Fig Tree Vineyard.

Spaghetti with Anchovy Carbonara

🕒 **TOTAL: 30 MIN • 4 SERVINGS**

- ¾ pound spaghetti
- ¼ cup extra-virgin olive oil
- 3 large garlic cloves, thinly sliced
- One 2-ounce can flat anchovies, drained and chopped
- Pinch of Aleppo pepper or crushed red pepper
- ½ teaspoon finely grated lemon zest
- 1 tablespoon chopped oregano
- ¼ cup chopped flat-leaf parsley
- 2 large egg yolks
- Salt and freshly ground black pepper

1. In a large pot of boiling salted water, cook the spaghetti until al dente. Drain the pasta, reserving ½ cup of the cooking water.

2. In a large, deep skillet, heat the oil with the garlic and anchovies and cook over moderately high heat until the anchovies have dissolved, about 2 minutes. Add the red pepper, zest, oregano and parsley, then add the pasta and toss to coat. Remove from the heat.

3. In a bowl, whisk the yolks with the reserved cooking water; add to the pasta. Cook over low heat, tossing, until the pasta is coated in a creamy sauce, 1 minute. Season with salt and pepper; serve. —*Chris Cosentino*

WINE Citrusy, herbal Sauvignon Blanc: 2010 Veramonte Reserva.

Spaghetti with Bottarga and Almond Bread Crumbs

📷 PAGE 87

ACTIVE: 25 MIN; TOTAL: 1 HR 20 MIN
8 SERVINGS ●

- ½ cup large salt-packed capers
- 1 cup whole blanched almonds
- 1½ cups coarse fresh bread crumbs
- ¼ cup finely chopped flat-leaf parsley
- 4 tablespoons unsalted butter
- ¾ cup plus 2 tablespoons extra-virgin olive oil
- 1 tablespoon crushed red pepper
- 1½ ounces *bottarga*, preferably mullet, finely grated (¾ cup), see Note
- 1 pound spaghetti

1. Soak the capers in a small bowl of cold water for 1 hour, then drain and finely chop the capers.

2. Meanwhile, preheat the oven to 350° and toast the almonds on a baking sheet for 10 minutes, until golden brown. Let the almonds cool, then coarsely chop them; transfer to a food processor and finely grind.

3. Spread the bread crumbs on the baking sheet and toast in the oven until crisp. Let cool, then toss with the almonds and parsley.

4. In a large pot, melt the butter in ½ cup plus 2 tablespoons of the oil. Add the capers, crushed red pepper and half of the *bottarga* and cook over moderate heat until sizzling, about 5 minutes. Remove from the heat.

5. In another large pot of boiling salted water, cook the spaghetti, stirring, until al dente. Drain the spaghetti, reserving ¾ cup of the pasta cooking water. Add the pasta to the *bottarga* sauce. Stir in the reserved cooking water, 2 tablespoons at a time, until the pasta is coated with a rich sauce.

6. Scatter one-fourth of the bread crumb mixture in a large, shallow bowl. Top with one-third of the pasta. Repeat the layering twice more, ending with the bread crumb mixture. Sprinkle the remaining *bottarga* over the pasta and drizzle with the remaining ¼ cup of olive oil. Serve right away.
—*Piero Incisa della Rocchetta*

NOTE *Bottarga* is cured roe from either mullet (which is slightly waxy and mildly fishy) or tuna (which has a pronounced anchovy flavor); it's sold at specialty food stores.

WINE Light-bodied Pinot Noir: 2009 Bodega Chacra Barda.

Buckwheat Pasta with Summer Squash, Tomatoes and Ricotta

🕒 **TOTAL: 45 MIN • 8 SERVINGS** ●

- 6 tablespoons extra-virgin olive oil
- 1 pound mixed yellow summer squash and zucchini, sliced ¼ inch thick
- 1 medium red onion, thinly sliced
- 1 pint grape tomatoes, halved
- Pinch of crushed red pepper
- Sea salt
- ¼ cup dry white wine
- 1½ pounds dried buckwheat pasta, such as *pizzoccheri* (see Note)
- 4 cups baby spinach
- 1 cup fresh ricotta cheese

1. In a large, deep skillet, heat ¼ cup of the olive oil until nearly smoking. Add the squash mix and onion and cook over high heat, stirring, until the vegetables are lightly charred in spots and crisp-tender, about 8 minutes. Add the tomatoes, crushing them lightly with your hands as you add them. Add the crushed red pepper, season with salt and cook over high heat, stirring occasionally, until softened, about 5 minutes. Add the wine and cook until nearly evaporated.

2. Meanwhile, cook the pasta in a large pot of boiling salted water until al dente. Drain the pasta, reserving ¾ cup of the cooking water.

3. Add the pasta to the skillet along with the spinach, ricotta and the reserved cooking water. Toss over moderately high heat until the spinach is wilted and the sauce is thickened and clings to the pasta. Transfer the pasta to a platter and drizzle with the remaining 2 tablespoons of olive oil, then serve.
—*Travis Lett*

NOTE Buckwheat pasta is available online at *pastacheese.com*.

WINE Lively, watermelony rosé: 2010 Robert Sinskey Vineyards Vin Gris of Pinot Noir.

Pappardelle with Duck Ragù

⏱ TOTAL: 45 MIN • 4 SERVINGS ●

At Terroir in New York City, chef Marco Canora braises duck for this pasta dish. The simplified version here calls for duck confit.

4 store-bought duck confit legs
¼ cup extra-virgin olive oil
½ cup minced onion
¼ cup minced carrot
¼ cup minced celery
Salt and freshly ground black pepper
12 Niçoise olives, pitted and halved
½ tablespoon rosemary leaves
1 garlic clove, minced
½ cup dry red wine
2 cups chicken stock
6 tablespoons unsalted butter
½ pound pappardelle
½ cup freshly grated Parmigiano-Reggiano cheese

1. Microwave the duck legs at high power for 1 minute, until warm. Remove the skin from the legs and reserve it for another use. Remove the meat from the bones and cut it into bite-size pieces; discard the bones.
2. In a large, deep skillet, heat the oil. Add the onion, carrot and celery and season lightly with salt and pepper. Cook over moderately high heat, stirring, until slightly softened, 1 minute. Reduce the heat to moderate and cook, stirring, until browned, about 8 minutes.

ingredient tip

mafaldine These long strands of pasta, shaped like a curled ribbon on both sides, are named in honor of Princess Mafalda of Savoy—and so are also known as *reginette* ("little queens" in Italian). Try these noodles instead of spaghetti or pappardelle with meat ragù.

Add the olives, rosemary and garlic and cook over high heat, stirring, until fragrant, about 1 minute. Add the duck and stir gently to coat with the vegetables. Add the wine and simmer for 1 minute. Add the stock and simmer until the liquid is reduced to ¾ cup, about 10 minutes. Remove from the heat and stir in half of the butter. Cover and keep warm.
3. In a large pot of boiling salted water, cook the pappardelle until al dente; drain. Add the pasta to the duck ragù and cook over moderate heat, stirring gently, until simmering. Remove from the heat and stir in the Parmigiano-Reggiano cheese and the remaining 3 tablespoons of butter. Season with salt and black pepper and serve.
—*Marco Canora*

WINE Firm, earthy red: NV Cornelissen Mun-Jebel 6 Rosso.

Goat Ragù with Fresh Spaghetti

ACTIVE: 30 MIN; TOTAL: 4 HR 25 MIN
8 SERVINGS ● ● ●

Chef Chris Pandel of The Bristol in Chicago mixes a savory, slow-cooked goat-and-olive ragù with fresh spaghetti.

4 pounds whole goat shoulder, on the bone
Salt and freshly ground pepper
2 teaspoons fennel seeds
1 teaspoon coriander seeds
1 teaspoon black peppercorns
3 tablespoons vegetable oil
2 medium onions, coarsely chopped
2 medium carrots, coarsely chopped
1 celery rib, coarsely chopped
1 fennel bulb, cored and chopped
1 cup dry white wine
6 cups chicken stock
1 bay leaf
1 rosemary sprig
1 cup pitted Picholine olives—½ cup left whole, ½ cup coarsely chopped
½ teaspoon crushed red pepper
¼ cup small mint leaves
3 tablespoons fresh lemon juice
2 pounds fresh spaghetti or linguine
2 tablespoons extra-virgin olive oil

1. Preheat the oven to 350°. Season the goat with salt and pepper. Heat a large, enameled cast-iron casserole. Add the fennel and coriander seeds and the peppercorns and toast over moderate heat until fragrant, about 1 minute; transfer the spices to a plate to cool. Add the oil to the hot casserole and swirl to coat the bottom. Add the goat and cook over moderately high heat until richly browned all over, about 4 minutes per side. Transfer the goat to a plate.
2. Add the onions, carrots, celery and fennel to the casserole and cook over moderate heat, stirring occasionally, until softened, about 8 minutes. Add the wine and boil over high heat until reduced by half, scraping up any browned bits on the bottom of the casserole, about 3 minutes. Add the chicken stock and bring to a boil. Return the goat to the casserole. Add the bay leaf, rosemary sprig and the ½ cup of whole olives. Put the toasted spices and the crushed red pepper in a tea ball and submerge it in the liquid. Cover and bake, turning the goat once, until the meat is very tender, about 3 hours. Let the goat cool to room temperature in the cooking liquid.
3. Discard the bay leaf, rosemary sprig and the contents of the tea ball. Transfer the goat shoulder to a large rimmed baking sheet and remove all of the meat, breaking it up into 2-inch pieces. Remove any fat, bones and gristle and discard.
4. Pass the vegetables and cooking liquid through the coarse disk of a food mill and return the sauce to the casserole. Add the goat meat pieces and the remaining ½ cup of chopped olives. Simmer over low heat for 3 minutes. Stir in the mint leaves and lemon juice and season with salt and pepper.
5. Bring a large pot of salted water to a boil. Add the spaghetti and cook until almost al dente. Drain the spaghetti and add it to the ragù in the casserole. Bring to a simmer and cook for 2 minutes, stirring gently. Add the olive oil, toss well and serve. —*Chris Pandel*
MAKE AHEAD The goat ragù can be refrigerated for up to 3 days.
BEER Crisp black IPA: Goose Island A Beer Named Sue.

● HEALTHY ● MAKE AHEAD ● VEGETARIAN ● STAFF FAVORITE

pappardelle with duck ragù

Herbed Fazzoletti with Asparagus and Burrata

ACTIVE: 45 MIN; TOTAL: 1 HR
6 TO 8 SERVINGS ● ●

The *fazzoletti* (literally, "handkerchiefs") for this recipe are easy to make by cutting sheets of fresh pasta into squares.

- ¾ cup parsley leaves, plus more for garnish
- 2 tablespoons snipped chives, plus more for garnish
- 2 tablespoons tarragon leaves, plus more for garnish
- 2 tablespoons chervil leaves, plus more for garnish
- 1½ teaspoons fresh lemon juice
- ½ cup extra-virgin olive oil

Salt and freshly ground pepper

- 1 pound asparagus, cut into ½-inch pieces
- 1 pound fresh pasta sheets, cut into 3-inch squares (*fazzoletti*)
- ¼ cup pine nuts, preferably Italian
- 10 ounces burrata or buffalo mozzarella, cut into cubes

1. In a blender or food processor, combine the ¾ cup of parsley with the 2 tablespoons each of chives, tarragon and chervil. Pulse until chopped. Add the lemon juice and ¼ cup plus 2 tablespoons of the oil and puree until smooth. Season with salt and pepper.
2. Bring a large pot of salted water to a boil. Put the asparagus in a colander and ease it into the boiling water. Blanch the asparagus just until bright green, about 2 minutes. Shake dry. Boil the pasta until al dente. Drain, reserving ¼ cup of the pasta cooking water.
3. In a large, deep skillet, heat the remaining 2 tablespoons of oil. Add the pine nuts and toast over moderate heat until golden; transfer to a plate. Add the pasta, herb puree, asparagus and the pasta water to the skillet. Cook over moderate heat, tossing well. Toss in the cheese and pine nuts. Transfer to bowls and garnish with whole herbs.
—*Grace Parisi*

WINE Steely Italian white: 2010 Bollini Trentino Pinot Grigio.

Penne with Cabbage and Potatoes

TOTAL: 40 MIN • 4 SERVINGS ●

This classic Lombardian peasant dish is traditionally made with buckwheat pasta. Here, easy-to-find whole wheat penne stands in for the buckwheat, but the sauce is just as rustic and garlicky as the original.

- ¾ pound whole wheat penne
- ¾ pound green cabbage, chopped
- 1 large Yukon Gold potato (¾ pound), peeled and cut into ½-inch dice
- 2 tablespoons unsalted butter
- 2 tablespoons extra-virgin olive oil
- 2 garlic cloves, thinly sliced
- ½ teaspoon chopped rosemary
- ½ teaspoon chopped thyme

Salt and freshly ground pepper

- 4 ounces Italian Fontina cheese, shredded (1 cup)
- ¼ cup freshly grated Parmigiano-Reggiano, plus more for serving

1. In a large pot of boiling salted water, cook the penne until al dente. Drain the pasta, reserving 1 cup of the cooking water.
2. Fill the pasta pot with 1 inch of water. Spread the chopped cabbage in a steamer basket set over the pasta pot and top with the diced potato. Steam the vegetables until they are very tender, stirring once or twice, about 10 minutes. Pour off the water and wipe out the pot.
3. In the same pot, melt the butter in the olive oil. Add the sliced garlic and cook over moderately high heat, stirring, until lightly browned, about 2 minutes. Add the cabbage and potato along with the rosemary and thyme and season with salt and pepper. Cook until slightly dry, about 2 minutes. Add the pasta with its cooking water and cook, stirring and breaking up the potato, until the sauce is creamy and thick, about 2 minutes. Remove from the heat and stir in the Fontina and the ¼ cup of Parmigiano. Transfer the pasta to bowls and serve, passing extra grated cheese at the table. —*Marc Vetri*
WINE Zesty Sauvignon Blanc: 2010 Bernardus Monterey County.

Buttered Noodles with Toasted Sage

TOTAL: 25 MIN • 10 SERVINGS

While Parmigiano-Reggiano is wonderful on these simple egg noodles, locavore chef Tory Miller of L'Etoile restaurant in Madison prefers to use Wisconsin's own SarVecchio Parmesan cheese, which is made according to many of the Italian original's exacting standards. Another idea he borrows from Italy: adding leftover Parmesan rinds to the stock used here for added flavor.

- 1 stick unsalted butter, cut into tablespoons, at room temperature
- ½ cup thinly sliced sage leaves
- 2 garlic cloves, minced
- 2 teaspoons chopped rosemary
- 2½ cups chicken stock
- 1 pound wide egg noodles
- ½ cup plus 2 tablespoons freshly grated Parmesan cheese, preferably SarVecchio brand (see Note)

Salt and freshly ground black pepper

1. Bring a pot of salted water to a boil. In a skillet, melt 4 tablespoons of the butter. Add the sage leaves and cook over moderate heat until crisp; with a slotted spoon, transfer the toasted sage to a small bowl. Add 1 more tablespoon of the butter to the skillet. Add the garlic and rosemary and cook until fragrant, about 1 minute. Add the stock and boil until reduced to 1 cup, 8 minutes. Cover the skillet and remove from the heat.
2. Cook the noodles until al dente; drain. Return the noodles to the pot. Add the reduced stock and the remaining 3 tablespoons of butter and toss well. Stir in the ½ cup of grated cheese and season with salt and pepper.
3. Transfer the noodles to a bowl, top with the toasted sage and remaining 2 tablespoons of grated cheese and serve.
—*Tory Miller*
NOTE SarVecchio Parmesan can be purchased online at *shopsartori.com*.
WINE Aromatic, pear-scented white: 2009 Sartori di Verona Ferdi.

● HEALTHY ● MAKE AHEAD ○ VEGETARIAN ● STAFF FAVORITE

herbed fazzoletti with asparagus and burrata

Bucatini with Cauliflower and Brussels Sprouts

⏱ TOTAL: 40 MIN • 4 SERVINGS

Philadelphia chef Marc Vetri sautés cauliflower and brussels sprouts until they're charred and flavorful, then tosses them with long, thick strands of bucatini. The best part: the crispy bread crumb topping.

¾ pound bucatini or perciatelli
½ cup plus 2 tablespoons extra-virgin olive oil
½ pound cauliflower florets, cut into 1-inch pieces
½ pound brussels sprouts, halved or quartered if large
Salt and freshly ground black pepper
1 small onion, finely chopped
2 large garlic cloves, thinly sliced
4 plump oil-packed anchovies, minced
½ teaspoon crushed red pepper
1 teaspoon chopped rosemary
1 teaspoon chopped thyme
½ cup dry bread crumbs
½ cup freshly grated Parmigiano-Reggiano, plus more for serving

1. In a large pot of boiling salted water, cook the bucatini until al dente. Drain the pasta, reserving ½ cup of the cooking water.
2. Meanwhile, in a large, deep skillet, heat ¼ cup of the oil. Add the cauliflower and brussels sprouts and season with salt and black pepper; cover and cook over moderately high heat, stirring occasionally, until lightly charred and crisp-tender, about 5 minutes. Add ¼ cup of oil to the skillet along with the onion, garlic, anchovies, crushed red pepper, rosemary and thyme; cook, stirring, until the onion is slightly softened, about 3 minutes. Cover and cook over low heat until the cauliflower and sprouts are tender, about 3 minutes. Keep warm.
3. In a small skillet, heat the remaining 2 tablespoons of olive oil. Add the bread crumbs and cook over moderately high heat, stirring, until golden and crisp, about 4 minutes. Season with salt and transfer to a bowl.
4. Add the pasta and the reserved cooking water to the vegetables and cook over moderate heat, tossing, until the water is nearly absorbed. Remove from the heat and stir in the ½ cup of grated cheese. Serve the pasta in wide bowls, passing the bread crumbs and additional cheese at the table. —*Marc Vetri*
WINE Rich white: 2010 Seghesio Fiano.

Orecchiette with Greens, Mozzarella and Chickpeas

⏱ TOTAL: 40 MIN • 4 SERVINGS ● ●

½ pound orecchiette
Vegetable oil, for frying
1 cup drained canned chickpeas, patted dry
⅛ teaspoon ground cumin
⅛ teaspoon ground coriander
Kosher salt and ground black pepper
¼ cup extra-virgin olive oil
4 garlic cloves, thinly sliced
½ teaspoon crushed red pepper
1 cup grape tomatoes, halved
½ pound Swiss chard, stemmed and leaves coarsely chopped
4 ounces fresh mozzarella, cut into ½-inch cubes
8 large basil leaves, torn

1. In a large pot of boiling salted water, cook the orecchiette until al dente. Drain, reserving ¼ cup of the cooking water.
2. Meanwhile, in a medium, deep skillet, heat ¼ inch of vegetable oil until shimmering. Add the chickpeas and cook over high heat until crisp, 4 minutes. Transfer them to a paper towel–lined plate, sprinkle with the cumin and coriander and season with salt and black pepper. Discard the oil and wipe out the skillet.
3. Add the olive oil, garlic and crushed red pepper to the skillet. Cook over moderately high heat until fragrant, 30 seconds. Add the tomatoes and cook until softened, 3 minutes. Add the chard and cook, stirring, until wilted, 5 minutes. Season with salt and black pepper.
4. Add the pasta and reserved cooking water to the skillet and cook over moderate heat, stirring until incorporated. Add the mozzarella and basil and toss. Spoon the pasta into bowls, sprinkle with the chickpeas and serve. —*Marcie Turney*
WINE Fruit-forward Pinot Gris: 2010 Elk Cove.

Orecchiette with Sausage and Cherry Tomatoes

⏱ TOTAL: 30 MIN • 4 SERVINGS

Using sausage in place of ground meat is a good shortcut for making pasta sauce because it's already seasoned. Provolone cheese is stirred in before serving for a salty, creamy finish.

1 pound orecchiette
¼ cup extra-virgin olive oil
¾ pound sweet Italian sausage, casings removed
1 pint cherry tomatoes, halved
½ teaspoon crushed red pepper
Salt
2 ounces aged provolone cheese, shredded

1. In a large pot of boiling salted water, cook the orecchiette until al dente. Drain the pasta, reserving ¾ cup of the cooking water.
2. Meanwhile, in a large, deep skillet, heat 1 tablespoon of the olive oil until shimmering. Add the sausage in 1-inch clumps and cook over moderately high heat, turning once, until browned and cooked through, about 8 minutes. Using a slotted spoon, transfer the sausage to a plate.
3. Add 2 tablespoons of the olive oil to the skillet along with the cherry tomatoes and crushed red pepper; cook over moderately high heat, pressing the tomatoes until they are slightly softened, about 4 minutes. Add the reserved pasta cooking water, season with salt and cook over moderate heat, scraping up any browned bits and crushing the tomatoes, until the liquid is reduced by half and the tomatoes are nearly broken down, about 5 minutes.
4. Add the pasta to the skillet along with the cooked sausage and the remaining 1 tablespoon of olive oil and cook, stirring, until the pasta is evenly coated, about 3 minutes. Remove from the heat and stir in the shredded provolone cheese. Transfer the pasta to bowls and serve right away. —*Marc Vetri*
WINE Bold, cherry-dense Merlot: 2009 Avalon Napa Valley.

● HEALTHY ● MAKE AHEAD ● VEGETARIAN ● STAFF FAVORITE

bucatini with cauliflower and brussels sprouts

Spicy Tonnarelli with Clams

⏱ **TOTAL: 25 MIN • 4 SERVINGS** ● ●

- ¼ cup extra-virgin olive oil
- 1 ounce hot *coppa* or soppressata, cut into ¼-inch dice (¼ cup)
- 4 garlic cloves, thinly sliced
- ½ teaspoon crushed red pepper
- 6 tablespoons dry white wine
- 32 Manila or littleneck clams, scrubbed
- ¾ pound *tonnarelli* or linguine

Freshly ground black pepper

- 2 tablespoons each of thinly sliced mint and basil

1. In a deep skillet, heat the olive oil. Add the *coppa*, garlic and crushed red pepper; cook over moderately low heat until the garlic is golden, 1½ minutes. Add the wine and bring to a boil over moderately high heat. Add the clams, cover and cook for 5 to 8 minutes; as they open, transfer them to a covered bowl. **2.** In a large pot of boiling salted water, cook the *tonnarelli* (or linguine) until almost al dente. Drain, reserving ¾ cup of the cooking water. Add the pasta to the skillet. Stir in the cooking water over low heat, tossing until the pasta is al dente, about 1 minute. Season with black pepper. Add the clams to the pasta, garnish with the herbs and serve. —*Marcie Turney*

WINE Crisp Italian white: 2010 Sartarelli Classico Verdicchio.

Cavatelli with Mussels, Lillet and Dill

⏱ **TOTAL: 30 MIN • 4 SERVINGS** ●

- 2 pounds mussels, scrubbed
- ¼ cup dry white wine
- 2 dill sprigs, plus 1 tablespoon chopped dill
- ¼ cup Lillet or dry vermouth
- ¾ cup crème fraîche
- 1 small shallot, minced
- 1 teaspoon finely grated lemon zest
- 1 teaspoon finely grated grapefruit zest (optional)
- ¾ pound fresh cavatelli

Freshly ground pepper

1. In a large saucepan, combine the mussels, wine, dill sprigs and 2 tablespoons of the Lillet and bring to a boil. Cover and steam until the mussels open, about 4 minutes. Transfer the mussels to a bowl and strain the juices into a medium bowl. Remove the mussels from their shells; discard any mussels that don't open. Rinse out the saucepan. **2.** Return the juices to the saucepan and simmer until reduced to ¾ cup, about 5 minutes. Stir in the crème fraîche, shallot and the lemon and grapefruit zests. **3.** Meanwhile, in a large pot of boiling salted water, cook the pasta until nearly al dente; drain. Add the pasta to the saucepan along with the remaining 2 tablespoons of Lillet. Cook over high heat, stirring frequently, until the sauce is thick and creamy, about 4 minutes. Stir in the mussels and chopped dill and season the pasta with pepper. Serve right away. —*Kerry Heffernan*

WINE Briny, crisp Loire Valley white: 2008 Michel Delhommeau Cuvée St. Vincent Muscadet Sèvre et Maine Sur Lie.

Rigatoni with Sea Bass and Tomatoes

⏱ **TOTAL: 30 MIN • 4 SERVINGS** ●

- ¾ pound rigatoni
- ¼ cup extra-virgin olive oil
- 2 small onions, finely chopped
- 2 large garlic cloves, thinly sliced
- ½ teaspoon crushed red pepper

One 28-ounce can peeled Italian tomatoes, chopped, juices reserved
- 1 cup bottled clam juice
- 1 pound skinless fish fillets, such as sea bass, halibut, snapper or swordfish, cut into ¾-inch dice

Salt
- ¼ cup chopped flat-leaf parsley

1. In a large pot of boiling salted water, cook the pasta until al dente. Drain the pasta. **2.** Meanwhile, in a large, deep skillet, heat the olive oil until shimmering. Add the onions and garlic and cook over moderate heat until softened, about 5 minutes. Add the crushed red pepper and tomatoes with their juices and bring to a boil. Cook over moderately high heat, stirring occasionally, for about 8 minutes, until the sauce is very thick. Add the clam juice and simmer until the sauce is thickened and slightly reduced, about 5 minutes. Season the fish with salt and stir it into the sauce. Simmer for 2 minutes, until the fish is nearly cooked through. **3.** Add the rigatoni to the sauce along with the parsley and cook for 1 minute, stirring to coat the pasta. Serve. —*Marc Vetri*

WINE Juicy, light-bodied red: 2008 Domenico Clerico Langhe Visadi Dolcetto.

Sea Urchin Linguine

⏱ **TOTAL: 25 MIN**

4 FIRST-COURSE SERVINGS ● ●

This pasta from F&W Best New Chef 2011 Carlo Mirarchi of Roberta's restaurant in Brooklyn, New York, evokes the chef's childhood vacations in Calabria, Italy, where he dove for fresh sea urchins.

- 4 ounces fresh sea urchin (see Note)
- ¼ cup extra-virgin olive oil
- ½ pound linguine
- 1 cup ramp greens, coarsely chopped, or 3 tablespoons chopped chives (see Note)

1. In a blender, puree the sea urchin with 2 tablespoons of the olive oil until smooth. **2.** In a pot of heavily salted boiling water, cook the linguine until al dente. Meanwhile, in a deep skillet, heat the remaining 2 tablespoons of oil. Add the ramps and cook over moderately high heat until wilted, 1 minute. **3.** Drain the linguine, reserving 5 tablespoons of the cooking water. Add the linguine to the skillet with the sea urchin puree and 2 tablespoons of the cooking water and toss over moderate heat for 30 seconds. Off the heat, add the remaining 3 tablespoons of cooking water and toss. Transfer to bowls and serve. —*Carlo Mirarchi*

NOTE Look for *uni* (sea urchin) at Japanese markets. If using chives, toss them with the pasta at the end.

WINE Minerally Muscadet: 2009 Domaine de la Louvetrie.

● HEALTHY ● MAKE AHEAD ● VEGETARIAN ● STAFF FAVORITE

cavatelli with mussels, lillet and dill

Potato Gnocchi with Garlic Butter, Mushrooms and Snails

ACTIVE: 45 MIN; TOTAL: 1 HR 35 MIN
8 SERVINGS ●

At The Modern in New York City, chef Gabriel Kreuther makes potato gnocchi using *fromage blanc,* a fresh French cheese that creates a light texture and lovely tang; sour cream is a fine replacement. Snails add an earthy flavor to the dish (though the recipe is also delicious without them).

GNOCCHI
Rock salt
¾ pound Yukon Gold potatoes
1 cup sour cream
1 large egg, lightly beaten
1 cup all-purpose flour, plus more for dusting
2 teaspoons kosher salt
¼ teaspoon freshly grated nutmeg
SAUCE
6 tablespoons unsalted butter, softened
6 small garlic cloves, minced
⅓ cup finely chopped parsley
Salt and freshly ground black pepper
¾ cup dry white wine
One 12-ounce can small Burgundy snails, drained and rinsed
2 tablespoons extra-virgin olive oil
1 pound oyster mushrooms, stems trimmed and large caps halved
1 teaspoon sherry vinegar
¼ cup freshly grated Parmigiano-Reggiano cheese
2 cups small watercress sprigs

1. PREPARE THE GNOCCHI Preheat the oven to 450°. Spread ¼ inch of rock salt in a pie plate. Arrange the potatoes on top of the salt, cover with foil and bake for about 40 minutes, until they are tender. When the potatoes are cool enough to handle, peel and pass them through a ricer into a bowl. Add the sour cream, egg, the 1 cup of flour, the kosher salt and nutmeg to the potatoes and stir gently until incorporated.

2. Transfer the potato mixture to a resealable plastic bag and cut ½ inch off one of the corners. Line a baking sheet with parchment paper and dust with flour. Pipe 1-inch gnocchi onto the baking sheet and cover with plastic wrap.

3. PREPARE THE SAUCE In a small bowl, blend the butter with the garlic and parsley and season with salt and pepper.

4. In a small saucepan, bring the white wine to a simmer, add the snails and cook over low heat for about 5 minutes.

5. In a large, deep skillet, heat the olive oil. Add the oyster mushrooms and season with salt and pepper. Cover and cook over moderately high heat, stirring a few times, until starting to brown, about 3 minutes. Uncover and cook, stirring, until the mushrooms are browned and tender, about 4 minutes longer. Add the snails and ½ cup of the wine they were in and bring to a simmer. Stir in the garlic butter and sherry vinegar and remove from the heat.

6. In a large pot of boiling salted water, cook half of the gnocchi until they float to the surface. Using a slotted spoon, transfer the gnocchi to the sauce. Repeat with the remaining gnocchi, gently folding them all into the sauce. Transfer the gnocchi to bowls. Sprinkle with the Parmigiano-Reggiano cheese and watercress and serve.
—*Gabriel Kreuther*

MAKE AHEAD The gnocchi can be boiled, chilled in ice water, tossed in oil and refrigerated overnight. Reheat the gnocchi in a pot of boiling water. The garlic butter can be frozen for up to 2 weeks. Bring the butter to room temperature before using.
WINE Pinot Noir: 2009 Babcock Rita's Earth.

Butternut Squash and Sage Wontons

TOTAL: 1 HR 15 MIN • MAKES 2 DOZEN
WONTONS ● ● ●

"Wonton wrappers are terrific for making ravioli when you don't have time to make homemade pasta," says Jill Donenfeld of The Culinistas, a bicoastal private-chef service. The wontons here, filled with mashed butternut squash and roasted garlic, get nicely crispy when sautéed in a touch of oil, but they're also excellent simply steamed.

4 large garlic cloves, unpeeled
2 sage leaves—1 whole, 1 minced
2 tablespoons plus 1 teaspoon extra-virgin olive oil
¼ cup walnuts
¾ pound butternut squash—peeled, seeded and cut into 1-inch cubes
1 medium shallot, minced
Salt and freshly ground pepper
24 wonton wrappers
1 tablespoon freshly grated Parmigiano-Reggiano cheese

1. Preheat the oven to 400°. Arrange the garlic cloves and the whole sage leaf on a piece of foil and drizzle with 1 teaspoon of the olive oil. Wrap in the foil and roast for about 40 minutes, until the garlic cloves are very soft. Let cool, then peel the garlic.

2. Meanwhile, spread the walnuts in a pie plate and toast for about 5 minutes, until golden brown. Let the walnuts cool, then coarsely chop them.

3. In a medium saucepan, cover the squash with water. Bring to a boil and simmer over moderate heat until tender, about 15 minutes. Drain well and transfer to a bowl. Add the roasted garlic and the sage leaf to the squash and mash with a fork.

4. In a large nonstick skillet, heat 1 tablespoon of the oil. Add the shallot and minced sage and cook over moderate heat until the shallot is softened, 3 minutes. Mix the shallot and sage into the squash and season with salt and pepper. Wipe out the skillet.

5. Working with 4 wonton wrappers at a time, mound a rounded teaspoon of squash filling in the center of each wrapper. Brush the edges of the wrappers with water and fold each one into a triangle, pressing the edges to seal, then bring the pointed edges together and press to seal. Transfer the stuffed wontons to a baking sheet and cover them with plastic wrap. Repeat with the remaining wonton wrappers and filling.

6. Oil a steamer basket and set it over simmering water. Arrange half of the wontons in the basket, cover and steam for 5 minutes. Transfer the steamed wontons to a large plate. Repeat with the remaining wontons.

● HEALTHY ● MAKE AHEAD ○ VEGETARIAN ● STAFF FAVORITE

7. In the large nonstick skillet, heat the remaining 1 tablespoon of olive oil until shimmering. Add the wontons and cook over moderate heat, turning once, until they are lightly browned and crisp, about 2 minutes per side. Transfer the wontons to a platter, sprinkle with the toasted walnuts and the cheese and serve. —*Jill Donenfeld*

MAKE AHEAD Freeze the uncooked stuffed wontons on a baking sheet, then store in a plastic bag for up to 1 month. Steam however many you want at a time. The steamed wontons can be refrigerated for up to 2 days. Bring to room temperature before sautéing.

WINE Minerally northern Italian white: 2009 Kellerei Andrian Pinot Bianco.

Ricotta Gnudi with Chanterelles

⏱ **TOTAL: 45 MIN • 6 SERVINGS** ●

These tender *gnudi*—essentially cheesy mounds of ravioli filling—from chef and cookbook author Nancy Silverton are fantastic with buttery chanterelles.

GNUDI

 1 pound whole cow-milk ricotta
 ¼ cup freshly grated Parmigiano-Reggiano cheese, plus more for serving
 1 large egg, lightly beaten
 2 teaspoons unsalted butter, melted
 ¼ teaspoon freshly grated nutmeg
 1 cup all-purpose flour, plus more for dusting and rolling

CHANTERELLES

 ½ cup extra-virgin olive oil, plus more for drizzling
 1 pound chanterelle mushrooms, thickly sliced

Salt

 8 large garlic cloves, thinly sliced
 2 teaspoons thyme leaves
 1 stick unsalted butter, diced

1. PREPARE THE GNUDI In a large bowl, combine the ricotta, ¼ cup of Parmigiano, egg, butter and nutmeg. Sprinkle the 1 cup of flour over the mixture and fold it in. Dust the dough lightly with more flour and shape into a ball. On a lightly floured work surface, roll the dough out to a rope and cut it into 36 pieces. Gently roll the pieces into balls and transfer to a floured baking sheet.

2. PREPARE THE CHANTERELLES In a large skillet, heat the ½ cup of oil. Add the chanterelles, season with salt and cook over high heat until the liquid evaporates and the mushrooms are lightly browned, 10 to 12 minutes. Add the garlic and thyme and stir over low heat for 30 seconds. Add ½ cup of water and the butter, raise the heat to moderate and stir until the butter is melted. Season with salt.

3. In a large pot of boiling salted water, boil the *gnudi* until tender and cooked through, about 6 minutes; drain. Add the *gnudi* to the skillet and stir gently to coat with the sauce. Cook over moderate heat for 2 minutes. Spoon the *gnudi* and sauce into bowls. Drizzle with oil, sprinkle with cheese and serve. —*Nancy Silverton (Adapted from* The Mozza Cookbook: Recipes from Los Angeles's Favorite Italian Restaurant and Pizzeria *by Nancy Silverton with Matt Molina and Carolynn Carreño, published by Alfred A. Knopf/A Division of Random House, Inc.)*

WINE Fragrant Alto Adige white: 2010 Alois Lageder Beta Delta.

Chicken-Liver Ravioli

ACTIVE: 1 HR; TOTAL: 3 HR 20 MIN

6 TO 8 SERVINGS ● ●

 ½ pound chicken livers, trimmed
 1 shallot, thinly sliced
 1 large garlic clove, thinly sliced
 1 teaspoon chopped sage, plus 10 whole leaves
 ½ teaspoon chopped thyme
 5 tablespoons balsamic vinegar
 7 tablespoons unsalted butter

Salt and freshly ground pepper

 1 package wonton wrappers (48)

All-purpose flour, for dusting

 ½ cup chicken stock or broth

1. In a nonreactive bowl, toss the livers, shallot, garlic, chopped sage, thyme and 1 tablespoon of the vinegar; refrigerate for 2 hours.

2. In a medium skillet, heat 2 tablespoons of the butter. Add the livers and marinade and cook over moderately high heat, turning, until lightly browned, about 8 minutes.

3. Scrape the mixture into a food processor and pulse until chopped. Add 1 tablespoon of the butter and puree until smooth. Season with salt and pepper. Scrape the puree into a resealable plastic bag and refrigerate until cooled slightly and firm, about 20 minutes. Snip off one corner of the bag.

4. Arrange 4 wontons on a work surface and brush the edges with water. Pipe a rounded teaspoon of the liver onto each wrapper and fold the wrapper over to create a triangle. Press out any trapped air and press the edges to seal. Transfer the ravioli to a wax paper–lined baking sheet dusted with flour. Repeat with the remaining wrappers and filling.

5. Bring a large pot of salted water to a boil. Add the ravioli and cook until al dente, 3 to 4 minutes. Drain and gently shake dry.

6. Heat the remaining 4 tablespoons of butter in a large skillet. Add the sage leaves and cook over high heat until crisp, 4 minutes. Transfer to a plate. Add the remaining ¼ cup of vinegar to the skillet; simmer until syrupy, 3 minutes. Add the stock and bring to a boil. Add the cooked ravioli; gently stir to coat with the sauce. Transfer the ravioli and sauce to bowls, crumble the fried sage on top and serve. —*Chris Cosentino*

WINE Smooth Pinot Noir: 2008 Dashwood.

best pasta pot

two-in-one Calphalon's hard-anodized pot has two inserts: one for cooking and draining pasta, another for steaming vegetables. *$100; pans.com.*

Stovetop Mac and Cheese with Cheese Crisps

⏱ **TOTAL: 45 MIN • 4 SERVINGS** ●

Paprika adds a smoky flavor to this super-creamy mac and cheese that includes Fontina, extra-sharp cheddar and mascarpone. Golden cheese crisps replace the usual bread crumbs on top.

- 8 ounces extra-sharp cheddar cheese, coarsely shredded (about 2 cups)
- 4 tablespoons unsalted butter
- ¼ cup all-purpose flour
- 1 teaspoon smoked paprika
- 2 cups milk
- 4 ounces imported Fontina cheese, coarsely shredded (about 1 cup)
- ½ cup mascarpone cheese

Salt

- ½ pound elbow macaroni

ingredient tip

The author of five books on the subject (including two on grilled cheese sandwiches; the latest is Grilled Cheese, Please!*), Laura Werlin is America's top expert at cooking with cheese. Admittedly obsessive, she confesses that she dreams about it. Here, Werlin's tips for buying cheese and the best ways to use the different varieties.*

best all-around supermarket cheese At a store with few good options, Gruyère rarely disappoints.

best melting cheeses Werlin's favorite varieties are Monterey Jack, Fontina, Muenster, Gouda, mild cheddar and Gruyère.

best uses for sharp cheddar Sharp cheddar is drier than the mild kind, so it stays firmer when heated. Use this variety for its flavor, not meltiness.

1. Sprinkle half of the cheddar onto an extra-large nonstick skillet in four 4-inch mounds. Cook over moderate heat until the cheese is lacy and golden, about 4 minutes. Using a flexible spatula, carefully flip each crisp and cook until golden, about 1 minute longer. Drain on a paper towel–lined plate and break into large pieces.

2. In a very large saucepan, melt the butter. Whisk in the flour and paprika and cook over moderate heat until bubbling, about 2 minutes. Add the milk and whisk until smooth. Cook over moderate heat, whisking constantly, until thick and creamy, about 5 minutes. Stir in the remaining cheddar and the Fontina and cook over low heat until melted. Off the heat, stir in the mascarpone and season with salt.

3. Meanwhile, cook the macaroni in a large pot of boiling salted water until al dente. Drain and add to the cheese sauce. Cook over low heat, stirring constantly, until hot and bubbling, about 2 minutes. Spoon the mac and cheese into bowls, top with the cheese crisps and serve.

—*Laura Werlin*

MAKE AHEAD The cheese crisps can be kept in an airtight container at room temperature for up to 2 days. Recrisp before serving if necessary.

WINE Berry-rich Pinot Noir: 2009 Poppy.

White Lasagna Cupcakes

ACTIVE: 45 MIN; TOTAL: 2 HR
MAKES 8 CUPCAKES ●

These extra-rich mini lasagnas are part of a savory cupcake trend. Inspired by the lasagna cupcakes created by Heirloom-L.A. caterers, F&W's Grace Parisi came up with her own white version (made without tomato sauce) flavored with Fontina and prosciutto.

- 4 tablespoons unsalted butter, plus more for buttering the ramekins
- ¾ cup freshly grated Parmigiano-Reggiano cheese, plus more for sprinkling
- ½ pound fresh lasagna noodles
- ½ cup all-purpose flour
- 2 cups milk
- 1 large egg
- ¼ cup snipped chives
- 2 tablespoons chopped parsley
- 8 ounces Fontina cheese, shredded
- 6 ounces thinly sliced prosciutto, finely diced

Freshly ground pepper

1. Preheat the oven to 350°. Butter eight 6-ounce ramekins and coat with Parmigiano; tap out the excess. Place the ramekins on a sturdy rimmed baking sheet.

2. In a large pot of lightly salted boiling water, cook the lasagna noodles until al dente. Drain the noodles and cool under running water. Pat dry. Using a 3¼-inch biscuit cutter, stamp out 24 rounds (they should fit neatly inside the ramekins).

3. In a large saucepan, melt the 4 tablespoons of butter. Add the flour and whisk over moderately high heat for 1 minute. Add the milk and whisk over moderate heat until the sauce is bubbling and thickened, about 5 minutes. Remove the saucepan from the heat and whisk in the egg, chives, parsley and ½ cup of the Parmigiano. Let cool slightly, then stir in the Fontina and prosciutto. Season the filling with pepper.

4. Arrange 1 pasta round in the bottom of each ramekin. Spoon a scant ¼ cup of the filling into each ramekin and top with another noodle; press to flatten slightly. Top with the remaining filling and pasta rounds. Sprinkle the tops with the remaining ¼ cup of Parmigiano and cover loosely with foil.

5. Bake the cupcakes for about 20 minutes, until the filling is just bubbling. Remove the foil and bake for about 30 minutes longer, until slightly puffed and the tops and sides are golden. Let cool for 20 minutes. Run a knife around the lasagna cupcakes, then invert onto plates, tapping firmly to release them. Serve hot or warm.

—*Grace Parisi*

MAKE AHEAD The unmolded baked lasagna cupcakes can be refrigerated overnight. Reheat in a 325° oven.

WINE Bright, rich Chardonnay: 2009 Patz & Hall Dutton Ranch.

● HEALTHY ● MAKE AHEAD ● VEGETARIAN ● STAFF FAVORITE

stovetop mac and cheese with cheese crisps

Pappardelle with Clams, Turmeric and Habaneros

ACTIVE: 35 MIN; TOTAL: 1 HR 15 MIN
6 SERVINGS

"I've always loved the flavors of garlic and turmeric with shellfish," says chef Zakary Pelaccio of New York City's Fatty Crab. Here, he warms those flavorings along with chiles in olive oil before adding fresh basil, clam juice and a splash of gin, then tosses it all with littleneck clams and pappardelle.

- 8 large garlic cloves, unpeeled
- 2 tablespoons extra-virgin olive oil
- ½ teaspoon ground turmeric
- 2 habanero chiles—1 chopped with seeds, 1 seeded and thinly sliced
- 2 cups packed whole basil leaves, plus ½ cup chopped basil
- 1 tablespoon coarsely cracked black pepper
- ¼ cup gin
- 1 cup bottled clam juice
- 4 dozen littleneck clams, scrubbed
Finely grated zest of 1 lime
- 2 tablespoons fresh lime juice
- ¾ pound pappardelle
- 4 tablespoons unsalted butter

ingredient tip

anchovy paste A small amount of this paste can give an umami boost to salad dressing, marinara or meaty ragùs. It can also be used in place of Asian fish sauce in Thai curries or noodle dishes like the pad thai at right.

1. Preheat the oven to 400°. Loosely wrap the garlic cloves in aluminum foil and bake them for about 25 minutes, until they are very soft. Peel the garlic cloves.

2. In a medium saucepan, heat the olive oil. Add the roasted garlic cloves, turmeric and chopped habanero and cook over moderate heat until fragrant, about 2 minutes. Add the basil leaves, coarsely cracked black pepper, gin and clam juice, cover and cook over low heat until the liquid has reduced to ½ cup, about 10 minutes. Strain the reduction into a large pot, pressing on the solids.

3. Bring the strained liquid to a boil. Add the clams, cover and cook, shaking the pot a few times, until they start to open, 3 minutes; as the clams open, transfer them to a bowl and keep covered. When all of the clams have opened, boil the broth over high heat until reduced to 2 cups, about 5 minutes. Stir in the lime zest and lime juice.

4. Meanwhile, in a large pot of boiling salted water, cook the pappardelle until al dente. Drain the pasta.

5. Add the pappardelle to the pot with the reduced clam broth and toss to coat. Add the butter, 1 tablespoon at a time, tossing well over moderate heat, until melted. Transfer the pappardelle to bowls, then top with the clams, chopped basil and sliced habanero and serve right away.
—*Zakary Pelaccio*

WINE Fresh, minerally Italian white: 2010 Fontana Candida Frascati Superiore.

Quick Shrimp Pad Thai

TOTAL: 30 MIN • 4 SERVINGS ●

This is a great, fast take on American-style pad thai, with an appealing combination of sweet, sour and spicy flavors. Look for the pad thai noodles (also called rice sticks) at Asian grocery stores or in the Asian section of supermarkets.

- 8 ounces pad thai noodles, preferably A Taste of Thai or Thai Kitchen brands
- 2 tablespoons Asian fish sauce
- ¼ cup fresh lime juice, plus lime wedges for serving
- 3 tablespoons light brown sugar
- 2 Thai bird chiles or 1 serrano chile with seeds, stemmed and thinly sliced
- ¼ cup plus 1 tablespoon canola oil
- 3 large shallots, thinly sliced (1 cup)
- 3 large garlic cloves, minced
- 12 ounces shelled and deveined medium shrimp
- 2 large eggs, beaten
- 4 scallions, thinly sliced
Roasted peanuts, chopped cilantro and bean sprouts, for serving

1. Put the pad thai noodles in a large bowl and cover them with very hot water. Let the noodles soak until they are just pliable, about 5 minutes. Transfer the noodles to a colander and let them drain, shaking and tossing the noodles once or twice.

2. Meanwhile, in a small bowl, whisk the fish sauce with the lime juice, light brown sugar and sliced chiles.

3. In a large nonstick skillet, heat 3 tablespoons of the canola oil until shimmering. Add the shallots and garlic and cook over high heat, stirring occasionally, until lightly browned, about 3 minutes. Add the pad thai noodles and stir-fry with the shallots and garlic until the noodles are heated through, about 2 minutes. Add the shrimp and cook, stirring occasionally, until they begin to curl and turn pink, about 2 minutes.

4. Scrape the noodles and shrimp to one side of the pan and add the remaining 2 tablespoons of canola oil to the empty side of the skillet. Add the beaten eggs and cook, stirring occasionally, until nearly set, about 1 minute. Add the sliced scallions and toss everything together, keeping the eggs relatively intact. Add the fish sauce mixture and stir-fry until the noodles are evenly coated, about 2 to 3 minutes.

5. Transfer the pad thai to a platter. Top with roasted peanuts, cilantro and bean sprouts and serve right away, with lime wedges.
—*Grace Parisi*

WINE Ripe, lime-scented Pinot Gris from Oregon: 2009 O'Reilly's.

● HEALTHY ● MAKE AHEAD ○ VEGETARIAN ● STAFF FAVORITE

Bizarre Foods *host Andrew Zimmern transforms his international travel experiences into simple, delicious dishes like soy-ginger-glazed chicken yakitori,* OPPOSITE; *recipe, page 116.*

poultry

Thai Chicken and Watermelon Salad

ACTIVE: 30 MIN; TOTAL: 1 HR
4 SERVINGS ● ●

- 2 stalks of fresh lemongrass, pale inner core only, minced
- ¼ cup vegetable oil
- Salt and freshly ground pepper
- 1½ pounds skinless, boneless chicken breast halves, butterflied
- 2 Thai chiles, thinly sliced
- 2 garlic cloves, thinly sliced
- 2 tablespoons light brown sugar
- 3 tablespoons fresh lime juice
- 3 tablespoons Asian fish sauce
- 2 tablespoons water
- 2½ pounds seedless watermelon, sliced and stamped into rounds (3 cups)
- ¼ cup each of chopped cilantro and mint

1. In a bowl, combine the lemongrass, oil and a pinch each of salt and pepper. Add the chicken breast and turn to coat. Let marinate at room temperature for 30 minutes.
2. Light a grill and oil the grates or preheat a grill pan and brush with oil. Grill the chicken over moderately high heat, turning once, until cooked through and lightly charred, about 6 minutes. Let cool slightly, then slice.

quick asian rub for grilled poultry

This quick and easy spice mixture is great on chicken, duck and other birds. Massage the rub onto the meat before grilling.

In a skillet, combine 10 white peppercorns with ¼ cup Szechuan peppercorns, 2 tablespoons chile powder and 1 tablespoon each of garlic powder and dried lemon peel. Toast until fragrant. Let cool, then grind. Stir in 1 tablespoon kosher salt. —*Pete Evans*

3. In a mini food processor, combine the Thai chiles with the garlic, brown sugar, lime juice, fish sauce and water and pulse until the chiles and garlic are finely chopped.
4. Arrange the watermelon in shallow bowls and top with the chicken, dressing, cilantro and mint. Serve. —*Grace Parisi*
VARIATION Dice the chicken. Cut the watermelon into balls. Pour the dressing over the chicken. Stir in the watermelon, cilantro and mint. Serve in Chinese soup spoons.
WINE Lively rosé: 2010 Palmina Botasea.

Winter Chicken Salad with Citrus and Celery

ACTIVE: 45 MIN; TOTAL: 1 HR 30 MIN
6 SERVINGS

- 7 tender celery ribs, 6 thinly sliced
- 2 unpeeled smashed garlic cloves
- ½ teaspoon black peppercorns
- 3 blood oranges
- Salt
- Four 12-ounce chicken breast halves on the bone
- 3 tablespoons red wine vinegar
- ½ cup extra-virgin olive oil
- Freshly ground pepper
- 2 cups shaved Grana Padano cheese
- ⅔ cup chopped marcona almonds

1. In a large saucepan, combine the whole celery rib, garlic and peppercorns with 6 cups of water. Using a peeler, remove the zest from 2 of the oranges and add the zest to the pot. Season lightly with salt and bring to a boil. Add the chicken and simmer over low heat for 16 minutes. Remove from the heat and let the chicken stand for exactly 30 minutes. Remove the chicken and pull the meat from the bones, discarding the skin. Shred the chicken and let cool. Reserve the broth for another use.
2. Meanwhile, using a sharp knife, peel the oranges, removing all of the bitter white pith. Working over a strainer set over a large bowl, cut in between the membranes to release the sections. Squeeze the juice from the membranes into the bowl. Whisk in the vinegar and oil and season with salt and pepper.

3. Add the shredded chicken, sliced celery, orange sections and cheese to the bowl; toss well. Mound the salad on a platter, sprinkle with the almonds and serve. —*Mindy Fox*
WINE Fragrant white: 2010 Jelu Torrontés.

Indian Barbecue Chicken

⏱ TOTAL: 35 MIN • 4 SERVINGS ●
For this sweet and tangy chicken, Philadelphia chef Marcie Turney blends tamarind and other Indian flavors into her molasses barbecue sauce.

- 3 tablespoons vegetable oil, plus more for rubbing
- 1 medium onion, finely diced
- 3 garlic cloves, minced
- 3 tablespoons minced peeled fresh ginger
- 1 cup ketchup
- ⅓ cup distilled white vinegar
- ⅓ cup tamarind puree (see Note)
- ⅓ cup unsulfured molasses
- Pinch of sugar
- 3 tablespoons whole-grain mustard
- ¼ teaspoon cayenne pepper
- 2 teaspoons garam masala
- Salt and freshly ground black pepper
- Four 6-ounce skinless, boneless chicken breast halves

1. In a skillet, heat the 3 tablespoons of oil. Add the onion and cook over moderate heat until translucent, 4 minutes. Add the garlic and ginger and cook until fragrant. Add the ketchup, vinegar, tamarind, molasses, sugar, mustard and cayenne and simmer over low heat, stirring, until reduced to 1¾ cups, 5 minutes. Stir in the garam masala and season with salt and black pepper.
2. Light a grill or preheat a grill pan. Rub the chicken with oil and season with salt. Grill over moderately high heat, turning once, until almost cooked, about 7 minutes. Brush with the sauce and grill over low heat, brushing and turning, until glazed, 4 minutes, then serve. —*Marcie Turney*
NOTE Tamarind puree is available at Indian and Latin markets.
WINE Juicy, full-bodied rosé: 2010 Muga.

● HEALTHY ● MAKE AHEAD ● VEGETARIAN ● STAFF FAVORITE

thai chicken and watermelon salad

Tomato-and-Cilantro-Marinated Chicken Shashlik

TOTAL: 40 MIN PLUS OVERNIGHT MARINATING • MAKES 8 SKEWERS ●

Serve these ultra-easy chicken kebabs with Georgian Grilled Tomato Sauce and Walnut-Yogurt Sauce for dipping (recipes follow).

- 2 large plum tomatoes, coarsely grated on a box grater
- 2 garlic cloves, minced
- ½ cup pure olive oil
- ½ cup chopped cilantro
- 4 pounds skinless, boneless chicken breasts, cut into 2-inch pieces
- Vegetable oil, for brushing
- Salt and freshly ground pepper

1. In a large bowl, combine the grated tomatoes, garlic, olive oil and cilantro. Add the chicken and coat thoroughly with the marinade. Cover and refrigerate overnight.

russian-cottage grilling menu

These recipes were inspired by the summer weekends Moscovites spend at their cottages (dachas) in the Russian countryside—gardening, foraging and grilling.

boston lettuce with cilantro and walnuts (page 42)

cranberry bean salad with celery, basil and mint (page 282)

grilled eggplant salad with walnuts (page 56)

herb-and-chile-marinated fish shashlik (page 206)

tomato-and-cilantro-marinated chicken shashlik (above)

pork shashlik with spicy red wine marinade (page 177)

2. Light a grill or preheat a grill pan. Thread the chicken onto 8 metal skewers, leaving a small space between each piece. Brush the chicken with vegetable oil and season with salt and pepper. Grill over moderate heat, turning occasionally, until lightly charred and just cooked through, about 15 minutes.
—*Dmitry Leonov*

WINE Vibrant, tropical fruit–scented Sauvignon Blanc: 2010 Babich Marlborough.

GEORGIAN GRILLED TOMATO SAUCE

TOTAL: 20 MIN • MAKES 2½ CUPS ● ● ●

- 4 medium tomatoes, halved
- 1 large jalapeño
- 1 small red onion, coarsely chopped
- 1 garlic clove, minced
- ¼ cup chopped parsley
- ¼ cup chopped cilantro
- Salt and freshly ground black pepper

1. Light a grill or preheat a grill pan. Grill the tomatoes and jalapeño over high heat, turning, until charred, about 4 minutes. Halve the jalapeño and discard the stem and seeds. Coarsely chop the tomatoes.
2. Transfer the jalapeño and tomatoes to a food processor. Add the onion, garlic, parsley and cilantro and process until smooth. Season with salt and pepper and let stand for 10 minutes before serving. —*DL*

WALNUT-YOGURT SAUCE

TOTAL: 10 MIN PLUS OVERNIGHT CHILLING • MAKES 3½ CUPS ● ● ●

- 1½ cups walnuts (½ pound)
- 1½ cups plain whole-milk yogurt
- 2 teaspoons Sriracha sauce
- 1 small garlic clove, minced
- ½ small onion, minced
- Salt
- ½ cup thinly sliced basil leaves

In a food processor, puree the walnuts with the yogurt and Sriracha; transfer to a bowl. Fold in the garlic and onion, season with salt and refrigerate overnight. Just before serving, garnish the sauce with the basil. —*DL*

MAKE AHEAD The walnut-yogurt sauce can be refrigerated for up to 5 days.

Chicken Breasts with Artichoke-Olive Sauce

TOTAL: 20 MIN • 4 SERVINGS ●

Chef Marcie Turney has three restaurants in Philadelphia, each devoted to a different place (the Mediterranean, India and Mexico). This fast chicken recipe was influenced by her trips to Italy.

- ¼ cup plus 1 tablespoon extra-virgin olive oil
- 3 tablespoons freshly squeezed lemon juice
- 2 teaspoons finely grated lemon zest
- 3 garlic cloves, minced
- 1 tablespoon chopped oregano
- One 10-ounce box frozen artichoke hearts, thawed and patted dry
- 8 pitted kalamata olives, halved
- ½ cup coarsely crumbled feta cheese
- Salt and freshly ground pepper
- Four 6-ounce skinless, boneless chicken breast halves
- 2 tablespoons chopped flat-leaf parsley

1. Preheat the oven to 400°. In a medium bowl, whisk ¼ cup of the olive oil with the lemon juice, lemon zest, garlic and oregano. Fold in the artichokes, olives and feta; season the sauce with salt and pepper.
2. Season the chicken breasts with salt and pepper. In an ovenproof skillet, heat the remaining 1 tablespoon of olive oil. Add the chicken, skinned side down, and cook over moderately high heat until browned, about 3 minutes; turn the chicken over and transfer the skillet to the oven.
3. Roast the chicken for about 10 minutes, until white throughout. Transfer the chicken to plates and spoon the sauce on top. Garnish with the parsley and serve.
—*Marcie Turney*

WINE Crisp, medium-bodied Greek white: 2010 Domaine Skouras Moschofilero.

● HEALTHY ● MAKE AHEAD ● VEGETARIAN ● STAFF FAVORITE

Chicken Parmesan with Pepperoni

⏱ ACTIVE: 30 MIN; TOTAL: 45 MIN

4 SERVINGS ●

Chef Bryan Vietmeier of Take 5 Urban Market in Seattle merges two Italian-American favorites here: chicken parm and pepperoni.

- 2 large eggs
- ¼ cup milk
- ½ cup all-purpose flour
- 2 cups *panko* (Japanese bread crumbs), finely crushed in a food processor
- Four 8-ounce skinless, boneless chicken breast halves, pounded ¾ inch thick
- Salt and freshly ground pepper
- ¾ cup canola oil
- 1½ cups tomato sauce
- ¼ cup freshly grated Parmigiano-Reggiano cheese
- 1 cup shredded mozzarella
- 2 ounces sliced pepperoni
- 2 tablespoons chopped flat-leaf parsley

1. Preheat the oven to 450°. In a pie plate, beat the eggs with the milk. Spread the flour and crushed *panko* in 2 separate pie plates. Season the chicken breasts all over with salt and freshly ground pepper and dust in the flour. Dip the chicken in the egg mixture and then in the *panko;* press to help the crumbs adhere to the chicken.

2. In a large skillet, heat the canola oil until shimmering. Add the chicken and fry over moderately high heat, turning once, until cooked through, about 7 minutes. Drain the chicken on paper towels, then transfer to a rimmed baking sheet. Top the chicken with the tomato sauce, Parmigiano, mozzarella and pepperoni slices.

3. Bake the chicken for about 15 minutes, until the cheese is melted and bubbling. Transfer the chicken to plates, sprinkle with the parsley and serve. —*Bryan Vietmeier*

WINE Black cherry–scented, light-bodied red: 2008 Giuseppe Mascarello e Figlio Santo Stefano di Perno Dolcetto d'Alba.

Chicken Breasts with Anchovy-Basil Pan Sauce

⏱ TOTAL: 40 MIN • 4 SERVINGS

F&W's Marcia Kiesel likes to pair this basil-flecked chicken recipe with Soave, the lightly herbal white wine from Italy's Veneto region that's fantastic for drinking in the warm summer months.

- 4 boneless chicken breast halves with skin
- Salt and freshly ground black pepper
- 1 tablespoon extra-virgin olive oil
- 2 medium shallots, thinly sliced
- 4 large anchovy fillets, minced
- ¼ teaspoon crushed red pepper
- ¼ cup dry white wine
- ½ cup slivered basil
- 1 tablespoon freshly squeezed lemon juice
- 1 tablespoon cold unsalted butter

1. Preheat the oven to 400° and season the chicken breasts with salt and black pepper. In a large ovenproof skillet, heat the olive oil. Add the chicken breasts, skin side down, and cook over moderately high heat until they are richly browned, about 3 minutes. Turn the chicken breasts and transfer the skillet to the oven. Roast for about 10 minutes, until just cooked through. Transfer the chicken to warmed plates.

2. Set the skillet over moderately high heat and add the shallots; cook until softened, about 3 minutes. Stir in the minced anchovies and crushed red pepper. Add the white wine and boil for 1 minute, scraping up any browned bits from the bottom of the pan. Add ⅓ cup of water and boil until the liquid is reduced to 3 tablespoons, about 1 minute. Remove the skillet from the heat and stir in the basil and lemon juice. Swirl in the butter and season the pan sauce with salt and freshly ground black pepper.

3. Pour the anchovy-basil pan sauce over the roasted chicken breasts, spooning the shallots all around, and serve right away. —*Marcia Kiesel*

SERVE WITH Fried zucchini blossoms.

WINE Lightly herbal Soave: 2010 Tedeschi.

Yucatán-Spiced Chicken

⏱ TOTAL: 45 MIN • 4 SERVINGS

These roasted bone-in chicken breasts are rubbed with a light orange-lime puree that is common in Mexico's Yucatán region.

- Finely grated zest of 1 orange, plus ¾ cup fresh orange juice
- Finely grated zest of 2 limes, plus ¼ cup fresh lime juice
- 4 garlic cloves, chopped
- 3 tablespoons ancho chile powder
- 2 tablespoons chopped fresh oregano
- ¼ cup extra-virgin olive oil, plus more for drizzling
- Salt and freshly ground pepper
- Four 8-ounce chicken breast halves on the bone, with skin
- 1 large chayote—halved lengthwise, pitted and cut into 12 wedges
- 1 seeded poblano, cut into thin rings
- 1 red onion, thinly sliced into rings
- 2 tablespoons each of thinly sliced cilantro and mint

1. Preheat the oven to 425°. In a blender, puree the orange zest and orange juice, lime zest and lime juice, garlic, ancho powder, oregano and the ¼ cup of olive oil. Season the puree with salt and pepper.

2. Arrange the chicken breasts in a shallow baking dish, skin side up, and make 3 deep, crosswise cuts in each breast half. Season the chicken with salt and cover it with the puree, rubbing it into the slits. Spread the chayote, poblano and onion on a rimmed baking sheet, drizzle with olive oil and season with salt. Roast the chicken in the upper third of the oven for about 30 minutes, basting a few times, until just white throughout; rotate the pan once halfway through roasting. At the same time, roast the vegetables for about 30 minutes, until browned and the chayote is crisp-tender.

3. Preheat the broiler. Broil the chicken 6 inches from the heat until well glazed, 2 minutes. Garnish with the herbs and serve the chicken and vegetables with the pan juices. —*Marcie Turney*

WINE Rich Chardonnay: 2009 Hanging Vine.

Lemongrass-Cilantro Chicken with Honey Dipping Sauce

TOTAL: 35 MIN PLUS OVERNIGHT
MARINATING • 4 SERVINGS ●

The juicy grilled chicken breasts here are a great example of *pings*, simple grilled dishes that are very popular all over Laos. Bruising the lemongrass is an essential step that helps release its flavor into the marinade, which can also be used for fish or pork.

SAUCE

⅓ cup water
1½ teaspoons sugar
2 teaspoons honey
¼ teaspoon crushed red pepper
1 tablespoon white vinegar
1 tablespoon Asian fish sauce
Salt and freshly ground black pepper

CHICKEN

2 large stalks of fresh lemongrass, cut into 1-inch pieces
1 cup packed chopped cilantro
4 large shallots, coarsely chopped
½ cup vegetable oil
4 boneless chicken breast halves with skin
Salt and freshly ground black pepper
1 cup small mint leaves
Lime wedges, for serving

1. MAKE THE SAUCE In a small saucepan, combine the water, sugar and honey and cook over moderate heat, stirring until the sugar has dissolved, about 1 minute. Pour the mixture into a heatproof bowl and add the crushed red pepper. Let the sauce cool to room temperature, then add the white vinegar and fish sauce and season with salt and freshly ground black pepper.

2. PREPARE THE CHICKEN Using the side of a chef's knife or a rolling pin, bruise the pieces of lemongrass. Transfer the pieces to a large, shallow dish. Add the chopped cilantro, shallots and vegetable oil and mix well to incorporate the ingredients. Add the chicken breasts to the dish and coat them thoroughly with the marinade. Cover and refrigerate the chicken overnight. Bring to room temperature before grilling.

3. Light a grill or preheat a grill pan. Scrape the marinade off the chicken breasts. Season the chicken with salt and freshly ground black pepper and grill, skin side down, over moderately high heat until the skin is lightly charred and crisp, about 3 minutes. Move the chicken to a cooler part of the grill or reduce the heat to moderate and grill for 2 minutes longer. Turn the chicken and cook until white throughout, about 5 minutes longer. Transfer the chicken to a cutting board and let rest for 5 minutes.

4. Slice the chicken crosswise ⅓ inch thick and transfer to plates. Sprinkle the chicken with the mint leaves and serve with lime wedges. Pass the dipping sauce at the table. —*Sebastien Rubis*

SERVE WITH Steamed sticky black rice.

MAKE AHEAD The honey dipping sauce can be refrigerated for up to 2 days. Serve the sauce at room temperature.

BEER Crisp, citrusy lager: Beerlao.

Chicken Milanese with Sage and Lemon Butter Sauce

🕐 TOTAL: 45 MIN • 8 SERVINGS

These pounded, breaded and fried chicken cutlets, with their crisp golden crust, were a staple in designer Linda Meyers's house while growing up. "We'd eat them plain—but if guests were coming over, my mom would add a butter sauce," she says. Here, she creates her own butter sauce, made with fresh sage and lemon, and serves the dish alongside a simple salad with Italian vinaigrette. (For Meyers's salad recipe, see page 44.)

SAUCE

6 tablespoons cold unsalted butter, cut into tablespoons
2 medium shallots, minced
1 cup heavy cream
1 cup dry white wine
1 cup chicken stock or low-sodium broth
2 tablespoons chopped fresh sage
2 teaspoons fresh lemon juice
Pinch of cayenne pepper
Salt and freshly ground white pepper

CHICKEN

1 cup seasoned dry bread crumbs
½ cup *panko* (Japanese bread crumbs)
¼ cup freshly grated Parmigiano-Reggiano cheese
Finely grated zest of 1 lemon
1½ teaspoons dried thyme
2 large eggs
Eight 6-ounce chicken breast cutlets, pounded ¼ inch thick
Salt and freshly ground black pepper
Vegetable oil, for frying
¼ cup chopped parsley

1. PREPARE THE SAUCE In a medium saucepan, melt 1 tablespoon of the butter. Add the shallots and cook over moderate heat until softened, 4 minutes. Add the cream, wine and stock and bring to a boil. Simmer over moderate heat until reduced to 1½ cups, 20 minutes. Remove from the heat and whisk in the remaining 5 tablespoons of butter, 1 tablespoon at a time. Add the sage, lemon juice and cayenne pepper. Season with salt and white pepper and cover.

2. MEANWHILE, PREPARE THE CHICKEN In a shallow bowl, combine the bread crumbs, *panko*, grated cheese, lemon zest and thyme. In another shallow bowl, beat the eggs. Season the eggs and chicken cutlets with salt and black pepper. Dip each cutlet in the egg mixture and let the excess drip off, then dredge in the bread crumbs. Transfer the breaded cutlets to a baking sheet lined with parchment paper.

3. Preheat the oven to 325°. In each of 2 large skillets, heat ¼ inch of oil until shimmering. Working in batches, add the breaded cutlets and cook over moderately high heat for 1 minute. Lower the heat to moderate and fry, turning once, until the cutlets are browned and crisp, 4 minutes. Transfer to paper towels to drain, then keep warm in the oven on another baking sheet while you fry the rest.

4. Rewarm the sauce over moderate heat, stirring constantly. Arrange the cutlets on plates, sprinkle with the parsley and serve with the sauce. —*Linda Meyers*

WINE Light-bodied, red fruit–inflected Beaujolais: 2009 Potel-Aviron Chénas.

● HEALTHY ● MAKE AHEAD ○ VEGETARIAN ○ STAFF FAVORITE

lemongrass-cilantro chicken with honey dipping sauce

Cider Vinegar–Braised Chicken Thighs

ACTIVE: 40 MIN; TOTAL: 1 HR 45 MIN
6 SERVINGS ●

2 tablespoons extra-virgin olive oil
3 pounds chicken thighs, fat trimmed
Salt and freshly ground pepper
5 carrots, sliced ½ inch thick
5 garlic cloves, thinly sliced
1 leek, white and light green parts only, thinly sliced
2 tablespoons all-purpose flour
1 cup cider vinegar
3 cups low-sodium chicken broth
3 tablespoons unsalted butter
2 tablespoons chopped parsley
2 tablespoons snipped chives

1. Preheat the oven to 350°. In a large enameled cast-iron casserole, heat the oil. Season the chicken with salt and pepper and add to the casserole, skin side down. Cook over moderately high heat, in batches if necessary, turning once, until golden brown, about 12 minutes. Transfer to a platter.
2. Spoon off all but 2 tablespoons of the fat in the casserole. Add the carrots, garlic and leek and cook over low heat until crisp-tender, 5 minutes. Add the flour and stir for 1 minute. Add the vinegar and stir, scraping up any browned bits from the bottom of the pot. Bring the sauce to a boil and cook until thickened, 3 minutes. Add the broth, season with salt and pepper and bring to a boil. Nestle the chicken in the sauce, skin side up. Transfer to the oven and braise the chicken for 50 minutes, until cooked through.
3. Preheat the broiler. Transfer the chicken to a baking sheet, skin side up. Broil on the middle rack of the oven until the skin is golden and crisp, about 4 minutes.
4. Simmer the sauce over moderate heat until reduced to about 4 cups, 10 minutes. Stir in the butter until melted. Add the herbs and season the sauce with salt and pepper. Return the chicken to the casserole, skin side up, and serve. —*James Boyce*
WINE Rich, barrel-aged California Chardonnay: 2009 Franciscan.

Spice-Rubbed Chicken Thighs

ACTIVE: 40 MIN; TOTAL: 1 HR 45 MIN
4 SERVINGS ●

1½ teaspoons coriander seeds
¼ star anise pod
1½ teaspoons cracked black peppercorns
1¼ teaspoons crushed red pepper
1 tablespoon kosher salt
8 meaty chicken thighs
¼ cup canola oil
1 large Spanish onion, thinly sliced
1 large leek, white and tender green parts only, thinly sliced
2 plum tomatoes, chopped
3 thyme sprigs
3 oregano sprigs
1 cup dry red wine
1 tablespoon red wine vinegar
1 tablespoon honey
Chopped parsley and chives, for garnish

1. Preheat the oven to 350°. In a small skillet, toast the coriander seeds, star anise, cracked peppercorns and crushed red pepper over moderate heat, shaking the pan, until fragrant, about 2 minutes. Transfer to a spice grinder and let cool, then pulse until coarsely ground. Add the salt. Rub the spices all over the chicken thighs.
2. In a large skillet, heat the oil. Add the chicken and cook over high heat, turning once, until deep golden, 10 minutes. Arrange the chicken in a roasting pan, skin side up. Pour off most of the oil from the skillet and add the onion and leek. Cook over moderate heat, stirring, until softened, 5 minutes. Add the tomatoes, thyme and oregano and cook until the tomatoes just begin to break down, 3 minutes. Add the red wine and cook until reduced to ¼ cup, scraping up any bits stuck to the pan, 5 minutes. Stir in 1 cup of water and pour the mixture into the roasting pan.
3. Cover the pan with foil and braise the chicken in the oven for about 1 hour, until cooked through. Transfer the chicken to a plate. Strain the sauce into a saucepan. Boil until the sauce is reduced to 1 cup, 5 minutes. Stir in the vinegar and honey; keep warm.

4. Preheat the broiler. Return the chicken to the roasting pan, skin side up, and broil 8 inches from the heat for 2 minutes, until the skin is crisp. Sprinkle the chicken with the parsley and chives and serve with the sauce. —*Tre Wilcox*
WINE Bright, fruit-forward Côtes-du-Rhône: 2009 J.L. Chave Mon Coeur.

Crispy Chicken Thighs with Golden Raisin Compote

TOTAL: 40 MIN • 4 SERVINGS ●

2 tablespoons unsalted butter
5 ounces butternut squash, peeled and cut into ½-inch dice (1 cup)
1 large shallot, minced
½ Granny Smith apple—peeled, cored and cut into ½-inch dice
¼ teaspoon cinnamon
¼ teaspoon cayenne pepper
1¼ cups golden raisins (½ pound)
½ cup dry white wine
2 tablespoons honey
2 teaspoons chopped thyme
Salt and freshly ground black pepper
1 tablespoon vegetable oil
Eight 6-ounce bone-in chicken thighs

1. Preheat the oven to 350°. In a skillet, melt the butter. Add the squash, cover and cook over moderate heat until almost tender, 3 minutes. Add the shallot and cook for 1 minute. Add the apple, cinnamon and cayenne and cook for 1 minute. Add the raisins, wine, honey and thyme and cook until the wine is almost evaporated. Season the compote with salt and black pepper.
2. In an ovenproof nonstick skillet, heat the oil. Season the chicken with salt and black pepper and add to the skillet, skin side down. Cook over high heat until the skin is crisp, 5 minutes. Turn the chicken, transfer the skillet to the oven and roast for 6 minutes, until cooked through; serve with the compote. —*Doug Svec*
SERVE WITH Buttered farro with chives.
WINE Oxidized, sherry-like white from the Jura region of France: 2007 Jacques Puffeney Cuvée Sacha Arbois Blanc.

● HEALTHY ● MAKE AHEAD ● VEGETARIAN ● STAFF FAVORITE

crispy chicken thighs with golden raisin compote

Pan-Roasted Chicken with Tarragon Crème Fraîche

ACTIVE: 30 MIN; TOTAL: 1 HR 20 MIN
4 SERVINGS

This recipe was inspired by a dish at Paris's Coinstot Vino. Key to the recipe is the fragrant spice mixture that seasons the chicken breasts before they're sautéed; Coinstot Vino buys a blend from the excellent spice merchant Thiercelin that includes mustard seeds, black pepper and coriander seeds. Don't reduce the crème fraîche that finishes the dish; just make sure it's heated through before serving.

- 1 teaspoon coriander seeds
- 1 teaspoon yellow mustard seeds
- 1 teaspoon black peppercorns
- 1 teaspoon dried summer savory or dried oregano
- 4 medium fingerling potatoes, halved lengthwise
- 2 medium carrots, sliced diagonally 1 inch thick
- ¼ head of cauliflower, cut into 1½-inch florets
- ¼ pound haricots verts or thin green beans
- 5 tablespoons unsalted butter
- 1 tablespoon fresh lemon juice
Salt and freshly ground pepper
- 4 boneless chicken breast halves with skin
- ¼ cup chicken stock or low-sodium broth
- ½ cup crème fraîche
- ¼ cup chopped tarragon

1. In a spice grinder, combine the coriander and mustard seeds with the peppercorns and summer savory and grind to a powder.
2. Set a steamer basket in a wide pot and bring 1 inch of water to a simmer. Layer the vegetables in the basket starting with the potatoes, then the carrots, cauliflower and beans. Cover and steam over moderate heat until the beans are just tender, 3 minutes; transfer to a bowl. Steam until the cauliflower is tender, 3 minutes more; add to the bowl. Steam the carrots and potatoes until tender, 10 minutes longer; add to the bowl.
3. In a large skillet, melt 2 tablespoons of the butter. Add the steamed vegetables and cook over moderately high heat, tossing, until heated through and coated with butter, about 1 minute. Add the lemon juice and season with salt and pepper.
4. Season the chicken breasts with salt and pepper and coat all over with the ground spices. In another large skillet, melt the remaining 3 tablespoons of butter. Add the chicken breasts skin side down and cook over moderately low heat until the skin is well browned, about 12 minutes. Turn the chicken and cook, basting a few times, until just cooked through, about 7 minutes longer. Transfer the chicken to a platter.
5. Rewarm the vegetables. Add the chicken stock to the skillet and boil over high heat for 2 minutes, scraping up any browned bits. Add the crème fraîche and bring to a boil, stirring. Remove from the heat and stir in the tarragon. Season the sauce with salt and pepper. Spoon the sauce over the chicken, mound the vegetables alongside and serve.
—*Jane Sigal*

MAKE AHEAD The recipe can be prepared 1 day ahead through Step 2. Refrigerate the steamed vegetables; keep the spice mixture at room temperature.

WINE Bright, minerally Chablis: 2009 Gilbert Picq et ses Fils Chablis.

General Tso's Chicken

TOTAL: 45 MIN • 4 SERVINGS ●

This sweet-spicy Chinese-American restaurant staple is often heavily battered and deep-fried. The version here, created by F&W's Grace Parisi, is healthier than take-out because the chicken is only lightly coated in cornstarch and then pan-fried.

- 1½ teaspoons toasted sesame oil
- 1 large egg white
- ¼ cup plus 1 tablespoon soy sauce
- ¼ cup plus 3 tablespoons cornstarch
- 1 pound skinless, boneless chicken thighs, trimmed and cut into 1½-inch pieces
- 1 cup low-sodium chicken broth
- 1 teaspoon Chinese chile-garlic sauce
- 3 tablespoons sugar
- 1 tablespoon vegetable oil, plus more for frying
- 2 tablespoons minced fresh ginger
- 2 large garlic cloves, minced
- 4 scallions, thinly sliced
Steamed broccoli and white rice, for serving

1. In a medium bowl, combine the toasted sesame oil with the egg white, 1 tablespoon of the soy sauce and ¼ cup plus 2 tablespoons of the cornstarch. Add the chicken, stirring to coat. Let stand at room temperature for 20 minutes.
2. Meanwhile, in a small bowl, whisk the chicken broth with the chile-garlic sauce, sugar and the remaining ¼ cup of soy sauce and 1 tablespoon of cornstarch.
3. In a large saucepan, heat the 1 tablespoon of oil. Add the ginger and garlic and cook over high heat until fragrant, about 1 minute. Stir the broth mixture, add it to the pan and cook until thickened and glossy, about 3 minutes. Keep the sauce warm over low heat.

tips for roasting chicken

pan juices Don't let pan juices go to waste. Instead, add cubes of bread to the roasting pan once the chicken is finished, then toss with butter and bake until the bread is crispy.

brine Use a small, clean garbage bag to brine chicken; this helps enormously with refrigerator space. Make sure to remove as much excess air as possible and to tie the bag securely to prevent leaking.

stock Save the chicken necks in a resealable bag in the freezer and use to make chicken stock.
—*Floyd Cardoz*

● HEALTHY ● MAKE AHEAD ○ VEGETARIAN ● STAFF FAVORITE

4. In a large, deep skillet, heat ½ inch of oil until shimmering. Carefully add the chicken, one piece at a time, and fry over high heat, turning once or twice, until very browned and crisp, about 4 minutes. Drain the chicken on paper towels and immediately add to the sauce along with the scallions. Cook just until coated, about 30 seconds. Serve right away, with steamed broccoli and rice.
—*Grace Parisi*

WINE Bright Italian sparkling wine: NV Mionetto Prosecco di Valdobbiadene.

Korean Chicken Tacos

TOTAL: 1 HR 30 MIN PLUS OVERNIGHT MARINATING • MAKES 12 MINI TACOS
These clever "tacos" from Dennis Lee of Namu in San Francisco use squares of nori (the dried seaweed that wraps sushi) instead of conventional tortillas. Also unexpected are the toppings: a mouthwatering mix of rice, charbroiled chicken, cracklings, kimchi mayonnaise and kimchi salsa.

1½ **pounds boneless chicken thighs—lightly pounded, skin reserved**
1 **tablespoon minced garlic**
1 **tablespoon minced fresh ginger**
1 **cup soy sauce**
1 **cup mirin**
¼ **cup toasted sesame oil**
1½ **pounds tomatoes, diced**
2 **large scallions, thinly sliced**
¼ **cup finely diced pickled daikon (see Note) or fresh daikon**
¾ **cup kimchi, finely chopped**
Kosher salt
2 **teaspoons Tabasco**
1 **cup mayonnaise**
3 **cups cooked sushi rice**
3 **sheets of plain nori (see Note), cut into quarters with scissors**
12 **mini sheets of seasoned roasted nori (see Note)**
3 **tablespoons teriyaki sauce**
Toasted sesame seeds

1. In a bowl, toss the chicken, garlic, ginger, soy sauce, mirin and 2 tablespoons of the sesame oil. Cover and refrigerate overnight.

2. Preheat the oven to 350°. In a small saucepan, cover the chicken skin with water and simmer for 15 minutes; drain and pat dry. Arrange the chicken skin on a parchment paper–lined baking sheet and roast until golden and crisp, about 30 minutes; drain the cracklings on paper towels, then cut them into ½-inch pieces. Discard the parchment.

3. Preheat the broiler. Drain the chicken and arrange on the baking sheet. Broil, turning once, until lightly charred, about 6 minutes. Cut the chicken into ¼-inch pieces.

4. In a large bowl, toss the tomatoes, scallions, daikon and ¼ cup of the kimchi; season with salt. In a small bowl, whisk the Tabasco, mayonnaise and the remaining ½ cup of kimchi; season with salt. In a medium bowl, toss the rice with the remaining 2 tablespoons of sesame oil.

5. Top each plain nori square with a seasoned nori sheet. Spoon on the rice, flattening slightly, and drizzle with the teriyaki. Top with the kimchi mayonnaise, chicken, sesame seeds, cracklings and kimchi salsa. Serve. —*Dennis Lee*

NOTE Pickled daikon and nori are available at Asian markets. Seasoned nori is available at markets like Trader Joe's.

BEER Zesty pale ale: Abita Restoration.

Chicken Tinga Tacos

ACTIVE: 30 MIN; TOTAL: 2 HR 30 MIN
MAKES 24 TACOS ● ● ●
"The chicken is braised in the oven, but you can make it in a slow cooker or completely on the stove, in a casserole," says Jenn Louis, the chef at Sunshine Tavern in Portland, Oregon. There are many versions of *tinga*, the spicy, smoky Mexican tomato sauce. This one is especially easy, calling for only a few simple ingredients.

¼ **cup plus 2 tablespoons extra-virgin olive oil**
2½ **pounds trimmed, skinless, bone-in chicken thighs**
Salt and freshly ground black pepper
1 **large onion, thinly sliced**
3 **large garlic cloves, minced**
One 28-ounce can diced tomatoes
2 **canned chipotles in adobo, coarsely chopped**
1 **cup chicken broth**
24 **corn tortillas**
2 **ounces Cotija cheese, crumbled**
Sliced scallions and chopped cilantro, for garnish

1. Heat 3 tablespoons of the olive oil in a large nonstick skillet. Season the chicken thighs all over with salt and freshly ground black pepper, add them to the skillet and cook over moderately high heat, turning once, until browned, about 12 minutes. Transfer the chicken to a 9-by-13-inch baking dish and pour off the fat in the skillet.

2. Add the remaining 3 tablespoons of olive oil to the skillet along with the sliced onion. Cook over moderately high heat, stirring occasionally, until the onion is lightly browned and softened, about 5 minutes. Add the minced garlic and cook until fragrant, about 2 minutes. Add the can of diced tomatoes and their juices, the chipotles and the chicken broth and bring the mixture to a boil. Simmer the sauce over moderate heat, stirring occasionally, until thickened and slightly reduced, about 20 minutes.

3. Preheat the oven to 350°. Transfer the sauce to a food processor and let cool for about 15 minutes. Puree until smooth and season with salt and freshly ground black pepper. Pour the sauce over the chicken. Bake the chicken uncovered in the center of the oven for about 45 minutes, until the meat is tender and the sauce is very thick and darkened around the edges. Wrap the tortillas in foil and warm them in the oven for about 10 minutes.

4. Remove the chicken from the sauce and shred the meat; discard the bones. Return the chicken meat to the sauce. Spoon about 3 tablespoons of chicken onto each tortilla and sprinkle with the crumbled cheese. Garnish the tacos with the scallions and cilantro and serve hot. —*Jenn Louis*

MAKE AHEAD The *tinga* can be refrigerated for up to 3 days and reheated gently.

WINE Vibrant, citrusy Sauvignon Blanc: 2009 Yellow + Blue.

Fried Chicken Tacos

TOTAL: 35 MIN PLUS 2 HR MARINATING
4 SERVINGS ●

"Right in Tijuana's red-light district sits Kentucky Fried Buches, where cooks fry chicken necks, skin on, to fill soft corn tortillas. I can't stop eating them," says *Bizarre Foods* TV host Andrew Zimmern. "At home, I fry skin-on chicken thighs until they're supercrisp, then eat them with avocado-tomatillo salsa."

¼ cup fresh lime juice
Kosher salt
4 large boneless chicken thighs with skin (about 5 ounces each), pounded ⅓ inch thick
½ pound tomatillos, husked and quartered
2 garlic cloves, chopped
2 serrano chiles or 1 large jalapeño with seeds, chopped
1 small onion, coarsely chopped
3 tablespoons cilantro leaves
1 Hass avocado, cut into ½-inch dice
⅓ cup all-purpose flour
½ teaspoon freshly ground black pepper
Large pinch of cayenne pepper
Vegetable oil, for frying
Warm corn tortillas, for serving

1. In a large bowl, combine 2 tablespoons of the lime juice with 1 teaspoon of salt, stirring to dissolve the salt. Add the chicken thighs and turn to coat. Refrigerate for 2 hours.
2. In a food processor, combine the tomatillos, garlic, serranos, onion and cilantro and process to a coarse puree. Transfer the salsa to a bowl and stir in the avocado and the remaining 2 tablespoons of lime juice. Season with salt.
3. Pat the chicken dry with paper towels. In a shallow bowl, combine the flour, black pepper, cayenne and ½ teaspoon of salt.
4. In a large skillet, heat ⅓ inch of oil until shimmering. Dredge the chicken in the flour, shaking off any excess. Fry the chicken over moderately high heat until well browned and crisp, about 3½ minutes per side. Transfer to paper towels to drain.

5. Cut the fried chicken into thin strips and serve with the tomatillo salsa and warm corn tortillas. —*Andrew Zimmern*
NOTE Zimmern likes trimming away some of the chicken thigh so there's as much crispy skin as there is meat. If you opt to do the same, fry the chicken for 3 minutes per side.
WINE Sweet-berried Beaujolais: 2009 Villa Ponciago Fleurie La Réserve.

Sweet-and-Spicy Chicken

ACTIVE: 15 MIN; TOTAL: 1 HR
4 TO 6 SERVINGS
Chef Bill Kim of Chicago's Urbanbelly prefers using frozen lemongrass to fresh in the marinade for this chicken because he finds the flavor sweeter and more intense.

4 garlic cloves, smashed and peeled
2 tablespoons snipped chives
1 tablespoon chopped fresh ginger
1 large stalk of frozen or fresh lemongrass, tender pale inner core only, minced
2 tablespoons toasted sesame oil
½ cup Thai sweet chile sauce
3 tablespoons *sambal oelek* or other Asian chile sauce
2 pounds skinless, boneless chicken thighs, trimmed

1. In a mini food processor, combine the garlic, chives, ginger, lemongrass and sesame oil and pulse until finely chopped. Add the sweet chile sauce and *sambal oelek* and pulse to blend.
2. Spread the marinade all over the chicken thighs and let them stand at room temperature for at least 30 minutes or refrigerate for up to 24 hours.
3. Light a grill or preheat a grill pan. Lift the chicken thighs from the marinade, letting the excess drip off. Grill over moderately high heat, turning occasionally, until browned and cooked through, about 15 minutes. —*Bill Kim*
VARIATION The marinade is also delicious with pork chops or pork tenderloin.
SERVE WITH Steamed rice and bok choy.
WINE Medium-bodied Chilean Pinot Noir: 2010 Cono Sur Visión.

Chicken Yakitori

📷 PAGE 105
ACTIVE: 45 MIN; TOTAL: 1 HR 30 MIN
4 TO 6 SERVINGS ● ●

1½ cups water
¼ cup kombu (½ ounce), broken into small pieces (see Note)
¼ cup bonito flakes (see Note)
3 cups sake
1 cup soy sauce
¾ cup mirin
½ cup light brown sugar
3 pounds skinless, boneless chicken thighs, cut into 1½-inch pieces
2 bunches of scallions (about 12), cut into 1-inch lengths
One 4-inch piece of fresh ginger, peeled
Vegetable oil, for brushing

1. In a small saucepan, bring the water and kombu to a simmer. Add the bonito flakes and return to a simmer. Remove the pan from the heat and let stand for 3 minutes. Strain the broth into a large saucepan. Add the sake, soy sauce, mirin and brown sugar to the broth and boil over moderately high heat, stirring occasionally, until slightly thickened, about 45 minutes.
2. Meanwhile, soak 16 bamboo skewers in water for 20 minutes; drain. Alternately thread the chicken and scallions onto the skewers.
3. Finely grate the ginger into a small, fine strainer set over a bowl. Press the juice from the ginger; you should have 2 tablespoons.
4. Light a grill or preheat a grill pan. Brush the chicken and scallions with vegetable oil and grill the skewers over moderate heat, turning, until just cooked through, about 10 minutes. Just before removing them from the grill, brush the skewers with the ginger juice and soy glaze. Serve the yakitori, passing more glaze for dipping.
—*Andrew Zimmern*
NOTE Kombu is dried seaweed. Bonito flakes are made from smoked bonito or tuna. Both are available at Japanese markets.
WINE Bold, berry-inflected Oregon Pinot Noir: 2008 Sokol Blosser's Big Tree Block.

● HEALTHY ● MAKE AHEAD ● VEGETARIAN ● STAFF FAVORITE

fried chicken tacos

Chicken with Candied Cashews

⏱ **TOTAL: 45 MIN • 2 SERVINGS**

Chefs Rich Torrisi and Mario Carbone often find inspiration in New York City's Chinatown. At their restaurant Torrisi Italian Specialties, they transform Chinese cashew chicken into a fancy appetizer featuring the chicken "oyster"—the succulent piece of meat that's between the thigh and backbone, prized by French chefs. Torrisi and Carbone's recipe below substitutes chicken thigh meat for the oysters and turns the dish into a main course served with steamed white rice.

- ¼ cup granulated sugar
- ¾ cup unsalted roasted cashews
- 2 tablespoons vegetable oil
- 2 garlic cloves, minced
- 1 scallion, minced
- 1 tablespoon minced fresh ginger
- 3 tablespoons soy sauce
- 1 tablespoon light brown sugar
- ¾ teaspoon cornstarch dissolved in 2 teaspoons of water
- 1 tablespoon plus ½ teaspoon fresh lemon juice

Kosher salt

- 2 tablespoons unsalted butter
- ¼ cup extra-virgin olive oil, plus more for drizzling
- 4 large skinless, boneless chicken thighs, trimmed of fat and cut into 1-inch pieces

Freshly ground pepper

- ¼ teaspoon onion powder
- ¼ teaspoon garlic powder
- ½ teaspoon celery seeds
- ¼ cup thinly sliced tender celery ribs
- ¼ cup celery leaves

Steamed white rice, for serving

1. Line a small baking sheet with parchment paper. In a small saucepan, combine the granulated sugar and ¼ cup of water. Boil over moderately high heat, swirling the pan, until a rich brown caramel forms, 4 minutes. Stir in the cashews until coated. Quickly spread the nuts on the baking sheet, keeping them separate. Let cool. Break off any large pieces of caramel and reserve for a snack.

2. In a small saucepan, combine the vegetable oil, garlic, scallion and ginger. Cover and cook over low heat for 1 minute. Remove from the heat and let stand, covered, for 10 minutes. Strain the oil through a coarse strainer into a medium skillet, pressing on the solids. Add the soy sauce, brown sugar and ¼ cup of water and bring to a simmer over moderate heat. Whisk in the cornstarch mixture and simmer over low heat, whisking, until thickened, about 30 seconds. Remove from the heat, add 1 tablespoon of the lemon juice and lightly season the sauce with salt.

3. In a medium saucepan, melt the butter in the ¼ cup of olive oil. Season the chicken with salt and pepper and add to the saucepan. Cook over moderate heat, turning, until white throughout, about 5 minutes.

4. In a small bowl, combine the onion and garlic powders, celery seeds and ½ teaspoon of salt. In another small bowl, toss the sliced celery and leaves with the remaining ½ teaspoon of lemon juice and a small drizzle of olive oil and season with salt and pepper.

5. Transfer the chicken to shallow bowls, spooning the sauce over the chicken. Top with the candied cashews and season with the celery salt. Scatter the celery salad on top and serve with rice. Alternatively, arrange the chicken on cocktail forks and season with the celery salt. Serve with the sauce, candied cashews and celery salad.
—*Mario Carbone and Rich Torrisi*

MAKE AHEAD The candied cashews can be stored in an airtight container at room temperature for 1 day. Reheat briefly in a 350° oven if they are sticky. The sauce can be refrigerated overnight; reheat gently.

WINE Spicy, honey-scented Gewürztraminer: 2009 Montinore Estate.

Spice-Braised Chicken Legs with Red Wine and Tomato

ACTIVE: 30 MIN; TOTAL: 1 HR 40 MIN
6 SERVINGS ● ●

Maria Guarnaschelli, the legendary cookbook editor at W.W. Norton, made a version of this lightly spicy dish when her daughter, Alexandra, was a kid. Alex has adapted the recipe by adding red wine.

- 3 tablespoons canola oil
- 6 whole chicken legs, split into drumsticks and thighs, skin and fat removed

Salt and freshly ground pepper

- ½ teaspoon cumin seeds
- 2 large onions, thinly sliced
- 3 garlic cloves, smashed
- 2 tablespoons grated fresh ginger

One 3-inch cinnamon stick, broken in half

- ½ teaspoon crushed red pepper
- 2 bay leaves
- 1 cup dry red wine
- 1 cup chicken stock or low-sodium broth

One 28-ounce can whole tomatoes, chopped, with their juices

1. In a large, deep skillet, heat 2 tablespoons of the canola oil until shimmering. Season the chicken with salt and pepper and add half to the skillet. Cook over moderately high heat until browned, about 3 minutes per side. Transfer the browned chicken to a plate and repeat with the remaining chicken. Pour off the fat in the skillet.

2. Add the remaining 1 tablespoon of oil to the skillet. Add the cumin seeds and cook over moderately high heat for about 10 seconds, until fragrant. Add the onions and cook over moderately high heat, stirring occasionally, until softened, about 5 minutes. Add the garlic, ginger, cinnamon stick, crushed red pepper and bay leaves and cook, stirring, until the garlic is golden, about 3 minutes. Add the wine and simmer over moderately low heat for 5 minutes. Add the stock and the tomatoes with their juices and simmer for 10 minutes.

3. Add the chicken to the sauce along with any accumulated juices and simmer over low heat, turning a few times, until the chicken is cooked through and the sauce is flavorful, about 50 minutes. Discard the cinnamon stick and bay leaves, season with salt and pepper and serve. —*Alexandra Guarnaschelli*

SERVE WITH Steamed white or brown rice.
MAKE AHEAD The braised chicken can be refrigerated overnight. Reheat gently.
WINE Substantial, dark-berried Tempranillo: 2008 Mano a Mano.

● HEALTHY ● MAKE AHEAD ● VEGETARIAN ● STAFF FAVORITE

chicken with candied cashews

Crisp Spiced Chicken with Hummus Vinaigrette

⏱ TOTAL: 45 MIN • 4 SERVINGS

Adam and Andrew Erace offer a carefully curated selection of local, sustainable foods at their Green Aisle Grocery in Philadelphia. Among their excellent prepared items is chef Michael Solomonov's hummus, which Adam uses in this creamy, complex-tasting vinaigrette for roasted chicken.

- 4 chicken drumsticks
- 4 chicken thighs
- ¼ cup plus 2 tablespoons extra-virgin olive oil
- 2 tablespoons ground coriander

Salt and freshly ground pepper

- 4 cups cooked couscous
- ½ cup coarsely chopped roasted pistachios
- ½ cup pomegranate seeds
- 1½ cups coarsely chopped flat-leaf parsley
- 1 cup prepared hummus
- ¼ cup white wine vinegar

1. Preheat the oven to 450°. In a large bowl, toss the chicken drumsticks and thighs with 2 tablespoons of the olive oil and the coriander; season with salt and pepper. Arrange the chicken on a rack set over a baking sheet, skin side up. Roast in the upper third of the oven for about 35 minutes, turning twice, until the chicken is cooked through. Turn on the broiler and broil for 2 minutes, until the skin is crisp and golden.

2. Meanwhile, in another large bowl, toss the couscous with the pistachios, pomegranate seeds and ½ cup of the parsley. In a blender, puree the hummus and vinegar with the remaining 1 cup of parsley and ¼ cup of olive oil. Add 2 tablespoons of water and puree until smooth. Season the hummus dressing with salt and pepper.

3. Stir one-third of the hummus dressing into the couscous and transfer to a platter. Arrange the chicken on top and serve, passing the extra dressing on the side.
—*Adam Erace*

WINE Spicy, citrusy Verdejo: 2009 Shaya.

Chicken and Rice with Fresh Chorizo

ACTIVE: 45 MIN; TOTAL: 2 HR
4 SERVINGS

- 2 tablespoons extra-virgin olive oil
- 4 links fresh chorizo or hot Italian sausage
- 4 whole chicken legs

Salt and freshly ground pepper

- 2 garlic cloves, minced
- 1 medium red onion, coarsely chopped
- 1 red bell pepper, coarsely chopped
- ½ teaspoon ground turmeric
- ¼ cup dry white wine

One 28-ounce can whole tomatoes, drained and chopped

- 6 cups chicken stock
- 1½ cups long-grain rice
- 1 cup frozen peas, thawed
- 3 scallions, coarsely chopped
- 2 tablespoons chopped cilantro
- 1 jalapeño, seeded and minced

1. In a large enameled cast-iron casserole, heat 1 tablespoon of the olive oil. Add the chorizo, cover and cook over moderate heat, turning once, until richly browned and just cooked through, 10 minutes; transfer to a plate. Season the chicken legs with salt and pepper and add them to the casserole, skin side down. Cook over moderately high heat until browned, 5 minutes per side. Transfer the chicken to the plate with the chorizo.

2. Pour off all but 2 tablespoons of fat from the casserole. Add the garlic, onion and bell pepper and cook over moderate heat, stirring occasionally, until softened, 8 minutes. Add the turmeric and cook, stirring, until fragrant, 30 seconds. Add the wine and boil over high heat until almost evaporated, 3 minutes. Add the chopped tomatoes and chicken stock and bring to a boil. Return the chorizo and chicken to the casserole along with any accumulated juices. Simmer over low heat until the chicken is cooked through, about 45 minutes.

3. In a medium saucepan, heat the remaining 1 tablespoon of olive oil. Add the rice and cook over moderate heat, stirring, until coated with oil. Stir 5 cups of the chicken cooking liquid into the rice. Cover partially and cook over moderately low heat, stirring often, until the rice is just tender and has absorbed most of the cooking liquid, about 25 minutes. Stir in the peas, scallions, cilantro and jalapeño and warm over low heat. Season with salt and pepper.

4. Cut each chorizo link into 3 pieces and return them to the casserole. Gently reheat the chicken and chorizo. Spoon the rice onto large plates and top with the chorizo pieces and chicken. Spoon some of the remaining cooking liquid on top and serve.
—*Pedro Miguel Schiaffino*

WINE Pinot Noir: 2008 Saintsbury Garnet.

Classic Southern Fried Chicken

⏱ TOTAL: 45 MIN • 4 SERVINGS ●

In the 2011 movie *The Help,* the food plays a starring role. The character Minny uses Crisco to fry chicken to perfection, admiring the way the vegetable shortening "bubbles up like a song" as it cooks.

One 4-pound chicken, cut into 8 pieces
- 2 large eggs
- ½ cup whole milk
- 1½ cups all-purpose flour
- 1 tablespoon each seasoned salt and seasoned pepper, such as Lawry's
- 24 ounces solid vegetable shortening, such as Crisco

1. Pat the chicken pieces dry and line a baking sheet with wax paper. In a large bowl, whisk the eggs with the milk, then add the chicken pieces. In another bowl, whisk the flour with the seasoned salt and seasoned pepper. Dredge the chicken in the seasoned flour and transfer to the baking sheet.

2. In a 12-inch cast-iron skillet, heat the vegetable shortening to 365°. Add all of the chicken and fry over moderate heat, turning occasionally, until the chicken is deeply golden brown and an instant-read thermometer inserted nearest the bone registers 170°, 20 to 24 minutes. Drain the chicken on paper towels and serve right away. —*Chris Ubick*

WINE Light, dry California rosé: 2010 Lorenza.

● HEALTHY ● MAKE AHEAD ● VEGETARIAN ● STAFF FAVORITE

Chicken al Forno with Salsa Verde

ACTIVE: 45 MIN; TOTAL: 1 HR 30 MIN
4 SERVINGS ●

In his book *Italian, My Way,* chef Jonathan Waxman of Barbuto in New York City recommends using a mortar for the salsa verde here, but a food processor also works well.

CHICKEN

One 4-pound chicken
Salt and freshly ground black pepper
¼ cup extra-virgin olive oil
1 lemon, halved

SALSA VERDE

¼ cup salt-packed capers, soaked in cold water for 1 hour and drained
4 oil-packed anchovy fillets, soaked in cold water for 15 minutes and patted dry
3 garlic cloves, coarsely chopped
½ cup chopped arugula
½ cup chopped flat-leaf parsley
½ cup chopped basil
½ cup chopped cilantro
¼ cup chopped tarragon
¼ cup chopped sage
¼ cup snipped chives
¼ teaspoon crushed red pepper
1 cup extra-virgin olive oil
Salt

1. **PREPARE THE CHICKEN** Preheat the oven to 450°. Using kitchen scissors, cut out the backbone. Flatten the chicken and pull out the breast bone. Cut the chicken in half through the breast and season with salt and pepper. Set the chicken skin side up in a roasting pan and drizzle with the oil; add the lemon halves to the pan and roast for 40 minutes, basting every 10 minutes, until just cooked through.
2. **MEANWHILE, MAKE THE SALSA VERDE** In a food processor, pulse the capers with the anchovies and garlic until finely chopped. Add all of the remaining ingredients and pulse to combine. Season with salt. Serve the chicken with the salsa verde and the roasted lemon. —*Jonathan Waxman*

WINE Lean, tangy Austrian Pinot Noir: 2008 Stadlmann Classic.

Pan-Roasted Chicken with Corn Relish

ACTIVE: 45 MIN; TOTAL: 5 HR • 4 SERVINGS

One 4-pound chicken, cut into 8 pieces
2 heads of garlic, cloves peeled
12 bay leaves, preferably fresh
4 ears of corn, shucked
2 tablespoons extra-virgin olive oil, plus more for brushing
Salt and freshly ground pepper
1 cup roasted red pepper strips, finely chopped
1 large jalapeño, seeded and minced
2 tablespoons chopped basil
1 tablespoon chopped mint
1 tablespoon fresh lime juice
½ cup sherry vinegar
½ cup chicken stock
2 tablespoons unsalted butter

1. In a large bowl, toss the chicken, garlic and bay leaves and refrigerate for at least 4 hours or overnight.
2. Preheat the oven to 350°. Brush the corn with oil and season with salt and pepper. Wrap in foil and roast until tender, about 1 hour. Cut the kernels from the cobs and transfer to a bowl. Add the roasted peppers, jalapeño, basil, mint and lime juice; season the relish with salt and pepper.
3. In a large ovenproof skillet, heat the 2 tablespoons of oil. Season the chicken with salt and pepper. Cook skin side down over moderately high heat until golden, about 5 minutes. Turn the chicken, add the garlic and bay leaves and cook until the garlic begins to brown, about 3 minutes. Transfer the skillet to the oven and roast the chicken for about 25 minutes, until cooked through.
4. Set the skillet over high heat and cook until the pan juices are nearly evaporated. Transfer the chicken and garlic to a platter; pour off any fat. Add the vinegar and stock to the skillet and cook, scraping up browned bits, until reduced by half, 2 minutes. Whisk in the butter. Serve the chicken with the sauce and relish. —*Cathal Armstrong*

WINE Herbal South African Chenin Blanc: 2009 Raats Family Wines Original.

Honey-and-Lemon-Glazed Roast Chicken

ACTIVE: 20 MIN; TOTAL: 1 HR 45 MIN
8 SERVINGS ●

"I'm crazy for chicken," says winemaker Piero Incisa della Rocchetta. "I regularly eat a whole one by myself." Inspired by beautifully browned Peking duck, he brushes lemon-and-herb-stuffed chickens with a mixture of lemon juice, soy sauce and honey from the beehives in his Patagonia vineyards. The soy sauce gives the chicken skin a lovely mahogany glaze and a salty, earthy edge.

¼ cup plus 1 teaspoon honey
2 tablespoons plus 1 teaspoon fresh lemon juice
2 tablespoons soy sauce
Three 3-pound chickens
Salt
9 large rosemary sprigs
9 garlic cloves, quartered
1 lemon, cut into 12 wedges

1. Preheat the oven to 450°. In a small bowl, combine the honey, lemon juice and soy sauce. Set the chickens on a large rimmed baking sheet and tuck the wing tips underneath. Season the cavities with salt and stuff each one with 3 rosemary sprigs, 3 quartered garlic cloves and 4 lemon wedges. Brush two-thirds of the honey glaze over the chickens and season them lightly with salt. Roast the chickens in the middle of the oven for 30 minutes.
2. Reduce the oven temperature to 325°. Rotate the chickens on the baking sheet and brush them with the remaining honey glaze. Roast the chickens for about 45 minutes longer, until the juices run clear when the thighs are pierced with a skewer; turn the baking sheet halfway through roasting. Transfer the chickens to a carving board and let them rest for 15 minutes. Carve the chickens and serve.
—*Piero Incisa della Rocchetta*

SERVE WITH Incisa della Rocchetta's Twice-Cooked Potatoes (page 270).

WINE Burgundy: 2007 Nicolas Potel Pommard Les Vignots.

Balinese Grilled Chicken

ACTIVE: 35 MIN; TOTAL: 2 HR PLUS
4 HR MARINATING • 4 SERVINGS

Australian chef Pete Evans tried a version of this chicken roasted over an open fire while traveling in Indonesia. "I stole that dish from a housekeeper I met on a surfing trip to Bali," he says. The turmeric, chiles, shallots and ginger in the marinade are popular flavors in Indonesian cooking.

10 garlic cloves, halved
 3 fresh long red chiles, halved
    and seeded
 6 small shallots, halved
 2 tablespoons chopped fresh ginger
 1 teaspoon ground turmeric
¼ cup vegetable oil, plus more
    for brushing
Salt and freshly ground pepper
One 4-pound chicken, butterflied
 4 fresh bay leaves
 4 limes, halved

1. In a food processor, combine the garlic, chiles, shallots, ginger and turmeric and pulse until finely chopped. Add the ¼ cup of vegetable oil and pulse to a fine paste. Transfer the paste to a small skillet and cook over moderate heat, stirring, until fragrant and lightly browned, about 5 minutes. Let the paste cool completely and season with salt and pepper.
2. Set the butterflied chicken in a baking dish and rub the paste all over it. Place the bay leaves on top. Cover and refrigerate for at least 4 hours or overnight.
3. Light a grill. Line the grate with a double sheet of heavy-duty aluminum foil brushed lightly with oil. Transfer the chicken to the foil, skin side up. Cover and grill over moderate heat (350° to 375°) for about 1 hour, until nearly cooked through. Add the limes to the foil and grill the chicken until the juices run clear when an inner thigh is pierced, about 15 minutes longer. Carve the chicken, transfer to a platter and serve with the limes.
—Pete Evans

WINE Fruity, lush Australian Viognier: 2009 Yalumba The Y Series.

Butter-Roasted Chicken with Cilantro and Mint

ACTIVE: 40 MIN; TOTAL: 2 HR 15 MIN
PLUS 4 HR MARINATING • 6 SERVINGS

New York chef Floyd Cardoz rubs chickens with butter, then lets them rest in the fridge for extra-crispy skin and moist breast meat.

 2 cups small cilantro sprigs
 2 cups mint leaves
 6 garlic cloves, chopped
 3 tablespoons chopped fresh ginger
 2 serrano chiles, thinly sliced
    (with seeds)
½ cup fresh lime juice
 3 tablespoons unsalted butter, melted
 2 tablespoons ground cumin
 1 tablespoon freshly ground
    black pepper
¼ teaspoon ground cloves
Kosher salt
Two 3½-pound chickens, backbones and
    wing tips removed

1. In a food processor, combine the cilantro, mint, garlic, ginger, chiles and lime juice and process until smooth. Transfer to a bowl and stir in the butter, cumin, black pepper, cloves and 1 teaspoon of kosher salt.
2. Set the chickens breast side down on a large rimmed baking sheet and spread with some of the herb butter. Turn the chickens over and splay them out. Loosen the skin on the breasts and legs and spread some of the butter on the chicken underneath the skin. Rub the remaining butter over the top of the skin. Cover and refrigerate for 4 hours.
3. Preheat the oven to 425°. Let the chickens stand at room temperature for 20 minutes.
4. Roast the chickens in the upper third of the oven for about 1 hour, until they are richly browned and the juices run clear when a thigh is pierced. Transfer the chickens to a carving board and let rest for 10 minutes.
5. Pour the pan juices into a glass measuring cup and skim the fat from the surface. Carve the chickens and serve with the pan juices.
—Floyd Cardoz

WINE Fresh, red-berried Chianti Classico: 2007 Il Molino di Grace.

Big Bob Gibson's Chicken with White Barbecue Sauce

ACTIVE: 15 MIN; TOTAL: 50 MIN
4 SERVINGS

At Big Bob Gibson Bar-B-Q restaurants in Decatur, Alabama, and Monroe, North Carolina, chef Chris Lilly butterflies a whole chicken, smokes it over hickory wood chips, then dunks the bird into a vat of tangy white barbecue sauce. This easier, simplified version of the recipe calls for chicken pieces, which home cooks can grill until crispy and nicely charred, then serve with Lilly's terrific five-minute white sauce.

½ cup hickory wood chips
One 3½-pound chicken,
    cut into 8 pieces
Vegetable oil, for brushing
Salt and freshly ground black pepper
 1 cup mayonnaise
½ cup distilled white vinegar
¼ cup apple juice
 1 teaspoon prepared horseradish
 1 teaspoon fresh lemon juice
¼ teaspoon cayenne pepper

1. Light a gas grill. Wrap the hickory wood chips in heavy-duty foil and pierce the packet all over with a skewer. Add the foil packet to the grill. Cover and let the wood chips begin to smoke, about 5 minutes.
2. Brush the chicken with vegetable oil and season generously with salt and freshly ground black pepper. Grill the chicken, covered, over moderately high heat, turning and shifting the pieces occasionally, until lightly charred and cooked through, about 35 to 40 minutes. Transfer to a platter.
3. In a medium bowl, whisk the mayonnaise with the vinegar, apple juice, horseradish, lemon juice and cayenne and season with 1 teaspoon of black pepper and ½ teaspoon of salt. Transfer the white barbecue sauce to a pitcher and serve with the chicken.
—Chris Lilly

MAKE AHEAD The barbecue sauce can be refrigerated for up to 1 week.

BEER Hoppy, grapefruity India Pale Ale: Samuel Adams Latitude 48.

● HEALTHY ● MAKE AHEAD ● VEGETARIAN ● STAFF FAVORITE

big bob gibson's chicken with white barbecue sauce

Brined Roast Chicken with Olive Bread Panzanella

ACTIVE: 30 MIN; TOTAL: 2 HR 30 MIN PLUS
OVERNIGHT BRINING • 6 SERVINGS ●

- 3 quarts plus 3 cups tepid water (15 cups)
- 2 cups dry white wine
- 3 heads of garlic, halved crosswise
- ½ cup kosher salt, plus more for seasoning
- 2 tablespoons coarsely ground black pepper, plus more for seasoning
- 2 lemons, thinly sliced
- 1 orange, thinly sliced
- 9 rosemary sprigs, plus 2 teaspoons chopped rosemary

Two 3½-pound chickens
- 1 pound olive bread, cut into cubes
- 2 tablespoons bacon fat or melted butter

1. In a very large pot, combine the water, wine, garlic, ½ cup of kosher salt, 2 tablespoons of pepper, lemons, orange and 3 rosemary sprigs. Stir to dissolve the salt. Put the chickens in the brine, breast side down. Cover and refrigerate overnight.
2. Preheat the oven to 425°. Remove the chickens from the brine and pat dry. Put the chickens in a roasting pan, breast sides up. Stuff the remaining 6 rosemary sprigs in the cavities and tie the legs together. Season lightly with salt and pepper and sprinkle with the chopped rosemary. Roast for 30 minutes. Add ½ cup of water to the pan and roast at 375° for 1 hour and 15 minutes longer, rotating the pan, until the juices run clear.
3. Lift the chickens and tilt them to let the cavity juices run into the pan. Transfer the chickens to a carving board and keep warm. Increase the oven temperature to 425°. Add the bread cubes and the bacon fat to the pan; toss well. Spread the bread in an even layer and bake in the upper third of the oven for about 20 minutes, until crisp on top and moist underneath. Carve the chickens and serve with the panzanella. —*Floyd Cardoz*
WINE Lemony, floral Greek white: 2010 Tselepos Mantinia Moschofilero.

Aleppo-Pepper-and-Mint-Roasted Chicken
📷 COVER

ACTIVE: 30 MIN; TOTAL: 2 HR
4 SERVINGS ●

- 5 small red onions, peeled, each cut through the roots into 8 wedges
- 1 tablespoon extra-virgin olive oil
- 1½ tablespoons plus 2 teaspoons dried mint, crumbled

Sea salt and freshly ground black pepper
- 4 tablespoons unsalted butter, softened
- 4 large garlic cloves, thinly sliced
- 2 scallions, thinly sliced
- 1 tablespoon plus 2 teaspoons Aleppo pepper flakes
- 2 lemons—zests removed in strips, 1 lemon cut lengthwise into wedges

One 4-pound chicken

1. Preheat the oven to 425°. In a medium bowl, toss the onions, olive oil and the 2 teaspoons of mint. Season the onions with salt and black pepper.
2. In a small bowl, mash the butter with the garlic, scallions, Aleppo pepper, lemon zest and the remaining 1½ tablespoons of mint; season with salt. Rub the seasoned butter evenly under the skin of the chicken. Tie the legs together with kitchen string and set the chicken in a medium roasting pan.
3. Season the chicken with salt and black pepper and roast for 20 minutes. Add the onions to the pan, reduce the oven temperature to 375° and roast for 20 minutes longer. Squeeze the lemon wedges over the chicken and add to the pan. Roast for 35 minutes longer, basting, until an instant-read thermometer inserted in the thigh registers 165°. Transfer the chicken to a surface. Let rest for 10 minutes.
4. Return the pan with the onions and lemon to the oven; roast for 10 minutes. Remove the string and carve the chicken. Serve with the onions, lemon wedges and pan juices. —*Mindy Fox*
WINE Lively, red-berried Pinot Noir: 2009 Healdsburg Ranches.

Lyon-Style Chicken with Vinegar Sauce

ACTIVE: 25 MIN; TOTAL: 1 HR
4 SERVINGS ●

New York chef April Bloomfield adds a hefty amount of vinegar to the sauce for her tangier take on classic chicken *lyonnaise.*

- 3 tablespoons extra-virgin olive oil
One 4-pound chicken, cut into 10 pieces
Salt and freshly ground pepper
- 3 tablespoons unsalted butter
- 12 large garlic cloves, unpeeled
- 1 bay leaf
- 1 cup Banyuls vinegar or red wine vinegar
- 2 cups chicken stock
- ¼ cup crème fraîche
Herbed Steamed Rice (page 272), for serving

1. Preheat the oven to 450°. In a large, deep skillet, heat the oil. Season the chicken with salt and pepper, add to the skillet and cook over moderately high heat until browned. Add 1 tablespoon of the butter to the skillet and swirl to coat the chicken. Turn the chicken skin side up and add the garlic and bay leaf.
2. Transfer the skillet to the oven and bake the chicken for 8 minutes, until the breast pieces are just white throughout. Transfer the breast pieces to a plate. Add the vinegar to the skillet, return to the oven and bake the remaining chicken, basting a few times, until cooked through, 15 minutes longer. Transfer the chicken and garlic to the plate.
3. Add the chicken stock to the skillet and boil, scraping up the browned bits, until the mixture is reduced to 1¼ cups, about 10 minutes. Whisk in the crème fraîche and the remaining 2 tablespoons of butter. Return the chicken to the skillet along with any accumulated juices. Simmer over moderately high heat, basting a few times, until the sauce thickens slightly and the chicken is heated through, about 3 minutes. Season with salt and pepper and serve with the Herbed Steamed Rice. —*April Bloomfield*
WINE Focused red Burgundy: 2008 Domaine Faiveley Mercurey Rouge.

● HEALTHY ● MAKE AHEAD ● VEGETARIAN ● STAFF FAVORITE

brined roast chicken with olive bread panzanella

Simplest Chicken and Leek Stew

⏱ TOTAL: 45 MIN • 4 SERVINGS ●

- 2 tablespoons extra-virgin olive oil
- 2 medium leeks, white and tender green parts only, thinly sliced
- ½ pound cremini mushrooms, thinly sliced

Salt and freshly ground pepper
- 1 pound skinless, boneless chicken breast halves, cut into 2-inch pieces

All-purpose flour, for dusting
- 1½ cups chicken stock or low-sodium broth
- 1 tablespoon chopped thyme
- 2 tablespoons sour cream
- 2 teaspoons Dijon mustard

1. In a skillet, heat 1 tablespoon of the oil. Add the leeks and cook over moderate heat, stirring, until softened, about 7 minutes. Add the mushrooms and season with salt and pepper. Cover and cook, stirring, until the mushrooms are tender, about 4 minutes. Scrape the leeks and mushrooms onto a plate.

2. Season the chicken with salt and pepper and lightly dust with flour, shaking off any excess. Heat the remaining 1 tablespoon of oil in the skillet. Add the chicken and cook over moderate heat until golden brown, about 2 minutes per side. Add the chicken stock and thyme and simmer over moderate heat until the chicken is just cooked through, about 1 minute. Using a slotted spoon, transfer the chicken to the plate with the vegetables.

3. Simmer the stock over moderately high heat until reduced by half, about 2 minutes. Return the chicken, leeks and mushrooms to the skillet and simmer over low heat until warmed through, about 1 minute.

4. In a bowl, blend the sour cream with the mustard and stir into the stew. Remove the skillet from the heat. Season the stew with salt and pepper and serve.
—*Jamie Oliver*

SERVE WITH Steamed rice.
WINE Rich, vanilla-tinged California Chardonnay: 2008 Buehler Russian River Reserve.

Dhaba Chicken Curry

⏱ ACTIVE: 25 MIN; TOTAL: 40 MIN
4 SERVINGS ● ●

"You'll find this curry at practically all of the *dhabas* [roadside restaurants] that line the highways in northern India," says Indian star chef Sanjeev Kapoor. "Economical and tasty, it gives you a taste of simple Punjabi cooking."

- 3 onions, coarsely chopped
- 2 garlic cloves

One 1-inch piece of fresh ginger, peeled and chopped
- ¼ cup vegetable oil
- 1 tablespoon ground coriander
- ½ teaspoon ground cumin
- ½ teaspoon cayenne pepper
- ¼ teaspoon cinnamon

Pinch of ground cloves
Pinch of ground cardamom
- ¼ teaspoon turmeric
- 1 cup tomato sauce

Four 6-ounce chicken breast halves on the bone, skinned
Salt
- 1 cup water

Garam masala, for sprinkling
- 2 tablespoons chopped cilantro

1. In a food processor, chop the onions. Add the garlic and ginger and process until they are finely chopped.

2. In a medium enameled cast-iron casserole, heat the vegetable oil. Add the coriander, cumin, cayenne, cinnamon, cloves and cardamom and cook over low heat until fragrant, about 1 minute. Add the onion mixture and cook over high heat, stirring occasionally, until the mixture is golden brown, about 6 minutes. Add the turmeric and tomato sauce and simmer over moderately high heat, stirring occasionally, until slightly thickened, about 3 minutes.

3. Season the chicken breasts with salt and add them to the casserole. Coat the chicken with the sauce. Add the water, cover and bring to a boil. Simmer over low heat, turning a few times, until the chicken is white throughout, about 10 minutes. Season the chicken curry with salt.

4. Transfer the chicken and sauce to a serving bowl. Sprinkle the garam masala on top, garnish with the cilantro and serve.
—*Sanjeev Kapoor*

SERVE WITH Basmati rice or naan.
WINE Baking spice–scented Beaujolais: 2009 Joseph Drouhin Moulin-à-Vent.

Southern Baked Chicken Casserole

ACTIVE: 45 MIN; TOTAL: 1 HR 45 MIN
8 SERVINGS ●

- 2 tablespoons unsalted butter
- 1 tablespoon vegetable oil
- 1 small onion, finely chopped
- 1 red bell pepper, finely chopped
- 1 celery rib, finely chopped
- ¼ cup all-purpose flour
- 1½ cups milk

Salt and freshly ground pepper
Tabasco
- ½ cup mayonnaise
- 4 cups shredded rotisserie chicken
- ½ cup finely chopped pimientos (from a 4-ounce jar)
- 1 sleeve Ritz crackers, crushed (4 ounces)

1. Preheat the oven to 350°. In a large saucepan, melt the butter in the oil. Add the onion, bell pepper and celery and cook over moderately high heat, stirring, until softened, about 6 minutes. Add the flour and cook, stirring, for 2 minutes. Add the milk and whisk until combined. Simmer until thickened, 3 minutes. Season the mixture with salt, pepper and Tabasco. Remove from the heat and stir in the mayonnaise, chicken and pimientos.

2. Transfer the chicken mixture to a 1½-quart shallow baking dish. Scatter the crushed crackers on top. Bake for about 45 minutes, until the casserole is golden and bubbling. Let rest for 15 minutes before serving.
—*Jennifer Nettles*

SERVE WITH Crackers and toasts.
MAKE AHEAD The baked chicken casserole can be refrigerated overnight.
WINE Full-bodied, pear-scented Chardonnay: 2009 Chateau St. Jean Sonoma County.

● HEALTHY ● MAKE AHEAD ● VEGETARIAN ● STAFF FAVORITE

Chicken Tagine with Artichoke Hearts and Peas

ACTIVE: 25 MIN; TOTAL: 1 HR 15 MIN

4 SERVINGS ● ●

To give this Moroccan stew flavor without much fat, legendary French chef Joël Robuchon simmers the chicken in a spiced broth. Artichoke hearts add a lovely spring flavor; they are also one of the best vegetable sources of antioxidants.

One 4-pound chicken—legs separated into drumsticks and thighs, breasts halved crosswise, skin and visible fat removed

Salt and freshly ground black pepper

2 medium onions—1 coarsely chopped, 1 minced

1½ cups chicken stock or low-sodium broth

6 saffron threads, crumbled

½ teaspoon ground ginger

½ teaspoon ground coriander

½ teaspoon ground cumin

½ teaspoon hot paprika

¼ teaspoon turmeric

2 medium tomatoes, cut into eighths

¼ preserved lemon, rind only, minced (see Note)

8 frozen artichoke hearts, thawed and quartered

1 cup frozen petite peas, thawed

1. Season the chicken pieces with salt and pepper. In a medium enameled cast-iron casserole, combine the chicken with the coarsely chopped onion and the chicken stock and bring to a boil. In a small bowl, mix the saffron threads with the ginger, coriander, cumin, paprika and turmeric. Stir the spice mixture into the broth. Cover and simmer over low heat, turning the chicken pieces once, until the breast pieces are just white throughout, about 25 minutes; transfer the breast pieces to a bowl and cover. Continue to simmer the drumsticks and thighs, covered, until done, about 15 minutes longer; transfer to the bowl with the breast pieces and keep covered.

2. Add the minced onion, the tomatoes, preserved lemon and artichoke hearts to the casserole and simmer over moderate heat until the broth is richly flavored, about 5 minutes. Season with salt and pepper and add the peas. Return the chicken to the casserole and simmer gently, turning a few times, until heated through. Serve the tagine in shallow bowls. —*Joël Robuchon*

SERVE WITH Couscous.

NOTE Preserved lemons are a Moroccan staple made from lemons that have been cured in lemon juice and salt. Look for them at specialty food stores.

MAKE AHEAD The chicken tagine can be refrigerated overnight. Reheat gently.

WINE Lemony Grüner Veltliner from Austria: 2008 Prager Federspiel Hinter der Burg.

Persian Chicken Stew

ACTIVE: 30 MIN; TOTAL: 1 HR 45 MIN

4 SERVINGS ●

Khoresht fesenjan is a Persian stew made with pomegranate juice and walnuts. Chef Matthew Dillon serves this version at his Sitka & Spruce restaurant in Seattle's Melrose Market. His rule No. 1 for making this dish: "Use a thoughtfully and responsibly raised whole chicken."

One 4-pound chicken—quartered, backbone and neck reserved, wings saved for another use

Salt and freshly ground black pepper

2 tablespoons extra-virgin olive oil

1 onion, cut into ½-inch dice

3 garlic cloves, peeled and smashed

¼ cup raisins

1 cup chopped walnuts

Pinch of saffron threads soaked in ¼ cup water

2 cups low-sodium chicken broth

1 cup pomegranate juice

3 cardamom pods, lightly crushed

4 allspice berries

1 dried lime (see Note) or one 3-inch piece of lime zest

One 2-inch cinnamon stick

½ tablespoon red wine vinegar

Couscous, for serving

1. Preheat the oven to 350°. Season the chicken with salt and pepper. In a large enameled cast-iron casserole, heat the olive oil. Add half of the chicken along with the backbone and neck and cook over moderately high heat until browned, about 4 minutes per side. Transfer the chicken to a plate and repeat with the remaining pieces.

2. Pour off all but 2 tablespoons of the fat in the casserole. Add the onion, smashed garlic cloves, raisins and chopped walnuts to the casserole and cook over moderate heat, stirring occasionally, until the onion is softened and golden brown, about 7 minutes. Add the saffron water, chicken broth, pomegranate juice, cardamom, allspice, dried lime and cinnamon stick and bring to a boil over moderately high heat. Return the chicken pieces to the casserole, skin side up, along with any accumulated juices. Cover and braise the chicken in the oven for about 35 minutes, until the breasts are cooked through.

3. Transfer the chicken breasts to a medium bowl and keep them warm. Continue braising the dark meat pieces for about 15 minutes, until the legs are cooked through, then transfer the legs to the bowl. Discard the chicken back and neck.

4. Boil the braising liquid over high heat until it is reduced to ¾ cup, about 15 minutes. Discard the lime, cardamom, allspice and cinnamon stick. Add the red wine vinegar and season the sauce with salt and pepper. Return the chicken pieces to the sauce and simmer them gently until they are heated through, about 3 minutes. Transfer the chicken stew to shallow bowls and serve right away, with couscous.
—*Matthew Dillon*

SERVE WITH Sliced pink or red grapefruits and oranges, sprinkled lightly with rose water and cinnamon.

NOTE Dried lime is a sour, tangy Middle Eastern ingredient made by boiling fresh lime in salt water, then drying it in the sun. It's available at Middle Eastern markets or online at *kalustyans.com*.

WINE Fruit-forward Spanish red: 2009 Bodegas Borsao Monte Oton Garnacha.

Curried-Coconut Chicken Rendang

ACTIVE: 45 MIN; TOTAL: 1 HR 30 MIN
PLUS 4 HR MARINATING • 6 SERVINGS ● ●

In this Malaysian classic, chicken thighs are flavored with fragrant ginger-chile paste, then slow-cooked in coconut milk.

3 tablespoons Madras curry powder
2 teaspoons freshly ground pepper
2 lemongrass stalks, bottom two-thirds only, bruised and cut into 4-inch pieces
2 tablespoons fresh lime juice
⅓ cup plus 2 tablespoons canola oil
Salt
3 pounds chicken thighs
8 small shallots
1 small red onion, quartered
5 garlic cloves
Six ¼-inch slices of peeled fresh ginger
3 macadamia nuts
5 dried Asian chiles, stemmed
1 can unsweetened coconut milk
1 tablespoon light brown sugar
1½ tablespoons shredded unsweetened coconut, toasted

1. In a bowl, combine the curry powder, pepper, lemongrass, lime juice and 2 tablespoons of the oil. Season with salt. Add the chicken, turn to coat and refrigerate for 4 hours.
2. In a food processor, puree the shallots, onion, garlic, ginger, nuts and chiles.
3. In a deep skillet, heat the remaining ⅓ cup of oil. Fry the chile paste over moderately high heat, stirring, until lightly browned, 5 minutes. Add the chicken with its marinade; cook over moderate heat until the chicken is browned and nearly cooked through, 20 minutes. Add the coconut milk, sugar and coconut and simmer over moderate heat, stirring, until the chicken is tender and the sauce is very thick, 25 minutes. Spoon off as much oil as possible; discard the lemongrass. Season with salt and serve. —*Zang Toi*
MAKE AHEAD The *rendang* can be refrigerated for 2 days. Rewarm before serving.
WINE Fresh, berry-scented rosé Champagne: NV Nicolas Feuillatte Brut Rosé.

Swamp Chili (Poblano and Spinach Posole)

ACTIVE: 1 HR; TOTAL: 1 HR 30 MIN
6 TO 8 SERVINGS ● ●

Spinach and pureed poblanos give this chili a swamp-like look that's fun on Halloween.

1½ pounds poblano chiles
¼ cup extra-virgin olive oil
1 large white onion, finely chopped
1½ teaspoons ground cumin
1½ teaspoons ground coriander
5 large garlic cloves, minced
One 10-ounce package frozen chopped spinach, thawed and squeezed dry
1 quart low-sodium chicken broth
Kosher salt
1 slice of white sandwich bread
¼ cup milk
½ pound ground chicken
½ pound ground pork
1 teaspoon pure ancho chile powder
One 15-ounce can white hominy, drained
2 tablespoons chopped cilantro

1. Roast the poblanos directly over a gas flame or under a broiler until charred all over. Transfer the chiles to a bowl, cover with plastic wrap and let cool. Peel, stem and seed the chiles. Transfer to a blender and puree until smooth.
2. In an enameled cast-iron casserole, heat the oil. Add the onion, cumin, coriander and 4 of the garlic cloves. Cook over low heat until the onion is soft, about 8 minutes. Add the pureed poblanos and cook, stirring, until the mixture thickens, about 5 minutes. Add the spinach and broth and season with salt. Simmer over low heat until slightly reduced and the spinach begins to break down, 15 minutes.
3. Meanwhile, in a bowl, mash the bread to a paste with the milk. Add the chicken, pork, chile powder, the remaining garlic and 1 teaspoon of salt and gently knead to combine. Roll tablespoons of the mixture into meatballs and add to the chili with the hominy. Simmer until the meatballs are cooked through, about 15 minutes. Stir in the cilantro and serve. —*Grace Parisi*
WINE Juicy, spicy Grenache: 2008 Yalumba Bush Vine.

Chicken Dijon

⏱ **ACTIVE: 20 MIN; TOTAL: 45 MIN**
4 SERVINGS ● ●

Cookbook author Melissa Clark likes using only drumsticks in this mustardy stew, thickened with tangy crème fraîche, so that all the meat cooks at the same rate.

1 teaspoon coriander seeds
2 tablespoons extra-virgin olive oil
8 medium chicken drumsticks (about 3 pounds)
Salt and freshly ground pepper
¼ cup finely chopped onion
4 garlic cloves, minced
1½ cups low-sodium chicken broth
2 tablespoons whole-grain mustard
3 tablespoons crème fraîche or sour cream
2 teaspoons chopped tarragon
Crusty bread, for serving

1. In a large skillet, toast the coriander seeds over moderately high heat until they are fragrant, about 2 minutes. Transfer the seeds to a mortar, let cool and then crush the seeds coarsely with a pestle.
2. In the same skillet, heat the olive oil until shimmering. Season the chicken drumsticks with salt and pepper, add them to the skillet and cook over moderately high heat, turning, until golden brown all over, about 10 minutes. Add the onion and cook, stirring occasionally, until softened, about 3 minutes. Add the garlic and cook for 1 minute. Add the broth and crushed coriander and bring to a boil. Cover and cook over moderately low heat until the chicken is cooked through, about 15 minutes.
3. Transfer the chicken to a platter, cover and keep warm. In a small bowl, whisk the mustard with the crème fraîche and tarragon. Whisk the mixture into the skillet and simmer the sauce over moderate heat until thickened, about 5 minutes. Return the chicken to the skillet and turn to coat. Serve the chicken with crusty bread.
—*Melissa Clark*
WINE Full-bodied, fruity California Chardonnay: 2009 Wyatt.

● HEALTHY ● MAKE AHEAD ● VEGETARIAN ● STAFF FAVORITE

chicken dijon

Pot-Roasted Chicken with Mushrooms

ACTIVE: 30 MIN; TOTAL: 1 HR 30 MIN

4 SERVINGS

20 thyme sprigs
4   bay leaves
2   tablespoons dried chamomile flowers (see Note)
One 3½-pound chicken, patted dry
Salt and freshly ground pepper
4   tablespoons unsalted butter, softened
1½ pounds fresh or thawed frozen pizza dough
¾   pound brussels sprouts, thinly sliced
¼   cup extra-virgin olive oil
4   large garlic cloves, smashed
¾   pound mixed wild mushrooms, such as shiitake and oyster, stemmed and thickly sliced
½   cup veal demiglace mixed with ½ cup of water

1. Preheat the oven to 375° and spread the thyme, bay leaves and chamomile in the bottom of a large, deep, enameled cast-iron casserole. Season the chicken inside and out with salt and pepper and set it directly on the aromatics. Rub the top of the bird with 3 tablespoons of the butter.

2. Roll the pizza dough into a rope that is long enough to encircle the casserole. Press the dough onto the rim of the casserole and cover with the lid, pressing it into the dough. Pinch the dough up onto the lid slightly to seal the pot completely. Roast the chicken in the center of the oven for 1 hour and 10 minutes. Remove the lid, cracking the dough, and pierce the thigh to make sure the bird is cooked through. Replace the lid and let the chicken rest for 5 minutes.

3. Meanwhile, in a large skillet, melt the remaining 1 tablespoon of butter. Add the brussels sprouts, season with salt and pepper and cook over moderate heat until just wilted. Transfer the brussels sprouts to a platter.

4. Heat the olive oil in the skillet. Add the garlic and cook over moderate heat until golden, about 5 minutes; discard the garlic. Add the mushrooms, season with salt and pepper and cook over moderately low heat until softened and lightly browned, about 10 minutes. Add the demiglace mixture and simmer until slightly reduced, about 5 minutes.

5. Transfer the chicken to a cutting board and strain the pan juices into a measuring cup. Discard the fat from the juices, then add the juices to the mushrooms. Remove the chicken skin and slice the breast meat. Cut off the legs, cutting them into two pieces each. Arrange the chicken on the brussels sprouts on the platter, spoon the mushrooms and sauce on top and serve with chunks of the baked pizza dough, for dipping.
—*David Bouley*

NOTE Chamomile flowers are available at specialty food shops. Alternatively, the contents of 4 chamomile tea bags can be used in place of the dried flowers.

WINE Medium-bodied, dark-berried Spanish red: 2008 Silvano García Viñahonda Jumilla.

Honey-Chile Chicken Wings

ACTIVE: 10 MIN; TOTAL: 1 HR

4 SERVINGS

Tim Wood, the chef at Carmel Valley Ranch in California, avoids the deep fryer and opts to broil or grill his chicken wings, which turns them supercrispy. A soy-and-honey glaze makes them sweet, sticky and salty.

4   pounds chicken wings
¼   cup extra-virgin olive oil
Salt and freshly ground pepper
¼   cup unseasoned rice vinegar
1   teaspoon crushed red pepper
½   cup honey
2   tablespoons soy sauce
2   scallions, thinly sliced

1. Preheat the broiler and set a rack in the center of the oven. In a large bowl, toss the chicken wings with the olive oil and season with salt and pepper. Arrange the wings on a wire rack set over a large, sturdy baking sheet. Broil for 45 to 50 minutes, turning once or twice, until the wings are cooked through and crisp.

2. Meanwhile, in a small saucepan, combine the vinegar and crushed red pepper and simmer for 1 minute. Let cool, then whisk in the honey and soy sauce.

3. In a large bowl, carefully toss the chicken wings with the honey-soy mixture. Transfer the wings to a platter, sprinkle with the scallions and serve. —*Tim Wood*

WINE Merlot: 2007 Estancia Central Coast.

Spicy Apricot Wings

TOTAL: 40 MIN • 6 SERVINGS

½   cup hickory, apple or apricot wood chips
½   cup apricot preserves
2   tablespoons Worcestershire sauce
2   tablespoons light brown sugar
1   tablespoon soy sauce
1   tablespoon Dijon mustard
1   tablespoon kosher salt
2   teaspoons freshly ground black pepper
1   teaspoon garlic powder
1   teaspoon sweet paprika
½   teaspoon cayenne pepper
¼   teaspoon ground ginger
3   pounds chicken wings, wing tips removed and wings cut into 2 pieces

1. Light a gas grill. Wrap the wood chips in heavy-duty foil, pierce the packet with a skewer and add it to the grill. Cover and let the wood chips begin to smoke, 5 minutes.

2. Meanwhile, in a large bowl, combine the preserves with the Worcestershire, brown sugar, soy sauce, mustard, salt, black pepper, garlic powder, sweet paprika, cayenne and ginger. Scrape half of the mixture into a small bowl. Add the chicken wings to the large bowl and toss to coat well in the sauce. Let the chicken wings stand for 5 minutes.

3. Grill the chicken wings, covered, over moderately high heat, turning them occasionally, until they are charred in spots and cooked through, 22 to 25 minutes. Transfer the chicken wings to a platter and serve the reserved sauce on the side. —*Chris Lilly*

BEER Citrusy wheat beer from Georgia: SweetWater Sch'Wheat.

● HEALTHY ● MAKE AHEAD ● VEGETARIAN ● STAFF FAVORITE

Spice-Rubbed Poussins

ACTIVE: 30 MIN; TOTAL: 1 HR PLUS OVERNIGHT MARINATING • 4 SERVINGS

Ma Cuisine, a restaurant in a small square in Beaune, France, features delicious, wine-friendly dishes like these *poussins* that are coated with a mix of spices, then roasted until browned and juicy. If you can't find *poussins,* substitute Cornish hens or two small chickens and adjust the cooking time.

1 small shallot, minced
2 teaspoons chopped thyme
1 teaspoon sweet paprika
1 teaspoon curry powder
½ teaspoon ground ginger
½ teaspoon freshly grated nutmeg
½ teaspoon freshly ground white pepper
¼ teaspoon ground cloves
2 tablespoons extra-virgin olive oil
Kosher salt
Four 1-pound *poussins,* backbones
     and wing tips removed
½ cup dry white wine
1 garlic clove, minced
1 tablespoon soy sauce
1 tablespoon Worcestershire sauce

1. In a bowl, combine the shallot, thyme, paprika, curry, ginger, nutmeg, white pepper and cloves. Stir in the oil and season with a large pinch of salt. Set the *poussins* on a rimmed baking sheet, breast side up; press down to flatten the birds. Spread the spice paste all over, then refrigerate overnight.
2. Preheat the oven to 425°. In a small saucepan, boil the white wine, garlic, soy sauce and Worcestershire sauce over high heat until reduced by a third, about 5 minutes.
3. Season the *poussins* with salt and roast for 10 minutes. Increase the oven temperature to 450° and baste the *poussins* with the wine mixture. Roast for about 20 minutes longer, basting 3 more times with the wine mixture, until the birds are nicely browned and the inner thigh juices run clear. Let the *poussins* rest for 10 minutes, then serve.
—*Fabienne Escoffier*
WINE Light red: 2008 Domaine de L'Arlot Côte de Nuits Villages Clos du Chapeau.

Roast Capon with Mushroom-Armagnac Sauce

ACTIVE: 30 MIN; TOTAL: 3 HR
8 SERVINGS

Capons are very large, neutered roosters that are prized for their intense chicken flavor and tender texture. In this recipe, master chef Jacques Pépin roasts the bird simply, then makes a mushroom-Armagnac sauce enriched with cream, vermouth and the pan juices from the capon.

One 8½- to 9½-pound capon
Salt and freshly ground
     black pepper
2 teaspoons herbes de Provence
3 tablespoons unsalted butter
1 pound white mushrooms,
     sliced ⅛ inch thick
½ pound shiitake mushrooms,
     stems discarded and caps sliced
     ⅛ inch thick
½ cup dry vermouth or white wine
1½ cups chicken stock or
     low-sodium broth
1 cup heavy cream
2 tablespoons Armagnac or Cognac
2½ teaspoons potato starch dissolved
     in 2 tablespoons of water
1 tablespoon chopped tarragon

1. Preheat the oven to 400°. In a large roasting pan, season the capon inside and out with salt, pepper and the herbes de Provence. Roast the capon breast side up for about 30 minutes, then turn it breast side down and roast for about 1 hour. Turn the capon breast side up and roast for about 1 hour longer, until an instant-read thermometer inserted in the inner thigh registers 160°.
2. Meanwhile, in a large, deep skillet, melt the butter. Add the white and shiitake mushrooms and season lightly with salt and pepper. Cover and cook over moderate heat, stirring occasionally, until the mushrooms are lightly browned, about 15 minutes. Add the vermouth and cook until it's almost evaporated. Add the chicken stock and simmer over moderate heat for about 5 minutes. Add the cream and Armagnac and simmer until the sauce has reduced to 3 cups, about 4 minutes. Remove from the heat and whisk in the potato starch mixture until incorporated. Cook over low heat, whisking, until thickened, about 1 minute. Remove from the heat, stir in the tarragon and season with salt and pepper.
3. Lift the capon from the roasting pan, letting the cavity juices drain into the pan; transfer the capon to a carving board and let rest for 15 to 20 minutes.
4. Pour the pan juices into a glass measuring cup and skim the fat from the surface. Strain the juices into the mushroom sauce and reheat gently. Carve the capon at the table and serve with the mushroom sauce.
—*Jacques Pépin*
WINE Red Burgundy: 2006 Domaine Jean-Marc Morey Beaune Grèves Premier Cru.

fast flavor for roast chicken

garlic confit Fresh summer garlic has large cloves that are especially sweet and juicy. To preserve them, simmer the cloves in oil with chiles and thyme until soft and silky, then store in jars until needed. Slip the garlic confit under chicken skin before roasting or mash into butter and spread on bread.

Peel the cloves from 6 heads garlic (you will have about 2 cups). In a medium saucepan, combine the garlic cloves with 6 thyme sprigs, 3 small bay leaves, 3 dried red chiles and 2 cups olive oil. Simmer over low heat until the garlic is tender but not browned, about 30 minutes. Let cool. Using a slotted spoon, transfer the garlic, herbs and chiles to three ½-pint canning jars. Pour the cooking oil on top, seal and refrigerate for up to 4 months. —*Grace Parisi*

Confit of Guinea Hen Legs with Prunes and Honey

ACTIVE: 30 MIN; TOTAL: 4 HR 30 MIN
4 SERVINGS ●

Kosher salt
- ¼ cup light brown sugar
- 8 garlic cloves, smashed
- 2 tablespoons rosemary leaves
- 2 tablespoons cracked black peppercorns
- 2 bay leaves, crushed
- 8 guinea hen legs (see Note)
- 1 cup pitted prunes

Boiling water
- 1 cup honey
- ¼ cup cider vinegar
- 1 teaspoon ground ginger
- ½ teaspoon crushed red pepper
- 1 quart vegetable oil
- 1 cup rendered duck fat (see Note)

1. In a small bowl, combine ⅓ cup of salt with the brown sugar, garlic, rosemary, peppercorns and bay leaves. Put the hen legs in a large, shallow dish and rub all over with the salt mixture. Cover and refrigerate for 3 hours.

2. In a heatproof bowl, cover the prunes with boiling water and let stand until softened, 10 minutes; drain and transfer to a saucepan. Add the honey and vinegar and simmer over low heat for 30 minutes. Stir in the ginger and red pepper; remove from the heat. Season with salt and let cool to room temperature.

3. Preheat the oven to 325°. Rinse the legs and pat dry with paper towels. Set the legs in a small flameproof roasting pan, skin side up. Pour in the oil, add the duck fat and bring to a simmer over moderate heat to melt the duck fat. Transfer the pan to the oven and bake the legs for 1 hour, until just cooked, turning them halfway through.

4. Transfer the legs to a platter. Heat a nonstick skillet over moderate heat. Add half of the legs, skin side down, and cook until browned, 5 minutes. Turn the legs and cook until browned on the other side, 3 minutes. Repeat with the remaining legs. Serve with the prunes and sauce.
—David McMillan and Frédéric Morin

SERVE WITH Watercress salad.
NOTE Guinea hen legs and rendered duck fat can be ordered from *dartagnan.com*.
WINE Elegant white Burgundy: 2008 Dominique Cornin Pouilly-Fuissé Les Chevrières.

Puerto Rican–Style Turkey

ACTIVE: 15 MIN; TOTAL: 45 MIN
4 TO 6 SERVINGS ●

The inspiration for this curry-and-chile-spiced marinade was *lechón*, a slow-roasted Puerto Rican pork dish that Chicago chef Bill Kim learned from his mother-in-law. Because the flavors are intense, it's best to scrape off the marinade before grilling.

- 8 garlic cloves, smashed and peeled
- 2 tablespoons dried oregano
- 1 tablespoon sweet paprika
- 1 tablespoon pure ancho chile powder
- ¾ teaspoon curry powder
- ½ tablespoon kosher salt
- 2 tablespoons distilled white vinegar
- 3 tablespoons extra-virgin olive oil
- 2 pounds turkey cutlets

Vegetable oil, for brushing

1. In a mini food processor, combine the garlic cloves, oregano, paprika, chile powder, curry and salt and process until the garlic is chopped. Add the vinegar and olive oil and process to a paste.

2. Rub the marinade onto the turkey cutlets and let stand at room temperature for at least 30 minutes or refrigerate the turkey for up to 24 hours.

3. Light a grill or preheat a grill pan. Scrape the marinade off the turkey cutlets. Brush the cutlets with vegetable oil and grill over moderately high heat, turning once, until lightly charred and cooked through, about 5 minutes total. Serve right away.
—Bill Kim

VARIATION The marinade is also great for pork chops and pork tenderloin.
SERVE WITH Black beans and yellow rice.
MAKE AHEAD The marinade can be refrigerated for up to 3 days.
WINE Tropical South African Chenin Blanc: 2010 Mulderbosch.

Ground Turkey Laap

TOTAL: 35 MIN • 4 SERVINGS ●

In Laos, this *laap* (a ground meat dish) is usually made with duck and can be eaten alone or with sticky rice. The recipe here substitutes ground turkey, which is more readily available in the US and less expensive. But to make it the authentic way, use an equal amount of duck breast trimmed of fat, freeze it for 10 minutes and then finely chop by hand.

- 1 tablespoon long-grain white rice
- 1 tablespoon vegetable oil
- 1 pound ground turkey
- ¼ cup plus 2 tablespoons chicken stock or low-sodium broth
- 1 tablespoon plus 1 teaspoon Asian fish sauce

Salt and freshly ground black pepper
- 1 tablespoon fresh lime juice
- 2 large stalks of lemongrass—tender pale inner core only, minced
- 2 scallions, thinly sliced
- 1 medium shallot, thinly sliced and separated into rings
- ½ cup chopped cilantro
- ½ cup chopped mint
- ¼ teaspoon crushed red pepper

Small romaine or Belgian endive leaves and lime wedges, for serving

1. In a small skillet, toast the rice over high heat, shaking the skillet a few times, until the rice is golden brown, about 3 minutes. Transfer the rice to a spice grinder and let cool completely. Grind the rice to a powder.

2. In a large skillet, heat the oil. Add the turkey and cook over moderately high heat, breaking up the meat evenly, until no pink remains, about 4 minutes. Add the stock and cook, stirring, until bubbling. Remove from the heat and stir in the fish sauce. Season with salt and black pepper and stir in the lime juice. Let stand for 5 minutes, then stir in the lemongrass, scallions, shallot rings, cilantro, mint, crushed red pepper and rice powder.

3. Arrange the lettuce and lime wedges on a platter. Spoon the *laap* on the lettuce and serve. *—Sebastien Rubis*

WINE Riesling: 2009 Rolf Binder Highness.

● HEALTHY ● MAKE AHEAD ● VEGETARIAN ● STAFF FAVORITE

ground turkey laap

Barbecue-Glazed Turkey Burgers

TOTAL: 20 MIN • 4 SERVINGS

Turkey burgers are a popular lunch at actress and cookbook author Gwyneth Paltrow's house. Jarred barbecue sauce adds a ton of flavor to the burgers and helps keep them from drying out.

- 1 pound ground turkey
- Kosher salt and freshly ground pepper
- ¼ cup plus 2 tablespoons sweet-smoky jarred barbecue sauce
- Canola oil, for brushing
- 4 brioche buns, split and toasted
- Pickled jalapeño slices, Swiss cheese slices and pickle chips, for serving

Light a grill or preheat a grill pan. In a bowl, season the turkey with salt and pepper and gently knead in ¼ cup of the barbecue sauce. Shape the meat into four 4-inch patties, about ¾ inch thick. Brush with oil and grill over moderate heat, turning them once, until

nearly cooked through, 7 minutes. Brush with the remaining 2 tablespoons of barbecue sauce and cook for about 1 minute longer, until cooked through and lightly glazed. Transfer the burgers to the buns, top with pickled jalapeños, Swiss cheese and pickle chips and serve. —*Gwyneth Paltrow*

WINE Juicy California red blend: 2009 Beckmen Cuvée Le Bec.

Black-Bean Turkey Chili

ACTIVE: 20 MIN; TOTAL: 1 HR 30 MIN
4 SERVINGS ● ●

- 2 tablespoons extra-virgin olive oil
- 1 pound lean ground turkey (white meat only)
- Salt and freshly ground pepper
- 3 garlic cloves, minced
- 1 medium onion, finely chopped
- 2 tablespoons ancho chile powder
- 1 tablespoon New Mexico chile powder
- 1 teaspoon ground cumin
- One 14-ounce can chopped tomatoes
- One 15-ounce can tomato sauce
- One 15-ounce can black beans, drained and rinsed
- 4 corn tortillas

1. In a saucepan, heat the oil. Add the turkey, season with salt and pepper and cook over moderate heat, breaking up the meat, until white throughout, 4 minutes. Add the garlic, onion, chile powders and the cumin; cook, stirring, until fragrant, 5 minutes. Stir in the tomatoes, tomato sauce and 1 cup of water; bring to a simmer. Cook over low heat, stirring occasionally, until thickened, 45 minutes. Add the beans and simmer for 15 minutes.

2. Meanwhile, light a grill or preheat a grill pan. Grill the corn tortillas over moderate heat until they are soft, 30 seconds per side; wrap them in a towel.

3. Season the chili with salt and pepper and serve with the tortillas. —*Ronnie Killen*

SERVE WITH Low-fat sour cream.

MAKE AHEAD The chili can be refrigerated for up to 3 days. Reheat gently.

WINE Juicy, not-too-tannic Montepulciano: 2008 Farnese Montepulciano d'Abruzzo.

Kung Pao Turkey Drumsticks

TOTAL: 45 MIN • 4 SERVINGS ●

- ⅓ cup honey
- ¼ cup minced fresh ginger
- 1 quart plus 2 tablespoons canola oil
- 1 medium shallot, minced
- 3 garlic cloves, minced
- 2 tablespoons mirin
- 3 tablespoons unseasoned rice vinegar
- 3 tablespoons low-sodium soy sauce
- 3 tablespoons dark soy sauce (or *kecap manis*)
- 2 tablespoons hoisin sauce
- 1 tablespoon *sambal oelek*
- 4 small turkey drumsticks
- ¼ cup salted roasted peanuts, chopped
- 2 scallions, minced

1. In a small saucepan, bring the honey and 1 tablespoon of the ginger to a simmer. Let cool, then strain the honey into a bowl.

2. In a medium saucepan, heat the 2 tablespoons of canola oil. Add the shallot and cook over low heat, stirring, until softened, about 4 minutes. Add the garlic and the remaining 3 tablespoons of ginger and cook over low heat until softened, about 2 minutes. Stir in the mirin and vinegar and simmer until slightly reduced, 2 minutes. Add both soy sauces and the hoisin and simmer just until slightly thickened, about 1 minute. Stir in the *sambal oelek*.

3. In a large, deep skillet, heat the 1 quart of canola oil to 350° on a deep-fry thermometer. Add the drumsticks and fry over moderate heat, turning occasionally, until they are crisp and golden and an instant-read thermometer inserted near the bone registers 160°, 20 to 25 minutes; be sure to maintain the oil temperature at 350°. Drain the drumsticks and blot with paper towels.

4. Transfer the drumsticks to a large bowl, add the sauce and toss to coat. In a pie plate, combine the peanuts and scallions. Roll the turkey legs in the peanut-scallion mixture, drizzle with the ginger honey and serve. —*Graham Elliot Bowles*

WINE Spicy Alsace Gewürztraminer: 2007 Schlumberger Les Princes Abbés.

supereasy turkey sandwich spread

bacon jam *This signature condiment from Skillet Street Food in Seattle is a meaty hit of smoke and sweetness in a jar. It's great spread on turkey or cheese sandwiches.* $14 for 10.5 oz; skillet baconjam.com.

Cook jam for a minute or two, until hot and glistening. Spread goat cheese on toasted baguette and top with minced hot cherry peppers or jalapeños and dollops of the hot bacon jam. Cover with a little salad made with shredded radicchio, baby arugula and toasted walnuts dressed in cider vinegar and extra-virgin olive oil. —*Tina Ujlaki*

● HEALTHY ● MAKE AHEAD ● VEGETARIAN ● STAFF FAVORITE

kung pao turkey drumsticks

poultry

thanksgiving leftover ideas

Because chef Michael Symon tends to overdo the cooking on Thanksgiving (he generally buys five turkeys, one or two just for making stock), there is invariably a lot of extra food. Here, three of his favorite dishes for leftovers.

turkey sandwiches

"I love having these the day after Thanksgiving," says Symon. He piles toasted sourdough bread with sliced turkey, chunks of avocado and lime mayonnaise (mayo mixed with a little lime juice and lime zest). He finishes the sandwiches with Sriracha and a handful of cilantro leaves.

turkey and dumpling soup

Symon uses leftover turkey stock and meat to make this soothing soup. He cooks sautéed carrots, parsnips, celery root and onion in the stock, then adds leftover turkey. He also adds dumplings made with flour, eggs, milk, turkey fat and tarragon; the dumplings cook in the simmering soup right before serving. For the complete recipe, go to *foodandwine.com/ symon-leftovers.*

quick breakfast bread pudding

Symon sees breakfast potential in leftover stuffing—either butternut squash with corn bread or lemony mushroom with pine nuts (both recipes on page 290). He dices the stuffing, whisks up a bunch of eggs with strips of dark turkey meat and some whole milk, then bakes the bread pudding in a deep skillet. "I have it right out of the oven, before anyone wakes up," says Symon. "Then everyone else eats it all morning."

Cider-Glazed Turkey with Lager Gravy

ACTIVE: 45 MIN; TOTAL: 4 HR 30 MIN PLUS OVERNIGHT SALTING • 10 TO 12 SERVINGS ●

Lots of people brine their turkeys. Not star chef Michael Symon, who thinks brining makes the texture of the bird a little rubbery. He salts his bird well and refrigerates it overnight to season it. Before roasting, he covers the breast and legs with cheesecloth that's been soaked in a cider-infused butter. For his beer-spiked gravy, Symon recommends the German-style Dortmunder Gold, made by Great Lakes Brewing Company, from his home state of Ohio.

TURKEY

One 12- to 13-pound turkey—
  neck and giblets reserved, wing tips cut off and reserved
2 tablespoons kosher salt
1 unpeeled head of garlic, halved crosswise
1 jalapeño, halved
1 Granny Smith apple, quartered
12 sage leaves
⅓ cup apple cider
1 stick unsalted butter

GRAVY

2 tablespoons vegetable oil
Reserved turkey neck, wing tips and giblets
Salt and freshly ground pepper
⅓ cup all-purpose flour
½ cup apple cider
One 12-ounce bottle lager
1 bay leaf

1. PREPARE THE TURKEY Season the turkey inside and out with the kosher salt. Cover with plastic wrap and refrigerate overnight.
2. Uncover the turkey and let it return to room temperature before proceeding. Stuff the cavity with the garlic, jalapeño, apple and 6 of the sage leaves. Transfer the turkey to a large roasting pan.
3. Preheat the oven to 350°. In a small saucepan, combine the cider with the butter and the remaining 6 sage leaves and cook over low heat until the butter has melted and the sage is fragrant, about 4 minutes. Dampen a 32-by-20-inch piece of cheesecloth with water and squeeze dry. Immerse the cheesecloth in the cider butter until the liquid is absorbed. Drape the soaked cheesecloth over the turkey breast and legs.
4. Roast the turkey for 30 minutes. Add 2 cups of water to the roasting pan and continue to roast for about 2 hours longer, rotating the pan a few times, until an instant-read thermometer inserted in the inner thigh registers 165°.
5. MEANWHILE, PREPARE THE GRAVY In a large saucepan, heat the vegetable oil. Add the turkey neck, wing tips and giblets except for the liver (reserve the liver) and season with salt and pepper. Cook the parts over moderate heat, turning them a few times, until nicely browned, about 12 minutes. Remove the turkey parts and reserve. Off the heat, stir the flour into the fat in the saucepan to make a paste. Gradually whisk in the cider until smooth, then whisk in the lager. Add 3 cups of water and bring to a boil over moderately high heat, whisking until thickened. Return the turkey parts to the saucepan and add the bay leaf. Cover and cook over low heat, whisking occasionally, until the gravy is flavorful, about 1½ hours. Discard the turkey parts and bay leaf.
6. Carefully peel the cheesecloth off the turkey and discard. Transfer the turkey to a cutting board and let rest for about 30 minutes. Pour the pan juices into a glass measuring cup and skim the fat from the surface. Add the pan juices to the gravy and bring to a simmer over moderate heat. Season the reserved liver with salt and pepper, add to the gravy and simmer until pink in the center, about 5 minutes. Remove the liver and cut it into small pieces.
7. In a blender, puree the liver with 1 cup of the gravy. Whisk the liver puree into the gravy and season with salt and pepper. Rewarm the gravy if necessary. Carve the turkey and serve with the gravy.
—Michael Symon
WINE Cherry-rich Pinot Noir from Oregon: 2008 Scott Paul La Paulée Pinot Noir.

136

● HEALTHY ● MAKE AHEAD ● VEGETARIAN ● STAFF FAVORITE

cider-glazed turkey with lager gravy

Duck à l'Orange

ACTIVE: 1 HR 30 MIN; TOTAL: 3 HR
4 TO 6 SERVINGS ●

Because a single duck rarely has enough meat to feed more than two or three people, master chef Jacques Pépin prepares two ducks side by side when serving this classic dish to guests. And because he's roasting whole ducks, he cooks them until they're well done, which results in the crispiest skin and best flavor.

Two 5½- to 6-pound Pekin ducks, trimmed of excess fat—necks, gizzards and hearts reserved
Salt and freshly ground black pepper
- 1 cup water
- 1 tablespoon vegetable oil
- 2 medium carrots, coarsely chopped
- 2 medium tomatoes, coarsely chopped
- 2 celery ribs, coarsely chopped
- 1 small leek, white and pale green parts only, coarsely chopped
- 1 small onion, coarsely chopped
- 2 garlic cloves, crushed but not peeled
- 2 bay leaves
- 1 teaspoon dried thyme
- 3 tablespoons all-purpose flour
- 2 tablespoons tomato paste
- 1 quart chicken stock or low-sodium broth
- 1 cup dry white wine
- 5 navel oranges
- ⅓ cup sugar
- ⅓ cup cider vinegar
- 2 tablespoons currant jelly
- 2 tablespoons Grand Marnier
- 2 tablespoons cold unsalted butter

1. Preheat the oven to 450°. Cut off the first two wing joints of the ducks and reserve. Chop the necks into 2-inch lengths.
2. Prick the ducks around the thighs, backs and breasts, then season them inside and out with salt and pepper. Set a rack in a very large roasting pan. Set the ducks breast up on the rack as far apart as possible. Add the water to the pan and roast the ducks in the center of the oven for 20 minutes. Reduce the oven temperature to 350°. Turn the ducks on their sides, propping them up by placing 2 large balls of foil between them, and roast for 30 minutes. Turn the ducks to their other sides and roast for 30 minutes longer.
3. Meanwhile, in a large saucepan, heat the oil. Add the hearts, gizzards, wing joints and necks and season with salt and pepper. Cook over moderately high heat, stirring, until richly browned, 10 minutes. Add the carrots, tomatoes, celery, leek, onion, garlic, bay leaves and thyme and cook, stirring, until softened, 5 minutes. Stir in the flour and tomato paste, then gradually stir in the stock and wine. Bring to a boil, stirring, then reduce the heat to moderately low and simmer for 1 hour. Strain the sauce into a bowl, pressing on the solids.
4. Meanwhile, remove the zest in strips from 1 of the oranges. Cut the zest into a very fine julienne. In a small saucepan of boiling water, blanch the julienne for 1 minute. Drain and rinse under cold water; pat dry.
5. Halve and squeeze 2 of the oranges; you will need 1 cup of juice. Peel the remaining oranges (including the one you stripped the zest from) with a knife, removing all of the bitter white pith. Cut in between the membranes to release the sections into a bowl.
6. In a medium saucepan, boil the sugar and vinegar over moderately high heat until the syrup is a pale caramel color, 4 minutes. Gradually add the 1 cup of orange juice, then the currant jelly and bring to a boil. Add the strained duck sauce and simmer over moderate heat to reduce slightly, 8 minutes. Season with salt and pepper. Add the Grand Marnier and remove from the heat. Swirl in the butter, 1 tablespoon at a time.
7. Pour off the fat in the roasting pan. Turn the ducks breast side up and roast for 40 minutes longer. Remove the ducks from the oven and preheat the broiler. Broil the ducks 6 inches from the heat, rotating the pan a few times, until richly browned, about 3 minutes.
8. Insert a wooden spoon into the cavities and tilt the ducks, letting the juices run into the pan. Transfer the ducks to a platter and keep warm. Scrape the pan juices into a fat separator and pour the juices back into the roasting pan. Simmer over moderate heat, scraping up any browned bits and coagulated juices. Strain the contents of the roasting pan into the orange sauce.
9. Garnish the duck platter with the reserved orange sections and scatter the blanched zest over the ducks. Carve the ducks at the table and pass the sauce separately.
—*Jacques Pépin*

MAKE AHEAD The base for the orange duck sauce (Step 3) can be prepared up to 2 days ahead and refrigerated.
WINE Smooth, Grenache-based Côtes-du-Rhône: 2009 Féraud-Brunel.

Duck Breasts and Orzo Salad with Herb-Infused Olive Oil

TOTAL: 45 MIN PLUS 3 WEEKS TO MAKE THE INFUSED OIL • **4 SERVINGS** ●

"Infusing olive oil is a great way to add more herbs to your life," says Jovial King, the Vermont-based herbalist behind Urban Moonshine, a line of bitters and tonics. F&W's Marcia Kiesel rubs King's herb-infused oil on duck breasts and shallots before grilling them and also uses it in a vinaigrette for this hearty main-course salad.

- ¼ cup plus 2 teaspoons Herb-Infused Olive Oil (recipe follows)
- 2 Pekin duck breasts, skin removed
Salt and freshly ground black pepper
- 2 large shallots, sliced crosswise ¼ inch thick
- 2½ tablespoons red wine vinegar
- ¼ teaspoon cayenne pepper
- ¼ pound yellow wax beans
- 1 cup orzo
- 6 small radishes, thinly sliced
- 1 teaspoon chopped thyme

1. Rub 1 teaspoon of the Herb-Infused Olive Oil on the duck breasts; season with salt and black pepper. In a small bowl, gently toss the shallots with 1 more teaspoon of the herb oil; season with salt and black pepper.
2. In another bowl, whisk the remaining ¼ cup of Herb-Infused Olive Oil with the vinegar and cayenne. Season the vinaigrette with salt and black pepper.

● HEALTHY   ● MAKE AHEAD   ● VEGETARIAN   ● STAFF FAVORITE

3. In a large saucepan of boiling salted water, cook the beans until just tender, about 3 minutes. Using a slotted spoon, transfer the beans to a work surface and pat dry. Slice the beans on the diagonal 1 inch thick.
4. Add the orzo to the boiling water and cook until al dente. Drain and transfer the orzo to a large bowl. Let cool slightly, stirring a few times. Add all but 1 teaspoon of the vinaigrette to the orzo and season with salt and pepper. Let cool to room temperature, tossing occasionally.
5. Light a grill. Grill the duck breasts over moderately high heat, turning once, until well browned on the outside and medium-rare within, about 4 minutes per side. Transfer the duck breasts to a carving board and let rest for 5 minutes. Grill the shallots on a perforated grill pan until browned and charred in spots, about 3 minutes per side.
6. Add the beans, shallots and radishes to the orzo and toss. Transfer to plates. Slice the duck crosswise and arrange next to the orzo. Drizzle the duck with the reserved 1 teaspoon of vinaigrette, sprinkle with the chopped thyme and serve. —*Marcia Kiesel*
WINE Medium-bodied, cherry-rich Pinot Noir: 2008 Cambria Julia's Vineyard.

HERB-INFUSED OLIVE OIL

ACTIVE: 10 MIN; TOTAL: 1 HR 10 MIN
PLUS 3 WEEKS STEEPING
MAKES ABOUT 1 CUP ● ● ○

- ½   cup packed parsley leaves
- ½   cup packed basil leaves
- ¼   cup chopped chives
- 2   cups extra-virgin olive oil
- 4   large thyme sprigs
- 2   rosemary sprigs

1. In a food processor, process the parsley, basil, chives and ½ cup of the olive oil to a loose paste. Let stand for 1 hour. Pour the oil through a fine sieve into a tall, narrow jar, stopping when you reach the sediment at the bottom. Add the remaining 1½ cups of olive oil. Submerge the thyme and rosemary sprigs in the oil. Cover and let stand for 3 to 4 weeks in a cool, dark place.

2. Funnel the oil into a glass bottle, discarding the thyme and rosemary sprigs. Store the infused oil in a cool, dark place for up to 2 months. —*Jovial King*

Dry-Aged Duck Breasts with Golden Beet Panzanella

ACTIVE: 45 MIN; TOTAL: 1 HR 30 MIN
PLUS 4 DAYS AGING (OPTIONAL)
4 SERVINGS
Chef Paul Kahan of Blackbird and The Publican in Chicago has a great trick for heightening the flavor of duck breasts: He ages them on the bone in the refrigerator for up to one week. Boneless duck breasts can be aged using the same method, although the results won't be as dramatic; if you're short on time, you can substitute unaged duck.

- 1   whole bone-in Pekin duck breast (see Note) or 2 boneless Pekin duck breast halves
- 1   pound medium golden beets, trimmed
- ¼   cup extra-virgin olive oil, plus more for drizzling
- 4   thick slices of bacon, cut into ½-inch dice
- ½   pound peasant bread, cut into 1-inch cubes (6 cups)
- Salt and freshly ground pepper
- 1   pint yellow cherry tomatoes, halved
- 4   scallions, thinly sliced
- 1   teaspoon dried oregano
- ¼   cup red wine vinegar

1. If aging the duck breast, set it skin side up on a plate and keep in the refrigerator uncovered for at least 4 days and up to 7.
2. Preheat the oven to 400°.
3. Put the beets in a baking dish and drizzle lightly with olive oil; cover with aluminum foil and roast until just tender, about 1 hour. When the beets are cool enough to handle, peel off the skins and slice the beets into ¼-inch-thick rounds.
4. Meanwhile, in a large ovenproof skillet, cook the diced bacon over moderate heat until crisp, about 5 minutes. Using a slotted

spoon, transfer the bacon to paper towels to drain. Add the cubes of bread to the skillet and stir well to coat with the bacon fat. Transfer the skillet to the oven and bake, stirring a few times, until the bread is crisp, about 15 minutes. Season lightly with salt and freshly ground pepper.
5. If using bone-in duck breast, remove the breast halves from the bone. Trim the skin to just cover the meat. Heat a medium-sized skillet until hot. Season the duck breasts with salt and freshly ground pepper and cook skin side down over moderate heat until the skin is richly browned and crisp, about 12 minutes. Turn the duck and cook until medium-rare, about 4 minutes longer. Transfer the duck to a carving board and let rest for about 5 minutes. Slice the duck breasts crosswise ⅛ inch thick.
6. In a large bowl, toss the beets with the bacon, croutons, tomatoes, scallions and oregano. In a small bowl, stir the ¼ cup of olive oil with the vinegar and season with salt and pepper. Pour the dressing over the salad and toss well. Mound the salad on plates, top with the sliced duck and serve. —*Paul Kahan*
NOTE For a whole bone-in duck breast, ask a butcher to remove the legs and cut the back off a whole duck.
MAKE AHEAD The peeled roasted beets can be refrigerated overnight in an airtight container. Bring the beets to room temperature before serving.
BEER Bright, slightly tart Belgian-style ale: Goose Island Golden Jet.

equipment tip

roasting pan Le Creuset's flame-proof enameled cast-iron roasters are super-versatile. Use them for casseroles, vegetables or poultry. *From $125; lecreuset.com.*

Thai-Style Duck and Green Papaya Salad

⏱ **TOTAL: 45 MIN • 4 SERVINGS** ●

- 1 tablespoon raw long-grain rice
- 2 tablespoons dried shrimp, chopped (optional)
- 1 garlic clove, chopped
- 1 Thai chile, chopped
- 1 tablespoon unsalted roasted peanuts
- 1 tablespoon light brown sugar
- 1 tablespoon granulated sugar
- 4 small plum tomatoes, chopped
- 3 tablespoons fresh lime juice
- 2 tablespoons Asian fish sauce
- 1½ pounds green papaya, peeled and cut into long, thin strands on a mandoline (see Note)
- 1 large carrot, cut into long strands on a mandoline
- 2 shallots, thinly sliced
- 3 tablespoons cilantro leaves
- 3 tablespoons mint leaves
- 4 ounces dried rice vermicelli, soaked in water for 20 minutes and drained

Two 6-ounce boneless Pekin duck breasts—fat trimmed, skin scored in a crosshatch pattern

Salt

ingredient tip

fish sauce Popular in Southeast Asia, this pleasantly funky sauce has a rich, salty flavor. It adds a wonderful savoriness to stir-fries, fish and meat marinades, soup stocks and dressings, as in the Thai-Style Duck and Green Papaya Salad, above.

1. In a small skillet, toast the rice over moderate heat, tossing, until lightly browned, about 4 minutes. Transfer the rice to a mortar or spice grinder and let cool completely. Pound or grind to a powder. Set the toasted rice powder aside.

2. In a large mortar (or food processor), pound the chopped dried shrimp until it is coarsely ground. Add the garlic, chile and peanuts and pound coarsely. Add both sugars and pound to a paste. Add the tomatoes and pound to coarsely crush them. Stir in the lime juice and fish sauce.

3. In a large bowl, toss the green papaya, carrot, shallots, cilantro and mint leaves. Add the tomato dressing and toss well.

4. In a saucepan of boiling water, add the drained rice vermicelli. Cook until just al dente, about 30 seconds. Drain and return the vermicelli to the saucepan. Fill the saucepan with cold water and swirl. Drain and repeat 3 times to prevent the noodles from sticking together. Drain the vermicelli in a colander and lift the strands up a few times to release excess water.

5. Heat a medium skillet. Season the duck breasts with salt and add them to the hot skillet, skin side down. Cook over moderately high heat for about 2 minutes. Reduce the heat to moderate and cook until the skin is browned and crisp, about 2 minutes longer. Turn the duck and cook until medium-rare, about 4 minutes longer. Transfer the duck to a carving board to rest for 5 minutes. Thinly slice the duck breasts crosswise.

6. Add the rice noodles to the green papaya salad and toss well. Transfer to a platter. Arrange the duck slices on top, sprinkle with the toasted rice powder and serve.
—*Andrew Zimmern*

NOTE Green (unripe) papayas have dark green skin and are very firm to the touch. They are available at Indian and Southeast Asian markets.

MAKE AHEAD The toasted rice powder, tomato dressing and cooked duck breast can be prepared up to 1 day in advance. Gently rewarm the duck before proceeding.

WINE Brisk, zippy sparkling wine: NV German Gilabert Cava.

Duck Confit Tacos

⏱ **TOTAL: 45 MIN • 4 SERVINGS** ●

"If Mexico hadn't shared its chiles with China, would we have spicy Chinese food?" asks chef José Andrés. His Las Vegas restaurant China Poblano, with dishes like these Asian duck tacos, shows how more and more chefs are combining seemingly unrelated cuisines. Store-bought confit duck legs make these tacos really easy.

- 1 large poblano
- ½ pound plum tomatoes
- ¼ pound tomatillos, husked
- 1 large garlic clove, unpeeled
- 1 fresh red chile, seeded and chopped
- 1 large scallion, chopped
- 2 teaspoons fresh lime juice
- Salt
- 4 confit duck legs
- ½ cup low-sodium chicken broth
- 3 tablespoons soy sauce
- ½ teaspoon Chinese five-spice powder
- 8 corn tortillas, warmed
- Cilantro sprigs, for serving

1. Roast the poblano under the broiler or directly over a gas flame, turning, until it is charred. Let cool. Peel, seed and chop.

2. Preheat a cast-iron skillet. Add the tomatoes, tomatillos and garlic and cook over moderate heat, turning, until charred. Peel the garlic; transfer to a food processor. Add the tomatoes, tomatillos, poblano, red chile and scallion and pulse until chunky. Add the lime juice and season the salsa with salt.

3. Microwave the duck at high power for 1½ minutes, until the skin is warm. Remove the skin from the legs in 1 piece. Line a plate with paper towels and lay the skins on top. Microwave at high power for about 5 minutes, until the skin is browned and sizzling. Remove the skin from the paper towels and let cool completely. Cut the crisp skin into thin strips.

4. Shred the duck meat. In a skillet, simmer the broth, soy sauce and five-spice powder. Add the duck and toss until heated through.

5. Serve the tortillas with the salsa, duck, cracklings and cilantro.
—*José Andrés*

● HEALTHY   ● MAKE AHEAD   ● VEGETARIAN   ● STAFF FAVORITE

duck confit tacos

Medlock Ames Winery in Sonoma, California, hosts an artisans' dinner in their tasting room. The main course: garlic-crusted roast rack of lamb, OPPOSITE; *recipe, page 162.*

beef and lamb

Grilled Steaks with Onion Sauce and Onion Relish

ACTIVE: 40 MIN; TOTAL: 3 HR
6 SERVINGS

Cleveland chef Jonathon Sawyer makes a tangy sauce for grilled meat by simmering red onions and jalapeños with water and vinegar, then pureeing them until silky.

- 2 tablespoons cracked black pepper
- 2 dry bay leaves, crumbled
- 1 tablespoon Asian fish sauce
- ¼ cup extra-virgin olive oil
- Six 12- to 14-ounce rib eye steaks (about ¾ inch thick)
- 4 tablespoons unsalted butter
- 1 pound red onions, thinly sliced
- 2 pickled jalapeños, seeded
- 1 tablespoon dry red wine
- 2 tablespoons red wine vinegar
- Salt and freshly ground pepper
- ½ cup drained cocktail onions, coarsely chopped
- ¼ cup oil-cured Moroccan olives, pitted and chopped
- ¼ cup torn mint leaves

1. In a large, shallow dish, mix the cracked pepper with the bay leaves, fish sauce and 2 tablespoons of the olive oil. Add the steaks to the dish and rub all over with the mixture. Let stand at room temperature for 2 hours or refrigerate for 4 hours.

2. Meanwhile, in a saucepan, melt the butter. Add the onions and jalapeños and cook over moderate heat until the onions are just softened, 5 minutes. Add the wine and 1 tablespoon of the vinegar and season with salt and ground pepper. Add 2 cups of water and bring to a simmer. Cover and cook over low heat until the onions are very tender, 40 minutes.

3. Uncover the onions and cook over moderate heat, stirring frequently, until the liquid is evaporated, about 10 minutes. Transfer the onions to a blender. Add the remaining 1 tablespoon of vinegar and puree until very smooth. Season with salt and ground pepper.

4. In a medium bowl, toss the cocktail onions, olives and mint leaves with the remaining 2 tablespoons of olive oil.

5. Preheat a grill pan or light a grill. Grill the steaks over moderate heat, turning them once or twice, until lightly charred, about 7 minutes for medium-rare meat. Let the steaks rest for 5 minutes, then serve with the onion sauce and pickled onion relish.
—*Jonathon Sawyer*

SERVE WITH French fries.

WINE Rich, blackberry-scented Cabernet Sauvignon: 2009 Wyatt.

Grilled Rib Eyes with Mushrooms and Fish Sauce

TOTAL: 35 MIN • 4 SERVINGS

- 2 tablespoons unsalted butter
- 2 tablespoons extra-virgin olive oil, plus more for brushing
- 2 large shallots, thinly sliced
- 2 pounds mixed mushrooms, such as cremini, oyster and shiitake, stemmed and thinly sliced
- 2 to 3 tablespoons Asian fish sauce
- Pinch of cayenne pepper
- 2 tablespoons chopped tarragon
- 2 tablespoons snipped chives
- Four 10-ounce rib eye steaks (about ¾ inch thick)
- Salt and freshly ground black pepper

1. In a large nonstick skillet, melt the butter in the 2 tablespoons of olive oil. Add the shallots and mixed mushrooms and cook over high heat, stirring occasionally, until the mushrooms are browned and their liquid is evaporated, about 8 minutes. Add the fish sauce and cayenne pepper and cook for 1 minute. Stir in the tarragon and chives, cover and keep warm.

2. Preheat a grill pan. Brush the steaks with olive oil and season them with salt and black pepper. Grill over moderately high heat for 3 to 4 minutes per side for medium-rare meat. Transfer the steaks to plates. Top with the mushrooms and serve.
—*Grace Parisi*

MAKE AHEAD The cooked mushrooms can be refrigerated overnight. Reheat gently.

WINE Inky, black currant–scented Cabernet Sauvignon: 2006 Arrowood.

Grilled Steak with Cucumber and Daikon Salad

TOTAL: 40 MIN • 4 SERVINGS

- 2 tablespoons soy sauce
- 1 tablespoon fresh lemon juice
- 1 tablespoon unseasoned rice vinegar
- 1 garlic clove, minced
- ¼ cup canola oil, plus more for rubbing
- Salt and freshly ground pepper
- ½ seedless cucumber, very thinly sliced
- 8 ounces daikon, peeled and very thinly sliced
- Four 8- to 10-ounce strip steaks (¾ inch thick)
- 1 tablespoon minced lemon zest
- 1 teaspoon minced fresh chile
- 4 ounces baby arugula
- 1 cup radish or daikon sprouts (optional)
- 2 tablespoons toasted sesame seeds

1. In a small bowl, whisk the soy sauce with the lemon juice, vinegar and garlic. Whisk in the ¼ cup of oil until emulsified. Season with salt and pepper. Transfer half of the dressing to a medium bowl, add the cucumber and daikon and toss to coat. Let stand at room temperature for 30 minutes, then drain and squeeze out any excess liquid. Return the cucumber and daikon to the bowl.

2. Light a grill or preheat a grill pan. Rub the steaks with oil and season with salt and pepper. Grill the steaks over moderate heat, turning once, until lightly charred on both sides and medium-rare within, about 7 minutes. Transfer the steaks to a work surface and let rest for 5 minutes.

3. In a small bowl, combine the lemon zest and chile and season with salt and pepper; transfer the steaks to plates and spoon the gremolata on top. Add the arugula, sprouts and the remaining dressing to the cucumber and daikon and toss. Serve the salad with the steaks, garnished with the sesame seeds.
—*David Myers*

WINE Concentrated, full-bodied Portuguese red: 2007 Vale do Bomfim.

● HEALTHY ● MAKE AHEAD ○ VEGETARIAN ● STAFF FAVORITE

grilled rib eye with mushrooms and fish sauce

Rib Eye Steaks with Pete's Barbecue Sauce

⏱ TOTAL: 45 MIN • 4 SERVINGS ●

1   cup red wine vinegar
½   teaspoon dry mustard
¼   teaspoon ground cloves
2   tablespoons vegetable oil,
    plus more for grilling
¼   cup finely chopped onion
2   garlic cloves, minced
1   teaspoon cumin seeds
2   tablespoons light brown sugar
2   plum tomatoes, coarsely chopped
1   cup smoky barbecue sauce
1   teaspoon *sambal oelek*
Salt and freshly ground pepper
Four 1-pound rib eye steaks on the bone,
    cut ¾ inch thick
Rosemary sprigs, for garnish

1. In a medium saucepan, combine the vinegar, dry mustard and cloves and simmer over moderate heat until reduced by half, about 10 minutes. Transfer the vinegar to a heatproof bowl. Wipe out the saucepan.
2. Add the 2 tablespoons of oil to the saucepan along with the onion, garlic and cumin. Cook over moderately low heat until the onion is softened and fragrant, about 5 minutes. Add the brown sugar and tomatoes and cook until softened, about 5 minutes. Add the reduced vinegar and the barbecue sauce and simmer until reduced to 2 cups, about 5 minutes. Transfer the sauce to a blender and puree until smooth. Add the *sambal oelek* and season with salt and pepper.

ingredient tip

sambal oelek This fiery sauce made with fresh red chiles, brown sugar and salt adds heat to marinades like the one for chef Bill Kim's Spicy Thai Steak, at right.

3. Light a grill or preheat a grill pan. Rub the steaks with oil and season generously with salt and pepper. Grill over moderately high heat, turning once, until the steaks are lightly charred and medium-rare, about 6 minutes total. Let the steaks rest for 5 minutes, then garnish with rosemary and serve with the barbecue sauce. —*Pete Evans*
WINE Bold Shiraz: 2009 Jip Jip Rocks.

Spicy Thai Steak

ACTIVE: 20 MIN; TOTAL: 1 HR
8 SERVINGS ●

Any leftover steak is perfect for serving over a salad or in sandwiches. The marinade is also great for shrimp and chicken.

¼   cup basil leaves
¼   cup cilantro leaves
8   peeled garlic cloves
2   tablespoons *sambal oelek* or other
    Asian chile sauce
2   tablespoons Asian fish sauce
1   teaspoon finely grated lemon zest
1   teaspoon finely grated lime zest
½   cup vegetable oil
3   pounds skirt steak, cut into 5-inch
    lengths, or flank steak left whole

1. In a mini food processor, combine the basil, cilantro, garlic, *sambal oelek* and fish sauce and pulse until finely chopped. Add the lemon and lime zests and oil and pulse until fairly smooth.
2. Rub the marinade on the steak and let stand at room temperature for at least 30 minutes or refrigerate for up to 24 hours.
3. Light a grill or preheat a grill pan. Grill the steak over moderately high heat, turning occasionally, until medium-rare, about 6 minutes for skirt steak and 12 minutes for flank. Let the steak rest for 5 minutes, then thinly slice across the grain and serve. —*Bill Kim*
MAKE AHEAD The marinade can be kept in the refrigerator for up to 3 days. The grilled steak can be refrigerated overnight. Thinly slice and serve cold.
WINE Vibrant, cherry-rich Montepulciano d'Abruzzo: 2009 Nicodemi.

Ethiopian Spiced Steak

ACTIVE: 50 MIN; TOTAL: 1 HR 30 MIN
4 TO 6 SERVINGS

One 1½-pound sirloin steak
1½ tablespoons berbere spice
    (see Note)
1   pint red cherry tomatoes, halved
1   pint yellow cherry tomatoes, halved
2   tablespoons extra-virgin olive oil
Salt and freshly ground black pepper
2   tablespoons freshly squeezed
    lemon juice
3   large celery ribs, thinly sliced,
    plus ½ cup celery leaves
2   tablespoons chopped
    flat-leaf parsley
2   tablespoons capers,
    drained and chopped
2   teaspoons red wine vinegar
½   red onion, thinly sliced
4   tablespoons unsalted butter
3   cups vegetable oil
1   large baking potato—peeled, cut
    into 3-by-¼-inch sticks, rinsed and
    dried completely
1   head of Boston or green leaf lettuce,
    separated into leaves

1. Sprinkle the sirloin steak with 1 tablespoon of the berbere spice and let stand at room temperature for 1 hour.
2. Meanwhile, preheat the oven to 350°. On a large rimmed baking sheet, toss the halved red and yellow tomatoes with the olive oil. Season with salt and pepper and bake for about 45 minutes, until the tomatoes are sizzling and just starting to brown.
3. In a medium bowl, mix the lemon juice with the remaining ½ tablespoon of berbere spice. Add the celery ribs and leaves, the parsley, capers, vinegar and onion and toss well. Season with salt and pepper.
4. In a large skillet, melt the butter. Season the steak with salt and pepper and cook over moderately high heat until richly browned, about 5 minutes. Turn the steak and cook over moderate heat until medium-rare, about 6 minutes longer. Transfer the steak to a carving board to rest for 10 minutes.

● HEALTHY   ● MAKE AHEAD   ○ VEGETARIAN   ○ STAFF FAVORITE

5. Meanwhile, in a medium saucepan, heat the vegetable oil to 375°, then add half of the potato sticks and fry, stirring occasionally, until browned and crisp, about 5 minutes. Drain on paper towels and repeat with the remaining potatoes.

6. Thinly slice the steak across the grain. Arrange the lettuce leaves on a platter. Add the tomatoes and their juices to the bowl with the celery and toss. Spoon the tomato salad onto the lettuce leaves. Top with the sliced steak and crisp potatoes and serve. —*Andrew Zimmern*

NOTE Berbere is an Ethiopian spice mix that includes chiles, allspice, ginger and *ajwain,* a thyme-like spice. Look for it at specialty food markets and *kalustyans.com.*

MAKE AHEAD The roasted-tomato salad can be made up to 3 hours ahead.

WINE Juicy, blackberry-rich Malbec from Argentina: 2007 Melipal.

Roast Beef with Root Vegetable and Green Peppercorn Salad

ACTIVE: 30 MIN; TOTAL: 1 HR 30 MIN
6 SERVINGS ● ●

F&W's Kristin Donnelly loves brined green peppercorns in this garlicky dressing for sweet roasted fall vegetables and roast beef.

- 1 pound sweet potatoes, scrubbed and cut into 1-inch pieces
- 1 pound parsnips, peeled and cut into ¾-inch pieces
- 1 pound celery root, peeled and cut into ¾-inch pieces
- 1 pound golden beets, peeled and cut into ¾-inch pieces
- 4 large unpeeled garlic cloves
- ¼ cup extra-virgin olive oil
- Salt
- One 1½-pound eye of round beef roast, trimmed of visible fat
- Freshly ground black pepper
- 2 tablespoons balsamic vinegar
- 1½ teaspoons brined green peppercorns, chopped, plus 1 tablespoon of brine
- 1 teaspoon honey
- 4 cups baby arugula (about 3 ounces)

1. Preheat the oven to 425° and line a large, rimmed baking sheet with parchment paper. In a large bowl, toss the sweet potatoes, parsnips, celery root, golden beets and unpeeled garlic cloves with 3 tablespoons of the olive oil and season with salt. Spread the vegetables on the baking sheet and roast on the bottom rack of the oven for about 1 hour, stirring occasionally, until browned and very tender. Let cool slightly.

2. Meanwhile, in a medium ovenproof skillet, heat the remaining 1 tablespoon of olive oil until shimmering. Season the beef roast with salt. Add it to the skillet and cook over moderately high heat, turning, until browned all over, about 5 minutes. Transfer the roast to a plate and pour off the fat in the skillet, then add 2 tablespoons of water to the skillet and cook, scraping up the browned bits on the bottom of the pan. Pour the pan juices into the large bowl.

3. Return the eye of round beef roast to the skillet and roast in the oven for about 25 minutes, until an instant-read thermometer inserted in the thickest part registers 115° for medium-rare meat. Transfer the roast to a board, then season the meat with freshly ground black pepper.

4. Squeeze the roasted garlic cloves from their skins into the meat juices in the large bowl and mash with a fork. Whisk in the balsamic vinegar, green peppercorns, brine and honey. Add the roasted vegetables to the bowl and toss with the dressing, then add the arugula and toss again.

5. Carve the roast into thin slices and serve warm or at room temperature with the salad. —*Kristin Donnelly*

WINE Peppery Loire Valley Cabernet Franc: 2009 Bernard Baudry Chinon Les Granges.

Rare Roast Beef with Fresh Herbs and Basil Oil

ACTIVE: 20 MIN; TOTAL: 1 HR
6 SERVINGS ●

Adapted from a recipe in author and culinary legend Patricia Wells's cookbook *Salad as a Meal,* this rosy roast beef topped with herbs and basil oil seems decadent, but contains only two grams of saturated fat per serving.

One 1½-pound beef eye of round roast
- ½ cup mixed finely chopped rosemary, mint and tarragon
- Salt and freshly ground black pepper
- ½ cup plus 1 tablespoon extra-virgin olive oil
- 2 cups fresh basil leaves

1. Preheat the oven to 475°. Generously coat the roast with half of the chopped herb mixture and season with salt and pepper.

2. In an ovenproof skillet, heat 1 tablespoon oil over moderately high heat. Add the roast; lightly brown it on all sides, 3 minutes. Wipe out the skillet, return the meat to it and roast in the oven until an instant-read thermometer inserted in the center registers 110°, 25 minutes. Transfer the roast to a cutting board and season again with salt and pepper. Cover loosely with foil; let rest for 20 minutes.

3. Meanwhile, bring a large saucepan of salted water to a boil and fill a bowl with ice water. Blanch the basil in the saucepan for 15 seconds. Transfer the basil to the ice water; drain well and squeeze out all of the excess water. Transfer the basil to a blender. Add the remaining ½ cup extra-virgin olive oil and a pinch of salt and blend thoroughly.

4. Thinly slice the roast beef and drizzle each portion with ½ tablespoon of the basil oil. Sprinkle with the remaining ¼ cup of chopped herbs and serve. —*Patricia Wells*
WINE Cassis-scented, spicy California Cabernet: 2008 Obsidian Ridge.

ingredient tip

grainy mustard Whisked into oil and vinegar, it makes a terrific salad dressing; mixed with stock and cream, it becomes a luscious sauce for roasts and other meats.

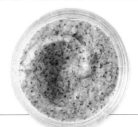

Stuffed Flatiron Steak

ACTIVE: 40 MIN; TOTAL: 1 HR 40 MIN
4 TO 6 SERVINGS

The flatiron steak (also known as the top blade steak) is a marbled cut of beef from the shoulder. Uniform in thickness and rectangular in shape (just like an old-fashioned iron), it's extremely lean yet remains tender and flavorful after braising—unlike other cuts, which can get stringy.

- Five ⅓-inch-thick slices of white Pullman bread
- 1 tablespoon plus 1 teaspoon extra-virgin olive oil, plus more for brushing
- 10 pitted prunes
- 1¼ cups dry red wine
- One 5-ounce piece of pancetta, cut into ¼-inch dice
- 4 large garlic cloves, very finely chopped
- 4 ounces vacuum-packed cooked chestnuts, coarsely crumbled
- 1 tablespoon chopped rosemary, plus 2 large rosemary sprigs
- 1 tablespoon freshly grated pecorino cheese
- ¼ teaspoon cayenne pepper
- Salt and freshly ground black pepper
- 2 large eggs, lightly beaten
- Two 1¼-pound flatiron steaks, each pounded to a ⅓-inch thickness
- 2½ cups beef broth
- 2 large shallots, coarsely chopped
- 2 tablespoons all-purpose flour

1. Preheat the oven to 400°. Put the bread on a large baking sheet and brush all over with olive oil. Bake for about 20 minutes, until very crisp and golden brown. Let cool. Break up the toasts and transfer to a food processor. Process to coarse crumbs.

2. In a large glass measuring cup, cover the prunes with ½ cup of the wine. Microwave at high power for 1 minute, or until the prunes are soft. Cut the prunes into ½-inch pieces and transfer them to a large bowl along with the soaking wine.

3. In a large, deep ovenproof skillet, heat 1 teaspoon of the olive oil. Add one-third of the pancetta and cook over moderate heat until crisp, about 7 minutes. With a slotted spoon, add the pancetta to the prunes. Add the garlic to the skillet and cook over low heat for 1 minute. Scrape the garlic into the bowl. Add the bread crumbs, crumbled chestnuts, chopped rosemary, pecorino and cayenne and season with salt and black pepper. Stir the eggs into the stuffing.

4. Put the steaks on a work surface and season both sides with salt and black pepper. Press half of the stuffing over each steak. Roll up the steaks lengthwise and tie them at 2-inch intervals with kitchen string.

5. Turn the oven temperature down to 350°. Heat the remaining 1 tablespoon of olive oil in the ovenproof skillet until shimmering. Add the steaks and cook over moderately high heat until browned all over, about 8 minutes. Turn the steaks seam side down. Add the remaining ¾ cup of wine and pancetta to the skillet along with the beef broth, rosemary sprigs and shallots; bring to a boil. Transfer the skillet to the oven and braise the steaks for about 25 minutes, turning them once, until a thermometer inserted in the steaks registers 130° for medium-rare to medium meat.

6. Transfer the steaks to a carving board to rest for about 5 minutes. Whisk the flour into the pan juices and simmer over moderately high heat, whisking a few times, until the gravy is thickened and slightly reduced, about 3 minutes. Strain the gravy into a small saucepan, pressing on the solids. Season with salt and freshly ground black pepper and keep the gravy warm.

7. Untie the steaks and slice them crosswise ¼ inch thick. Serve with the gravy.
—Marcia Kiesel

WINE Concentrated, lively Zinfandel: 2009 Sobon Fiddletown.

Flank Steak with Herbed Salsa

⏱ **TOTAL: 30 MIN • 4 SERVINGS** ●

TV chef Jamie Oliver likes to chop all the salsa ingredients together on a large cutting board so that the tomatoes, scallions, garlic, jalapeño and herbs get well combined. He even seasons the salsa and adds a splash of olive oil on the board.

- 2 medium tomatoes, finely chopped
- 4 scallions, finely chopped
- 1 cup cilantro leaves, finely chopped
- ½ cup mint leaves, finely chopped
- 1 large jalapeño, seeded and minced
- 1 garlic clove, minced
- Juice of 1 lemon
- Salt and freshly ground pepper
- One 1-pound flank steak
- 2 teaspoons extra-virgin olive oil

1. Light a grill or preheat a grill pan. In a medium bowl, combine the tomatoes with the scallions, cilantro, mint, jalapeño, garlic and lemon juice. Season the salsa with salt and freshly ground pepper.

2. Rub the flank steak with the olive oil and season with salt and pepper. Grill over high heat until nicely charred outside and medium-rare within, 3 minutes per side. Transfer the steak to a carving board; let rest for 5 minutes. Thinly slice the steak across the grain and serve with the herbed salsa.
—Jamie Oliver

WINE Herb-scented Cabernet Sauvignon: 2009 Lapostolle Cuvée Alexandre.

equipment tip

chopping mats Super-durable flexible silicone mats protect work surfaces from knife marks. They can be used to chop all the salsa ingredients for Jamie Oliver's flank steak, far right. *$6 for 4; bedbathandbeyond.com.*

● HEALTHY ● MAKE AHEAD ● VEGETARIAN ● STAFF FAVORITE

stuffed flatiron steak

Short Ribs with Mushrooms and Spring Vegetables

ACTIVE: 1 HR 30 MIN;
TOTAL: 4 HR 15 MIN PLUS OVERNIGHT
MARINATING • 4 SERVINGS ●

RIBS

One 750-milliliter bottle dry red wine
 1 medium leek, white and pale green
    parts only, coarsely chopped
 1 small onion, coarsely chopped
 2 carrots, coarsely chopped
 3 garlic cloves, smashed
10 parsley sprigs
 2 thyme sprigs
 2 bay leaves
Eight ½-pound beef short ribs on the
    bone, excess fat trimmed
 2 tablespoons vegetable oil
Salt and freshly ground black pepper
All-purpose flour, for dusting
 2 cups chicken stock or
    low-sodium broth
 2 cups beef stock or low-sodium broth
SAUCE AND VEGETABLES
 2 tablespoons vegetable oil
 ½ pound shiitake mushrooms,
    stems discarded and caps sliced
    ¼ inch thick
Salt and freshly ground black pepper
 2 large shallots, thinly sliced
 2 teaspoons thyme leaves
 1 garlic clove, minced
 ½ cup dry red wine
 2 tablespoons chopped flat-leaf
    parsley, plus more for garnish
20 red pearl onions
 4 medium turnips, cut into wedges
 2 medium carrots,
    cut into 2-inch sticks
12 fingerling potatoes, scrubbed

1. PREPARE THE RIBS In a large bowl, combine the red wine with the leek, onion, carrots, garlic, parsley sprigs, thyme sprigs and bay leaves. Put the beef short ribs in 2 large resealable plastic bags and then pour half of the marinade into each bag. Seal the bags, transfer them to a sturdy baking sheet and refrigerate overnight.

2. Preheat the oven to 300°. Remove the short ribs from the marinade and pat dry with paper towels. Using a slotted spoon, remove the vegetables from the marinade.
3. In a large skillet, heat the vegetable oil. Season the short ribs with salt and pepper and dust with flour, shaking off the excess. Add half of the ribs to the skillet and cook over moderately high heat until browned and crusty, about 3 minutes per side. Transfer the ribs to a large roasting pan. Repeat with the remaining ribs, lowering the heat if the ribs get too dark.
4. Add the vegetables to the skillet and cook over moderately high heat until they start to brown, about 4 minutes; transfer to the roasting pan. Add the marinade to the skillet and bring to a boil, skimming the surface. Add the chicken and beef stock and bring to a boil, scraping up any browned bits from the bottom of the skillet. Pour the liquid over the ribs. Cover the pan with aluminum foil and braise the ribs in the oven for about 3 hours, until the meat is very tender.
5. Remove the ribs from the roasting pan. Strain the braising liquid and skim off the fat. Discard the vegetables.
6. PREPARE THE SAUCE AND VEGETABLES In a medium saucepan, heat the vegetable oil. Add the shiitake mushrooms and season them with salt and freshly ground black pepper. Cover and cook over moderate heat, stirring a few times, until the mushrooms are browned, about 5 minutes. Add the shallots and thyme and cook until the shallots are softened, about 4 minutes. Add the garlic and cook until fragrant, about 1 minute. Add the red wine and boil over high heat until reduced to 3 tablespoons, about 2 minutes. Add the skimmed braising liquid and boil over moderately high heat for 5 minutes; season the sauce with salt and pepper. Stir in the 2 tablespoons of chopped parsley.
7. Preheat the oven to 350°. In a large saucepan of boiling salted water, cook the vegetables separately until tender: about 3 minutes for the pearl onions; 4 minutes for the turnips; 5 minutes for the carrots and 12 minutes for the potatoes. Trim and peel the onions. Slice the potatoes lengthwise.

8. Remove the bones from the rib meat and return the meat to the roasting pan. Add the cooked vegetables and pour the sauce on top. Cover with foil and bake for about 15 minutes, until heated through. Serve the stew in shallow bowls, garnished with parsley.
—*Rory Herrmann*
MAKE AHEAD The braised short ribs can be refrigerated in the braising liquid with the mushrooms for up to 3 days. The blanched spring vegetables can be refrigerated separately from the short ribs overnight.
WINE Robust, floral Italian red: 2008 Avignonesi Vino Nobile di Montepulciano.

Robb Walsh's Texas Barbecue Brisket

ACTIVE: 1 HR; TOTAL: 10 HR PLUS
OVERNIGHT MARINATING
10 SERVINGS ●

One 9-pound whole beef brisket
Sea salt and freshly ground black pepper
 4 tablespoons unsalted butter
 3 large garlic cloves, smashed
 1 teaspoon ground coriander
 1 cup barbecue sauce
 1 cup low-sodium beef broth

1. Generously season the brisket all over with salt and pepper. Place the brisket on a large rimmed baking sheet, cover with plastic wrap and refrigerate overnight.
2. Light a charcoal fire in a starter chimney. Add the lit coals to the firebox of a smoker and heat the smoker to 275°. Place oak or other hardwood chips, chunks or logs around the coals so that the wood smolders but does not flare. Set the brisket on the grill, fat side down. Cover and smoke for 2 hours. Monitor the smoker throughout the smoking process and add more lit coals and/or wood as needed to maintain the temperature and smoke level.
3. Meanwhile, in a small saucepan, combine the butter with the garlic and coriander and cook over moderate heat for about 2 minutes, until fragrant. Add the barbecue sauce and beef broth and simmer the mop for 5 minutes. Season with salt and pepper.

● HEALTHY ● MAKE AHEAD ● VEGETARIAN ● STAFF FAVORITE

4. After 2 hours, brush the brisket all over with the mop. Turn the brisket fat side up. Continue to cook, mopping every 30 minutes, until an instant-read thermometer inserted in the thickest part registers 165°, about 6½ hours longer.

5. Transfer the brisket to a large sheet of heavy-duty foil. Brush the remaining mop and garlic all over the brisket and wrap it in the foil. Put the wrapped brisket in a large, disposable aluminum roasting pan. Set the pan in the smoker and cook the brisket until it reaches 185°, about 1 hour longer.

6. Slice the brisket thinly across the grain and serve it with its cooking juices.
—*Robb Walsh*

SERVE WITH Sliced white bread, chili beans, coleslaw and pickles.

WINE Smoky, full-bodied Washington Syrah: 2007 Snoqualmie.

Meat Loaf with Creamy Onion Gravy

ACTIVE: 45 MIN; TOTAL: 2 HR
12 SERVINGS ●

- 1 tablespoon canola oil
- 1 large onion, finely chopped
- 2 large carrots, finely chopped
- 1 celery rib, finely chopped
- 2 garlic cloves, minced
- 1½ cups *panko* bread crumbs
- 4 large eggs
- 2 tablespoons Dijon mustard
- 2 tablespoons ketchup
- 2 tablespoons Worcestershire sauce
- 1 teaspoon Tabasco
Kosher salt and freshly ground black pepper
- 3 pounds ground beef chuck
- 1 pound ground pork
- ½ pound Monterey Jack cheese, cut into ½-inch cubes
Creamy Onion Gravy (recipe follows), for serving

1. Preheat the oven to 400°. In a medium skillet, heat the oil. Add the onion, carrots, celery and garlic and cook over moderate heat, stirring occasionally, until softened,

about 8 minutes. Scrape the mixture into a very large bowl and let cool. Add the *panko*, eggs, mustard, ketchup, Worcestershire sauce, Tabasco, 1½ tablespoons of salt and 1 teaspoon of pepper and stir to form a paste. Using your hands, work in the ground meats and cheese until combined.

2. Line a large roasting pan with parchment paper. Firmly pat the meat mixture into 2 loaves, about 10 inches long. Arrange the loaves 3 inches apart on the parchment and roast in the lower third of the oven for about 1 hour, until lightly browned and an instant-read thermometer inserted in the center of the loaves registers 150°. Let the meat loaves rest for 15 minutes, then cut into thick slices and serve with the Creamy Onion Gravy.
—*Andrew Curren*

WINE Balanced, medium-bodied Rhône-style red blend: 2009 Unti Petit Frere.

CREAMY ONION GRAVY
⏱ TOTAL: 45 MIN • MAKES 5 CUPS ●

- 2 tablespoons unsalted butter
- 2 tablespoons extra-virgin olive oil
- 2 large white onions, thinly sliced (about 6 cups)
- ¼ cup all-purpose flour
- 1 quart chicken stock or low-sodium broth
- 1 cup heavy cream
Salt and freshly ground black pepper

1. In a large saucepan, melt the butter in the olive oil. Add the sliced white onions and stir to coat. Cover and cook over moderate heat until the onions are very soft but not browned, 10 to 12 minutes. Stir in the flour and cook for about 2 minutes. Add the chicken stock and cook, whisking frequently, until the gravy is thickened, 7 to 8 minutes. Stir in the heavy cream and simmer the onion gravy over moderate heat for about 5 minutes.

2. Transfer the onion gravy to a blender and puree until smooth. Season with salt and black pepper. Return the onion gravy to the saucepan and simmer until it is reduced to 5 cups, about 5 minutes. —*AC*

Kale and Scallion Negimaki

ACTIVE: 35 MIN; TOTAL: 1 HR 30 MIN
4 SERVINGS

For her revamp of Japanese *negimaki* (grilled beef and scallion rolls), F&W's Marcia Kiesel adds blanched kale. She also stirs miso into the traditional teriyaki marinade and glaze.

- ¼ cup tamari
- ¼ cup mirin
- 1½ tablespoons red miso
- 1 tablespoon sugar
- ½ teaspoon toasted sesame oil
Eight ¼-inch-thick slices of tenderloin steak (1½ pounds), pounded ⅛ inch thick
- ½ pound kale, stems discarded
- 8 scallions, quartered lengthwise
Vegetable oil, for brushing
Toasted sesame seeds, for garnish

1. In a small bowl, whisk together the tamari, mirin, red miso, sugar and sesame oil. Spread 1 teaspoon of the mixture on each side of the beef slices. Refrigerate for 1 hour. Reserve the remaining marinade.

2. In a saucepan of boiling salted water, cook the kale until bright green, 2 minutes. Drain and lightly squeeze out the excess water.

3. On a work surface, lay out a slice of beef with a long side facing you. Place 1 scallion slice across the lower edge. Top with one-eighth of the kale; some of the kale should extend beyond the short sides of the meat. Roll the meat up over the filling very tightly. Secure the roll with 2 toothpicks. Repeat with the remaining meat, scallions and kale.

4. Light a grill or preheat a grill pan. Brush the rolls with oil. Oil the grill grate. Grill the rolls over high heat until charred, 2 minutes. Brush the rolls with some marinade and grill for a few seconds more, until glazed.

5. Transfer the rolls to a work surface. Discard the toothpicks. Cut the *negimaki* into 1-inch lengths. Transfer to a platter, cut side up, and drizzle with the remaining marinade. Sprinkle with sesame seeds and serve.
—*Marcia Kiesel*

WINE Earthy, minerally Pinot Noir: 2009 Thierry Puzelat Touraine.

mastering griddle burgers

For superjuicy burgers with a delicious sear, pros know a griddle beats a grill. Here, L.A.'s Umami Burger founder **Adam Fleischman** shares his recipes and tips for perfect patties.

Umami Burgers with Port and Stilton

⏱ **TOTAL: 40 MIN** • **MAKES 4 BURGERS** ●

Resist the urge to pile on any of the usual toppings—lettuce, tomato, ketchup. "The port is your condiment," explains Fleischman.

- 1 cup ruby port
- 2 pounds mixed ground beef brisket, skirt steak and sirloin steak (20 percent fat)
- Salt and freshly ground pepper
- ½ cup Stilton cheese (3 ounces), softened
- Umami dust, for sprinkling (optional, recipe below)
- 4 brioche hamburger buns, buttered and toasted

1. In a small saucepan, cook the port over moderate heat until reduced to 2 tablespoons, about 15 minutes.

2. Heat a cast-iron griddle until very hot. Form the meat into four 4-by-1-inch patties without packing too tightly. Season generously with salt and pepper. Add the patties to the griddle and cover with a roasting pan; cook over moderately high heat until very crusty, 4 minutes. Flip the patties and cook, covered, 2 minutes longer. Top with the Stilton; cook uncovered 1 minute. Transfer to a plate; sprinkle with umami dust. Let rest for 2 minutes, then set on the buns. Drizzle with the reduced port, top with the buns and serve. **BEER** Malty brown ale: Brooklyn Brewery.

secret seasoning

To make simplified umami dust, use a spice grinder to pulse 3 tablespoons bonito flakes and ½ ounce each of crumbled dried kombu and dried shiitake mushrooms into a powder. Also available soon at umamiburger.com.

Cheddar-and-Onion Smashed Burgers

⏱ **TOTAL: 30 MIN** • **MAKES 4 BURGERS** ●

Inspired by the sliders at White Manna in Hackensack, New Jersey, Fleischman flattens balls of meat on the griddle to make patties.

- 16 thin bread-and-butter pickle slices, patted dry
- Four 4-inch potato buns, buttered and toasted
- 1¼ pounds ground beef chuck (30 percent fat)
- Salt and freshly ground pepper
- 2 small onions, sliced paper-thin
- 4 ounces sharp cheddar cheese, sliced
- Umami dust, for sprinkling (optional, recipe below)

1. Heat a cast-iron griddle until very hot. Layer the bread-and-butter pickle slices on the bottom buns.

2. Without overworking the meat, loosely form it into 4 balls and place them on the griddle. Cook the meatballs over moderately high heat for 30 seconds. Using a large sturdy spatula, flatten each ball into a 5-inch round patty. Season the patties with salt and pepper and cook for 2 minutes, until well seared. Press a handful of sliced onions onto each patty. Using the spatula, carefully flip each burger so the onions are on the bottom. Top with the cheese and cook for 2 minutes. Cover with a roasting pan and cook just until the cheese is melted, 1 minute more. Transfer the burgers with the onions to the buns and sprinkle with umami dust. Top with the buns and serve. **WINE** Juicy, peppery California Zinfandel: 2008 Edmeades Mendocino County.

making the smashed burgers

smash loosely formed balls of meat into flat patties on the griddle.

add sliced onions on top of each patty, then carefully flip the burgers.

top with cheddar and brown the onions as the cheese melts.

umami burger with port and stilton

Bacon Hamburgers with Catalina Dressing

⏱ TOTAL: 45 MIN • 4 SERVINGS

In Saint-Pascal, a village near Kamouraska, Quebec, the burger topping of choice is Kraft Catalina dressing. Here, Montreal's Joe Beef chefs Frédéric Morin and David McMillan create a tangy homemade version.

1 large beefsteak tomato, halved crosswise and seeded
¼ cup vegetable oil, plus more for rubbing
¼ cup red wine vinegar
1 tablespoon sweet smoked paprika
1 tablespoon tomato paste
1 small garlic clove, chopped
1 teaspoon sugar
Salt and freshly ground black pepper
Hot sauce
½ pound sliced bacon, coarsely chopped and frozen for 15 minutes
1 pound ground beef chuck
Butter, for spreading
4 sesame-topped hamburger buns, split and toasted
4 thick slices of sweet onion

1. Preheat the oven to 425°. Put the tomato in a small baking dish and rub with oil. Turn the halves cut side down and bake for 20 minutes, until they start to soften. Let cool, then peel and chop the tomato. Transfer to a blender; add the vinegar, paprika, tomato paste, garlic, sugar and the ¼ cup of oil and blend. Season with salt, pepper and hot sauce.
2. In a food processor, pulse the bacon until very finely chopped. In a large bowl, using your hands, blend the ground chuck with the bacon. Form the mixture into 4 patties.
3. Heat a large skillet. Season the burgers with salt and pepper; cook over moderate heat until well browned on the outside and barely pink in the center, 4 minutes per side. Butter the buns; place an onion slice on the bottom halves. Top with the burgers and some dressing, close the burgers and serve.
—David McMillan and Frédéric Morin

WINE Red Burgundy: 2008 Domaine Dublère Volnay Les Pitures 1er Cru.

Beef Tenderloin with Tomatoes, Shallots and Maytag Blue

ACTIVE: 30 MIN; TOTAL: 1 HR 30 MIN
4 SERVINGS ●

2 pints cherry tomatoes, halved
1½ pounds medium shallots, peeled
1 cup dry red wine
3½ tablespoons extra-virgin olive oil
4 thyme sprigs
Salt and freshly ground black pepper
One 2-pound center-cut beef tenderloin
2 tablespoons vegetable oil
4 ounces Maytag blue cheese, crumbled into ½-inch chunks (1 cup)

1. Preheat the oven to 350°. Spread the tomatoes and shallots on separate rimmed baking sheets. Add ½ cup of the wine, 2 tablespoons of the oil and 2 thyme sprigs to the tomatoes. Add the remaining 1½ tablespoons of olive oil and 2 thyme sprigs to the shallots. Season the tomatoes and shallots with salt and pepper, toss well and spread in even layers. Bake for about 40 minutes, until the tomatoes and shallots are very tender. Discard the thyme.
2. Increase the oven temperature to 425°. Season the tenderloin with salt and pepper. In a large ovenproof skillet, heat the vegetable oil until shimmering. Add the tenderloin and cook over high heat until browned, about 4 minutes, then turn and cook for about 3 minutes longer. Transfer the skillet to the oven and roast the tenderloin for about 10 minutes. Turn and roast for 10 minutes longer, until an instant-read thermometer inserted in the thickest part of the meat registers 125° for medium-rare. Transfer to a carving board and let rest for 10 minutes.
3. Pour off the fat in the skillet. Add the remaining ½ cup of red wine and boil until reduced by half, scraping up the browned bits, 3 minutes. Remove the skillet from the heat and stir in the baked tomatoes, shallots and their juices.
4. Slice the beef ⅓ inch thick and transfer to plates; spoon the tomatoes, shallots and sauce on top. Dot with the cheese and serve.
—Marcia Kiesel

WINE Argentinean red: 2008 Tercos Bonarda.

Peruvian Steak and Potato Stir-Fry

⏱ TOTAL: 35 MIN • 4 SERVINGS

F&W's Grace Parisi came up with this fast take on one of Midtown Lunch blogger Zach Brooks's favorite dishes: the Peruvian meat-and-fries combo called *lomo saltado*. "Anytime you put french fries into the dish, I'm in," Brooks says. "What's better than that? Nothing, that's what."

¼ cup extra-virgin olive oil
1 teaspoon ground cumin
1 teaspoon ground coriander
1 garlic clove, minced
Salt and freshly ground black pepper
1 pound skirt steak
1 red onion, halved and slivered
Vegetable oil, for frying
8 ounces frozen french fries
¼ cup sliced pickled jalapeños
1 large tomato, chopped
¼ cup cilantro
Hot sauce, for serving

1. In a large bowl, combine the olive oil with the cumin, coriander, garlic and a generous pinch each of salt and black pepper. Cut the steak into 4-inch pieces; slice the steaks across the grain ½ inch thick and add to the bowl along with the red onion. Let marinate for about 10 minutes.
2. Meanwhile, in a large skillet, heat ½ inch of vegetable oil until shimmering. Add the frozen french fries and fry over high heat until golden and crisp, about 3 minutes; drain the fries on paper towels.
3. Heat a large griddle until very hot. Add the steak and onion along with the pickled jalapeños and stir-fry over high heat until the meat and onion are cooked through and lightly charred, 3 to 4 minutes. Add the tomato and cook until softened and beginning to char, about 1 minute. Add the french fries and cilantro and flip with a spatula to combine. Serve right away, with hot sauce.
—Grace Parisi

WINE Peppery, full-bodied Zinfandel from Sonoma: 2009 Cline.

● HEALTHY ● MAKE AHEAD ● VEGETARIAN ● STAFF FAVORITE

Beef Tenderloin with Cilantro-Wine Sauce and Mashed Yucca

ACTIVE: 40 MIN; TOTAL: 1 HR 30 MIN
4 SERVINGS ●

"We have a stew in Peru called *seco*, made with beef or lamb, yellow chiles and lots of cilantro," says Lima-based chef Pedro Miguel Schiaffino. The dish inspired him to make a wine sauce with cilantro, which he serves with beef tenderloin.

SAUCE
- 2 tablespoons extra-virgin olive oil
- 1 medium red onion, coarsely chopped
- 2 garlic cloves, chopped
- 1 long fresh red chile, seeded and chopped
- 2 medium tomatoes, coarsely chopped
- 2 whole cloves
- 2 bay leaves
- 1 teaspoon dried oregano
- 1 teaspoon ground cumin
- ¼ cup dry red wine
- 2 tablespoons red wine vinegar
- 1 cup chopped cilantro
- 2 cups low-sodium beef broth
- 4 tablespoons cold unsalted butter, cut into tablespoons

Salt and freshly ground pepper

YUCCA AND MEAT
- 1 pound yucca, peeled and cut into 1-inch cubes
- ½ cup warm milk
- 3 tablespoons unsalted butter

Salt and freshly ground pepper
- 1 tablespoon vegetable oil

Four 8-ounce beef tenderloins

1. PREPARE THE SAUCE In a large saucepan, heat the oil. Add the onion, garlic and chile and cook over moderate heat until softened, 5 minutes. Add the tomatoes and cook over moderately high heat, stirring a few times, until starting to brown, 4 minutes. Add the cloves, bay leaves, oregano and cumin and stir for 1 minute. Add the wine and vinegar and stir to release any browned bits on the bottom of the saucepan. Stir in the cilantro and beef broth. Simmer over low heat until the liquid is reduced to 2 cups, 20 minutes. Strain the sauce into a small saucepan and whisk in the butter, 1 tablespoon at a time. Season with salt and pepper.

2. PREPARE THE YUCCA AND MEAT In a medium saucepan, cover the yucca with water and boil over moderately high heat until tender, 25 minutes. Drain well. Return the yucca to the saucepan and shake over moderate heat for 10 seconds to dry it out. Remove from the heat and mash the yucca with a potato masher. Mash in the milk and then the butter. Season with salt and pepper; keep warm.

3. In a large skillet, heat the vegetable oil. Season the tenderloins with salt and pepper and cook over moderately high heat until richly browned on the bottom, about 3 minutes. Reduce the heat to moderate and cook for 4 minutes longer. Turn the tenderloins and cook until medium-rare, about 5 minutes.

4. Spoon the yucca onto plates and top with the tenderloins. Spoon the sauce over the meat and serve. —*Pedro Miguel Schiaffino*
WINE Fresh, herbal Tempranillo from Spain's Rioja: 2007 Pinturas Crianza.

Rosemary-Pepper Beef Rib Roast with Porcini Jus

ACTIVE: 30 MIN; TOTAL: 4 HR
PLUS OVERNIGHT MARINATING
12 TO 14 SERVINGS ●

"When entertaining at home, I'm always hard-pressed for stove space," says chef Floyd Cardoz of New York City's North End Grill. To save room, he sears the meat in a preheated pan in the oven, which also helps the meat cook more quickly.

- ¼ cup coarsely chopped fresh rosemary
- 3 tablespoons fresh coarsely ground black pepper, plus more for seasoning
- 3 tablespoons vegetable oil

One 6-rib standing beef rib roast (14 to 15 pounds), ½-inch fat cap left on the meat

Salt
- 3 tablespoons unsalted butter
- 1 medium shallot, very finely chopped
- 2 large garlic cloves, thinly sliced
- ¼ cup dry red wine
- 1 quart beef stock or broth
- ¼ cup sherry vinegar
- 4 thyme sprigs
- 1 ounce dried porcini (1 cup), ground to a powder in a spice grinder or blender

1. In a small bowl, combine the rosemary with the 3 tablespoons of black pepper and the vegetable oil and rub all over the roast. Cover and refrigerate overnight.

2. Put a large roasting pan in the middle of the oven and preheat to 375°. Let the rib roast stand at room temperature for 30 minutes.

3. Season the rib roast with salt and put it in the hot roasting pan, fat side down. Roast for 30 minutes. Turn the rib roast over and cook at 350° for about 3 hours, rotating the pan 2 or 3 times. The rib roast is done when an instant-read thermometer inserted in the thickest part of the meat registers 130° for medium-rare. Transfer the rib roast to a carving board to rest for at least 20 minutes.

4. Meanwhile, in a saucepan, melt the butter. Add the shallot and garlic and cook over moderate heat until lightly browned, 5 minutes. Add the wine and boil for 2 minutes. Add the stock, vinegar and thyme and bring to a boil. Simmer over moderate heat until reduced to 2½ cups, about 20 minutes. Strain the sauce and return it to the saucepan. Whisk in the porcini powder and simmer for 1 minute. Cover, remove from the heat and let stand for about 5 minutes. Season with salt and pepper. Carve the roast and serve with the porcini jus. —*Floyd Cardoz*
WINE Approachable, peppery California Cabernet Sauvignon: 2009 Mandolin.

ingredient tip

cilantro This zesty herb with a lively, pungent flavor is great for garnishing dishes like Grace Parisi's Peruvian Steak and Potato Stir-Fry, opposite.

Beef Brasato with Pappardelle and Mint

ACTIVE: 45 MIN; TOTAL: 4 HR PLUS
OVERNIGHT MARINATING

8 SERVINGS ● ●

At Incanto restaurant in San Francisco, chef Chris Cosentino braises beef shank and oxtail in red wine to make a brasato that he serves with house-made mint pappardelle. For this easy home version, the dish uses just beef shank, and fresh pappardelle from the store replaces house-made pasta.

2¾ pounds trimmed boneless beef shank, cut into 2-inch pieces
One 750-milliliter bottle dry red wine
15 mint sprigs, stems reserved
Salt and freshly ground pepper
¼ cup extra-virgin olive oil
One 35-ounce can peeled Italian tomatoes, crushed
1 pound fresh pappardelle
4 large garlic cloves, thinly sliced
Freshly grated Parmigiano-Reggiano cheese, for serving

1. In a large resealable plastic bag, combine the beef with the wine, mint stems and a generous pinch of salt and pepper. Seal the bag and refrigerate overnight.

2. Preheat the oven to 325°. Drain the beef, reserving the marinade; discard the mint stems. Pat the beef dry. In a large enameled cast-iron casserole, heat 2 tablespoons of the olive oil. Add half of the meat to the casserole and cook over moderately high heat, turning occasionally, until well browned all over, about 12 minutes. Transfer the meat to a plate. Brown the remaining meat over moderate heat.

3. Return all of the meat to the casserole. Add the marinade and bring to a boil. Add the tomatoes, season with salt and pepper and bring to a boil. Cover and braise in the oven for about 2 hours and 15 minutes, until the meat is very tender.

4. Using a slotted spoon, transfer the meat to a plate and shred with 2 forks. Boil the braising liquid until it is reduced to 2½ cups, about 20 minutes.

5. Meanwhile, in a large pot of boiling salted water, cook the pappardelle until al dente. Drain and return the pasta to the pot. Add the shredded meat and the reduced braising liquid and cook over moderate heat, stirring, until the pasta is well coated with the *brasato*, about 2 minutes.

6. In a small skillet, heat the remaining 2 tablespoons of olive oil until shimmering. Add the garlic and cook until lightly golden, about 1 minute. Add the mint leaves and cook for 10 seconds. Pour the garlic-mint oil over the pasta and toss. Serve in shallow bowls, passing the cheese alongside.
—Chris Cosentino

WINE Blackberry-rich Washington state Syrah: 2008 Owen Roe Ex Umbris.

Spiced-Coriander-and-Mustard-Crusted Rib Roast of Beef

ACTIVE: 30 MIN; TOTAL: 4 HR
PLUS OVERNIGHT MARINATING

12 TO 14 SERVINGS

A spice grinder is a key tool, because freshly ground spices have the most vibrant flavor. The spice crust on this roast is peppery, fragrant and so delicious you'll want to pick it off and eat it while the roast rests.

1 tablespoon allspice berries
3 tablespoons black peppercorns
3 tablespoons yellow mustard seeds
3 tablespoons coriander seeds
2 tablespoons cumin seeds
3 tablespoons kosher salt, plus more for seasoning
One 6-rib standing beef rib roast (14 to 15 pounds), ½-inch fat cap left on the meat
2 cups plain Greek yogurt
¼ cup plus 2 tablespoons drained horseradish
2 tablespoons grated fresh ginger
1 tablespoon freshly ground black pepper
1 teaspoon sugar

1. Put the allspice berries in a spice grinder and finely grind. Pass through a fine strainer into a bowl. Put the coarse bits left in the strainer back in the grinder. Add the peppercorns and coarsely grind them. Transfer to the bowl. Coarsely grind the mustard seeds and add to the bowl. Coarsely grind the coriander and then the cumin seeds; add to the bowl. Stir in the 3 tablespoons of salt. Rub the spice blend all over the meat. Cover the roast and refrigerate overnight.

2. Put a large roasting pan in the middle of the oven and preheat the oven to 375°. Let the rib roast stand at room temperature for about 30 minutes.

3. Season the rib roast with salt and place it in the hot roasting pan, fat side down. Cook for 30 minutes. Turn the rib roast over and cook at 350° for about 3 hours, rotating the pan 2 or 3 times. The rib roast is done when an instant-read thermometer inserted in the thickest part of the meat registers 130° for medium-rare. Transfer to a carving board to rest for about 20 minutes.

4. Meanwhile, in a bowl, stir the yogurt with the horseradish, ginger, black pepper and sugar and season with salt. Refrigerate until 20 minutes before serving.

5. Carve the roast and serve with the yogurt sauce. —Floyd Cardoz

WINE Bright, red cherry–inflected Syrah: 2008 Boxcar Sonoma Coast.

rib roast tips

New York chef Floyd Cardoz shares tips for preparing his two rib roasts at right and on page 155.

preheat To save stovetop space, preheat your roasting pan in the oven, then sear the meat (fat side down) right in the oven.

spices All spices contain oils that lose their potency as soon as they're ground. Grinding spices right before using ensures they have the most flavor and aroma.

leftovers Cut only the meat you'll need so you can have fresh roast beef for sandwiches the next day.

● HEALTHY ● MAKE AHEAD ● VEGETARIAN ● STAFF FAVORITE

beef brasato with pappardelle and mint

Classic Pot-au-Feu

ACTIVE: 45 MIN; TOTAL: 5 HR
6 TO 8 SERVINGS ● ●

In this recipe for the wintry French stew, two cuts of beef—shank and rump roast—are braised with marrow bones until they're deeply flavorful and tender.

- 1 large onion, quartered
- 6 large leeks, white and pale green parts only, cut into 2½-inch lengths
- 12 celery ribs, halved crosswise
- 6 medium carrots, peeled and halved crosswise
- 4 meaty beef shanks (about 3 pounds), 1½ inches thick
- One 3-pound beef rump roast or bottom round, tied
- 4 parsley sprigs
- 4 thyme sprigs
- 2 bay leaves
- 1 teaspoon whole black peppercorns
- Kosher salt
- Eight to ten 2-inch marrow bones (optional)
- 8 quarts water
- 6 medium parsnips, peeled and cut into 2-inch lengths
- 6 medium turnips, peeled and quartered
- 1 pound rutabagas, peeled and cut into eighths
- 1½ pounds unpeeled small potatoes, about 1½ inches, scrubbed
- Freshly ground black pepper
- Horseradish, whole-grain mustard and sour cream, for serving

1. In a large pot, combine the onion and half each of the leeks, celery and carrots. Set the beef shanks and rump roast on top of the vegetables. Wrap the parsley, thyme and bay leaves in moistened cheesecloth and tie into a bundle, then add to the pot along with the peppercorns and 1 tablespoon of salt. Add 2 of the marrow bones and the water. Bring to a boil over high heat, then reduce the heat to low, cover partially and simmer, skimming occasionally, until the rump roast is very tender, about 2½ hours.

2. Transfer the beef shanks and rump roast to a large bowl and cover. Strain the broth and return it to the pot. Boil over high heat until reduced to 10 cups, about 45 minutes; skim off the fat from the surface.

3. Add the remaining leeks, celery and carrots to the broth along with the parsnips, turnips and rutabagas. Cover and simmer over low heat until the vegetables are just tender, about 30 minutes. Add the remaining 6 to 8 marrow bones and the potatoes. Cover and simmer the pot-au-feu until the potatoes are tender, about 40 minutes.

4. Untie the rump roast and cut it across the grain into 6 to 8 slices. Cut the shank meat into 2-inch chunks; add the meats to the pot and simmer until heated through. Season with salt and pepper. Ladle the broth into shallow bowls. Add the meats, marrow bones and vegetables and serve, passing horseradish, mustard and sour cream at the table. —David Duband

WINE Powerful red Burgundy: 2008 David Duband Gevrey-Chambertin.

Vietnamese Caprese

TOTAL: 50 MIN PLUS OVERNIGHT CHILLING • 4 SERVINGS

For this noodle salad, Anthony Myint, the chef at Mission Chinese Food in San Francisco, combines the Italian trinity of tomato, basil and mozzarella with rice noodles and a version of the classic Vietnamese noodle sauce *nuoc mam*, made with fresh tomato juice. You could also call the dish an Asian-inflected take on spaghetti and meatballs.

- 1 pound ground beef chuck
- 4 red or green Thai chiles, minced
- 3 garlic cloves, minced
- ¼ cup Asian fish sauce
- Salt
- 1 pound large tomatoes, coarsely chopped
- 2 tablespoons freshly squeezed lime juice
- 1 teaspoon sugar
- 2 tablespoons extra-virgin olive oil
- ¼ pound dried wide rice noodles
- ¼ pound fresh mozzarella, cut into ¼-inch-thick sticks
- 1 cup grape tomatoes, halved
- 4 ounces cucumber, cut into ¼-inch-thick sticks (about 1 cup)
- ½ cup small Thai basil sprigs

1. In a large bowl, break up the beef. Add the chiles, two-thirds of the garlic, 2 tablespoons of the fish sauce and a pinch of salt and gently work the seasonings into the meat. Form the meat into 16 balls, transfer to a baking sheet and refrigerate overnight.

2. In a food processor, combine the coarsely chopped tomatoes with the remaining garlic and a large pinch of salt and pulse until the tomatoes are finely chopped. Strain the tomatoes through a coarse strainer into a large bowl, pressing on the solids; you should have about ¾ cup of juice. (To make a nearly clear tomato water, let the tomato mixture drain through a fine strainer overnight.) Whisk the fresh lime juice, sugar, 1 tablespoon of the olive oil and the remaining 2 tablespoons of fish sauce into the strained tomato juice.

3. In a large bowl, cover the dried rice noodles with water and let stand for about 20 minutes. Meanwhile, bring a medium saucepan of salted water to a boil.

4. In a large skillet, heat the remaining 1 tablespoon of olive oil until shimmering. Add the seasoned meatballs and cook over moderate heat until the meatballs are browned all over and nearly cooked through, 6 to 8 minutes. Let rest for 5 minutes.

5. Drain the rice noodles and add them to the boiling water. Cook the noodles, stirring, until al dente, about 40 seconds. Drain the rice noodles and return them to the pan. Fill the pan with cold water. When the noodles are cool, drain them again. Lightly pat the noodles dry, then add them to the tomato dressing and toss.

6. Transfer the dressed rice noodles to shallow bowls and top with the meatballs. Garnish with the fresh mozzarella, grape tomatoes, cucumber sticks and Thai basil sprigs and serve. —Anthony Myint

WINE Substantial, fruity Italian rosé: 2010 Castello di Ama.

● HEALTHY ● MAKE AHEAD ○ VEGETARIAN ● STAFF FAVORITE

classic pot-au-feu

Carbonnade à la Flamande (Flemish Beef Stew)

ACTIVE: 45 MIN; TOTAL: 3 HR
8 SERVINGS ●

This classic Belgian beef stew is known for its sweet-sour combination of caramelized onions and beer. Any dark Belgian-style ale would be a good choice here. As with most stews, the dish will taste even better a day or two after it's made.

- 4 tablespoons unsalted butter
- 3 pounds beef flatiron or blade steaks, cut into ⅓-inch-thick slices, about 3 inches wide
- Salt and freshly ground pepper
- 3 cups thickly sliced onions
- ½ cup all-purpose flour
- Three 12-ounce bottles beer
- ½ teaspoon dried thyme
- 2 bay leaves
- Chopped parsley, for garnish
- Boiled carrots and potatoes, for serving

1. In an enameled cast-iron casserole, melt 2 tablespoons of the butter. Season the beef with salt and pepper and add one-third of it to the casserole. Cook over moderate heat until lightly browned, 3 minutes per side. Transfer to a bowl. Repeat with 2 more batches of meat, using the remaining 2 tablespoons of butter.
2. Add the onions to the casserole, cover and cook over low heat, stirring, until browned, 8 minutes. Stir in the flour until the onions are well coated, then slowly add the beer. Return the meat to the casserole along with any accumulated juices. Add the thyme and bay leaves, cover and simmer over low heat, stirring, until the beef is tender, 2 hours.
3. Uncover and transfer the meat to a bowl. Simmer the sauce over moderate heat until thickened slightly. Discard the bay leaves. Return the meat to the casserole and season with salt and pepper. Sprinkle with parsley and serve with boiled carrots and potatoes.
—*Jacques Pépin*

WINE Curranty Cabernet Sauvignon: 2008 Château Fantin Bordeaux Supérieur.

Slow-Grilled Rack of Lamb with Mustard and Herbs

ACTIVE: 25 MIN; TOTAL: 1 HR
8 SERVINGS ●

"The one bad thing to do with lamb is a fast roast: It leaves the interior pretty much raw and the exterior charred," explains Hugh Acheson, the chef at Five & Ten in Athens, Georgia, and Empire State South in Atlanta. Quickly searing the racks and then grilling them over low heat makes the lamb perfectly browned outside and pink within.

- 2 racks of lamb (2½ pounds each), chine bones removed and excess fat trimmed
- Salt and freshly ground black pepper
- 2 tablespoons Dijon mustard
- 1 tablespoon chopped flat-leaf parsley
- 2 teaspoons chopped fresh rosemary
- 2 teaspoons chopped fresh thyme
- Caramelized Onion Jam (recipe follows), for serving

1. Light a grill or preheat a grill pan. If using charcoal, let the coals burn until white, then push them to one side of the grill. Season the racks of lamb with salt and freshly ground pepper. Spread the meaty sides of the racks with the Dijon mustard and then press the chopped parsley, rosemary and thyme onto the meat to help the herbs adhere.
2. Sear the racks of lamb over high heat, or directly over the coals, meaty side down, until they are nicely browned, about 6 minutes. Turn the racks so that they are leaning against each other with the bones pointing up and grill until the meaty sides are nicely browned on the bottom, about 3 minutes. Turn the racks bone side down and lower the heat to moderately low, or move the racks to the cooler side of the grill. Cover the grill and continue cooking until an instant-read thermometer inserted in the center of the meat registers 130° for medium-rare meat, about 20 minutes. Transfer the racks of lamb to a carving board and let them rest for about 10 minutes.

3. Using a sharp slicing knife, carve the racks of lamb into chops and serve them with the Caramelized Onion Jam.
—*Hugh Acheson*

WINE Red from France's Loire Valley: 2009 Jean-Maurice Raffault Les Galuches Chinon.

CARAMELIZED ONION JAM

🕑 TOTAL: 45 MIN
MAKES 2 CUPS ● ● ●

This easy-to-make sweet-tart caramelized onion jam from Acheson is excellent with his juicy rack of lamb. It would also be great with roasted meats or poultry, grilled salmon or even fresh goat cheese.

- ¼ cup extra-virgin olive oil
- 3 large sweet onions, cut into ¼-inch dice
- 2 parsley sprigs
- 2 bay leaves
- 1 rosemary sprig
- 1 cup sugar
- ¾ cup white balsamic vinegar
- Salt

1. In a large, heavy-bottomed pot, heat the olive oil until shimmering. Add the diced onions and cook them over moderately high heat, stirring occasionally, until they are golden brown, about 15 minutes.
2. Tie the parsley sprigs, bay leaves and rosemary sprig together with kitchen twine. Add the herb bundle to the diced onions and cook over low heat, stirring a few times, until fragrant, about 3 minutes. Sprinkle the sugar over the onions and cook, without stirring, until the sugar melts, about 5 minutes. Increase the heat to high and cook, without stirring, until an amber-brown caramel forms, about 6 minutes. Stir in the white balsamic vinegar and simmer over low heat, stirring a few times, until the jam is thick, about 5 minutes longer. Remove the herb bundle from the pot and discard. Season the Caramelized Onion Jam with salt and let cool to warm, then serve. —*HA*

MAKE AHEAD The Caramelized Onion Jam can be refrigerated for up to 5 days. Serve warm or at room temperature.

● HEALTHY ● MAKE AHEAD ● VEGETARIAN ● STAFF FAVORITE

roast rack of lamb three ways

An elegant dinner strategy: Roast a rack of lamb, then use the pan with the drippings to make one of three delectable sauces. FOOD & WINE's **Marcia Kiesel** has a pan and a plan.

olive-prune
In the skillet the lamb was cooked in, cook 1 minced garlic clove in 2 teaspoons oil. Add ¼ cup red wine, 8 quartered prunes and 8 halved Picholine olives; simmer for 1 minute. Add ¼ cup chicken stock and 1 teaspoon chopped rosemary. Off the heat, swirl in 2 tablespoons butter, 1 at a time.

tangerine-chile
In the skillet the lamb was cooked in, combine ½ cup tangerine juice, 1 teaspoon grated tangerine zest and 1 small fresh red chile. Boil until reduced by half. Add ¼ cup chicken stock and boil until slightly reduced. Off the heat, swirl in 2 tablespoons butter, 1 at a time.

mustard-shallot
In the skillet the lamb was cooked in, cook 2 sliced shallots in 2 teaspoons oil until soft. Add ¼ cup white wine and simmer for 2 minutes. Add ¼ cup chicken stock and bring to a simmer. Off the heat, add 1 tablespoon whole-grain mustard and 2 teaspoons each of Dijon mustard and thyme leaves.

Pan-Roasted Rack of Lamb
ACTIVE: 15 MIN; TOTAL: 45 MIN • 2 SERVINGS

Preheat the oven to 400°. In an ovenproof skillet, heat 1 tablespoon vegetable oil until shimmering. Season a 2½-pound frenched rack of lamb with salt and pepper. Add the lamb to the pan, fat side down, and cook over moderately high heat until browned, 3 minutes. Turn the lamb fat side up and cook for 2 minutes longer. Transfer the skillet to the oven and roast the lamb for 20 minutes, until an instant-read thermometer inserted in the center of the meat registers 125° for medium-rare. Transfer the lamb to a carving board and let rest for 10 minutes. Pour off the fat in the skillet and make one of the pan sauces above.

go-to wine pairing

tuscan red The 2009 Casamatta Rosso, a Sangiovese from Tuscany's Bibi Graetz, has the earthiness, dried-fruit notes and juiciness to go with the sauces above.

Garlic-Crusted Roast Rack of Lamb

📷 PAGE 143

ACTIVE: 10 MIN; TOTAL: 1 HR 45 MIN
8 SERVINGS ●

Kenny Rochford, the general manager of Medlock Ames Winery in Sonoma, California, likes to make a rack of lamb by simply rubbing it with plenty of garlic, rosemary, olive oil and salt before roasting.

    1 head of garlic, cloves peeled
    ¼ cup rosemary leaves
    ¼ cup extra-virgin olive oil
    2 racks of lamb, frenched
       (2 pounds each)
Salt and freshly ground pepper

1. In a mini food processor, combine the garlic, rosemary and olive oil and process until the garlic is finely chopped. Season the lamb racks with salt and freshly ground pepper and rub the garlic-rosemary oil all over them. Set the racks fat side up on a large rimmed baking sheet and let stand for 1 hour.
2. Preheat the oven to 450°. Roast the lamb in the upper third of the oven for 15 minutes. Turn the racks and roast for 10 minutes longer for medium-rare meat. Transfer the racks to a carving board, stand them upright and let rest for 10 minutes.
3. Carve the racks in between the rib bones and transfer to plates. Serve right away.
—*Kenny Rochford*
WINE Smooth, black cherry–rich Sonoma Merlot: 2006 Medlock Ames.

ingredient tip

cumin This spice is great mixed with ginger and garlic to add Indian flavor to lamb, or with oregano and cilantro for a Mexican flair.

Rack of Lamb with Pasilla Chiles

ACTIVE: 45 MIN; TOTAL: 3 HR 15 MIN
4 SERVINGS ●

Inspired by the great lamb he had in Valle de Guadalupe, a vineyard-filled stretch of the Baja peninsula, Mexican cuisine specialist Rick Bayless marinates meat with a sweet, spicy sauce made with fruity *pasilla* chiles, serving more alongside. Be sure not to buy frenched racks of lamb; the sauce forms an especially nice crust around the little bits of meat left on the bones.

    6 unpeeled garlic cloves
    6 *pasilla* chiles, seeded (see Note)
    ¼ cup honey
    2 tablespoons balsamic vinegar
    1 teaspoon Mexican dried oregano
    ⅛ teaspoon ground cumin
Kosher salt and freshly ground pepper
Two 8-bone racks of lamb
       (not frenched), fat trimmed
Olive oil, for grilling
Chopped red onion and parsley and
       queso añejo (see Note), for garnish

1. Heat a cast-iron skillet or griddle. Add the garlic and toast over moderate heat until the skin is blackened in spots, 10 minutes.
2. Meanwhile, toast the *pasillas* in the skillet: Press with a spatula and turn once, until pliable and fragrant, 1 minute. Transfer the chiles to a heatproof bowl and cover with hot water. Microwave at high power for 1 minute, until the chiles are completely rehydrated.
3. Transfer the chiles to a blender and add ⅓ cup of their soaking liquid. Peel the garlic and add to the blender with the honey, vinegar, oregano, cumin, 1 teaspoon of salt and ¼ teaspoon of pepper. Puree, then strain.
4. In a shallow baking dish, rub the lamb with ⅓ cup of the puree. Let stand at room temperature for 2 hours or refrigerate overnight.
5. In a small saucepan, simmer the remaining puree with ¼ cup of water; keep warm.
6. Light a grill and oil the grates or preheat a grill pan and brush with oil. Grill the lamb over moderately high heat, turning and rotating the racks, until the lamb is lightly charred

outside and an instant-read thermometer inserted in the center of the meat registers 135° for medium-rare, 30 minutes; move the meat to moderate heat if it starts to burn. Transfer the lamb to a carving board; let rest for about 5 minutes. Carve the lamb into chops and garnish with chopped red onion, parsley and *queso añejo*. Serve with the *pasilla* sauce. —*Rick Bayless*
NOTE *Pasillas* are long, black dried chiles. *Queso añejo* is a dry grating cheese; *cotija* or *ricotta salata* are good substitutes.
WINE Smoky, berry-rich Argentinean Malbec: 2009 Altos Las Hormigas.

Grilled Lamb Chops with Garlic, Chiles and Anchovies

📷 PAGE 4

TOTAL: 30 MIN PLUS OVERNIGHT
MARINATING • 8 SERVINGS

    ¾ cup pure olive oil
One 2-ounce can oil-packed anchovies,
       oil reserved
    3 red jalapeños, thinly sliced
    8 garlic cloves, thinly sliced
    ¼ cup packed mint leaves
    1 tablespoon packed marjoram leaves
    24 baby lamb rib chops
       (about 3 ounces each)
Salt and freshly ground black pepper

1. In a bowl, combine the olive oil, anchovy oil and jalapeños. On a cutting board, chop the anchovies with the garlic, mint and marjoram until minced; add to the bowl. Arrange the lamb chops in a baking dish, top with the marinade and turn to coat. Cover with plastic wrap and refrigerate overnight. Bring to room temperature before grilling.
2. Light a grill or preheat a grill pan. Scrape the marinade off the lamb and season the chops with salt and black pepper. Grill over high heat, turning once or twice, until nicely charred outside and medium-rare within, about 6 minutes. Transfer the chops to a platter and let rest for 5 minutes before serving.
—*Ethan Stowell*
WINE Deep, rich Syrah from Washington's Columbia Valley: 2009 Barnard Griffin.

● HEALTHY ● MAKE AHEAD ○ VEGETARIAN ● STAFF FAVORITE

rack of lamb with pasilla chiles

Double-Cut Lamb Chops with Spicy Red Wine Gastrique

ACTIVE: 45 MIN; TOTAL: 1 HR 30 MIN
4 SERVINGS ●

When chef Omri Aflalo serves this dish at Michael Mina's Bourbon Steak in San Francisco, he makes the *gastrique* (a sweet-and-sour sauce) with a slow-cooked lamb stock. The simplified recipe below substitutes a 30-minute sauce made with store-bought beef stock or broth.

¼   cup vegetable oil
4   garlic cloves, sliced ¼ inch thick
2   medium shallots, thinly sliced
¼   cup red wine vinegar
1½   cups dry red wine
1   fresh red chile, thinly sliced
3   tablespoons sugar
2   tablespoons sherry vinegar
1   cup beef stock or low-sodium broth
Salt and freshly ground black pepper
Eight double-rib lamb chops, about 5 ounces each (see Note)

fast meat rub

spicy herb salt *This lightly spicy salt is delicious rubbed over big cuts of meat, like leg of lamb or thick rib eye steaks.*

In a food processor, pulse 1 cup rosemary leaves and 1 cup thyme leaves with 2 large, thinly sliced garlic cloves until chopped. Add ½ cup coarse sea salt and pulse until finely chopped. Add 1 teaspoon crushed red pepper and pulse to blend. Spread the herb salt in an even layer on a large rimmed baking sheet and let stand, stirring occasionally, until dried, about 2 days. Transfer the mixture to a jar or manual spice grinder.
—*Grace Parisi*

1. In a medium saucepan, heat 1 tablespoon of the vegetable oil. Add the garlic and half of the shallots and cook over moderate heat until browned, about 7 minutes. Add the red wine vinegar and boil until almost evaporated, about 2 minutes. Add the red wine and boil over high heat until reduced to ½ cup, about 10 minutes. Strain the red wine reduction into a bowl.

2. In a small saucepan, heat 1 tablespoon of the vegetable oil. Add the chile and the remaining shallots. Cook over moderate heat until softened, about 4 minutes. Add the sugar and 1 tablespoon of water and cook over moderate heat, without stirring, until the water has evaporated and the caramel is richly browned, about 10 minutes. Carefully add the sherry vinegar, stirring, until incorporated. Add the beef stock and boil over high heat until reduced to ¾ cup, about 8 minutes. Add the red wine reduction and boil over high heat until reduced to 1 cup, about 5 minutes. Season the *gastrique* with salt and pepper.

3. Preheat the oven to 450°. In each of 2 large ovenproof skillets, heat 1 tablespoon of the vegetable oil. Season the lamb chops with salt and freshly ground black pepper and add them to the skillets, fat side down. Cook over moderately high heat until browned, about 2 minutes. Turn the chops and brown them on the other side, about 2 minutes longer. Turn the chops fat side up. Transfer the skillets to the upper and bottom thirds of the oven. Roast the lamb chops for about 7 minutes, or until an instant-read thermometer inserted in the center of a chop registers 130° for medium-rare meat.

4. Let the chops rest for 5 minutes, then transfer to plates. Drizzle with the *gastrique* and serve right away. —*Omri Aflalo*

SERVE WITH Moroccan Carrots (page 258).
NOTE Cut from a rack of lamb, double-rib chops include two ribs, resulting in a thicker and juicier steak.
MAKE AHEAD The red wine *gastrique* can be kept in the refrigerator overnight in an airtight container. Reheat gently.
WINE Napa Valley red: 2007 Once Wines The Table Cabernet Sauvignon.

Grilled Lamb Shoulder Chops with Manischewitz Glaze

⏱ **TOTAL: 35 MIN • 4 SERVINGS**

The sweet wine glaze for these chops started as a joke. "Someone kiddingly told me to try Manischewitz, so I bought a bottle," says New York chef Rich Torrisi. At Torrisi Italian Specialties, he and co-chef Mario Carbone serve the lamb with fried Jerusalem artichokes.

Two 1½-pound lamb shoulder chops, cut 1½ inches thick
Salt and freshly ground pepper
1½   cups Manischewitz Concord wine or other Concord grape wine
2   tablespoons grape jelly, preferably Concord grape
2   tablespoons red wine vinegar
Vegetable oil, for frying
1   cup mint leaves, patted dry
½   cup celery leaves
1   teaspoon ground coriander
1   teaspoon celery seeds
1   whole matzo cracker, crushed
Finely grated zest of 1 lemon

1. Light a grill or preheat a grill pan. Season the lamb chops with salt and pepper and grill over moderate heat, turning a few times, until nicely charred outside and medium within, 15 minutes per side. Transfer to a platter.

2. Meanwhile, in a medium saucepan, boil the wine over high heat until reduced to ¼ cup, 15 minutes. Whisk in the grape jelly and simmer for 1 minute. Remove from the heat and stir in the vinegar.

3. In a small saucepan, heat ½ inch of oil until shimmering. Add the mint and fry over high heat until crisp, 15 seconds. Using a slotted spoon, transfer to paper towels to drain. Add the celery leaves and fry until crisp, 30 seconds. Drain on paper towels.

4. Generously brush the hot lamb chops with the glaze. Sprinkle the chops with the coriander and celery seeds. Coat the fat edge of the chops with the matzo. Scatter the fried mint and celery leaves and the lemon zest over the lamb. Each chop serves two people.
—*Mario Carbone and Rich Torrisi*

WINE Bright Barbera d'Alba: 2010 Seghesio.

● HEALTHY   ● MAKE AHEAD   ○ VEGETARIAN   ● STAFF FAVORITE

Slow-Cooked Leg of Lamb with Spiced Yogurt and Herbs

ACTIVE: 1 HR; TOTAL: 4 HR 30 MIN
8 SERVINGS ● ●

"We have wood-burning ovens that retain a lot of heat after a day of cooking pizzas," explains chef Travis Lett of Gjelina restaurant in Los Angeles. "So we often use them overnight for things like this slow-cooked leg of lamb." While Lett cooks his lamb for up to 10 hours, this version in a conventional oven cuts the cooking time by more than half.

LAMB

- 1 quart chicken stock or low-sodium broth
- 2 cups dry white wine
- 1 cup fresh lemon juice
- ¼ cup honey
- 1 teaspoon whole allspice berries
- ½ teaspoon whole cloves
- 1 tablespoon ground coriander seeds
- 2 tablespoons smoked paprika
- 2 tablespoons fresh oregano leaves
- 2 tablespoons thyme leaves
- 1 tablespoon whole black peppercorns
- 2 onions, sliced crosswise ¼ inch thick
- 15 garlic cloves, peeled and lightly smashed
- 3 jalapeños, seeded and quartered

One 5-pound semi-boneless leg of lamb (aitchbone removed), tied
Sea salt and freshly ground pepper

SPICED YOGURT

- 2 cups plain Greek yogurt
- ¼ cup extra-virgin olive oil
- 1 cup packed cilantro leaves
- 1 tablespoon ground cumin
- 1 tablespoon ground coriander
- 1 tablespoon fresh lemon juice

Salt and freshly ground pepper

HERB SALAD

- ¾ cup packed parsley leaves
- ¾ cup packed cilantro leaves
- ½ cup packed tarragon leaves
- ½ cup snipped chives
- 1 jalapeño—halved, seeded and very thinly sliced crosswise
- ½ cup very thinly sliced red onion
- 2 tablespoons extra-virgin olive oil
- 2 tablespoons freshly squeezed lemon juice

Salt and freshly ground pepper
Cooked couscous, for serving

1. MAKE THE LAMB Preheat the oven to 425°. In a roasting pan large enough to hold the lamb, whisk the chicken stock with the wine, lemon juice, honey, allspice, cloves, coriander, paprika, oregano, thyme and peppercorns. Add the onions, garlic and jalapeños in an even layer. Season the lamb all over with salt and pepper and place it in the roasting pan, fat side up.

2. Braise the leg of lamb, uncovered, until it just starts to brown, about 45 minutes. Reduce the oven temperature to 325° and braise the lamb for about 2 hours and 30 minutes longer, until the meat is nicely browned and starting to pull away from the bone. Transfer the leg of lamb to a carving board and let stand for about 10 minutes.

3. Strain the braising liquid into a medium saucepan and skim off the fat. Boil the liquid until it is slightly reduced, about 10 minutes. Season the jus with salt and freshly ground black pepper and keep it warm.

4. MEANWHILE, MAKE THE SPICED YOGURT In a food processor, combine the yogurt with the olive oil, cilantro, cumin, coriander and lemon juice and puree until smooth. Season the mixture with salt and pepper. Transfer the spiced yogurt to a bowl.

5. MAKE THE HERB SALAD In a medium bowl, combine the parsley, cilantro and tarragon leaves with the chives, jalapeño, onion, olive oil and lemon juice and toss well. Season the salad with salt and pepper.

6. Cut the strings off of the lamb and carve the meat into ½-inch-thick slices. Arrange the lamb on a bed of couscous on a large, deep platter, then drizzle the jus and spiced yogurt over the lamb. Top with the herb salad and serve. —*Travis Lett*

MAKE AHEAD The lamb can be refrigerated with its reduced jus overnight. Reheat and slice before serving.

WINE Dark, blackberry-scented Syrah: 2009 Qupé Central Coast.

Sautéed Liver with Indian Spices

TOTAL: 40 MIN • 4 SERVINGS

- 1 onion, chopped
- 2 garlic cloves, halved
- 2 tablespoons chopped fresh ginger
- 1 teaspoon cumin seeds
- 1 serrano chile, chopped
- ¼ teaspoon turmeric
- 2 cardamom pods—seeds removed and crushed, pods discarded

Freshly ground black pepper

- 3 tablespoons water
- 2 tablespoons unsalted butter
- 1 cup lamb or beef stock or canned beef broth
- 1 tablespoon vegetable oil
- 1 pound lamb liver, cut into 1½-inch pieces, or chicken livers, trimmed and cut into 1½-inch pieces

Salt

- 1 tablespoon fresh lemon juice
- 3 tablespoons chopped cilantro

Steamed white rice, for serving

1. In a food processor, finely chop the onion, garlic cloves, ginger, cumin seeds, chile, turmeric, crushed cardamom seeds and ½ teaspoon of black pepper. Add the water and pulse to make a soupy paste.

2. In a medium skillet, melt the butter. Add the spice paste and cook over moderate heat, stirring, until almost dry, 5 minutes. Add the lamb or beef stock and simmer over low heat, stirring, until the sauce is thickened, about 8 minutes.

3. In a large nonstick skillet, heat the oil. Season the liver with salt and pepper and cook over moderately high heat until browned on the bottom, about 2 minutes. Reduce the heat to moderate, turn the liver and cook until medium within, about 2 minutes. Add the liver to the sauce and simmer for 1 minute. Add the lemon juice and season with salt and pepper. Sprinkle with the cilantro and serve with steamed white rice.
—*Jennifer McLagan*

WINE Concentrated, blackberry-inflected Malbec: 2008 Clos Siguier Cahors.

Spiced Leg of Lamb with Olives, Apricots and Lemons

ACTIVE: 30 MIN; TOTAL: 5 HR 30 MIN

10 TO 12 SERVINGS ●

One 8-pound semi-boneless leg of lamb (aitch bone removed)
4 small garlic cloves, thinly sliced
Kosher salt
¼ cup harissa (see Note)
½ cup extra-virgin olive oil
10 thyme sprigs
2 tablespoons sugar
1 lemon, very thinly sliced
1 cup pitted oil-cured black olives
12 ounces dried apricots, quartered

1. Using a sharp paring knife, poke small slits all over the lamb and insert a garlic slice in each one. Season the meat all over with salt and rub with the harissa and ¼ cup of the olive oil, working it into the slits. Set the lamb on a rack in a roasting pan and top with the thyme sprigs. Let stand at room temperature for 2 hours or marinate in the refrigerator overnight (bring the lamb to room temperature before roasting).

2. Meanwhile, sprinkle 1 tablespoon of salt and 1 tablespoon of the sugar on a large plate. Arrange the lemon slices on top and sprinkle with 1 tablespoon of salt and the remaining sugar. Drizzle the remaining ¼ cup of olive oil on top and cover with plastic wrap. Let stand at room temperature for 4 hours or refrigerate overnight. Drain the lemon slices, then rinse and pat dry.

3. Preheat the oven to 325°. Pour 2 cups of water in the bottom of the roasting pan and roast the lamb for 2 hours, adding water to the pan as it evaporates. Transfer the lamb to a platter and remove the rack. Add the olives, apricots and cured lemon to the pan. Return the lamb to the pan and roast for 30 minutes longer, until an instant-read thermometer inserted in the thickest part of the meat registers 130° to 135°. Stir the olives, apricots and lemon slices occasionally and add a little water if the pan juices get too dry. Transfer the lamb to a cutting board, tent with foil and let stand for 45 minutes.

4. Scrape the olives, apricots and lemons into a bowl along with any pan juices. Skim off the fat. Slice the lamb and serve with the lemon, olives and apricots. —*Jeff Cerciello*

NOTE Harissa is available at specialty food shops or from *chefshop.com*.

WINE Decadent, berry-rich Italian red: 2008 Alois Lageder Merlot.

Provençal Lamb Stew with Basil

ACTIVE: 40 MIN; TOTAL: 1 HR 30 MIN

4 SERVINGS ●

1½ pounds trimmed boneless lamb shoulder, cut into 1-inch pieces
Salt and freshly ground pepper
5 tablespoons extra-virgin olive oil
2 large shallots, finely chopped
3 anchovy fillets, chopped
1 tablespoon minced rosemary
5 garlic cloves, minced
1 pound baby red potatoes, halved
1 cup dry rosé
½ cup pitted green olives
3 tablespoons chopped basil

1. Season the lamb with salt and pepper. In a large, heavy Dutch oven, heat 3 tablespoons of the oil. Add the lamb and cook over moderately high heat until browned, 12 minutes; using a slotted spoon, transfer to a plate.

2. Add the shallots, anchovies, rosemary and most of the garlic to the Dutch oven and cook over moderate heat, stirring, until the shallots are softened, 5 minutes. Stir in the potatoes and cook just until browned in spots, about 2 minutes. Add the rosé and cook until nearly evaporated, scraping up any browned bits, 5 minutes. Add the lamb and any accumulated juices, the olives and 2 cups of water and bring to a boil. Cover and simmer over moderately low heat until the lamb is tender and the potatoes are cooked through, 50 minutes.

3. In a bowl, mash the remaining garlic to a paste. Stir in the basil and the remaining 2 tablespoons of olive oil. Stir the mixture into the stew and serve. —*Melissa Clark*

WINE Lively, medium-bodied red: 2009 Eric Texier Côtes-du-Rhône.

Spicy Spring-Lamb Crépinettes

TOTAL: 50 MIN

MAKES 10 CRÉPINETTES ●

1½ tablespoons fennel seeds
1 tablespoon black peppercorns
2½ pounds ground lamb
¼ cup dry red wine
5 garlic cloves, minced
1 tablespoon finely chopped rosemary
1 tablespoon finely chopped thyme
1 tablespoon finely chopped tarragon
1 tablespoon kosher salt
1 teaspoon crushed red pepper
1 sheet caul fat, soaked and rinsed (see Note)
1 tablespoon canola oil

1. Preheat the oven to 400°. In a small skillet, toast the fennel seeds and black peppercorns over moderately high heat until fragrant, about 2 minutes; transfer the toasted spices to a grinder and let cool completely. Finely grind the spices and transfer them to a large bowl. Add the lamb, red wine, garlic, rosemary, thyme, tarragon, salt and crushed red pepper and knead until the ingredients are thoroughly blended. Form the meat into ten 3-inch patties, about 1 inch thick.

2. Spread the sheet of caul fat on a work surface and cut into ten 8-inch squares. Form the *crépinettes* by wrapping each lamb patty in a square of caul fat, pressing to create a smooth package.

3. Heat the oil in a very large ovenproof skillet until shimmering. Add the *crépinettes* and cook over moderately high heat until golden on the bottom, 3 minutes. Flip and cook for 2 minutes longer. Transfer the skillet to the oven and roast the *crépinettes* until cooked through, 6 minutes longer. Let rest for 3 minutes, transfer to a platter and serve.
—*Russell Flint*

NOTE Caul fat, a fatty membrane from pigs and sheep used to wrap meats and pâtés, is available at specialty butchers.

MAKE AHEAD The uncooked *crépinettes* can be refrigerated overnight.

WINE Smooth, spicy Syrah: 2009 Charles Smith Boom Boom!

● HEALTHY   ● MAKE AHEAD   ● VEGETARIAN   ● STAFF FAVORITE

spiced leg of lamb with olives, apricots and lemons

Braised Lamb with Potatoes

ACTIVE: 30 MIN; TOTAL: 3 HR 15 MIN
4 SERVINGS

One 3-pound boneless lamb shoulder
  roast, well trimmed
Salt and freshly ground black pepper
  2 tablespoons vegetable oil
  4 slices of bacon,
    cut into 1-inch pieces
  2 large onions, thinly sliced
  1 cup dry white wine
  2 cups chicken stock or
    low-sodium broth
  2 thyme sprigs
  2 unpeeled garlic cloves
  1 bay leaf
  4 Yukon Gold potatoes (1½ pounds),
    peeled and sliced ½ inch thick
Chives, for garnish

1. Preheat the oven to 375°. Season the lamb all over with salt and pepper and roll it into a neat roast. With cotton twine, tie the roast at 1½-inch intervals.

2. In a medium enameled cast-iron casserole, heat 1 tablespoon of the oil until shimmering. Add the lamb and cook over moderately high heat until richly browned all over, about 4 minutes per side. Transfer the lamb to a plate and pour off the fat in the casserole.

3. Add the remaining 1 tablespoon of oil to the casserole and add the bacon. Cook over moderate heat, stirring a few times, until the bacon is lightly browned, about 3 minutes. Add the onions and cook, stirring a few times, until softened. Add the wine and boil over high heat until slightly reduced, about 2 minutes. Add the stock, thyme, garlic and bay leaf. Return the lamb to the casserole along with any accumulated juices. Cover with a sheet of parchment paper and the lid. Braise in the oven for 1 hour.

4. Remove the casserole from the oven and transfer the lamb to a plate. Nestle the potato slices into the cooking liquid. Turn the lamb over and set it on top of the potatoes. Replace the parchment paper and the lid and bake for 1½ hours longer, until the lamb and potatoes are very tender.

5. Transfer the lamb to a cutting board, cover loosely with foil and let rest for 15 minutes. Discard the thyme sprigs and bay leaf and season the braising liquid with salt and pepper. Discard the strings from the roast and cut the lamb into thick slices. Serve in shallow bowls with the potatoes and braising liquid, garnished with chives.
—*David McMillan and Frédéric Morin*
WINE Spicy Rhône red: 2008 Domaine de la Vieille Julienne Côtes du Rhône.

Lamb Shawarma

TOTAL: 40 MIN • 4 SERVINGS

  2 teaspoons ground cumin
  ½ teaspoon dried oregano
  2 garlic cloves, minced
  3 tablespoons fresh lemon juice
  ¼ cup extra-virgin olive oil
Kosher salt
  1 pound lamb shoulder, visible fat
    trimmed and meat thinly sliced
  1 white onion, halved and cut
    into thin slivers
  ½ cup tahini (sesame paste)
  ½ cup mayonnaise
Hot sauce, lettuce, sliced tomatoes, rice
  and warmed pita, for serving

1. In a large bowl, combine the cumin and oregano with half of the garlic and 1 tablespoon of the lemon juice. Stir in the oil and a generous pinch of salt. Add the lamb and onion and let stand for 15 minutes.

2. Meanwhile, in a blender or mini food processor, combine the tahini with ½ cup of water and the remaining garlic and 2 tablespoons of lemon juice and puree until smooth. Add the mayonnaise and puree until creamy. Season the white sauce with salt.

3. Heat a large griddle or 2 skillets until very hot. Add the lamb and onion and cook over high heat, turning occasionally, until the meat and onion are charred and tender, 6 to 7 minutes. Transfer to plates and serve with the tahini sauce, hot sauce, lettuce, tomatoes, rice and pita. —*Grace Parisi*
WINE Spicy Santa Barbara Syrah: 2007 Three Saints Santa Ynez Valley.

Lemon-and-Fennel-Roasted Lamb with Polenta

ACTIVE: 1 HR; TOTAL: 1 HR 30 MIN PLUS
OVERNIGHT MARINATING • 8 SERVINGS

  2 large lemons,
    scrubbed and thinly sliced
  6 garlic cloves
  1 tablespoon ground fennel
  ¾ cup extra-virgin olive oil
  1 tablespoon freshly ground black
    pepper, plus more for seasoning
3½ pounds butterflied boneless
    leg of lamb
Salt
  4 cups water
  1 cup coarse polenta (not instant)
  1 cup milk
  2 tablespoons unsalted butter
  ½ cup mascarpone cheese
  1 cup freshly grated Pecorino
    Romano cheese
  ¼ cup chopped flat-leaf parsley
  2 tablespoons prepared horseradish

1. In a food processor, puree the lemons with the garlic, fennel, olive oil and the 1 tablespoon of black pepper. Set the lamb in a glass baking dish and coat with the marinade. Cover the dish with plastic wrap and refrigerate overnight.

2. Preheat the oven to 350°. Scrape off some of the marinade and transfer the lamb to a roasting pan. Season with salt. Roast for about 45 minutes, until an instant-read thermometer inserted in the thickest part registers 125°. Transfer the lamb to a cutting board and let rest for 15 minutes.

3. Meanwhile, in a large saucepan, combine the water with the polenta, whisking until smooth. Cook over moderate heat, stirring, until the polenta is slightly thickened, about 5 minutes. Whisk in the milk and cook over moderate heat, whisking constantly, until the polenta is almost tender, about 25 minutes. Whisk in the butter and mascarpone and cook for about 15 minutes longer, until the polenta is creamy and tender. Stir in the Pecorino Romano and season the polenta with salt and freshly ground pepper.

● HEALTHY ● MAKE AHEAD ● VEGETARIAN ● STAFF FAVORITE

4. Spoon the polenta onto dinner plates. Thinly slice the roasted lamb and arrange the slices over the polenta. In a small bowl, combine the parsley and horseradish. Sprinkle the mixture over the lamb and serve. —*Chris Cosentino*

WINE Juicy, cherry-scented Montepulciano d'Abruzzo: 2007 Cataldi Madonna.

Chinese Black Bean and Brandy Lamb Kebabs

ACTIVE: 30 MIN; TOTAL: 1 HR
4 TO 6 SERVINGS

- 4 garlic cloves, smashed and peeled
- 2 tablespoons basil leaves
- 2 tablespoons cilantro leaves
- 2 tablespoons chopped fresh ginger
- ½ small shallot, coarsely chopped
- ½ scallion, coarsely chopped
- ¼ cup Chinese black bean sauce
- 2 tablespoons brandy
- 2 tablespoons hoisin sauce
- ¾ teaspoon *sambal oelek*
- ½ tablespoon Asian fish sauce
- 2 pounds trimmed lamb shoulder, cut into 1-inch pieces

1. In a mini food processor, combine the garlic, basil, cilantro, ginger, shallot and scallion and pulse until finely chopped. Add the black bean sauce, brandy, hoisin, *sambal oelek* and fish sauce and pulse to blend.

2. In a bowl, toss the lamb with the marinade until completely coated. Thread the lamb onto skewers, leaving a little space between each piece of meat. Let stand at room temperature for at least 30 minutes or refrigerate for up to 24 hours.

3. Light a grill or preheat a grill pan. Grill the kebabs over moderately high heat, turning occasionally, until the meat is lightly charred outside and just cooked through, about 8 to 10 minutes. —*Bill Kim*

VARIATION The black bean and brandy marinade is also delicious with salmon.

MAKE AHEAD The marinade can be refrigerated for up to 3 days.

WINE Juicy, peppery California Zinfandel: 2009 Marietta Cellars.

Norwegian Meatballs

TOTAL: 1 HR • 8 SERVINGS ●

MEATBALLS
- ¾ cup milk
- 1 tablespoon plain whole-milk yogurt
- 3 slices of white sourdough bread, crusts removed
- 1 tablespoon vegetable oil
- 1 medium onion, finely chopped
- 1 tablespoon ground allspice
- ½ teaspoon ground ginger
- ½ teaspoon freshly grated nutmeg
- 1 pound ground lamb
- 1 pound ground veal
- 1 large egg yolk
- 1 tablespoon kosher salt
- ½ teaspoon freshly ground black pepper

GRAVY
- 1 quart beef stock
- ⅓ cup brandy
- 1½ cups crème fraîche (12 ounces)
- 3 ounces *gjetost* cheese, shredded (1 cup), see Note
- 1 tablespoon unsweetened cocoa powder

Mashed potatoes and rutabagas, for serving

1. PREPARE THE MEATBALLS In a medium bowl, mix the milk and yogurt. Add the bread and press to submerge. Let stand until saturated, about 10 minutes.

2. Meanwhile, in a medium skillet, heat the oil. Add the onion and cook over moderate heat until softened, 8 minutes. Add the allspice, ginger and nutmeg and cook for 1 minute.

3. In a large bowl, combine the ground lamb and veal with the bread mixture, onion and egg yolk. Sprinkle with the salt and pepper and blend thoroughly. Form into 80 rounded-teaspoon-size meatballs.

4. Preheat a grill pan. Oil the pan and grill the meatballs in batches over moderate heat, turning, until lightly charred, about 5 minutes per batch.

5. MAKE THE GRAVY In a large, deep skillet, boil the beef stock over high heat until reduced to 2 cups, about 10 minutes. Add the brandy and boil for 2 minutes. Whisk in the crème fraîche, *gjetost* cheese and cocoa powder and bring to a simmer.

6. Add the grilled meatballs and simmer them over low heat, stirring occasionally, until the meatballs are cooked through and the gravy is slightly thickened, about 10 minutes. Serve the meatballs with mashed potatoes and rutabagas. —*Signe Johansen*

NOTE *Gjetost*, a sweet, semifirm Scandinavian cheese, is available at cheese shops and online at *igourmet.com*.

WINE Spicy, berried Rhône red: 2009 Delas Freres Saint-Esprit Côtes-du-Rhône.

Provençal Grilled Lamb

ACTIVE: 15 MIN; TOTAL: 45 MIN PLUS
1 HR 30 MIN MARINATING
4 TO 6 SERVINGS

Winemaker Mathilde Dalle and chef Patrick Thibaud of Château de Campuget, a winery and inn in France's Rhône Valley, use the quintessentially Provençal combination of rosemary, thyme and garlic to flavor lamb.

- 4 garlic cloves, minced
- 1 tablespoon chopped rosemary
- 1 tablespoon chopped thyme
- ¼ cup extra-virgin olive oil
- 2½ pounds boneless butterflied leg of lamb

Salt and freshly ground black pepper

1. In a bowl, mix the garlic, rosemary, thyme and oil. Season the lamb with salt and pepper and rub the herb oil all over. Let the lamb stand at room temperature for 1½ hours or refrigerate for at least 3 hours or overnight.

2. Bring the lamb to room temperature if necessary. Light a grill or preheat a grill pan. Grill the lamb over moderate heat, turning once, until browned outside and an instant-read thermometer inserted in the meat registers 125° for medium-rare, about 8 minutes per side. Transfer the lamb to a carving board and let rest for 10 minutes, then thinly slice across the grain and serve. —*Mathilde Dalle and Patrick Thibaud*

WINE Herb-scented Syrah blend: 2007 Château de Campuget Tradition Rouge.

L.A.'s food, wine and style tastemakers gather for a holiday party. The meal prepared by Farmshop chef Jeff Cerciello features fennel-garlic pork roast, OPPOSITE; recipe, page 181.

**pork
and veal**

Cider-Maple Pork Chops with Woodland Bitters Compote

ACTIVE: 45 MIN; TOTAL: 3 HR 15 MIN
4 SERVINGS

This pork recipe is also delicious using store-bought Angostura bitters in place of the home-made Woodland Bitters; both have a woodsy, spiced flavor.

MARINATED PORK CHOPS
- 1 cup apple cider
- ½ cup pure maple syrup
- ¼ cup bourbon
- 2 tablespoons light brown sugar
- 1 tablespoon Woodland Bitters (page 391) or Angostura bitters
- 2 thyme sprigs
- 2 garlic cloves, smashed

Four ¾-pound pork rib chops
GLAZE
- 1 cup apple cider
- 1 cup pure maple syrup
- 1 teaspoon Woodland Bitters (page 391) or Angostura bitters

Kosher salt and freshly ground pepper

quick spice blend

This fast and smoky spice mixture is terrific on pork chops, flank steak, skirt steak and other quick-cooking meats. Massage the rub onto the meat before grilling.

In a skillet, combine 2 tablespoons dried oregano with 1 teaspoon ground cumin, 1 teaspoon onion powder, 1 teaspoon dried orange peel and 1 teaspoon ground chipotle chile pepper. Toast all of the spices over low heat until they become fragrant. Let the spice mixture cool completely, then stir in 3 tablespoons dark brown sugar and 1 tablespoon kosher salt. Use the spice blend immediately or store in a jar for up to 3 months. —*Pete Evans*

COMPOTE
- 4 Granny Smith apples, peeled and cut into ½-inch dice
- ½ cup apple cider
- ¼ cup dark brown sugar
- 1 tablespoon bourbon
- 1 tablespoon butter
- 1 teaspoon fresh lemon juice
- 1 teaspoon Woodland Bitters (page 391) or Angostura bitters
- 1 cinnamon stick
- 1 tablespoon vegetable oil

Kosher salt and freshly ground pepper

1. MARINATE THE CHOPS Mix all of the marinade ingredients and pour into a resealable plastic bag. Add the pork chops and refrigerate for 2 hours.
2. MEANWHILE, MAKE THE GLAZE In a saucepan, boil the apple cider, maple syrup and bitters over moderately high heat until reduced by half, about 10 minutes. Season with salt and pepper and let cool.
3. MAKE THE COMPOTE Combine the apples with the apple cider, dark brown sugar, bourbon, butter, lemon juice, bitters and cinnamon stick in a medium saucepan and bring to a boil. Cook over moderately high heat until the apples just begin to soften, about 5 minutes. Reduce the heat to moderately low and simmer until the liquid has thickened, about 25 minutes. Keep the apple compote warm.
4. Remove the pork chops from the marinade and pat dry. In a large cast-iron skillet, heat the vegetable oil until shimmering. Season the chops with salt and freshly ground pepper and cook over moderately high heat, turning, until nicely browned, about 7 minutes. Reduce the heat to moderately low and brush with the glaze. Cook for about 7 minutes, turning and brushing with additional glaze, until an instant-read thermometer inserted in the chops near the bone registers 140°. Transfer the chops to a platter and let stand for about 5 minutes. Serve the pork chops with the apple compote.
—*Brad Thomas Parsons*
WINE Herbal, berry-scented Chilean Syrah: 2008 Chono Reserva.

Caribbean Jerk Pork Chops

ACTIVE: 20 MIN; TOTAL: 1 HR 15 MIN
4 SERVINGS

To make his spiced jerk pork at Big Bob Gibson Bar-B-Q in Alabama and North Carolina, Chris Lilly cooks a picnic shoulder for eight hours. The chops in the easier version here, rubbed with a vibrant jerk paste, require just 20 minutes on the grill.

- 1 habanero chile, seeded and chopped
- 1 small onion, coarsely chopped
- 1 scallion, thinly sliced
- 1 garlic clove, thinly sliced
- 1 teaspoon ground allspice
- ¾ teaspoon dried thyme
- ¼ teaspoon ground ginger
- ¼ teaspoon freshly grated nutmeg
- ¼ teaspoon cinnamon

Kosher salt and freshly ground pepper
- 1 tablespoon vegetable oil, plus more for brushing
- 1 cup store-bought Kansas City–style barbecue sauce

Four 12-ounce pork rib chops
- ½ cup hickory, pecan or oak chips

1. In a mini food processor, combine the habanero, onion, scallion, garlic, allspice, thyme, ginger, nutmeg and cinnamon. Add 1½ teaspoons of salt and 1 teaspoon of pepper. Process until finely chopped. Add the 1 tablespoon of oil and process to a smooth paste.
2. In a small bowl, whisk 1 tablespoon of the paste with the barbecue sauce. Spread the remaining paste all over the chops and let stand at room temperature for 30 minutes.
3. Light a gas grill. Wrap the wood chips in heavy-duty foil, pierce the packet all over with a skewer and add to the grill. Cover and let the chips begin to smoke, about 5 minutes.
4. Lightly brush the chops with oil and season with salt. Grill the chops, covered, over moderately high heat, turning and shifting the chops occasionally, until they are lightly charred and a meat thermometer inserted nearest the bone registers 140°, 18 to 20 minutes. Transfer the chops to a platter; serve with the spiced barbecue sauce. —*Chris Lilly*
BEER Pale ale: Deschutes Mirror Pond.

● HEALTHY ● MAKE AHEAD ● VEGETARIAN ● STAFF FAVORITE

caribbean jerk pork chops

Grilled Root Beer Pork Ribs
ACTIVE: 45 MIN; TOTAL: 2 HR 45 MIN
PLUS OVERNIGHT MARINATING
6 SERVINGS

Four 12-ounce bottles root beer
1 cup Asian fish sauce
1 head of garlic, cloves crushed
¼ cup black peppercorns, cracked
2 large shallots, thinly sliced
16 cups ice
2 large racks of pork spare ribs
   (about 5 pounds each)
1 vanilla bean, split and seeds scraped
2 tablespoons finely ground long
   pepper (see Note) or black pepper
¼ cup fresh lime juice,
   plus lime wedges for serving

1. In a medium saucepan, bring 2 bottles of the root beer to a boil with the fish sauce, garlic, cracked black peppercorns and shallots. Remove from the heat, cover and let steep for 25 minutes. Transfer the mixture to a large roasting pan and add the ice. Add the rib racks, cover and refrigerate overnight.
2. Preheat the oven to 325°. Remove the ribs from the marinade and scrape off most of the solids. Transfer the ribs to a large rimmed baking sheet. Cover with foil and bake for about 2 hours, until the meat is very tender but not falling off the bones.
3. Meanwhile, in a medium saucepan, combine the remaining 2 bottles of root beer with the vanilla bean and seeds and long pepper and boil over moderately high heat until reduced to ⅔ cup, about 25 minutes. Add the lime juice and simmer for 2 minutes. Discard the vanilla bean.
4. Light a grill. Grill the ribs over high heat until richly browned, about 4 minutes per side. Transfer the racks to a carving board and cut in between the ribs. Serve the ribs with lime wedges, passing the root beer sauce at the table. —*Zakary Pelaccio*
NOTE Long pepper, a fragrant Indonesian relative of black pepper, can be found at specialty food stores and *salttraders.com*.
WINE Robust Australian Shiraz: 2010 The Chook Shiraz-Viognier.

Grilled Chile Pork Chops with Tortilla-Tomatillo Salsa
ACTIVE: 45 MIN; TOTAL: 4 HR
4 SERVINGS

1 tablespoon ancho chile powder
1 tablespoon ground coriander
1 teaspoon Mexican oregano
4 garlic cloves, minced
2 limes—1 zested and juiced,
   1 cut into wedges
¼ cup plus 2 tablespoons
   extra-virgin olive oil
Salt and freshly ground pepper
Four 1-inch-thick, bone-in pork rib chops
4 tomatillos, husked and halved
1 serrano chile, halved and seeded
¼ cup chopped cilantro
1 Hass avocado, diced
1 cup tortilla chips, lightly crushed

1. In a large, shallow bowl, combine the chile powder with the coriander, oregano, minced garlic, lime zest, lime juice and ¼ cup of the olive oil. Season with salt and pepper. Add the pork chops and turn to coat. Cover and refrigerate the chops for 3 hours. Bring to room temperature before grilling.
2. Set a cast-iron grill pan over high heat. In a bowl, toss the tomatillos and serrano with 1 tablespoon of the oil; season with salt and pepper. Grill over high heat until the tomatillos are lightly charred, 4 minutes. Transfer the tomatillos and serrano to a work surface. Coarsely chop the tomatillos and mince the serrano. Transfer to a bowl and add the cilantro, avocado and the remaining 1 tablespoon of oil. Season the salsa with salt and pepper.
3. Lower the heat under the grill pan to moderate. Scrape the marinade off the chops. Grill the chops until they are lightly charred and an instant-read thermometer inserted near the bone registers 135°, about 12 minutes. Transfer the pork chops to a platter and cover loosely with foil. Let rest for 5 minutes.
4. Stir the tortilla chips into the salsa, then spoon the salsa over the pork chops. Serve right away, with lime wedges. —*Grace Parisi*
WINE Smoky, blueberry-scented Spanish red: 2009 Juan Gil Jumilla.

Cumin-Glazed Ribs with Avocado-Pineapple Salsa
ACTIVE: 40 MIN; TOTAL: 4 HR
6 SERVINGS ●

¼ cup ancho chile powder
¼ cup plus 1 tablespoon ground cumin
Kosher salt and freshly ground pepper
2 racks baby back ribs (5 pounds total)
4 jalapeños, seeded and thinly sliced
8 garlic cloves, smashed
½ cup plus 2 tablespoons fresh lime
   juice
½ cup honey
1 pound peeled, cored fresh pineapple,
   cut into ½-inch-thick rings
2 tablespoons light brown sugar
¼ cup finely diced red onion
½ cup chopped cilantro
1 large Hass avocado, diced

1. In a bowl, combine the ancho powder with ¼ cup of the cumin, 2 tablespoons of salt and ½ teaspoon of pepper. Set the ribs on a rimmed baking sheet and rub with the spice mix. Cover with plastic wrap and refrigerate for at least 2 hours or up to 10 hours.
2. Preheat the oven to 350°. Add ¼ inch of water to the sheet; bake the ribs for 45 minutes, until barely tender. Cover with foil; bake until tender, 30 minutes. Pour off the juices.
3. In a blender, puree three-fourths of the jalapeños with the garlic and ½ cup of the lime juice. Blend in the honey and remaining cumin. Transfer the glaze to a saucepan; simmer over low heat until thickened, 15 minutes.
4. Raise the oven temperature to 450°. Brush the ribs with half of the glaze. Roast until well glazed, turning once, about 20 minutes. Brush with the remaining glaze.
5. Light a grill or preheat the broiler. Grill the pineapple over high heat, turning once, until lightly charred, 5 minutes. Finely dice; transfer to a bowl. Add the brown sugar, onion, cilantro, avocado and remaining jalapeño and lime juice. Season with salt and pepper.
6. Grill or broil the ribs over high heat, turning once, until caramelized, about 5 minutes. Cut between the bones and serve with the salsa. —*Susan Feniger*

● HEALTHY ● MAKE AHEAD ○ VEGETARIAN ● STAFF FAVORITE

grilled root beer pork ribs

Country-Style Ribs with Apple-Bourbon Barbecue Sauce

TOTAL: 45 MIN • 6 SERVINGS

- ½ cup hickory, apple or maple wood chips
- 2 tablespoons light brown sugar
- 1 tablespoon kosher salt
- 1 tablespoon sweet paprika
- ¾ teaspoon garlic powder
- ¾ teaspoon onion powder
- ¾ teaspoon ground cumin
- ½ teaspoon freshly ground black pepper

Pinch of cinnamon

Pinch of ground ginger

- 4 pounds meaty country-style pork ribs (about 6 ribs total)

Apple-Bourbon Barbecue Sauce (recipe follows)

1. Light a gas grill. Wrap the wood chips in heavy-duty foil, pierce the packet all over with a skewer and add to the grill. Cover and let the chips begin to smoke, about 5 minutes. **2.** Meanwhile, in a small bowl, combine the brown sugar, salt, paprika, garlic powder, onion powder, cumin, black pepper, cinnamon and ginger. Rub the spice mixture all over the ribs and let stand for 5 minutes. **3.** Grill the ribs, covered, over moderately high heat for 20 minutes, turning occasionally, until they are lightly charred and cooked through. Brush the ribs liberally with some of the barbecue sauce and grill, turning once, until nicely glazed, about 5 minutes. Transfer the ribs to a platter and serve, passing more barbecue sauce on the side. —*Chris Lilly* **WINE** Syrah: 2008 Hogue Genesis.

APPLE-BOURBON BARBECUE SAUCE

TOTAL: 20 MIN • MAKES 2½ CUPS ● ●

- 2 tablespoons unsalted butter
- ¼ cup finely chopped onion
- 1 Granny Smith apple, peeled and coarsely shredded
- 3 tablespoons bourbon
- 2 cups store-bought smoky Kansas City–style barbecue sauce

In a medium saucepan, melt the butter. Add the onion and cook over moderate heat, stirring occasionally, until softened, about 5 minutes. Add the apple and cook until the moisture has evaporated, about 3 minutes. Add the bourbon and cook until nearly evaporated, about 3 minutes. Stir in the sauce and bring to a boil. Simmer over low heat for 5 minutes. Use or refrigerate for up to 1 month. —*CL*

Smoked Pork Tenderloin with Bourbon-Rosemary Sauce

ACTIVE: 15 MIN; TOTAL: 2 HR 15 MIN
4 SERVINGS ●

Jason Alley, the chef at Comfort in Richmond, Virginia, uses wood chips and an indoor smoker (it resembles a covered roasting pan) to smoke the pork here in less than a minute on the stove, then finishes cooking it in the oven. Because stovetop smoking is so fast, lean pork tenderloin won't become too dry. (Wood chips and stovetop smokers are available at *cameronscookware.com*.)

- ½ cup bourbon
- ½ cup soy sauce
- ½ cup light brown sugar

Juice of 1 lemon

- 3 large rosemary sprigs, bruised, plus 1 teaspoon chopped rosemary

Two 1-pound pork tenderloins

- 1 tablespoon vegetable oil

Salt and freshly ground pepper

- ½ cup low-sodium beef broth
- 2 tablespoons unsalted butter

Smoked-Onion Soubise (recipe follows), for serving

1. In a glass dish, mix the bourbon, soy sauce, sugar, lemon juice and rosemary sprigs. Add the pork and turn to coat. Let stand for 1½ hours, turning the pork every 30 minutes. **2.** Preheat the oven to 375°. To set up a stovetop smoker, see the Smoker Tip on page 194. In a well-ventilated area, set the smoker over high heat. When smoke rises from all sides, set the pork on the rack; reserve ½ cup of the marinade. Cover and smoke for 40 seconds; remove from the smoker.

3. In an ovenproof skillet, heat the oil until shimmering. Add the pork and season with salt and pepper. Cook over moderate heat until browned all over. Transfer the pork to the oven and roast until pale pink in the center, 15 minutes. Transfer the meat to a carving board and let rest for 5 minutes. **4.** Pour off the oil and set the skillet over high heat. Add the reserved marinade and the broth and boil, scraping up any browned bits in the skillet, until reduced to ⅔ cup, 5 minutes. Remove from the heat, swirl in the butter and season with salt and pepper. Stir in the chopped rosemary. **5.** Slice the pork ⅓ inch thick. Serve with the pan sauce and the Smoked-Onion Soubise. —*Jason Alley* **WINE** Lush Malbec: 2008 Durigutti Classico.

SMOKED-ONION SOUBISE

ACTIVE: 25 MIN; TOTAL: 1 HR
4 SERVINGS ● ● ●

- 1¼ pounds onion, thinly sliced
- 2½ tablespoons white rice
- 2 tablespoons unsalted butter
- ½ cup heavy cream
- ½ teaspoon freshly grated nutmeg
- ½ cup shredded Gruyère cheese

Salt and freshly ground pepper

- 1 tablespoon minced chives

1. Preheat the oven to 325°. To set up a stovetop smoker, see the Smoker Tip on page 194. Place a sheet of foil on the smoker rack; poke holes all over. In a well-ventilated area, set the smoker over high heat. When smoke rises from all sides, spread the onion over the foil. Cover and smoke for 45 seconds. Remove the onion. **2.** In a saucepan of boiling water, cook the rice for 3 minutes; drain. In an enameled cast-iron casserole, melt the butter. Add the onion; cook over moderate heat until softened. Add the rice, cream and nutmeg; bring to a boil. Cover and bake until the onion is tender, 30 minutes. Increase the oven temperature to 400°. Stir the cheese into the onion; bake for 5 minutes. Season with salt and pepper; garnish with the chives. —*JA*

● HEALTHY ● MAKE AHEAD ● VEGETARIAN ● STAFF FAVORITE

Pork Shashlik with Spicy Red Wine Marinade

TOTAL: 45 MIN PLUS OVERNIGHT
MARINATING • MAKES 8 SKEWERS

- 4 garlic cloves, minced
- 4 plum tomatoes, coarsely grated on a box grater
- 1 medium onion, coarsely grated on a box grater
- 1 cup dry red wine
- ¼ cup chopped cilantro, plus cilantro sprigs for garnish
- 1 teaspoon crushed red pepper
- 1 teaspoon dried oregano
- 1 teaspoon paprika
- 4 pounds trimmed boneless pork shoulder, cut into 2-inch pieces

Vegetable oil, for brushing
Salt and freshly ground pepper
Grilled flatbread and Spicy Plum Sauce (recipe follows), for serving

1. In a bowl, combine the garlic, tomatoes, onion, wine, chopped cilantro, crushed red pepper, oregano and paprika. Add the pork; toss to coat. Cover and refrigerate overnight.
2. Light a grill or preheat a grill pan. Thread the pork onto 8 metal skewers; leave a small space between each piece. Brush with oil; season with salt and pepper. Grill over moderate heat, turning occasionally, until nicely browned and cooked through, 30 minutes. Serve with cilantro sprigs, grilled flatbread and Spicy Plum Sauce. —*Dmitry Leonov*
WINE Juicy red: 2008 El Chaparral Garnacha from Vega Sindoa.

SPICY PLUM SAUCE

ACTIVE: 20 MIN; TOTAL: 40 MIN
MAKES ABOUT 1 CUP ● ● ●

- 3 red or black plums (about ¾ pound), quartered and pits reserved
- 2 teaspoons sugar
- 1 long red chile, seeded and minced
- 2 tablespoons chopped cilantro
- 1 tablespoon chopped dill
- 1 teaspoon red wine vinegar

Salt

1. In a small saucepan, cover the plums and pits with 2½ cups of water and bring to a boil. Cover partially and simmer over moderately low heat until the plums are very soft, about 20 minutes. Drain the plums, reserving ¼ cup of the water; discard the pits.
2. Transfer the plums to a blender. Add the sugar, half of the chile and the reserved cooking liquid and puree. Strain the puree through a fine-mesh strainer into a bowl. Stir in the cilantro, dill, vinegar and the remaining chile. Season with salt and serve. —*DL*

Pork Tenderloin Braised with Elderflower and Fennel

TOTAL: 30 MIN • 6 SERVINGS ●

- 2 tablespoons canola oil

Two 12-ounce pork tenderloins, sliced crosswise 1½ inches thick and lightly pounded

- 1 teaspoon fennel seeds, chopped
- 1 teaspoon cracked black peppercorns

Salt

- 2 fennel bulbs, cored and thinly sliced
- 1 large onion, halved and thinly sliced
- 1½ cups dry white wine
- ½ cup elderflower cordial
- 5 thyme sprigs
- 2 bay leaves

1. In a skillet, heat 1 tablespoon of the oil. Sprinkle the pork with the fennel seeds and peppercorns and season with salt. Add the pork to the skillet and cook over high heat, turning once, until lightly browned, 5 minutes. Transfer the pork to a plate.
2. Add the remaining 1 tablespoon of oil to the skillet. Add the sliced fennel and onion; cover and cook over moderate heat, stirring occasionally, until softened, 7 minutes. Add the wine, cordial and herbs and cook until the liquid is reduced by half, 5 minutes.
3. Return the pork and any accumulated juices to the skillet. Cover and simmer over low heat until the pork is cooked through, 10 minutes. Discard the herbs and serve. —*Trina Hahnemann*
WINE Smooth, cassis-scented French red: 2008 Hecht & Bannier Minervois.

Za'atar-Rubbed Pork Tenderloin

ACTIVE: 30 MIN; TOTAL: 1 HR
4 SERVINGS ●

Za'atar is a Middle Eastern blend of sesame seeds, herbs and sumac, a tangy powder made from a dried berry. The blend gives this pork tenderloin a bold flavor. Make it in a pan that browns well and has slightly higher sides, if possible.

- 2 tablespoons za'atar (or 2 teaspoons dried thyme and 2 teaspoons sesame seeds)
- ¼ cup canola oil

Kosher salt

Two 12-ounce pork tenderloins, sliced crosswise 1½ inches thick and pounded ½ inch thick

- 2 poblano peppers
- 1 small onion, finely chopped
- 1 pint grape tomatoes, halved

1. In a medium bowl, combine the za'atar with the canola oil and a generous pinch of kosher salt. Add the pork tenderloins, turn to coat and let stand at room temperature for about 30 minutes.
2. Meanwhile, roast the poblano peppers directly over a gas flame or under a broiler, turning frequently, until blackened all over; transfer to a bowl, cover with plastic wrap and let cool slightly. Peel and seed the chiles; cut into thin strips.
3. In a large nonstick skillet, heat 1 tablespoon of the oil from the pork marinade. Add the pork tenderloins and cook over high heat, turning once, until white throughout and lightly browned, about 5 minutes. Transfer the pork to a platter.
4. Add any remaining marinade oil to the skillet. Add the onion and poblano strips and cook over moderately high heat, stirring, until the onion is softened, about 5 minutes. Add the grape tomatoes and toss. Add ½ cup of water and cook until the tomatoes are just softened, about 4 minutes. Spoon the sauce over the pork and serve. —*Grace Parisi*
WINE Berry-rich Spanish red: Bodegas San Isidro Gémina Monastrell.

Pork Loin with Tea and Prunes

ACTIVE: 35 MIN; TOTAL: 2 HR 45 MIN
4 SERVINGS ●

12   pitted prunes
2   tablespoons balsamic vinegar
2   English Breakfast tea bags
4   medium carrots, cut into 1-inch dice
4   medium Yukon Gold potatoes, peeled and cut into 1-inch dice
4   medium turnips, peeled and cut into 1-inch dice
3   celery ribs, cut into 1-inch chunks
2   small red onions, cut into 1-inch dice
4   tablespoons unsalted butter
Salt and freshly ground black pepper
1   tablespoon vegetable oil
One 4-rib, bone-in pork loin roast (about 3 pounds)
One 3-inch cinnamon stick, broken in half
1   cup low-sodium vegetable broth

1. In a saucepan, add the prunes, vinegar and ¾ cup of water; bring to a boil. Simmer over low heat for 10 minutes. Off the heat, add the tea and let steep for 1 hour; discard the tea.
2. Preheat the oven to 375°. In a pot of boiling salted water, cook the carrots, potatoes, turnips and celery for 2 minutes; drain and transfer to a roasting pan. Add the onions and stir in the butter. Season with salt and pepper.

wine pairing tip

With lighter meats like pork or veal, pair the wine with the sauce.

The hearty tea-and-balsamic reduction for the pork loin above pairs well with a rich, dry red wine like Amarone, whereas the brighter mustard-and-lemon glaze on the pork at right actually works quite well with a full-bodied white wine such as Chenin Blanc. In each case, the sauce dictates the pairing choice, since the simply cooked protein is fairly neutral-tasting.

3. In an ovenproof skillet, heat the oil until shimmering. Season the pork with salt and pepper and cook, fat side down, over moderately high heat until browned, 4 minutes. Turn the pork and cook until browned, 3 minutes.
4. Set the pork in the center of the roasting pan, fat side up. Pour off the fat from the skillet. Roast the pork for 1 hour and 20 minutes, until it is almost done; return to the skillet. Increase the oven temperature to 450°. Roast the vegetables for 15 minutes, until tender.
5. Add the prunes and their liquid to the skillet with the cinnamon; bring to a boil. Spoon the liquid over the pork. In the upper third of the oven, roast the pork for 8 minutes, until an instant-read thermometer inserted into the thickest part reads 140°. Transfer the pork to a carving board and let rest for 10 minutes.
6. Add the broth to the skillet and simmer, reducing the sauce to ¾ cup. Discard the cinnamon; season with salt and pepper. Carve the pork into chops; serve. —*Bruno Loubet*
WINE Amarone: 2006 Masi Costasera.

Mustard-and-Lemon-Glazed Pork with Roasted Vegetables

ACTIVE: 30 MIN; TOTAL: 2 HR PLUS
2 HR MARINATING • 8 SERVINGS ●

Chef Alexandra Guarnaschelli roasts carrots and shallots along with pork, then uses the drippings for a sauce. "The idea is that you never throw flavor away," she says.

¼   cup Dijon mustard
¼   cup whole-grain mustard
Finely grated zest of 1 lemon
1   tablespoon chopped thyme
1   tablespoon unsalted butter, softened
One 3-pound boneless pork loin roast, trimmed of all fat
Salt and freshly ground pepper
1   pound baby carrots, peeled
16   large shallots, peeled
½   cup dry white wine
12   garlic cloves, unpeeled
¼   teaspoon crushed red pepper
1¼   cups chicken stock or low-sodium broth
2   tablespoons extra-virgin olive oil
1   tablespoon sherry vinegar

1. In a small bowl, whisk the Dijon and whole-grain mustards with the grated lemon zest, thyme and butter. Set 2 tablespoons of the mustard mixture aside. Season the pork loin roast with salt and pepper and spread the rest of the mustard mixture all over it. Let stand at room temperature for 2 hours or refrigerate overnight.
2. Preheat the oven to 350°. In a medium saucepan of boiling salted water, blanch the carrots for about 2 minutes. Using a slotted spoon, transfer the carrots to a bowl. Add the shallots to the saucepan and cook for about 4 minutes. Drain and halve the shallots lengthwise and add them to the carrots. Add the white wine, garlic, crushed red pepper, ¼ cup of the chicken stock and 1 tablespoon of the olive oil to the vegetables and toss well. Spread the vegetables around the edge of a shallow roasting pan, setting the shallots cut side down. Leave enough room in the center for the pork.
3. In a large nonstick skillet, heat the remaining 1 tablespoon of olive oil. Add the pork loin roast and cook over moderately high heat until browned on 2 sides, about 6 minutes total. Transfer the pork to the roasting pan and nestle it in the vegetables, then roast in the oven for about 45 minutes. Turn the pan 180 degrees, add ½ cup of the chicken stock and roast for about 20 minutes longer, until an instant-read thermometer inserted into the thickest part of the pork loin roast registers 140°.
4. Transfer the pork roast to a board. Roast the vegetables on the bottom shelf of the oven for 15 about minutes longer, until they are very tender; transfer to a bowl and keep warm. Set the roasting pan over moderately high heat on the stove, add the remaining ½ cup of stock and simmer for about 1 minute, scraping up the browned bits. Add the sherry vinegar and bring to a simmer. Off the heat, whisk in the reserved 2 tablespoons of the mustard mixture and season with salt and pepper. Slice the pork and serve with the roasted vegetables and sauce.
—*Alexandra Guarnaschelli*
WINE Fruity, zesty Chenin Blanc: 2008 Monmousseau Ammonite Vouvray.

● HEALTHY ● MAKE AHEAD ● VEGETARIAN ● STAFF FAVORITE

mustard-and-lemon-glazed pork with roasted vegetables

do-it-yourself tamales

A veteran of America's most avant-garde kitchens shifts his intense focus to making extraordinary tamales. **Alex Stupak** of New York's Empellón shares his recipes and tips.

make the dough and prepare the filling

Masa for Tamales

⏱ TOTAL: 15 MIN • MAKES ENOUGH FOR ABOUT 18 TAMALES

- 2½ cups masa harina (see Note)
- 1½ cups hot water
- 1 cup cold lard
- 2 teaspoons baking powder
- 1½ teaspoons kosher salt
- 1 cup cold chicken stock or low-sodium broth

In a large bowl, stir the masa harina with the water until evenly moistened; let cool. In the bowl of a standing electric mixer fitted with the paddle, beat the lard with the baking powder and salt at medium speed until fluffy, about 3 minutes. With the machine on, add the masa in golf-ball-size lumps, then drizzle in the chicken stock and beat the masa until completely smooth. Increase the speed to high and beat until fluffy, about 3 minutes; the texture should resemble soft hummus. **NOTE** Masa harina (nixtamalized corn flour) is available at supermarkets, specialty food shops and online at *mexgrocer.com*.

Red-Chile-Braised Pork

ACTIVE: 30 MIN; TOTAL: 3 HR 30 MIN
MAKES ENOUGH FOR ABOUT 18 TAMALES
● ●

- 10 guajillo chiles, stemmed and seeded
- 10 garlic cloves
- 2 canned chipotles in adobo sauce
- 1 teaspoon freshly ground black pepper
- ½ teaspoon cinnamon
- ½ teaspoon dried oregano
- 3 pounds boneless pork shoulder

Kosher salt

1. Using tongs, briefly toast the guajillo chiles over an open flame or in a cast-iron skillet until fragrant, 5 seconds per side. Transfer the guajillos to a blender. Add 2 cups of hot water and let stand for 15 minutes.

2. Add the garlic, chipotles, black pepper, cinnamon and oregano to the blender and puree. Strain the sauce into a large enameled cast-iron casserole, pressing on the solids. Add the pork and 6 cups of hot water to the casserole; bring to a boil. Cover partially and simmer over low heat until the pork is tender, 2 hours.

3. Using a slotted spoon, transfer the pork to a bowl and let cool slightly. Boil the sauce until it is reduced to 4 cups, about 20 minutes.

4. Shred the pork with 2 forks and return it to the sauce. Simmer uncovered until the sauce is reduced and just coats the pork, about 20 minutes. Season the pork with salt and let cool slightly.

assemble and steam

1. PREP THE LEAVES Using a sharp knife, cut off the stringy tops and bottoms of each banana leaf. Cut the leaves into 8-inch squares; you'll need about 18. Set aside any torn leaves to line the steamer.

2. ADD THE FILLING Spread ¼ cup masa in a slightly off-center 4-by-6-inch rectangle on a banana leaf square. Spread 2 tablespoons of the pork filling over the masa.

3. FOLD THE TAMALES Fold the bottom edge of the square up and over so that the masa encloses the filling. Fold the top edge of the leaf down, then fold in the sides to close the packet. Tie the packet with kitchen string. Repeat to form the remaining tamales.

4. STEAM AND SERVE THE TAMALES Line a large steamer with a layer of banana-leaf scraps. Add the tamales in 2 loose layers. Steam over boiling water for 1 hour and 20 minutes; replenish the water as needed. Remove from the heat and let the tamales stand in the covered steamer for 30 minutes. Transfer the tamales to a platter and pass scissors at the table.

NOTE Banana leaves can be purchased at specialty food stores or online at *store.gourmetsleuth.com*.

two more takes on tamales

Two tamale variations from chef Alex Stupak:

tamal pie *Baked in a skillet, this savory pie known as* tamal de cazuela *is easy to assemble and a great way to feed a group.*

Preheat the oven to 300° and grease a 10-inch cast-iron skillet with lard. Spoon two-thirds of the Masa for Tamales (at far left) into the skillet, mounding it slightly up the side. Spread 2½ cups Red-Chile-Braised Pork (at left) evenly over the masa and top with the remaining masa. Bake the tamal pie for about 30 minutes, until nearly set. Increase the oven temperature to 375° and bake until firm and lightly browned, about 35 minutes longer. Let the pie stand for 30 minutes, then cut into wedges and serve.

crispy fried tamales *Leftover tamales can be revived by frying them in oil for a hot, crispy snack.*

Dust unwrapped tamales with rice flour. In a large skillet, heat ½ inch vegetable oil to 350°. Carefully add the tamales in batches and fry them, turning once, until golden, about 5 minutes. Drain the fried tamales on paper towels.

Pork Confit Tacos with Grilled Pineapple Salsa

ACTIVE: 40 MIN; TOTAL: 3 HR PLUS
OVERNIGHT MARINATING • 6 SERVINGS ●

- ¼ cup kosher salt, plus more for seasoning
- 3 tablespoons sugar
- 2 tablespoons juniper berries, crushed
- 1 tablespoon coarsely ground white pepper
- 10 garlic cloves, minced
- 8 thyme sprigs
- 6 tablespoons chopped cilantro
- 2½ pounds boneless pork shoulder, cut into 1½-inch pieces
- 2 cups vegetable oil, plus more for brushing
- 12 ounces sliced fresh pineapple (½ inch thick)
- 1 yellow onion, sliced ½ inch thick
- 4 plum tomatoes, halved lengthwise
- 3 tablespoons chopped mint
- 2 tablespoons minced red onion
- 2 canned chipotle chiles, chopped
- Juice of 1 lime
- Warm corn tortillas, for serving

1. In a bowl, combine the ¼ cup of salt with the sugar, juniper, white pepper, garlic, thyme and half of the cilantro. Add the pork and toss to coat. Refrigerate overnight or for up to 16 hours.

2. Preheat the oven to 300°. Scrape the seasonings off the pork and transfer to a large enameled cast-iron casserole. Pour the 2 cups of oil over the meat and bring to a simmer over moderately high heat. Cover and bake for 2½ hours, until very tender.

3. Light a grill or preheat a grill pan. Brush the pineapple, yellow onion and tomatoes with oil and grill over moderately high heat until charred, 2 minutes per side. Cut into ½-inch dice; transfer to a bowl. Stir in the mint, red onion, chipotles, lime juice and the remaining cilantro; season with salt.

4. Lift the pork pieces from the oil. Grill over moderately high heat until charred all over. Transfer to a plate and shred. Serve with the salsa and tortillas. —*Andrew Zimmern*

Fennel-Garlic Pork Roast
📷 PAGE 171

ACTIVE: 45 MIN; TOTAL: 4 HR PLUS
OVERNIGHT BRINING • 8 TO 10 SERVINGS

BRINE
- ¼ cup honey
- 2 tablespoons black peppercorns
- 18 fresh bay leaves (⅓ ounce)
- 10 thyme sprigs
- 10 flat-leaf parsley sprigs
- 2 heads of garlic, halved horizontally
- 1 cup kosher salt
- One 4-pound boneless pork loin, tied

RUB
- 2 tablespoons fennel seeds, chopped
- 1 teaspoon crushed red pepper
- 6 garlic cloves, thinly sliced
- 1 teaspoon finely grated lemon zest
- Pinch of salt
- ¼ cup extra-virgin olive oil
- 2 tablespoons canola oil

1. MAKE THE BRINE In a saucepan, combine the honey, peppercorns, bay leaves, thyme, parsley, garlic and salt with 1 quart of cold water; bring to a boil, stirring to dissolve the salt. Pour into a large bowl; let cool. Add another 2 quarts of cold water along with the pork; refrigerate for 12 to 18 hours. Drain and pat dry, picking off any seasonings.

2. MAKE THE RUB In a mini food processor or a mortar, combine the fennel seeds, red pepper, garlic, lemon zest and salt; process or pound to a paste. Stir in the olive oil. Rub half of the paste on the lean side of the pork; let stand at room temperature for 2 hours.

3. Preheat the oven to 350° and set a rack on a large rimmed baking sheet. On a large griddle, heat the canola oil until shimmering. Add the pork fat side down; cook over moderately high heat until browned, 5 minutes. Transfer the pork to the rack, fat side up; slather with the remaining garlic paste. Roast the pork for about 1 hour, until an instant-read thermometer inserted in the thickest part registers 140° to 145°. Let rest for 20 minutes before slicing. —*Jeff Cerciello*
WINE Aromatic Pinot Noir from Oregon: 2008 Domaine Serene Yamhill Cuvée.

Slow-Cooked Sweet-and-Sour Pork Shoulder with Pineapple

ACTIVE: 30 MIN; TOTAL: 5 HR PLUS 2 HR MARINATING • 8 TO 10 SERVINGS ●

Inspired by the retro combination of ham and pineapple, star chef Jean-Georges Vongerichten created this Asian twist by mixing the pineapple with vinegar for a sweet-sour effect, and marinating the pork with paprika and Sriracha chile sauce. "Chile is my condiment of choice: A little here, a little there, really makes the food sing," he says.

- 2 tablespoons kosher salt
- 1 tablespoon hot smoked paprika
- 1 tablespoon onion powder
- 1 tablespoon garlic powder

One 7-pound trimmed boneless pork shoulder, at room temperature

- ¼ cup Sriracha sauce

One 2-pound ripe pineapple—peeled, cored and cut into 1-inch pieces

- 1 cup light brown sugar
- 1 cup apple cider vinegar

1. In a small bowl, combine the salt, paprika and onion and garlic powders. Set the pork fat side down on a work surface. Using a boning knife, cut between the natural separations in the meat in about 4 places. Sprinkle the spice mixture all over the pork, then rub all over with the Sriracha. Roll up the roast and tie it at 1-inch intervals with kitchen twine; let marinate at room temperature for 2 hours.

ingredient tip

smoked paprika Also called pimentón, it gives dishes like the pork shoulder above mild heat and an appealing smokiness.

aleppo pepper This mildly hot spice used in the braised pork at right has a fruity, raisin-like flavor.

crushed red pepper Made from a variety of peppers, it has a high ratio of seeds, intensifying the heat.

2. Preheat the oven to 325°. In a roasting pan, toss the pineapple with the brown sugar and vinegar. Spread the pineapple in the pan and set the pork roast on top, fat side up. Roast for 4 hours, basting every 30 minutes, until an instant-read thermometer inserted in the thickest part of the meat registers 165°. Transfer to a carving board to rest for 20 minutes.
3. Set the roasting pan with the pineapple over high heat and boil the pan juices until slightly thickened, 2 minutes. Remove the strings from the pork, carve into ½-inch-thick slices and arrange on a platter. Add carving juices to the pan and season with salt. Serve the pork with the pineapple and pan juices. —*Jean-Georges Vongerichten*

SERVE WITH Bibb lettuce wraps, Barley and Rice with Sesame Oil and Chives (page 274), and Almost-Instant Hot Kimchi (page 254).
WINE Generous, juicy Australian Grenache: 2008 d'Arenberg The Custodian.

Braised Pork Shoulder with Rhubarb and Peas

ACTIVE: 1 HR; TOTAL: 3 HR 30 MIN 8 SERVINGS ●

- 1 tablespoon freshly ground black pepper, plus more for seasoning
- 1 teaspoon salt, plus more for seasoning
- 1 tablespoon ground coriander
- 1 tablespoon ground fennel
- 1½ teaspoons Aleppo pepper or crushed red pepper

One 3-pound boneless pork shoulder roast

- ¼ cup extra-virgin olive oil
- 1 onion, thinly sliced
- 1 carrot, thinly sliced
- 1 fennel bulb—halved, cored and thinly sliced
- 2 celery ribs, thinly sliced
- 6 garlic cloves, smashed, plus 3 sliced cloves
- 3 bay leaves
- 2 cups dry red wine
- 1 quart chicken stock or low-sodium broth

- 1 pound rhubarb, cut into ½-inch pieces
- 2 tablespoons sugar

Two 1-inch strips of lemon zest

- 2 tablespoons fresh lemon juice
- 6 thyme sprigs
- 2 cups frozen baby peas, thawed

1. In a bowl, combine the black pepper and salt with the coriander, fennel and red pepper. Rub the spices all over the pork.
2. In a large enameled cast-iron casserole, heat 2 tablespoons of the olive oil until shimmering. Add the pork and cook over moderately high heat until browned all over, about 15 minutes. Transfer the pork to a plate.
3. Preheat the oven to 325°. Add the onion, carrot, fennel, celery, smashed garlic and 1 of the bay leaves to the pot, cover and cook over low heat until the onion is softened, 3 minutes. Uncover and cook over high heat until golden, about 3 minutes longer. Add the wine and boil until reduced to ¼ cup, about 15 minutes. Add the stock and bring to a boil.
4. Return the pork to the pot. Cover and braise the pork in the oven for about 2 hours and 15 minutes, until very tender. Transfer the pork to a cutting board. Strain the braising liquid and discard the solids. Spoon off as much fat as possible from the liquid.
5. Meanwhile, in a 9-by-13-inch glass or ceramic baking dish, combine the rhubarb, sugar, lemon zest and juice, thyme and the remaining 2 bay leaves. Season with salt and pepper. Cover with parchment paper and foil and bake for 30 minutes, until the rhubarb is tender but not broken down. Discard the lemon zest, thyme and bay leaves.
6. In a medium skillet, heat the remaining 2 tablespoons of olive oil. Add the sliced garlic and peas and cook over moderate heat until the garlic is tender, about 4 minutes. Season with salt and pepper.
7. Slice the pork; transfer to plates. Drizzle with the braising liquid. Spoon the rhubarb and peas alongside; serve. —*Chris Cosentino*
MAKE AHEAD The pork and rhubarb can be refrigerated separately for up to 2 days.
WINE Lively, berry-scented sparkling rosé: NV Graham Beck Brut.

● HEALTHY ● MAKE AHEAD ○ VEGETARIAN ● STAFF FAVORITE

slow-cooked sweet-and-sour pork shoulder

Roast Pork Loin with Fennel Salad

ACTIVE: 30 MIN; TOTAL: 1 HR 45 MIN
PLUS OVERNIGHT MARINATING
10 SERVINGS

PORK

- 1 tablespoon each of whole fennel seeds, coriander seeds, cloves, black peppercorns, star anise pods, allspice berries and juniper berries
- 1 cup kosher salt
- ½ cup light brown sugar
- 4 bay leaves
- One 10-rib, bone-in pork loin roast (about 7 pounds)

SALAD

- 1 large red grapefruit
- ⅓ cup fresh orange juice
- 2 tablespoons red wine vinegar
- 2 tablespoons extra-virgin olive oil
- 1 tablespoon honey
- Salt and freshly ground pepper
- 2 large fennel bulbs, cored and very thinly sliced on a mandoline
- 1 small red onion, thinly sliced

1. PREPARE THE PORK In a large pot, toast all of the spices over moderately high heat until fragrant, about 1 minute. Add 1 gallon of water, the salt, sugar and bay leaves; bring to a boil, stirring to dissolve the salt and sugar. Pour the brine into a large roasting pan and let cool to room temperature. Put the pork roast in the brine, meaty side down. Cover the roasting pan and refrigerate overnight. Bring the pork roast to room temperature in the brine before roasting.

2. Preheat the oven to 350°. Set the pork roast on a large rimmed baking sheet, meaty side up. Roast the pork in the upper third of the oven for about 1 hour and 15 minutes, until an instant-read thermometer inserted in the thickest part registers 145°. Transfer the roast to a carving board; let rest for 15 minutes.

3. MAKE THE SALAD Using a small, sharp knife, peel the grapefruit, removing all of the bitter white pith. Working over a large bowl, cut in between the membranes, releasing the grapefruit sections into the bowl.

4. In a small bowl, combine the orange juice, red wine vinegar, olive oil and honey; season the dressing with salt and pepper. Add the sliced fennel and red onion to the grapefruit sections in the large bowl.

5. Carve the pork roast into chops and transfer to plates. Toss the fennel salad with the dressing, mound the salad alongside the chops and serve. —*Tory Miller*

WINE Vibrant, crisp Spanish white: 2009 Doña Rosa Albariño.

Pressure-Cooker Pork Carnitas

TOTAL: 1 HR • 5 TO 6 SERVINGS ●
Braising pork shoulder in a pressure cooker makes it tender in just 35 minutes.

- 2¼ pounds boneless pork shoulder, cut into ¾-inch pieces
- 1 teaspoon achiote paste
- 1 teaspoon pure ancho chile powder
- 1 teaspoon pure chipotle chile powder
- Salt
- Vegetable oil for frying
- Warm corn tortillas, cilantro and lime wedges, for serving

1. Pour ¼ inch of water into a pressure cooker and add the pork. Cover and cook at 15 PSI (see Note) for 25 minutes, regulating the heat to prevent excessive steam from escaping through the valve. Turn off the heat and wait for the pressure cooker to depressurize so that the lid can be removed without force, about 10 minutes. Using a slotted spoon, transfer the meat to a strainer. Stir the achiote paste and both chile powders into the pan juices and season with salt.

2. In a medium skillet, heat ½ inch of oil until shimmering. Working in batches, fry the pork over high heat, turning once, until crispy, 3 minutes. Season with salt. Add the meat to the sauce and stir to coat. Serve the carnitas with tortillas, cilantro and lime wedges. —*Maxime Bilet and Nathan Myhrvold*

NOTE Fifteen pounds per square inch (PSI) is the most common setting for pressure cookers. Products vary, however, so be sure to consult the owner's manual.

BEER Citrusy white ale: Allagash White.

Braised Pork with Clams

ACTIVE: 45 MIN; TOTAL: 2 HR 30 MIN
6 SERVINGS

- 2 tablespoons extra-virgin olive oil
- 1½ pounds trimmed boneless pork shoulder, cut into 1-inch pieces
- Salt and freshly ground pepper
- 1 small onion, finely chopped
- 1 carrot, thinly sliced
- 1 celery rib, thinly sliced
- 1 tablespoon tomato paste
- ½ cup dry white wine
- 3 cups low-sodium chicken broth
- 4 thyme sprigs
- 4 parsley sprigs, plus 2 tablespoons chopped parsley
- 1 bay leaf
- 1½ dozen littleneck clams, scrubbed
- 1 cup jarred pickled Italian vegetables, drained and chopped
- 2 tablespoons chopped cilantro

1. Preheat the oven to 325°. In a large, deep ovenproof skillet, heat the oil until shimmering. Season the pork with salt and pepper; add it to the skillet in a single layer. Cook over moderately high heat, turning once, until the pork is browned, 12 minutes. Transfer to a plate. Add the onion, carrot and celery and cook over low heat until softened, 5 minutes.

2. Stir in the tomato paste and return the pork to the skillet. Add the wine and cook until evaporated. Add the chicken broth and bring to a boil. Using kitchen string, tie the thyme, parsley sprigs and bay leaf into a bundle; add the bundle to the skillet. Cover tightly and braise in the oven until the meat is tender, about 1 hour and 15 minutes.

3. Return the skillet to the stove. Discard the herb bundle. Simmer the pork uncovered over moderate heat until the liquid is reduced by half, 15 minutes. Arrange the clams in the liquid, cover and cook until they open, about 6 minutes. Transfer the pork and clams to bowls and ladle the braising liquid on top. Garnish with the pickled vegetables, chopped parsley and cilantro; serve. —*George Mendes*

WINE Robust, full-bodied Portuguese red: 2007 José Maria da Fonseca Domini.

● HEALTHY ● MAKE AHEAD ● VEGETARIAN ● STAFF FAVORITE

braised pork with clams

Crisp-Skinned Porchetta with Lemon and Chile

ACTIVE: 30 MIN; TOTAL: 5 HR 30 MIN
12 TO 14 SERVINGS

Porchetta, a traditional Italian street food, is a moist and fatty fresh ham covered with skin that's generously seasoned with salty garlic, rosemary, ground fennel and lemon. F&W Best New Chef 2011 James Lewis of Bettola in Birmingham, Alabama, adds some heat to his version with crushed red pepper.

6 ounces thinly sliced pancetta, chopped (1 cup)
16 large garlic cloves, chopped
Finely grated zest of 4 lemons
2 tablespoons chopped rosemary
1 tablespoon plus 2 teaspoons crushed red pepper
1 tablespoon ground fennel
2 teaspoons freshly ground black pepper
Kosher salt
1 tablespoon extra-virgin olive oil
One 18-pound, bone-in fresh ham with shank and skin (see Note)

three ideas for leftover ham

panini Stack slices of smoky ham and extra-sharp cheddar cheese between 2 slices of sturdy bread spread with mango chutney. Heat in a panini press or on a griddle.

ham salad Combine diced ham with shredded Gruyère cheese and pickled onions. Toss with grainy mustard and mayonnaise.

white bean soup In a pot, heat canned white beans and julienned ham with chicken broth, garlic and rosemary. Ladle into bowls; serve with crusty bread. —*Grace Parisi*

1. Preheat the oven to 325°. In a food processor, process the chopped pancetta until finely ground. Transfer the pancetta to a plate. Add the garlic, lemon zest, rosemary, crushed red pepper, ground fennel, black pepper, 2 teaspoons of kosher salt and the olive oil to the food processor and pulse until the garlic is finely chopped. Add the pancetta and pulse until the paste is well blended.
2. Set the ham skin side down on a work surface. Using a sharp knife, slash the meat at regular intervals. Season the meat lightly with kosher salt. Spread the spice paste all over the meat and in the slashes. Fold the leg back together, and with long, thick bamboo skewers, thread the leg closed at 2-inch intervals to keep the leg sealed. Set the leg skin side up. Cut a crosshatch pattern in the skin and fat. Season the skin and fat generously with kosher salt and transfer the ham to a large roasting pan.
3. Bake the ham in the lower third of the oven for 2 hours and 45 minutes, rotating the roasting pan twice. Increase the oven temperature to 375° and continue to roast the ham for about 2 hours longer, rotating the roasting pan twice more. The ham is done when an instant-read thermometer inserted in the thickest part of the meat registers 170° and the skin is very crisp. Transfer the ham to a carving board to rest for 25 to 30 minutes.
4. Pour the pan juices into a small saucepan and skim off the fat; keep warm.
5. Carve the porchetta into ⅓-inch-thick slices and serve with the crunchy skin. Pass the warm pan juices at the table.
—*James Lewis*

SERVE WITH Roasted potatoes and greens.
NOTE Have your butcher remove the hip and leg bone, leaving the shank bone in. There should be a layer of skin covering about two-thirds of the leg on top and a layer of exposed fat covering the rest of the leg.
MAKE AHEAD The uncarved porchetta can be refrigerated for up to 3 days and eaten in sandwiches, salads or soups. Alternatively, reheat the ham, slice and serve with eggs.
WINE Berry-rich Montepulciano d'Abruzzo: 2009 Quattro Mani.

Veal Scaloppine with Wilted Parsley, Lemon and Sesame

TOTAL: 45 MIN • 4 SERVINGS

¼ cup extra-virgin olive oil
2 medium shallots, minced
4 garlic cloves, minced
4 anchovy fillets, minced
6 cups small flat-leaf parsley sprigs
3 tablespoons fresh lemon juice
4 tablespoons unsalted butter
Salt and freshly ground black pepper
1¼ pounds veal scaloppine (8 pieces), pounded ⅛ inch thick
All-purpose flour, for dusting
Vegetable oil, for frying
2½ tablespoons Japanese crushed roasted sesame seeds (see Note)

1. In a medium skillet, heat the olive oil. Add the shallots and cook over moderate heat until softened, 3 minutes. Add the garlic and anchovies and cook over moderately low heat until fragrant, 4 minutes. Add the parsley and cook over moderate heat, tossing, until wilted, 2 minutes. Add the lemon juice and the butter and stir until melted. Remove the parsley from the heat and season with salt and pepper.
2. Set a rimmed baking sheet near the stove. Season the veal with salt and pepper and dust with flour, shaking off the excess. In a large skillet, heat ⅛ inch of vegetable oil until shimmering. Add 3 of the scaloppine; cook over high heat until browned, 1 minute. Turn; cook for 30 seconds longer, until browned. Transfer to the baking sheet. Repeat with the remaining veal, adding more oil and adjusting the heat as necessary. Discard the oil.
3. Pour any accumulated veal juices into the parsley and reheat. Transfer the veal to plates and spoon the parsley and sauce on top; sprinkle with the sesame seeds and serve.
—*Marcia Kiesel*

SERVE WITH Roasted potatoes.
NOTE Find seasoned Japanese sesame seeds (*gomashio*) at Asian markets or substitute crushed toasted sesame seeds and salt.
WINE Light-bodied, fragrant Beaujolais: 2009 Terres Dorées Fleurie.

● HEALTHY ● MAKE AHEAD ○ VEGETARIAN ● STAFF FAVORITE

veal scaloppine with wilted parsley, lemon and sesame

Roasted Rack of Veal with Root Vegetables

ACTIVE: 30 MIN; TOTAL: 2 HR 45 MIN
4 SERVINGS ●

Frasca Food and Wine restaurant in Boulder, Colorado, is inspired by the Friuli region of Italy; co-owner and wine director Bobby Stuckey serves a number of eccentric Friulian wines. This roasted veal dish from Frasca chef Lachlan Mackinnon-Patterson is particularly good with slightly tannic "orange" wines like Gravner's Ribolla Gialla.

½   pound pearl onions
1¼ pounds fingerling potatoes
2   large parsnips, peeled and cut into
    ¾-inch pieces
2   large carrots, cut into small pieces
1   head of garlic, cloves peeled
3   tablespoons extra-virgin olive oil
Salt and freshly ground black pepper
One 4-bone rack of veal, left untrimmed
    (about 5 pounds)
1   tablespoon chopped rosemary
1   tablespoon chopped thyme
2   cups chicken stock
3   tablespoons cold unsalted butter
1   tablespoon sherry vinegar

1. Preheat the oven to 375°. In a saucepan of boiling water, blanch the pearl onions for 30 seconds. Drain the onions. Trim the tops and bottoms and let the loose skins slide off.
2. In a large roasting pan, toss the pearl onions, fingerling potatoes, parsnips, carrots and garlic cloves with the olive oil. Season with salt and pepper and spread the vegetables in an even layer.
3. Season the veal with salt and pepper and rub the chopped rosemary and thyme into the layer of fat. Nestle the veal in the vegetables in the roasting pan, fat side up. Roast for 1 hour and 45 minutes, until an instant-read thermometer inserted in the thickest part of the meat registers 140°.
4. Transfer the veal to a carving board and let rest for 15 minutes. Spoon the vegetables into a bowl; keep warm. Pour off the fat from the roasting pan and reserve. Set the pan over moderately high heat, add the chicken stock and bring to a boil. Cook over high heat for 2 minutes, scraping up the browned bits. Strain the pan juices into a small saucepan and boil over high heat until reduced to ¾ cup, about 7 minutes. Remove the pan juices from the heat and let cool for 2 minutes. Whisk in the butter, 1 tablespoon at a time. Season the sauce with salt and pepper and stir in the vinegar.
5. Carve the rack of veal into 4 chops and transfer them to plates. Spoon a little of the reserved fat from the roasting pan over the meat and serve with the roasted vegetables, passing the sauce at the table.
—Lachlan Mackinnon-Patterson
SERVE WITH Tossed green salad.
WINE Complex, slightly tannic Italian white: 2004 Gravner Ribolla Gialla.

Chilled Veal Roast with Herbes de Provence and Fennel Salad

ACTIVE: 40 MIN; TOTAL: 1 HR 30 MIN
PLUS 3 HR CHILLING • 4 SERVINGS ●

Picholine olives and herbes de Provence give this luscious cold veal roast a distinctly southern French feel.

One 2½-pound boneless veal
    leg roast
¼   cup Picholine olives, pitted
    and chopped
1   tablespoon plus 1 teaspoon
    herbes de Provence
¼   cup plus 2 tablespoons extra-
    virgin olive oil
1   large scallion, minced
½   teaspoon finely grated
    lemon zest
Salt and freshly ground black pepper
¼   cup white wine
3½ tablespoons freshly squeezed
    lemon juice
1   large garlic clove, minced
2   fennel bulbs—
    very thinly sliced on a
    mandoline, soaked in ice water
    for 1 hour and drained
1   pint cherry tomatoes, halved
2   tablespoons chopped
    flat-leaf parsley

1. Preheat the oven to 375°. Set the roast on a work surface. Using a sharp knife, slice the roast lengthwise about two-thirds of the way through. In a small bowl, combine the olives with 1 teaspoon of the herbes de Provence, 1 tablespoon of the oil and the scallion and lemon zest. Rub the roast all over with the remaining 1 tablespoon of herbes de Provence and season with salt and black pepper. Pack the olive mixture into the slit and tie the roast closed with butcher's twine at 2-inch intervals.
2. In a large ovenproof skillet, heat 2 tablespoons of the oil. Add the veal roast and cook over moderately high heat until browned all over, 2 minutes per side. Transfer the skillet to the oven and roast the veal for about 30 minutes, turning once, until an instant-read thermometer inserted in the thickest part registers 145°. Transfer the veal roast to a plate and let it cool to room temperature. Wrap the veal roast in plastic and refrigerate until it is chilled, at least 3 hours or overnight.
3. Meanwhile, set the skillet over high heat and add the wine. Boil for 1 minute, scraping up any browned bits. Add ¼ cup of water and boil for 30 seconds. Remove the skillet from the heat and pour in any accumulated juices from the cooling veal. Let the pan sauce cool to room temperature. Stir in 1 tablespoon of the oil and ½ tablespoon of the lemon juice and season the sauce with salt and black pepper.
4. In a bowl, combine the remaining 2 tablespoons of oil, 3 tablespoons of lemon juice and the garlic; season with salt and black pepper. Pat the fennel dry with paper towels and add to the bowl along with the tomatoes and parsley. Toss the salad well.
5. Remove the twine from the veal. Carve the roast into ⅓-inch-thick slices and transfer to plates. Spoon the pan sauce over the meat and serve the fennel salad alongside.
—Marcia Kiesel
MAKE AHEAD The cooked veal and pan sauce can be refrigerated separately for up to 2 days. Serve the veal lightly chilled and the pan sauce at room temperature.
WINE Dry, crisp Provençal rosé: 2010 Chateau Miraval Pink Floyd.

● HEALTHY ● MAKE AHEAD ● VEGETARIAN ● STAFF FAVORITE

roasted rack of veal with root vegetables

Braised Veal Shoulder with Spring Vegetables

ACTIVE: 1 HR; TOTAL: 4 HR

6 SERVINGS ●

At Edi & the Wolf in New York City, chefs Eduard Frauneder and Wolfgang Ban serve goat-cheese-and-herb-stuffed veal in individual-size portions. Prepared as a whole roast, as in the recipe here, it's a great way to feed a group. To give the veal braising liquid an even richer flavor, substitute 1 cup of veal demiglace for 1 cup of the beef stock.

- ½ cup fresh goat cheese, softened (3 ounces)
- ¼ cup chopped celery leaves
- 1 tablespoon chopped marjoram
- 1 teaspoon chopped rosemary
- Salt and freshly ground pepper
- One 3-pound butterflied veal shoulder roast
- 2 tablespoons extra-virgin olive oil
- 2 shallots, thinly sliced
- 1 large carrot, thinly sliced
- 1 small celery rib, thinly sliced
- 1 cup dry red wine
- 4 cups beef stock
- 1 bay leaf
- 1 garlic clove, smashed
- 2 tablespoons chopped parsley
- 2 tablespoons chopped tarragon
- 2 tablespoons chopped dill
- Spring Vegetables with Pickled Onions (recipe follows), for serving

1. Preheat the oven to 300°. In a small bowl, mix the goat cheese with the celery leaves, marjoram and rosemary and season with salt and pepper. Lay the veal shoulder on a work surface, boned side up, and season with salt and pepper. Spread the goat cheese mixture over the meat, then roll it up and tie at 1-inch intervals with kitchen string. Season with salt and pepper.

2. In a large enameled cast-iron casserole, heat the olive oil. Add the veal roast and cook over moderately high heat, turning, until browned all over, about 10 minutes. Transfer the veal to a plate. Add the shallots, carrot and celery to the pan and cook over low heat until the vegetables are softened, about 5 minutes. Add the wine and simmer until syrupy, about 10 minutes. Return the veal roast to the casserole. Add the beef stock, bay leaf and garlic and bring to a boil.

3. Cover the casserole and braise the veal in the oven until tender, 2½ to 3 hours, turning once or twice.

4. Transfer the braised veal to a carving board and cover loosely with aluminum foil. Strain the cooking liquid into a saucepan and spoon off the fat. Boil the liquid until reduced to 2 cups, about 15 minutes. Stir in the parsley, tarragon and dill and season with salt and freshly ground pepper.

5. Remove the strings from the roast and slice it ¾ inch thick. Serve with the jus and the Spring Vegetables with Pickled Onions. *—Wolfgang Ban and Eduard Frauneder*

WINE Light-bodied, spicy Austrian red: 2008 Moric Blaufränkisch.

SPRING VEGETABLES WITH PICKLED ONIONS

TOTAL: 45 MIN PLUS 4 HR BRINING

6 SERVINGS ● ● ●

New York chefs Eduard Frauneder and Wolfgang Ban pickle ramps for this dish, but cipollini are easier to find and work nicely as well. The recipe makes more pickled onions than you'll need, but they keep for several weeks in the refrigerator and are delicious as a garnish for meat or cocktails.

- 1 pound cipollini onions
- 1 tablespoon fennel seeds
- 1 tablespoon black peppercorns
- 1 tablespoon coriander seeds
- 1 bay leaf
- 1½ cups red wine vinegar
- ¾ cup water
- ¾ cup sugar
- Kosher salt
- 16 baby carrots
- 1 tablespoon unsalted butter
- 1 tablespoon extra-virgin olive oil
- 6 scallions, dark green parts only, cut into 3-inch lengths
- 1 cup frozen baby peas
- Freshly ground pepper

1. In a large saucepan of boiling salted water, cook the cipollini for 5 minutes. Drain well and peel the onions, then transfer them to a clean 1-quart heatproof jar.

2. Put the fennel seeds, peppercorns, coriander seeds and bay leaf in a tea ball or tie in a cheesecloth bundle. In a saucepan, cover the ball or spice bundle with the vinegar, water, sugar and ¼ cup of kosher salt; bring to a boil, stirring to dissolve the sugar and salt. Pour the brine and the spice bundle over the onions; let stand at room temperature for at least 4 hours or refrigerate overnight.

3. Meanwhile, in a large pot of boiling salted water, cook the carrots until tender, about 10 minutes. Drain and pat dry.

4. In a large, deep skillet, melt the butter in the olive oil. Add the scallion greens and cook over moderately high heat until softened and lightly browned, about 1 minute. Add the baby carrots and peas and cook until heated through, about 3 minutes. Drain and thinly slice half of the pickled onions and add them to the vegetables (reserve the remaining onions for another use). Cook until just heated through, season with salt and freshly ground pepper and serve. *—WB and EF*

Meat-Stuffed Cabbage Cakes

ACTIVE: 45 MIN; TOTAL: 1 HR 30 MIN

4 SERVINGS ●

- 1 pound ground veal
- ½ pound sweet Italian sausage, casings removed
- 1½ cups fresh white bread crumbs
- 4 medium shallots, minced
- 2 garlic cloves, minced
- 2 large eggs, lightly beaten
- ¼ cup chopped parsley
- Kosher salt and freshly ground pepper
- ½ teaspoon freshly grated nutmeg
- One 1½-pound head of Savoy cabbage, cored
- 2 tablespoons unsalted butter
- 1 large onion, finely diced
- 1 medium carrot, thinly sliced
- ½ cup dry white wine
- 2 cups chicken stock or low-sodium broth

● HEALTHY ● MAKE AHEAD ● VEGETARIAN ● STAFF FAVORITE

1. In a large bowl, combine the veal, sausage, bread crumbs, shallots, garlic, eggs, 2 tablespoons of the parsley, 1½ teaspoons of salt, ½ teaspoon of pepper and the nutmeg.

2. In a medium saucepan of boiling water, submerge the cabbage, cored side up. Simmer until the leaves are softened, about 1 minute. Using tongs, transfer the 16 largest intact cabbage leaves to paper towels and pat dry. Cut out the ribs; reserve the other cabbage leaves for another use.

3. Line a small bowl or coffee cup with an 8-by-10-inch piece of plastic wrap. Overlap 2 cabbage leaves in the bowl. Spoon ½ cup of the stuffing in the center of the leaves and fold the leaves over to enclose the stuffing. Cover with the overhanging plastic wrap and twist to form a compact, round cake. Unwrap the cake. Repeat with the remaining cabbage leaves and stuffing.

4. Preheat the oven to 350°. In an enameled cast-iron casserole, melt the butter. Add the onion and carrot and cook over moderately low heat until softened, about 10 minutes. Add the white wine and bring to a boil. Add the chicken stock and season with salt and pepper. Add the cabbage cakes, seam side down. Cover and bake for about 35 minutes, until the filling is cooked through. Transfer the cabbage cakes to shallow bowls and ladle in the broth. Sprinkle with the remaining 2 tablespoons of chopped parsley and serve. —*Hubert Keller*

WINE Bright, red-berried Russian River Pinot Noir: 2009 Foppiano.

Creole Stuffed Tofu
TOTAL: 50 MIN • 4 FIRST-COURSE SERVINGS

Chef Anthony Myint of Mission Chinese Food in San Francisco wants to change the image of tofu as only an Asian ingredient or a health food. Most stuffed tofu contains only a small morsel of filling, but he cuts out a large rectangle in the tofu, fills it with sausage, then fries and serves it over a warm scallion sauce along with shrimp and roasted tomatoes. Creole hot sausage matches the Louisiana flavors in this multi-culti mashup, but any fresh sausage would be great.

One 14-ounce block of soft tofu, drained and quartered
Salt
3 tablespoons unsalted butter
2 bunches of scallions (about 12), sliced crosswise ¼ inch thick
¼ cup half-and-half
½ pound fresh sausage, such as Creole hot sausage, fresh chorizo or other fresh spicy sausage, casings removed
Vegetable oil, for frying
Celery leaves, lemon wedges and Tabasco, for serving

1. Using a small knife, gently scoop out a ⅓-inch deep rectangle in each piece of tofu, leaving a ⅓-inch border. Salt the tofu pieces all over and set them cut side down on paper towels to drain for 30 minutes.

2. Meanwhile, in a medium skillet, melt the butter. Add the scallions and a pinch of salt, cover and cook over moderately low heat, stirring occasionally, until the scallions are very soft, about 10 minutes; transfer to a blender. Add the half-and-half and puree. Season the scallion sauce with salt.

3. Pat the tofu dry and mound the sausage in the cutouts. In a skillet, heat ¼ inch of vegetable oil. Add the tofu, sausage side up, cover with a splatter screen and cook over moderately high heat until browned. Cover the skillet with a lid, reduce the heat to moderate and cook until the sausage is cooked through, about 5 minutes.

4. In a small skillet, warm the scallion sauce over moderately low heat and spoon it onto 4 plates. Top with the fried sausage-stuffed tofu. Garnish with the celery leaves and serve the tofu right away, with the lemon wedges and Tabasco. —*Anthony Myint*

SERVE WITH Oven-roasted cherry tomatoes and sautéed shrimp.

NOTE Creole hot sausage gets its distinctive heat from a Cajun-style spice blend, typically cayenne pepper, black pepper, paprika and ground bay leaf. It is available to purchase online at *vaucressonsausage.com.*

WINE Fresh, apricot-scented German Riesling: 2010 Leitz Dragonstone.

Chile-Cumin Spice Paste
TOTAL: 30 MIN • MAKES 1½ CUPS

Terrific with pork, this versatile seasoning paste is fruity, smoky and spicy. Use ancho chiles for more heat, *guajillo* for less.

4 ounces dried chiles, such as ancho, *pasilla* or *guajillo*, stemmed and seeded
4 canned chipotles in adobo, seeded
3 large garlic cloves, finely chopped
1 tablespoon ground cumin
1 teaspoon caraway seeds
1 teaspoon dried oregano, crumbled
¼ cup extra-virgin olive oil
2 large shallots, minced (½ cup)
Salt and freshly ground black pepper

1. In a large microwave-safe bowl, cover the dried chiles with 2 cups of hot water. Cover the bowl with plastic wrap and microwave at high power for 2 to 3 minutes, until the chiles are slightly softened. Let stand at room temperature until the chiles are fully softened, about 5 minutes.

2. Drain the chiles, reserving ⅔ cup of the soaking liquid. Transfer the chiles and their reserved soaking liquid to a blender or food processor. Add the chipotles and puree until very smooth. Strain, pressing hard to remove the skin and any seeds.

3. On a work surface, combine the garlic, cumin, caraway and oregano and chop until the caraway seeds are minced. In a medium skillet, heat the oil. Add the garlic paste and shallots and cook over moderate heat, stirring occasionally, until the shallots are softened, about 6 minutes. Add the chile puree and cook over low heat, stirring occasionally, until thick, about 10 minutes. Season with salt and black pepper. Let cool, then transfer to a jar and refrigerate. —*Grace Parisi*

USES Rub the spice paste on pork chops before grilling; blend it with butter and serve with grilled steak; mix it with yogurt as a dip for naan; mix it with mayonnaise and use as a sandwich spread.

MAKE AHEAD The Chile-Cumin Spice Paste can be refrigerated for up to 3 months.

fish

Grilled Salmon Gravlax

TOTAL: 25 MIN PLUS 36 HR CURING
6 SERVINGS ● ●

2½ pounds whole salmon fillet with skin
  3 tablespoons aquavit
2½ tablespoons light brown sugar
  2 tablespoons kosher salt
  1 teaspoon ground coriander seeds
  ½ teaspoon ground cardamom
Vegetable oil, for rubbing

smoker tip

smoking meat or fish *(as in the recipe at right) doesn't require a pit or a lot of time. Jason Alley, chef at Comfort in Richmond, Virginia, uses an inexpensive stovetop smoker. (Order stovetop smokers at cameronscookware.com.)*

prepare the smoker Spread ½ cup small, dry hardwood chips over the bottom of the smoker, then place the drip tray and rack directly on the chips.

to jury-rig a smoker Line a wok or disposable aluminum baking pan with heavy-duty foil, spread with dry wood chips, then top with another layer of foil (to catch drips) and a rack. Seal the wok or pan with a lid or sheet of foil.

1. Set the salmon skin side down on a large rimmed baking sheet and rub with the aquavit. Let the salmon stand for about 10 minutes. In a small bowl, combine the brown sugar, salt, coriander and cardamom. Rub the sugar mixture all over the salmon. Cover and refrigerate for 36 hours.
2. Light a grill or preheat a grill pan. Pat the salmon dry; cut into 6 portions. Rub the grill and salmon skin with oil. Grill the fish skin side down over moderately high heat until the skin is crisp, about 1 minute. Cover the grill. Cook the fish over moderate heat until rare within, 6 minutes. Serve hot or chilled.
—*Jeremy Daniels and Megan Walhood*

SERVE WITH Horseradish mayonnaise and a radish salad.

WINE Clean, medium-bodied white: 2010 Tenuta Beltrame Tocai Friulano.

Smoked and Cured Salmon with Orange Zest

TOTAL: 15 MIN PLUS 3 DAYS CURING
MAKES 2 POUNDS ● ● ●

One 2-pound center-cut salmon fillet
2½ tablespoons kosher salt
  2 tablespoons light brown sugar
  1 teaspoon ground coriander
Finely grated zest of 1 orange
  2 tablespoons vodka

1. Follow the Smoker Tip at left. In a well-ventilated area, set the smoker over high heat. After about 1 minute, when smoke rises from all sides, put the salmon on the rack, skin side down. Cover and smoke for about 20 seconds. Move off the heat; smoke for about 30 seconds longer.
2. Set the salmon skin side up in a glass baking dish. Mix the salt, brown sugar, coriander and orange zest; rub the spice mix and the vodka over both sides of the salmon. Cover and refrigerate for 3 days, turning daily.
3. Rinse the salmon fillet and pat dry. Using a sharp knife, thinly slice the salmon on an angle, cutting toward the tail, and serve.
—*Jason Alley*

WINE Fragrant, citrusy Vermentino: 2009 Tenuta Guado al Tasso.

Salmon and Spinach Cakes

ACTIVE: 40 MIN; TOTAL: 1 HR
MAKES 12 CAKES

1½ pounds large Yukon Gold potatoes
  5 ounces baby spinach
  ½ cup mayonnaise
  1 jalapeño, seeded and minced
  3 tablespoons chopped dill, plus
    dill sprigs for garnish
Salt
1½ pounds skinless salmon fillet,
    cut into ½-inch pieces
  ¼ cup plus 2 tablespoons heavy cream
  ¼ cup minced onion
Vegetable oil, for frying

1. In a medium saucepan, cover the potatoes with water. Simmer over moderately high heat until the potatoes are tender, about 30 minutes. Drain and let them cool. Peel the potatoes and cut them into ¼-inch dice. Transfer them to a large bowl.
2. Meanwhile, in a large skillet, heat 2 tablespoons of water over moderately high heat. Add the baby spinach in batches and cook until wilted. Drain, squeeze dry and coarsely chop the spinach.
3. In a small bowl, mix the mayonnaise, jalapeño and chopped dill and season with salt.
4. Put the salmon in a food processor and pulse a few times, until chopped. Pulse in the cream until incorporated. Add the salmon to the potatoes in the large bowl. Stir in the baby spinach and onion and season with salt. Form the mixture into 12 patties.
5. In a large nonstick skillet, heat ⅛ inch of oil. Add half of the cakes and fry over high heat until lightly browned on the bottom, 1 minute. Reduce the heat to moderately high and cook until well browned, 2 minutes. Turn and cook for 3 minutes, until browned. Repeat with the remaining cakes; add more oil to the skillet as needed. Garnish the cakes with the dill sprigs and serve with the sauce.
—*Marcia Kiesel*

MAKE AHEAD The sauce can be refrigerated overnight in an airtight container.

BEER Crisp, floral India Pale Ale: Elysian Avatar Jasmine IPA.

● HEALTHY ● MAKE AHEAD ○ VEGETARIAN ● STAFF FAVORITE

Gingered Salmon with Grilled Corn and Watercress Salad

TOTAL: 40 MIN • 4 SERVINGS ● ●

Chef Quinn Hatfield of Hatfield's in L.A. stuffs pickled ginger into slits in salmon fillets to infuse them with flavor. To keep the sliced fish intact and the ginger in place, he cleverly skewers the fillets before cooking.

- ½ cup plus 2 tablespoons balsamic vinegar
- ¼ cup plus 2 tablespoons canola oil
- 5 small ears of corn, shucked
- Four 6-ounce salmon fillets with skin
- 20 small slices of pickled ginger (about 1 ounce)
- Salt and freshly ground pepper
- 2 teaspoons Dijon mustard
- ½ teaspoon honey
- 1 bunch of watercress, thick stems discarded (about 8 ounces)

1. Preheat the oven to 375°. In a small saucepan, boil ½ cup of the balsamic vinegar until reduced to 3 tablespoons, about 5 minutes. Let the reduction cool, then stir in 1 tablespoon of the canola oil.

2. Heat a grill pan. Grill the corn over high heat, turning, until nicely charred all over, about 5 minutes. Let cool. Using a serrated knife, cut the kernels from the cobs.

3. Arrange the salmon fillets skin side down on a work surface. Using the tip of a sharp knife, make five ½-inch-deep slits crosswise in the flesh of each fillet. Stuff 1 slice of ginger into each slit, then thread each fillet lengthwise with a short skewer.

4. In a large ovenproof nonstick skillet, heat 1 tablespoon of the canola oil. Season the salmon fillets with salt and pepper and add them to the skillet, skin side down. Cook over moderately high heat until the skin is lightly golden, about 3 minutes. Transfer the skillet to the oven and roast the salmon for about 6 minutes, turning once halfway through, until the skin is very crisp and the fish is just cooked through.

5. In a large bowl, whisk the remaining 2 tablespoons of balsamic vinegar with the mustard and the honey. Gradually whisk the remaining ¼ cup of canola oil into the dressing. Add the grilled corn kernels and watercress to the bowl and toss to coat. Transfer the salad to plates and top with the skewered salmon. Drizzle the fish and salad with the balsamic vinegar reduction and serve right away. —*Quinn Hatfield*

VARIATION Stuff the salmon with small slices of prosciutto instead of ginger.

NOTE To make a larger batch of the balsamic reduction in Step 1, start with at least 1 cup of vinegar and boil until syrupy and reduced by more than half. Refrigerate without the canola oil for up to 2 weeks. Drizzle the balsamic reduction over grilled vegetables or fresh fruit, or add to sparkling water.

WINE Vibrant, herb-scented Grüner Veltliner: 2009 Domäne Wachau Federspiel Terrassen.

Triple-Mustard Salmon

TOTAL: 20 MIN • 4 SERVINGS ● ●

A coating of Dijon mustard, mustard seeds and toasted wheat germ creates a crisp crust for these salmon fillets.

- 3 tablespoons toasted wheat germ
- 1 tablespoon yellow mustard seeds, crushed
- Four 6-ounce skinless salmon fillets
- Salt and freshly ground pepper
- 2½ tablespoons Dijon mustard
- 1½ teaspoons dry mustard
- 1 tablespoon canola oil

1. In a shallow dish, combine the wheat germ and mustard seeds. Season the salmon fillets with salt and pepper. In a bowl, blend the Dijon mustard with the dry mustard and spread it over the skinned side of the fillets. Dip the mustard side of the fillets in the wheat germ mixture until thickly coated.

2. In a nonstick skillet, heat the oil until shimmering. Add the fillets, crust side down, and cook over moderately high heat until browned and crisp, 3 minutes. Turn the fillets and cook over moderate heat until barely cooked in the center, 3 minutes longer. Transfer the salmon to plates and serve crust side up. —*Marcia Kiesel*

WINE Fragrant Vermentino: 2009 Prelius.

Salmon with Red Wine–Balsamic Sauce

TOTAL: 30 MIN • 4 SERVINGS ●

Chef Alfred Portale of Gotham Bar and Grill in New York City serves his salmon with a peppery riff on beurre rouge, a French butter sauce made with red wine.

- 2 tablespoons extra-virgin olive oil
- 1 small shallot, minced
- 1 thyme sprig
- ½ teaspoon cracked black pepper
- 2 cups dry red wine
- ¼ cup balsamic vinegar
- 2 tablespoons heavy cream
- 4 tablespoons cold unsalted butter, cut into tablespoons
- Salt and freshly ground black pepper
- Four 6-ounce skinless salmon fillets

1. In a medium saucepan, heat 1 tablespoon of the olive oil. Add the minced shallot and cook over moderate heat until softened, about 4 minutes. Add the thyme sprig, black pepper, red wine and balsamic vinegar and boil the mixture over high heat until reduced to 2 tablespoons, about 12 minutes. Remove the saucepan from the heat and whisk in the heavy cream, then whisk in the butter, 1 tablespoon at a time. Season the sauce with salt and freshly ground black pepper, then strain into a bowl and keep warm.

2. In a large nonstick skillet, heat the remaining 1 tablespoon of olive oil until shimmering. Season the salmon fillets with salt and pepper and add them to the skillet, skinned side up. Cook over moderately high heat until the fillets are browned, about 4 minutes. Turn and cook over moderate heat until the fish is just opaque throughout, about 3 minutes longer. Transfer the salmon to plates, spoon the red wine–balsamic sauce over the fish and garnish with ground black pepper. Serve the salmon immediately. —*Alfred Portale*

SERVE WITH Steamed baby turnips or braised fennel.

WINE Cranberry-inflected Pinot Noir from Oregon: 2008 Village Parcel American.

Salmon Steaks with Curried Fennel-Wine Sauce

⏱ TOTAL: 40 MIN • 4 SERVINGS ●

F&W's Marcia Kiesel cooks fennel until silky over long, low heat, then serves it in a curry-laced wine sauce over broiled salmon.

 3 tablespoons vegetable oil
 2 large fennel bulbs—bulbs halved, cored and sliced lengthwise ¼ inch thick, plus a few fronds for garnish
Salt and freshly ground pepper
 4 scallions, cut into 1-inch lengths
1½ teaspoons medium-hot curry powder
 ¼ cup dry white wine
 1 cup bottled clam juice
 4 salmon steaks (about ¾ inch thick)
 ½ tablespoon fresh lemon juice
 2 tablespoons cold unsalted butter

1. In a deep 10-inch skillet, heat 2 tablespoons of the oil. Add the fennel and season lightly with salt and pepper. Cover and cook over low heat, stirring, until lightly browned and tender, 20 minutes. Add the scallions, cover and cook until they are just tender, 2 minutes. Transfer to a bowl. Add the remaining 1 tablespoon of oil to the skillet and add the curry powder. Cook over low heat, stirring, until fragrant, about 1 minute. Add the wine and boil over high heat until reduced by half, about 1 minute. Add the clam juice and boil until reduced by half, about 3 minutes. Cover and remove the skillet from the heat.
2. Preheat the broiler. Arrange the salmon steaks on a large rimmed baking sheet and season with salt and pepper. Broil about 6 inches from the heat for 3 to 4 minutes, until just opaque throughout.
3. Meanwhile, scrape the fennel and scallions into the sauce and reheat; stir in the lemon juice. Remove the skillet from the heat and stir in the butter, 1 tablespoon at a time, until incorporated. Season with salt and pepper.
4. Transfer the salmon to plates and spoon the sauce on top. Garnish the salmon with fennel fronds and serve right away.
—*Marcia Kiesel*

WINE Citrusy, full-bodied Chardonnay: 2009 Talbott Kali Hart.

Slow-Roasted Salmon with Tarragon and Citrus

📷 PAGE 193

ACTIVE: 30 MIN; TOTAL: 1 HR 30 MIN
6 SERVINGS

 4 tablespoons unsalted butter, melted
 4 garlic cloves, very thinly sliced
 3 medium shallots, minced
 2 tablespoons fennel seeds, coarsely ground in a spice grinder
Finely grated zest of 3 lemons, plus
  1½ tablespoons fresh lemon juice
Finely grated zest and juice of 1 orange
 2 tablespoons chopped tarragon
 1 tablespoon coarsely ground black pepper
 2 teaspoons chopped thyme
Extra-virgin olive oil, for the baking dish
2½ pounds whole skinned salmon fillet
Kosher salt
 ½ teaspoon cayenne pepper
Flaky sea salt, for sprinkling

1. In a bowl, combine the melted butter with the garlic, shallots, fennel seeds, zests, tarragon, black pepper and thyme.
2. Preheat the oven to 300°. Brush a large glass or ceramic baking dish with olive oil. Lightly season the salmon fillet with kosher salt. Spread half of the seasoning mixture on the skinned side of the fish. Place the salmon skinned side down in the baking dish and fold the thin tail end under itself to make the fillet an even thickness. Stir the cayenne pepper into the remaining seasoning mixture and spread it over the salmon. Let the salmon stand at room temperature for about 20 minutes.
3. Carefully pour the fresh orange juice into the baking dish and cover tightly with aluminum foil. Bake the salmon fillet for about 35 minutes, until the fish is barely opaque in the center.
4. Sprinkle the salmon with the lemon juice and sea salt and serve. —*Floyd Cardoz*

MAKE AHEAD The seasoning mixture can be refrigerated overnight.

WINE Herb-scented, citrusy Pinot Gris: 2009 Margerum Klickitat.

Barbecued Salmon with Green Mango Salad

⏱ TOTAL: 35 MIN • 4 SERVINGS ●

Australian chef and television personality Pete Evans uses green mango—which is firm and a little crunchy—for the fresh, bright salad that accompanies these grilled salmon fillets.

 1 teaspoon finely grated lime zest
 3 tablespoons fresh lime juice
 2 tablespoons unseasoned rice vinegar
 1 tablespoon light brown sugar
 1 tablespoon low-sodium soy sauce
 ¼ cup vegetable oil, plus more for brushing
Salt and freshly ground pepper
 1 large unripe mango (1¼ pounds), peeled and very thinly sliced
 ½ seedless cucumber, thinly sliced
 ¼ cup chopped cilantro
 2 tablespoons chopped mint
 2 tablespoons roasted sesame seeds
Four 7-ounce salmon fillets with skin

1. In a large bowl, whisk the lime zest and lime juice with the rice vinegar, brown sugar and soy sauce. Whisk in the ¼ cup of vegetable oil and season with salt and freshly ground pepper. Add the sliced green mango, cucumber, cilantro, mint and 1 tablespoon of the roasted sesame seeds.
2. Light a grill or preheat a grill pan. Brush the salmon fillets with vegetable oil and season them with salt and pepper. Grill the salmon skin side down over moderate heat, turning once, until the skin is very crisp and the fish is slightly opaque in the center, 10 to 12 minutes. Transfer the salmon fillets to plates, sprinkle them with the remaining 1 tablespoon of roasted sesame seeds and serve with the green mango salad.
—*Pete Evans*

MAKE AHEAD The green mango salad can be covered with plastic wrap and refrigerated for up to 4 hours. Add the chopped cilantro and mint just before serving.

WINE Dry, lime-scented Australian Riesling: 2009 Pewsey Vale Eden Valley.

● HEALTHY ● MAKE AHEAD ○ VEGETARIAN ○ STAFF FAVORITE

salmon steak with curried fennel-wine sauce

Slow-Roasted Salmon with Tamarind, Ginger and Chipotle

ACTIVE: 35 MIN; TOTAL: 1 HR 30 MIN

6 SERVINGS ● ●

Top Chef Masters Season 3 winner Floyd Cardoz looks to big flavors—tart tamarind, spicy ginger, sweet maple syrup and smoky chipotles—to create a vibrant and delicious seasoning paste for salmon.

- 2 dried chipotle chiles
- 2 cloves
- 1 tablespoon cumin seeds
- 1 teaspoon black peppercorns
- 3 tablespoons vegetable oil, plus more for the baking dish
- 4 large garlic cloves, minced
- 3 medium shallots, minced
- 2 tablespoons minced fresh ginger
- 2 tablespoons jarred tamarind puree
- 2 tablespoons pure maple syrup

Kosher salt

2½ pounds whole skinned salmon fillet

Flaky sea salt, for sprinkling

1. In a medium skillet, cook the dried chipotle chiles over moderate heat, turning, until they are toasted, about 4 minutes. Let cool, then break up the chipotles and discard the stems and seeds.

2. In a spice grinder, combine the toasted chipotles with the cloves, cumin seeds and peppercorns and grind to a powder.

3. In the same skillet, heat the 3 tablespoons of vegetable oil. Add the garlic, shallots and ginger and cook over moderate heat, stirring occasionally, until softened, about 5 minutes. Stir in the ground spices and cook until fragrant, about 2 minutes. Add the tamarind puree and maple syrup and season with a big pinch of kosher salt.

4. Preheat the oven to 300°. Lightly season the salmon with kosher salt. Oil a large glass or ceramic baking dish. Spread the spice paste on both sides of the salmon and set the salmon skinned side down in the dish. Fold the thin tail end under itself to make the fillet an even thickness. Let the salmon stand at room temperature for 20 minutes.

5. Cover the baking dish with foil and bake the salmon for about 35 minutes, until barely opaque in the center. Sprinkle with sea salt and serve. —*Floyd Cardoz*

MAKE AHEAD The spice paste can be refrigerated overnight.

WINE Spicy, raspberry-rich Pinot Noir: 2009 Adelsheim Willamette Valley.

Samoan-Style Tuna and Cucumber Salad

TOTAL: 30 MIN • 4 SERVINGS

"In Samoa, insanely good tuna is cheap and plentiful; a 20-pound fish might go for $5," says Andrew Zimmern, host of *Bizarre Foods* on the Travel Channel. "Samoans season raw tuna with coconut milk, lime and fermented sea cucumber intestine, called *se'e*. At home I skip the *se'e* in favor of fish sauce to give the dish a salty balance."

- ½ teaspoon sesame-chile oil
- 1 teaspoon soy sauce
- 1 pound fresh sushi-grade tuna, cut into ½-inch dice
- ¼ cup unsweetened dried coconut flakes
- 1 cup unsweetened coconut milk
- 3 tablespoons fresh lime juice
- 2 tablespoons Asian fish sauce
- 1 tablespoon light brown sugar

One 12-ounce seedless cucumber, cut into julienne

Lime wedges, for serving

1. In a large bowl, combine the chile oil and soy sauce. Add the tuna and toss well. Cover and refrigerate for 20 minutes.

2. Meanwhile, preheat the oven to 350°. Put the coconut flakes in a pie plate and bake for about 5 minutes, until golden brown.

3. In a small bowl, whisk the coconut milk with the lime juice, fish sauce and light brown sugar until combined.

4. Mound the cucumber julienne on plates. Top with the tuna, then drizzle with the coconut dressing. Sprinkle the salad with the toasted coconut and serve right away, with lime wedges. —*Andrew Zimmern*

WINE Zippy, green apple–scented Vinho Verde: 2009 Quinta da Aveleda.

Seared Tuna Steaks with Citrusy Soy Sauce

TOTAL: 20 MIN • 4 SERVINGS ●

The savory citrus-soy glaze drizzled over the tuna here has deep umami flavors.

- ½ cup soy sauce
- ¼ cup mirin
- 1 small shallot, thinly sliced
- ½ jalapeño, seeded and chopped
- 2 tablespoons fresh orange juice

One 3-inch strip of lemon zest plus 1 tablespoon fresh lemon juice

- 1 teaspoon sugar
- ¼ teaspoon ground coriander
- 1 tablespoon vegetable oil

Four 4-ounce tuna steaks (1 inch thick)

Salt and freshly ground pepper

1. In a small saucepan, mix the soy sauce, mirin, shallot, jalapeño, orange juice, lemon zest and juice, sugar and coriander. Simmer over moderate heat until reduced by half, about 8 minutes. Strain the sauce.

2. In a large nonstick skillet, heat the oil until shimmering. Season the tuna with salt and pepper. Cook over high heat for 1 minute per side. Transfer the tuna to a platter and let rest for 1 minute; thickly slice and serve with the sauce. —*Santos Majano*

WINE Passion fruit–scented orange wine: 2009 The Scholium Project Farina Vineyards The Prince in His Caves.

ingredient tip

soy sauce Terrific in marinades for fish and meat, this Asian staple can also be reduced to create a thick, savory glaze, as in the seared tuna steaks at far right.

● HEALTHY ● MAKE AHEAD ● VEGETARIAN ● STAFF FAVORITE

samoan-style tuna and cucumber salad

Hot Niçoise Salad

⏱ **TOTAL: 45 MIN • 4 SERVINGS** ● ●

"One cold day in London, I was dreaming about Niçoise salad," says actress and cookbook author Gwyneth Paltrow. "But it didn't seem right to eat something so chilly in the dead of winter." She created this hot version with the classic recipe's basic ingredients.

- ½ pound green beans
- 1 cup grape tomatoes, halved
- ½ cup pitted Niçoise olives (3 ounces)
- 1 cup roasted red or yellow bell peppers, cut into strips
- Two 2-ounce cans flat anchovies packed in olive oil, drained and chopped
- ½ cup torn basil leaves
- ½ cup plus 2 tablespoons extra-virgin olive oil
- Salt and freshly ground pepper
- Four 6-ounce tuna steaks (1 inch thick)
- 4 large eggs
- 2 tablespoons fresh lemon juice

1. Preheat the oven to 400°. Put the beans in a steamer basket and steam over 1 inch of boiling water until crisp-tender, 4 minutes; transfer to a large roasting pan.
2. Lightly squeeze the tomatoes and add to the pan. Add the olives, roasted peppers, anchovies and basil, toss with ¼ cup of the oil and season with salt and pepper. Brush the tuna steaks with 1 tablespoon of the oil and season with salt and pepper. Set the tuna on the vegetables. Nestle 4 ramekins among the vegetables and crack an egg into each one. Drizzle the eggs with 1 tablespoon of the oil and season with salt and pepper.
3. Roast the tuna, vegetables and eggs in the center of the oven for 15 minutes, until the fish is slightly rare in the center and the egg whites are set but the yolks are still runny.
4. Meanwhile, in a small bowl, whisk the remaining ¼ cup of oil with the lemon juice and season with salt and pepper. Drizzle the dressing over the vegetables and tuna steaks, transfer to plates and serve immediately. —*Gwyneth Paltrow*

WINE Fragrant, strawberry-inflected Provençal rosé: 2009 Mas de Gourgonnier.

Swordfish Piccata

⏱ **TOTAL: 30 MIN • 6 SERVINGS** ●

- Six 6- to 7-ounce skinless swordfish steaks
- Salt and freshly ground black pepper
- 6 thin slices of serrano ham or prosciutto
- ½ cup all-purpose flour, plus more for dusting
- ½ cup freshly grated Parmigiano-Reggiano cheese
- 1 large egg, beaten
- ½ cup milk
- 2 tablespoons extra-virgin olive oil
- 1 stick unsalted butter
- ½ cup sliced almonds
- 2 tablespoons freshly squeezed lemon juice
- 2 tablespoons drained capers
- 2 tablespoons chopped flat-leaf parsley
- Sautéed kale, creamy polenta and lemon wedges, for serving

1. Preheat the oven to 350°. Season the fish with salt and black pepper and wrap a slice of ham around each steak. Lightly dust the swordfish all over with flour.
2. In a pie plate, combine the ½ cup of flour with the Parmigiano-Reggiano cheese. In another pie plate, whisk the beaten egg with the milk. Dip the swordfish steaks in the egg mixture, allowing the excess to drip off, then press the steaks into the flour-cheese mixture so that it adheres.
3. In a large ovenproof nonstick skillet, heat the olive oil until shimmering. Add the swordfish steaks and cook over moderately high heat until lightly browned, about 3 minutes. Flip the steaks over. Transfer the skillet to the oven and roast the swordfish for about 5 minutes, until cooked through.
4. Meanwhile, in a medium skillet, melt the butter. Add the sliced almonds and cook over moderate heat, stirring, until the almonds are toasted and the butter is lightly browned, about 4 minutes. Remove the sauce from the heat and add the lemon juice, capers and parsley. Transfer the swordfish steaks to plates and spoon the sauce on top. Serve right away, with sautéed kale, creamy polenta and lemon wedges. —*John Besh*

WINE Fresh, citrusy Riesling: 2009 Frankland Estate Isolation Ridge.

Grilled Swordfish with Lima Bean and Herb Butter

⏱ **ACTIVE: 20 MIN; TOTAL: 40 MIN**
10 SERVINGS

Fresh lima beans and herbs add a green hue to the butter for the grilled swordfish here. For a neat presentation, roll the lima bean and herb butter in plastic wrap into a cylinder and refrigerate until firm. Slice off rounds of butter as you need them.

- ½ cup shelled lima beans (from about 1 pound in the pod)
- Salt
- 1½ sticks unsalted butter, softened
- 2 tablespoons chopped chives
- 2 tablespoons chopped parsley
- 1 tablespoon chopped dill
- Hot sauce
- Ten 6-ounce swordfish steaks (about 1 inch thick)
- Extra-virgin olive oil, for rubbing
- Freshly ground black pepper

1. In a small saucepan, cover the shelled lima beans with water and bring to a boil. Add a pinch of salt, cover and simmer over moderately low heat until tender, about 10 minutes. Drain and let cool.
2. Puree the lima beans in a mini food processor. Add the butter, chives, parsley and dill and process until smooth. Season with salt and hot sauce.
3. Light a grill or preheat a grill pan. Rub the swordfish steaks with oil and season with salt and pepper. Grill the fish over moderately high heat until nicely browned outside and just opaque throughout, about 4 minutes per side. Top the fish with the lima bean butter and serve right away. —*Lee Woolver*
MAKE AHEAD The lima bean butter can be refrigerated overnight.

WINE Floral, wild strawberry–scented rosé: 2010 Domaine Houchart.

● HEALTHY ● MAKE AHEAD ○ VEGETARIAN ● STAFF FAVORITE

grilled swordfish with lima bean and herb butter

Whole Grilled Fish with Crispy Garlic and Red Chiles

⏱ TOTAL: 45 MIN • 6 SERVINGS ●

Six 18-inch-long banana leaves, rinsed (see Note)
3 tablespoons minced fresh ginger
6 scallions, white and green parts thinly sliced separately
Two 2-pound whole red snappers
¼ cup sherry
¼ cup low-sodium soy sauce
½ cup vegetable oil
8 large garlic cloves, thinly sliced
2 fresh long red chiles, seeded and thinly sliced
Salt
½ cup cilantro leaves
Lime wedges, for serving

1. Light a grill and line the grate with lightly oiled heavy-duty aluminum foil. Arrange the banana leaves in 2 stacks of 3 and sprinkle each with one-fourth of the ginger and scallion whites. Cut 3 gashes into the flesh on both sides of each fish, cutting to the bone. Set the fish on the banana leaves and scatter the remaining ginger and scallion whites on top. Sprinkle with the sherry and soy sauce. Fold the leaves over the fish and tie each packet in 3 places with kitchen string.

mediterranean rub for seafood

This quick and easy spice mixture is terrific on fish and shellfish. Massage the rub onto the seafood before throwing it on the grill.

In a skillet, combine 2 tablespoons fennel seeds with 1 tablespoon each of coriander seeds, celery salt and lemon zest. Toast until fragrant. Let cool, then grind. Stir in 1 tablespoon coarse sea salt. —*Pete Evans*

2. Place the packets on the grate, close the grill and cook over high heat for 25 minutes, turning the packets once, until a thermometer inserted in the thickest part of the fish registers 140°. Carefully transfer the packets to a platter and let rest for 2 minutes. Cut them open and peel back the banana leaves.
3. In a skillet, heat the oil. Add the garlic and chiles and cook over low heat, stirring, until the garlic is crisp, 2 minutes. Spoon the oil, garlic and chiles over the fish; season with salt. Scatter the cilantro and scallion greens on top; serve with lime wedges. —*Pete Evans*
NOTE Banana leaves are available at Latin and Asian markets.

WINE Lemony Australian white: 2009 Torbreck Woodcutter's Semillon.

Grilled Opah with Olives

⏱ TOTAL: 20 MIN • 4 SERVINGS

1 tablespoon unsalted butter
Extra-virgin olive oil
1 anchovy fillet, chopped
¼ teaspoon crushed red pepper
1 tablespoon Italian pine nuts
4 teaspoons chopped capers
2 Picholine olives, pitted and chopped
1 tablespoon fresh lemon juice
Salt
Four 6-ounce opah or swordfish steaks (1 inch thick), see Note

1. In a saucepan, melt the butter in 1 tablespoon of olive oil. Cook over moderate heat until the butter browns slightly and smells nutty, 2 minutes. Add the anchovy, crushed red pepper, pine nuts, capers, olives and lemon juice and cook for 1 minute. Season with salt and remove from the heat.
2. Light a grill or preheat a grill pan. Rub the fish with oil and season with salt. Grill over high heat until just cooked through, 1½ minutes per side. Slice each steak into 4 pieces. Spoon the topping over the fish and serve. —*Erik Anderson*
NOTE Opah is available at specialty fish markets or *honolulufish.com.*

WINE Vibrant, medium-bodied Italian white: 2010 Argiolas Costamolino Vermentino.

Halibut and Summer Vegetables en Papillote

ACTIVE: 30 MIN; TOTAL: 1 HR 30 MIN
4 SERVINGS ● ●

1 pint cherry tomatoes, halved
1 tablespoon extra-virgin olive oil
1 tablespoon balsamic vinegar
1 tablespoon thyme leaves
Kosher salt and freshly ground pepper
3 tablespoons unsalted butter
Four 6-ounce halibut steaks (about 1 inch thick)
2 tablespoons fresh lemon juice
1 lemon, thinly sliced into 12 rounds
¼ cup Niçoise olives
5 baby zucchini, quartered lengthwise
1 teaspoon ground coriander seeds

1. Preheat the oven to 350°. On a small baking sheet, toss the halved cherry tomatoes with the olive oil, balsamic vinegar and thyme. Arrange the tomatoes cut side up and season with salt and pepper. Bake the tomatoes for 45 minutes, until slightly dried.
2. In a large skillet, melt 1 tablespoon of the butter. Season the halibut steaks with salt and freshly ground pepper and add to the skillet. Cook over moderately high heat until lightly browned on one side, about 3 minutes; transfer the halibut to a plate.
3. Add the remaining 2 tablespoons of butter to the skillet and cook over moderate heat until it just starts to brown, about 2 minutes. Remove from the heat, stir in the lemon juice and season with salt and pepper.
4. Lay four 15-inch-long sheets of parchment paper on a work surface. Arrange 3 lemon slices in the center of each sheet and top with a halibut steak, seared side up. Scatter the tomatoes, olives and zucchini evenly around the fish, spoon on the butter sauce and sprinkle with the coriander. Fold the parchment over the fish and vegetables and fold the edge over itself in small pleats to seal.
5. Transfer the papillotes to a baking sheet. Bake for 15 minutes, until slightly puffed. Snip the parchment open with scissors and serve. —*Nikole Herriott*

WINE Unoaked Chardonnay: 2009 A to Z.

● HEALTHY ● MAKE AHEAD ● VEGETARIAN ● STAFF FAVORITE

Roasted Halibut with Wine-Braised Fennel

⏲ TOTAL: 40 MIN • 6 SERVINGS ●

Chef and Food Network star Alexandra Guarnaschelli loves to serve her raisin-studded braised fennel with a meaty white fish like halibut. Roasting the large fish fillet whole is a great way to serve a small crowd.

- 3 tablespoons extra-virgin olive oil
- 3 fennel bulbs, cut through the cores into 1-inch-thick wedges
- Salt and freshly ground black pepper
- ¼ teaspoon crushed red pepper
- 1 cup plus 1 tablespoon dry white wine
- 2 bay leaves
- ¼ cup golden raisins
- 1 small shallot, minced
- One 2½-pound skinless halibut or striped bass fillet

1. Preheat the oven to 450°. In a large skillet, heat 2 tablespoons of the oil. Add the fennel cut side down, season with salt and black pepper and sprinkle with the crushed red pepper. Cover and cook over moderate heat until browned, about 12 minutes, turning the wedges halfway through. Add 1 cup of the wine, ¼ cup of water, the bay leaves and raisins and simmer over low heat, turning a few times, until most of the wine has evaporated and the fennel is tender, about 15 minutes. Discard the bay leaves; season the fennel with salt and black pepper.

2. Meanwhile, spread the minced shallot in the shape of the fish fillet on a rimmed baking sheet and drizzle with the remaining 1 tablespoon of wine. Season the skinned side of the fillet with salt and black pepper and set it down on the minced shallot. Rub the top of the fish with the remaining 1 tablespoon of olive oil and season with salt and black pepper. Roast the halibut on the top shelf of the oven for about 12 minutes, until it is barely opaque in the center.

3. Transfer the halibut and its cooking juices to a platter, spoon the braised fennel alongside and serve. —*Alexandra Guarnaschelli*
WINE Crisp, salty Spanish white: 2009 Salneval Albariño.

Whole Fish Roasted with Potatoes and Thyme

ACTIVE: 30 MIN; TOTAL: 1 HR 20 MIN
6 SERVINGS ● ●

F&W's Kristin Donnelly became a convert to cooking whole fish, which she says is "amazingly easy, delicious and cheaper than fillets."

- 2 pounds baby Yukon Gold potatoes, halved
- 18 small cipollini onions or large shallots, peeled and quartered
- 3 tablespoons extra-virgin olive oil
- 12 thyme sprigs
- Salt and freshly ground pepper
- Two 2-pound cleaned whole black bass, striped bass or other sea bass
- 1 lemon, thinly sliced, plus 1 lemon half for squeezing
- 2 tablespoons finely chopped flat-leaf parsley

1. Preheat the oven to 425° and line a large, rimmed baking sheet with parchment paper.
2. In a large bowl, toss the potatoes and onions with 1½ tablespoons of the olive oil and 4 thyme sprigs and season with salt and freshly ground pepper. Spread on a large rimmed baking sheet and roast for about 20 minutes, until the potatoes are blistered in spots and barely tender.
3. Rub both fish all over with the remaining 1½ tablespoons of oil; season generously with salt. Stuff the cavities with the lemon slices and the remaining 8 thyme sprigs. Stir the potatoes and onions, pushing them toward the sides, and set the fish on the baking sheet. Roast for 30 minutes, until the fish are just cooked through and the potatoes and onions are tender.
4. Transfer the potatoes and onions to a platter. Using 2 forks, pull the skin off the top of the fish and discard. Remove the fillets from the bones and transfer the fish to the platter. Squeeze the lemon juice over the fish, potatoes and onions, sprinkle with the chopped parsley and serve.
—*Kristin Donnelly*
WINE Minerally Sauvignon Blanc: 2010 Philippe Raimbault Les Godons Sancerre.

Grilled Striped Bass with Indian-Spiced Tomato Salad

⏲ TOTAL: 30 MIN • 4 SERVINGS ● ●

This summery grilled bass with ginger-spiced tomatoes is a favorite of New York chef Floyd Cardoz, an avid fisherman.

- 1 tablespoon whole black peppercorns
- 1 tablespoon coriander seeds
- ¼ cup plus 2 tablespoons extra-virgin olive oil
- ¼ cup chopped basil
- 2 tablespoons red wine vinegar
- 1 medium shallot, minced
- 1 tablespoon minced fresh ginger
- ½ teaspoon sugar
- 2 pounds assorted heirloom tomatoes, cut into 1-inch dice
- Salt
- 1 teaspoon chopped rosemary
- Four 6-ounce wild striped bass fillets with skin
- Freshly ground pepper

1. In a small skillet, toast the peppercorns and coriander seeds over moderately high heat until fragrant, 30 seconds. Transfer to a spice grinder and let cool completely. Grind the peppercorns and coriander to a powder.
2. In a large bowl, combine ¼ cup of the olive oil with the ground spices, basil, red wine vinegar, shallot, ginger and sugar. Add the tomatoes and toss to coat with the dressing. Season the tomatoes with salt.
3. Light a grill or preheat a grill pan. In a shallow baking dish, combine the remaining 2 tablespoons of olive oil with the rosemary. Season the bass with salt and pepper and coat with the rosemary oil. Grill the bass over moderately high heat, skin side down, until nicely charred and crisp on the bottom, 3 minutes. Turn the bass and cook until just opaque in the center, 3 minutes longer.
4. Using a slotted spoon, transfer the tomato salad to plates. Set the bass fillets on the tomatoes, spoon the tomato dressing over and around the fish and serve.
—*Floyd Cardoz*
WINE Robust, juicy rosé from Spain: 2010 Bodegas Olivares.

Salt-Crusted Snapper with Eggplant-Raisin Puree

ACTIVE: 30 MIN; TOTAL: 1 HR 45 MIN
4 SERVINGS ●

According to *Top Chef* Season 6 winner Michael Voltaggio, "There's something sexy about baking a whole fish in a big pile of salt. And then cracking into the salt crust to reveal a fish that's perfectly cooked and seasoned inside."

Three 4-inch cinnamon sticks
1 medium eggplant (1 pound)
¼ cup golden raisins
2 tablespoons extra-virgin olive oil
Sea salt
Cayenne pepper
3 pounds kosher salt
2 cups water
One 2-pound cleaned red snapper
2 bay leaves
½ lemon, preferably Meyer lemon, cut into wedges

1. Preheat the oven to 400°. Poke the cinnamon sticks into the eggplant. Roast the eggplant on a baking sheet until it is tender, about 50 minutes. Transfer the eggplant to a bowl, cover with plastic wrap and let cool slightly. Discard the cinnamon sticks and then peel the eggplant.
2. In a microwave-safe bowl, cover the raisins with water and microwave at high power until plumped, about 30 seconds. Drain the raisins and transfer them to a blender. Add the roasted eggplant and the olive oil and puree until smooth. Season the puree with sea salt and cayenne.
3. In a large bowl, mix the kosher salt with the water until it is the consistency of moist sand. On a parchment paper–lined baking sheet, mound one-fourth of the salt slightly larger than the fish. Lay the fish on the salt and fill its cavity with the bay leaves and lemon wedges. Poke a short skewer into the thickest part of the fish, just behind the head. Pack the remaining kosher salt over and around the fish to enclose it; leave the skewer visible in the salt mixture.
4. Bake the fish until an instant-read thermometer inserted in the skewer hole registers 135°, about 35 minutes. Let the fish rest for 5 minutes; crack and remove the salt crust. Serve the fish without the skin, with the eggplant puree alongside.
—*Michael Voltaggio*
SERVE WITH Arugula salad.
WINE Aromatic, dry Provençal rosé: 2010 Commanderie de la Bargemone.

Steamed Snapper with Mustard Greens

⏱ **TOTAL: 40 MIN • 4 SERVINGS** ●

½ cup coarsely shredded daikon
½ cup *ponzu* sauce (see Note)
2 tablespoons canola oil
6 ounces shiitake mushrooms, stems discarded and caps thinly sliced
½ small head napa cabbage, thinly sliced crosswise (4 cups)
4 ounces mustard greens—stems discarded, leaves coarsely chopped
Salt and freshly ground pepper
1½ tablespoons soy sauce
1½ tablespoons mirin
1½ tablespoons water
Four 4-ounce red snapper fillets

1. In a small bowl, toss the shredded daikon with the *ponzu* sauce.
2. In a large nonstick skillet, heat the oil until shimmering. Add the shiitake and cook over high heat until lightly browned, about 6 minutes. Add the cabbage and greens and season with salt and pepper. Cook, stirring occasionally, until wilted, 3 minutes. Stir in the soy sauce, mirin and water. Arrange the fish over the greens and season with salt and pepper. Cover and cook over moderate heat until the snapper flakes with a fork, about 8 minutes. Transfer to plates and serve with the daikon and *ponzu* sauce.
—*David Myers*
NOTE Japanese *ponzu* is a soy-based citrus sauce available at Japanese markets and the Asian section of most supermarkets.
WINE Tangy, unoaked Oregon Chardonnay: 2009 Chehalem Inox.

Hibiscus-and-Mezcal-Cured Snapper

ACTIVE: 25 MIN; TOTAL: 2 HR 5 MIN
6 SERVINGS ● ●

½ tablespoon poppy seeds
½ cup dried hibiscus flowers (see Note)
1 cup boiling water
¼ cup mezcal
2 tablespoons kosher salt
2 tablespoons light brown sugar
Finely grated zest of ½ grapefruit
Finely grated zest of 1 lime
Six 4-ounce skinless red snapper fillets (¾ inch thick)
1 large, ripe passion fruit, halved
1 tablespoon fresh lime juice
1 medium shallot, minced
2 teaspoons Asian fish sauce
2 European cucumbers—peeled, seeded and cut into a julienne
¼ cup chopped cilantro

1. In a skillet, toast the poppy seeds over high heat, stirring, until they smell slightly nutty, about 2 minutes.
2. In a heatproof bowl, cover the hibiscus flowers with the boiling water and let steep for 1 hour. Strain into a bowl.
3. Add the mezcal to the hibiscus liquid along with the salt, brown sugar and grapefruit and lime zests. Put the snapper fillets in a large, resealable plastic bag and add the hibiscus liquid. Refrigerate, turning the fish often, until red and lightly cured, 45 minutes.
4. Meanwhile, scoop the passion fruit pulp and seeds into a large bowl and add the lime juice, shallot and fish sauce. Add the cucumbers and cilantro and toss the salad well.
5. Using a sharp knife, thinly slice the fillets and fan the slices out on plates. Arrange the cucumber salad alongside. Sprinkle with the toasted poppy seeds and serve.
—*Zakary Pelaccio*
NOTE Dried hibiscus flowers are available at health-food stores, Latin and Caribbean markets and tea shops.
WINE Tropical fruit–scented, lively Sauvignon Blanc: 2010 Indaba.

● HEALTHY ● MAKE AHEAD ○ VEGETARIAN ● STAFF FAVORITE

salt-crusted snapper with eggplant-raisin puree

Herb-and-Chile-Marinated Fish Shashlik

TOTAL: 45 MIN PLUS 4 HR MARINATING
MAKES 8 SKEWERS ●

Russians usually make these kebabs with sturgeon. Since most wild sturgeon is now endangered, look for some that is sustainably farmed, or try black cod or swordfish.

 2 medium onions, finely chopped
 2 large garlic cloves, finely chopped
 1 jalapeño, finely chopped
 1 fresh red chile, finely chopped
 1 cup chopped dill
 1 cup chopped parsley
 1 cup dry white wine
 4 pounds firm, full-flavored skinless
     fish fillets, cut into 2-inch pieces
Vegetable oil, for brushing
Salt and freshly ground pepper
Lemon wedges and grilled flatbread,
     for serving

1. In a large bowl, toss the onions with the garlic, jalapeño, red chile, dill, parsley and wine. Add the fish and stir to coat thoroughly. Cover and refrigerate for 4 hours.
2. Light a grill. Thread the fish onto 8 metal skewers, leaving a small space between each piece. Brush with oil and season with salt and pepper. Grill over high heat, turning, until lightly charred and just opaque throughout, about 12 minutes. Serve with lemon wedges and grilled flatbread. *—Dmitry Leonov*
WINE Citrusy Vermentino: 2009 Bisson Golfo del Tigullio Vignaerta.

ingredient tip

curry powder The sweet spice blend adds depth to dishes like Curried Cod and Mussels (right) and Ocean Trout with Curried Lentils (opposite).

Curried Cod and Mussels

:D **TOTAL: 30 MIN • 4 SERVINGS**

French superchef Alain Ducasse cooks mussels, then removes the top half of each shell before serving them with haddock and a curry sauce with mussel jus. Home cooks can serve the mussels with both of their shells and replace the haddock with easier-to-find cod.

 ¼ cup dried porcini mushrooms
 ¾ cup boiling water
 1 tablespoon extra-virgin olive oil
 ¼ cup minced shallots (about 1 large)
 1 Granny Smith apple, finely diced
 1 garlic clove, minced
 1 tablespoon Madras curry powder
 2 thyme sprigs
Salt and freshly ground pepper
 2 pounds mussels, scrubbed
 ½ cup dry white wine
 ½ cup heavy cream
 1 pound skinless cod fillets—bones
     removed, fish cut into 2-inch chunks
Crusty bread, for serving

1. Soak the dried porcini mushrooms in the boiling water until they are softened, about 10 minutes. Strain the mushrooms, reserving the soaking liquid, and rinse to remove any grit. Finely chop the mushrooms.
2. In a large pot, heat the oil. Add the shallots, apple, garlic, curry powder, thyme sprigs and porcini and season with salt and pepper. Cook over moderate heat, stirring, until the shallots are softened, about 5 minutes.
3. Add the mussels and toss. Add the wine. Bring to a boil, cover and cook over high heat until the mussels have opened, 3 minutes. Discard any mussels that do not open. Add the cream and ½ cup of the porcini soaking liquid, stopping before you reach the grit. Bring to a simmer. Nestle the cod in the broth, cover and cook until the fish lightly flakes, 4 minutes. Discard the thyme sprigs. Transfer the cod and mussels to large bowls and spoon the broth on top. Serve with crusty bread. *—Alain Ducasse*
WINE Ripe, citrusy Sauvignon Blanc from California: 2010 Brander.

Cod with Fresh Tomato Sauce and Arborio Rice

ACTIVE: 30 MIN; TOTAL: 1 HR
4 SERVINGS ●

 6 tablespoons extra-virgin olive oil
 5 large garlic cloves, minced
 ¼ teaspoon crushed red pepper
 3 pounds tomatoes, coarsely chopped
 ⅛ teaspoon saffron threads, crumbled
 5 oregano sprigs
Salt and freshly ground black pepper
Zest of 1 orange, in 1-inch-wide strips,
     plus finely grated zest for garnish
 5 bay leaves
 3 whole cloves
 1 cup arborio rice
Four 4-ounce skinless cod or
     halibut fillets
Chopped parsley, for garnish

1. In a large, deep skillet, heat ¼ cup of the olive oil. Add the garlic and crushed red pepper and cook over moderate heat until the garlic is golden, about 1 minute. Add the tomatoes and saffron and cook over moderate heat until the tomatoes just begin to soften, about 5 minutes. Add the oregano and season with salt and black pepper. Cook the sauce over moderately low heat, stirring and crushing the tomatoes with a spoon, until the sauce is thickened and the liquid is reduced, about 35 minutes. Discard the oregano.
2. Meanwhile, in a large pot of boiling salted water, combine the orange zest strips, bay leaves, cloves, rice and 1 tablespoon of the olive oil and cook until the rice is al dente, about 15 to 18 minutes. Drain the rice, discarding the zest, bay leaves and cloves. Return the rice to the pot. Add the remaining 1 tablespoon of olive oil and season with salt.
3. Nestle the cod in the tomato sauce and cook, turning the fillets once, until just opaque throughout, about 12 minutes.
4. Spoon the rice into bowls and top with the cod and sauce. Sprinkle with parsley and finely grated orange zest and serve. *—Jessica Theroux*
WINE Zippy, lemony Sauvignon Blanc: 2010 75 Wine Company.

● HEALTHY ● MAKE AHEAD ● VEGETARIAN ● STAFF FAVORITE

Ten-Minute Salt Cod with Corn and Littleneck Clams

🕐 **TOTAL: 40 MIN • 4 SERVINGS** ●

Instead of using salt cod, a classic Portuguese ingredient that takes days to soak, George Mendes, the chef at New York City's Aldea and an F&W Best New Chef 2011, quick-cures fresh cod by standing it in kosher salt for only 10 minutes. He says cod is naturally soft and flaky ("as well as bland," he adds), so salting gives it a firmer texture and a more pronounced flavor.

Four 5-ounce skinless center-cut
    cod fillets
½ cup kosher salt
2 ears of corn, shucked
1 tablespoon unsalted butter
1 teaspoon fresh lemon juice
Freshly ground white pepper
¼ cup extra-virgin olive oil
Wondra flour, for dusting
20 littleneck clams, scrubbed
2 garlic cloves, minced
2 cilantro sprigs
1 thyme sprig
½ cup dry white wine
½ teaspoon sweet smoked paprika
1 tablespoon chopped parsley
Crusty bread, for serving

1. Set the cod on a plate and cover all over with the salt. Let stand for exactly 10 minutes. Rinse off the salt and pat the cod dry.
2. Meanwhile, bring a medium saucepan of water to a boil. Add the corn and cook for 2 minutes; drain and pat dry. Cut the kernels off the cobs. In a small skillet, toss the corn with the butter and lemon juice and season with white pepper. Cook the corn until heated through, about 1 minute.
3. In a large, deep nonstick skillet, heat the olive oil. Dust the cod with Wondra flour and season with white pepper. Add the fish to the pan, skinned side down, and cook over high heat until golden, about 4 minutes. Flip the cod and cook over moderate heat for 1 minute. Add the clams, garlic, cilantro and thyme and season with pepper. Add the wine, cover and cook over moderate heat until the

clams open and the fish is cooked through, about 6 minutes. Discard the herb sprigs and any clams that do not open.
4. Rewarm the corn and spoon it into 4 shallow bowls. Top with the cod and sprinkle with the smoked paprika. Spoon the clams and broth all around and garnish with the parsley. Serve right away, with crusty bread.
—*George Mendes*

WINE Juicy Portuguese white: 2010 Luis Pato Maria Gomes.

Ocean Trout with Curried Lentils and Spring Onions

ACTIVE: 30 MIN; TOTAL: 1 HR
4 SERVINGS ●

Vadouvan is a spice blend of curry leaves, mustard seeds, shallots and garlic. At GT Fish & Oyster in Chicago, chef Giuseppe Tentori tops *vadouvan* lentils with Tasmanian ocean trout and caramelized spring onions.

3 tablespoons vegetable oil
1 small onion, finely diced
1 carrot, finely diced
1 large celery rib, finely diced
1½ tablespoons *vadouvan* (see Note)
    or curry powder
¼ cup dry white wine
1½ cups French green lentils
Salt and freshly ground pepper
3 tablespoons extra-virgin olive oil
8 spring onions with small 1-inch
    bulbs, halved lengthwise through
    the bulbs and greens
Four 6-ounce Tasmanian ocean trout
    fillets with skin

1. In a medium saucepan, heat 2 tablespoons of the vegetable oil until shimmering. Add the onion, carrot and celery, cover and cook over moderate heat, stirring, until softened, 5 minutes. Add the *vadouvan* and cook, stirring, until fragrant, 1 minute. Add the wine and boil for 1 minute. Add the lentils and 2½ cups of water and bring to a boil. Cover and cook over moderately low heat until the lentils are almost tender, 20 minutes. Uncover and simmer the lentils until slightly saucy, 5 minutes longer. Season with salt and pepper.

2. Preheat the oven to 350°. In large ovenproof skillet, heat the olive oil. Add the spring onions cut side down and cook until browned, about 4 minutes. Turn the onions over and bake them in the oven until tender and caramelized, about 10 minutes.
3. In a large skillet, heat the remaining 1 tablespoon of vegetable oil. Season the trout with salt and pepper and add to the skillet, skin side down. Cook over moderately high heat until the skin is browned and crisp, about 2 minutes. Turn the trout and cook until medium-rare, about 1 minute longer.
4. Spoon the lentils onto plates. Top with the trout fillets and spring onions and serve.
—*Giuseppe Tentori*

NOTE *Vadouvan* can be purchased online at *thespicehouse.com.*
MAKE AHEAD The curried lentils can be made up to 2 days ahead.
BEER Belgian-inspired black saison: Goose Island Squid Ink Saison.

healthy dinner in an hour

This light, satisfying three-course menu from Cooking with Italian Grandmothers *author Jessica Theroux is ready and on the table in 60 minutes.*

mixed greens and herb salad with figs and walnuts (page 42)
"Toss it with your hands," says Theroux, so you don't bruise the delicate salad leaves.

cod with fresh tomato sauce and arborio rice (opposite)
A garlic-tomato sauce for cod gets Sicilian flavor from orange zest and saffron threads.

honey-roasted apricots with amaretti cookies (page 342)
Roasting apricots turns them into "sticky versions of themselves."

Trout with Preserved Lemons, Raisins and Pine Nuts

⏱ **TOTAL: 45 MIN • 4 SERVINGS** ●

In Morocco, the mountains of the Middle Atlas region are the only source for trout. "It's so high up, you can go skiing there," says legendary cookbook author and Moroccan cuisine expert Paula Wolfert. "Parts of the region look like Switzerland." This light, brothy dish reminded her of one she had at famed French chef Michel Bras's restaurant in southwestern France. In fact, Wolfert uses his method here, poaching the fish gently in a preserved-lemon broth so the texture stays silky.

Two 8-ounce skinless trout fillets,
    cut into 1-inch pieces
Salt and freshly ground black pepper
Cayenne pepper
  3 tablespoons coarsely chopped
     cilantro
  2 tablespoons golden raisins
  6 scallions, halved lengthwise
     and sliced ⅛ inch thick on the
     diagonal (1 cup)
  2 medium carrots, sliced
     ⅛ inch thick on the diagonal
  1 teaspoon honey
  1 preserved lemon—pulp removed,
     peel rinsed and minced (see Note)
  1 tablespoon pine nuts
  1 tablespoon extra-virgin olive oil

1. In a shallow dish, season the fish with salt, black pepper and cayenne; spread in a single layer. Sprinkle the fish with 1 tablespoon of the cilantro. Cover with plastic wrap and refrigerate while you prepare the rest of the dish.
2. In a small bowl, cover the golden raisins with warm water and let stand until plump, about 10 minutes. Drain.
3. Meanwhile, in a large, deep skillet, combine the scallions and carrots with 4 cups of water and simmer over moderate heat until the carrots are tender, about 10 minutes. Add the honey, preserved lemon peel, raisins and pine nuts, season with salt and black pepper and simmer for 10 minutes longer.
4. Slip the trout into the broth, cover and simmer over moderately low heat until the fish is just barely cooked through, about 10 minutes. Drizzle the fish with the olive oil, garnish with the remaining 2 tablespoons of cilantro and serve. —*Paula Wolfert*

NOTE Preserved lemons are cured in salt and lemon juice. They are available at specialty food markets and *chefshop.com*.

WINE Zesty California Sauvignon Blanc: 2010 Teira.

Trout with Warm Pine Nut Dressing and Fennel Puree

ACTIVE: 35 MIN; TOTAL: 1 HR
4 SERVINGS

  1 medium fennel bulb, cut into
     thin wedges
  6 garlic cloves, peeled
  ¼ cup plus 2 teaspoons canola oil
Salt and freshly ground black pepper
  ¼ cup dried porcini mushrooms
     (about ¼ ounce)
  ½ cup boiling water
  ¼ cup pine nuts, preferably Italian
  1½ tablespoons balsamic vinegar
Four 4-ounce trout fillets, pin bones
     removed
  2 ounces mesclun

1. Preheat the oven to 425°. Arrange the fennel wedges and 5 of the garlic cloves on a 12-inch sheet of foil and drizzle with 1 tablespoon of the canola oil. Fold the foil into a packet and roast for about 45 minutes, until the packet is sizzling and the fennel and garlic cloves are tender. Transfer the fennel and garlic to a food processor and puree until smooth; season with salt and pepper.
2. Meanwhile, in a microwave-safe container, combine the dried porcini with the boiling water. Microwave on high power for 2 minutes, until the porcini are plumped. In a medium skillet, heat 1 tablespoon of the oil. Add the pine nuts and the remaining 1 clove of garlic and cook over moderate heat until the nuts are golden, about 3 minutes. Remove from the heat and strain the porcini liquid into the skillet, stopping before you reach the grit at the bottom. (Reserve the porcini for another use.) Add the balsamic vinegar and simmer over moderate heat until the liquid is reduced to 2 tablespoons, about 5 minutes; discard the garlic. Add 2 tablespoons of the oil and season the dressing with salt and pepper.
3. Heat the remaining 2 teaspoons of oil in a large nonstick skillet. Season the trout fillets with salt and pepper. Add one fillet at a time to the skillet, skin side down; press with a spatula to flatten for 30 seconds. Repeat with the remaining fillets until the pan is full. Cook over moderately high heat until the trout is browned on the bottom and nearly cooked through, about 3 minutes. Flip the fish and cook for 30 seconds longer.
4. Spread the fennel puree on plates and top with the trout. Drizzle half of the dressing on top. Add the greens to the remaining dressing in the skillet and toss to coat. Mound the greens on the fish and serve. —*David Bouley*

WINE Smooth, pear-scented Oregon Pinot Gris: 2009 Bethel Heights Vineyard.

Smoked Trout Salad with Mustard Dressing

⏱ **TOTAL: 20 MIN • 4 SERVINGS** ● ●

  1 medium shallot, chopped
  1½ tablespoons sherry vinegar
  1½ tablespoons red wine vinegar
  1 tablespoon Dijon mustard
  2½ tablespoons vegetable oil
  1½ tablespoons walnut oil
Salt and freshly ground pepper
  2 Belgian endives, leaves separated
  1 Granny Smith apple—halved,
     cored and very thinly sliced on
     a mandoline
  ½ cup walnuts, coarsely chopped
  ½ pound boneless smoked trout
     or whitefish, broken into pieces
  1 cup small watercress sprigs

1. In a blender, puree the shallot, both vinegars and the mustard. Gradually blend in the oils. Season with salt and pepper.
2. Arrange the endives, apple, walnuts, trout and watercress on plates. Drizzle with the dressing and serve. —*DJ Olsen*

WINE Apricoty, amphora-aged white: 2006 Vinoterra Kisi.

● HEALTHY ● MAKE AHEAD ● VEGETARIAN ● STAFF FAVORITE

smoked trout salad with mustard dressing

Smoked Mackerel Salad with Crunchy Vegetables

⏱ **TOTAL: 25 MIN • 4 SERVINGS** ● ● ●

"The fish we eat in Denmark—mackerel, herring, salmon—have beneficial omega-3 oils," says Trina Hahnemann, author of *The Nordic Diet*. Any smoked fish will work well here.

- ½ cup 2 percent plain Greek yogurt
- 3 tablespoons grated fresh horseradish
- 1½ tablespoons fresh lemon juice
- 1½ teaspoons apple cider vinegar
- ½ teaspoon sugar
- 9 ounces smoked mackerel, skinned and flaked (2 cups)
- One 12-ounce seedless cucumber, peeled and finely diced (2 cups)
- 5 large radishes, cut into matchsticks
- 1 large Granny Smith apple, diced
- 2 tablespoons snipped chives
- Salt and freshly ground pepper
- 1 head of romaine lettuce

In a large bowl, whisk the yogurt with the horseradish, lemon juice, vinegar and sugar. Fold in the fish, cucumber, radishes, apple and chives; season with salt and pepper. Top the lettuce leaves with the salad and serve. —*Trina Hahnemann*

Grilled Sardines with Piquillo Pepper Sauce

ACTIVE: 30 MIN; TOTAL: 1 HR 4 SERVINGS

Sardines have very low levels of mercury relative to larger fish. Here, they're grilled and served with smoky piquillo pepper sauce for a bold Spanish flavor.

- 12 fresh large sardines, cleaned (have your fishmonger do this)
- ¾ cup extra-virgin olive oil
- 3 garlic cloves, very finely chopped
- Salt and freshly ground black pepper
- ½ cup jarred piquillo peppers (4 ounces)
- 2 tablespoons sherry vinegar
- Pinch of cayenne pepper
- Grilled peasant bread, for serving

1. Arrange the sardines in a shallow baking dish. Pour ½ cup of the olive oil over the sardines and top with two-thirds of the chopped garlic. Season with salt and black pepper. Let the sardines stand at room temperature for 30 minutes.

2. Meanwhile, in a mini food processor, combine the piquillo peppers with the sherry vinegar, cayenne pepper and the remaining chopped garlic; puree until smooth. Add the remaining ¼ cup of olive oil and puree until incorporated. Season the piquillo pepper sauce with salt and pepper.

3. Light a grill or preheat a grill pan. Oil the grill and cook the sardines, flipping them once, until they are lightly charred and cooked through, about 4 minutes. Transfer the sardines to a large platter and serve right away with the piquillo pepper sauce and grilled peasant bread. —*Grace Parisi*

WINE Vibrant, medium-bodied white: 2009 Occhipinti SP68 Bianco.

Fish Grilled in Banana Leaves with Chile-Lime Sauce

⏱ **TOTAL: 30 MIN • 6 SERVINGS** ● ●

For this quick and bold sauce, New York chef Zakary Pelaccio purees fresh lemongrass and ginger with chiles and fish sauce. The sauce goes with any grilled or roasted fish, with or without the banana leaves.

- ¼ cup plus 1 tablespoon palm sugar (see Note) or light brown sugar
- 4 large stalks of fresh lemongrass, tender inner cores of the bottom third only, chopped
- 2 medium shallots, sliced
- 2 garlic cloves, sliced
- 2 tablespoons chopped fresh ginger
- 1 fresh long red chile, chopped
- ⅓ cup fresh lime juice
- 2 tablespoons Asian fish sauce
- ½ cup chopped cilantro
- Six 6-ounce Spanish, Boston or king mackerel fillets with skin
- Vegetable oil, for rubbing
- Salt and freshly ground pepper
- 6 banana leaves, each cut into a 12-by-10-inch piece (see Note)

1. In a blender or mini food processor, combine the palm sugar, lemongrass, shallots, garlic, ginger, chile and lime juice; pulse to make a slightly coarse puree. Transfer to a bowl and stir in the fish sauce and cilantro.

2. Light a grill or preheat a grill pan. Score the skin side of each mackerel fillet 3 or 4 times, rub with oil and season with salt and pepper. Place a fillet skin side up in the center of each banana leaf. Fold up each leaf like an envelope to enclose the fish.

3. Grill the banana leaf packets over moderately high heat until the fish is barely opaque in the center, about 3 minutes per side. Place a packet on each plate and pass the sauce at the table. —*Zakary Pelaccio*

NOTE Palm sugar is available at Asian markets and *amazon.com*. Frozen banana leaves can be purchased in specialty food stores or at *store.gourmetsleuth.com*.

WINE Fruity, concentrated rosé: 2010 Crios de Susana Balbo.

fast fish condiment

vietnamese peach relish

This savory peach relish, which has the flavor of a Vietnamese dipping sauce, is delicious with fish. Use peaches firm enough to hold their shape once diced.

In a mortar (or use a mini food processor), pound 1 minced garlic clove and 1 seeded, minced serrano or jalapeño chile with 2 tablespoons light brown sugar to form a paste. Add 3 tablespoons Asian fish sauce and 2 tablespoons each of fresh lime juice and water. Transfer the mixture to a medium bowl. Stir in 3 peeled, diced peaches. Add ¼ cup chopped cilantro and 2 tablespoons chopped mint. Serve with halibut or shrimp. —*Grace Parisi*

● HEALTHY ● MAKE AHEAD ● VEGETARIAN ● STAFF FAVORITE

grilled sardines with piquillo pepper sauce

Greek Fish Stew

⏱ **TOTAL: 45 MIN • 4 SERVINGS** ●

"On the Greek island of Kalymnos, fishermen make a stew with shellfish, whole fish, lemon and water," says *Bizarre Foods* host Andrew Zimmern. "They eat it straight from the pot with their hands—no bowls. It tastes of sweat and iodine, but it is easily one of the best soups I've ever had. I make my version with halibut, throwing in mussels at the end."

- 6 tablespoons extra-virgin olive oil
- 1 onion, thinly sliced
- 1 medium leek, halved lengthwise and thinly sliced crosswise
- 2 large garlic cloves, minced
- 5 large celery ribs, thinly sliced, plus ¼ cup leaves
- 2 parsley sprigs
- 2 thyme sprigs

Salt and freshly ground pepper

- 1 small lemon, scrubbed and quartered
- 3 cups dry white wine
- 2 cups chicken stock or low-sodium broth

One 1½-pound halibut steak on the bone

- 2 pounds mussels, scrubbed

Crusty bread, for serving

1. In a large enameled cast-iron casserole, heat ¼ cup of the oil. Add the onion, leek, garlic, celery ribs and leaves, parsley and thyme and season with salt and pepper. Cook over moderate heat, stirring occasionally, until the vegetables are softened, about 8 minutes. Add the lemon and wine and simmer over moderately high heat until the wine is reduced by half, about 4 minutes. Add the stock and simmer over moderate heat until reduced by one-third, about 5 minutes.

2. Season the halibut steak with salt and freshly ground pepper and add it to the casserole. Cover and simmer over low heat for about 5 minutes. Turn the halibut and add the mussels. Cover and cook over moderate heat until the mussels open, about 4 minutes. Discard any mussels that don't open. Season with salt and pepper and drizzle with the remaining 2 tablespoons of olive oil. Transfer the stew to a deep dish and serve with crusty bread. —*Andrew Zimmern*

WINE Fragrant Greek white: 2010 Gai'a Notios.

Catalan Fish Stew with Pimentón Mayonnaise

⏱ **TOTAL: 40 MIN • 4 SERVINGS** ●

Grating plum tomatoes for Catalan fish stew makes an instant puree. Cooking the tomato puree with serrano ham and olives adds layers of flavors to the dish.

- 1½ pounds plum tomatoes, halved crosswise
- 3 tablespoons extra-virgin olive oil
- 1 large onion, thinly sliced
- 2 garlic cloves, minced
- 1 cup bottled clam juice
- 4 ounces sliced serrano ham, cut into thin strips
- ⅓ cup pitted green olives, chopped
- 1½ pounds halibut fillet, cut into 2-inch chunks

Kosher salt

- ½ cup mayonnaise
- ½ teaspoon sweet Pimentón de la Vera (smoked Spanish paprika)

1. Using a box grater set in a bowl, carefully grate the cut sides of the tomatoes, stopping when you reach the skin. You should have about 2 cups of tomato pulp.

2. In a large, deep skillet, heat 1 tablespoon of the olive oil. Add the onion and half of the garlic and cook over moderate heat, stirring frequently, until they are softened and just beginning to brown, about 6 minutes. Add the tomato pulp and cook over high heat until it is thickened, about 5 minutes. Add the clam broth and boil until it is reduced by half, about 5 minutes.

3. Add the serrano, olives and halibut and simmer over moderate heat, stirring occasionally, until the fish is cooked through and the stew is thick, about 5 minutes longer.

4. Meanwhile, in a small bowl, using the back of a spoon, mash the remaining garlic to a paste with a pinch of salt. Whisk in the mayonnaise, pimentón and the remaining 2 tablespoons of olive oil.

5. Serve the fish stew in shallow bowls with a dollop of the pimentón mayonnaise. —*Grace Parisi*

SERVE WITH Crusty bread.

WINE Lively, medium-bodied Spanish white: 2009 Finca OS Cobatos Monterrei Godello.

Baked Seafood Dumplings with Saffron Sauce and Swiss Chard

ACTIVE: 1 HR 15 MIN; TOTAL: 3 HR 30 MIN
4 SERVINGS ●

These elegant fish dumplings, also known as *quenelles*, from New York chef April Bloomfield are a hallmark of Lyonnaise cooking. "The word *quenelles* made me think these would be a lot of work," says Bloomfield. "But actually they're fun to make."

DUMPLINGS

- 6 tablespoons unsalted butter, at room temperature
- 2 tablespoons all-purpose flour
- ½ cup milk

Kosher salt

- ½ pound skinless white fish fillets, such as sole, flounder or cod, cut into ½-inch pieces
- 1 large egg white
- 3 large eggs
- ¼ teaspoon freshly ground white pepper
- ¼ teaspoon freshly grated nutmeg

ingredient tip

bottled clam juice With a nice briny flavor similar to homemade fish stock, store-bought clam juice can be used in recipes like Catalan Fish Stew with Pimentón Mayonnaise (right) and Baked Seafood Dumplings with Saffron Sauce and Swiss Chard (far right). Look's Atlantic is a good and widely available brand.

● HEALTHY ● MAKE AHEAD ○ VEGETARIAN ● STAFF FAVORITE

SAFFRON SAUCE AND CHARD

- 1 tablespoon extra-virgin olive oil
- 2 garlic cloves, thinly sliced
- ½ cup dry white wine
- ¼ teaspoon saffron threads
- 2 cups fish stock or bottled clam juice
- 2 cups heavy cream
- 1 tablespoon fresh lemon juice

Salt and freshly ground white pepper

- 1 pound Swiss chard—stems cut into 1-inch pieces, leaves left whole
- 3 tablespoons minced chives

1. MAKE THE DUMPLINGS In a small saucepan, melt 2 tablespoons of the butter. Stir in the flour over low heat to form a paste, then slowly whisk in the milk until smooth. Simmer, whisking often, until thickened, about 7 minutes. Season lightly with salt; transfer the *panade* to a bowl, press plastic wrap directly onto the surface and let it cool to room temperature.

2. In a food processor, puree the fish to a paste. Add the egg white and process until blended and very smooth. Refrigerate the fish paste in the processor bowl until thoroughly chilled, about 20 minutes.

3. Add the *panade* to the fish paste and process until blended. With the machine on, alternately add the eggs and the remaining 4 tablespoons of butter, scraping down the bowl after each addition. Transfer the mixture to a stainless steel bowl and stir in the white pepper, nutmeg and 1¼ teaspoons of salt. Refrigerate the dumpling mixture until thoroughly chilled, about 30 minutes.

4. Bring a large, wide pot of salted water to a boil. Line a large baking sheet with parchment paper. Using a ⅓-cup measure or ice cream scoop, gently shape the mixture into 8 round dumplings. Set the dumplings on the parchment and refrigerate for 5 minutes. Set a large bowl of ice water near the stove.

5. Lower the parchment with the dumplings into the boiling water; discard the paper. Simmer the dumplings over moderate heat, turning once, until firm, 12 minutes. Using a slotted spoon, transfer the dumplings to the ice water and let cool for 10 minutes. Drain the dumplings and pat dry with paper towels.

6. MAKE THE SAFFRON SAUCE AND CHARD In a saucepan, heat the oil. Add the garlic and cook over moderate heat until golden brown, 1 minute. Add the wine and crumble in the saffron. Simmer over moderate heat until the wine has reduced by one-third, 3 minutes. Add the fish stock and boil over high heat until reduced to ½ cup, 15 minutes. Add the cream and simmer over low heat until reduced to 2 cups, 10 minutes. Add the lemon juice; season with salt and pepper.

7. Preheat the oven to 375°. Lightly butter a 9-by-13-inch baking dish. In a large pot of boiling salted water, cook the chard stems until tender, 4 minutes. Using a slotted spoon, transfer the stems to paper towels to dry, then arrange in the prepared dish. Arrange the dumplings on top. Pour the saffron sauce over the dumplings and bake for 20 minutes.

8. Meanwhile, add the Swiss chard leaves to the boiling water and cook until bright green and just tender, about 2 minutes. Drain and squeeze out any excess water. Cut the leaves into small pieces. Sprinkle the dumplings with the chard leaves and baste with the sauce. Bake for about 20 minutes, until the dumplings are nicely glazed. Sprinkle with the chives and serve. —*April Bloomfield*

WINE Vibrant, grassy Sauvignon Blanc: 2010 Morgan Monterey.

Polenta-Crusted Fish Cakes with Spicy Tomato Sauce

⏱ **TOTAL: 45 MIN • 4 SERVINGS** ●

"Fish cakes are perceived as being quite British, and they're always a little dull," says Yotam Ottolenghi, chef and owner of Ottolenghi, a London take-out chain. To make the cakes more vibrant, he adds plenty of herbs and serves them with a tarragon-infused tomato sauce spiked with fresh red chile.

SAUCE

- 1 tablespoon extra-virgin olive oil
- 6 garlic cloves, minced
- 1 large fresh red chile, minced
- 4 large plum tomatoes, chopped
- 1 tablespoon tomato paste
- 1½ tablespoons chopped tarragon

Salt

FISH CAKES

- ¾ pound Yukon Gold potatoes, peeled and cut into 1-inch chunks
- ¼ cup instant polenta
- 1½ pounds skinless cod or halibut fillets, cut into 1-inch chunks
- 4 garlic cloves, minced
- 2 tablespoons chopped parsley
- 2 tablespoons chopped cilantro
- 2 teaspoons kosher salt
- 1½ teaspoons ground cumin
- 1 large egg, lightly beaten
- ½ teaspoon crushed red pepper
- 2 tablespoons canola oil

1. MAKE THE SAUCE In a large skillet, heat the olive oil. Add the garlic and chile and cook over moderately low heat until fragrant, about 3 minutes. Add the tomatoes and cook over moderate heat until thickened, 10 minutes. Stir in the tomato paste and ⅓ cup of water and simmer for 2 minutes longer. Add the tarragon and season with salt.

2. MEANWHILE, MAKE THE FISH CAKES In a saucepan, cover the potatoes with water and bring to a boil. Boil over moderately high heat until tender, about 7 minutes. Drain well and lightly mash the potatoes with a fork.

3. Spread the polenta in a pie plate. In a food processor, combine the fish, garlic, parsley, cilantro, salt, cumin, egg and crushed red pepper and pulse until the fish is coarsely chopped. Transfer to a bowl and fold in the potatoes. Form the mixture into twelve 2-inch cakes (½ inch thick); coat with the polenta.

4. In a large nonstick skillet, heat 1 tablespoon of the canola oil. Add half of the fish cakes and pan-fry over moderately high heat until golden brown and just cooked through, about 3 minutes per side. Transfer the fish cakes to a platter. Repeat with the remaining 1 tablespoon of canola oil and fish cakes, adjusting the heat if the cakes get too dark. Serve the fish cakes hot or at room temperature with the warm tomato sauce. —*Yotam Ottolenghi*

MAKE AHEAD The tomato sauce can be refrigerated overnight. Reheat gently.

WINE Full-bodied southern Italian white: 2009 Librandi Cirò Bianco.

In Duxbury Bay, Massachusetts, Island Creek Oysters founder Skip Bennett (left) and chef Jeremy Sewall prep for a seafood feast including oysters on the half shell with rosé mignonette, OPPOSITE; *recipe, page 225.*

shellfish

Warm Shrimp Salad with Kamut, Red Chile and Tarragon

ACTIVE: 30 MIN; TOTAL: 1 HR 30 MIN
4 SERVINGS ● ●

Kamut is an heirloom variety of wheat with a sweet, almost buttery flavor. F&W's Kristin Donnelly loves using it in this main-course shrimp salad scented with tarragon.

- 1 cup dried kamut or spelt berries (see Note)
- 4 ounces haricots verts, cut into thirds
- 1 tablespoon unsalted butter
- 1 tablespoon extra-virgin olive oil
- 1 large shallot, halved and thinly sliced

Salt

- 2 teaspoons minced fresh red chile
- 1 pound medium shrimp, shelled and deveined
- ¼ cup dry white wine or dry vermouth
- 1½ tablespoons finely chopped tarragon

Lemon wedges, for serving

1. In a heavy, medium saucepan, toast the kamut over moderately high heat until fragrant, 3 to 4 minutes. Add 4 cups of water and bring to a boil. Cover and simmer over moderately low heat until the grains are tender, 1 hour 10 minutes; drain off any excess water.
2. In a medium, deep skillet, combine the haricots verts with ¼ cup of water. Cover and steam over moderately high heat, stirring, until crisp-tender, 3 to 4 minutes. Drain.
3. Wipe out the skillet. Melt the butter in the oil over moderately high heat. Add the shallot, season with salt and cook, stirring, until softened, 2 minutes. Add the chile and cook, stirring, until fragrant. Add the shrimp, season with salt and cook, stirring, until just pink, 3 minutes. Add the wine and cook, stirring, for 1 minute. Stir in the kamut and haricots verts and cook until hot. Stir in the tarragon, season with salt and serve with lemon wedges.
—*Kristin Donnelly*

NOTE Kamut and spelt berries are available at health-food stores.
WINE Strawberry-scented Provençal rosé: 2010 Domaine Sainte Lucie MiP.

Shrimp Slaw with Cilantro-Lime Vinaigrette

⏱ **TOTAL: 40 MIN • 6 SERVINGS** ●

Chef Kent Rathbun's weight loss prompted him to create healthy dishes for his Dallas restaurants. At Rathbun's Blue Plate Kitchen, he makes his jalapeño-spiced coleslaw with crab, shrimp and lobster, but this shrimp-only version is also delicious.

- 1½ pounds medium shrimp, shelled and deveined
- ⅓ cup fresh lime juice
- 3 tablespoons extra-virgin olive oil
- 1 jalapeño, seeded and minced
- 1 garlic clove, minced

Salt and freshly ground pepper

- ½ pound green cabbage, cored and finely shredded (4 cups)
- ¼ pound red cabbage, finely shredded (1½ cups)
- ¼ pound jicama, peeled and cut into thin matchsticks
- 1 medium carrot, coarsely grated
- 1 cup cilantro leaves

1. In a large saucepan of boiling salted water, cook the shrimp until just white throughout, about 1½ minutes. Drain and let cool.
2. In a large bowl, whisk the lime juice with the olive oil, jalapeño and garlic and season with salt and pepper.
3. Add the green and red cabbages, jicama, carrot and cilantro to the bowl and toss well. Add the shrimp, toss again and serve right away. —*Kent Rathbun*

Grilled Shrimp with Apple and Charred Scallions

⏱ **TOTAL: 30 MIN**
8 FIRST-COURSE SERVINGS ● ●

"Shrimp come from all over the world, but I think the kind from coastal Georgia and the Gulf is the best—and it's pretty much a sustainable product," says Hugh Acheson, an F&W Best New Chef 2002 and the chef and co-owner of Five & Ten in Athens, Georgia. Here, he prepares the shrimp as a light appetizer with green apple, charred scallions, sesame seeds and a paprika vinaigrette.

- ¼ cup plus 2½ tablespoons extra-virgin olive oil
- 1 tablespoon sherry vinegar
- 1 tablespoon freshly squeezed lime juice
- ½ teaspoon sweet smoked paprika
- ½ teaspoon Dijon mustard

Salt and freshly ground pepper

- 6 scallions
- 1 pound medium shrimp, shelled and deveined
- 1 Granny Smith apple—peeled, cored and julienned
- 1 tablespoon toasted sesame seeds

1. In a small bowl, whisk ¼ cup plus 1 tablespoon of the olive oil with the vinegar, fresh lime juice, sweet smoked paprika and Dijon mustard. Season the dressing with salt and freshly ground pepper.
2. In a large saucepan of boiling salted water, blanch the scallions until bright green, about 1 minute. Drain the scallions, rinse under cold water and pat dry.
3. Light a grill or preheat a grill pan. Rub the scallions with ½ tablespoon of the olive oil and season with salt and pepper.
4. In a bowl, toss the shrimp with the remaining 1 tablespoon of olive oil and season with salt and pepper.
5. Grill the scallions over high heat until lightly charred, about 30 seconds per side. Grill the shrimp until lightly charred and white throughout, about 1 minute per side. In a medium bowl, toss the apple with 1 tablespoon of the dressing.
6. Cut the scallions into 2-inch lengths. Scatter the scallions and julienned apple on a platter. Arrange the grilled shrimp on top of the scallions and apple.
7. Drizzle the remaining dressing over the grilled shrimp, then sprinkle with the toasted sesame seeds and serve right away.
—*Hugh Acheson*

MAKE AHEAD The dressing in Step 1 and blanched scallions in Step 2 can be prepared and kept in the refrigerator in separate containers for up to 2 days.
WINE Zesty Austrian Riesling: 2009 Schloss Gobelsburg Gobelsburger.

● HEALTHY ● MAKE AHEAD ● VEGETARIAN ● STAFF FAVORITE

warm shrimp salad with kamut, red chile and tarragon

Grilled Shrimp with Sweet Chile Sauce

TOTAL: 30 MIN • 4 FIRST-COURSE SERVINGS ●

Australian chef Pete Evans is especially fond of Thai, Chinese and Indonesian flavors, as evidenced by this grilled shrimp with a sweet-and-sour sauce that mixes ketchup with fish sauce, hoisin, cilantro and mint.

- ¼ cup vegetable oil, plus more for grilling
- 4 garlic cloves, minced
- 2 fresh long red chiles, seeded and minced
- 2 tablespoons julienned fresh ginger
- ½ cup ketchup
- ¼ cup Thai sweet chile sauce
- ¼ cup hoisin sauce
- 1 tablespoon Asian fish sauce
- 1 tablespoon sugar
- 1 scallion, minced
- 2 tablespoons chopped cilantro
- 2 tablespoons chopped mint
- 1 cup halved grape tomatoes
- 12 jumbo shrimp in the shells, butterflied and deveined

Salt and freshly ground pepper

1. In a large saucepan, heat the ¼ cup of oil. Add the garlic, chiles and ginger and cook over moderate heat, stirring, until fragrant, 2 minutes. Add the ketchup, chile sauce, hoisin sauce, fish sauce, sugar and ¼ cup of water. Simmer until slightly thickened, 5 minutes. Spoon 1 cup of the sauce into a bowl and let cool slightly, then stir in the scallion, cilantro, mint and tomatoes.

2. Light a grill or preheat a grill pan. In a bowl, toss the shrimp with oil; season with salt and pepper. Grill over moderately high heat, turning once, until cooked through, 6 minutes. Transfer the shrimp to a large bowl. Add the sauce from the saucepan; toss. Return the shrimp to the grill and cook, turning once, until glazed, 1 minute. Serve the shrimp with the sweet chile sauce. —*Pete Evans*

SERVE WITH Steamed rice.

WINE Lime-scented Riesling from Tasmania: 2009 Frogmore Creek.

Garlic and Paprika Shrimp

ACTIVE: 45 MIN; TOTAL: 2 HR 15 MIN 6 SERVINGS

When he makes this dish at his New York City restaurant Aldea, F&W Best New Chef 2011 George Mendes creates a rich sauce with shrimp heads, then thickens it with xanthan gum. The simpler alternative here is flavored with shrimp shells and thickened with strained vegetables.

- ¼ cup plus 2 tablespoons extra-virgin olive oil
- 1½ pounds large shrimp— shelled and deveined, shells reserved
- 1 small onion, thinly sliced
- 1 fennel bulb, thinly sliced
- 2 inner celery ribs, thinly sliced
- 6 garlic cloves—2 smashed, 4 minced

Pinch of saffron threads, crumbled

- ¼ cup Pernod
- ¼ cup brandy
- 1 teaspoon tomato paste
- 2 tarragon sprigs
- 2 parsley sprigs, plus 1 tablespoon finely chopped parsley
- 3 tablespoons unsalted butter

Salt and freshly ground pepper

- 1½ teaspoons sweet paprika
- 1 tablespoon chopped cilantro
- 2 tablespoons fresh lemon juice

1. In a large pot, heat 2 tablespoons of the oil. Add the shrimp shells and cook over moderate heat until they turn pink, 3 minutes. Add the onion, fennel, celery, smashed garlic and saffron and cook until softened, 5 minutes. Add the Pernod and brandy and cook until evaporated. Stir in the tomato paste, add 6 cups of water and bring to a boil. Simmer until the broth is reduced to 4 cups, 45 minutes. Add the tarragon and parsley sprigs and let stand off the heat for 15 minutes.

2. Strain the liquid, pressing the vegetables to mash them through the sieve. Alternatively, pass the mixture through a food mill. Discard the shrimp shells. Transfer the liquid to a saucepan and simmer until reduced to 2 cups, 30 minutes. Swirl in the butter and season the sauce with salt and pepper.

3. In a large skillet, heat 1 tablespoon of the oil until shimmering. Season the shrimp with salt and pepper, then sauté over high heat, turning once, until nearly cooked, 2 minutes. Transfer the shrimp to a plate. Add the remaining 3 tablespoons of oil to the skillet. Add the minced garlic and cook over low heat until softened and golden, 1 minute. Stir in the paprika. Return the shrimp to the skillet and add the chopped herbs and the lemon juice. Cook for 1 minute longer, until the shrimp are white throughout.

4. Ladle the sauce into bowls and top with the shrimp. Drizzle any garlic oil over the shrimp and serve. —*George Mendes*

WINE Zippy Vinho Verde: 2010 Fâmega.

Spicy Grilled Shrimp with Yuzu Kosho Pesto

TOTAL: 25 MIN • 4 SERVINGS ●

Yuzu *kosho* is a spicy and aromatic Japanese condiment made from hot chiles and ultra-citrusy yuzu zest. It's the key to this super-simple and utterly delicious recipe from F&W Best New Chef 2011 Ricardo Zarate of Mo-Chica in Los Angeles.

- 1½ tablespoons yuzu *kosho* (see Note)
- 1½ teaspoons minced peeled ginger
- 1 garlic clove, minced
- 1 large stalk of fresh lemongrass, pale inner bulb only, minced
- 1½ tablespoons chopped cilantro
- ½ cup extra-virgin olive oil
- 12 jumbo shrimp (about ¾ pound), butterflied in the shell

1. In a small bowl, combine the yuzu *kosho* with the ginger, garlic, lemongrass, cilantro and olive oil. Spread half of the pesto on the shrimp and let stand for 10 minutes.

2. Light a grill or preheat a grill pan. Grill the shrimp over high heat, turning once, until lightly charred and cooked through, 4 minutes. Transfer the shrimp to plates and serve with the remaining pesto. —*Ricardo Zarate*

NOTE Yuzu *kosho* is available at Japanese markets and *chefshop.com*.

WINE Fragrant, medium-bodied Torrontés from Argentina: 2009 Inacayal.

● HEALTHY ● MAKE AHEAD ● VEGETARIAN ● STAFF FAVORITE

Easy Grilled Paella

TOTAL: 1 HR • 6 SERVINGS

- 3 cups fish stock or low-sodium chicken broth
- ½ pound large shrimp, shelled and deveined, shells reserved

Pinch of saffron threads, crumbled

- ½ lemon
- 2 tablespoons extra-virgin olive oil
- 6 ounces fresh chorizo (2 small links), sliced ½ inch thick
- 2 ripe tomatoes, finely chopped
- 2 garlic cloves, minced
- 1 teaspoon smoked paprika
- 1½ cups Calasparra or arborio rice (about 10 ounces)
- ½ pound cleaned squid—bodies halved lengthwise, scored in a crosshatch pattern and cut into 2-inch pieces
- 1 pound cockles, scrubbed
- ½ pound jumbo lump crabmeat
- 1 cup roasted red peppers (5 ounces), cut into strips
- 2 tablespoons chopped parsley

Hot sauce and lemon wedges, for serving

1. In a large saucepan, combine the stock with the shrimp shells and saffron. Squeeze in the lemon, add the half to the saucepan and bring to a simmer. Remove from the heat and let stand for 10 minutes. Strain the broth and discard the solids.

2. Meanwhile, light a grill. Place a large flameproof skillet on the grill and heat the olive oil in it. Add the chorizo, cover the skillet and close the grill. Cook over high heat until the chorizo is sizzling and lightly browned, about 5 minutes. Add the tomatoes, garlic and smoked paprika, cover the skillet, close the grill and cook, stirring once or twice, until the tomatoes are softened, about 5 minutes. Add the rice and stir to coat with the tomato mixture. Stir in the shrimp broth. Cover the skillet, close the grill and cook until half of the broth has been absorbed, about 10 minutes. Stir in the shrimp, squid and cockles. Cover the skillet, close the grill and cook until the rice is al dente and has formed a crust on the bottom and side of the skillet and the

seafood is cooked, about 8 minutes. Fold in the crab, peppers and parsley and cook just until heated through. Serve with hot sauce and lemon wedges. —*Pete Evans*

WINE Bright Australian Pinot Gris: 2009 Innocent Bystander.

Goan Shrimp Curry

TOTAL: 20 MIN • 4 SERVINGS ●

- 3 dried red chiles
- ¼ cup dried unsweetened coconut flakes
- 1½ teaspoons coriander seeds
- 1 teaspoon cumin seeds

One 1-inch piece of fresh ginger, peeled and chopped

- 4 garlic cloves, chopped
- 1 teaspoon tamarind concentrate (see Note) or 1 tablespoon fresh lemon juice
- 1 tablespoon vegetable oil
- 1 small onion, cut into ¼-inch dice
- 2 jalapeños, halved lengthwise
- 1 pound shelled and deveined medium shrimp
- 1 tablespoon malt or cider vinegar

Salt

1. In a large nonstick skillet, cook the dried chiles, coconut, coriander and cumin over moderately high heat, shaking the skillet, until the coconut starts to brown, 1 minute; transfer to a blender. Add the ginger, garlic, tamarind and ½ cup of water and puree.

2. In the same skillet, heat the oil. Add the onion and jalapeños and cook over moderately high heat until the onion is golden brown, about 3 minutes. Add the puree and bring to a boil. Add the shrimp and cook over moderately low heat, turning a few times, until just white throughout, about 2 minutes. Remove the skillet from the heat and stir in the vinegar. Season with salt and serve right away. —*Sanjeev Kapoor*

SERVE WITH Basmati rice.

NOTE Tamarind concentrate is available at specialty food stores.

WINE Vibrant, zippy Albariño: 2009 Bonny Doon Vineyard Ca' del Solo Estate.

Marseille-Style Shrimp Stew

TOTAL: 45 MIN • 4 SERVINGS ●

- 6 garlic cloves, minced

Salt

- ½ cup mayonnaise
- 1 teaspoon fresh lemon juice
- ½ teaspoon paprika

Pinch of cayenne pepper

- 3 tablespoons extra-virgin olive oil
- 1 medium fennel bulb, cored and finely chopped
- 1 onion, finely chopped

Three 1-inch strips of orange zest

Pinch of ground cloves

- ½ cup dry white wine
- 1 cup bottled clam juice
- 1 cup canned whole tomatoes, chopped
- ¼ teaspoon saffron threads, crumbled

Freshly ground pepper

- 1½ pounds jumbo shrimp, peeled and deveined

Toasted baguettes, for serving

1. In a bowl, mash one-third of the garlic with a pinch of salt. Whisk in the mayonnaise, lemon juice, paprika and cayenne. Whisk in 1 tablespoon of the oil. Set the rouille aside.

2. In a large, deep skillet, heat the remaining 2 tablespoons of oil until shimmering. Add the fennel and onion and cook over moderately high heat, stirring, until softened, 7 minutes. Add the remaining garlic, the orange zest and ground cloves and cook until fragrant, 1 minute. Add the wine and cook until nearly evaporated, 5 minutes. Add the clam juice, tomatoes, saffron and 1 cup of water and bring to a boil. Season with salt and pepper and simmer until the sauce is reduced by half, about 10 minutes.

3. Add the shrimp to the skillet, cover and cook over moderate heat, turning once, until cooked, 5 minutes. Discard the zest. Spread the rouille on toasts and serve with the stew. —*Melissa Clark*

WINE Crisp Provençal rosé: 2010 Commanderie de la Bargemone.

Gingered Stir-Fry with Shrimp and Snow Peas

⏱ **TOTAL: 30 MIN • 4 SERVINGS** ●

Stir-fries are best made in large nonstick skillets that can create a sear. For this recipe, F&W's Grace Parisi builds layers of flavor with Chinese chile-garlic sauce and matchsticks of fresh ginger.

½ cup chicken stock or low-
sodium broth
2 tablespoons low-sodium soy sauce
1 teaspoon Chinese chile-garlic sauce
1 teaspoon cornstarch
2 tablespoons vegetable oil
¼ cup fresh ginger,
cut into fine matchsticks
½ pound snow peas
1 pound medium shrimp, shelled
and deveined
4 small scallions, thinly sliced
on the diagonal
Steamed rice, for serving

nonstick pans do's and don'ts

use plastic The first rule of nonstick: Pick plastic or wooden tools, never metal, which can scratch coatings.

season pans Periodically rub oil on cool pans to maintain the nonstick coating.

go for heft Heavy pans are less likely to overheat than flimsy ones.

shun scratches Eating flakes of nonstick coating can be harmful: Toss out any scratched skillets.

avoid high heat Excessive heat (from the broiler, for example) can damage coatings.

pay for quality Great pans can last for years—they're a smart investment for the kitchen.

1. In a small bowl, whisk the chicken stock with the low-sodium soy sauce, Chinese chile-garlic sauce and cornstarch.
2. In a large nonstick skillet, heat the vegetable oil until shimmering. Add the ginger matchsticks and stir-fry over moderately high heat until they are softened, about 1 minute. Add the snow peas and stir-fry until they are crisp-tender and the ginger is beginning to brown, about 2 minutes. Add the shrimp and stir-fry for about 1 minute. Add the scallions and stir-fry for 30 seconds. Whisk the chile sauce, add it to the skillet and stir-fry until the shrimp are opaque throughout and the sauce is thickened, about 1 minute longer. Serve with steamed rice. —*Grace Parisi*
WINE Tart, citrusy Sauvignon Blanc from Chile: 2010 Las Mulas.

Shrimp with Spicy Chipotle-Tomato Sauce

ACTIVE: 25 MIN; TOTAL: 1 HR
4 SERVINGS ●

While in Ensenada in Mexico's Baja region, superchef and Mexican cuisine specialist Rick Bayless had *salsa negra* (black salsa), a smoky chipotle-based sauce, over raw oysters. Here, he blends it with tomatoes to serve with grilled shrimp.

One 15-ounce can diced tomatoes,
drained
2 tablespoons canola oil, plus more
for grilling
¼ cup Salsa Negra with Chipotle
(recipe follows)
⅓ cup water
Salt and freshly ground pepper
1¼ pounds large shrimp, shelled
and deveined
Chopped cilantro, for garnish

1. In a blender, puree the diced tomatoes. In a medium saucepan, heat the 2 tablespoons of oil until shimmering. Add the tomato puree and cook over moderately high heat, stirring frequently, until very thick, about 7 minutes. Add the Salsa Negra and the water and simmer until slightly thickened, about 10 minutes. Season the sauce with salt and pepper.

2. Light a grill or preheat a grill pan. Brush the shrimp with oil and season with salt and pepper. Grill over moderately high heat, turning once, until lightly charred and cooked through, about 5 minutes. Drizzle the shrimp with the sauce, sprinkle with cilantro and serve. —*Rick Bayless*
MAKE AHEAD The chipotle-tomato sauce can be refrigerated for up to 5 days.
WINE Bright, juicy rosé: 2010 Robert Oatley Rosé of Sangiovese.

SALSA NEGRA WITH CHIPOTLE
⏱ **TOTAL: 35 MIN • MAKES 1 CUP** ● ● ●

Balsamic vinegar might seem like an unusual ingredient in Mexican food, but it is common in Baja, perhaps because there are so many wineries in the region. This recipe makes more salsa than is used in the Shrimp with Spicy Chipotle-Tomato Sauce above, but it keeps in the refrigerator for weeks and can add an intense, smoky heat to grilled meats, stews and tacos.

¾ cup chipotles in adobo sauce
(from a 7-ounce can), stemmed
and coarsely chopped
1 tablespoon molasses, preferably
unsulfured
3 tablespoons balsamic vinegar
2 tablespoons dark brown sugar
½ cup water
2 tablespoons soy sauce

1. In a blender, combine the chipotle chiles with the molasses, balsamic vinegar, dark brown sugar and ¼ cup of the water. Blend until the mixture is smooth.
2. Strain the sweet chipotle puree through a fine strainer into a small saucepan, pressing on the solids with a spatula to extract as much of the puree as possible.
3. Simmer the chipotle sauce over moderately low heat, stirring frequently with a heatproof rubber spatula, until it is very thick, pasty and reduced to ¾ cup, about 20 minutes. Remove the salsa from the heat. Stir in the soy sauce and remaining ¼ cup of water. Serve the *salsa negra* hot or at room temperature. —*RB*

● HEALTHY ● MAKE AHEAD ● VEGETARIAN ● STAFF FAVORITE

gingered stir-fry with shrimp and snow peas

Dashi-Poached Scallop Salad with Wasabi Dressing

◔ TOTAL: 30 MIN
4 FIRST-COURSE SERVINGS ●

- 2 tablespoons fresh lemon juice
- 1 teaspoon wasabi paste
- ¼ cup canola oil

Salt and freshly ground pepper
- 2 teaspoons instant dashi
- 12 sea scallops, sliced into thirds
- 4 ounces mesclun

1. In a large bowl, whisk the lemon juice with the wasabi paste and oil. Season the dressing with salt and pepper.

2. In a large saucepan, bring the dashi and 4 cups of water to a simmer. Add the scallops and poach just until opaque, 1½ to 2 minutes. Drain and pat dry. Transfer the scallops to a bowl and toss with half of the dressing.

3. Add the greens to the dressing in the large bowl and toss to coat. Season with salt and pepper. Arrange the scallops on plates, top with the greens and serve. —*David Myers*
WINE Sauvignon Blanc: 2009 Noble Hill.

Scallops with Warm Tomato-Basil Dressing

◔ TOTAL: 30 MIN • 4 FIRST-COURSE
SERVINGS ● ●

- 1 teaspoon coriander seeds
- ½ teaspoon fennel seeds
- ¼ cup extra-virgin olive oil, plus more for brushing
- 1 tablespoon fresh lemon juice
- 2 tomatoes—peeled, seeded and diced
- 2 tablespoons minced fresh fennel
- 1 tablespoon chopped chervil or tarragon
- 1 tablespoon finely shredded basil, plus baby leaves for garnish

Salt and freshly ground pepper
- 16 jumbo sea scallops (about 1 pound)

1. In a saucepan, toast the coriander and fennel seeds over moderate heat until fragrant, about 2 minutes; transfer to a mortar and let cool. Pound until coarsely ground.

2. Warm the ¼ cup of oil in the same saucepan. Add the spices and the lemon juice; let stand for 1 minute. Add the tomatoes, fennel, and herbs; season with salt and pepper.

3. Light a grill or preheat a grill pan. Brush the scallops with oil and season with salt and pepper. Grill over high heat, turning once, until browned and just firm, 4 minutes. Transfer to plates and spoon the dressing on top. Garnish with basil and serve. —*Pete Evans*
WINE Ripe, tropical Sauvignon Blanc: 2009 Buitenverwachting Beyond.

Scallops with Yogurt and Fennel

◔ TOTAL: 35 MIN • 4 SERVINGS ●

- 2 tablespoons extra-virgin olive oil
- 2 fennel bulbs, each cut into 8 wedges through the core

Salt and freshly ground pepper
- 1 large shallot, minced
- 1 garlic clove, minced
- 1 thyme sprig

Pinch of saffron threads
- ½ cup vegetable stock
- 1 tablespoon vegetable oil
- 16 medium sea scallops
- ¼ cup plain whole-milk yogurt, seasoned with salt

1. In a large skillet, heat 1 tablespoon of the olive oil. Add the fennel, cut side down, season with salt and pepper and cook over moderately high heat, turning once, until browned on 2 sides, 6 minutes. Add the remaining 1 tablespoon of olive oil and the shallot, garlic, thyme and saffron; cook, stirring, until the shallot is softened, 1 minute. Add the stock, cover and simmer over low heat, turning once, until the fennel is tender, 12 minutes. Season with salt and pepper; discard the thyme.

2. In another large skillet, heat the vegetable oil. Season the scallops with salt and pepper and add to the skillet. Cook over high heat until richly browned outside but barely cooked within, about 1 minute per side.

3. Using a slotted spoon, transfer the fennel to plates. Serve the scallops, salted yogurt and fennel juices alongside. —*Urs Bieri*
WINE Citrusy Verdejo: 2009 Bodegas Naia.

Warm Scallop Salad with Mushrooms and Zucchini

◔ TOTAL: 35 MIN • 4 SERVINGS ● ●

- 2 anchovies, minced
- 1 teaspoon finely grated lemon zest
- 1½ tablespoons fresh lemon juice
- 5 tablespoons extra-virgin olive oil

Salt and freshly ground pepper
- 1 medium zucchini, halved lengthwise and sliced crosswise ¼ inch thick
- ½ pound oyster mushrooms
- 16 large sea scallops
- 1 large shallot, thinly sliced
- ¼ cup dry white wine
- 1 tablespoon unsalted butter
- 1 small head of Boston lettuce, torn into pieces
- 2 tablespoons minced chives
- 2 teaspoons chopped tarragon

Finely grated *bottarga* (optional, see Note on page 89)

1. In a small bowl, combine the anchovies, lemon zest, lemon juice and 2 tablespoons of the olive oil. Season with salt and pepper.

2. In a large skillet, heat 1 tablespoon of the olive oil. Add the zucchini, season with salt and cook over high heat until browned in spots; transfer to a large plate. Add 1 tablespoon of the olive oil and the mushrooms to the skillet; season with salt and pepper, cover and cook over moderate heat until starting to brown. Uncover and cook until tender and browned; transfer to the plate.

3. Season the scallops with salt and pepper. Heat the remaining 1 tablespoon of olive oil in the skillet until shimmering. Add the scallops and cook over moderately high heat until browned on the bottom. Turn the scallops and cook for 1 minute longer; transfer to a small plate. Add the shallot to the pan and cook until softened. Add the wine and simmer, then stir in the zucchini and mushrooms and reheat. Swirl in the anchovy dressing, any scallop juices and the butter.

4. Arrange the lettuce on plates; top with the scallops and vegetables. Garnish with the herbs and *bottarga;* serve. —*Marcia Kiesel*
WINE Sancerre: 2009 Domaine Vacheron.

● HEALTHY ● MAKE AHEAD ● VEGETARIAN ● STAFF FAVORITE

dashi-poached scallop salad with wasabi dressing

Andouille, Crab and Oyster Gumbo

ACTIVE: 30 MIN; TOTAL: 1 HR 30 MIN
8 SERVINGS ●

½ cup all-purpose flour
½ cup vegetable oil
1 pound andouille sausage, sliced ¼ inch thick
3 large celery ribs, cut into ½-inch dice
1 onion, cut into ½-inch dice
1 red bell pepper, cut into ½-inch dice
1 habanero chile, minced and most seeds discarded
3 garlic cloves, minced
½ pound okra, sliced ¼ inch thick
2 teaspoons dried thyme
1 bay leaf
3 tablespoons *filé* powder (see Note)
5 cups chicken stock or low-sodium broth
3 cups bottled clam juice
3 tablespoons Worcestershire sauce
3 large tomatoes, finely chopped
1 pound lump crabmeat, picked over
2 dozen shucked oysters and their liquor
Salt and freshly ground pepper
Steamed rice or crusty bread, for serving

how to shuck an oyster

step one Set the oyster flat side up on a work surface. Be sure to wear shucking gloves.

step two Near the hinge, carefully insert an oyster knife between the shells; twist the knife to pop open.

step three Scrape the oyster from the top shell, then lift off the shell.

step four Run the knife along the bottom shell to release the oyster.

1. In a large pot, stir the flour and oil until smooth. Cook over moderate heat, stirring every 45 seconds, until the roux turns a rich brown color, about 15 minutes. Add the andouille, celery, onion, red pepper, habanero, garlic, okra, thyme, bay leaf and half of the *filé* powder and cook over moderate heat, stirring occasionally, until the onion is translucent, about 5 minutes. Add the stock, clam juice, Worcestershire and tomatoes and bring to a boil. Reduce the heat to low and simmer for 1 hour, stirring occasionally.
2. Stir in the remaining *filé* powder and add the crab, oysters and their liquor. Season with salt and pepper and simmer gently for 1 minute to just cook the oysters. Serve the gumbo with rice or bread.
—*Andrew Zimmern*
NOTE *Filé* powder, made from the ground dried leaves of the sassafras tree, is used as a thickener. Look for it in the spice section of most supermarkets.
BEER Fresh, balanced pale ale: Anchor Steam Liberty Ale.

Oysters Rocafella

TOTAL: 30 MIN • 4 FIRST-COURSE SERVINGS ●

2 teaspoons sugar
2 teaspoons water
½ cup Champagne or sparkling wine
¼ cup fresh grapefruit juice
2 teaspoons fresh lemon juice
¼ cup Champagne vinegar
1 small shallot, minced
Freshly ground pepper
2 dozen bluepoint or other East Coast oysters, shucked on the half shell
Crushed ice and coarse salt, for serving
1 tablespoon dried egg-white powder (see Note)
1 to 2 bunches of Champagne grapes or small seedless red grapes, frozen until solid, halved if large

1. In a microwave-safe cup, combine the sugar and water. Cook at high power for 20 seconds. Stir until the sugar dissolves, then let the sugar syrup cool.

2. In a small stainless steel bowl, combine the sugar syrup, Champagne and citrus juices. Set the bowl over a larger bowl of ice and keep cold. In another small bowl, combine the vinegar and shallot and season with pepper.
3. Arrange the shucked oysters on a bed of crushed ice and coarse salt. Add the egg-white powder to the Champagne–citrus juice mixture and beat with a handheld mixer or immersion blender until thick and frothy.
4. Spoon a little of the vinegar-shallot mixture over the oysters and a little of the Champagne froth on top. Garnish with the frozen Champagne grapes and serve right away.
—*Mario Carbone and Rich Torrisi*
NOTE Egg-white powder is available at health-food stores and most supermarkets.
WINE Dry, crisp Champagne: Domaine Chandon NV Brut Classic.

Grilled Oysters with Tabasco-Leek Butter

TOTAL: 35 MIN
MAKES 2 DOZEN OYSTERS

6 tablespoons unsalted butter
1 medium leek, white and tender green parts only, very thinly sliced
1 teaspoon sherry vinegar
1 large garlic clove, minced
1 tablespoon fresh lemon juice
½ tablespoon Tabasco
Salt
2 dozen oysters on the half shell

1. In a skillet, melt 2 tablespoons of the butter. Add the leek and cook over moderate heat, stirring, until softened and lightly browned, 8 minutes. Stir in the vinegar, transfer to a bowl and let cool. Stir in the garlic, lemon juice and Tabasco. Soften the remaining 4 tablespoons of butter and combine thoroughly with the leek mixture. Season with salt.
2. Light a grill. Place a dollop of leek butter on each oyster. Grill the oysters over high heat until they are just cooked through and the butter is melted, about 1 minute. Serve right away. —*James Holmes*
WINE Herb-scented Sonoma Sauvignon Blanc: 2009 Benziger.

● HEALTHY ● MAKE AHEAD ● VEGETARIAN ● STAFF FAVORITE

Oysters on the Half Shell with Rosé Mignonette

📷 PAGE 215

⏱ TOTAL: 10 MIN • 8 FIRST-COURSE SERVINGS ●

Great oysters are delicious "naked," says Island Creek Oysters founder Skip Bennett. But Jeremy Sewall, the chef at Boston's Island Creek Oyster Bar, sometimes dresses them up with a mignonette (vinegar sauce) like this one, made with sparkling rosé.

- ½ cup sparkling rosé
- 2 shallots, minced
- 1 tablespoon white wine vinegar
- ¼ teaspoon freshly ground pepper
- 2 dozen shucked oysters

Shaved ice, for serving

In a small bowl, combine the rosé, shallots, vinegar and pepper. Arrange the oysters on a bed of ice and serve with the mignonette. —*Jeremy Sewall*

WINE Toasty, berried sparkling rosé: 2006 Soter Brut Rosé from Oregon.

Fragrant Gigante Beans with Garlic Confit and Mussels

ACTIVE: 1 HR; TOTAL: 2 HR 30 MIN PLUS OVERNIGHT SOAKING • 4 SERVINGS ● ●

BEANS

- ½ pound dried gigante beans or large limas, soaked overnight and drained
- ½ small onion
- 1 small celery rib
- 1 bay leaf
- 8 cloves of Garlic Confit with Thyme plus 1 teaspoon of the confit oil (recipe follows)

MUSSELS

- 1½ tablespoons extra-virgin olive oil
- 3 garlic cloves, minced
- 2 large shallots, minced
- 6 scallions, thinly sliced
- 3 plum tomatoes, chopped
- 1 cup dry white wine
- 3 tablespoons fresh lemon juice
- 1 teaspoon dried oregano
- 2 pounds mussels, scrubbed

- 2 tablespoons chopped dill
- 2 tablespoons minced chives

Salt and freshly ground pepper

- ½ cup crumbled feta cheese

1. PREPARE THE BEANS In a large saucepan, cover the beans with 2 inches of water. Add the onion, celery and bay leaf and bring to a boil. Cover partially and simmer, stirring occasionally, until tender, about 1½ hours. Add more water as necessary to keep the beans covered by 2 inches. Drain the beans and discard the onion, celery and bay leaf. **2.** In a large bowl, mash the cloves of Garlic Confit with the oil. Fold in the drained beans. **3. PREPARE THE MUSSELS** Set a large, warmed bowl near the stove. In a large pot, heat the oil. Add the garlic, shallots and scallions and cook over moderately high heat until softened, 3 minutes. Add the tomatoes and cook until they release their juices, 2 minutes. Add the wine, lemon juice and oregano and bring to a boil over high heat. Add the mussels, cover and cook until they open, 3 minutes. Using a large slotted spoon, scoop out the mussels and add to the warmed bowl. **4.** Add the beans, dill and chives to the pot and simmer, stirring, until the beans are hot. Season with salt and pepper. Off the heat, stir in the feta. Pour the beans into a deep platter and serve with the mussels. —*Michael Psilakis*

WINE Vibrant white Burgundy: 2008 Domaine de la Cadette La Châtelaine.

GARLIC CONFIT WITH THYME

ACTIVE: 20 MIN; TOTAL: 1 HR 40 MIN

MAKES 3 HEADS OF GARLIC CONFIT ● ● ●

- 3 large heads of garlic, cloves separated and peeled
- 3 large thyme sprigs
- 1 fresh bay leaf
- ½ cup extra-virgin olive oil
- ½ cup canola oil

Kosher salt and freshly ground pepper

1. Preheat the oven to 300°. In a small enameled cast-iron casserole, cover the garlic cloves, thyme sprigs and bay leaf with the

olive and canola oils. Transfer the casserole to the oven and braise for 50 minutes, until the garlic is very tender. Season with salt and pepper and let cool. Discard the herbs. **2.** Transfer the garlic and its cooking oil to a clean, resealable jar and refrigerate for up to 3 weeks. —*MP*

Shellfish in Brodetto

⏱ TOTAL: 30 MIN • 4 SERVINGS ● ●

- 4 thick slices of rustic bread
- ¼ cup extra-virgin olive oil, plus more for brushing and drizzling
- 5 garlic cloves—4 smashed, 1 whole
- 4 small dried red chiles, smashed
- ½ cup dry white wine
- ½ cup bottled clam juice
- 2 dozen littleneck clams, scrubbed
- 1 pint cherry tomatoes, halved
- 2 pounds mussels, scrubbed
- ¾ pound sea scallops, halved horizontally
- ½ cup small basil leaves

Salt

1. Preheat the oven to 375°. On a baking sheet, toast the bread for 8 minutes, until golden. Brush the toasts with olive oil and rub them all over with the whole garlic clove. Put 1 toast in the bottom of each of 4 bowls. **2.** In a deep skillet, heat the ¼ cup of oil. Add the smashed garlic and the chiles and cook over moderate heat for 2 minutes. Add the wine and cook over moderately high heat for 2 minutes. Add the clam juice and bring to a boil. Add the clams and tomatoes, cover and cook for 2 minutes. Stir in the mussels and scallops, cover and cook over high heat until the clams and mussels open and the scallops are just cooked, 3 minutes. Discard any clams or mussels that don't open. With a slotted spoon, transfer the seafood to the bowls. Boil the broth for 1 minute, until slightly reduced. Add the basil, season lightly with salt and pour the broth into the bowls. Drizzle with oil and serve. —*Dave Pasternack*

WINE Tropical, fruity South African Chenin Blanc: 2010 Indaba.

Crab Louie

⏱ TOTAL: 40 MIN • 4 TO 6 SERVINGS ● ●

Evening Land Vineyards president and sommelier Larry Stone is a stellar cook. One of his favorite dishes is this hearty Crab Louie, which he insists "is not a salad course. It's an entire meal." Stone prefers to make it with the classic Dungeness crab, but any crabmeat can be substituted.

DRESSING

1 cup mayonnaise
3 tablespoons ketchup
1 tablespoon sweet pickle relish
1 tablespoon fresh lemon juice
1 garlic clove, minced
1 teaspoon Tabasco
½ teaspoon Worcestershire sauce
¼ teaspoon sweet smoked paprika
¼ teaspoon chile powder
Salt and freshly ground pepper

SALAD

¾ pound asparagus
Two 6-ounce romaine hearts, cut crosswise ½ inch thick
One 6-ounce seedless cucumber, thinly sliced or cut into spears
4 large radishes, thinly sliced
4 medium tomatoes, cut into wedges (optional)
4 hard-boiled eggs, cut into wedges
1 pound crabmeat, preferably Dungeness

1. PREPARE THE DRESSING In a bowl, whisk the mayonnaise with the ketchup, relish, lemon juice, garlic, Tabasco, Worcestershire sauce, paprika and chile powder and season with salt and pepper. Let stand at room temperature for 15 minutes.

2. MEANWHILE, PREPARE THE SALAD In a medium saucepan of boiling salted water, cook the asparagus until just tender, 3 minutes. Drain and cool.

3. Arrange the romaine, cucumber, radishes, tomatoes, eggs and asparagus on a platter. Top with large chunks of the crabmeat and serve, passing the dressing at the table.

—*Larry Stone*

WINE Chardonnay: 2008 A to Z Oregon.

King Crab Salad with Grapefruit and Avocado

TOTAL: 1 HR • 8 SERVINGS ● ●

This lovely seafood salad was an improvisation. "I made it with what I had in the house," says winemaker Piero Incisa della Rocchetta. "Scarcity breeds creativity." He uses grapefruit juice both to glaze the crab and to make the sweet-tangy salad dressing.

3 large red grapefruits
½ small red onion, very thinly sliced
1 tablespoon soy sauce
1 tablespoon fresh lemon juice
¼ cup plus 2 tablespoons extra-virgin olive oil
Salt
1½ pounds cooked shelled king crab meat (2½ pounds in the shell), cut into 3-by-½-inch pieces
2 Hass avocados—peeled, halved lengthwise and very thinly sliced
16 unsalted roasted almonds, cracked
2 tablespoons cilantro leaves

1. Using a sharp paring knife, peel off the skin and bitter white pith from the grapefruits. Working over a bowl, cut in between the membranes to release the grapefruit sections. Set the sections aside. Squeeze the juice from the membranes into the bowl; there should be ½ cup of juice.

2. In a bowl, mix the onion, soy sauce and lemon juice with 4 tablespoons of the oil. Stir in ¼ cup of grapefruit juice from the bowl and season with salt. Let stand for 10 minutes.

3. In a skillet, heat the remaining 2 tablespoons of olive oil until shimmering. Add the crab and cook over high heat, turning once, 30 seconds. Add the remaining ¼ cup of grapefruit juice and cook until the crab is lightly caramelized, about 10 seconds. Remove from the heat.

4. Arrange the grapefruit in shallow bowls. Layer the avocado on top, then the crab. Spoon the dressing over the crab, garnish with the almonds and cilantro and serve.

—*Piero Incisa della Rocchetta*

WINE Dry, crisp sparkling wine: NV Bollinger Special Cuvée Champagne.

Crisp Crab Cakes with Chipotle Mayonnaise

ACTIVE: 25 MIN; TOTAL: 1 HR
4 SERVINGS ●

CRAB CAKES

¼ pound skinless cod or flounder fillet, cut into ½-inch pieces
5 scallions, thinly sliced
3 jalapeños, seeded and minced
3 tablespoons fresh lemon juice
1 tablespoon chopped parsley
½ teaspoon cayenne pepper
¾ teaspoon kosher salt
¼ teaspoon freshly ground black pepper
½ cup mayonnaise
1 pound lump crabmeat, picked over
1½ cups *panko* bread crumbs

CHIPOTLE MAYONNAISE

¾ cup mayonnaise
1 chipotle chile in adobo, seeded and minced
1 tablespoon fresh lemon juice
1 teaspoon Old Bay Seasoning
1 teaspoon Dijon mustard
Salt and freshly ground black pepper
Pure olive oil, for frying

1. MAKE THE CRAB CAKES In a mini food processor, puree the fish. Transfer to a bowl and add the scallions, jalapeños, lemon juice, parsley, cayenne, salt, pepper and mayonnaise and mix thoroughly. Gently fold in the crabmeat. Form the mixture into 8 cakes. Coat the cakes with the *panko* and refrigerate for 30 minutes.

2. MEANWHILE, MAKE THE CHIPOTLE MAYONNAISE In a small bowl, combine the mayonnaise, chipotle, lemon juice, Old Bay and mustard and season with salt and black pepper. Cover and refrigerate.

3. In a large nonstick skillet, heat ¼ inch of oil until shimmering. Add the crab cakes and cook over moderate heat until browned and heated through, 3 minutes per side. Serve with the chipotle mayonnaise.

—*Preston Clark*

WINE Tangy Chardonnay: 2009 Joel Gott.

● HEALTHY ● MAKE AHEAD ● VEGETARIAN ● STAFF FAVORITE

crisp crab cakes with chipotle mayonnaise

Steamed Lobster with Lemon Thyme Butter

⏱ **TOTAL: 30 MIN • 8 SERVINGS** ●

These lobsters are steamed over seaweed, but if that's hard to get, use large leaves of romaine lettuce (or even just a metal colander) to keep the lobsters from becoming submerged in the water.

2 sticks unsalted butter
Finely grated zest and juice of 2 lemons
8 large lemon thyme sprigs
¼ cup kosher salt, plus more for seasoning
2 quarts water
2 pounds seaweed or 4 large heads of romaine, large outer leaves only
Eight 1½-pound live lobsters

1. In a small saucepan, combine the butter with the lemon zest, lemon juice and lemon thyme and melt the butter slowly over low heat. Season the butter lightly with salt, then cover the pan and set aside.

2. In each of 2 large pots, bring 1 quart of the water to a boil. Add 2 tablespoons of the salt and enough seaweed to each pot to form a bed that rises above the water. Arrange half of the lobsters in each pot on top of the seaweed. Cover and steam over high heat until the lobsters are bright red all over, 8 to 10 minutes.

3. Transfer the lobsters to a platter. Reheat the butter and discard the thyme. Serve the lobsters with the butter for dipping.
—*Jeremy Sewall*

WINE Minerally Spanish white: 2009 Javier Sanz Villa Narcisa.

Butter-Poached Lobster with Kimchi Butter Sauce

TOTAL: 1 HR • 6 SERVINGS ●

"My fiancée, Jori Jayne Emde, makes a lot of kimchi, and she brings it down to St. John every time we go," says New York chef Zakary Pelaccio. On the island, he tops local spiny lobster with a beurre blanc (butter sauce) flavored with rhubarb kimchi. Maine lobsters and classic cabbage kimchi are equally delicious in this recipe.

Four 1½-pound live lobsters
¼ cup chopped kimchi plus ¼ cup kimchi liquid from the jar
¼ cup rice vinegar
1 medium shallot, minced
1 stick plus 2 tablespoons cold unsalted butter
4 green cardamom pods, seeds removed and lightly crushed
2 tablespoons yellow mustard seeds
1½ tablespoons chopped tarragon
Salt and freshly ground pepper

1. Bring a large pot of water to a boil. Plunge the lobsters in head first, then cover and cook until they are bright red all over, about 8 minutes. Transfer the lobsters to a large rimmed baking sheet and let cool slightly. Twist off the tails and claws. Crack the shells and remove the meat from the tails, claws and knuckles. Halve the tail meat lengthwise and discard the intestinal veins.

2. In a small saucepan, combine the kimchi and kimchi liquid, rice vinegar and shallot and boil over moderately high heat until the liquid has reduced to 3 tablespoons, about 3 minutes. Remove from the heat and whisk in 6 tablespoons of the butter, 1 tablespoon at a time, to form a smooth, creamy sauce. Cover and set aside.

3. In a large skillet, toast the crushed cardamom seeds and the mustard seeds over moderately high heat until fragrant, about 30 seconds. Add the remaining 4 tablespoons of butter and remove from the heat. When the butter has melted, add the lobster meat and stir to coat with butter. Cover and set the skillet over low heat, turning the lobster a few times, until just heated through, about 3 minutes.

4. Very gently rewarm the kimchi butter sauce over low heat, whisking constantly. Whisk in the tarragon and season with salt and freshly ground pepper.

5. Transfer the lobster to plates, spoon the kimchi butter sauce on top and serve.
—*Zakary Pelaccio*

WINE Crisp, zesty Sancerre: 2010 Domaine Vincent Delaporte.

Curry Lobster Cocktail

**ACTIVE: 45 MIN; TOTAL: 1 HR 30 MIN
4 SERVINGS**

Two 1¼-pound live lobsters
8 fresh or frozen kaffir lime leaves
1 tablespoon vegetable oil, plus more for rubbing
1 large shallot, minced
3 oil-packed anchovy fillets, minced
¾ teaspoon curry powder
¾ cup mayonnaise
2 teaspoons fresh lime juice
1 tablespoon chopped dill
Salt
2 cups mesclun greens
1 Kirby cucumber, thinly sliced

1. Preheat the oven to 300°. In a large pot of boiling water, cook the lobsters until they turn bright red, 8 minutes. Drain and let cool.

2. Twist the bodies from the tails. Using scissors, cut along the underside of the shells and remove the meat. Halve the tails lengthwise and discard the dark intestines. Crack the claws and remove the meat in one piece. Remove the knuckle meat. Transfer the lobster to a bowl and refrigerate until chilled.

3. Holding a lime leaf, pull off the stem to divide the leaf in half. Repeat with the remaining leaves. Rub the leaves with oil; transfer to a baking sheet. Bake for 8 minutes, until crisp.

4. In a small skillet, heat the 1 tablespoon of oil. Add the shallot and cook over moderately low heat until softened, 2 minutes. Mash the anchovies with the shallot. Add the curry powder and cook until fragrant, 1 minute. Scrape the mixture into a bowl and let cool. Stir in the mayonnaise, lime juice and dill and season with salt. Refrigerate for 15 minutes.

5. Fold the curry mayonnaise into the lobster. Serve the lobster salad over the greens; top with the lime leaves and cucumber.
—*Marcia Kiesel*

CURRY LOBSTER ROLLS Spoon the lobster salad into 4 split hot dog buns or hero rolls, then top with the crisped lime leaves and cucumber slices.

WINE Aromatic, fruity German white: 2009 Schloss Mühlenhof Müller-Thurgau Trocken.

● HEALTHY   ● MAKE AHEAD   ● VEGETARIAN   ● STAFF FAVORITE

curry lobster cocktail

Grilled Baby Octopus with Roasted Peppers and Potatoes

ACTIVE: 45 MIN; TOTAL: 1 HR 15 MIN
4 SERVINGS

Houston sommelier Antonio Gianola got the idea for this recipe from *Wine Bar Food* by Tony and Cathy Mantuano. He poaches baby octopus slowly in olive oil before grilling until crisp, then serves it on a salad of silky roasted peppers and potatoes.

OCTOPUS
2¼ cups extra-virgin olive oil
5 garlic cloves, coarsely chopped
3 medium shallots, coarsely chopped
1½ pounds cleaned baby octopus
Salt
SALAD
1 red bell pepper (see Note)
1 yellow bell pepper (see Note)
1¼ pounds Yukon Gold potatoes, peeled and cut into 1-inch cubes
2 garlic cloves, thinly sliced
1 medium shallot, thinly sliced
½ teaspoon sweet smoked paprika, plus more for sprinkling
1½ tablespoons fresh lemon juice
Salt and freshly ground black pepper
2 tablespoons finely chopped flat-leaf parsley

1. PREPARE THE OCTOPUS In a medium saucepan, heat ¼ cup of the olive oil. Add the chopped garlic and shallots and cook over moderately high heat, stirring a few times, until golden brown, about 4 minutes. Add the octopus, the remaining 2 cups of olive oil and a pinch of salt and bring to a simmer. Cook over low heat, skimming a few times, until the octopus is tender, about 45 minutes. Using tongs, transfer the octopus to a large plate and cover with plastic wrap. Strain and reserve ½ cup of the olive oil.

2. MEANWHILE, PREPARE THE SALAD Roast the bell peppers over a gas flame or under a preheated broiler, turning, until they are charred all over. Transfer the roasted peppers to a large plate and let cool, then rub off the skins and discard the seeds. Slice the roasted peppers into thin strips.

3. In a medium saucepan, cover the cubed potatoes with water by 3 inches and boil over moderately high heat until tender, about 10 minutes. Drain the potatoes and return them to the pan. Shake the saucepan over the heat for about 10 seconds to dry out the potatoes.

4. In a large skillet, heat 2 tablespoons of the reserved octopus oil. Add the sliced garlic and shallot and cook over moderately high heat until softened, about 2 minutes. Add the roasted pepper strips and the ½ teaspoon of paprika and cook, stirring, until the peppers are hot. Add the potatoes and cook, tossing gently, until heated through. Drizzle the roasted pepper–potato salad with ½ tablespoon of the lemon juice and season with salt and freshly ground black pepper.

5. Light a grill or preheat a grill pan. Brush the octopus with some of the reserved octopus oil and season with salt and black pepper. Grill over high heat, turning once, until the octopus are nicely charred and crisp, about 3 minutes per side.

6. Arrange the roasted pepper–potato salad on a platter and top with the grilled octopus. Drizzle with the remaining reserved octopus oil and the remaining 1 tablespoon of lemon juice. Sprinkle with smoked paprika and the parsley and serve right away.
—Antonio Gianola

NOTE To simplify this recipe, buy roasted peppers from the supermarket.
WINE Earthy, minerally rosé: 2000 R. López de Heredia Viña Tondonia Gran Reserva.

Watermelon and Squid Salad

TOTAL: 30 MIN • 6 SERVINGS

This salad would never be found in San Francisco chef Hoss Zaré's native Iran, but its dusting of ground sumac—a tart dried berry—is distinctly Persian.

⅓ cup rice vinegar
⅓ cup Champagne vinegar
3 scallions, thinly sliced
2 jalapeños, seeded and minced
1 tablespoon finely grated lime zest
2 tablespoons lime juice
Salt and freshly ground pepper
1 pound baby squid, bodies and tentacles separated but left whole
¼ cup extra-virgin olive oil
1 teaspoon finely grated orange zest
½ teaspoon crushed red pepper
1 small seedless watermelon (about 3½ pounds)—halved, rind removed, flesh sliced ½ inch thick
⅓ cup chopped tarragon
⅓ cup chopped mint
Ground sumac, for sprinkling (optional, see Note)

1. In a small bowl, whisk the rice vinegar with the Champagne vinegar, scallions, jalapeños, 2 teaspoons of the lime zest and 1 tablespoon of the lime juice. Season the dressing with salt and pepper.

2. Light a grill or preheat a grill pan. In a medium bowl, toss the squid with the olive oil, orange zest, crushed red pepper and the remaining 1 tablespoon of lime juice and 1 teaspoon of lime zest; season with salt and pepper. Grill the squid over high heat until lightly charred, 4 minutes.

3. Arrange the watermelon slices on a platter. Drizzle with the dressing and sprinkle with the chopped tarragon and mint. Top the watermelon with the grilled squid, sprinkle with sumac and serve right away.
—Hoss Zaré

NOTE Find sumac at specialty food stores or *kalustyans.com*.
WINE Fruit-forward California Chardonnay: 2009 Five Rivers.

ingredient tip

smoked paprika This rich, smoky spice gives seafood and vegetable dishes a meaty flavor. Blended with ketchup, it's great on burgers.

● HEALTHY ● MAKE AHEAD ● VEGETARIAN ● STAFF FAVORITE

grilled baby octopus with roasted peppers and potatoes

shellfish

Warm Squid Salad with Pimentón Vinaigrette

⏱ TOTAL: 30 MIN

4 FIRST-COURSE SERVINGS ● ●

Inspired by a meal that she had at a Japanese restaurant, F&W's Marcia Kiesel slices the squid into rings while keeping the shape of the squid bodies intact.

- 2 teaspoons sweet pimentón de la Vera (Spanish smoked paprika)
- ½ teaspoon hot paprika
- 2 tablespoons sherry vinegar
- ¼ cup extra-virgin olive oil
- Salt and freshly ground black pepper
- 1 small red bell pepper, cut into ⅛-inch dice
- ¼ green bell pepper, cut into ⅛-inch dice
- 1 large shallot, minced
- 8 cleaned 6-inch squid bodies (about 1 pound total)
- 8 cups packed mesclun (5 ounces)

1. In a bowl, combine both paprikas with the vinegar and olive oil and season with salt and pepper. In another bowl, combine both bell peppers with the shallot and ¼ cup of the paprika vinaigrette; reserve the remaining vinaigrette. Let the pepper mixture stand at room temperature for 15 minutes.

2. Using a very sharp knife, slice the squid bodies crosswise ⅛ inch thick. Oil a large rimmed baking sheet and, using a long spatula, carefully transfer the squid to the baking sheet, keeping the shape of the squid as intact as possible.

3. Preheat the broiler. Brush the squid generously with some of the reserved vinaigrette and season with salt and pepper. Broil the squid 4 inches from the heat for about 2 minutes, until just tender and glazed.

4. Meanwhile, toss the mesclun with the remaining vinaigrette and arrange on plates. Transfer the squid to the plates, keeping the shape intact. Dot the pepper mixture around the salad and serve. —*Marcia Kiesel*

WINE Light-bodied Spanish red from the Bierzo region: 2008 Descendientes de José Palacios Pétalos Mencía.

Squid in Tamarind Brown Butter with Green Mango

ACTIVE: 25 MIN; TOTAL: 1 HR

6 SERVINGS

Zakary Pelaccio uses local squid and tamarind to make this dish at his Fatty Crab restaurant on St. John in the US Virgin Islands, but the flavors are primarily Asian. Yuzu *kosho,* a spicy Japanese condiment made from yuzu zest and chiles, adds fragrant citrus notes and heat, while *kecap manis* (an Indonesian soy sauce) gives the sauce a touch of saltiness and sweetness.

- 2 pounds whole cleaned squid
- Salt
- 2 teaspoons yuzu *kosho* paste (see Note)
- 1½ tablespoons orange-infused olive oil
- 1½ tablespoons fresh lime juice
- 1 small garlic clove, minced
- 4 tablespoons unsalted butter
- ¼ cup tamarind puree (see Note)
- 1 tablespoon *kecap manis* (see Note)
- 1 tablespoon water
- Freshly ground pepper
- 1 large unripe mango, peeled and cut into julienne strips
- 4 scallions, thinly sliced on a wide diagonal

1. In a large saucepan, cover the squid with water. Add 1 teaspoon of salt and simmer over low heat until tender, about 30 minutes. Drain the squid, then score each squid body in a crosshatch pattern.

2. In a bowl, combine the yuzu *kosho* with the olive oil, lime juice and minced garlic.

3. In a large skillet, melt the butter over moderately high heat, about 1 minute. Add the squid and sear over high heat until browned, about 2 minutes. Stir in the tamarind puree, *kecap manis* and water and remove from the heat. Season with salt and pepper and transfer to a platter.

4. In a medium bowl, mix the julienned mango and sliced scallions with the yuzu *kosho* dressing. Toss the salad with the squid and serve right away.

—*Zakary Pelaccio*

NOTE Yuzu *kosho,* tamarind puree and *kecap manis* are available at specialty food stores and online at *amazon.com.*

MAKE AHEAD The boiled squid can be tossed lightly in vegetable oil and refrigerated overnight. Proceed with Step 2.

WINE Rich, ripe Chardonnay from Australia: 2009 Paringa.

Citrus-Soy Squid

⏱ TOTAL: 45 MIN • 4 SERVINGS

Although the squid here is tasty after just 30 minutes of marinating, an extra half hour makes a big difference in the flavor. This supereasy marinade keeps for several days in the refrigerator, so it's great to make a large batch and save half for later.

- 1 cup mirin (see Note)
- 1 cup soy sauce
- ⅓ cup yuzu juice or fresh lemon juice (see Note)
- 2 cups water
- 2 pounds squid, tentacles left whole, bodies cut crosswise 1 inch thick

1. In a large bowl, combine the mirin with the soy sauce, yuzu juice and water.

2. Pour half of the marinade into an airtight container and refrigerate for later use. Add the squid to the large bowl with the remaining marinade and let stand at room temperature for 30 minutes to 1 hour, or refrigerate for up to 4 hours.

3. Light a grill or preheat a grill pan. Drain the squid. Grill over moderately high heat, turning once, until tender and white throughout, about 3 minutes. Serve hot.

—*Bill Kim*

VARIATION The marinade is also delicious with tofu or pork belly.

SERVE WITH Grilled whole scallions and lemon wedges.

NOTE Mirin is available at Asian markets; sweet sherry is a good substitute. Yuzu is available at specialty markets.

MAKE AHEAD The marinade can be refrigerated for up to 5 days.

WINE Citrusy Riesling from California's Mendocino region: 2009 Breggo.

● HEALTHY ● MAKE AHEAD ● VEGETARIAN ● STAFF FAVORITE

citrus-soy squid

Star Moscow restaurateur Katya Drozdova hosts a grilling party in the countryside with classics like green beans with eggs, chiles and cilantro, OPPOSITE; *recipe, page 237.*

vegetables and tofu

Asparagus with Watercress and Brown Butter Potatoes

⏱ **ACTIVE: 30 MIN; TOTAL: 45 MIN**
6 SERVINGS ●

- 1 pound large fingerling potatoes, peeled and cut into ½-inch coins
- 4 tablespoons unsalted butter
- Pinch of freshly grated nutmeg
- Salt and freshly ground pepper
- 2 cups *panko* (Japanese bread crumbs)
- 1½ pounds medium asparagus
- ¼ cup all-purpose flour
- 3 large eggs, beaten
- 2 cups canola oil, for frying
- 7 tablespoons extra-virgin olive oil
- 1 small shallot, minced
- ½ teaspoon tomato paste
- 3 tablespoons white wine vinegar
- ½ cup chopped flat-leaf parsley
- ½ cup chopped chervil or tarragon
- ½ cup snipped chives
- 1 teaspoon chopped thyme
- 3 large hard-boiled eggs, finely chopped
- 1 bunch of watercress, thick stems discarded

1. Preheat the oven to 225°. Bring a medium saucepan of water to a boil. Add the potatoes and boil over high heat until tender, about 10 minutes. Drain well. Pass the potatoes through a ricer into a bowl.
2. In the same saucepan, cook the butter over moderate heat until browned and nutty, about 4 minutes. Stir in the potatoes and nutmeg and season with salt and pepper. Keep the potato puree warm over low heat.
3. In a food processor, pulse the *panko* until fine. Dust all but the asparagus tips with the flour. In a pie plate, beat the eggs. In another pie plate, add the *panko* and season with salt and pepper. Dip the floured part of the asparagus in the egg, then dredge in the *panko*.
4. In a deep skillet, heat the canola oil until shimmering. Fry the asparagus in batches over moderately high heat, turning, until golden and crisp, about 3 minutes. Drain on paper towels and sprinkle with salt. Keep the asparagus warm in the oven.

5. In a small skillet, heat 1 tablespoon of the olive oil until shimmering. Add the shallot and cook over moderate heat until softened, about 3 minutes. Scrape the shallot into a bowl. Whisk in the tomato paste and vinegar, then whisk in the remaining 6 tablespoons of olive oil. Add the herbs and chopped eggs to the dressing and season with salt and pepper. Add the watercress and toss to coat.
6. Spoon the potato puree onto plates, top with the asparagus and salad and serve.
—*Wolfgang Ban and Eduard Frauneder*

Parmesan Asparagus with Poached Eggs

⏱ **TOTAL: 30 MIN • 4 SERVINGS** ●

This simple, surprisingly elegant recipe by actress Gwyneth Paltrow combines three foods that she adores: fresh spring asparagus, Parmesan cheese and poached eggs.

- 1 pound thick asparagus, trimmed
- 2 tablespoons unsalted butter, melted
- Salt and freshly ground pepper
- ¼ cup freshly grated Parmigiano-Reggiano cheese
- 1 tablespoon white wine vinegar
- 4 large eggs
- Toast, for serving

1. Preheat the broiler. Blanch the asparagus in a large, deep skillet of boiling salted water until crisp-tender, 3 minutes. Using a slotted spoon, transfer to a paper towel–lined plate and pat dry; reserve the liquid in the skillet. Arrange the asparagus in 4 individual shallow baking dishes. Brush with the butter and season with salt and pepper. Sprinkle with the cheese and broil 6 inches from the heat until golden, about 1 minute.
2. Add the vinegar to the asparagus blanching liquid and return to a simmer. Crack the eggs into the simmering water, leaving plenty of space between them, and poach until the whites are set but the yolks are runny, about 3 minutes. Using a slotted spoon, carefully remove each egg from the water, blot thoroughly dry with a paper towel and set on the asparagus. Serve with toast.
—*Gwyneth Paltrow*

Asparagus with Eggs and Pumpernickel Crumbs

⏱ **TOTAL: 40 MIN • 4 SERVINGS** ● ●

- 2 teaspoons unsalted butter, softened
- 1 thick slice of pumpernickel bread
- 2 tablespoons extra-virgin olive oil, plus more for drizzling
- ½ medium white onion, minced
- 2 tablespoons capers, drained and coarsely chopped
- 1 teaspoon raspberry vinegar
- 3 tablespoons chopped parsley
- Salt and freshly ground pepper
- 16 medium asparagus spears, trimmed
- 4 large eggs

1. Preheat the oven to 375°. Spread the butter on the slice of bread. Bake in the oven for about 4 minutes, until crisp. Let cool, then break the toast into ½-inch pieces.
2. In a small skillet, heat the 2 tablespoons of olive oil. Add the onion and cook over moderate heat until softened, about 7 minutes. Add the capers and vinegar and cook, stirring, for about 30 seconds. Remove from the heat. Stir in the parsley and season the onion relish with salt and pepper.
3. Light a grill or preheat a grill pan. Drizzle the asparagus with olive oil and season with salt and pepper. Grill the asparagus over medium heat, turning, until lightly charred and crisp-tender, about 5 minutes.
4. Meanwhile, bring a saucepan of water to a boil. Add the eggs and simmer over moderate heat for 4½ minutes. Transfer the eggs to a bowl of ice water; keep the water simmering. Gently crack the eggs all over and carefully remove the shells, keeping the eggs whole.
5. Return the shelled eggs to the simmering water until heated through, 30 seconds. Arrange the asparagus on plates and top with the onion relish and the eggs. Season with salt and pepper. Scatter the pumpernickel crumbs on top and serve.
—*Richard Blais*

MAKE AHEAD The crumbs, onion relish and grilled asparagus can be prepared up to 4 hours ahead. Reheat the relish and asparagus before serving.

● HEALTHY ● MAKE AHEAD ● VEGETARIAN ● STAFF FAVORITE

Braised Cucumbers with Dill

⏱ **TOTAL: 20 MIN • 10 SERVINGS** ● ● ○

Fresh cucumbers are excellent when gently braised in butter and served warm. This dish is best with thin-skinned cucumbers, like English, Japanese and Persian varieties.

- 1½ tablespoons unsalted butter
- 1 medium leek, white and pale green parts only, cut into ½-inch dice
- 3 pounds tender-skinned cucumbers—peeled in stripes, halved, seeded and cut crosswise ½ inch thick
- 2 tablespoons water
- Salt
- 2 tablespoons chopped dill

In a large skillet, melt 1 tablespoon of the butter. Add the leek and cook over moderately low heat, stirring, until tender, 4 minutes. Stir in the cucumbers, the remaining ½ tablespoon of butter and the water. Season with salt. Cover and cook over moderate heat, stirring, until the cucumbers are crisp-tender, 3 minutes. Uncover and cook over moderately high heat until any liquid has evaporated, 1 minute. Transfer the cucumbers to a bowl, stir in the dill and serve. —*Brent Ridge and Josh Kilmer-Purcell*

Green Beans with Eggs, Chiles and Cilantro

📷 **PAGE 235**

⏱ **TOTAL: 30 MIN • 8 SERVINGS** ● ● ● ○

This tasty Georgian dish called *lobio* (bean dish) is typically served cool in the Caucasus, but with its buttery scrambled eggs and tender green beans, it's equally delicious hot. Serve as part of a family-style menu or as a light main course.

- 1 pound green beans, cut into 2-inch pieces
- 1 tablespoon unsalted butter
- 1 tablespoon vegetable oil
- 1 small onion, finely chopped
- 5 large eggs, lightly beaten
- Salt and freshly ground pepper
- 1 cup chopped cilantro, plus small cilantro sprigs for garnish
- 2 tablespoons chopped walnuts
- 1 garlic clove, minced
- 1 small jalapeño, seeded and minced
- 1 small red chile, seeded and minced
- ½ teaspoon dill seeds

1. In a saucepan of boiling salted water, cook the green beans until tender, 6 minutes. Drain and let cool. Transfer to a bowl.
2. In a large nonstick skillet, melt the butter in the oil. Add the onion and cook over moderate heat, stirring, until softened, about 6 minutes. Add the eggs and season with salt and pepper. Cook over moderate heat, stirring, until the eggs are scrambled, about 3 minutes. Add the eggs to the beans.
3. Stir in the chopped cilantro, walnuts, garlic, jalapeño, red chile and dill seeds. Season with salt and pepper. Garnish with cilantro sprigs just before serving. —*Dmitry Leonov*

Spring Vegetable Stew

ACTIVE: 30 MIN; TOTAL: 1 HR
4 SERVINGS ● ○ ○

F&W's Marcia Kiesel created this lovely vegetable stew to highlight a favorite Austrian ingredient, white asparagus. When fresh fava beans are available, use them in place of the cranberry beans.

- ¼ pound thin white asparagus, cut into 1-inch lengths
- 1 cup shelled fresh cranberry beans (4 ounces or 1 pound in the pod)
- 2 tablespoons extra-virgin olive oil
- 20 thin scallions, white and pale green parts only
- ¼ pound *Hon Shimeji* or beech mushrooms (available at Asian or specialty food markets)
- Salt
- 6 white turnips, about 2 inches in diameter, peeled and cut into wedges
- 2 medium carrots, cut into 1-inch-long sticks
- 2¼ cups vegetable stock
- One 6-ounce zucchini, halved lengthwise and sliced crosswise ¼ inch thick
- ½ teaspoon finely grated lemon zest
- 1 teaspoon fresh lemon juice
- 1 romaine heart, cut into 2-inch pieces
- 2 tablespoons crème fraîche
- 1 tablespoon small chervil leaves
- 1 tablespoon minced chives

1. In a pot of simmering salted water, cook the asparagus over moderately high heat until tender, about 4 minutes. Using a slotted spoon, transfer the asparagus to a large bowl. Add the cranberry beans to the water and simmer over moderate heat until tender, about 40 minutes. Drain the beans and transfer to the bowl.
2. Meanwhile, in a medium enameled cast-iron casserole, heat ½ tablespoon of the olive oil. Add the scallions and cook over moderate heat until barely tender, about 1 minute. Transfer the scallions to the bowl with the asparagus and cranberry beans. Add another ½ tablespoon of the olive oil to the casserole. Add the mushrooms, season with salt, cover and cook over moderate heat, stirring a few times, until they are lightly browned and tender, about 3 minutes. Transfer the mushrooms to the bowl.
3. Heat the remaining 1 tablespoon of olive oil in the casserole. Add the turnips and carrots, season with salt and cook over moderate heat for 1 minute. Add 1 cup of the stock, cover and cook over low heat, stirring occasionally, for 15 minutes. Add another ½ cup of the stock, cover and cook until the turnips and carrots are tender, about 10 minutes longer. Add the zucchini and ½ cup of the stock and simmer until the zucchini is just tender, about 4 minutes. Add the remaining ¼ cup of stock to the casserole along with the lemon zest, lemon juice and lettuce and cook, stirring, until the lettuce just wilts, about 20 seconds. Stir in the crème fraîche.
4. Add the asparagus, beans, scallions and mushrooms to the stew. Simmer briefly, until heated through, about 30 seconds. Add the chervil and chives, transfer the stew to bowls and serve right away. —*Marcia Kiesel*
SERVE WITH Spaetzle.
WINE Tart cherry–scented, peppery Austrian red: 2008 Nigl Blauer Zweigelt.

Curried Spaghetti Squash and Chickpea Toasts

ACTIVE: 30 MIN; TOTAL: 1 HR
6 SERVINGS ● ● ●

      1   small spaghetti squash
            (about 3 pounds), halved and seeded
   ¼   cup plus 2 tablespoons
            extra-virgin olive oil
Salt and freshly ground black pepper
      1   onion, chopped
      1   carrot, finely chopped
      1   tablespoon ground coriander
   1½   teaspoons ground cumin
   ½   teaspoon crushed red pepper
   ½   teaspoon finely grated orange zest
   1½   teaspoons Madras curry paste
            or curry powder
One 15-ounce can chickpeas, drained
   ½   cup water
   ½   cup chopped cilantro
Grilled peasant bread and toasted
      pumpkin seeds, for serving

1. Preheat the oven to 350°. Place the halved spaghetti squash cut side up on a baking sheet and brush it with 2 tablespoons of the olive oil. Season with salt and black pepper. Roast the spaghetti squash for about 45 minutes, until the flesh is tender and lightly browned in spots. Let cool slightly.
2. Meanwhile, in a large skillet, heat the remaining ¼ cup of olive oil. Add the chopped onion and carrot and cook over moderate heat, stirring, until they are just softened, about 5 minutes. Add the coriander, cumin, crushed red pepper, grated orange zest and curry paste and cook, stirring, until fragrant, about 1 minute. Add the drained chickpeas and the water and simmer until the vegetables are very tender and the liquid has evaporated, about 5 minutes.
3. Using a fork, rake the squash into strands; you should have about 2½ cups of squash. Add the cilantro and squash to the curry and season with salt. Serve the curried squash over grilled peasant bread, garnished with toasted pumpkin seeds. —*Jonathon Sawyer*
WINE Tropical fruit–scented Chenin Blanc: 2009 Raats Family Original.

Sugar Snap Peas with Soffrito, Hot Pepper and Mint

:) TOTAL: 30 MIN • 8 SERVINGS ● ● ●

   ¼   cup plus 2 tablespoons
            extra-virgin olive oil
      2   medium carrots, finely chopped
      2   medium celery ribs, finely chopped
      1   medium onion, finely chopped
   ½   medium red bell pepper,
            finely chopped
   1½   pounds sugar snap peas,
            halved crosswise
   ½   teaspoon crushed red pepper
   ¼   cup water
   ½   cup torn mint leaves
Sea salt

1. In a medium skillet, heat ¼ cup of the olive oil. Add the carrots, celery, onion and bell pepper and cook over moderate heat, stirring occasionally, until the *soffrito* is tender and lightly browned, about 8 minutes.
2. In a large skillet, heat the remaining 2 tablespoons of olive oil until shimmering. Add the snap peas and cook over high heat just until they are bright green, about 2 minutes. Add the *soffrito* and cook until the snap peas are lightly browned in spots, about 2 minutes. Add the crushed red pepper and water and cook until the snap peas are crisp-tender, about 2 minutes longer. Add the torn mint and season with salt. Serve hot or at room temperature. —*Travis Lett*

Artichokes with Smoked-Herb Mayonnaise

:) ACTIVE: 10 MIN; TOTAL: 35 MIN
4 SERVINGS ● ● ●

      4   large artichokes, stems trimmed
      1   cup mayonnaise
      3   tablespoons chopped dill
      2   tablespoons chopped capers
      1   teaspoon finely grated lemon zest
      2   teaspoons fresh lemon juice
   ½   teaspoon smoked sea salt
   ¼   teaspoon sweet smoked paprika
Hot sauce
Freshly ground pepper

1. Set a steamer basket in a large pot over ½ inch of boiling water. Arrange the artichokes stem side down in the basket. Cover and steam over moderate heat until a knife easily pierces the stems, about 30 minutes. Transfer the artichokes to a platter.
2. In a medium bowl, whisk the mayonnaise with the dill, capers, lemon zest and juice, salt and paprika. Add a few dashes of hot sauce and season the mayonnaise with pepper. Serve the artichokes warm or lightly chilled with the mayonnaise. —*Richard Blais*

Zucchini-Ricotta Fritters

:) TOTAL: 30 MIN
MAKES 20 FRITTERS ● ●

      2   medium zucchini (about 7 ounces
            each), coarsely shredded
      2   garlic cloves, very thinly sliced
      3   large scallions, very thinly sliced
   ½   cup fresh sheep-milk ricotta cheese
      2   large eggs
      2   teaspoons finely grated lemon zest
Kosher salt and freshly ground pepper
   ¾   cup all-purpose flour
Olive oil, for frying
Lemon wedges, for serving

1. In a large bowl, combine the zucchini with the garlic, scallions, ricotta cheese, eggs, lemon zest and 1 teaspoon each of salt and freshly ground pepper. Stir the mixture well, then stir in the flour just until the ingredients are incorporated.
2. Line a large baking sheet with paper towels. In a large skillet, heat ¼ inch of olive oil until shimmering. Working in batches, add 2-tablespoon mounds of the zucchini batter to the hot oil, spreading them to form 3-inch fritters. Fry over moderately high heat, turning once, until browned and crisp, about 3 minutes. Drain the fritters on the paper towels and serve right away, with lemon wedges. —*Mario Batali*
MAKE AHEAD The Zucchini-Ricotta Fritters can be kept at room temperature for up to 2 hours and recrisped in a 325° oven.
WINE Citrusy, spritzy Spanish white: 2010 Ameztoi Txakolina.

● HEALTHY ● MAKE AHEAD ● VEGETARIAN ● STAFF FAVORITE

curried spaghetti squash and chickpea toasts

Grilled Squash Ribbons and Prosciutto with Mint Dressing

⏲ **TOTAL: 30 MIN • 4 SERVINGS** ● ●

- 1 teaspoon finely grated lime zest
- ¼ cup fresh lime juice
- ¼ cup chopped mint
- 2 garlic cloves, very finely chopped
- ¼ cup extra-virgin olive oil, plus more for brushing

Salt and freshly ground pepper

- 2 medium zucchini, very thinly sliced lengthwise on a mandoline
- 2 medium yellow squash, very thinly sliced lengthwise on a mandoline
- 6 ounces thinly sliced prosciutto

1. Light a grill or preheat a grill pan. In a small bowl, combine the lime zest and juice with the mint, garlic and the ¼ cup of olive oil. Season the dressing with salt and pepper.

2. Alternately thread the zucchini, yellow squash and prosciutto onto 4 pairs of 12-inch bamboo skewers. Lightly brush the vegetables and prosciutto with olive oil and season generously with salt and pepper.

3. Grill the skewers over high heat until the zucchini and yellow squash slices are lightly charred, about 1½ minutes per side. Serve with the mint dressing on the side.
—*Marcia Kiesel*

VARIATION This dish is also excellent as a pasta salad. Boil the pasta of your choice until it is al dente, then toss with olive oil and let cool slightly. Meanwhile, coarsely chop

vegan tip

When they're seasoned and pureed with water, raw cashews become spreadable and creamy just like a soft cheese, as in the eggplant *involtini* at right. Mix in nutritional yeast or rejuvelac (the strained liquid from fermented grains) for buttery, funky notes.

the grilled zucchini, yellow squash and prosciutto and transfer to a serving bowl. Add the pasta and mint dressing and toss. Season with salt and pepper.

WINE Zesty, affordable Spanish sparkling wine: NV Castellroig Cava Brut.

Eggplant Involtini with Grilled Ratatouille

TOTAL: 1 HR 30 MIN • 6 SERVINGS ● ●

Faux cheeses made with nuts are a cornerstone of vegan cooking. To stuff these *involtini* (little Italian rolls), chef Sean Baker of Gather restaurant in Berkeley re-creates the flavor of ricotta by combining pureed raw cashews with nutritional yeast, which has a very savory, almost cheese-like flavor.

INVOLTINI
- 2 cups raw cashews (10 ounces)
- 1 teaspoon nutritional yeast (see Note)
- ½ cup water
- ¼ cup pitted kalamata olives, finely chopped

Salt and freshly ground pepper

Two 1-pound eggplants, sliced lengthwise ¼ inch thick

Extra-virgin olive oil, for brushing

RATATOUILLE
- 1 pound tomatoes, sliced crosswise ½ inch thick
- 2 medium red onions, sliced crosswise ½ inch thick
- 4 Italian frying peppers
- 1 eggplant (1 pound), sliced crosswise 1 inch thick
- 2 small zucchini (1 pound), halved lengthwise
- 2 tablespoons extra-virgin olive oil, plus more for brushing

Salt and freshly ground pepper
- 2 garlic cloves, thinly sliced
- 1 bay leaf
- 1 teaspoon chopped thyme
- 1 teaspoon dried oregano, crumbled
- ½ cup dry white wine
- ½ cup water
- ½ cup shredded basil

Harissa, for serving

1. MAKE THE INVOLTINI In a food processor, combine the cashews with the nutritional yeast and water and process to a fine paste. Transfer the paste to a bowl, stir in the olives and season with salt and pepper.

2. Light a grill or preheat a grill pan. Brush the eggplant slices (there should be about 24) with oil and grill over moderately high heat, turning once, until tender and lightly charred, 2 to 3 minutes. Arrange them on a work surface and season with salt and pepper. Spoon 1 tablespoon of the cashew filling onto one end of each eggplant slice. Roll into tight cylinders. Cover with plastic wrap.

3. MAKE THE RATATOUILLE Brush all of the vegetables with olive oil and season with salt and pepper. Grill the vegetables in batches until tender and lightly charred, about 3 minutes for the tomatoes and 6 minutes for the onions, peppers, eggplant and zucchini. Transfer the grilled tomatoes to a blender and puree until smooth.

4. Peel, seed and dice the peppers and chop the onions. Add them to a large, deep skillet along with the 2 tablespoons of oil and the garlic, bay leaf, thyme and oregano. Cook over moderately high heat until tender, 5 minutes. Add the wine and boil until evaporated, 2 minutes. Add the tomato puree and water, season with salt and pepper and simmer until the sauce is slightly reduced, 15 minutes. Cut the eggplant and zucchini into ½-inch pieces and add to the skillet. Simmer 10 minutes longer. Discard the bay leaf and stir in the basil.

5. Spoon the grilled ratatouille into shallow bowls and top with the eggplant *involtini*. Spoon a dollop of harissa on top and serve right away. —*Sean Baker*

NOTE Nutritional yeast is a type of yeast that is high in vitamin B12. The savory butter-yellow flakes can help make lighter foods more satisfying. It is available at well-stocked specialty and natural-food stores or online at *vitaminshoppe.com*.

MAKE AHEAD The *involtini* and ratatouille can be refrigerated in separate containers for up to 2 days.

WINE Light-bodied Piedmontese red: 2009 Prunotto Dolcetto d'Alba.

● HEALTHY ● MAKE AHEAD ● VEGETARIAN ● STAFF FAVORITE

grilled squash ribbons and prosciutto with mint dressing

Mushroom-Stuffed Eggplant
ACTIVE: 30 MIN; TOTAL: 1 HR 45 MIN
4 SERVINGS ● ● ●

4 Italian eggplants (2½ pounds)
Salt
Extra-virgin olive oil
1 pound oyster mushrooms, sliced lengthwise ¼ inch thick
Freshly ground pepper
4 garlic cloves, minced
1 medium red onion, finely diced
1 teaspoon ground cumin
2 tablespoons unsalted butter
4 ounces stale baguette, cut into ½-inch dice, soaked in ½ cup red wine
2 ounces young pecorino, diced
¾ cup low-sodium vegetable broth
2 tablespoons chopped parsley

1. Halve the eggplants lengthwise and cut out the flesh, leaving ¼-inch shells. Cut the flesh into ½-inch dice. Salt the eggplant shells and let them stand for about 30 minutes. Pat the shells dry.
2. Preheat the oven to 350°. Rub the eggplants with oil; set them on a rimmed baking sheet, cut side down. Add ¼ cup of water, cover with foil and bake for 45 minutes.
3. Meanwhile, in a skillet, heat 2 tablespoons of olive oil. Add the mushrooms. Season with salt and pepper, cover and cook over moderate heat until tender; transfer to a bowl. Heat 1 tablespoon of olive oil in the skillet. Add the diced eggplant. Season with salt and pepper, cover and cook until tender and browned, 3 minutes; add to the mushrooms.
4. Add the garlic, onion and 2 tablespoons of olive oil to the skillet. Cover and cook, until softened. Add the cumin and 1 tablespoon of the butter and stir until fragrant, about 1 minute; add to the mushrooms. Stir in the wine-soaked bread, cheese and broth and season the filling with salt and pepper.
5. Increase the oven temperature to 425°. Turn the eggplant shells cut side up and fill with the bread stuffing. Dot the tops with the remaining 1 tablespoon of butter and bake in the upper third of the oven for 10 minutes.
6. Preheat the broiler. Broil the eggplant 4 inches from the heat until browned, 2 minutes. Top with the parsley and serve. —*Marcia Kiesel*
WINE Earthy Greek red: 2006 Kir-Yianni Ramnista Xinomavro.

Speedy Ratatouille with Goat Cheese
TOTAL: 1 HR • 4 SERVINGS ● ● ●

½ cup extra-virgin olive oil, plus more for drizzling
1 pound eggplant, peeled and cut into 1-inch dice
5 large garlic cloves, minced
Salt and freshly ground black pepper
1 zucchini, cut into ½-inch dice
1 yellow squash, cut into ½-inch dice
1 large onion, cut into ½-inch dice
1 red bell pepper, cut into ½-inch dice
2 pounds tomatoes, cored and finely chopped
1 cup loosely packed shredded basil leaves
½ teaspoon finely grated lemon zest
½ teaspoon fresh lemon juice
½ cup crumbled aged goat cheese

1. In a large enameled cast-iron casserole or Dutch oven, heat ¼ cup of the olive oil until shimmering. Add the eggplant and cook over moderately high heat, stirring occasionally, until almost tender, about 5 minutes. Add one-third of the garlic, season with salt and black pepper and cook for 1 minute. Using a slotted spoon, transfer the eggplant to a plate.
2. Add 2 tablespoons of the olive oil to the casserole along with the zucchini and yellow squash and cook over moderate heat until lightly browned in spots, about 5 minutes. Add another one-third of the garlic, season with salt and black pepper and cook for 1 minute. Add the vegetables to the eggplant.
3. Add the remaining 2 tablespoons of oil to the casserole along with the onion and bell pepper. Cook over moderate heat until softened, about 7 minutes. Add the remaining minced garlic, season with salt and black pepper and cook for about 1 minute. Add the tomatoes, two-thirds of the basil and the reserved vegetables and cook over moderate heat until the tomatoes have broken down and the vegetables are tender, about 15 minutes. Stir in the remaining basil along with the lemon zest and juice. Transfer to bowls and sprinkle with the goat cheese. Drizzle with olive oil and serve. —*Melissa Clark*
MAKE AHEAD The ratatouille can be refrigerated overnight.
WINE Citrusy Chenin Blanc: 2009 François Chidaine Montlouis Clos du Breuil.

Eggplant Compote
🕓 **ACTIVE: 15 MIN; TOTAL: 30 MIN**
MAKES 3½ CUPS ● ● ● ●
"Usually, eggplant absorbs so much oil and becomes full of fat," says star chef Joël Robuchon. For this healthy dish, he ingeniously steams eggplant instead of sautéing in oil.

1½ pounds eggplant, peeled and cut into ½-inch dice
3 medium tomatoes, coarsely grated on a box grater
2 garlic cloves, minced
¾ teaspoon ground cumin
½ teaspoon sweet Hungarian paprika
¼ cup tomato sauce, such as marinara or canned tomato puree
1 tablespoon white wine vinegar
Salt and freshly ground pepper
¼ teaspoon finely grated lemon zest
2 tablespoons chopped cilantro
1 tablespoon chopped parsley

1. Set the diced eggplant in a steamer basket. Set the basket over 1 inch of water and bring to a simmer. Cover and steam the eggplant until tender, 12 minutes; drain well.
2. In a large skillet, combine the tomatoes, garlic, cumin and paprika and simmer over moderate heat until thickened, 5 minutes. Add the tomato sauce and the eggplant and simmer, gently stirring a few times, until the eggplant is flavored with the sauce, 3 minutes. Remove from the heat and stir in the vinegar. Season with salt and pepper; add the zest, cilantro and parsley. Serve warm or at room temperature. —*Joël Robuchon*

Warm Grilled Corn with Pancetta and Red Pepper

🕐 TOTAL: 45 MIN • 8 SERVINGS ●

Chef Jeremy Sewall of Boston's Island Creek Oyster Bar created this side dish to accompany seafood. The corn gets a great porky flavor from the pancetta, which is simmered in water and then fried in the same pan to make it extra-crisp.

- 16 ears of corn, shucked
- Vegetable oil, for drizzling
- ½ pound pancetta, sliced ½ inch thick and cut into ½-inch dice
- ½ cup water
- 2 tablespoons minced garlic
- 2 small red bell peppers, cut into ½-inch dice
- 2 tablespoons sherry vinegar
- Salt and freshly ground black pepper
- 2 tablespoons small oregano leaves

1. Light a grill or preheat a grill pan. Drizzle the corn with oil and rub to coat thoroughly. Grill over moderate heat, turning often, until lightly charred all over and just tender, about 15 minutes, working in batches if necessary. Transfer the corn to a work surface and, when cool enough to handle, cut the kernels from the cobs.

2. In a large, deep skillet, combine the pancetta with the water and bring to a boil. Simmer over moderate heat until the water evaporates, about 4 minutes. Fry the diced pancetta, stirring occasionally, until crisp, about 8 minutes. Pour off all but 2 tablespoons of the fat in the skillet.

3. Add the garlic and red bell peppers to the skillet and cook over moderate heat, stirring, until the garlic is fragrant, about 2 minutes. Stir in the corn kernels and sherry vinegar and cook briefly to heat through. Remove from the heat and season with salt and black pepper. Stir in the oregano leaves, transfer to a bowl and serve.
—*Jeremy Sewall*

MAKE AHEAD The recipe can be made ahead through Step 1. The grilled corn kernels can be refrigerated overnight. Bring the corn to room temperature before proceeding.

Grilled Corn and Tomatoes with Vegan Tonnato Sauce

🕐 TOTAL: 45 MIN

6 SERVINGS ● ● ○ ○

"I have a huge affinity for Italian cooking," says Berkeley chef Sean Baker. "I just love *tonnato* [tuna] sauce and wanted vegans to have a sense of what it would taste like." To evoke the briny flavor of tuna, Baker adds seaweed to a puree of tofu and olive oil.

TONNATO SAUCE
- 2 loose tablespoons dried wakame (see Note)
- Boiling water
- ¼ cup silken tofu (about 3 ounces)
- 1 tablespoon capers, drained
- 1 small garlic clove
- 1 teaspoon yellow miso paste
- 1 teaspoon Dijon mustard
- 1 teaspoon nutritional yeast (see Note)
- 2 tablespoons freshly squeezed lemon juice
- ¼ cup plus 2 tablespoons extra-virgin olive oil
- Salt and freshly ground black pepper

SALAD
- 4 ears of corn, shucked
- 2 tablespoons extra-virgin olive oil, plus more for brushing
- Salt and freshly ground black pepper
- 1 tablespoon freshly squeezed lemon juice
- 2 tablespoons chopped basil
- 6 heirloom tomatoes, thinly sliced
- One 8-inch square sheet of nori, finely shredded (see Note)

1. MAKE THE SAUCE In a small heatproof bowl, soak the wakame in the boiling water until softened, about 5 minutes. Drain, rinse and press out any excess water; pat dry. Transfer the wakame to a mini food processor and add the tofu, capers, garlic, miso, mustard, nutritional yeast and lemon juice. Process to a paste. Add the olive oil and process until fairly smooth; the wakame won't break down completely. Season the sauce with salt and pepper.

2. MAKE THE SALAD Light a grill or preheat a grill pan. Brush the ears of corn with olive oil and season with salt and pepper. Grill over high heat, turning, until tender and lightly charred all over, about 5 minutes. When the corn is cool enough to handle, cut the kernels from the cobs into a medium bowl. Add the 2 tablespoons of olive oil, the lemon juice and basil and season the corn salad with salt and freshly ground black pepper.

3. Spread the sauce on plates and top with the tomatoes. Season with salt and pepper. Spoon the corn salad over the tomatoes and garnish with the shredded nori.
—*Sean Baker*

NOTE Dried wakame and nori, varieties of seaweed, are available at Asian markets, natural-food stores or at *shesellsseaweed. com*. Nutritional yeast is available at well-stocked specialty and natural-food stores or online at *vitaminshoppe.com*.

MAKE AHEAD The *tonnato* sauce can be stored in an airtight container in the refrigerator for up to 2 days. Bring to room temperature before serving.

WINE Rich California Chardonnay: 2009 La Follette Sangiacomo Vineyard.

fast corn salads

tomato-sausage Toss corn with blanched sugar snap peas, grilled andouille sausage, onion slices and halved cherry tomatoes. Dress with chopped cilantro, red wine vinegar and olive oil.

southwest-inspired Toss corn with diced roasted jalapeños, black beans, diced celery and chopped cilantro. Dress with lime juice, sour cream and canola oil.

summer succotash Toss corn with cooked baby lima beans and diced red and yellow bell peppers. Dress with freshly squeezed lemon juice and olive oil.

Stuffed Baby Peppers with Yogurt and and Floral Honey

TOTAL: 25 MIN PLUS 2 WEEKS
IF STEEPING HONEY • 4 SERVINGS ● ●

F&W's Marcia Kiesel uses flower-infused honey in savory dishes like these yogurt-stuffed baby peppers.

20 small sweet peppers, such as
    baby bell peppers
 1 cup plain low-fat yogurt
 1 garlic clove, minced
Salt and freshly ground black pepper
10 pitted kalamata olives, thinly sliced
 2 small jalapeños, very thinly
    sliced crosswise
Lavender-Rose Honey (recipe follows),
    for drizzling

1. Light a grill or preheat a grill pan. Grill the peppers over moderately high heat, turning, until lightly charred and crisp-tender, 3 minutes. Peel off any charred parts and halve the peppers lengthwise. Cut out the cores and scrape the seeds. Arrange the peppers cut side up on plates.
2. In a bowl, mix the yogurt with the garlic; season with salt and black pepper. Fill each pepper half with the yogurt. Scatter the olives and jalapeños on top. Drizzle each plate with 2 teaspoons of the honey and serve.
—*Marcia Kiesel*

LAVENDER-ROSE HONEY

TOTAL: 15 MIN PLUS 2 WEEKS STEEPING
MAKES ABOUT 3½ CUPS ● ● ●

 1 quart mild raw honey,
    such as wildflower
¾ cup dried organic rose petals
½ cup dried lavender flowers

In a large jar, mix the honey with the rose petals and lavender. Close and let stand in a sunny window for 2 weeks, turning every few days. Warm the jar in a microwave or under hot water until the honey is runny. Strain through a sieve into a clean jar. Discard the flowers. Store the honey in a cool, dark place for several months. —*Jovial King*

Stuffed Peppers with Thai Curry Rice and Mushrooms

ACTIVE: 40 MIN; TOTAL: 1 HR 30 MIN
4 SERVINGS ● ●

Heirloom seed specialists Emilee and Jere Gettle make this hearty vegetarian dish when bell peppers are at their peak, in late summer.

 4 large bell peppers
 2 tablespoons unsalted butter
    or grapeseed oil
 2 medium shallots, minced
 4 garlic cloves, minced
Salt
¾ cup long-grain white rice
½ cup unsweetened coconut milk
 1 tablespoon minced fresh ginger
 1 tablespoon Thai red curry paste
 1 large jalapeño, finely chopped,
    with seeds
¾ pound oyster mushrooms, cut into
    ½-inch pieces
 4 cups chopped spinach
¼ cup chopped Thai basil, plus basil
    leaves for garnish
 1 tablespoon fresh lemon juice

1. Bring a pot of water to a boil. Slice the tops off the peppers and cut the tops into ¼-inch dice; discard the cores and stems. Boil the hollowed-out peppers until just tender, 4 minutes. Using tongs, carefully transfer the peppers to paper towels to drain, cut side down. Reserve 1½ cups of the cooking water.
2. In a saucepan, melt 1 tablespoon of the butter. Add the shallots and garlic, season with salt and cook over moderate heat until softened, 3 minutes. Add the rice and cook, stirring, until toasted, 4 minutes. Stir in the coconut milk, ginger, curry paste and the 1½ cups of reserved pepper water and bring to a simmer. Cover and cook over low heat until the liquid is absorbed, 25 minutes.
3. Meanwhile, preheat the oven to 350°. In a large skillet, heat the remaining 1 tablespoon of butter. Add the diced bell pepper tops and the jalapeño and cook over moderate heat, stirring, until tender, about 5 minutes. Add the mushrooms, cover and cook, stirring a few times, until tender, about 5 minutes.

Uncover and cook, stirring, until the mushrooms are browned, about 4 minutes longer. Add the spinach and cook, stirring, until wilted, about 1 minute.
4. Add the vegetable mixture to the rice and stir in the chopped basil and lemon juice. Season with salt. Fill the peppers with the rice mixture and set them in a shallow glass or ceramic baking dish. Cover with aluminum foil and bake for about 45 minutes, until the rice filling is heated through. Garnish with basil and serve. —*Emilee and Jere Gettle*
WINE Bright, tropical California Sauvignon Blanc: 2009 Turnbull.

Corn on the Cob with Seasoned Salts

⏱ **TOTAL: 30 MIN • 4 SERVINGS** ● ●

"Walk to pick it, run to cook it," was the mantra in the days when corn turned starchy within hours of harvesting. New varieties stay sweet and tender longer. Flavoring the ears here is a trio of seasoned salts.

1½ tablespoons Maldon
    or Halen Môn Welsh sea salt
 2 teaspoons finely grated orange zest
1½ tablespoons kosher salt
 1 teaspoon hot smoked paprika
1½ tablespoons coarse smoked salt
 1 tablespoon coarsely ground
    black pepper
 8 ears of corn, shucked
Vegetable oil, for drizzling
Unsalted butter, for serving

1. Prepare the salts in 3 small bowls: Mix the Maldon salt with the orange zest, the kosher salt with the paprika and the smoked salt with the black pepper.
2. Light a grill or preheat a grill pan. Drizzle the ears of corn with vegetable oil and rub to coat them thoroughly. Grill over moderate heat, turning often, until the corn is lightly charred all over and just tender, about 15 minutes. Transfer the corn to a large platter and serve with butter and the seasoned salts. —*Marcia Kiesel*
MAKE AHEAD The salts can be stored separately in airtight containers for up to 1 week.

corn on the cob with seasoned salts

Provençal Vegetable Tart

ACTIVE: 45 MIN; TOTAL: 2 HR 30 MIN
MAKES ONE 4-BY-14-INCH TART OR TWO
10-INCH ROUND TARTS • 6 SERVINGS ● ●

Before she opened her Vermont bakery Vergennes Laundry, Julianne Jones sold savory tarts at the local farmers' market. This one, which she calls "tart-a-touille," is made with the vegetables that are in ratatouille.

TART SHELL

1¾ cups all-purpose flour
½ teaspoon salt
1 stick plus 2 tablespoons cold unsalted butter, cubed
¼ cup ice water

FILLING

3½ tablespoons extra-virgin olive oil, plus more for drizzling
1 small yellow bell pepper—cored, seeded and sliced ¼ inch thick
1 medium onion, cut into ¼-inch wedges
Salt and freshly ground black pepper
1 small Japanese eggplant, sliced ¼ inch thick
1 small zucchini, sliced ¼ inch thick
½ cup grape tomatoes
2 teaspoons Champagne vinegar
1 teaspoon fresh thyme leaves
1 teaspoon chopped basil
2 ounces thinly sliced Tomme de Savoie or imported Fontina cheese

super-simple ratatouille

Salt diced eggplant for 20 minutes. Pat dry, then sauté in olive oil for 5 minutes; set aside. Sauté chopped onion and garlic in more oil until fragrant. Stir in diced bell pepper and zucchini and chopped thyme; cook for 10 minutes. Add diced tomatoes; simmer for 5 minutes. Add the eggplant and fresh basil, then season with salt and pepper.

1. MAKE THE TART SHELL In a food processor, combine the flour and salt. Add the butter and pulse 5 times in 1-second bursts. Add the ice water and pulse until the dough comes together. Turn the dough out onto a floured work surface and knead briefly. Flatten the dough into a disk, wrap in plastic and chill for about 30 minutes, until firm.
2. Preheat the oven to 375°. On a floured work surface, roll out the dough to a 6-by-16-inch rectangle, a scant ¼ inch thick. Ease the pastry into a 4-by-14-inch tart mold and trim the overhang to ½ inch. Fold the overhang over to reinforce the edges. Refrigerate the tart shell for about 15 minutes, until firm.
3. Line the tart shell with parchment and pie weights and bake in the center of the oven for 35 minutes, until set. Remove the parchment and weights and bake for about 10 minutes longer, until golden. Let cool.
4. MEANWHILE, MAKE THE FILLING Line a baking sheet with parchment paper and drizzle with oil. In a bowl, toss the bell pepper and onion with ½ tablespoon of the oil, season with salt and pepper and arrange on one-quarter of the baking sheet. Add the eggplant to the bowl, toss with ½ tablespoon of the oil, season with salt and pepper and arrange on another quarter of the baking sheet. Repeat with the zucchini and tomatoes, using ½ tablespoon of oil for each.
5. Roast the vegetables for about 45 minutes, turning once, until tender. Let them cool slightly, then return them to the bowl. Add the vinegar, herbs and the remaining 1½ tablespoons of olive oil and toss; season with salt and pepper. Scrape the roasted vegetables into the tart shell, tuck in the cheese slices and serve. —*Julianne Jones*
WINE Herb-scented Pinot Noir: 2008 Anthill Farms Anderson Valley.

Provençal Vegetable Casserole

ACTIVE: 30 MIN; TOTAL: 2 HR 15 MIN
6 SERVINGS ● ● ●

Guests at Château de Campuget, an 18th-century winery and inn in France's Rhône Valley, adore this casserole of vegetables baked in a ceramic pot until soft, sweet and glazed in their own juices.

3 tablespoons extra-virgin olive oil, plus more for drizzling
2 large beefsteak tomatoes, sliced ¼ inch thick
Salt and freshly ground pepper
1 large onion, thinly sliced
2 garlic cloves, minced
2 teaspoons chopped thyme
One 1½-pound eggplant, sliced lengthwise ¼ inch thick
Two ½-pound zucchini, sliced lengthwise ¼ inch thick
2 tablespoons chopped parsley

1. Preheat the oven to 350°. In a large skillet, heat 1 tablespoon of the olive oil. Add half of the tomatoes, season with salt and pepper and cook over high heat for about 10 seconds per side. Transfer the tomatoes to a large plate; repeat with the remaining slices.
2. Add the remaining 2 tablespoons of olive oil to the skillet. Add the onion, garlic and thyme, cover and cook over moderate heat, stirring occasionally, until the ingredients are softened. Season with salt and pepper; remove the skillet from the heat.
3. Oil a 9-by-13-inch ceramic or glass baking dish. Arrange one-third of the eggplant on the bottom, drizzle with oil; season with salt and pepper. Scatter half of the onions on top, followed by half of the zucchini. Drizzle the zucchini with oil, season with salt and pepper and sprinkle with half of the parsley. Arrange half of the tomatoes and their cooking juices over the zucchini. Repeat the layering, ending with a layer of eggplant. Drizzle with oil; season with salt and pepper.
4. Cover the casserole with aluminum foil; bake in the upper third of the oven for 1 hour. Remove the foil, tilt the baking dish and baste the top of the casserole with the juices. Continue baking for 30 minutes, until very tender.
5. Preheat the broiler. Tilt the baking dish and pour off all but ¼ cup of the juices. Broil the casserole 4 inches from the heat until the top is nicely browned. Let the casserole rest for at least 15 minutes, then serve. —*Mathilde Dalle and Patrick Thibaud*
WINE Herbal Rhône rosé: 2010 Château de Campuget Tradition.

● HEALTHY ● MAKE AHEAD ○ VEGETARIAN ● STAFF FAVORITE

provençal vegetable tart

Endive Tarte Tatin

ACTIVE: 25 MIN; TOTAL: 2 HR
6 SERVINGS ● ○

This buttery, flaky pastry (made in a food processor) topped with endives is extremely adaptable: Try asparagus or fennel in place of the endives.

PASTRY

- 1½ cups all-purpose flour
- 1 teaspoon kosher salt
- 1½ sticks cold unsalted butter, cubed
- ⅓ cup ice water

TOPPING

- 2 tablespoons unsalted butter
- 4 medium Belgian endives, halved lengthwise
- Salt and freshly ground pepper
- ⅓ cup fresh orange juice

1. MAKE THE PASTRY In a food processor, pulse the flour and salt. Add the butter pieces and pulse to the size of small peas. Sprinkle the ice water over the flour mixture and pulse until the pastry starts to come together.

2. Scrape the pastry out onto a work surface and knead gently a few times to form a cohesive dough. Flatten into a disk, wrap in plastic and refrigerate until thoroughly chilled and firm, about 1 hour.

3. PREPARE THE TOPPING Preheat the oven to 350°. In a 12-inch ovenproof skillet, melt the butter. Add the endives, cut side down, and cook over moderately high heat until sizzling, about 2 minutes. Cover the skillet, transfer to the oven and bake for 25 minutes. Turn the endives cut side up and season with salt and pepper. Cover and bake for about 20 minutes longer, until very tender.

4. Turn the endives cut side down. Cook over moderately high heat until browned, 2 minutes. Add the orange juice to the skillet and bring to a boil, then remove from the heat. Increase the oven temperature to 425°.

5. On a lightly floured work surface, roll the pastry out to a 12-inch round, about ¼ inch thick. Lay the pastry over the endives in the skillet. Trim any overhang. Bake in the upper third of the oven for about 35 minutes, until the pastry is richly browned and crisp.

6. Set the skillet over high heat and shake gently to loosen the endives. Set a large plate upside-down on top of the pan, then carefully invert the tart onto the plate. Let cool slightly, then cut into wedges and serve warm.
—*Chantal Leroux*

WINE Citrusy French white: 2009 Alain Gras Saint-Romain Blanc.

Gin-and-Orange-Juice-Braised Endives

◔ **ACTIVE: 15 MIN; TOTAL: 40 MIN**
10 SERVINGS ● ○

- 3 tablespoons extra-virgin olive oil
- 10 medium Belgian endives, halved lengthwise
- ½ cup gin
- Salt and freshly ground black pepper
- 1 cup fresh orange juice
- 4 tablespoons unsalted butter
- 2 tablespoons honey
- 2 scallions, white and pale green parts only, thinly sliced
- 2 tablespoons salted roasted pumpkin seeds
- Balsamic vinegar, for drizzling

1. In each of 2 large skillets, heat 1½ tablespoons of the extra-virgin olive oil. Add the endive halves, cut side down, and cook over moderate heat until richly browned, about 5 minutes. Slowly pour ¼ cup of the gin into each skillet and cook until it's reduced by half. Turn the endives over, season with salt and freshly ground black pepper and add ½ cup of the orange juice to each skillet. Cover and cook over low heat, turning once, until the endives are tender, about 15 minutes.

2. Transfer the braised endives to a warm platter, cut side up. Pour the liquid from one of the skillets into the other. Add the butter and honey and boil over high heat until syrupy, about 4 minutes. Season with salt and freshly ground pepper. Pour the sauce over the endives and garnish with the sliced scallions and roasted pumpkin seeds. Drizzle the endives with the balsamic vinegar and serve at once. —*Tory Miller*

Swiss Chard and Leek Gratin

ACTIVE: 45 MIN; TOTAL: 1 HR 15 MIN
10 TO 12 SERVINGS ● ● ●

- 3 pounds Swiss chard, large stems discarded
- 3 tablespoons extra-virgin olive oil
- 6 medium leeks, white and tender green parts only, sliced ¼ inch thick
- Salt
- 3 garlic cloves, minced
- 6 tablespoons unsalted butter
- ⅔ cup all-purpose flour
- 1 quart whole milk
- ½ cup shredded Gruyère cheese
- ½ cup freshly grated Parmigiano-Reggiano cheese
- ¼ teaspoon freshly grated nutmeg
- Freshly ground pepper

1. In a large pot of boiling water, blanch the chard in batches until wilted, about 1 minute. Drain the chard, squeeze dry and chop it.

2. Heat the oil in the pot. Add the leeks and a pinch of salt. Cover and cook over moderately low heat, stirring, until tender, 7 minutes. Uncover, add the garlic and cook, stirring, until fragrant, 2 minutes. Add the chard, season with salt and remove from the heat.

3. Preheat the oven to 425°. Butter a 10-by-15-inch baking dish. In a large saucepan, melt the butter. Stir in the flour over moderate heat to form a paste. Gradually whisk in one-third of the milk and cook, whisking, until the mixture starts to thicken. Repeat two more times with the remaining milk. Bring the sauce to a boil, whisking constantly. Reduce the heat to low and cook, whisking often, until thickened and no floury taste remains, 15 minutes. Whisk in the cheeses and the nutmeg; season with salt and pepper. Mix the sauce into the leeks and chard. Season with salt and pepper.

4. Transfer the mixture to the prepared baking dish. Bake in the upper third of the oven for about 25 minutes, until bubbling and golden brown on top. Let rest for at least 10 minutes before serving. —*Michael Symon*
MAKE AHEAD The unbaked gratin can be refrigerated overnight. Bring to room temperature before baking.

● HEALTHY ● MAKE AHEAD ○ VEGETARIAN ○ STAFF FAVORITE

gin-and-orange-juice-braised endives

Braised Collard Greens

ACTIVE: 30 MIN; TOTAL: 1 HR 30 MIN
8 SERVINGS ● ● ○ ○ ●

Mississippi soul food specialist Mary Hoover braises these collard greens until they're supertender and silky, but she cautions that "younger people" tend to prefer their collards crunchier. She recommends drinking the collards' cooking liquid, which she says is very healthful.

vegetable sides for a party

These fantastic vegetable sides from New York City chef Floyd Cardoz are versatile enough to go with either of his slow-roasted salmons (pages 196 and 198), roast chickens (pages 122 and 124) or rib roasts (pages 155 and 156)—or any main course you choose.

braised escarole In a large pot, heat ¼ cup canola oil until shimmering. Add 1 tablespoon yellow mustard seeds and cook until they pop. Add ½ tablespoon cumin seeds, 1 dried chipotle chile, 1 diced onion and 2 tablespoons minced fresh ginger and cook until the onion is translucent. Add 2 heads cleaned escarole and 1 cup chicken stock or broth and simmer until the escarole is tender. Season with salt and freshly ground pepper.

roasted squash In a large pot, heat ¼ cup oil. Add 4 cloves, 2 star anise pods, 2 dried chipotle chiles, 2 rosemary sprigs and ½ cup chopped fresh ginger; cook for 2 minutes, stirring. Stir in 10 cups 1-inch-cubed peeled winter squash; roast at 375° until tender. Discard the cloves, star anise, chiles and rosemary. Season with honey, lime juice, salt and pepper.

- ¼ cup vegetable oil
- 1½ tablespoons table salt
- 1 tablespoon sugar
- 5 pounds collard greens, thick stems and inner ribs discarded

Vinegar, for drizzling

In a large pot, combine the vegetable oil, salt and sugar with 3 quarts of water and bring to a vigorous boil. Add the collards in large handfuls, allowing each batch to wilt slightly before adding more. Return to a boil. Reduce the heat and simmer the collards over moderate heat, gently turning the greens occasionally, until they are very tender, about 1 hour. Using tongs, transfer the collards to a medium bowl, drizzle with vinegar and serve. *—Mary Hoover*

Cumin-Braised Swiss Chard

⏱ **TOTAL: 40 MIN • 8 SERVINGS** ● ● ●

"I could eat braised greens with every meal," says Jenn Louis, the chef at Lincoln restaurant and Sunshine Tavern in Portland, Oregon. The cumin here makes the chard a nice match with the Mexican flavors in her Chicken Tinga Tacos (page 115).

- 6 tablespoons extra-virgin olive oil
- 1 large onion, halved and thinly sliced
- 4 large garlic cloves, thinly sliced
- 1½ tablespoons ground cumin
- ½ teaspoon crushed red pepper
- 2½ pounds Swiss chard—stems thinly sliced, leaves cut into 1-inch ribbons
- ½ cup chicken stock
- 2 teaspoons unsalted butter

Salt

In a deep skillet, heat the olive oil. Add the onion, garlic, cumin and red pepper. Cover and cook over moderate heat, stirring occasionally, until the onion is softened, about 5 minutes. Add the chard stems and leaves and cook, stirring, until the leaves are wilted. Add the chicken stock, cover and cook over high heat, stirring occasionally, until the stems are tender, about 6 minutes. Swirl in the butter, season with salt and serve. *—Jenn Louis*

Kimchi-Creamed Collard Greens

ACTIVE: 40 MIN; TOTAL: 2 HR 15 MIN
8 SERVINGS ● ●

"I don't think a cuisine should ever stop growing," says chef Hugh Acheson of Five & Ten in Athens, Georgia. In this updated version of creamed spinach, the classic Southern side, he substitutes firm collard greens for the spinach and adds chopped kimchi to the cream sauce for a racy kick.

- 3 tablespoons extra-virgin olive oil
- 1 large onion, cut into ¼-inch dice
- ½ pound bacon cut into ¼-inch dice
- 2 pounds stemmed collard greens, leaves cut into 2-inch pieces
- ¼ cup sherry vinegar
- 1 tablespoon sorghum syrup (see Note)
- 2 cups chicken stock
- 2 cups water
- ½ teaspoon crushed red pepper

Salt

- 1 cup heavy cream
- 1 cup kimchi, finely chopped

1. In a large pot, heat the olive oil. Add the onion and cook over moderate heat, stirring occasionally, until golden brown, about 7 minutes. Add the bacon and cook, stirring occasionally, until the fat has rendered, about 10 minutes. Add the collards and cook over moderately high heat, stirring a few times, until it begins to wilt, about 4 minutes. Add the vinegar and boil for 1 minute. Add the sorghum syrup, stock, water, crushed red pepper and a large pinch of salt. Cover and cook, stirring a few times, until the collards are very tender, about 1½ hours. **2.** Meanwhile, in a small saucepan, simmer the cream over moderate heat until reduced by one-third, about 10 minutes. Add the kimchi and remove from the heat. **3.** When the collards are done, stir in the kimchi cream. Season with salt and serve. *—Hugh Acheson*

NOTE Sorghum syrup, sometimes referred to as sorghum molasses, is available online at *zingermans.com*. Alternatively, pure maple syrup can be used as a substitute.

● HEALTHY ● MAKE AHEAD ● VEGETARIAN ● STAFF FAVORITE

Asian Steamed Buns with Bok Choy and Chinese Chives

ACTIVE: 1 HR 15 MIN; TOTAL: 2 HR

MAKES 16 BUNS ● ● ●

DOUGH

½ cup warm water

1 tablespoon honey

2¼ teaspoons active dry yeast

3½ cups all-purpose flour

½ teaspoon salt

1 cup plain almond milk or soy milk, at room temperature

FILLING

½ pound trimmed mustard greens

¼ cup extra-virgin olive oil

10 ounces shiitake mushrooms, stems discarded and caps thinly sliced

6 garlic cloves, minced

2 large shallots, minced

½ pound baby bok choy, cut into ½-inch pieces

½ cup chopped Chinese chives

½ cup chopped basil

2 tablespoons soy sauce

2 tablespoons sweet chile sauce

Salt and freshly ground pepper

1. PREPARE THE DOUGH In a large bowl, combine the warm water, honey and yeast and let stand until foamy, 10 minutes. In another bowl, whisk the flour with the salt. Stir the almond milk into the yeast mixture, then stir in the flour. Knead the dough gently until smooth but still slightly sticky; transfer to an oiled bowl, cover and let rise until doubled in bulk, 50 minutes.

2. MEANWHILE, PREPARE THE FILLING In a medium saucepan of boiling salted water, cook the mustard greens until just tender, 1 minute. Drain well, let cool and squeeze dry. Coarsely chop the mustard greens.

3. In a large skillet, heat 3 tablespoons of the olive oil. Add the mushrooms, cover and cook over moderate heat, stirring occasionally, until tender, about 4 minutes. Add the garlic and shallots and the remaining 1 tablespoon of olive oil and cook, stirring, until softened, about 3 minutes. Add the bok choy, cover and cook, stirring occasionally, until tender, about 5 minutes. Stir in the mustard greens, chives, basil, soy sauce and sweet chile sauce and remove from the heat. Season with salt and pepper and let cool.

4. Cut out sixteen 3½-inch parchment paper squares. Punch down the dough and transfer to a floured work surface. Form it into a rectangle and cut into 16 equal pieces. Using floured hands, roll each piece of dough into a ball. Sprinkle the balls with flour, cover with plastic wrap and let rest for 10 minutes.

5. Working with 4 pieces of dough at a time, roll the balls out to 4-inch rounds, dusting with flour as needed. Fill each round with about 3 tablespoons of the filling. Bring the edge of the round up and over the filling and pinch the seam closed in pleats. Set the buns seam side down on the parchment squares and transfer to a baking sheet in the refrigerator until all of the buns are filled.

6. In a deep skillet or wok, bring 1½ inches of water to a boil, then set a bamboo or metal steamer over the water. Arrange 4 buns paper side down in the steamer. Cover and steam over moderately high heat until tender and cooked through, 10 minutes. Steam the remaining buns. —*Emilee and Jere Gettle*

SERVE WITH Sriracha sauce.

Chopped Kale with Hot Pepper Vinegar

ACTIVE: 15 MIN; TOTAL: 30 MIN

PLUS OVERNIGHT MARINATING

4 SERVINGS ● ● ● ●

1 cup white vinegar

2 serrano chiles, thinly sliced

¼ cup extra-virgin olive oil

1 medium onion, minced

10 garlic cloves, thinly sliced

2 teaspoons ground caraway

¾ pound kale, stems discarded and leaves coarsely chopped

Salt and freshly ground pepper

1. In a small saucepan, bring the vinegar to a simmer. Put the serranos in a small heatproof bowl; pour the hot vinegar over them. Let cool, cover and refrigerate overnight.

2. In a skillet, heat the oil. Add the onion and cook over moderate heat until softened, about 7 minutes. Add the garlic and cook over moderately low heat, stirring, until golden, about 5 minutes. Add the caraway and stir in the kale. Cover and cook over moderate heat until the kale is sizzling, about 2 minutes. Uncover and cook, stirring, until the kale is just tender, about 2 minutes. Season with salt and pepper and toss with 3 tablespoons of the vinegar; reserve the remaining vinegar for another use. Serve the kale hot or warm. —*Richard Blais*

Indian-Style Mustard Greens

⏲ TOTAL: 35 MIN • 4 TO 6 SERVINGS

● ● ● ●

1¼ pounds mustard greens, stemmed, or broccoli rabe, trimmed and chopped

½ pound cleaned spinach

2 tablespoons cornmeal

6 garlic cloves, chopped

4 jalapeños, seeded and finely chopped

One 2-inch piece of fresh ginger, peeled and chopped

2 red onions, finely chopped

¼ cup vegetable oil

Salt

1. Bring a large pot of salted water to a boil. Add the mustard greens and cook for 2 minutes. Add the spinach and cook for 30 seconds. Drain the greens, transfer to a food processor and puree. Sprinkle the cornmeal over the greens and pulse briefly to combine. Transfer the pureed greens to a bowl.

2. Add the garlic, jalapeños and ginger to the food processor and finely chop. Add the onions and finely chop.

3. In a large nonstick skillet, heat the oil. Add the garlic-onion mixture and cook over moderate heat, stirring occasionally, until lightly browned, about 7 minutes. Add the pureed greens and cook for about 4 minutes, stirring occasionally; add about ¼ cup of water if the greens look dry. Season with salt and serve. —*Sanjeev Kapoor*

SERVE WITH Naan or *makki ki roti*.

Grilled Brassicas with Mixed Grains and Bonito Broth

TOTAL: 1 HR • 4 SERVINGS

At Saison in San Francisco, F&W Best New Chef 2011 Joshua Skenes serves slow-roasted brassicas (plants in the mustard family, like broccoli, cauliflower, cabbage and rutabaga) with toasted puffed grains, foie gras fat, quail eggs and both a broth and an emulsion made from bonito (dried smoked fish) and local seaweeds. This is Skenes's streamlined version of that dish.

- ⅓ cup farro
- ⅓ cup pearled barley
- ⅓ cup wild rice
- One ½-ounce piece of dried kombu (see Note)
- One 5-gram package dried bonito flakes (see Note)
- ½ pound Broccolini or baby broccoli, stems peeled
- 4 large brussels sprouts, quartered
- 4 large cauliflower florets, quartered
- Extra-virgin olive oil, for drizzling
- Salt and freshly ground pepper
- 1 tablespoon soy sauce, preferably white soy (see Note)
- 4 tablespoons cold unsalted butter, cut into tablespoons
- 2 tablespoons plus 2 teaspoons fresh lemon juice (preferably Meyer lemon)
- 4 poached quail eggs (see Note)

1. In each of 3 small saucepans, toast the farro, barley and wild rice over moderately high heat, tossing, until they start to smell nutty, 2 minutes. Add water to each pan to cover the grains and rice by 2 inches; bring to a boil. Cover and cook until just tender, 25 minutes for the farro and barley and 35 minutes for the rice. Drain and transfer all the grains and rice to a medium saucepan.
2. Meanwhile, put the kombu in a small saucepan and add 2 cups of water. Cover and simmer over moderate heat for 5 minutes; do not boil. Remove from the heat and discard the kombu. Add the bonito flakes and let steep for 2 minutes, then strain the broth into a small saucepan.

3. Light a grill or preheat a grill pan. Toss the Broccolini, brussels sprouts and cauliflower with olive oil and season with salt and pepper. Grill on a perforated pan over moderate heat, turning often, until the vegetables are nicely charred and crisp-tender, 5 to 10 minutes.
4. Add ½ cup of the bonito broth, 2 teaspoons of the soy sauce and 1 tablespoon of the butter to the grains and heat, stirring often. Season lightly with salt.
5. Bring the remaining bonito broth to a boil. Transfer to a blender. Add the remaining 3 tablespoons of butter and 1 teaspoon of soy sauce and blend until frothy.
6. Spoon the grains into four bowls. Top with the grilled brassicas and sprinkle each serving with 2 teaspoons of the lemon juice. Top with the quail eggs and season with salt. Spoon the bonito butter froth over the eggs and grains and serve. —*Joshua Skenes*
NOTE Look for kombu, bonito flakes and white soy sauce at Asian markets. To poach quail eggs, carefully add to a pot of simmering water for 1 minute, then drain.
WINE Fruity, grassy New Zealand Sauvignon Blanc: 2010 Nobilo Icon Marlborough.

Grilled Turnips with Garlic

TOTAL: 20 MIN • 4 SERVINGS ● ● ●

- 1 pound turnips, sliced ¼ inch thick
- Extra-virgin olive oil
- Salt and freshly ground pepper
- 1 tablespoon minced garlic
- 2 tablespoons finely chopped Italian parsley
- Grated zest of 1 lemon

1. Light a grill or preheat a grill pan. Brush the turnips on both sides with 1 tablespoon of oil; season with salt and pepper. Grill the turnips over moderately high heat until tender, 2 minutes per side. Transfer to a platter.
2. In a skillet, cook the garlic in 2 tablespoons of olive oil over high heat just until sizzling. Reduce the heat to low and cook until the garlic is golden, 2 minutes. Off the heat, stir in the parsley and ½ teaspoon of pepper. Spoon the oil over the turnips and top with the lemon zest. —*Michael Schwartz*

Broccoli with Bacon, Blue Cheese and Ranch Dressing

⋅) **TOTAL: 30 MIN • 6 SERVINGS**

A quarter head of cooked and cooled broccoli with ranch dressing, blue cheese and bacon replaces the nutrition-free iceberg lettuce wedge beloved at steak houses. This salad would also be delicious with Broccolini, which is similar to broccoli but with smaller florets and longer stems.

- 1 large garlic clove, mashed
- Salt
- ¾ cup buttermilk
- ¾ cup plain low-fat Greek yogurt
- 1 tablespoon cider vinegar
- ¼ cup canola oil
- Freshly ground pepper
- 3 very large heads of broccoli, quartered lengthwise
- ½ pound sliced bacon
- ½ cup Roquefort cheese, crumbled (3 ounces)
- Snipped chives or chive blossoms, for garnish

1. On a work surface, mash the garlic with a generous pinch of salt until pasty. Scrape the garlic into a bowl and whisk in the buttermilk, yogurt and cider vinegar. Whisk in the canola oil and season the ranch dressing generously with pepper.
2. In a large, deep pot, bring 1 inch of water to a boil. Set the broccoli in a steamer basket; steam until bright green and crisp-tender, 4 to 5 minutes. Transfer the broccoli to a plate and refrigerate until cool.
3. Meanwhile, in a skillet, cook the bacon over moderate heat until golden and crisp, about 6 minutes. Drain on paper towels.
4. Arrange the bacon strips on plates and top with the broccoli wedges. Drizzle with the ranch dressing, top with the Roquefort cheese and sprinkle with chives. Serve any extra dressing on the side.
—*Grace Parisi*

MAKE AHEAD The dressing can be refrigerated for up to 4 days.
WINE Bright, full-bodied German Riesling: 2010 Leitz Leitz Out.

● HEALTHY ● MAKE AHEAD ● VEGETARIAN ● STAFF FAVORITE

broccoli with bacon, blue cheese and ranch dressing

Traditional Napa Cabbage Kimchi

ACTIVE: 30 MIN; TOTAL: 2 HR PLUS
3 DAYS FERMENTING • MAKES 3 QUARTS

● ● ●

This classic recipe for spicy Korean pickled cabbage is from Marja Vongerichten, host of PBS's *Kimchi Chronicles.*

- 2 large heads of napa cabbage (3¼ pounds each)—halved, cored and cut into 2-inch pieces
- ⅔ cup kosher salt
- 10 garlic cloves, halved
- ½ small onion, chopped
- One 1-inch piece of fresh ginger, peeled and chopped
- ¼ cup sugar
- ¼ cup plus 3 tablespoons Asian fish sauce
- ½ pound daikon, peeled and cut into matchsticks
- 1 bunch of scallions, cut into 2-inch lengths
- ¾ cup *gochugaru* (Korean red pepper powder), see Note at right

1. In each of 2 very large bowls, layer the cabbage with the salt. Let stand for 45 minutes. Toss the cabbage well and let stand for 45 minutes longer.
2. Fill a sink with cold water. Swirl the cabbage in it to remove the salt; drain and repeat. Drain the cabbage well, lightly pat dry with paper towels and transfer to a very large bowl.
3. In a mini food processor, puree the garlic, onion, ginger and sugar. Add the fish sauce and process until blended.
4. Add the daikon and scallions to the cabbage and toss. Add the garlic mixture and the red pepper powder and toss thoroughly. Pack the cabbage into three 1-quart jars. Press a piece of plastic wrap on the surface of the kimchi and put the lids on loosely. Let stand at room temperature for 3 days, until the cabbage is tangy and bubbling. Store the kimchi in the refrigerator.
—*Marja Vongerichten*
MAKE AHEAD The kimchi can be refrigerated for up to 6 months.

Almost-Instant Hot Kimchi

TOTAL: 20 MIN • 8 SERVINGS ●

Instead of slowly fermenting this kimchi, chef Jean-Georges Vongerichten uses vinegar for instant sourness. He serves it hot, like the sauerkraut from his native Alsace.

- 2 tablespoons vegetable oil
- 1 small red onion, thinly sliced
- 1 teaspoon coriander seeds
- 1 tablespoon *gochugaru* (Korean red pepper powder), see Note
- 2 tablespoons *gochujang* (Korean red chile paste), see Note
- 3 tablespoons sherry vinegar
- 3 tablespoons Asian fish sauce
- One 3¼-pound head of napa cabbage, cored and cut into 2-inch pieces
- 1 small Asian pear—peeled, cored and coarsely chopped
- 1 Kirby cucumber, sliced crosswise

In a large pot, heat the oil. Add the onion, coriander and pepper powder and cook over moderate heat, stirring, until the onion begins to brown, 4 minutes. In a small bowl, whisk together the pepper paste, sherry vinegar and fish sauce; add to the pot and cook over high heat, stirring, for 1 minute. Add the cabbage, pear and cucumber and cook, stirring, until the cabbage is just wilted, 3 minutes. Serve. —*Jean-Georges Vongerichten*
NOTE Korean red pepper paste and powder are available online at *hmart.com.*

Sparkling White Kimchi

ACTIVE: 30 MIN; TOTAL: 1 HR 30 MIN
PLUS OVERNIGHT MARINATING
MAKES 4 CUPS ● ● ●

"You see 7UP quite a bit in Korean recipes," says New York chef David Chang. He uses the soda in his quick "white" kimchi; it adds an appealing bubbliness to the cabbage.

- 1 pound napa cabbage—halved, cored and cut into 2-inch pieces
- 1 tablespoon kosher salt
- 1 tablespoon rice vinegar
- 2 scallions, white and tender green parts only, halved lengthwise
- 1 carrot, very thinly sliced
- 2 large red chiles, thinly sliced and seeded
- 1½ cups 7UP or ginger ale
- 1 bunch of watercress, thick stems discarded

In a bowl, toss the cabbage with the salt and squeeze to soften slightly. Cover with a small plate and a heavy can and let stand at room temperature for 1 hour. Pour off any liquid. Stir in the vinegar, scallions, carrot and chiles. Add the 7UP, cover with plastic and refrigerate overnight. Fold in the watercress just before serving. —*David Chang*

Pickled Wild Onions with Honey and Wild Rosemary

TOTAL: 30 MIN PLUS 6 HR PICKLING
6 TO 8 SERVINGS ● ● ● ●

- 10 ounces small wild onions, trimmed, or pearl onions, blanched, peeled and trimmed
- ½ cup white wine or Champagne vinegar
- ½ cup local honey
- ¼ cup water
- 2 tablespoons fresh lemon juice
- 5 whole black peppercorns
- Fine sea salt
- 6 wild rosemary sprigs
- 1 cup canola oil

1. Pack the onions into a heatproof glass jar. In a medium saucepan, combine the vinegar, honey, water, lemon juice, peppercorns, ¼ teaspoon of salt and 1 rosemary sprig and bring to a boil. Pour the hot liquid over the onions and place a plate on top to keep them submerged. Let stand for 6 hours at room temperature. Serve right away or refrigerate for up to 1 week.
2. Just before serving, snip the remaining 5 rosemary sprigs into 2-inch lengths. Heat the oil in a small skillet until shimmering. Add the rosemary and fry over moderately high heat for 30 seconds, until crisp and just beginning to brown around the edges. Drain on paper towels; sprinkle with salt. Serve with the onions. —*Joshua Skenes*

● HEALTHY ● MAKE AHEAD ● VEGETARIAN ● STAFF FAVORITE

do-it-yourself sauerkraut

It's more than just a topping for hot dogs and pork chops: Made the old-fashioned way, kraut is a health superfood. Fermentation pro **Alex Hozven** shares his recipes and tips.

Homemade Sauerkraut with Caraway and Apples

ACTIVE: 1 HR; TOTAL: 5 HR
PLUS UP TO 6 WEEKS FERMENTING
MAKES 2 QUARTS ● ● ○ ○

According to Hozven, owner of the Cultured Pickle Shop in Berkeley, the apple used here is a traditional component in many Eastern European sauerkraut recipes.

- 4 pounds green cabbage, very thinly sliced on a mandoline or finely shredded in a food processor
- 1 Granny Smith apple—peeled, cored and very thinly sliced on a mandoline
- 2 tablespoons plus 1 teaspoon fine sea salt
- 1 tablespoon caraway seeds
- ½ tablespoon juniper berries (optional)

Indian-Spiced Sauerkraut

ACTIVE: 1 HR; TOTAL: 5 HR
PLUS UP TO 6 WEEKS FERMENTING
MAKES 2 QUARTS ● ● ● ○

Hozven worked with an herbalist to create an ayurvedic spice blend, designed to improve digestion and balance within the body.

- 4 pounds green cabbage, very thinly sliced on a mandoline or finely shredded in a food processor
- 1 tablespoon each whole cumin seeds and coriander seeds
- ½ tablespoon each whole fennel seeds and black peppercorns
- 1 teaspoon each whole brown mustard seeds and fenugreek seeds
- 1 teaspoon each turmeric and paprika
- 2 tablespoons plus 1 teaspoon fine sea salt

Seakraut

ACTIVE: 1 HR; TOTAL: 5 HR
PLUS UP TO 6 WEEKS FERMENTING
MAKES 2 QUARTS ● ● ● ○

"Hijiki and arame seaweeds retain a good texture during fermentation," explains Hozven of this kraut inspired by the Japanese macrobiotic diet. If you can't find burdock, substitute another root vegetable, like carrot.

- 4 pounds green cabbage, very thinly sliced on a mandoline or finely shredded in a food processor
- One 4-inch piece of fresh burdock root, peeled and thinly sliced crosswise on a mandoline
- 1 small golden beet, finely shredded
- ¼ cup dry hijiki or arame seaweed
- 2 tablespoons plus 1 teaspoon fine sea salt

1. Combine all of the ingredients in a very large bowl. Squeeze the cabbage to release some liquid. Press a heavy plate on the cabbage to weigh it down and let stand at room temperature, tossing and squeezing the cabbage 4 or 5 more times, until it has released enough liquid to cover, about 4 hours.

2. Pour the cabbage and its liquid into a clean ceramic crock or tall glass container. Top the cabbage with a clean plate that just fits inside the crock. Place a glass or ceramic bowl on the plate and put a heavy can in the bowl; the cabbage should be completely submerged in its brine by at least ½ inch. Cover the crock with a clean kitchen towel and set it in a cool, dark place to ferment for about 6 weeks.

taste evolution
"Try the kraut at different stages to see its progression from one week to the next," says Hozven. "The longer it ferments, the more acidic—and shelf-stable—it gets."

3. Every 3 days, clean and replace the plate on the cabbage, skimming any foam or mold on the liquid. Discard the cabbage and its liquid if it's foul-smelling, or if anything brown, moldy or slimy has penetrated below what can easily be scraped off the surface. If too much liquid evaporates before the kraut is sufficiently fermented, dissolve ½ teaspoon of sea salt in 1 cup of spring water and add it to the crock. When the kraut is ready, it should have a light crunch and a bright, pleasantly tangy taste, with an acidity similar to that of a lemon.

Cabbage with Parsley Cream

⏲ TOTAL: 35 MIN • 4 SERVINGS ●

Cabbage-leaf rolls simulate the pointed cabbage heads that rising Danish chef Claus Henriksen uses at Dragsholm Slot, a restaurant inside a castle in Hørve, Denmark.

½ cup packed flat-leaf
    parsley leaves
1 hard-boiled egg, chopped
3 tablespoons cider vinegar
¼ cup vegetable oil
Salt
2 quarts water
4 tablespoons unsalted butter
8 large Savoy cabbage leaves,
    halved lengthwise and center ribs
    discarded
Thinly sliced scallions, assorted
    sprouts and extra-thin rye crisps,
    for serving

1. In a blender, combine the parsley leaves with the hard-boiled egg, cider vinegar and vegetable oil and puree. Season the parsley cream sauce with salt.

2. In a medium saucepan, combine the water, butter and a large pinch of salt and bring to a boil. Add the cabbage leaves, cover and simmer over moderate heat, shifting the leaves around for even cooking, until tender, about 4 minutes. Drain the cabbage leaves and pat dry with paper towels.

3. Tightly roll up the cabbage leaves and arrange the rolls on plates. Season them lightly with salt and top with the parsley cream sauce. Garnish the cabbage rolls with the sliced scallions and assorted sprouts and serve right away, with rye crisps.
—*Claus Henriksen*

ingredient tip

brussels sprouts Instead of cooking brussels sprouts, raw sprouts can be thinly sliced and tossed with olive oil, lemon juice and almonds for a quick salad.

Roasted Brussels Sprouts with Toasted Pecans and Avocado

⏲ ACTIVE: 20 MIN; TOTAL: 40 MIN
8 SERVINGS ● ● ●

New York City superstar chef Jean-Georges Vongerichten first created this recipe as an all-green dish, using pistachio nuts. "When I tried it with pecans, though, it was even better," he says. The unconventional combination plays with textures (crisp roasted brussels sprouts, creamy avocado) and flavors: "When you roast brussels sprouts, they get sweeter; but when you warm avocado, it gets a little more bitter."

½ cup pecans
2½ pounds brussels sprouts
¼ cup extra-virgin olive oil
Salt and freshly ground pepper
1 Hass avocado, cut into
    ½-inch dice
1 teaspoon chopped thyme
2 tablespoons balsamic vinegar

1. Preheat the oven to 400°. Spread the pecans in a pie plate and bake for about 5 minutes, until toasted. Let the pecans cool, then coarsely chop them.

2. Bring a large saucepan of salted water to a boil. Add the brussels sprouts and cook until bright green, about 3 minutes. Drain, cut the brussels sprouts in half and pat dry with paper towels.

3. On 2 large rimmed baking sheets, toss the brussels sprouts with the olive oil. Season with salt and freshly ground pepper and turn the brussels sprouts cut side down. Roast in the upper and lower thirds of the oven until nicely browned on the bottom, about 20 minutes; switch the baking sheets halfway through roasting.

4. In a large bowl, toss the roasted brussels sprouts with the pecans, diced avocado and thyme. Season with salt and pepper and transfer to a bowl. Drizzle with the balsamic vinegar and serve right away.
—*Jean-Georges Vongerichten*

MAKE AHEAD The blanched and halved brussels sprouts can be refrigerated overnight in an airtight container.

Roasted Brussels Sprouts with Capers, Walnuts and Anchovies

ACTIVE: 30 MIN; TOTAL: 1 HR 15 MIN
10 SERVINGS ● ● ●

The key to Michael Symon's deeply savory side is a dressing that includes capers and anchovies—Mediterranean touches inspired by the Cleveland chef's Greek and Italian heritage. Spiked with mustard and a little honey, the dressing nicely coats the brussels sprouts and toasted walnuts.

3 pounds brussels sprouts,
    quartered
¾ cup extra-virgin olive oil
Salt and freshly ground pepper
1 cup walnuts
¼ cup red wine vinegar
1 tablespoon grainy mustard
2 tablespoons honey
3 tablespoons capers, rinsed
    and chopped
2 garlic cloves, minced
2 shallots, minced
One 2-ounce tin of anchovies,
    drained and minced

1. Preheat the oven to 425°. In a large bowl, toss the brussels sprouts with ¼ cup of the oil and season with salt and pepper. Spread the brussels sprouts on 2 large rimmed baking sheets and roast for about 45 minutes, stirring once or twice, until they are tender and charred in spots; shift the pans halfway through roasting.

2. Spread the walnuts in a pie plate and toast for about 8 minutes, until golden. Let cool, then coarsely chop the nuts.

3. In the large bowl, whisk the vinegar with the mustard and honey. Whisk in the remaining ½ cup of olive oil until the dressing is emulsified. Add the capers, garlic, shallots and anchovies; season with salt and pepper. Add the brussels sprouts and toasted walnuts and toss well. Serve right away.
—*Michael Symon*

MAKE AHEAD The brussels sprouts and dressing can be made up to 4 hours ahead and kept at room temperature. Rewarm the brussels sprouts before serving.

● HEALTHY ● MAKE AHEAD ● VEGETARIAN ● STAFF FAVORITE

roasted brussels sprouts with capers, walnuts and anchovies

Roasted Beets and Carrots with Goat Cheese Dressing

ACTIVE: 30 MIN; TOTAL: 1 HR 15 MIN
6 SERVINGS ● ● ●

1½ pounds golden beets with tops
1½ pounds red beets with tops
  3 tablespoons extra-virgin olive oil
  3 large garlic cloves, halved
Salt and freshly ground pepper
  8 ounces fresh baby carrots
  1 tablespoon sherry vinegar
  1 large shallot, minced
  1 ounce soft goat cheese, crumbled

1. Preheat the oven to 425°. Peel the beets and cut them into 1-inch wedges. Discard the tough stems from the beet tops and coarsely chop the leaves.
2. In a large bowl, toss the golden beets with 1 teaspoon of the olive oil and 2 garlic clove halves and season with salt and pepper. Arrange in one-third of a large ovenproof skillet. Repeat with the red beets and then the baby carrots, using 1 teaspoon of olive oil and 2 garlic halves for each vegetable. Set the skillet over high heat and cook the vegetables without stirring until sizzling. Cover the skillet and roast in the oven for about 35 minutes, until tender. Transfer the roasted vegetables to a large platter.
3. In a small bowl, whisk the vinegar with 1 tablespoon of the olive oil and half of the shallot. Season with salt and pepper and whisk in the goat cheese.
4. In the skillet, heat the remaining 1 tablespoon of oil. Add the remaining shallot and cook over moderately high heat until softened, about 1 minute. Add the chopped beet greens and cook until just wilted, about 5 minutes. Season with salt and pepper.
5. Add half of the goat cheese dressing to the beet greens and toss. Add the roasted vegetables and toss once or twice. Transfer the salad to a platter and drizzle with the remaining dressing. Serve right away.
—*Grace Parisi*

MAKE AHEAD The roasted vegetables can be refrigerated for up to 3 days. Rewarm before assembling the salad.

Moroccan Carrots

⟳ ACTIVE: 10 MIN; TOTAL: 25 MIN
4 SERVINGS ◦

  4 medium carrots (¾ pound), thinly sliced on a mandoline
  1 cup fresh orange juice
  ¼ cup water
  ½ teaspoon ground coriander
  ½ teaspoon ground cumin
  ¼ teaspoon cinnamon
Large pinch of sugar
  1 tablespoon unsalted butter
Salt

1. In a medium saucepan of boiling salted water, cook the carrots for 1 minute. Drain.
2. In a large skillet, combine the carrots with the orange juice, water, coriander, cumin and cinnamon and simmer over moderate heat, stirring occasionally, until just tender, about 10 minutes. Remove the skillet from the heat and stir in the sugar and the butter. Season the carrots with salt and serve.
—*Omri Aflalo*

Roasted Beets and Celery Root with Goat Butter

ACTIVE: 30 MIN; TOTAL: 1 HR 30 MIN
4 SERVINGS ◦

1¼ pounds trimmed baby beets, preferably golden, scrubbed
  1 tablespoon extra-virgin olive oil
  3 tablespoons goat butter (see Note)
  1 pound celery root, peeled and cut into 2-by-½-inch batons
  2 thyme sprigs
Salt and freshly ground pepper
  1 cup vegetable stock

1. Preheat the oven to 350°. In a baking dish, toss the beets with the oil. Cover with foil and roast for 1 hour, until the beets are tender when pierced. Let cool slightly, then peel the beets and cut into small wedges.
2. In a large, deep skillet, heat 2 tablespoons of the butter. Add the celery root and thyme sprigs and season lightly with salt and freshly ground pepper. Cook over moderate heat, stirring occasionally, until lightly browned in spots, about 5 minutes. Add ¼ cup of the stock and simmer over moderate heat until nearly evaporated, about 2 minutes. Add the remaining stock, ¼ cup at a time, and cook until the celery root is tender, 8 to 10 minutes total. Stir in the beets and cook until heated through, 2 minutes. Discard the thyme. Swirl in the remaining 1 tablespoon of butter and season with salt and pepper. Serve right away.
—*Tyler Brown*

NOTE Goat butter is sold at specialty food stores. If it is unavailable, use regular butter.

Roasted Cauliflower with Golden Raisins

ACTIVE: 15 MIN; TOTAL: 1 HR
4 SERVINGS ● ● ●

"I love how sweet cauliflower gets when it's roasted," says Jill Donenfeld, founder of The Culinistas, a private-chef service in L.A., New York and Chicago. She adds a tablespoon of white balsamic vinegar to the cauliflower to help it caramelize even more.

  1 head of cauliflower, cut into small florets
2½ tablespoons extra-virgin olive oil
  1 tablespoon white balsamic vinegar
Salt and freshly ground pepper
  2 tablespoons golden raisins
  ¼ cup freshly grated Pecorino Romano cheese
  1 tablespoon chopped parsley

1. Preheat the oven to 375°. Spread the cauliflower on a large rimmed baking sheet. Drizzle with 2 tablespoons of the olive oil and the vinegar. Season with salt and pepper and toss well. Roast for about 40 minutes, until tender. Transfer to a bowl.
2. In a small skillet, heat the remaining ½ tablespoon of oil. Add the raisins and cook over moderate heat, tossing, until hot, 1 minute. Add the raisins to the cauliflower, sprinkle with the cheese and parsley and serve.
—*Jill Donenfeld*

MAKE AHEAD The roasted cauliflower can be refrigerated for up to 3 days. Reheat before proceeding with the recipe.

● HEALTHY ● MAKE AHEAD ◦ VEGETARIAN ◦ STAFF FAVORITE

roasted beets and celery root with goat butter

Grilled Baby Carrot Wraps with Poblano Cream

⏱ TOTAL: 45 MIN • 4 SERVINGS ● ● ●

About 15 slender baby carrots—grilled until charred, then tightly rolled inside a tortilla with poblano-spiked sour cream—make for a superb vegetable wrap.

- 2 poblano chiles
- ¼ cup sour cream
- 1½ teaspoons ground cumin
- ¼ cup chopped cilantro
- Green hot sauce
- Salt
- 60 assorted thin baby carrots (4 to 5 bunches), peeled
- Vegetable oil, for brushing
- Four 10-inch flour tortillas

1. Roast the poblanos directly over a gas flame or under a preheated broiler, turning, until charred all over. Let cool. Peel, seed and stem the chiles, then coarsely chop them. Transfer the poblanos to a blender. Add the sour cream, cumin and cilantro and puree. Season with hot sauce and salt.

2. In a large saucepan of boiling salted water, cook the carrots until crisp-tender, about 3 minutes. Drain and pat dry.

3. Light a grill or preheat a grill pan. Brush the carrots with oil. If using a grill, place the carrots in a perforated grill pan. Grill over moderately high heat, turning, until charred, about 5 minutes. Season lightly with salt.

4. Slice off the top third of each tortilla. Spread about 1 tablespoon of the poblano cream on each tortilla and arrange the carrots (about 15 for each wrap) in a row at the bottom. Tightly roll up the tortillas, folding in the sides as you go. Insert 2 toothpicks in each wrap to keep it closed. Brush the wraps all over with vegetable oil.

5. Grill the wraps over moderately high heat, turning, until charred and very crisp all over, about 2 minutes. Discard the toothpicks. Cut the wraps in half and serve right away, with the extra poblano cream on the side.
—*Marcia Kiesel*

MAKE AHEAD The poblano cream and boiled carrots can be refrigerated overnight.

Maple Root-Vegetable Stir-Fry with Sesame

⏱ TOTAL: 45 MIN • 8 SERVINGS ● ●

In Korea, cooks typically create stir-fries with just one kind of vegetable—lotus root, say, or potatoes. David Chang, the Korean-American chef of the Momofuku restaurants in New York City, decided to break tradition and stir-fry an assortment of vegetables, including Jerusalem artichokes, fingerling potatoes and parsnips. Also unconventional is the maple syrup he adds to sweeten the dish; there are maple trees all around South Korea but not much maple syrup.

- ¼ cup canola oil
- ¾ pound Jerusalem artichokes, scrubbed and sliced ⅓ inch thick
- 2 carrots, cut into ¾-inch pieces
- 2 parsnips, cut into ¾-inch pieces
- ½ pound fingerling potatoes, halved lengthwise
- 1 cup fresh lotus root, peeled and sliced (about 5 ounces), optional
- ¼ cup pure maple syrup
- ¼ cup soy sauce
- A few drops of toasted sesame oil
- 1 tablespoon toasted sesame seeds
- 2 scallions, thinly sliced

1. Preheat the oven to 375°. In a large ovenproof skillet, heat the canola oil until shimmering. Add the Jerusalem artichokes, carrots, parsnips and potatoes and cook over moderately high heat, stirring occasionally, until lightly browned, about 8 minutes. Transfer the skillet to the oven and roast for about 20 minutes, until all the vegetables are tender.

2. Add the sliced lotus root to the skillet along with the maple syrup and soy sauce. Cook the vegetables over moderate heat, stirring frequently, until the sauce becomes syrupy and the vegetables are glazed, about 8 minutes. Stir the sesame oil, sesame seeds and sliced scallions into the vegetables and serve immediately. —*David Chang*

WINE Light-bodied Piedmontese red: 2008 Flavio Roddolo Dolcetto d'Alba.

Sautéed Parsnips with Dates and Spiced Yogurt

ACTIVE: 40 MIN; TOTAL: 1 HR
10 SERVINGS ● ● ● ●

- ¾ cup plus 2 tablespoons extra-virgin olive oil
- 6 garlic cloves, smashed
- 3 pounds parsnips, peeled and sliced on the diagonal ½ inch thick
- 1½ cups sliced pitted Medjool dates (about 12)
- 5 marjoram sprigs
- Salt and freshly ground pepper
- 1 cup plain Greek yogurt
- 3 tablespoons fresh lemon juice
- 2 teaspoons ground sumac (see Note)

1. Preheat the oven to 350°. In a large skillet, heat the ¾ cup of olive oil with the garlic and cook over moderate heat until the garlic is golden. Using a slotted spoon, remove the garlic and reserve for another use. Add half of the parsnips to the skillet and cook over moderate heat, stirring occasionally, until golden and barely tender, about 12 minutes. Using a slotted spoon, transfer the parsnips to a roasting pan. Repeat with the remaining parsnips, then scrape the parsnips and any oil into the roasting pan. Add the dates and marjoram sprigs, season with salt and pepper and roast for about 8 minutes, just until the parsnips are tender and the dates are slightly caramelized. Transfer the parsnips and dates to a platter.

2. In a bowl, whisk the yogurt with the lemon juice, sumac and the remaining 2 tablespoons of olive oil. Season with salt. Serve the roasted parsnips and dates, passing the spiced yogurt at the table.
—*Jeff Cerciello*

NOTE Ground sumac is made from a tangy dried berry. It is available at specialty shops and Middle Eastern markets and online at *chefshop.com.*

MAKE AHEAD The cooked parsnips and spiced yogurt can be refrigerated in separate containers overnight. Rewarm the parsnips before serving.

● HEALTHY ● MAKE AHEAD ● VEGETARIAN ● STAFF FAVORITE

Parsi-Style Vegetable Stew

⏱ ACTIVE: 20 MIN; TOTAL: 35 MIN

4 SERVINGS ● ●

Worcestershire sauce may seem out of place in an Indian recipe, but some food historians believe that the condiment was created by the British when they ruled India, then named for the place where it was first bottled: Worcester, England.

- 3 tablespoons vegetable oil
- 3 dried red chiles, broken
- 1 teaspoon cumin seeds
- 2 onions, thinly sliced
- 5 garlic cloves, thinly sliced
- 2 jalapeños, halved lengthwise
- 2½ cups water
- 2 medium red-skinned potatoes, scrubbed and cut into ½-inch dice
- 1 sweet potato, peeled and cut into ½-inch dice
- 1 carrot, cut into ½-inch dice
- 1 large tomato, coarsely chopped
- ½ head cauliflower, cut into small florets
- 1 tablespoon Worcestershire sauce
- 1 teaspoon white vinegar
- 1 teaspoon sugar
- Salt

1. In a large saucepan, heat the vegetable oil. Add the dried chiles and cumin seeds and cook over moderately high heat until they are fragrant, about 1 minute. Add the sliced onions and cook, stirring them occasionally, until golden brown, about 4 minutes. Add the garlic and jalapeños and cook, stirring, until the garlic is golden, about 1 minute. Add the water, red and sweet potatoes, carrot, tomato and cauliflower and bring to a simmer. Cover and cook over moderately low heat until the vegetables are tender, about 10 minutes.

2. Stir in the Worcestershire sauce, vinegar and sugar and season with salt. Ladle the stew into bowls and serve right away. —*Sanjeev Kapoor*

MAKE AHEAD The vegetable stew can be refrigerated overnight.

WINE Fruit-forward, substantial white: 2009 Domaine Bernard Baudry Chinon Blanc.

Braised Root Vegetables and Cabbage with Fall Fruit

ACTIVE: 25 MIN; TOTAL: 1 HR

6 SERVINGS ● ● ●

This rustic stew is a simplified version of the more elaborate dish that legendary chef Alain Ducasse serves at Adour in Washington, DC.

- 2 tablespoons unsalted butter
- 2 tablespoons extra-virgin olive oil
- 1 small white onion, thinly sliced
- 4 carrots, sliced ⅓ inch thick
- 4 large radishes, quartered
- 4 baby turnips, peeled and quartered
- ¾ pound Savoy cabbage, cored and coarsely chopped
- 1 Golden Delicious apple—peeled, cored and cut into 1-inch pieces
- 2 garlic cloves, thinly sliced
- Salt and freshly ground pepper
- ½ cup low-sodium chicken broth
- 1 Bosc pear—peeled, cored and cut into 1-inch pieces

1. Preheat the oven to 350°. In a large, deep ovenproof skillet, melt the butter in the olive oil. When the foam subsides, add the onion, carrots, radishes, turnips, cabbage, apple and garlic. Season with salt and freshly ground pepper and cook over high heat, stirring, until the vegetables are lightly browned in spots, about 6 minutes. Add the chicken broth and bring to a boil. Cover and braise in the oven for 25 to 30 minutes, until the vegetables are tender.

2. Stir in the pear and cook over high heat until the liquid is evaporated and the pear is tender, 5 minutes; transfer to a bowl and serve. —*Alain Ducasse*

Ginger-Lime Baby Carrots

⏱ TOTAL: 20 MIN • 4 SERVINGS ● ●

"I just think carrots, particularly their tops and roots, are an artistic wonder," says *Top Chef: All-Stars* winner Richard Blais. "The color, the abstract shape—they're gorgeous." He cooks them in a tangy ginger sauce and then sprinkles them with the flavorful, seaweed-and-sesame-seed-based Japanese seasoning called *furikake*.

- 24 baby carrots, tops trimmed to 2 inches
- 1 tablespoon extra-virgin olive oil
- ½ tablespoon minced fresh ginger
- Pinch of cinnamon
- ½ cup chicken stock
- 1 tablespoon unsalted butter
- 2 teaspoons fresh lime juice
- ¼ teaspoon Sriracha sauce
- Salt
- 1 tablespoon *furikake* (see Note)

1. In a large saucepan of boiling salted water, cook the carrots until crisp-tender, about 2 minutes. Drain the carrots.

2. In a large skillet, heat the olive oil. Add the carrots, minced ginger and cinnamon and cook over moderate heat, tossing occasionally, until the ginger is fragrant, about 3 minutes. Add the chicken stock and boil over moderately high heat until the liquid is reduced by half, about 3 minutes. Remove the skillet from the heat and let cool for 30 seconds. Swirl in the butter, fresh lime juice and Sriracha sauce and season with salt. Arrange the carrots on a platter and spoon the ginger-lime sauce on top. Sprinkle with the *furikake* and serve right away. —*Richard Blais*

NOTE Furikake is available at Asian markets and many specialty food stores.

equipment tip

skillet All-Clad's workhorse skillets can be used for dishes that go from the stovetop directly into the oven, like David Chang's Maple Root-Vegetable Stir-Fry (opposite) and Alain Ducasse's Braised Root Vegetables and Cabbage with Fall Fruit (above left). *$140; metrokitchen.com.*

Honey-Soy-Glazed Vegetables with Crispy Mushrooms

⏱ TOTAL: 40 MIN • 4 SERVINGS ● ● ○

¼ cup plus 1 tablespoon canola oil
1 pound medium turnips, cut into
¾-inch wedges
1 pound medium radishes, quartered
¼ cup honey
2 tablespoons soy sauce
1 tablespoon fresh lemon juice
½ pound Swiss chard, stems
discarded and leaves coarsely
chopped
2 tablespoons molasses
2 tablespoons water
Salt
6 large shiitake mushrooms,
stemmed and caps quartered
½ pound Asian rice crackers,
pulverized

1. In a large skillet, heat 1 tablespoon of the oil until shimmering. Add the turnips and radishes and cook over moderately high heat, stirring, until lightly browned and crisp-tender, 10 minutes. Add the honey and cook over moderate heat, stirring, until the vegetables are glazed, 5 minutes. Add the soy sauce and cook until syrupy, 5 minutes longer. Add the lemon juice and the Swiss chard; cook until the chard is wilted, 2 minutes. Raise the heat to high and cook until all of the liquid has evaporated, 2 minutes longer; keep the vegetables warm.
2. In a medium bowl, whisk the molasses with the water and season with salt. Add the shiitake and toss to coat. Drain the mushrooms, squeezing out most of the excess liquid. In a separate bowl, toss the mushrooms with the rice cracker crumbs, pressing to help the crumbs adhere.
3. In a large skillet, heat the remaining ¼ cup of oil until shimmering. Add the coated mushrooms and cook them over high heat, turning once, until golden and crisp, 5 minutes. Transfer to paper towels to drain. Top the glazed vegetables with the crispy mushrooms and serve immediately.
—*David Chang*

Mushroom Kufteh with Green Harissa and Asparagus Pesto

ACTIVE: 45 MIN; TOTAL: 2 HR
6 SERVINGS ● ● ○ ○

2 tablespoons extra-virgin olive oil,
plus more for brushing
1½ pounds assorted wild mushrooms,
such as oyster and stemmed
shiitake, thinly sliced (8 cups)
Salt
1 cup *panko* (Japanese bread crumbs)
½ cup freshly grated Parmigiano-
Reggiano cheese (2 ounces)
½ cup chopped flat-leaf parsley
2 tablespoons chopped basil
2 tablespoons fresh lemon juice
¼ teaspoon cayenne pepper
2 large eggs
2 large egg whites
Green Harissa and Asparagus Pesto
(recipes follow), for serving

1. In a nonstick skillet, heat the 2 tablespoons of olive oil. Add the mushrooms, season with salt and cook over moderately high heat, stirring occasionally, until softened and lightly browned, about 12 minutes. Transfer the mushrooms to a work surface and let cool slightly, then coarsely chop and transfer to a large bowl. Add the *panko,* cheese, parsley, basil, lemon juice and cayenne and season with salt. Add the eggs and egg whites and knead the mixture to combine.
2. Line a large baking sheet with parchment paper. Using lightly moistened hands, form the mushroom mixture into six 1-inch-thick patties and set them on the baking sheet. Refrigerate until firm, about 1 hour.
3. Preheat the oven to 350°. Preheat a grill pan or a griddle, preferably nonstick, and brush with olive oil. Brush the *kufteh* with oil and grill over high heat, turning once, until browned, about 5 minutes. Return the *kufteh* to the baking sheet and bake for 10 minutes, until hot throughout. Serve the *kufteh* with Green Harissa and Asparagus Pesto.
—*Hoss Zaré*
WINE Zippy Grüner Veltliner: 2009 Schloss Gobelsburg Gobelsburger.

GREEN HARISSA

⏱ TOTAL: 20 MIN • MAKES 1 CUP ● ● ○ ○

½ cup packed baby spinach leaves
½ cup packed flat-leaf parsley leaves
1 teaspoon smoked paprika
¼ teaspoon ground cumin
⅛ teaspoon ground cardamom
1½ teaspoons ground coriander
2 small jalapeños, seeded and
coarsely chopped
2 garlic cloves
½ teaspoon finely grated lemon zest
½ teaspoon finely grated orange zest
2 tablespoons fresh lemon juice
1 tablespoon fresh orange juice
6 tablespoons extra-virgin olive oil
Salt and freshly ground pepper

In a blender, pulse the baby spinach, parsley, paprika, cumin, cardamom, coriander, jalapeños, garlic, lemon zest, orange zest, lemon juice and orange juice until the greens are chopped. With the machine on, add the oil and puree. Season with salt and pepper. —*HZ*
MAKE AHEAD The harissa can be refrigerated for up to 5 days.

ASPARAGUS PESTO

⏱ TOTAL: 20 MIN • MAKES 1 CUP ● ● ○

½ packed cup basil leaves
½ pound asparagus, trimmed and
coarsely chopped (1 cup)
¼ cup pine nuts
2 tablespoons fresh lemon juice
2 tablespoons freshly grated
Parmigiano-Reggiano cheese
6 tablespoons extra-virgin olive oil
Salt and freshly ground pepper

In a food processor, combine the basil leaves, asparagus, pine nuts, fresh lemon juice and Parmigiano-Reggiano cheese and pulse until the mixture is chopped. With the machine on, add the olive oil and process to a chunky puree. Season the Asparagus Pesto with salt and freshly ground pepper. —*HZ*
MAKE AHEAD The Asparagus Pesto can be refrigerated for up to 5 days.

● HEALTHY ● MAKE AHEAD ○ VEGETARIAN ● STAFF FAVORITE

honey-soy-glazed vegetables with crispy mushrooms

Grilled Hen-of-the-Woods Mushrooms with Sesame

◔ **TOTAL: 25 MIN • 8 SERVINGS** ● ●

"Hen-of-the-woods are often shredded and sautéed, but when you cook them whole, they become crispy outside and meaty and moist inside," says chef Jean-Georges Vongerichten of his preferred method of preparing the coral-like mushroom. "I'm a purist when it comes to beautiful ingredients, so serving the mushrooms in big clusters keeps them the way they grow in the woods."

- 1 tablespoon sesame seeds
- 2 pounds hen-of-the-woods mushrooms (*maitake*), separated into 8 wedges total

Extra-virgin olive oil, for brushing
Salt and freshly ground pepper

- 2 tablespoons thinly sliced parsley

Lime wedges, for serving

1. In a small skillet, toast the sesame seeds over moderate heat, stirring a few times, until golden, 3 minutes. Transfer to a plate.
2. Heat a grill pan and preheat the oven to 425°. Gently and generously brush the mushrooms with olive oil and season with salt and pepper. Grill in batches over moderately high heat, turning occasionally, until browned and crisp, about 8 minutes per batch. Transfer the mushroom wedges to a large rimmed baking sheet and reheat for about 4 minutes. Arrange the mushrooms on a platter. Sprinkle with the parsley and sesame seeds and serve with lime wedges.
—*Jean-Georges Vongerichten*

vegan tip

Dried mushrooms like porcini or shiitake are essential for creating deeply flavored vegetable stocks and broths. Adding smoked paprika and other dried chile powders can give dishes the fire-roasted smell of barbecue.

Mixed Mushroom Ragout

◔ **TOTAL: 45 MIN • MAKES 4 CUPS** ●

This rich, chunky mushroom ragout is great on everything from seared halibut to sautéed scallops and pasta. Instead of chicken stock, use vegetable stock to make it vegan.

- ¼ cup vegetable oil
- 1 pound shiitake mushrooms—stems discarded, caps sliced ¼ inch thick

Salt and freshly ground pepper

- 1 pound mixed mushrooms, such as cremini, sliced ⅛ inch thick, and oyster mushrooms, caps quartered
- 1 medium onion, finely diced
- 2 garlic cloves, minced
- ¼ cup dry white wine
- 1 cup chopped canned tomatoes, drained
- ½ cup unsweetened coconut milk
- 1 tablespoon Dijon mustard
- 1 tablespoon harissa
- 2 teaspoons white or blond miso
- 1 tablespoon golden raisins (optional)
- 1 tablespoon capers
- ½ cup chicken stock

1. In a large skillet, heat 2 tablespoons of the oil. Add the shiitake and season with salt and pepper. Cover and cook over moderate heat, stirring, until tender and starting to brown, about 7 minutes. Transfer to a bowl.
2. Heat 1 tablespoon of the vegetable oil in the skillet. Add the mixed mushrooms; cook over moderately high heat until any liquid has evaporated and the mushrooms start to brown, 5 minutes. Add the onion and remaining 1 tablespoon of oil; season with salt and pepper. Cover; cook over moderate heat, stirring, until the onion is softened, 5 minutes. Add the garlic, cover and cook over low heat, stirring a few times, until fragrant, 2 minutes. Add the wine; cook for 2 minutes. Add the tomatoes and simmer for 4 minutes.
3. In a bowl, whisk the coconut milk, mustard, harissa and miso. Add to the skillet along with the shiitake, raisins, capers and stock. Simmer over low heat, stirring, until thickened, about 4 minutes. Season with salt and pepper and serve. —*Stephanie Izard*

Korean Barbecue Portobellos

TOTAL: 1 HR • 6 SERVINGS ● ●

Chicago chef Bill Kim's mother makes a variation of the marinade here for *bulgogi,* thinly sliced Korean-style beef. The sweet-and-savory marinade is also great with meaty portobellos. The mushrooms need only 30 minutes of marinating, but the longer they marinate, the better. Wrap the grilled mushrooms in lettuce and serve with rice, as in traditional Korean barbecue.

- ½ small onion, halved
- ½ Asian pear, cored and quartered
- 1 small kiwi, peeled and quartered
- 8 garlic cloves, smashed and peeled
- ¼ cup chopped fresh ginger
- ½ cup light brown sugar
- ¼ cup granulated sugar
- 2 tablespoons toasted sesame oil
- ¾ cup soy sauce
- 1½ cups water

Six 6-ounce portobello mushrooms, stemmed and gills scraped

1. In a blender, combine the onion with the Asian pear, kiwi, garlic, ginger, light brown sugar, granulated sugar, sesame oil, soy sauce and water and puree until smooth.
2. Arrange the mushroom caps in a shallow baking dish and pour the marinade on top, then turn to coat them completely with the marinade. Let the mushrooms stand at room temperature for at least 30 minutes or refrigerate for up to 24 hours.
3. Light a grill or preheat a grill pan. Lift the mushrooms from the marinade, shaking off the excess. Grill the mushrooms over moderately high heat, turning occasionally, until they are tender, about 12 minutes.
—*Bill Kim*

VARIATION The marinade is great for thinly sliced flanken-style short ribs or steak. Marinate in the refrigerator overnight.

SERVE WITH Steamed rice, lettuce leaves and various kinds of kimchi.

MAKE AHEAD The marinade can be refrigerated for up to 3 days.

WINE Fresh, peppery Côtes-du-Rhône: 2009 M. Chapoutier Belleruche Rouge.

● HEALTHY ● MAKE AHEAD ● VEGETARIAN ● STAFF FAVORITE

do-it-yourself tofu

A chef's homemade tofu is surprisingly rich and indulgent, yet not at all heavy. Here, tofu advocate **Douglas Keane** shares his best recipes for the freshest, creamiest curds.

make soy milk *Homemade soy milk is the key to the best tofu (most store-bought versions won't work), but the origin of the soybeans isn't an issue: "I asked tofu makers in Kyoto, Japan, where their beans are from," says Keane, the chef at Cyrus restaurant in Sonoma, "and they said America." This recipe makes about 4 cups.*

1. In a large bowl, cover 1⅓ cups dried soybeans (8 ounces) with 3 inches cold water. Cover the soybeans and let stand overnight.
2. Drain the soybeans and transfer to a blender. Add 3 cups filtered water and puree at high speed until as smooth as possible.
3. Line a large sieve with a clean cotton napkin or 3 layers of cheesecloth and set the sieve over a heatproof bowl. In a large pot, boil 3 cups filtered water. Add the soybean puree and boil over moderately high heat for 8 minutes, stirring constantly with a heatproof rubber spatula to prevent sticking and scorching (be careful not to let it boil over).
4. Carefully pour the mixture into the prepared sieve. Let stand until just cool enough to handle, about 20 minutes. Gather the ends of the napkin or cheesecloth and squeeze to extract as much of the soy milk as possible; the remaining solids should be nearly dry. Discard the solids and skim off any foam from the soy milk.

for tofu skins *Tofu skin, known as yuba in Japan, forms on the surface of hot soy milk, similar to the skin that develops on warm cow milk.*

for silken tofu *To set the curd of this delicate tofu—which is delicious even plain—combine* nigari *(sea salts) with hot soy milk.*

for firm tofu *Solid tofu is silken tofu that's pressed into a block. One great improvised mold: a plastic berry basket lined with cheesecloth.*

In a large, clean saucepan, bring 4 cups of the homemade soy milk to just below a simmer. A skin will slowly form on the surface. When the skin is fully formed, use a paring knife to carefully detach it from the side of the saucepan. Carefully slide a chopstick or skewer under the skin and lift it from the milk. Let drain for a few seconds before transferring to a plate. Repeat, stacking the tofu skins, until the soy milk is depleted.
SERVE WITH Dashi, scallions and cilantro.
MAKE AHEAD Tofu skins can be wrapped in plastic and refrigerated overnight.

In a small bowl, dissolve 1 teaspoon *nigari* flakes (available online at *myworldhut.com*) in ¼ cup filtered water. Spoon 2 tablespoons plus 2 teaspoons of the *nigari* solution into a large heatproof glass bowl. In a large saucepan, heat 4 cups of the homemade soy milk to 185°. Pour into the bowl with the *nigari* solution and quickly stir, but only to combine thoroughly; it's easy to accidentally scramble the rapidly coagulating tofu. Cover and let stand undisturbed until fully set, 5 minutes. Discard the remaining *nigari* solution.
SERVE WITH Yuzu zest or fresh ginger.

Set a cheesecloth-lined sieve, colander or other mold with drainage over a bowl, and spoon freshly made silken tofu into it. Neatly fold the overhanging cheesecloth over the tofu and top with a small plate or other light weight to gently press out excess water. Let the tofu drain for at least 15 minutes or up to 2 hours, depending on the desired firmness. Unwrap and serve.
SERVE WITH Black radish slices and soy sauce, or a miso glaze.
MAKE AHEAD Firm tofu can be refrigerated for up to 3 days, covered in water.

Chile-Rubbed Tofu with Fried Potatoes and Tomato Sauce

ACTIVE: 45 MIN; TOTAL: 1 HR 30 MIN
PLUS OVERNIGHT MARINATING
4 SERVINGS ● ●

"I get this awesome tofu from a farm about an hour north of Chicago," says chef Ryan Poli of Tavernita. Inspired by the flavors of both Spain and Latin America, Poli created this substantial main-course vegan dish. He marinates the tofu with chiles and serves it alongside *patatas bravas* (crispy Spanish-style fried potatoes) and a tomato sauce flavored with smoked paprika.

TOFU

- 5 garlic cloves, unpeeled
- 2 ancho chiles, stemmed and seeded
- 2 dried guajillo chiles, stemmed and seeded
- 1 tablespoon vegetable oil, plus more for brushing
- 1 small onion, thinly sliced
- 1 cup pineapple juice
- 1 cup orange juice
- 1 teaspoon dried oregano

Salt

- 1 pound firm tofu, cut into 8 equal-sized pieces

POTATOES AND TOMATO SAUCE

- 4 medium red-skinned potatoes
- 6 tablespoons extra-virgin olive oil

Salt and freshly ground pepper

- 4 garlic cloves, thinly sliced
- 1 small red onion, minced
- ¾ teaspoon sweet smoked paprika
- ¼ teaspoon ground cumin

Pinch of crushed red pepper

One 14-ounce can diced tomatoes

- ¼ cup water
- 2 teaspoons white wine vinegar
- 1 teaspoon sugar

1. PREPARE THE TOFU In a small skillet, cook the garlic, anchos and guajillos over moderate heat, turning, until the chiles are toasted and the garlic is lightly charred, about 2 minutes for the chiles and 5 minutes for the garlic. Transfer to a plate.

2. Heat the 1 tablespoon of oil in the skillet until shimmering. Add the onion and cook over moderate heat until softened, about 5 minutes. Peel the garlic cloves and add them to the skillet along with the toasted chiles, the pineapple and orange juices and the oregano. Simmer over moderate heat until the juices have reduced to ½ cup, about 10 minutes. Transfer the mixture to a blender and puree. Season with salt. Spread half of the chile rub all over the tofu, cover and refrigerate overnight. Refrigerate the remaining chile rub separately.

3. PREPARE THE POTATOES AND TOMATO SAUCE In a saucepan, cover the potatoes with cold water and boil over moderately high heat until tender, about 20 minutes. Drain and let cool.

4. Preheat the oven to 425°. Cut the potatoes into ½-inch-thick wedges and transfer them to a large rimmed baking sheet. Drizzle 4 tablespoons of the olive oil over the potatoes and toss to coat. Arrange the potatoes in a single layer on the baking sheet, season with salt and pepper and bake for 20 minutes. Turn the potatoes and bake until crisp, about 15 minutes longer,

5. Meanwhile, in a medium skillet, heat the remaining 2 tablespoons of olive oil. Add the sliced garlic and minced onion and cook over moderate heat until softened, about 6 minutes. Add the paprika, cumin and crushed red pepper and cook, stirring, until fragrant, about 1 minute. Add the diced tomatoes and water and simmer over moderate heat, stirring occasionally, until thick, about 7 minutes. Add the vinegar and sugar and season the sauce with salt and pepper.

6. Light a grill or preheat a grill pan. Scrape the marinade off the tofu and generously brush the slices with vegetable oil. Grill the tofu over moderately high heat until nicely browned, about 3 minutes per side. Serve the tofu with the crisp potatoes and tomato sauce. Pass the reserved chile rub at the table. —*Ryan Poli*

MAKE AHEAD The chile rub and tomato sauce can be refrigerated for up to 3 days.
WINE Juicy, substantial rosé: 2010 Olga Raffault Chinon.

Spicy Green Bean and Tofu Stir-Fry with Ground Bison

🕐 TOTAL: 30 MIN • 4 SERVINGS ●

- ½ pound ground bison
- 2 large garlic cloves, minced
- 1 tablespoon minced fresh ginger
- 3 tablespoons soy sauce
- 1 tablespoon cornstarch
- 1 teaspoon sugar

Salt and freshly ground black pepper

- 2 tablespoons canola oil
- 1 pound green beans

One 12-ounce block silken firm tofu, cut into 1-inch cubes

- 1 cup low-sodium beef or chicken broth, preferably organic
- 1½ teaspoons Chinese chile-garlic sauce
- 2 scallions, thinly sliced

1. In a medium bowl, mix the bison with the garlic, ginger, 1 tablespoon of the soy sauce, 2 teaspoons of the cornstarch and the sugar. Season the meat lightly with salt and black pepper and let stand for about 20 minutes.

2. Meanwhile, in a nonstick skillet or well-seasoned wok, heat 1 teaspoon of the oil until shimmering. Add the seasoned meat, breaking it up into small bits with a spoon, and stir-fry over high heat until browned. Transfer to a bowl. Add the remaining 1 tablespoon plus 2 teaspoons of oil to the skillet, and when it is very hot, add the green beans and stir-fry until crisp-tender, about 3 minutes. Add the tofu cubes and stir-fry until the tofu is lightly browned in spots and the beans begin to blister, about 3 minutes longer. Return the meat to the skillet and stir gently to slightly break up the tofu.

3. In a bowl, whisk the broth with the Chinese chile-garlic sauce and the remaining 2 tablespoons of soy sauce and 1 teaspoon of cornstarch. Add the sauce to the skillet and bring to a boil. Simmer until the beans are tender and the sauce is thickened, about 5 minutes. Stir in the sliced scallions. Transfer the stir-fry to bowls and serve. —*Grace Parisi*

SERVE WITH Steamed rice.
WINE Juicy, fruit-forward red from Spain: 2009 Evodia Garnacha.

● HEALTHY ● MAKE AHEAD ○ VEGETARIAN ● STAFF FAVORITE

Seattle chef Ethan Stowell hosts a 4th of July party on Whidbey Island; he serves a grilled feast with side dishes like baby potato salad with radishes and celery, OPPOSITE; *recipe, page 270.*

potatoes, grains and beans

Brown Butter Mashed Potatoes

ACTIVE: 30 MIN; TOTAL: 1 HR
10 SERVINGS ● ●

Salt
3½ pounds white or all-purpose
  potatoes, peeled and cut into
  large chunks
  1 stick plus 2 tablespoons
  unsalted butter
  1 cup milk
  ¼ cup crème fraîche

1. In a large pot of boiling salted water, cook the potatoes over moderate heat until tender, about 25 minutes. Drain well. Return the potatoes to the pot and cook over high heat for about 1 minute to dry them out slightly. Pass the potatoes through a ricer and return them to the pot.
2. In a small saucepan, cook the butter over moderate heat until the milk solids turn dark golden, about 4 minutes. Add all but 2 tablespoons of the brown butter to the potatoes along with the milk and crème fraîche and stir well. Season with salt and stir over moderate heat until hot. Drizzle the remaining brown butter over the potatoes and serve.
—*Michael Symon*

MAKE AHEAD The mashed potatoes can be refrigerated overnight and rewarmed in the oven, covered with foil.

Twice-Cooked Potatoes

ACTIVE: 25 MIN; TOTAL: 2 HR
8 SERVINGS ● ●

Winemaker Piero Incisa della Rocchetta tosses boiled potatoes with a mixture of butter and olive oil, then roasts them until they're tender inside, crunchy outside.

  4 pounds baby or small Yukon Gold
  potatoes, scrubbed
  3 tablespoons extra-virgin olive oil
  1 tablespoon unsalted butter, melted
Salt and freshly ground pepper

1. Preheat the oven to 375°. In a pot of salted water, boil the potatoes over moderately high heat until tender, 25 minutes.

2. Drain the potatoes and let cool slightly, then peel and cut in halves or thirds. Combine the olive oil and butter and toss with the potatoes on a large rimmed baking sheet. Spread the potatoes in an even layer, season with salt and pepper and roast for about 1 hour, until browned. Serve hot.
—*Piero Incisa della Rocchetta*

Baby Potato Salad with Radishes and Celery

📷 PAGE 269

ACTIVE: 25 MIN; TOTAL: 1 HR 15 MIN
8 SERVINGS ● ● ●

Seattle chef Ethan Stowell lightens up traditional potato salad by adding plenty of radishes and celery and skipping the usual mayonnaise dressing in favor of a Champagne vinaigrette.

  3 pounds baby Yukon Gold
  potatoes or fingerling potatoes,
  scrubbed but not peeled
  1 cup extra-virgin olive oil
  ¼ cup Champagne vinegar
Kosher salt and freshly ground
  black pepper
  2 celery hearts, thinly sliced
  (about 4 cups)
  2 bunches of radishes, thinly sliced
  8 small scallions, white and
  light green parts only, thinly
  sliced (1 cup)

1. Bring a large pot of salted water to a boil. Add the potatoes and cook until tender, about 20 minutes. Drain and let cool slightly. Slice the potatoes ½ inch thick.
2. Meanwhile, in a large bowl, whisk the olive oil with the vinegar and season with salt and pepper. Gently fold in the potatoes and celery. Let stand at room temperature until cool, about 30 minutes. Just before serving, fold in the radishes and scallions and season with salt and pepper.
—*Ethan Stowell*

MAKE AHEAD The potato salad without the radishes and scallions can be refrigerated overnight. Bring to room temperature before adding the radishes and scallions.

Potatoes Lyonnaise with Lemon and Chile

ACTIVE: 20 MIN; TOTAL: 50 MIN
4 SERVINGS ●

New York City chef April Bloomfield says that the crisp potatoes and caramelized onions called potatoes *lyonnaise* are "the ultimate home fry." After traveling to France, she perfected this version by adding chopped garlic, lemon juice and crushed red pepper.

  1 tablespoon unsalted butter
  1 tablespoon extra-virgin olive oil
  2 medium onions, thinly sliced
Salt
  2 baking potatoes (1¾ pounds),
  peeled and sliced crosswise
  ½ inch thick
  ¼ cup rendered duck, goose or pork
  fat or melted unsalted butter
  1 large garlic clove, chopped
Freshly ground black pepper
Pinch of crushed red pepper
  2 teaspoons fresh lemon juice
  2 tablespoons chopped parsley

1. In a medium saucepan, melt the butter in the olive oil. Add the sliced onions and a large pinch of salt. Cover and cook over moderate heat, stirring occasionally, until the onions are very soft and golden, about 20 minutes.
2. Meanwhile, put the potatoes in a large saucepan of water, add a large pinch of salt and bring to a boil. Simmer over moderately high heat until just tender, about 5 minutes. Drain the potatoes and spread the slices in a single layer on a baking sheet; let cool to room temperature. Gently pat dry.
3. In a large nonstick skillet, heat the duck fat. Add the potato slices and cook over moderately high heat until they are browned and crisp, about 6 minutes on each side. Add the chopped garlic and shake it in the skillet until just golden, about 30 seconds. Add the cooked onions and season them with salt and black pepper. Gently stir in the crushed red pepper and lemon juice. Transfer the potatoes and onions to a platter, sprinkle with the chopped parsley and serve right away. —*April Bloomfield*

● HEALTHY ● MAKE AHEAD ● VEGETARIAN ● STAFF FAVORITE

potatoes lyonnaise with lemon and chile

potatoes, grains and beans

Peruvian Potato Salad with Shrimp Escabèche
TOTAL: 1 HR PLUS 6 HR MARINATING
6 SERVINGS ● ●

SHRIMP

3 tablespoons extra-virgin olive oil
1 pound large shrimp, shelled
and deveined
Kosher salt and freshly ground pepper
1 large red onion, thinly sliced
½ small red bell pepper, thinly sliced
2 garlic cloves, minced
1 teaspoon ground cumin
½ teaspoon turmeric
1 teaspoon chopped oregano
½ cup red wine vinegar
1 cup fish stock or clam juice
2 tablespoons chopped cilantro

POTATO SALAD

1 pound Yukon Gold potatoes, peeled
and cut into 2-inch chunks
3 tablespoons vegetable oil
3 tablespoons fresh lime juice
3 tablespoons jarred *ají amarillo*
paste (see Note)
Salt and freshly ground pepper
¼ cup mayonnaise
1 small ripe Hass avocado, sliced
lengthwise ¼ inch thick
2 tablespoons cilantro leaves

1. **PREPARE THE SHRIMP** In a large skillet, heat 2 tablespoons of the olive oil. Add the shrimp, season with salt and pepper and cook over moderately high heat until barely cooked, about 2 minutes. Using a slotted spoon, transfer the shrimp to a medium heat-proof bowl. Add the onion and red pepper to the skillet, cover and cook over moderate heat, stirring a few times, until softened, about 5 minutes. Transfer to the bowl. Heat the remaining 1 tablespoon of olive oil in the skillet. Add the garlic and cook until fragrant, about 1 minute. Add the cumin, turmeric and oregano and cook, stirring, for 30 seconds. Add the red wine vinegar and fish stock and boil over high heat until reduced to 1 cup, about 4 minutes. Stir in ½ teaspoon of salt until dissolved. Pour the marinade over the

shrimp and vegetables in the bowl and stir well. Let cool to room temperature. Stir in the cilantro. Cover the shrimp and refrigerate for at least 6 hours or overnight.

2. **PREPARE THE POTATO SALAD** In a medium saucepan, cover the potatoes with water and bring to a boil. Cook over moderately high heat until tender, about 8 minutes. Drain the potatoes and return them to the pan. Shake the pan over moderate heat to dry them out, about 10 seconds. Pass the potatoes through a ricer into a large bowl. Cover and refrigerate the potatoes until chilled.

3. Stir the vegetable oil, lime juice and *ají amarillo* paste into the chilled potatoes and season with salt and pepper.

4. Spread the potatoes on a rimmed platter in a 1-inch-thick layer and spread the mayonnaise on top. Arrange the avocado slices over the mayonnaise and season with salt. Spoon the marinated shrimp, vegetables and sauce over the avocado. Garnish with the cilantro leaves and serve. —*Pedro Miguel Schiaffino*
NOTE *Ají amarillo* paste, made from yellow chiles, is available at specialty food stores and online at *tienda.com.*

Two-Tone Potato Salad
ACTIVE: 30 MIN; TOTAL: 1 HR 15 MIN
10 SERVINGS ● ● ● ●

1 pound small blue potatoes,
scrubbed
4 pounds medium Yukon Gold
potatoes, scrubbed
2 cups mayonnaise, preferably vegan
Juice of 2 lemons
½ cup sweet pickle relish
One 3-ounce jar pickled cocktail
onions, drained and thinly sliced
2 teaspoons kosher salt
2 teaspoons fresh dill
¾ teaspoon freshly ground pepper
2 large celery ribs, cut into
¼-inch dice
½ cup minced red onion
½ cup minced chives, plus more
for garnish
Smoked paprika and lemon wedges,
for serving

1. Put the blue potatoes in a medium saucepan and the Yukon Golds in a large saucepan; cover both with water. Bring to a boil and simmer until just tender, 15 minutes for the blues, 20 minutes for the Yukon Golds. Drain the potatoes and let cool to room temperature. Peel and cut into ½-inch dice.

2. In a bowl, whisk the mayonnaise, lemon juice, relish, cocktail onions, salt, dill and pepper. Mix in the potatoes, celery, red onion and ½ cup of chives. Refrigerate until cold.

3. Spoon the potato salad onto a platter and garnish with chives and paprika. Serve cold or slightly chilled, with lemon wedges.
—*Emilee and Jere Gettle*

Herbed Steamed Rice
ACTIVE: 10 MIN; TOTAL: 1 HR
4 SERVINGS ●

When preparing this side dish, April Bloomfield, the chef and co-owner of three exceptional New York restaurants, advises: "You can mix up the herbs, but it's always good to add tarragon if you're serving the rice with chicken"—such as her Lyon-Style Chicken with Vinegar Sauce (page 124).

3 tablespoons unsalted butter
1 medium onion, diced
1 cup long-grain white rice, rinsed
and drained
1 garlic clove, minced
1½ cups water
Kosher salt
¼ cup chopped mixed herbs, such as
parsley, chives and tarragon

1. In a saucepan, melt the butter. Add the onion, cover and cook over low heat until translucent, 5 minutes. Stir in the rice and garlic. Add the water and 1 teaspoon of salt; bring to a boil over high heat. Cover and cook over moderately low heat for 10 minutes.

2. Replace the lid on the rice with a clean kitchen towel; remove from the heat. Let the rice stand, covered, for 5 minutes, until tender. Using 2 forks, lightly fluff the rice. Stir in the herbs, season with salt, cover with the towel and the lid and let stand for up to 30 minutes before serving. —*April Bloomfield*

● HEALTHY ● MAKE AHEAD ● VEGETARIAN ● STAFF FAVORITE

two-tone potato salad

Rice with Duck and Apricots

ACTIVE: 30 MIN; TOTAL: 1 HR 10 MIN
4 TO 5 SERVINGS

F&W Best New Chef 2011 George Mendes's signature dish at Aldea in New York includes poached duck breast and homemade duck confit. For this simplified recipe, buy the confit instead, and forgo the breast.

- 3 tablespoons extra-virgin olive oil
- ½ small onion, finely chopped
- 3 garlic cloves, minced
- 1 plum tomato, diced
- 1 tablespoon sweet paprika

Pinch of saffron threads, crumbled

- 1 cup arborio rice
- 2½ cups low-sodium chicken broth
- 2 confit duck legs, skinned and meat coarsely shredded
- ¼ cup thinly sliced chorizo
- ¼ cup sliced pitted kalamata olives
- ¼ cup diced dried apricots

Salt and freshly ground pepper

1. Preheat the oven to 375°. In a large oven-proof skillet, heat the oil until shimmering. Add the onion and garlic and cook over moderately low heat until softened, 5 minutes. Add the tomato and cook until softened, 5 minutes. Stir in the paprika and saffron. Add the rice and cook, stirring, for 2 minutes. Add half of the broth and gently simmer until absorbed, 8 minutes. Stir in the duck, chorizo, olives and apricots and season with salt and pepper. Add the remaining broth and bring to a boil. **2.** Bake the skillet uncovered until the rice is tender and absorbs the liquid, 16 minutes. —*George Mendes*
WINE Spicy, blackberry-rich Portuguese red: 2007 Álvaro Castro Tinto Dão.

Crisp Sushi-Rice Cakes

🙂 **TOTAL: 45 MIN • MAKES 8 CAKES** ● ●

- 1 cup sushi rice, rinsed
- ½ tablespoon mirin
- ½ teaspoon rice vinegar
- ½ teaspoon sugar

Salt
Vegetable oil, for frying

1. In a medium saucepan, combine the rice with 1½ cups of water, the mirin, vinegar and sugar; bring to a boil. Cover and cook over low heat for 20 minutes. Fluff the rice. Transfer to a bowl and let cool. Season with salt. **2.** Preheat the oven to 325°. In a large non-stick skillet, heat ¼ inch of oil until shimmering. For each cake, pack the rice into a ¼ cup measuring cup; unmold and flatten slightly. Cook the cakes over moderately high heat, pressing them, until golden brown, about 4 minutes. Turn and cook for 4 minutes longer. Serve hot. —*Santos Majano*

Barley and Rice with Sesame Oil and Chives

ACTIVE: 15 MIN; TOTAL: 1 HR
8 SERVINGS ● ●

Boribap, or barley with rice, is a popular Korean side dish that combines white rice with plump, nutty grains of barley. In their amped-up version, superchef Jean-Georges Vongerichten and his Korean-American wife, Marja, mix in toasted sesame oil and minced chives for more flavor.

- 1 cup pearled barley, rinsed
- 1 cup long-grain white rice, rinsed
- 2 tablespoons unsalted butter
- 1 teaspoon toasted sesame oil

Salt

- ½ cup thinly sliced chives

1. In a medium saucepan, cover the barley with 2 inches of water. Bring to a boil, cover and cook over low heat until just tender, about 45 minutes; add more water as needed to keep the barley covered. Drain well. **2.** Meanwhile, in a small saucepan, combine the rice with 1½ cups of room-temperature water. Bring to a boil, cover and cook over low heat for 14 minutes. Remove from the heat and let stand, covered, for 5 minutes. Uncover and fluff the rice with a fork. **3.** In a large skillet, melt the butter over moderate heat. Add the barley and rice and toss gently to mix. Remove from the heat. Stir in the sesame oil and season with salt. Fold in the chives. Transfer to a bowl and serve. —*Marja Vongerichten*

Grilled Polenta and Radicchio with Balsamic Drizzle

ACTIVE: 45 MIN; TOTAL: 2 HR 30 MIN
4 SERVINGS ● ●

- 2 cups water
- 2 cups soy milk
- 2 garlic cloves, smashed
- 1 rosemary sprig
- 1 thyme sprig
- 1 cup instant polenta

Salt and freshly ground pepper

- 1 cup balsamic vinegar
- 2 medium heads of radicchio, cut into 1-inch-thick wedges through the cores

Extra-virgin olive oil, for drizzling and brushing

1. Lightly oil a 9-inch square glass or ceramic baking dish. In a medium saucepan, combine the water, soy milk, garlic cloves, rosemary and thyme and bring to a boil. Remove from the heat and let steep for 10 minutes. **2.** Discard the garlic, rosemary and thyme and return the mixture to a boil. Gradually whisk in the polenta and simmer over low heat, whisking often, until very thick and no longer gritty, 10 minutes. Season with salt and pepper. Pour the polenta into the baking dish. Let cool to room temperature, then cover and refrigerate for at least 2 hours. **3.** Meanwhile, in a small saucepan, boil the balsamic vinegar over moderately high heat until reduced to ¼ cup, about 15 minutes. Let cool to room temperature. **4.** Light a grill. Drizzle the radicchio wedges with olive oil and season with salt and pepper. Grill over moderately high heat until lightly charred and just tender, about 3 minutes per side. Clean the grill with a wire brush. **5.** Carefully unmold the polenta and cut it into 8 wedges or squares. Brush all over with olive oil, then grill until the polenta is lightly charred on the bottom and releases easily, 4 minutes per side. Arrange the grilled polenta and radicchio on plates, drizzle with the balsamic reduction and serve. —*Ryan Poli*
MAKE AHEAD The cooked polenta and balsamic reduction can be made 1 day ahead.

● HEALTHY ● MAKE AHEAD ● VEGETARIAN ● STAFF FAVORITE

grilled polenta and radicchio with balsamic drizzle

Pea and Bacon Risotto

TOTAL: 50 MIN • 6 SERVINGS

When chef de cuisine James Tracey prepares this sweet pea risotto at Craft in Manhattan, he adds bacon for smokiness and a generous grating of Parmigiano-Reggiano cheese to make the dish extra-creamy.

- 6 ounces lean bacon, diced
- 2 cups frozen baby peas, thawed
- 2 tablespoons olive oil
- 1 small onion, minced
- 2 cups arborio rice
- ½ cup dry white wine
- 7 cups simmering chicken stock
- 1 tablespoon unsalted butter
- ½ cup freshly grated Parmigiano-Reggiano cheese
- 1 tablespoon fresh lemon juice
- Salt and freshly ground pepper
- 2 cups small pea shoots

1. In a skillet, cook the diced bacon over moderate heat until crisp, about 6 minutes. Drain the bacon on paper towels; reserve 1 tablespoon of the bacon fat.

2. In a food processor, puree half of the peas with 1 cup of water.

3. In a large saucepan, heat the oil. Add the onion and cook over moderate heat until softened, 5 minutes. Add the rice and cook, stirring, until the rice is evenly coated with the oil. Add the wine and simmer until almost evaporated, 3 minutes.

4. Add enough hot stock to just cover the rice and cook over moderate heat, stirring, until the stock has been absorbed. Add more stock to cover the rice. Continue cooking and stirring, adding more chicken stock as it is absorbed, until the rice is al dente and suspended in a creamy sauce, 25 minutes. Add the pea puree, the remaining peas and the bacon and cook, stirring, until hot. Remove the risotto from the heat and stir in the butter, reserved bacon fat, cheese and lemon juice. Season with salt and pepper. Garnish with the pea shoots and serve.

—*James Tracey*

WINE Dark-berried, concentrated Pinot Noir: 2008 Evening Land Seven Springs.

Farro with Artichokes and Herb Salad

TOTAL: 1 HR • 5 TO 6 SERVINGS ● ●

- 4 tablespoons unsalted butter
- 1 carrot, finely diced
- 1 small celery root, peeled and finely diced
- 1 small onion, finely diced
- 2 celery ribs—1 minced and 1 thinly sliced, plus ½ cup celery leaves
- 1 bay leaf
- 2 cups farro (14 ounces)
- 1 cup dry white wine
- 4 cups low-sodium chicken broth
- Salt and freshly ground pepper
- 3 tablespoons grated Grana Padano, plus shaved cheese for garnish
- 4 ounces marinated baby artichokes, drained and halved (¾ cup)
- ½ cup flat-leaf parsley leaves
- ¼ cup snipped chives
- 1 tablespoon tarragon leaves
- 1 teaspoon white wine vinegar
- 1 tablespoon extra-virgin olive oil

1. In a large saucepan, melt 2 tablespoons of the butter. Add the carrot, celery root, onion, minced celery and bay leaf and cook over moderate heat, stirring occasionally, until the vegetables are lightly browned, 5 minutes. Add the farro and cook, stirring, for 2 minutes. Add the wine and cook, stirring occasionally, until completely absorbed, 5 minutes. Add half of the chicken broth and cook, stirring occasionally, until completely absorbed, about 12 minutes. Season with salt and pepper. Add the remaining broth and cook, stirring occasionally, until completely absorbed, 12 minutes longer. Discard the bay leaf. Stir in the cheese along with the artichokes and the remaining 2 tablespoons of butter until creamy. Spoon into bowls.

2. In a medium bowl, toss the sliced celery and celery leaves with the parsley, chives and tarragon. Add the vinegar and oil, season with salt and pepper and toss. Mound the salad over the farro, garnish with cheese shavings and serve. —*Jonathon Sawyer*

WINE Vibrant white: 2010 Hirsch Veltliner #1.

Red Rice and Quinoa Salad with Orange and Pistachios

ACTIVE: 30 MIN; TOTAL: 1 HR
6 SERVINGS ● ● ● ●

This fluffy salad, which blends South American quinoa with nutty Camargue red rice from southern France, gets a fruity sweetness from orange juice and zest. It's delicious alongside roast chicken.

- 1 cup quinoa
- 1 cup Camargue red rice (see Note)
- ¼ cup extra-virgin olive oil
- 1 medium onion, thinly sliced
- Salt and freshly ground pepper
- ⅓ cup fresh orange juice
- 1½ teaspoons finely grated orange zest
- 1 tablespoon fresh lemon juice
- 1 garlic clove, minced
- ½ cup dried apricots, cut into ⅓-inch dice
- ½ cup roasted pistachios, chopped
- 4 scallions, thinly sliced
- 2 cups baby arugula leaves

1. Bring 2 medium saucepans of salted water to a boil. Add the quinoa to 1 saucepan and the red rice to the other. Cover and simmer over moderate heat until tender, about 12 minutes for the quinoa and 35 minutes for the rice. Drain the grains and spread them out on baking sheets to cool.

2. In a medium skillet, heat 1 tablespoon of the olive oil. Add the onion; season with salt and pepper. Cover and cook the onion over moderate heat, stirring occasionally, until golden brown, about 10 minutes. Let cool.

3. In a large bowl, combine the orange juice with the orange zest, lemon juice, garlic and the remaining 3 tablespoons of olive oil; season with salt and pepper. Add the grains, onion, apricots, pistachios and scallions and toss well. Serve with the arugula.

—*Yotam Ottolenghi*

NOTE Camargue red rice is available at specialty food and health-food stores. Brown rice makes an excellent substitute.

MAKE AHEAD The cooked quinoa and rice and the dressing can be refrigerated separately overnight.

● HEALTHY ● MAKE AHEAD ● VEGETARIAN ● STAFF FAVORITE

pea and bacon risotto

potatoes, grains and beans

Butter Beans in Miso Bagna Cauda

ACTIVE: 20 MIN; TOTAL: 4 HR PLUS OVERNIGHT SOAKING • 4 SERVINGS ● ●

Bagna cauda (literally, "hot bath") is a warm Piedmontese olive oil dip traditionally flavored with anchovies. Napa chef Jeremy Fox swaps out the anchovy for vegetarian-friendly miso, then tosses the garlicky sauce with warm baby potatoes and butter beans.

- 1 cup dried butter beans, soaked overnight and drained
- 12 baby potatoes
- 1 tablespoon plus 1 teaspoon red miso paste
- 1 teaspoon finely grated lemon zest plus juice of 2 lemons
- ½ cup extra-virgin olive oil
- 2 garlic cloves, minced
- 1 small onion, finely diced
- 2 tablespoons chopped parsley
- Salt
- 2 tablespoons chopped roasted almonds, for garnish
- Baby arugula and shaved Parmigiano-Reggiano cheese, for garnish

1. In a large saucepan, cover the drained butter beans with 2 inches of water. Cover partially and simmer over low heat until tender, about 3½ hours; add more water as needed to keep the beans covered by 2 inches. Drain the beans and reserve ½ cup of the cooking water.

2. In a medium saucepan, cover the potatoes with water and boil over moderately high heat until tender, about 15 minutes. Drain and let cool to warm, then break the potatoes open with your fingers.

3. Meanwhile, in a small bowl, whisk the miso paste with the lemon zest and juice. Whisk in the olive oil, then add the garlic, onion and parsley and season with salt.

4. In a large bowl, toss the beans and potatoes with the reserved bean cooking liquid. Add the miso dressing and toss. Season lightly with salt. Garnish with the almonds, arugula and cheese and serve.
—*Jeremy Fox*

Lima Bean and Sweet Pepper Gratin

ACTIVE: 30 MIN; TOTAL: 1 HR 8 SERVINGS ● ●

- 2 tablespoons unsalted butter, plus more for greasing the dish
- 1 shallot, minced
- 3 cups frozen baby lima beans
- 1 cup chicken stock
- 1 bay leaf
- Salt
- 1 tablespoon extra-virgin olive oil
- 1 large sweet onion, cut into 1-inch dice
- ¼ pound thick-cut bacon, cut into ½-inch pieces
- 4 garlic cloves, minced
- 2 roasted red peppers, cut into 1-inch pieces
- 1 tablespoon chopped parsley
- 1 teaspoon chopped thyme
- 1 cup freshly grated Parmigiano-Reggiano cheese
- Freshly ground pepper
- ½ cup torn basil leaves
- 1 cup fresh bread crumbs, made from a country-style bread

1. Butter a 9-by-13-inch baking dish. In a medium saucepan, melt 1 tablespoon of the butter. Add the shallot and cook over moderate heat until softened. Add the lima beans, stock, bay leaf, 1 cup of water and a large pinch of salt and bring to a boil. Cover and simmer over low heat until the beans are tender, 30 minutes; drain, reserving 1 cup of the cooking liquid. Discard the bay leaf.

2. Preheat the oven to 375°. In a large, deep skillet, heat the oil. Add the onion and bacon and cook over moderately high heat, stirring occasionally, until the onion is lightly caramelized, 10 minutes. Stir in the garlic, roasted peppers, parsley, thyme and lima beans; remove the skillet from the heat. Stir in the reserved 1 cup of cooking liquid and half of the cheese and season with salt and pepper.

3. Transfer the lima beans to the prepared baking dish. Sprinkle on the basil, followed by the remaining ½ cup of cheese and bread crumbs. Dot with the remaining 1 tablespoon of butter and bake in the upper third of the oven for 25 minutes, until golden brown on top. Let the gratin stand for 10 minutes, then serve. —*Hugh Acheson*

Fresh Lima Bean Gratins

ACTIVE: 45 MIN; TOTAL: 2 HR 6 SERVINGS ● ●

- 4 tablespoons unsalted butter, 1 tablespoon melted
- 3 tablespoons extra-virgin olive oil
- 1 pound small shallots, halved
- 8 thyme sprigs
- Salt and freshly ground pepper
- 4 cups shelled lima beans (1¼ pounds)
- 1½ tablespoons all-purpose flour
- 2 cups half-and-half
- 1½ cups cherry tomatoes, halved
- ½ cup *panko* (Japanese bread crumbs)
- 1 tablespoon chopped flat-leaf parsley

1. Preheat the oven to 425°. In a large, deep ovenproof skillet, melt 3 tablespoons of the butter in the oil. Add the shallots and thyme, season with salt and pepper and cook over high heat for 1 minute. Cover tightly and roast for about 30 minutes, until very tender.

2. Meanwhile, in a large saucepan of salted water, cook the limas until just tender, 5 minutes. Drain and cool under running water. Spread on paper towels and pat dry.

3. Transfer the shallots and thyme to a plate; leave as much fat in the pan as possible. Lower the oven to 375°. Strip the thyme leaves from the sprigs and return to the shallots. Add the flour to the skillet and cook over moderately high heat, whisking, for 1 minute. Add the half-and-half and simmer until thickened, 5 minutes. Remove from the heat. Stir in the limas, shallots, thyme and tomatoes; season with salt and pepper. Spoon into six 1½-cup ramekins and set on a baking sheet.

4. In a bowl, toss the *panko*, parsley and 1 tablespoon of melted butter; sprinkle over the gratins. Bake for 30 minutes, until bubbling. Turn on the broiler and broil for 2 minutes, just until browned. Let the gratins rest for 10 minutes before serving. —*Grace Parisi*

Veggie Burgers with Pomegranate Ketchup

ACTIVE: 45 MIN; TOTAL: 1 HR 25 MIN
6 SERVINGS ● ●

Eating vegan for a month led *Top Chef: All-Stars* winner Richard Blais to examine his pantry more closely. He discovered that ground porcini mushrooms add a meaty flavor to dishes like his veggie burger.

½ cup raisins
¼ cup roasted almonds, chopped
½ pound white mushrooms
1 cup steamed shelled edamame
2½ cups cooked green or brown lentils
2 cups cooked Israeli couscous
2½ teaspoons curry powder
1 tablespoon fresh lemon juice
2 teaspoons ground dried porcini
Kosher salt
1½ tablespoons canola oil
3 burger buns, split and toasted
½ cup ketchup mixed with 1 tablespoon of pomegranate molasses
Mesclun greens tossed with lemon juice and sautéed mushrooms, for serving

1. In a food processor, combine the raisins and almonds; process until finely chopped. Add the mushrooms and process until coarsely chopped. Add the edamame, lentils and half of the couscous and process until coarsely chopped. In a small bowl, dissolve the curry in the lemon juice and add to the processor along with the porcini and process to a coarse paste. Fold in the remaining couscous and season with salt. Form the mixture into 6 patties, about 1 inch thick.
2. In a large nonstick skillet, heat the canola oil. Add the patties and cook them over moderate heat, turning once, until they are browned, about 6 minutes.
3. Arrange the bun halves on plates and spread them with pomegranate ketchup. Set the burgers on the buns, top with the greens and sautéed mushrooms and serve.
—Richard Blais

WINE Bright, easygoing Beaujolais: 2009 Domaine des Terres Dorées L'Ancien.

Lentils with Garlic Sausage

TOTAL: 1 HR • 4 SERVINGS ●

For this quick weeknight stew, cookbook author Melissa Clark reinvents French lentils and sausage without hours of simmering or dirtying lots of pots.

¼ cup extra-virgin olive oil
1 pound French garlic sausage or kielbasa, cut into ¾-inch pieces
2 leeks, white and tender green parts only, thinly sliced
1 large carrot, diced
3 garlic cloves, minced
1½ cups French green lentils
3 thyme sprigs, 1 rosemary sprig and 1 fresh bay leaf, tied in a bundle
Salt
½ cup hazelnuts
2 tablespoons Dijon mustard
1 small head of escarole, chopped
1 tablespoon chopped parsley

1. In a large, heavy Dutch oven, heat 2 tablespoons of the olive oil. Add the garlic sausage and cook over moderately high heat, stirring, until browned, 5 minutes. Using a slotted spoon, transfer the sausage to a plate.
2. Add the leeks, carrot and garlic to the Dutch oven and cook over moderate heat until softened, about 7 minutes. Add the lentils, herb bundle and 5 cups of water and bring to a boil. Season with salt and simmer over low heat until the lentils are tender, about 35 minutes. Discard the herb bundle.
3. Meanwhile, preheat the oven to 350°. Spread the hazelnuts in a pie plate and toast for about 12 minutes, until golden. Let cool, then transfer the nuts to a kitchen towel and rub off the skins. Coarsely chop the nuts.
4. In a small bowl, combine the mustard with the remaining 2 tablespoons of olive oil. Add the escarole to the stew and cook until wilted, 6 minutes. Stir in the sausage pieces and cook until hot. Transfer the stew to bowls and drizzle with the mustard oil. Garnish with the nuts and parsley and serve.
—Melissa Clark

WINE Berry-rich Cabernet Franc: 2008 Catherine & Pierre Breton Beaumont Chinon.

Spiced Lentils with Mushrooms and Greens

TOTAL: 40 MIN • 2 MAIN-COURSE OR 4 SIDE-DISH SERVINGS ● ● ●

"I love lentils: They're packed with protein, very filling and a good source of iron," says Jill Donenfeld of The Culinistas, a bicoastal private-chef service. Eat these stewy lentils as a light lunch or serve with Roasted Cauliflower with Golden Raisins (page 258).

½ cup brown or green lentils
3 tablespoons extra-virgin olive oil
½ pound shiitake mushrooms, stems discarded and caps sliced ¼ inch thick
Salt
1 garlic clove, minced
¼ teaspoon ground cumin
¼ teaspoon ground coriander
¼ teaspoon freshly ground black pepper
⅛ teaspoon turmeric
½ pound Swiss chard or other tender greens, large stems discarded and leaves coarsely chopped
1 tablespoon chopped parsley

1. In a small saucepan, cover the lentils with 2½ cups of water and bring to a boil. Cover and cook over low heat until the lentils are tender, about 30 minutes.
2. Meanwhile, in a medium saucepan, heat 2 tablespoons of the olive oil. Add the shiitake and season with salt. Cover and cook over moderate heat, stirring, until the mushrooms are tender and starting to brown, 5 minutes. Add the remaining 1 tablespoon of olive oil along with the garlic, cumin, coriander, pepper and turmeric and cook, stirring, until fragrant, 1 minute. Add the greens and cook, stirring, until wilted, 2 minutes.
3. Add the lentils and their cooking liquid to the mushrooms and simmer for 3 minutes. Add up to ¼ cup of water if the lentils are too dry. Season with salt. Ladle the lentils into bowls, garnish with the parsley and serve.
—Jill Donenfeld

WINE Earthy, spicy southern Italian red: 2009 Argiolas Perdera.

Squash Stuffed with Quinoa and Wild Mushrooms

ACTIVE: 45 MIN; TOTAL: 1 HR 30 MIN

6 SERVINGS ● ●

"I love how out of control the vegetarian culture is in this city," says chef Kevin Kathman of Barbette in Minneapolis. To satisfy those diners, he stuffs maple-glazed roasted squash with quinoa and sautéed wild mushrooms. For a more substantial dish, serve the stuffed squash with roasted root vegetables brushed with the same glaze.

SQUASH

One 3½-pound kabocha or buttercup
    squash—halved lengthwise, seeded
    and cut into 6 wedges
Olive oil, for brushing
Kosher salt and freshly ground pepper
  2 tablespoons unsalted butter
  1 tablespoon light brown sugar
  2 tablespoons pure maple syrup
  3 thyme sprigs

SAUCE

  ½ cup heavy cream
  2 tablespoons maple syrup
  1 garlic clove, crushed
  2 thyme sprigs

FILLING

  3 tablespoons unsalted butter
  3 shallots—1 minced, 2 thinly
     sliced crosswise
  1 bay leaf
  4 thyme sprigs
2½ cups water
Salt and freshly ground pepper
1½ cups quinoa
  2 tablespoons extra-virgin olive oil
  ½ pound oyster mushrooms,
     cut into 1-inch chunks
  ½ pound shiitake mushrooms, stems
     discarded and caps sliced
  ⅓ cup chopped parsley

1. PREPARE THE SQUASH Preheat the oven to 350°. Brush the squash with oil and season with salt and pepper; arrange on a baking sheet cut side down and roast for about 20 minutes, until lightly browned. Flip the wedges and roast for 20 minutes, until just tender.

2. In a saucepan, melt the butter with the sugar, maple syrup and thyme. Cook over moderately low heat until the sugar has dissolved, about 3 minutes. Turn the squash skin side down and brush all over with the maple glaze. Roast for 10 minutes longer, until the squash is lightly browned and glazed.

3. MAKE THE SAUCE In a saucepan, whisk the cream with the maple syrup. Add the garlic and thyme and simmer over moderately high heat until reduced to ⅓ cup. Discard the garlic and thyme and keep warm.

4. MAKE THE FILLING In a medium saucepan, melt 2 tablespoons of the butter. Add the minced shallot and cook over moderate heat until softened, about 3 minutes. Add the bay leaf, thyme and water and bring to a boil. Season with salt and pepper, then add the quinoa. Cover and cook over moderately low heat until the quinoa is tender and the water has been absorbed, about 15 minutes.

5. In a large skillet, melt the remaining 1 tablespoon of butter in the oil. Add the sliced shallots and cook over moderately high heat, stirring, until lightly browned. Add the oyster and shiitake mushrooms and cook until browned on the bottom, 3 minutes. Continue cooking, stirring occasionally, until the mushrooms are browned and tender, about 6 minutes more. Stir in the quinoa and parsley and season with salt and pepper.

6. Arrange the roasted squash on plates. Fill each wedge with the quinoa stuffing, drizzle the sauce on top and serve right away.
—*Kevin Kathman*

WINE Lively, red berry–scented Barbera d'Asti: 2009 Michele Chiarlo Le Orme.

Quinoa Salad with Grilled Scallions, Favas and Dates

TOTAL: 1 HR • 4 SERVINGS ● ●

"One thing I've learned as a chef is not to overfeed your customers—a food coma is very unpleasant," says Charlie Parker of Plum restaurant in Oakland, California. This salad of grilled spring vegetables feels just filling enough, thanks to the addition of protein-rich quinoa and a puree of Medjool dates that are grilled first to soften them and intensify their natural sweetness.

  1 cup red quinoa, rinsed
  2 cups water
  8 soft Medjool dates, pitted
  2 tablespoons sherry vinegar
Salt
  1 pound fava beans in the pod
Finely grated zest and juice of 1 lemon
  ⅓ cup extra-virgin olive oil
Freshly ground pepper
 12 scallions
  6 stalks of green garlic or baby leeks
  2 tablespoons chopped mint
  1 cup small sorrel or arugula leaves

1. In a small saucepan, cover the quinoa with the water and bring to a boil. Cover and cook over moderately low heat until the water has been absorbed and the quinoa is tender, about 15 minutes. Uncover, fluff the quinoa and transfer to a large bowl.

2. Meanwhile, light a grill or preheat a grill pan. Grill the dates over moderate heat until lightly charred and very soft, about 2 minutes. Transfer the dates to a shallow bowl and mash to a puree with a fork. Stir in the vinegar and season the puree with salt.

3. Grill the fava bean pods over moderately high heat, turning occasionally, until the pods are softened and hot within, about 5 minutes. Transfer the pods to a bowl, cover with foil and let steam for 5 minutes.

4. In a small bowl, stir the lemon zest, juice and olive oil and season with salt and pepper. Shell and peel the fava beans and toss them with 1 tablespoon of the dressing.

5. Brush the scallions and green garlic with some of the dressing, season with salt and pepper and grill over moderately high heat, turning, until browned and tender, about 2 minutes. Transfer to a work surface and cut them into 2-inch lengths.

6. Mix the fava beans, scallions, green garlic and mint into the quinoa. Add the remaining dressing and toss well. Season with salt and pepper. Spread the date puree on the bottoms of 4 plates and spoon the quinoa salad on top. Garnish with the sorrel leaves and serve. —*Charlie Parker*

MAKE AHEAD The cooked quinoa can be refrigerated overnight.

● HEALTHY ● MAKE AHEAD ● VEGETARIAN ● STAFF FAVORITE

squash stuffed with quinoa and wild mushrooms

White Bean Stew

ACTIVE: 20 MIN; TOTAL: 2 HR PLUS
OVERNIGHT SOAKING

4 TO 6 SERVINGS ● ●

Mixing in a garlic mayonnaise and bitter greens at the table provides additional flavor and depth to this rustic stew.

- 2 tablespoons extra-virgin olive oil
- 3 garlic cloves, thinly sliced
- 2 celery ribs, cut into ¼-inch dice
- 1 carrot, cut into ¼-inch dice
- 1 onion, finely diced
- 1 bay leaf
- 1 teaspoon thyme leaves
- 6 cups water
- 1 large smoked ham hock
- ½ pound dried white beans, such as Great Northern or navy, soaked overnight and drained

Salt and freshly ground pepper

Garlic Mayonnaise and Sautéed Mustard Greens (recipes follow), for serving

1. In a large saucepan, heat the olive oil. Add the garlic, celery, carrot, onion, bay leaf and thyme leaves and cook over moderate heat, stirring occasionally, until softened, about 8 minutes. Add the water, ham hock and drained beans and bring to a boil. Simmer over low heat, stirring occasionally, until the beans are tender, about 1½ hours.

2. Remove the ham hock from the stew and chop the meat; discard the bones, skin and gristle. Discard the bay leaf. Add the ham hock meat to the beans, season with salt and pepper and serve with Garlic Mayonnaise and Sautéed Mustard Greens. —*Steven Satterfield*

GARLIC MAYONNAISE

TOTAL: 5 MIN

MAKES ABOUT ½ CUP ● ●

- ½ cup mayonnaise
- 2 garlic cloves, minced
- 1 tablespoon freshly squeezed lemon juice
- ½ teaspoon dry mustard

Salt

In a small bowl, whisk the mayonnaise with the minced garlic, freshly squeezed lemon juice and dry mustard; season the Garlic Mayonnaise with salt and serve. —*SS*

MAKE AHEAD The Garlic Mayonnaise can kept in the refrigerator in an airtight container for up to 2 days.

SAUTÉED MUSTARD GREENS

TOTAL: 20 MIN • 4 TO 6 SERVINGS ● ●

- 1¼ pounds mustard greens, stemmed
- 1 tablespoon unsalted butter
- 1 tablespoon extra-virgin olive oil
- 2 garlic cloves, minced
- ½ small red onion, finely diced
- ½ teaspoon crushed red pepper
- ¼ cup chicken stock

Salt

1. In a large saucepan of boiling salted water, cook the greens for 1 minute. Drain, squeeze out the excess water and coarsely chop.

2. In the same saucepan, melt the butter in the olive oil. Add the garlic, red onion and crushed red pepper and cook over moderate heat until softened, about 5 minutes. Add the mustard greens and cook over moderately high heat, stirring to coat with the flavored oil. Add the stock and season with salt. Transfer to a bowl to serve. —*SS*

Black-Eyed Peas

ACTIVE: 10 MIN; TOTAL: 1 HR 30 MIN

8 SERVINGS ● ● ●

Mary Hoover, who ran a soul food restaurant in Greenwood, Mississippi, for 30 years and was enlisted to prepare food for the 2011 film *The Help*, says that she can tell the black-eyed peas for a cool salad recipe are fully cooked when "their eyes pop out." To serve them as a warm side dish at dinner, as in the recipe here, she boils them longer, "until the cooking water turns gray."

- 1 pound dried black-eyed peas, picked over and rinsed
- ¼ cup vegetable oil
- 1½ teaspoons salt
- 1½ teaspoons sugar

1. In a large bowl, cover the black-eyed peas with room-temperature water and let soak for 20 minutes.

2. In a large saucepan, combine 2 quarts of water with the vegetable oil, salt and sugar and bring to a vigorous boil. Drain the black-eyed peas and add them to the saucepan. Simmer over moderate heat until the beans are tender but not mushy, 45 minutes to 1½ hours, depending on the freshness of the beans (older beans will need to cook longer). Add boiling water to the saucepan as it evaporates to keep the black-eyed peas covered. Drain the black-eyed peas in a colander, transfer them to a medium bowl and serve. —*Mary Hoover*

MAKE AHEAD The beans can be refrigerated in their cooking liquid for up to 4 days. Reheat gently before draining and serving.

Cranberry Bean Salad with Celery, Basil and Mint

ACTIVE: 20 MIN; TOTAL: 1 HR 30 MIN
PLUS OVERNIGHT SOAKING

8 SERVINGS ● ● ●

In Russia, people often make this red *lobio* with kidney beans. The recipe here substitutes cranberry beans because they have a creamier texture.

- 1 pound dried cranberry beans (2½ cups), soaked overnight and drained
- ¼ cup red wine vinegar
- ¼ cup vegetable oil
- 3 tablespoons Dijon mustard

Salt and freshly ground pepper

- 2 celery ribs, thinly sliced crosswise
- 1 jalapeño, seeded and minced
- 1 fresh red chile, seeded and minced
- ½ cup chopped basil
- ¼ cup chopped mint

1. In a large pot, cover the beans with 2 inches of water and bring to a boil. Cover the pot partially and simmer the beans over moderate heat, stirring occasionally, until tender, about 1 hour. Add more water as necessary to keep the beans covered. Drain the beans, reserving ½ cup of the cooking liquid.

2. In a small bowl, whisk the red wine vinegar, vegetable oil and Dijon mustard and season with salt and pepper.

3. Transfer the beans to a large bowl. Add the celery, jalapeño, red chile, the reserved bean cooking liquid and the dressing; toss well. Season with salt and pepper. Let the salad stand for 15 minutes, stirring occasionally. Stir in the basil and mint and serve. —*Dmitry Leonov*

Chickpeas in Spicy Tomato Gravy

⏲ **TOTAL: 35 MIN • 4 TO 6 SERVINGS**

● ● ●

This classic Punjabi dish called *masaledar cholay,* from superstar Indian chef Sanjeev Kapoor, is often served as part of a big Sunday lunch, along with raita, naan and salad. Vegans can omit the raita.

  8   garlic cloves, chopped
  2   jalapeños, chopped
One 2-inch piece of fresh ginger, peeled
      and chopped
  ¼   cup vegetable oil
  3   onions, cut into ¼-inch dice
  2   tablespoons ground cumin
  1   tablespoon ground coriander
  ¾   teaspoon cayenne pepper
1½   cups canned diced tomatoes
Two 15-ounce cans chickpeas,
      drained and rinsed
  2   cups water
Salt
  2   tablespoons cilantro leaves

1. In a mini food processor, combine the garlic, jalapeños and ginger and process to a paste. In a large nonstick skillet, heat the vegetable oil. Add the onions and cook over moderately high heat until sizzling, about 3 minutes. Reduce the heat to moderate and cook, stirring occasionally, until the onions are browned, about 7 minutes. Add the garlic paste and cook, stirring, until fragrant, about 2 minutes. Add the cumin, coriander and cayenne and cook, stirring, for 1 minute. Add the tomatoes and simmer over moderate heat until thickened, about 6 minutes.

Add the chickpeas and water and simmer until the chickpeas are flavored with the gravy, about 8 minutes. Season the chickpeas with salt.

2. Garnish the chickpeas with the cilantro and serve. —*Sanjeev Kapoor*

SERVE WITH Yogurt and naan.

MAKE AHEAD The chickpeas can be prepared through Step 1 and refrigerated in an airtight container for up to 2 days.

WINE Concentrated, fruity Italian rosato: 2009 Di Giovanna Gerbino.

Caraway-Spiced Chickpea Stew with Mint Yogurt

ACTIVE: 20 MIN; TOTAL: 2 HR PLUS OVERNIGHT SOAKING • 4 SERVINGS ● ● ●

Growing up in the Middle East absolutely influenced Yotam Ottolenghi's culinary approach, but the healthy, often vegetarian dishes served at Ottolenghi, his London chain specializing in take-out food, are eclectic in inspiration. "I like to add something unusual to a dish," says Ottolenghi. In this otherwise Mediterranean stew, for example, he includes caraway, a spice often used in northern and eastern European cooking. To give the dish a mellow sweetness, he adds roasted carrots.

  ½   cup dried chickpeas, soaked in
      water overnight and drained
  2   large carrots, cut into ½-inch dice
  ¼   cup plus 1 teaspoon extra-virgin
      olive oil
Salt and freshly ground pepper
  1   large onion, cut into ½-inch dice
  1   teaspoon caraway seeds
1½   teaspoons ground cumin
1½   pounds Swiss chard,
      stems discarded and leaves
      sliced ½ inch thick
  1   tablespoon fresh lemon juice
  ¾   cup plain low-fat yogurt
  1   teaspoon dried mint
  3   tablespoons cilantro leaves

1. Preheat the oven to 350°.

2. In a medium saucepan, cover the drained chickpeas by 2 inches of water and bring to

a boil. Cover and simmer over moderately low heat until tender, adding water as necessary to keep the chickpeas covered, about 1½ hours. Drain the chickpeas, reserving ½ cup of the cooking liquid.

3. Spread the diced carrots on a rimmed baking sheet, toss with 1 teaspoon of the olive oil and season with salt and freshly ground pepper. Roast in the oven for about 15 minutes, until barely tender.

4. In a large skillet, heat 3 tablespoons of the olive oil. Add the onion and caraway and season with salt and pepper. Cover and cook over moderate heat, stirring occasionally, until the onion is golden, about 10 minutes. Add the cumin and cook, stirring, until fragrant, about 1 minute. Add the Swiss chard leaves and cook over moderately high heat, stirring, until wilted, about 2 minutes. Add the carrots, chickpeas and their reserved cooking liquid and simmer over low heat for 3 minutes. Add the lemon juice and season the stew with salt and pepper.

5. In a small bowl, mix the yogurt with the mint and remaining 1 tablespoon of olive oil; season with salt and pepper. Transfer the stew to bowls and garnish with the cilantro. Pass the mint yogurt at the table. —*Yotam Ottolenghi*

SERVE WITH Grilled flatbread, steamed rice or couscous.

MAKE AHEAD The stew can be refrigerated overnight. Reheat gently. The mint yogurt can be refrigerated overnight.

WINE Minerally, citrusy Chardonnay: 2009 Domaine Rijckaert.

ingredient tip

coriander Often used with chickpeas, the spice is also great on everything from roasted chicken to grilled vegetables.

Montreal's Joe Beef co-chef Frédéric Morin at his rural retreat in Kamouraska, Quebec. A Joe Beef classic: their grilled cheese and bacon sandwich with cheese curds, OPPOSITE; *recipe, page 294.*

breads, pizzas and sandwiches

Tangier Street Bread (Kalinté)

ACTIVE: 20 MIN; TOTAL: 2 HR 45 MIN
PLUS OVERNIGHT RESTING
8 TO 12 SERVINGS ● ● ○ ○

This bread is Tangier's version of *socca*, the chickpea flour–based pancake of Nice, France, but it's quite a bit thicker and more custardy, like flan. Moroccans eat it by the slice on the street, sprinkled with cumin or smeared with harissa, but it's also delicious spread with cold salads.

1 large egg
¼ cup extra-virgin olive oil, plus more for brushing
2 teaspoons fine sea salt
4½ cups lukewarm water
2⅔ cups stone-ground chickpea flour, sifted
Ground cumin or harissa, for serving

1. In a blender or a large food processor, blend the egg with the ¼ cup of oil until foamy. Add the salt and half of the water and pulse for 3 seconds. Add half of the chickpea flour and process until smooth. Add the remaining flour and just enough water so the mixture is loose but not runny. Press the batter through a fine-mesh strainer set over a bowl and stir in the remaining water. Cover and refrigerate overnight or for up to 2 days.
2. At least 1½ hours before baking, set a pizza stone in the center of the oven and then preheat the oven to 500°. Lightly brush a 12-inch cast-iron skillet or deep-dish pizza pan with olive oil.
3. Whisk the batter until blended and pour it into the skillet. Bake the bread for 30 minutes. Brush the top of the bread with olive oil and cover two-thirds of it with a baking sheet. Turn the oven off and bake the bread in the residual heat for about 20 minutes longer, until deep golden brown and nicely glazed.
4. Using a spatula, loosen the edge and bottom of the bread, and slide it onto a work surface. Cut into small rectangles, sprinkle with cumin or harissa and serve hot or at room temperature. —*Paula Wolfert*
MAKE AHEAD The bread batter can be refrigerated for up to 2 days.

Two-Potato Flatbread with Olives and Feta

ACTIVE: 30 MIN; TOTAL: 1 HR 10 MIN
6 SERVINGS ●

Two ½-pound baking potatoes, peeled and sliced ⅛ inch thick
Extra-virgin olive oil, for brushing
Salt and freshly ground black pepper
Two ½-pound sweet potatoes, peeled and sliced ⅛ inch thick
12 ounces store-bought pizza dough
½ cup crumbled feta cheese
6 Picholine olives, pitted and quartered

1. Set a pizza stone on the bottom of the oven and preheat the oven to 400°. Spread the baking potato slices on a large rimmed baking sheet in a single layer. Brush with olive oil and season with salt and black pepper. Invert another rimmed baking sheet on top of the first one and bake the potatoes for about 5 minutes, until just tender; transfer to a plate. Repeat with the sweet potatoes, inverting the baking sheet on top and baking for 7 minutes, until just tender.
2. Increase the oven temperature to 500° and heat the pizza stone for 30 minutes.
3. On a lightly floured work surface, roll and stretch the pizza dough into a 10-by-12-inch rectangle, then transfer the rectangle to a floured pizza peel and brush the dough generously with olive oil. Arrange the potato slices on the dough and brush with olive oil. Top with the feta cheese and olives.
4. Slide the flatbread onto the hot pizza stone and bake for 7 minutes, until golden brown and crisp. Serve hot. —*Marcia Kiesel*
WINE Dry, berry-scented Provençal rosé: 2010 Mas de Gourgonnier.

Buckwheat Crackers with Smoked Fish

ACTIVE: 45 MIN; TOTAL: 4 HR
MAKES ABOUT 5 DOZEN CRACKERS ●

Using buckwheat flour in these incredibly crisp and buttery crackers gives them an appealing, earthy flavor. They're delightful with lemony crème fraîche and an assortment of smoked fish.

3 cups all-purpose flour, plus more for dusting
¼ cup buckwheat flour
1 teaspoon fine salt
1 stick cold unsalted butter, cut into small pieces
½ cup plus 2 tablespoons ice water
1 large egg, beaten
Sea salt flakes, for sprinkling
1 cup crème fraîche
1 tablespoon fresh lemon juice
½ teaspoon freshly ground black pepper
½ pound thinly sliced smoked salmon
½ pound smoked mackerel fillets, skinned and broken into pieces
¼ pound smoked shrimp
Sliced onions, for serving

1. In a large bowl, mix the all-purpose and buckwheat flours with the fine salt. Using a pastry cutter or 2 knives, cut in the butter until it resembles small peas. Sprinkle with the ice water and press gently with your hands to form a dough. Flatten the dough into an 8-by-6-inch rectangle, wrap in plastic and refrigerate for 1 hour.
2. Preheat the oven to 400°. Line a large rimmed baking sheet with parchment paper. Cut the dough into 4 equal rectangles. Working with 1 rectangle at a time and keeping the rest refrigerated, roll out the dough on a lightly floured surface to a 10-by-12-inch rectangle, about ¹⁄₁₆ inch thick. Transfer to the prepared baking sheet. Brush with the beaten egg and sprinkle with sea salt. Let stand for 3 minutes to let the egg wash dry. With a pastry wheel, cut the rectangle into 2-inch squares. Separate the squares, leaving about ½ inch between them. Top the squares with another sheet of parchment paper and another baking sheet. Bake for 25 minutes, until the crackers are golden brown. Transfer to a rack to cool. Repeat with the remaining dough, egg wash and salt.
3. In a small bowl, mix the crème fraîche, lemon juice and pepper. Arrange the smoked fish, shrimp and onions on a platter. Serve with the crackers and crème fraîche.
—*David McMillan and Frédéric Morin*

two-potato flatbread with olives and feta

do-it-yourself matzo

Cookbook author **Marcy Goldman** makes homemade whole-grain matzo year-round, topping it with a pungent horseradish relish. Here, she shares her recipes and tips for both.

roll the balls of dough as thinly as possible on a lightly floured surface into free-form ovals or rounds.

using a fork, prick holes all over the matzo to prevent air pockets (this is called "docking").

bake the matzo in a very hot oven until each piece is lightly browned, supercrisp and crackly.

Whole-Grain Matzo

⏱ TOTAL: 45 MIN • MAKES 12 MATZOS ● ● ○

Goldman started baking matzo with her sons after touring a temporary factory at a local synagogue that produced *shmura* matzo—the traditional, handmade variety. "As a baker and a Jewish mother, I thought, *I can do that*," she says. The whole-grain flours in this recipe create a more crackly, sandy texture than white-flour matzo.

- 1 cup all-purpose flour
- ½ cup spelt flour (available at natural-food stores)
- ½ cup oat flour (available at natural-food stores)
- ½ cup whole wheat flour
- About 1¼ cups water

1. Preheat the oven to 450°. Line 2 baking sheets with parchment paper. In a food processor, pulse the flours. With the machine on, pour in 1 cup plus 2 tablespoons of the water and process until a soft, evenly moistened dough forms. If necessary, add the remaining water, 1 tablespoon at a time. Divide the dough into 12 balls, cover with plastic wrap and let stand for 2 minutes.

2. On a lightly floured surface, roll out 4 balls of dough as thinly as possible; prick all over with a fork. Transfer to a baking sheet. Repeat with 4 more balls of dough. Bake in the upper and middle thirds of the oven until lightly browned and crisp, about 12 minutes; shift the sheets from top to bottom and front to back halfway through. Transfer the matzo to a rack. Repeat with the remaining 4 balls of dough.

Fresh Horseradish Relish with Apples and Cranberries

⏱ TOTAL: 40 MIN • MAKES 4 CUPS ● ● ○

At Passover, horseradish symbolizes the bitterness of the Israelites' slavery in Egypt. The version here is sweeter but still packs a punch.

- 1 pound horseradish root, peeled
- 1 large carrot
- 1 medium beet, peeled
- 1 large Granny Smith apple, peeled and cored
- 1 cup fresh or frozen cranberries
- ⅓ cup sugar
- ¾ cup distilled white vinegar
- Salt

In a food processor fitted with the shredding disk, separately shred the horseradish root, carrot, beet and apple; transfer the shredded fruit and vegetables to a large bowl. Using the blade of the food processor, pulse the cranberries with the sugar until the cranberries are finely chopped. Mix the cranberry mixture into the shredded fruit and vegetables along with the vinegar; season with salt. Allow to stand in the refrigerator for 3 days or up to 1 week before serving with matzo, gefilte fish, brisket or hard-boiled eggs.

> **fast food**
> One of the many kosher laws for matzo requires baking the dough within 18 minutes of mixing the flour and water, to prevent any leavening by wild yeasts.

whole-grain matzo with fresh horseradish relish

Lemony Mushroom and Pine Nut Stuffing Muffins

ACTIVE: 30 MIN; TOTAL: 1 HR 30 MIN
10 TO 12 SERVINGS ●

1 cup pine nuts (4½ ounces)
One 14-ounce brioche loaf—crust
    removed, bread cut into 1-inch dice
¼ cup extra-virgin olive oil
1 medium red onion, cut into
    ¼-inch dice
1 celery rib, cut into ¼-inch dice
1 pound assorted mushrooms—
    such as shiitake, oysters
    and chanterelles—shiitake stems
    trimmed, caps thinly sliced
Kosher salt and freshly ground pepper
1 cup heavy cream
2 large eggs
½ cup chicken stock or
    low-sodium broth
Finely grated zest of 1 lemon
Juice of 2 lemons
1 cup chopped parsley

1. Preheat the oven to 350°. Generously butter a 12-cup muffin tin. Spread the pine nuts in a pie plate. Toast the nuts for about 4 minutes, until golden.

2. Spread the brioche cubes on 2 large baking sheets. Bake for about 15 minutes, until toasted. Transfer to a large bowl and let cool. Increase the oven temperature to 375°.

3. In a large skillet, heat the oil. Add the onion and celery and cook over moderate heat until softened, 5 minutes. Add the mushrooms and season with salt and pepper. Cover and cook, stirring, until the mushrooms are tender and browned, 7 minutes. Let cool, then add to the brioche.

4. In a medium bowl, whisk the heavy cream with the eggs. Stir in the stock, lemon zest and juice and 2 teaspoons of salt. Add to the brioche along with the parsley and toasted pine nuts and stir well. Spoon the stuffing into the prepared muffin cups. Bake in the upper third of the oven for about 45 minutes, until crisp on top and heated through. Unmold the muffins and serve hot.
—*Michael Symon*

Butternut Squash and Corn Bread Stuffing Muffins

ACTIVE: 35 MIN; TOTAL: 2 HR 15 MIN
12 SERVINGS ●

One 2-pound butternut squash,
    halved lengthwise and seeded
Vegetable oil, for rubbing
Kosher salt and freshly ground pepper
1 pound prepared corn bread,
    cut into 1-inch cubes
½ pound thick-cut bacon, cut into
    1-inch pieces
1 medium red onion, cut into
    ¼-inch dice
1 celery rib, cut into ¼-inch dice
2 garlic cloves, minced
¼ cup chopped sage
2 teaspoons sugar
2 large eggs
½ cup chicken stock or low-
    sodium broth

1. Preheat the oven to 350°. Arrange the squash halves cut side up on a large rimmed baking sheet and rub with oil. Season with salt and pepper and turn the squash cut side down. Roast for about 1 hour, or until tender. Let cool slightly.

2. Increase the oven temperature to 375°. Spread the corn bread cubes on a large baking sheet and bake for about 20 minutes, until toasted. Let the bread cubes cool completely. Leave the oven on.

3. Generously butter a 12-cup muffin tin. In a medium skillet, cook the bacon over moderate heat until crisp. Using a slotted spoon, transfer the bacon to a paper towel–lined plate. Heat ¼ cup of the bacon fat in the skillet. Add the red onion and cook over moderate heat until softened, about 4 minutes. Add the celery, garlic and sage and cook, stirring occasionally, until the celery is softened, about 4 minutes. Stir in the bacon.

4. Peel the roasted squash. Scoop out and transfer 3 cups of the squash to a food processor, add the sugar and puree until smooth. Season the mixture with salt, add the eggs and process until incorporated. Add the chicken stock and process again.

5. In a large bowl, combine the toasted corn bread with the squash puree and let stand for 5 minutes. Stir lightly, add the onion-bacon mixture and 1 teaspoon of salt and stir again. Mound the stuffing in the prepared muffin cups. Wrap any extra stuffing in a piece of heavy-duty foil.

6. Bake the muffins and any extra foil-wrapped stuffing in the upper third of the oven for about 40 minutes, until crisp on top and heated through. Unmold the stuffing muffins and serve hot. —*Michael Symon*

Skillet Corn Bread with Figs, Feta and Rosemary

⏱ **ACTIVE: 15 MIN; TOTAL: 45 MIN**
MAKES ONE 9-INCH BREAD ● ●

1½ cups yellow stone-ground cornmeal
¾ cup all-purpose flour
2 tablespoons sugar
1 tablespoon baking powder
2 teaspoons chopped rosemary leaves
1 teaspoon kosher salt
1 cup plus 2 tablespoons buttermilk
2 large eggs
8 small, plump dried Black Mission
    figs, cut into ½-inch pieces
½ cup crumbled French feta cheese
3 tablespoons unsalted butter, melted
1 tablespoon vegetable oil

1. Preheat the oven to 425°. Heat a 9- or 10-inch cast-iron skillet in the oven for 10 minutes. In a large bowl, whisk the cornmeal with the flour, sugar, baking powder, rosemary and salt. In a medium bowl, whisk the buttermilk with the eggs; pour over the dry ingredients and mix gently. Using a rubber spatula, gently fold in the figs, feta and melted butter.

2. Remove the skillet from the oven. Add the oil and swirl to coat the bottom and halfway up the side. Scrape the batter into the skillet and lightly smooth the top. Bake for about 20 minutes, until the corn bread springs back when lightly pressed in the center. Invert the corn bread onto a rack and let it cool for about 10 minutes, then turn it right side up. Cut the corn bread into wedges and serve.
—*Marcia Kiesel*

● HEALTHY ● MAKE AHEAD ● VEGETARIAN ● STAFF FAVORITE

skillet corn bread with figs, feta and rosemary

Gorgonzola, Fig and Pancetta Pizza

ACTIVE: 1 HR; TOTAL: 3 HR • 4 SERVINGS

DOUGH

 1 tablespoon active dry yeast
 1 tablespoon sugar
 1 tablespoon extra-virgin olive oil
 1¼ cups warm water
 1 tablespoon kosher salt
 3 cups all-purpose flour, plus more for kneading and rolling

SAUCE AND TOPPINGS

 1 cup canned peeled Italian tomatoes
 Pinch of dried oregano, crumbled
 Salt and freshly ground pepper
 1 teaspoon extra-virgin olive oil, plus more for brushing
 2 tablespoons chopped parsley
 10 ounces fresh mozzarella, thinly sliced
 1 large plum tomato, very thinly sliced
 4 ounces very thinly sliced pancetta
 2 ounces Gorgonzola dolce
 2 cups baby arugula
 1 teaspoon balsamic vinegar
 8 fresh figs, quartered

1. MAKE THE DOUGH In a large bowl, combine the yeast, sugar, olive oil and water and let stand until foamy, about 5 minutes. Add the salt and 3 cups of flour and stir until a really stiff dough forms. Turn the dough onto a lightly floured work surface and knead until smooth, about 5 minutes. Oil the bowl, return the dough to it and let stand, covered, until doubled in bulk, about 2 hours.

2. Punch down the dough. Roll it into 4 balls. Transfer the balls to a work surface, cover with a towel and let rest for 15 minutes.

3. MEANWHILE, MAKE THE SAUCE In a blender, puree the canned tomatoes with the oregano; season with salt and pepper.

4. Light a grill. Work with 1 ball of dough at a time and keep the rest covered: Roll the dough out onto a floured work surface to a 10-inch round, ¼ inch thick. Transfer the round to a large, oiled baking sheet and brush with oil. Repeat with the remaining 3 balls of dough.

5. Set all of the toppings near the grill. Rub the grate with oil. Carefully drape two of the

pizza dough rounds over the grill and cook over low heat until golden on the bottom, about 3 minutes. Working quickly, flip the pizza crusts and top each with one-fourth of the tomato sauce, parsley, mozzarella, sliced tomato, pancetta and Gorgonzola. Close the lid and grill over low heat until the pizzas are lightly charred on the bottom, the cheese is bubbling and the pancetta is just beginning to brown, 4 minutes. Transfer the pizzas to a baking sheet. Repeat with the remaining dough and toppings. Return the pizzas to the grill, cover and rewarm until crisp, 1 minute.

6. In a bowl, toss the arugula with the remaining 1 teaspoon of oil and the balsamic vinegar and season with salt and pepper. Scatter the figs and arugula over the pizzas and serve. —*Pete Evans*

WINE Sparkling rosé: NV Jansz Premium.

Focaccia with Caramelized Onions, Pear and Blue Cheese

ACTIVE: 25 MIN; TOTAL: 2 HR 30 MIN
MAKES ONE 9-BY-13-INCH FOCACCIA

● ● ●

 1 cup warm water
 1 package active dry yeast
 ½ teaspoon honey
 2½ cups all-purpose flour
 ½ cup plus 1 tablespoon extra-virgin olive oil
 1 teaspoon kosher salt
 1 large onion, thinly sliced
 1 teaspoon light brown sugar
 1 large Bosc pear, cored and sliced
 ½ cup crumbled blue cheese

1. In a large bowl, combine the water, yeast and honey and let stand for 5 minutes. Stir in 1 cup of the flour and ¼ cup of the oil; let stand for 5 minutes. Stir in the remaining flour and the salt and knead until smooth. Transfer to an oiled bowl, cover with plastic and let stand for 1 hour.

2. Meanwhile, in a skillet, heat 1 tablespoon of the oil. Add the onion, cover and cook over moderate heat, stirring occasionally, for 10 minutes. Add the sugar, cover and cook, stirring occasionally, until browned, 10 minutes.

3. Preheat the oven to 450°. Oil a 9-by-13 inch rimmed baking sheet. Transfer the dough to the sheet and press it down to fit. Dimple the dough all over with your fingers and drizzle with 2 tablespoons of the olive oil. Let the dough rise until puffed, about 20 minutes.

4. Scatter the onions over the dough. Arrange the pear over the onions and sprinkle with the blue cheese. Drizzle the remaining 2 tablespoons of oil over the focaccia and bake for 20 minutes, until golden. Transfer to a rack to cool. Serve. —*Jill Giacomini Basch*

Tuna and Tomato Pizza with Aioli

ACTIVE: 45 MIN; TOTAL: 3 HR
MAKES TWO 12-INCH PIZZAS ●

DOUGH

 ¼ cup warm water
 1½ teaspoons active dry yeast
 ¾ cup cold water
 2¼ cups plus 3 tablespoons all-purpose flour, plus more for dusting
 3 tablespoons rye flour
 2 tablespoons extra-virgin olive oil
 1½ teaspoons fine sea salt

TOPPINGS

 1 garlic clove, mashed in a mortar
 1 tablespoon fresh lemon juice
 ⅓ cup mayonnaise
 Salt
 1 tablespoon extra-virgin olive oil, plus more for brushing
 1 medium onion, thinly sliced
 2 large plum tomatoes, thinly sliced
 ½ cup canned Italian tuna packed in olive oil, drained and coarsely flaked
 ¼ cup torn basil leaves
 1 cup torn arugula

1. MAKE THE DOUGH In a bowl, mix the warm water and yeast; let stand until foamy, 5 minutes. Stir in the cold water, 3 tablespoons of the all-purpose flour and the rye flour. Cover and let stand until bubbly, 30 minutes.

2. Stir in the remaining 2¼ cups of flour, the olive oil and salt. Turn the dough out onto a lightly floured work surface and knead until soft and smooth. Transfer the dough to a large

● HEALTHY ● MAKE AHEAD ○ VEGETARIAN ● STAFF FAVORITE

oiled bowl, cover with plastic wrap and let stand until doubled in bulk, about 1½ hours.

3. Preheat the oven to 500° and set a pizza stone on the bottom of the oven. On a floured work surface, punch the dough down and divide into thirds. Shape each piece into a ball. Cover 2 pieces with plastic wrap and let stand for 15 minutes. Wrap the remaining piece in plastic and freeze for later use.

4. PREPARE THE TOPPINGS In a small bowl, combine the garlic with the lemon juice and mayonnaise. Season the aioli with salt.

5. In a medium skillet, heat the 1 tablespoon of olive oil. Add the onion, cover and cook over moderate heat, stirring occasionally, until softened, 8 minutes. Season with salt.

6. Flour a pizza peel. On a lightly floured work surface, roll out or stretch 1 ball of dough to a 12-inch round. Transfer the round to the pizza peel and brush the dough with olive oil. Scatter half of the onion, tomatoes and tuna over the pizza and slide onto the hot stone. Bake the pizza for 7 minutes, until crisp and bubbling. Remove from the oven and drizzle the pizza with half of the aioli. Top with half of the basil and arugula, cut into wedges and serve. Repeat with the remaining dough and toppings. —*Mauricio Couly*
WINE Fragrant, lively white: 2010 Crios de Susana Balbo Torrontés.

Sweet Potato, Balsamic Onion and Soppressata Pizza

⏱ **ACTIVE: 30 MIN; TOTAL: 45 MIN**
4 SERVINGS

- 1 tablespoon unsalted butter
- 1 tablespoon extra-virgin olive oil
- 1 large white onion, thinly sliced
- 1 oregano sprig, plus 1 tablespoon oregano leaves
- 6 tablespoons balsamic vinegar

Kosher salt and freshly ground pepper
- 1 cup prepared mashed sweet potatoes

One 12-inch prebaked pizza crust
- 1½ cups shredded mozzarella (7 ounces)
- 4 ounces thinly sliced soppressata, cut into thin ribbons

1. Preheat the oven to 450° and set a pizza stone on the bottom of the oven (alternatively, the pizza can be baked directly on the oven rack).

2. In a large skillet, melt the butter in the olive oil. Add the onion and oregano sprig, cover and cook over moderately low heat, stirring occasionally, until softened, about 5 minutes. Add 2 tablespoons of water to the skillet and cook over moderate heat until the onion is caramelized, about 10 minutes; add a few tablespoons of water to the skillet if necessary. Add the balsamic vinegar and cook over moderate heat, stirring occasionally, until it has evaporated, about 10 minutes. Discard the oregano sprig and season the onion with salt and pepper.

3. Spread the sweet potatoes over the pizza crust. Top with the mozzarella, onion and soppressata. Scatter the oregano leaves on top. Slide the pizza onto the stone and bake for about 10 minutes, until bubbling and golden in spots. Cut into wedges and serve. —*Adam Erace*
WINE Juicy, medium-bodied Pinot Noir: 2009 McManis Family Vineyards.

Sun-Dried Tomato and Arugula Pizza

📷 PAGE 6
ACTIVE: 1 HR; TOTAL: 2 HR 30 MIN
MAKES EIGHT 8-INCH PIZZAS ● ●

DOUGH
- 4 cups all-purpose flour, plus more for dusting
- 1 tablespoon sugar
- 1 teaspoon active dry yeast
- 1¼ cups warm water
- 3 tablespoons extra-virgin olive oil
- 1 teaspoon salt

TOPPINGS
- 32 sun-dried tomato halves (not oil-packed)
- 4 garlic cloves, chopped
- ⅓ cup extra-virgin olive oil
- 1 pound fresh mozzarella, thinly sliced

Salt and freshly ground pepper
- 2 cups packed baby arugula

1. MAKE THE DOUGH In the bowl of a standing mixer fitted with the dough hook, mix the 4 cups of flour, the sugar and yeast at medium speed. At low speed, stir in half of the warm water, the olive oil and the salt, then add the remaining water and mix until a ball forms. Mix the dough for 2 minutes at low speed, 2 minutes at medium speed and 2 final minutes at low speed. Transfer the dough to a lightly oiled bowl, cover with plastic wrap and let stand in a warm place until doubled in bulk, about 1½ hours.

2. Put a pizza stone in the bottom of the oven and preheat the stone in the oven to 500° for about 45 minutes.

3. Punch down the dough and scrape it onto a floured work surface. Form the dough into a ball. Cut the ball into 8 equal-size pieces. Knead each piece into a ball and then flatten into disks. Cover with plastic wrap and let the dough rest for about 20 minutes.

4. MEANWHILE, MAKE THE TOPPINGS Put the sun-dried tomatoes in a small saucepan and cover with water. Cover and simmer over low heat until very soft, about 5 minutes. Drain and coarsely chop the tomatoes. In a mini food processor, puree the chopped garlic with the olive oil.

5. Generously flour a pizza peel. Using a rolling pin, roll out a disk of dough to an 8-inch round, about ⅛ inch thick. (Alternatively, pull and stretch the disk into an 8-inch round.) Transfer the round to the peel and brush with the garlic puree. Scatter with one-eighth of the sun-dried tomatoes and arrange one-eighth of the sliced cheese on top. Drizzle with a little of the garlic puree and season with salt and pepper. Bake on the hot stone for about 4 minutes, until the crust is crisp and the cheese is bubbling. Top with some baby arugula and serve. Repeat with the remaining dough and toppings. —*Kenny Rochford*
MAKE AHEAD The dough can be prepared through Step 1: Punch it down, cover with plastic wrap and refrigerate overnight. The chopped tomatoes and garlic oil can be refrigerated overnight. Bring everything to room temperature before proceeding.
WINE Earthy rosé: 2010 Medlock Ames.

Grilled Cheese and Bacon Sandwiches with Cheese Curds

📷 PAGE 285

⏱ TOTAL: 35 MIN • 4 SERVINGS ●

Cheese curds are small chunks of just-made cheese that haven't been pressed into a shape. They're milky and delicious in this grilled cheese sandwich from Joe Beef in Montreal. It's spread with the restaurant's signature "chicken glace mayo," made with chicken stock that co-chef Frédéric Morin says has been "reduced to oblivion." He suggests substituting beef bouillon to replicate his uniquely savory mayonnaise.

½ beef bouillon cube
  (about 1 teaspoon)
2 teaspoons hot water
¼ cup mayonnaise
2 teaspoons Sriracha sauce
Salt and freshly ground pepper
1 tablespoon vegetable oil
1 medium onion, thinly sliced
2 teaspoons cider vinegar
12 slices of bacon
2 tablespoons unsalted butter, softened
8 slices of white sandwich bread
½ pound sharp cheddar cheese, cut into 4 slices
3 ounces cheddar cheese curds (1 cup), see Note

1. In a small bowl, mash the bouillon cube into the hot water until dissolved. Whisk in the mayonnaise and Sriracha and season with salt and pepper.
2. In a medium skillet, heat the oil. Add the onion, cover and cook over moderate heat, stirring occasionally, until golden brown and softened, about 10 minutes. Stir in the vinegar and season with salt and pepper.
3. Meanwhile, in another skillet, cook the bacon over moderate heat, turning once, until crisp, 6 minutes. Drain on paper towels.
4. Set a griddle over 2 burners and turn the heat to moderate. Butter the bread slices on 1 side. Spread the other side of 4 bread slices with the spicy mayonnaise and top with the onion, cheddar, cheese curds and cooked bacon. Close the sandwiches buttered side out and griddle over moderately low heat until crisp, about 4 minutes per side. Cut the sandwiches in half and serve.
—*David McMillan and Frédéric Morin*
NOTE Cheese curds are available at specialty food shops and cheese shops.
WINE White Burgundy: 2007 Pierre-Yves Colin-Morey Saint-Aubin 1er Cru En Remilly.

Cucumber-Rye Tea Sandwiches

⏱ ACTIVE: 30 MIN; TOTAL: 45 MIN
MAKES 36 TEA SANDWICHES ●

Little slices of party rye are a Southern favorite for tea sandwiches: "You don't see regular rye down here every day," says Southern cookbook author Martha Hall Foose. If party rye isn't available, use a cookie cutter to create rounds from regular bread slices.

1 large seedless cucumber, peeled and cut into 3-inch lengths
3 tablespoons cider vinegar
1 tablespoon fresh lemon juice
1 tablespoon sugar
½ teaspoon salt
36 slices of party rye or 18 slices of rye bread
12 ounces cream cheese, softened
1 scallion, finely chopped
1 Persian cucumber, thinly sliced
Freshly ground black pepper

1. Using a box grater, coarsely grate the seedless cucumber lengthwise, stopping when you get to the seedy center. Transfer the grated cucumber to a medium bowl and stir in the vinegar, lemon juice, sugar and salt. Let stand for about 15 minutes.
2. If using rye bread slices, use a 2-inch-round cookie cutter to cut out 36 rounds from the bread. Cover with a slightly damp towel.
3. Transfer the grated cucumber to a colander to drain; squeeze out the excess liquid. Return it to the bowl and stir in the cream cheese and scallion. Spread the cucumber cream cheese on the bread rounds, top each with a Persian cucumber slice and arrange on a platter. Sprinkle with freshly ground black pepper and serve. —*Martha Hall Foose*

The New American Grilled Cheese

⏱ TOTAL: 40 MIN • 4 SERVINGS

The best grilled cheese sandwich is the gooiest one, says Laura Werlin, author of *Grilled Cheese, Please!* "After you bite into it, the cheese should stretch out past your face as far as your arm will reach. Otherwise, it's just not right."

4 cooked andouille sausages, sliced lengthwise in thirds
4 tablespoons butter, softened
6 ounces extra-sharp orange cheddar cheese, shredded (1½ cups)
8 large slices of sourdough bread
2 tablespoons Dijon mustard
4 ounces Monterey Jack, shredded (about 1 cup)
Cornichons, for serving

1. In a large nonstick skillet, cook the sliced sausages over moderate heat, turning once, until browned, about 8 minutes. Transfer the sausages to a plate and wipe out the pan.
2. In a large bowl, stir 2 tablespoons of the butter with the shredded cheddar cheese just until combined. Spread the remaining 2 tablespoons of butter on one side of each slice of bread; arrange them buttered side down on a work surface. Spread the cheddar mixture on the slices as evenly as possible. Spread the mustard over the cheddar. Sprinkle the shredded Monterey Jack over the mustard and top 4 slices with the sausages. Close the sandwiches, pressing lightly and tucking in any stray cheese.
3. Place the sandwiches in the skillet, cover and cook over moderately low heat until golden on the bottom, 3 minutes. Press with a spatula to flatten slightly, then flip the sandwiches, cover and cook until browned on the bottom, 3 minutes; lower the heat if the bread is browned before the cheese melts completely. Transfer the sandwiches to a cutting board and let rest for 2 minutes, then cut in half. Serve with cornichons.
—*Laura Werlin*
WINE Peppery, juicy Amador County Zinfandel: 2008 Sobon Estate Rocky Top.

● HEALTHY ● MAKE AHEAD ● VEGETARIAN ● STAFF FAVORITE

cucumber-rye tea sandwiches

Deluxe Lobster and Potato Chip Rolls

ACTIVE: 30 MIN; TOTAL: 1 HR 30 MIN
6 SERVINGS ●

- 1 cup mayonnaise
- 1 celery rib, finely diced
- 2 garlic cloves, finely grated
- 2 tablespoons fresh lemon juice
- 1½ teaspoons Worcestershire sauce
- 1½ teaspoons Tabasco
- 2 tablespoons snipped chives, plus more for garnish
- Kosher salt
- Three 1¼-pound live lobsters or 1¼ pounds cooked lobster meat
- 2 tablespoons unsalted butter
- 6 brioche hot dog buns
- One 4-ounce bag potato chips

1. In a bowl, whisk the mayonnaise, celery, garlic, lemon juice, Worcestershire sauce, Tabasco and the 2 tablespoons of chives; season with salt. Refrigerate until chilled.
2. Bring a very large pot of water to a boil and fill a large bowl with ice water. Add the lobsters to the boiling water, head first. Cover and cook until they're bright red, about 8 minutes. Transfer the lobsters to the ice water to stop the cooking. Drain the lobsters.
3. Twist off the lobster claws, knuckles and tails. Crack the claws and knuckles and remove the meat. Using kitchen scissors, cut along the underside of the tail shells and remove the meat. Discard the dark intestinal vein running lengthwise down each tail. Chop the lobster meat into ½-inch pieces and fold them into the dressing. Refrigerate until chilled, about 1 hour.
4. Meanwhile, melt the butter on a large griddle or in a large skillet. Add the closed buns and toast the outsides over high heat, turning frequently, until lightly browned, about 3 minutes. Transfer the buns to a platter, split the tops and fill with the lobster salad. Tuck the potato chips into the rolls, garnish with chives and serve right away.
—*Vinny Dotolo and Jon Shook*
WINE Fresh, citrusy Italian white: 2009 Sella & Mosca La Cala Vermentino.

Catfish Po'Boys with Pickle Remoulade

☺ **TOTAL: 40 MIN • MAKES 8 SANDWICHES** ●

Chef-owner Jay Foster of Farmerbrown's Little Skillet in San Francisco does brisk business in these fried-fish sandwiches at the Outside Lands music festival.

PICKLE REMOULADE
- 1 cup mayonnaise
- ¼ cup minced celery
- 1 small shallot, minced
- 1 garlic clove, minced
- 2 tablespoons Creole mustard
- 2 tablespoons sweet pickle relish
- 2 tablespoons chopped drained capers
- 2 tablespoons chopped flat-leaf parsley
- 1½ teaspoons smoked sweet paprika
PO'BOYS
- 1 cup cornmeal
- 1 cup *panko* (Japanese bread crumbs), crushed
- ½ cup all-purpose flour, plus more for dusting
- 1 teaspoon salt
- ½ teaspoon each of cayenne pepper, garlic powder and onion powder
- ¼ teaspoon each of dried thyme, dried sage, ground ginger and ground cumin
- 3 large eggs
- Eight 5-ounce skinless catfish fillets
- Vegetable oil, for frying
- 8 crusty hero rolls, split
- Shredded romaine, for serving

1. MAKE THE PICKLE REMOULADE In a bowl, combine all of the remoulade ingredients.
2. MAKE THE PO'BOYS In a pie plate, whisk the cornmeal with the *panko*, ½ cup of flour, the salt, cayenne pepper, garlic powder, onion powder, thyme, sage, ground ginger and cumin. In another pie plate, beat the eggs. Dust the catfish with flour, then dip in the beaten egg; coat in the *panko* mixture, pressing the crumbs to help them adhere. Transfer the catfish fillets to a baking sheet.
3. In a skillet, heat ¼ inch of vegetable oil. Fry the catfish in 2 batches over moderately high heat, turning once, until the crust is golden and crisp and the fish is cooked through, 4 minutes. Drain the fish on paper towels.
4. Spread the rolls with the remoulade. Top with the fish and romaine; serve. —*Jay Foster*
WINE Zippy Pinot Grigio: 2010 Palmina.

Curried-Egg Tea Sandwiches

ACTIVE: 20 MIN; TOTAL: 1 HR
MAKES 20 TEA SANDWICHES ●

In the early 1960s, *The Time Life Picture Cook Book* inspired Southern ladies to "go exotic" by adding ingredients like curry powder and orange zest to the egg salad in tea sandwiches like the ones here.

- 1 dozen large eggs, at room temperature
- ½ teaspoon finely grated orange zest (optional)
- 1 tablespoon freshly squeezed orange juice
- 1 teaspoon Madras curry powder
- ¼ teaspoon dry mustard
- ½ cup mayonnaise
- Salt and freshly ground pepper
- 20 slices of packaged white sandwich bread

1. Put the eggs in a large saucepan of cold water and bring to a vigorous boil. Cover, remove from the heat and let stand for 10 minutes. Drain the eggs and cool under running water, shaking the pan to lightly crack the shells. Transfer the eggs to a bowl of ice water and let them stand until they are completely cold, about 15 minutes.
2. Peel the eggs and pat dry. Finely chop the eggs and transfer to a large bowl. Add the orange zest and juice along with the curry, dry mustard and mayonnaise. Season with salt and pepper and mash with a fork.
3. Arrange 10 slices of sandwich bread on a work surface and divide the egg salad among them, spreading it to the edges. Top with the remaining bread and trim off the crusts. Cut each tea sandwich in half, then transfer them to a platter and serve. —*Martha Hall Foose*

● HEALTHY ● MAKE AHEAD ● VEGETARIAN ● STAFF FAVORITE

deluxe lobster and potato chip roll

Country Pâté Banh Mi

⏱ **TOTAL: 30 MIN • 4 SERVINGS**

Silken tofu blended with lemongrass and lime juice is a terrific dairy-free stand-in for mayonnaise in this riff on the Vietnamese *banh mi* sandwich.

- 2 ounces silken tofu
- 1 tablespoon Dijon mustard
- 2 tablespoons finely grated fresh lemongrass
- ½ teaspoon finely grated lime zest
- 1 tablespoon fresh lime juice
- 2 tablespoons vegetable oil
- Salt and freshly ground pepper
- 4 long soft hero rolls, split
- ½ pound country pâté, thinly sliced
- 1 bunch of cilantro (6 ounces), thick stems discarded
- 1 cup shredded carrots
- 16 slices of pickled jalapeño

1. In a mini food processor, combine the tofu, mustard, lemongrass, lime zest, lime juice and oil and process until smooth. Season with salt and pepper.

2. Spread the sauce on the cut sides of the rolls. Top with the pâté, cilantro, shredded carrots and pickled jalapeños. Close the sandwiches, cut in half and serve.
—*Adam Erace*

WINE Crisp, citrusy sparkling wine: NV Dibon Cava Brut Reserve.

Lao-Style Chicken Baguette Sandwiches with Watercress

⏱ **TOTAL: 30 MIN • 4 SERVINGS** ●

- 1 tablespoon vegetable oil
- 2 boneless chicken breast halves, with skin (6 ounces each)
- Salt and freshly ground black pepper
- Chile-Garlic Sauce (recipe follows)
- Four 6-inch lengths of baguette, split and toasted
- Mayonnaise
- 1 small bunch of watercress (4 ounces), thick stems discarded
- 2 medium tomatoes, sliced
- 1 cup coarsely shredded carrots

1. In a medium skillet, heat the oil. Season the chicken breasts with salt and pepper and add them to the skillet, skin side down. Cook over moderately high heat until the skin is browned and crisp, about 4 minutes. Reduce the heat to moderate. Turn the chicken breasts over and cook until white throughout, about 5 minutes longer. Transfer the chicken breasts to a carving board and let rest for 5 minutes. Slice the chicken crosswise ⅓ inch thick.

2. Spread the Chile-Garlic Sauce on the cut sides of the baguettes and spread mayonnaise on top. Fill the sandwiches with the watercress, chicken, tomatoes and carrots and serve. —*Sebastien Rubis*

WINE Lightly sweet sparkling wine: 2009 Marco Negri Moscato d'Asti.

CHILE-GARLIC SAUCE

⏱ **TOTAL: 15 MIN • MAKES ½ CUP** ● ●

This fiery condiment, known as *jaew bong*, is key in the recipe above and one of many *jaews* that are fundamental to Lao cuisine.

- ¼ cup plus 3 tablespoons vegetable oil
- 1 large shallot, thinly sliced and separated into rings
- 3 large garlic cloves, coarsely chopped
- 2½ tablespoons minced fresh ginger
- ¼ cup Korean coarse red pepper powder
- 2 tablespoons sugar
- 1½ tablespoons Asian fish sauce

In a small skillet, heat ¼ cup plus 2 tablespoons of the oil. Add the shallot rings and cook over moderate heat, stirring a few times, until golden brown and crisp, about 3 minutes. With a slotted spoon, transfer the shallot rings to a bowl. Add the garlic to the hot oil and cook over moderately low heat, stirring a few times, until golden, about 1 minute. With a slotted spoon, transfer the garlic to the bowl. Add the ginger to the skillet and cook until fragrant, 2 minutes. Add the red pepper powder and sugar and cook, stirring, for 30 seconds. Scrape the sauce into the bowl. Stir in the fish sauce and the remaining 1 tablespoon of oil. —*SR*

Moscow Banh Mi

TOTAL: 1 HR • MAKES 8 SANDWICHES ● ●

- 4 large carrots, finely julienned
- 1 tablespoon sugar
- 3 tablespoons cider vinegar
- Salt and freshly ground pepper
- 3 tablespoons canola oil
- 1 pound beets, peeled and finely julienned
- ½ small red onion, cut into thin slivers
- ¼ cup water
- ½ cup mayonnaise
- 3 tablespoons drained prepared horseradish, squeezed dry
- 1½ pounds skinless, boneless chicken breasts, pounded ½ inch thick
- 2 baguettes
- 8 large green lettuce leaves, torn

1. In a large skillet, cook the julienned carrots with the sugar and 2 tablespoons of the cider vinegar over moderate heat, tossing, until barely softened, about 2 minutes. Season with salt and pepper. Spread the carrots on a plate and refrigerate until chilled.

2. Wipe out the skillet and heat 1 tablespoon of the oil in it. Add the beets and onion and cook over moderate heat for 1 minute. Add the remaining vinegar and the water, cover and cook until the beets are crisp-tender and dry, 5 minutes. Spread the beets and onion on a plate, season with salt and pepper and refrigerate until chilled.

3. Preheat the oven to 350°. Light a grill or preheat a grill pan. In a bowl, whisk the mayonnaise and horseradish. Brush the chicken with the remaining oil and season with salt and pepper. Grill over high heat, turning once, until lightly charred, 5 minutes. Transfer to a cutting board and let cool slightly. Cut the chicken crosswise into strips.

4. Toast the baguettes in the oven for 5 minutes, until crusty. Split and cut each baguette into 4 lengths. Spread the mayonnaise on the bread and top with the beets and onion. Top with the chicken, carrots and lettuce. Close the sandwiches and serve.
—*Grace Parisi*

BEER Refreshing European lager: Peroni.

● HEALTHY ● MAKE AHEAD ● VEGETARIAN ● STAFF FAVORITE

moscow banh mi

Open-Face Steak Sandwich with Pickled Green Tomatoes

ACTIVE: 30 MIN; TOTAL: 2 HR 30 MIN
4 SERVINGS ●

2 garlic cloves, minced
Kosher salt
1 tablespoon minced rosemary
1½ teaspoons paprika
2 tablespoons extra-virgin olive oil
One 1-pound flank steak
Freshly ground pepper
Four ½-inch-thick slices of
   whole-grain bread
2 teaspoons mayonnaise
2 teaspoons Dijon mustard
8 slices of Flash-Pickled Green
   Tomatoes (recipe follows),
   plus 1 tablespoon pickling liquid
1 cup packed baby arugula

1. On a work surface, sprinkle the minced garlic with salt and, using the flat side of a knife, mash the garlic to a smooth paste. In a small bowl, whisk the garlic paste with the rosemary, paprika and olive oil. Rub the marinade all over the steak and let stand at room temperature for 2 hours or refrigerate for up to 2 days.

2. Preheat a grill pan. Season the flank steak with salt and pepper and grill over moderately high heat, turning once, until medium-rare, about 7 minutes. Transfer the steak to a board and let rest for 5 minutes. Thinly slice the steak across the grain.

3. Grill the bread until crisp and golden, about 2 minutes per side. Spread each slice with ½ teaspoon each of the mayonnaise and mustard. Arrange the steak on the bread and top with the pickled green tomatoes.

4. In a medium bowl, toss the arugula with the tomato pickling liquid and season with salt and pepper. Mound the arugula on the sandwiches and serve right away.
—Quinn Hatfield

MAKE AHEAD The grilled steak can be kept in the refrigerator for up to 2 days. Thinly slice the steak as needed.

WINE Juicy, medium-bodied Spanish red: 2008 Vinos de Terruños Siete 7.

FLASH-PICKLED GREEN TOMATOES

ACTIVE: 20 MIN; TOTAL: 3 HR 30 MIN
MAKES ABOUT 3 CUPS ● ● ●

¾ cup water
¾ cup apple cider vinegar
4 teaspoons kosher salt
1 tablespoon sugar
Freshly ground black pepper
1 teaspoon minced rosemary
2 garlic cloves, thinly sliced
1 pound green tomatoes,
   cored and sliced crosswise
   ¼ to ⅛ inch thick

1. In a small saucepan, combine the water with the vinegar, salt and sugar and bring to a boil, stirring. Let the pickling liquid cool to room temperature, then add the pepper, rosemary and garlic.

2. Layer the sliced tomatoes in a 1-quart glass jar and cover with the pickling liquid. Let stand at room temperature for 3 hours, then store in the refrigerator. Drain the pickles before serving. *—QH*

MAKE AHEAD The pickles can be refrigerated in their liquid for up to 1 week.

Italian Sausage and Fontina Biscuit Sandwiches

ACTIVE: 25 MIN; TOTAL: 50 MIN
4 SERVINGS

These buttery biscuits filled with spicy sausage, salty olives and rich cheese are intensely flavorful.

SAUSAGE FILLING
1 teaspoon extra-virgin olive oil
½ pound hot Italian sausages, pricked
   with a fork
1 roasted red bell pepper, cut into
   ½-inch dice
¼ cup sun-dried tomatoes in oil,
   drained and minced
6 scallions, cut into ½-inch pieces
⅓ cup chopped pitted kalamata olives
3 tablespoons freshly grated
   Parmigiano-Reggiano cheese
¾ cup shredded Italian Fontina cheese
Salt and freshly ground black pepper

BISCUITS
1¼ cups all-purpose flour
1 teaspoon baking powder
1 teaspoon sugar
½ teaspoon salt
¼ teaspoon baking soda
4 tablespoons unsalted butter,
   cut into small pieces and chilled
½ cup plus 2 tablespoons
   cold buttermilk
1 tablespoon heavy cream or milk
1 tablespoon freshly grated
   pecorino cheese

1. MAKE THE SAUSAGE FILLING In a skillet, heat the oil. Add the sausages, cover and cook over moderate heat until browned and cooked through, about 10 minutes. Drain the sausages and cut into ½-inch chunks.

2. Transfer the sausage to a microwave-safe bowl. Add the roasted red pepper, sun-dried tomatoes, scallions, olives, Parmigiano and ¼ cup of the Fontina to the sausage and season with salt and pepper. Mix well.

3. MAKE THE BISCUITS Preheat the oven to 375°. Lightly butter a baking sheet. In a bowl, whisk the flour, baking powder, sugar, salt and baking soda. Using a pastry cutter or your fingers, blend in the butter until the mixture resembles coarse meal. Gently stir in the buttermilk until almost incorporated. Using your hands, gently mix the dough until blended.

4. On a lightly floured work surface, form the dough into a square. Roll or pat the square into a ½-inch-thick rectangle. Cut the rectangle in half and cut each half in half again to make 4 biscuits; transfer to the prepared baking sheet. Brush the tops with the cream and sprinkle with the pecorino.

5. Bake the biscuits in the upper third of the oven for 10 minutes. Increase the oven temperature to 400° and bake for about 10 minutes longer, until the biscuits are pale golden and just cooked through. Let cool slightly.

6. Rewarm the sausage filling in the microwave. Split the biscuits; fill with the remaining ½ cup of Fontina and the sausage. Close the sandwiches and serve. *—Marcia Kiesel*

WINE Slightly spicy Sangiovese: 2008 Isole e Olena Chianti Classico.

● HEALTHY   ● MAKE AHEAD   ● VEGETARIAN   ● STAFF FAVORITE

do-it-yourself pretzels

Chefs now compete with sidewalk vendors to sell the best pretzels. (Chefs are winning—handily.) German-born L.A. chef **Hans Röckenwagner** shares his twist.

German-Style Pretzels

ACTIVE: 45 MIN; TOTAL: 4 HR • MAKES 8 PRETZELS ● ● ○

Röckenwagner's secret: Soaking the uncooked twists in a solution of lye (its high pH, which browns a pretzel's crust, gets neutralized).

- 3¾ cups bread flour (20 ounces), plus more for dusting
- 1½ cups warm water
- 1¼ teaspoons active dry yeast
- 2 teaspoons kosher salt
- 2 tablespoons unsalted butter, softened
- 10 cups lukewarm water
- ½ cup food-grade lye micro beads (see Note)
- Coarse salt or pretzel salt, for sprinkling

1. In the bowl of a standing electric mixer fitted with the dough hook, combine the 3¾ cups of bread flour with the warm water, yeast, kosher salt and butter and knead at medium speed until the flour is evenly moistened, 2 minutes. Increase the speed to high and knead until a smooth, elastic dough forms around the hook, 8 minutes.

2. Transfer the dough to a lightly floured surface. Cover loosely with a dry kitchen towel and let rest for 5 minutes. Cut the dough into 8 equal pieces and form each one into a ball. Cover the dough balls with the towel and let rest for another 5 minutes.

3. On an unfloured surface, roll each ball of pretzel dough into an 18-inch-long rope, tapering them slightly at both ends. To shape each pretzel, form the rope into a U shape. Cross the ends over each other twice to form the twist, then bring the ends to the bottom of the U and press the tips onto it. Arrange the pretzels on 2 large baking sheets lined with parchment paper and let stand uncovered in a

lye alternative
Dissolve ½ cup of baking soda in 2 quarts of boiling water. Boil the pretzels for 30 seconds, then drain on wire racks before salting and baking.

warm place for 45 minutes, or until slightly risen. Refrigerate the pretzels uncovered for at least 2 hours or overnight.

4. Preheat the oven to 400°. While wearing latex gloves, long sleeves and safety goggles, fill a large, deep ceramic, plastic or glass bowl with the lukewarm water. Carefully add the lye (always be sure to add lye to water, never the other way around) and, taking care not to splash, stir the solution occasionally until all the beads have fully dissolved, about 5 minutes. Using a slotted spatula, gently lower a pretzel into the solution for 15 seconds. Carefully turn the pretzel over and soak it for another 15 seconds. With the spatula, remove the pretzel from the lye solution and return it to the baking sheet.

5. Sprinkle the pretzels with coarse salt; bake on the top and middle racks until shiny-brown and risen, 17 minutes; shift the pans halfway through. Let cool slightly on the baking sheets before serving.

NOTE Food-grade lye can be ordered from *essentialdepot.com*.

MAKE AHEAD Pretzels baked without salt can be frozen for up to 1 month. Spray the frozen pretzels with water and sprinkle with salt; reheat in a 275° oven until warmed through, about 20 minutes.

the perfect twist

roll the dough into an 18-inch-long rope that tapers at both ends.

form a U shape, then cross the ends over each other twice to make the twist.

bring the ends to the bottom of the U and gently press down.

Aleppo-Pepper-Pork and Fennel Sandwiches

ACTIVE: 30 MIN; TOTAL: 3 HR 30 MIN
PLUS OVERNIGHT MARINATING
6 SERVINGS ●

PORK

3½ pounds boneless pork
    shoulder or leg
1 tablespoon fine sea salt
3 tablespoons minced garlic
¼ cup plus 1 tablespoon Aleppo pepper
¼ cup water
¼ cup white wine vinegar

SANDWICHES

¼ cup extra-virgin olive oil
3 tablespoons fresh lemon juice
Salt and freshly ground black pepper
1 large fennel bulb—trimmed,
    cored and very thinly sliced
4 cups packed arugula
6 toasted rolls, split, for serving

1. **PREPARE THE PORK** Make 6 cuts in the pork, 1 inch apart, cutting most of the way through the meat. Rub the pork all over with the salt. Rub the pork with the garlic and then with the Aleppo pepper, covering the meat completely. Wrap the pork in plastic and refrigerate overnight.

2. Preheat the oven to 325°. Set the pork in a baking dish just large enough to hold it; add the water. Cover the pork with parchment paper, then cover tightly with foil. Bake for about 2½ hours, until very tender.

3. Pour all but ¼ cup of the roasting juices into a bowl and reserve. Drizzle the pork with the vinegar, cover with foil and bake for 10 minutes. Remove the pork from the oven and let it rest, covered, for 10 minutes.

4. **PREPARE THE SANDWICHES** In a large bowl, stir the olive oil with the lemon juice and season with salt and black pepper. Add the fennel and arugula and toss.

5. Discard any fat and gristle from the pork. Shred the meat into large pieces and toss with the pan juices and reserved juices. Pile the meat on the rolls, top with the fennel salad and serve. —*Tony Mantuano*

WINE Juicy Garnacha: 2009 Viña Borgia.

Crispy Pork Belly Sandwiches with Meyer Lemon Relish

ACTIVE: 1 HR 15 MIN; TOTAL: 4 HR
PLUS 2 DAYS MARINATING • MAKES
8 SANDWICHES ●

1½ cups kosher salt
½ cup sugar
2 bay leaves
2 quarts boiling water
2 quarts ice water
4 pounds boneless, skinless,
    meaty fresh pork belly, fat trimmed
    to ¾ inch and scored
1 tablespoon coriander seeds
1 tablespoon fennel seeds
1 teaspoon black peppercorns
½ teaspoon cumin seeds
1 whole clove
1 allspice berry
6 garlic cloves, smashed
1 large onion, thinly sliced
1 celery rib, chopped
2 carrots, thinly sliced
1 cup dry white wine
3 cups chicken broth
Whole-grain mustard and chopped
    frisée, for serving
8 ciabatta rolls, split and toasted
Meyer Lemon Relish (recipe follows)

1. In a large pot, combine the salt, sugar, bay leaves and boiling water; stir to dissolve the salt and sugar. Add the ice water and let cool. Add the pork belly to the brine and refrigerate overnight.

2. Drain the pork belly and pat dry with paper towels. In a small skillet, combine the coriander seeds, fennel seeds, peppercorns, cumin, clove and allspice and toast over moderate heat until fragrant, about 3 minutes; transfer to a spice grinder and let cool completely. Coarsely grind the spices and rub them all over the pork belly. Transfer to a platter, cover and refrigerate overnight.

3. Preheat the oven to 325°. Rinse the pork, scraping off most of the spices, and pat dry. Heat a large, deep ovenproof skillet until hot. Add the pork, fatty side down, and cook over moderately high heat, turning once,

until browned on both sides, 8 minutes. Scatter the garlic, onion, celery and carrots on either side of the pork belly and cook until softened slightly, 5 minutes. Add the wine and boil until reduced to ¼ cup, 5 minutes. Add the broth and bring to a boil. Cover and braise in the oven for 2 hours, until the meat is very tender but not falling apart.

4. Transfer the pork belly to a platter and refrigerate for 30 minutes. Cut the meat into ½-inch-thick slices, then cut each slice in half so it will fit on the ciabatta.

5. In a large nonstick skillet, fry the pork slices in batches over moderately high heat, turning once, until crisp, about 4 minutes.

6. Spread mustard on the roll bottoms and top with the sliced pork belly, frisée and a generous dollop of Meyer Lemon Relish. Close the sandwiches, cut in half and serve. —*Rob Milliron*

MAKE AHEAD The whole braised pork belly can be refrigerated for up to 4 days.

WINE Lush Washington state Merlot: 2006 Novelty Hill Columbia Valley.

MEYER LEMON RELISH

◔ TOTAL: 20 MIN • MAKES ABOUT 1 CUP
● ● ● ●

1 large Meyer lemon—peeled,
    peel very thinly sliced
1 shallot—½ minced,
    ½ very thinly sliced
2 tablespoons fresh lemon juice
1 tablespoon white wine vinegar
1 garlic clove, minced
2 tablespoons minced chives
1 tablespoon finely chopped parsley
½ cup extra-virgin olive oil
Pinch of crushed red pepper
Salt and freshly ground black pepper

Finely chop the lemon pulp, discarding any seeds, and transfer to a bowl. Add the lemon peel, minced and sliced shallot, lemon juice, vinegar, garlic, chives, parsley, olive oil and crushed red pepper to the bowl. Season with salt and black pepper and serve. —*RM*

MAKE AHEAD The relish can be refrigerated for up to 3 days.

● HEALTHY ● MAKE AHEAD ● VEGETARIAN ● STAFF FAVORITE

crispy pork belly sandwich with meyer lemon relish

Pastrami and Mushroom "Hot Dogs"

⊘ TOTAL: 45 MIN • 4 SERVINGS

In this distinctive high-low recipe, Joe Beef co-chef and co-owner Frédéric Morin wanted to combine *girolles* (chanterelles) with something less highbrow. "As a good chef, you can't mix all expensive things in one dish," he says. So he stuffed the mushrooms inside hot dog buns with Montreal's famous smoked meat, a cured beef similar to pastrami.

- 3 tablespoons unsalted butter
- ¾ pound assorted mushrooms, such as chanterelles, stemmed shiitake and cremini, quartered
- Salt and freshly ground pepper
- ¼ cup dry sherry
- ½ cup veal demiglace (see Note)
- ¼ cup heavy cream
- 1 large shallot, minced
- 1 teaspoon cider vinegar
- 2 tablespoons chopped chives
- ½ pound sliced pastrami
- 4 hot dog rolls, split and toasted
- 1 ounce sharp cheddar or Mimolette cheese, shredded (¼ cup)

1. In a large skillet, melt 2 tablespoons of the butter. Add the mushrooms and season lightly with salt and pepper. Cover and cook over moderate heat, stirring a few times, until tender and browned, 8 minutes. Add the sherry and boil over high heat until reduced by half, 1 minute. Add the demiglace and simmer over moderate heat until slightly reduced, 3 minutes. Stir in the cream and simmer until thickened, 5 minutes. Add the shallot, vinegar and chives and season with salt and pepper.
2. Heat a nonstick skillet over moderate heat and melt the remaining 1 tablespoon of butter in it. Add the pastrami and cook until warmed through.
3. Fill the rolls with the pastrami. Top with the mushrooms and cheese and serve.
—*David McMillan and Frédéric Morin*
NOTE Veal demiglace, the rich, concentrated sauce, is available at specialty markets.
WINE Riesling: 2009 Domaines Schlumberger Les Princes Abbés.

Hot Dogs with Green Tomato Relish

ACTIVE: 45 MIN; TOTAL: 2 HR
8 SERVINGS

When Skip Bennett, founder of Island Creek Oysters in Massachusetts, steams lobsters on the Island Creek barge, he always tosses some hot dogs into the pot for the last few minutes to make his signature "steamer dogs." When he's steaming the franks on their own, he adds a little stout to the cooking water. He also steams the hot dog buns in the pot and tops the franks with a sweet-and-spicy green tomato relish.

RELISH
- 1 pound green (unripe) tomatoes, cut into ½-inch dice
- 1 red bell pepper, cut into ½-inch dice
- 1 onion, cut into ½-inch dice
- Kosher salt
- 6 tablespoons extra-virgin olive oil
- 1 cup distilled white vinegar
- 1 cup light brown sugar
- 2 teaspoons crushed red pepper
- ½ teaspoon ground cloves
- ½ teaspoon celery salt
- ½ teaspoon ground ginger
HOT DOGS
- 3 cups water
- One 12-ounce bottle stout or porter
- 1 tablespoon celery seeds
- 1 small onion, quartered
- 1 garlic clove, smashed
- 8 all-beef hot dogs
- 8 hot dog buns, split

1. MAKE THE RELISH In a colander, toss the green tomatoes, bell pepper and onion with 2 tablespoons of kosher salt and let stand for 1 hour to drain.
2. In a large, deep skillet, heat the olive oil. Add the drained vegetables and cook over moderate heat, stirring occasionally, until softened but not browned, about 7 minutes. Add the vinegar, brown sugar, crushed red pepper, cloves, celery salt and ginger and simmer until the mixture is thick, stirring occasionally, about 25 minutes. Let cool to room temperature and season with salt.

3. PREPARE THE HOT DOGS In a large saucepan, combine the water with the beer, celery seeds, onion and garlic and bring to a boil. Put a large steamer basket over the boiling water and add the hot dogs. Cover and steam over moderate heat for 8 minutes. Add the hot dog buns and steam for 30 seconds.
4. Put a hot dog in each bun, spread with green tomato relish and serve.
—*Skip Bennett and Jeremy Sewall*
BEER Crisp California pale ale: North Coast Brewing Acme Pale Ale.

Spicy Beer Mustard

ACTIVE: 15 MIN; TOTAL: 30 MIN
PLUS 2 DAYS CHILLING
MAKES ABOUT 5 CUPS ● ● ●

Chef Jeremy Nolen updates German classics at Brauhaus Schmitz in Philadelphia, including this intense mustard made with dark beer as an accompaniment to sausages.

- ½ cup black mustard seeds
- ½ cup yellow mustard seeds
- 1½ cups malt vinegar
- 2 cups dark beer, such as doppelbock
- 5 tablespoons honey
- ½ cup dark brown sugar
- 2 teaspoons salt
- 2 teaspoons ground allspice
- ¾ teaspoon turmeric
- 1 cup dry mustard

1. In a medium bowl, combine the black and yellow mustard seeds with the vinegar and 1½ cups of the beer. Cover and refrigerate overnight.
2. In a saucepan, combine the remaining ½ cup of beer with the honey, brown sugar, salt, allspice and turmeric and bring to a boil. Remove from the heat, transfer to a blender and let cool. Add the ground mustard and the mustard seeds with their soaking liquid to the blender and puree. Transfer the mustard to a glass jar. Cover and refrigerate overnight before serving.
—*Jeremy Nolen*
MAKE AHEAD The mustard can be refrigerated for up to 3 months.

● HEALTHY ● MAKE AHEAD ● VEGETARIAN ● STAFF FAVORITE

pastrami and mushroom "hot dogs"

The Mekong River runs through
Luang Prabang, Laos, a small city
with great Lao food like an omelet
with dill, scallion and Thai chile,
OPPOSITE; *recipe, page 312.*

breakfast
and brunch

Baked Eggs en Cocotte with Basil

⏱ TOTAL: 25 MIN • MAKES 8 EGGS ● ●

These baked eggs with melted butter are winemaker Piero Incisa della Rocchetta's go-to breakfast. The dish was also a favorite of his grandfather Mario, who founded the world-famous Sassicaia winery in Tuscany.

- 8 teaspoons extra-virgin olive oil
- 8 large eggs
- 4 tablespoons unsalted butter
- Salt and freshly ground pepper
- ¼ cup chopped basil
- Buttered toasted whole wheat or white bread

1. Preheat the oven to 350°. Coat the bottoms and sides of eight 4-ounce ramekins with 1 teaspoon of olive oil each. Arrange the ramekins around the sides of a roasting pan and crack 1 egg into each one. Top each egg with ½ tablespoon of butter and season with salt and pepper. Pour enough boiling water into the roasting pan to reach halfway up the sides of the ramekins.

2. Bake the eggs in the oven for about 15 minutes, turning the pan halfway through cooking, until the yolks are runny and the whites are just firm. Garnish the eggs with the basil and serve right away, with buttered toast. —*Piero Incisa della Rocchetta*

egg cooking tips

poached Crack an egg into a ramekin, then gently transfer to a saucepan of barely simmering water. Cook until the white is set and the yolk is runny, 4 minutes.

hard-boiled Cover an egg with cold water. Bring to a boil, then turn off the heat. Let sit, covered, for 10 minutes. Cool in cold water.

soft-boiled Lower an egg into boiling water. Reduce the heat to moderate and cook for 6 minutes.

Poached Eggs with Sunchokes and Comté Polenta

⏱ TOTAL: 45 MIN • 4 SERVINGS ●

- ½ pound sunchokes—scrubbed but not peeled, very thinly sliced (see Note)
- 3 tablespoons unsalted butter
- Salt and freshly ground pepper
- 1 cup whole milk
- ½ cup instant polenta
- 1½ cups shredded Comté cheese (6 ounces), plus more for garnish
- 4 large eggs
- Chervil sprigs and truffle salt, for garnish

1. In a deep skillet with a tight-fitting lid, combine the sunchokes with 1 tablespoon of the butter and stir over moderately high heat until the butter is melted. Add ½ cup of water, season with salt and pepper and bring to a boil. Cover and cook over moderate heat until the liquid is evaporated and the sunchokes are tender and lightly browned, 8 to 10 minutes. Transfer the sunchokes to a bowl and wipe out the skillet. Fill the skillet with water and bring to a simmer.

2. In a large saucepan, combine the milk with 1 cup of water, season with salt and bring to a boil. Whisk in the polenta and cook over moderate heat, whisking, until tender, about 5 minutes. Stir in the 1½ cups of shredded cheese and the remaining 2 tablespoons of butter until creamy; stir in a few tablespoons of water if the polenta is too stiff.

3. Crack the eggs into ramekins and gently pour them into the simmering water in the skillet, one at a time. Poach the eggs until the whites are set and the yolks are runny, about 4 minutes. Using a slotted spoon, transfer the eggs to a paper towel–lined plate.

4. Spoon the polenta and sunchokes into shallow bowls and top with the eggs. Garnish with chervil and cheese, sprinkle with truffle salt and serve right away. —*David Bouley*

NOTE Sunchokes, also called Jerusalem artichokes, are knobby relatives of the sunflower.

WINE Fresh, wild berry–scented Beaujolais: 2009 Château Thivin Brouilly.

Warm Bacon-and-Egg Salad

⏱ TOTAL: 35 MIN • 4 SERVINGS ●

"I like a fried egg," says New York City chef April Bloomfield about the topping on her arugula salad. "Especially when it's fried in bacon fat." She likes to use rich duck eggs when they are available.

- ¼ cup plus 3 tablespoons extra-virgin olive oil
- 2 garlic cloves, halved lengthwise
- 1 generous cup ½-inch crustless bread cubes
- 8 slices of lean bacon
- 4 anchovy fillets, chopped
- 2 tablespoons Banyuls vinegar or red wine vinegar
- 2 teaspoons Dijon mustard
- Salt
- 4 large eggs
- 5 ounces baby arugula
- ¼ cup chopped chives
- Freshly ground pepper

1. In a large nonstick skillet, heat 2 tablespoons of the olive oil. Add the garlic and cook over moderate heat until golden brown, about 2 minutes. Using a slotted spoon, transfer the garlic to a mini processor.

2. Add the bread cubes to the skillet and cook over moderate heat, stirring, until browned and crisp, 3 minutes; transfer to a plate.

3. Heat 1 tablespoon of the oil in the skillet. Add the bacon and cook over moderate heat until crisp. Transfer the bacon to a plate; keep warm. Reserve the bacon fat in the skillet.

4. Add the anchovies, vinegar, mustard and the remaining ¼ cup of oil to the garlic and process until smooth. Season with salt.

5. Heat the bacon fat in the skillet. Crack the eggs into the skillet and fry over moderately high heat until over easy, 1½ minutes on one side and 30 seconds on the other side.

6. In a large bowl, toss the the arugula and croutons with the dressing. Mound the salad on plates and sprinkle with the chives. Top with the bacon and the eggs, season with pepper and serve. —*April Bloomfield*

WINE Full-bodied, citrusy Pinot Gris: 2010 J Vineyards California.

● HEALTHY ● MAKE AHEAD ● VEGETARIAN ● STAFF FAVORITE

baked egg en cocotte with basil

Eggs Baked Over Sautéed Mushrooms and Spinach
⊙ **ACTIVE: 20 MIN; TOTAL: 45 MIN**
4 SERVINGS ● ●

- 1 tablespoon olive oil, plus more for the ramekins
- 1 large leek, white and light green parts only, cut into ½-inch pieces
- 1 tablespoon unsalted butter
- 1 pound white or cremini mushrooms, thinly sliced (about 6 cups)
- 1 tablespoon soy sauce
- ¼ cup dry red wine
- 5 ounces baby spinach
- Salt and freshly ground pepper
- 4 large eggs
- 4 slices of whole-grain toast

1. Preheat the oven to 350°. In a deep skillet, heat the 1 tablespoon of olive oil. Add the leek and cook over moderate heat, stirring, until softened, about 3 minutes. Stir in the butter and mushrooms. Cover and cook, stirring occasionally, until the mushrooms are softened and a lot of liquid is released, about 7 minutes. Uncover and add the soy sauce and red wine and cook over moderately high heat, stirring, until the liquid is reduced to 2 tablespoons, about 5 minutes. Add the spinach and stir until wilted, 2 minutes. Season with salt and pepper.

vegan tip

The following vegan essentials can substitute for eggs and dairy to create a satisfying brunch.

in place of eggs Crumbled tofu sautéed with turmeric (for color), cumin and coriander is a terrific vegan take on scrambled eggs.

in place of milk All sorts of nuts, grains and beans can be blended with water, then strained to create tasty non-animal milks.

2. Coat four 1-cup ramekins or small gratin dishes with olive oil. Transfer the mushroom-and-spinach mixture to the ramekins and crack an egg on top of each. Bake for 10 to 12 minutes, until the whites are barely set and the yolks are runny. Let stand for 2 minutes, then serve with the toasts.
—*Kristin Donnelly*

WINE Fruity, light-bodied Gamay: 2010 Marcel Lapierre Raisins Gaulois.

Salami-and-Egg Mishmash
⊙ **TOTAL: 15 MIN • 6 SERVINGS**
"I do love breakfast for dinner—for the record, I highly recommend it," says Noah Bernamoff, the chef-owner of Mile End, a Montreal-style Jewish delicatessen in Brooklyn, New York. For now, he serves this mishmash of scrambled eggs, house-cured fried salami and watercress only until noon, but it will appear in a sandwich on the all-day menu at Mile End Sandwich, the new restaurant he's opening in Manhattan.

- ¼ cup canola oil
- 1 large onion, thinly sliced
- 10 ounces thickly sliced Genoa salami, cut into ¼-inch-thick strips (2 cups)
- 4 cups torn watercress or baby arugula
- 1 dozen large eggs, lightly beaten
- Salt and freshly ground pepper
- Rye toast, for serving

Heat the canola oil in a large nonstick skillet. Add the sliced onion and cook over moderately high heat, stirring, until softened, about 5 minutes. Add the salami strips and cook, stirring occasionally, until lightly browned, about 2 minutes. Add the watercress and cook until just wilted, about 1 minute. Add the eggs, season with salt and pepper and cook, stirring gently, until the eggs are softly set, about 2 minutes longer. Transfer the salami-and-egg mishmash to plates and serve right away, with rye toast.
—*Noah Bernamoff*

WINE Light, fragrant red: 2009 Giacomo Fenocchio Dolcetto d'Alba.

Spinach-Arugula Frittata
⊙ **TOTAL: 25 MIN • 4 SERVINGS** ● ● ●
For this healthy vegetable-packed frittata, F&W's Marcia Kiesel blends whole eggs with egg whites to lighten the texture. She likes to make the dish in a nonstick, oven-safe skillet with sloped sides.

- ¼ cup water
- 5 ounces baby spinach
- 3 ounces baby arugula
- 4 large eggs
- 5 large egg whites
- 1½ tablespoons freshly grated Parmigiano-Reggiano cheese
- Salt and freshly ground black pepper
- 4 teaspoons vegetable oil
- 1 medium shallot, thinly sliced
- 1 medium frying pepper, thinly sliced
- 1 teaspoon chopped thyme

1. In a 9-inch ovenproof nonstick skillet, bring the water to a boil over moderately high heat. Add the baby spinach and cook, stirring, until wilted, about 1 minute. Using tongs, transfer the spinach to a colander. Repeat with the arugula. Gently squeeze the greens dry and then coarsely chop them. Wipe out the skillet.

2. Preheat the oven to 400°. In a medium bowl, whisk the eggs with the egg whites, Parmigiano-Reggiano cheese and a large pinch each of salt and black pepper.

3. Heat 3 teaspoons of the vegetable oil in the skillet. Add the sliced shallot and frying pepper and cook over moderate heat, stirring, until the pepper is just tender, about 4 minutes. Add the thyme and the chopped greens and cook, stirring, until hot. Season with salt and black pepper.

4. Add the remaining 1 teaspoon of oil to the vegetables, then pour in the egg mixture. Tilt the skillet to evenly distribute the eggs and cook over moderately low heat until set around the edge, 3 minutes. Bake the frittata on the top shelf of the oven for 4 minutes, until just set. Invert the frittata onto a plate and let cool slightly. Cut into wedges and serve. —*Marcia Kiesel*

WINE Fresh, zippy Prosecco: NV Astoria.

● HEALTHY ● MAKE AHEAD ○ VEGETARIAN ● STAFF FAVORITE

egg baked over sautéed mushrooms and spinach

Lao Omelet with Dill, Scallion and Thai Chile

📷 PAGE 307

⏱ TOTAL: 15 MIN • MAKES 1 OMELET ●

The dill, fish sauce and scallions in this round omelet may seem like an overly bold combination of flavors, but the result is surprisingly delicious. It's also adaptable: Eat it for breakfast or as a quick, light supper.

- 3 large eggs
- 2 tablespoons chopped dill
- 1 scallion, cut into 1-inch pieces
- 1 Thai red chile, sliced
- ½ teaspoon Asian fish sauce
- ¼ teaspoon freshly ground pepper

Pinch of salt

- 2 tablespoons vegetable oil
- 1 medium shallot, coarsely chopped

1. In a bowl, beat the eggs. Stir in the dill, scallion, Thai chile, fish sauce, pepper and salt.
2. In a nonstick skillet, heat 1 tablespoon of the oil. Add the shallot and cook over moderately high heat until softened, 2 minutes. Add the remaining 1 tablespoon of oil and, when it is hot, add the egg mixture. Cook, stirring, until the eggs are almost set, about 1 minute. Run a heatproof plastic spatula around the edge to loosen the omelet and cook undisturbed until golden brown on the bottom, about 30 seconds. Invert the omelet onto a plate and serve. —*Sebastien Rubis*
SERVE WITH Tomato-Coriander Sauce (recipe follows).
WINE Crisp Sauvignon Blanc: 2009 Domaine de Bellecours Sancerre.

TOMATO-CORIANDER SAUCE

⏱ TOTAL: 20 MIN • MAKES 1¼ CUPS ● ●

- 3 small shallots
- 3 large garlic cloves
- 1 or 2 red Thai chiles
- 3 scallions—2 cut into 1-inch pieces, 1 coarsely chopped
- 3 plum tomatoes—halved, seeded and coarsely chopped
- 2 tablespoons chopped cilantro

Salt

Heat a medium cast-iron skillet. Add the shallots, garlic and chiles and cook over moderate heat for about 3 minutes, stirring occasionally. Add the scallion pieces and cook, stirring occasionally, until everything is charred in spots, about 3 minutes longer. Transfer the contents of the skillet to a large mortar and pound to a coarse paste. Add the chopped tomatoes and pound until they are incorporated. Stir in the chopped scallion and cilantro, season with salt and serve. —*SR*

Omelet Soufflé

⏱ TOTAL: 15 MIN

MAKES ONE 8-INCH OMELET ●

Aki Kamozawa and H. Alexander Talbot, of the food science blog Ideas in Food, are beloved by chefs like Richard Blais for culinary innovations. Here, they share their method for creating a fluffy omelet—fold in beaten egg whites to make it puff up like a soufflé—from their book *Ideas in Food*.

- 3 large eggs, separated

Pinch of sea salt

- 1½ tablespoons unsalted butter
- ½ cup shredded Gruyère cheese

1. Preheat the broiler and position a rack in the center of the oven, about 8 inches from the heat. In a large bowl, using a whisk or a handheld electric mixer, beat the egg whites until soft peaks form.
2. In a small bowl, whisk the egg yolks with the sea salt and one-fourth of the beaten egg whites, then fold the egg yolk mixture into the remaining beaten egg whites until no streaks remain.
3. In an 8-inch ovenproof skillet, melt the butter. Scrape the omelet mixture into the skillet and shake gently to evenly distribute the eggs. Sprinkle the shredded Gruyère cheese all over and transfer the skillet to the oven. Broil the omelet for about 3 minutes, until lightly browned and very puffy. Carefully slide the omelet onto a plate, folding it in half. Serve right away.
—*Aki Kamozawa and H. Alexander Talbot*
WINE Light, minerally Champagne: NV Fleury Fleur de L'Europe Brut.

Best-Ever Cheese Soufflé

ACTIVE: 20 MIN; TOTAL: 1 HR

6 SERVINGS ● ●

This retro cheese soufflé was inspired by research that New York chef Alexandra Guarnaschelli did for her supper club, The Darby.

- ¼ cup plus 2 tablespoons freshly grated Parmigiano-Reggiano cheese
- 3 tablespoons unsalted butter
- 3 tablespoons all-purpose flour
- 1¼ cups heavy cream
- 4 large eggs, separated, plus 3 large egg whites
- 3 tablespoons dry sherry
- 6 ounces Gruyère cheese, shredded (2 packed cups)
- 2 tablespoons sour cream
- 1¼ teaspoons kosher salt
- 1 teaspoon Dijon mustard
- ½ teaspoon dry mustard
- ¼ teaspoon cayenne pepper
- ¼ teaspoon cream of tartar

1. Preheat the oven to 375°. Butter a 1½-quart soufflé dish and coat it with 2 tablespoons of the Parmigiano.
2. In a medium saucepan, melt the butter. Stir in the flour to make a paste. Gradually whisk in the cream and bring to a boil over moderate heat, whisking. Reduce the heat to low and cook, whisking, until very thick, 3 minutes. Transfer the base to a large bowl; let cool. Stir in the egg yolks, sherry, Gruyère, sour cream, salt, Dijon mustard, dry mustard, cayenne and the remaining ¼ cup of Parmigiano.
3. Put the 7 egg whites in a large stainless steel bowl. Add the cream of tartar. Using an electric mixer, beat the whites until firm peaks form. Fold one-third of the whites into the soufflé base to lighten it, then fold in the remaining whites until no streaks remain.
4. Scrape the mixture into the prepared dish. Run your thumb around the inside rim of the dish to wipe away any crumbs. Bake for about 35 minutes, until the soufflé is golden brown and puffed. Serve right away.
—*Alexandra Guarnaschelli*
WINE Fresh, white peach–inflected Pinot Grigio: 2009 Vezzo.

● HEALTHY   ● MAKE AHEAD   ● VEGETARIAN   ● STAFF FAVORITE

Double-Baked Cheese Soufflé with Parmesan Cream

ACTIVE: 30 MIN; TOTAL: 1 HR 15 MIN

4 SERVINGS ● ● ●

Superchef Alain Ducasse's ultrarich soufflé is baked twice: first until it's puffed and golden, then again to brown the top.

SOUFFLÉ

- 6 tablespoons unsalted butter, plus more for greasing
- ½ cup freshly grated Parmigiano-Reggiano cheese (2 ounces), plus more for dusting
- 6 tablespoons all-purpose flour
- 1 garlic clove, peeled
- 1 cup milk
- ½ cup shredded Comté cheese

Salt and freshly ground white pepper

- 4 large eggs, separated

PARMESAN CREAM

- ½ cup heavy cream
- ¼ cup milk
- ⅓ cup shredded Comté cheese
- ⅓ cup freshly grated Parmigiano-Reggiano cheese (1½ ounces)

Salt and freshly ground white pepper

1. MAKE THE SOUFFLÉ Preheat the oven to 375°. Butter an 8-inch square glass baking dish and dust with Parmigiano-Reggiano. In a medium saucepan, melt the 6 tablespoons of butter. Whisk in the flour and garlic and cook over moderate heat for about 2 minutes. Add the milk and whisk until thickened, about 2 minutes. Discard the garlic. Add the Comté cheese and the ½ cup of Parmigiano-Reggiano. Season with salt and white pepper. Transfer to a food processor and pulse until smooth. Add the egg yolks and pulse again; transfer the cheese mixture to a large bowl. Rinse out the food processor bowl.

2. In a clean medium bowl, using an electric mixer, beat the egg whites at high speed until soft peaks form. Thoroughly fold the egg whites into the cheese-and-egg-yolk mixture. Scrape the batter into the prepared dish and smooth the surface. Bake for about 30 minutes, until risen and golden. Let the soufflé cool for 10 minutes.

3. MEANWHILE, MAKE THE PARMESAN CREAM In a medium saucepan, bring the cream and milk to a boil; transfer to the food processor. Add the Comté and Parmigiano-Reggiano cheeses and let stand for 5 minutes. Process until smooth, then season with salt and white pepper.

4. Turn on the broiler. Invert the soufflé onto a baking sheet and broil 8 inches from the heat for about 30 seconds, until golden. Slice the soufflé and serve with the Parmesan cream. —*Alain Ducasse*

WINE Fresh, green apple–inflected sparkling wine: NV Jean-François Mérieau Bulles.

Three-Day Brined Lox with Anise-Herb Sauce

TOTAL: 1 HR PLUS 3 DAYS BRINING

MAKES 2 POUNDS ● ● ●

F&W Best New Chef 2007 Matthew Dillon loves this Nordic method of brining fish (known as *lenrimmad lax*). At Sitka & Spruce in Seattle, he serves the lox with an herb sauce made from blanched nettles. The recipe here calls for parsley and mint, easier-to-find substitutes.

WET-BRINED LOX

- 2 pounds whole salmon or halibut fillet, with skin
- 3 cups cold water
- ⅓ cup kosher salt
- 1 teaspoon dill seeds
- 1 teaspoon anise seeds
- 1 tablespoon coriander seeds, cracked
- 6 dill sprigs
- 6 parsley sprigs
- 6 cilantro sprigs
- 4 garlic cloves, sliced
- 1 small shallot, sliced

HERB SAUCE

- ½ cup freshly squeezed lemon juice
- 3 garlic cloves, thinly sliced
- 2 shallots, minced
- ½ cup chopped flat-leaf parsley
- ½ cup chopped mint
- ½ cup chopped dill
- ¼ cup chopped chervil
- 1½ teaspoons finely grated lemon zest
- 1 teaspoon anise seeds, toasted and coarsely crushed
- 1 teaspoon Aleppo pepper or crushed red pepper
- 1 cup grapeseed oil

Salt and freshly ground pepper

Crème fraîche, cornichons, dark bread and grainy mustard, for serving

1. MAKE THE LOX Rinse and dry the fish. Set the fillet in a deep 9-by-13-inch baking dish. In a large bowl, whisk the cold water with the kosher salt until the salt is dissolved, then add the dill seeds, anise seeds, coriander seeds, herb sprigs, garlic and shallot. Pour the brine over the fish and evenly distribute the aromatics. Top the fillet with a sheet of paper towel, pressing gently to moisten the sheet. Wrap the entire baking dish in plastic wrap. Refrigerate for 3 days, turning the fish in its brine, topping it with a fresh paper towel and rewrapping in plastic wrap after 36 hours.

2. Drain and discard the brine and scrape the aromatics off the fish fillet. Place the fillet skin side down on a rack set over a baking sheet and refrigerate uncovered until the surface is mostly dry but slightly tacky, about 2 hours.

3. MAKE THE HERB SAUCE In a bowl, combine the lemon juice with the garlic and shallots and let stand for 20 minutes. Stir in the parsley, mint, dill, chervil, lemon zest, anise seeds, Aleppo pepper and oil and season with salt and pepper.

4. Place the fish on a work surface. Using a very sharp, thin-bladed knife, cut the fish crosswise into very thin slices, running the blade horizontally once it reaches the skin to free each slice. Transfer the slices to a platter and serve with the herb sauce, crème fraîche, cornichons, dark bread and mustard. —*Matthew Dillon*

MAKE AHEAD The lox can be prepared through Step 2, wrapped in plastic and refrigerated for up to 4 days.

WINE Fresh, herb-scented Italian white: 2010 Jankara Vermentino di Gallura.

Swedish Caviar Cake

ACTIVE: 25 MIN; TOTAL: 2 HR 30 MIN
8 SERVINGS ● ●

This caviar "cake" is actually an easy chilled custard that's topped with crème fraîche, chopped onion and two types of fish roe.

1¾ cups whole milk
¾ teaspoon salt
Butter, for greasing the baking dish
5 large eggs
1 cup crème fraîche
½ cup finely chopped red onion
3 tablespoons red caviar, such as trout roe (about 2 ounces)
3 tablespoons black caviar, such as paddlefish roe (about 2 ounces)
1 tablespoon finely chopped fresh dill
Freshly ground pepper

1. In a small saucepan, bring the milk to a boil over moderately high heat. Immediately remove the saucepan from the heat, stir in the salt and let cool to warm.

2. Preheat the oven to 325° and butter an 11-by-7-inch glass or ceramic baking dish. Meanwhile, in a medium saucepan, bring 1 quart of water to a simmer.

caviar tip

Roe from trout, salmon, whitefish, paddlefish and domestic sturgeon can be outstanding on their own or in recipes like the Swedish Caviar Cake, above.

trout Small, juicy orange trout caviar has a subtle trout flavor.

paddlefish This black caviar from a sturgeon cousin has a delicate, earthy taste and silky texture.

hackleback Onyx-colored caviar from this Mississippi or Missouri river sturgeon is sweet and buttery.

3. In a large bowl, whisk the cooled milk with the eggs until smooth. Pour the mixture into the prepared baking dish and cover tightly with aluminum foil. Set the dish in a roasting pan and pour enough of the simmering water into the roasting pan to reach about halfway up the side of the baking dish. Transfer the roasting pan to the middle of the oven. Bake the custard for about 30 minutes, until a knife inserted into the center comes out clean. Transfer the baking dish to a rack and remove the aluminum foil. Let the custard cool completely, then keep in the refrigerator for about 1 hour, until chilled.

4. Spread the crème fraîche in an even layer over the cooled custard. Spoon the onion, the red caviar and the black caviar over the crème fraîche in alternating diagonal rows. Sprinkle the caviar cake with the dill, season with pepper and serve.
—Malin Elmlid

MAKE AHEAD The caviar cake can be made through Step 3, covered and kept in the refrigerator overnight.

English Muffins

ACTIVE: 30 MIN; TOTAL: 3 HR
MAKES 8 ENGLISH MUFFINS ● ● ●

At The Bakery, the new branch of Cakes & Ale in Decatur, Georgia, chef-owner Billy Allin serves his airy, chewy homemade English muffins all day long. In the morning he offers them with butter and jams, such as house-made peach preserves; later in the day he might use them for BLTs, melts and other sandwiches.

1 cup milk
½ cup water
2 envelopes active dry yeast
3¼ cups all-purpose flour, plus more as needed
2 tablespoons wheat germ
2 tablespoons wheat bran
2 tablespoons barley malt syrup (see Note)
1½ teaspoons salt
2 tablespoons unsalted butter, melted, plus more for the griddle
Cornmeal, for dusting
Butter and jam for serving at breakfast; ham and cheese for serving as a melt later in the day

1. In a large microwave-safe bowl, mix the milk and water and heat at high power in 30-second bursts until just warm to the touch. Stir in the yeast and 1¼ cups of the flour. Cover and let the mixture stand until billowy, about 30 minutes.

2. Stir in the the wheat germ, wheat bran, barley syrup, salt and the 2 tablespoons of butter. Stir in the remaining 2 cups of flour. Turn the dough out onto a well-floured work surface and knead until smooth, kneading in up to ⅓ cup of flour as necessary to make a silky, supple dough. Transfer the dough to a large oiled bowl. Cover the bowl with a kitchen towel and let the dough rise until it's doubled in volume, about 45 minutes. Punch down the dough and let rise until it is doubled again, 1 hour longer.

3. Preheat the oven to 350°. Heat a large cast-iron griddle on the stove over low heat. Dust a work surface with cornmeal, then pat out the dough ¾ inch thick. Using a floured 3-inch biscuit cutter, stamp out 7 rounds as close together as possible. Gently pat the scraps together and stamp out 1 more round. Brush the griddle with butter. Griddle the English muffins on moderately low heat, turning once, until golden on both sides, about 6 minutes total.

4. Transfer the English muffins to a parchment paper–lined baking sheet and bake for about 20 minutes, until they are risen and cooked through; an instant-read thermometer inserted in the center of the muffins should register 195°. Let cool completely. Using a fork, split the muffins horizontally and toast them until golden. Serve the English muffins with butter and jam or as a sandwich with ham and cheese.
—Billy Allin

NOTE Earthy barley malt syrup is a natural sweetener that's available at health-food stores and some specialty food stores.

MAKE AHEAD The English muffins can be frozen for up to 1 month.

● HEALTHY ● MAKE AHEAD ○ VEGETARIAN ○ STAFF FAVORITE

english muffin

Corned Beef Hash with Fried Eggs

⏱ TOTAL: 45 MIN • 6 SERVINGS

This tomato-spiked hash from Colby Garrelts, an F&W Best New Chef 2005, is a simplified take on the haute version he serves at Bluestem in Kansas City, Missouri. Made with peppers, onions and crisp potatoes, it's superb topped with a runny fried egg.

- ¼ cup plus 1 tablespoon vegetable oil
- 3 baking potatoes (about 2 pounds), peeled and cut into ½-inch dice
- 1 medium onion, thinly sliced
- 1 red bell pepper, thinly sliced

Salt and freshly ground pepper

- 1½ pounds cooked corned beef, fat trimmed and meat cut into ½-inch dice
- 4 garlic cloves, minced
- 1 cup canned tomato sauce
- 1 tablespoon hot sauce, plus more for serving
- 6 large eggs

Snipped chives, for serving

1. In a very large nonstick skillet, heat 3 tablespoons of the vegetable oil. Add the diced potatoes and cook them over moderately high heat, stirring occasionally, until golden, about 10 minutes.
2. Add the onion and bell pepper and season with salt and pepper. Cook over moderately high heat, stirring occasionally, until softened, about 2 minutes. Add the corned beef and cook, stirring occasionally, until browned, about 8 minutes. Add the garlic and cook until fragrant, about 1 minute. Add the tomato sauce and 1 tablespoon of hot sauce and simmer over moderate heat, stirring occasionally, until the sauce is very thick, about 15 minutes.
3. In another large nonstick skillet, heat the remaining 2 tablespoons of oil. Crack the eggs into the skillet and fry sunny-side up or over-easy. Spoon the hash onto plates and top with the eggs. Sprinkle the hash with chives and serve right away.
—*Colby Garrelts*

Spinach Bread Pudding with Lemon and Feta

ACTIVE: 30 MIN; TOTAL: 4 HR

8 SERVINGS ●◐

Heidi Swanson, who blogs about healthy food on her excellent website 101 Cookbooks, shares this lightened whole wheat bread pudding in her cookbook *Super Natural Every Day: Well-Loved Recipes from My Natural Foods Kitchen.*

- 3 tablespoons extra-virgin olive oil, plus more for greasing the dish
- 8 ounces whole wheat bread, cut into ½-inch cubes
- 5 ounces baby spinach, finely chopped
- ½ cup crumbled feta cheese
- 2 teaspoons Dijon mustard
- ½ teaspoon finely grated lemon zest
- 1 tablespoon fresh lemon juice
- 6 large eggs, beaten
- 2 cups milk

Kosher salt and freshly ground pepper

- 1 teaspoon chopped oregano

1. Preheat the oven to 350°. Lightly oil a medium baking dish. Spread the bread cubes on a baking sheet and bake for about 10 minutes, until dry but not browned. Let cool, then transfer to a large bowl. Stir in the spinach and ¼ cup of the feta.
2. In another bowl, whisk 2 tablespoons of the olive oil with the mustard, lemon zest and lemon juice. Add the eggs and beat until blended. Add the milk and season with 1 teaspoon of salt and ½ teaspoon of pepper. Pour the egg mixture over the bread cubes; stir until they are evenly moistened. Transfer the bread mixture to the prepared baking dish and let stand at room temperature for 2 hours or refrigerate overnight.
3. Sprinkle the remaining feta on the bread pudding and bake in the center of the oven until risen and set, about 40 minutes. Turn on the broiler. Drizzle with the remaining 1 tablespoon of oil and broil until the bread pudding is golden and crispy on top, about 2 minutes. Scatter the oregano on top, cut the bread pudding into squares and serve.
—*Heidi Swanson*

Breakfast Biscuit Sandwiches

TOTAL: 1 HR

MAKES 10 BREAKFAST BISCUITS ●

A giant step up from fast-food breakfast sandwiches, these biscuits from Peels in New York City are topped with fried eggs, cheddar cheese and country ham. Raspberry jam is optional.

- 4 cups all-purpose flour, plus more for dusting
- 2 tablespoons kosher salt
- 1½ tablespoons baking powder
- 1 teaspoon baking soda
- 2 sticks unsalted butter, cubed and chilled, plus more for spreading
- 1½ cups buttermilk
- 10 ounces sliced country ham, 10 ounces sliced cheddar cheese and 10 fried eggs, for serving

Raspberry jam, for serving (optional)

1. Preheat the oven to 400° and position racks in the upper and lower thirds. Line 2 baking sheets with parchment paper. In a large bowl, whisk the 4 cups of flour with the salt, baking powder and baking soda. Using a pastry blender or 2 knives, cut in the 2 sticks of cubed butter until it is the size of small peas. Add the buttermilk and stir until a shaggy dough forms.
2. Turn the dough out onto a floured surface; knead until it comes together. Pat the dough ¾ inch thick. Using a 3½-inch round cutter, stamp out as many biscuits as possible. Reroll the scraps and stamp out more biscuits. You should have 10.
3. Transfer the biscuits to the baking sheets and bake for about 30 minutes, until golden and risen, shifting the pans halfway through baking. Let the biscuits cool.
4. Split the biscuits and spread with butter. Preheat a griddle and cook the biscuits, cut side down, until golden. Fill the biscuits with ham, cheddar and fried eggs and spread with jam, if desired. Close and serve.
—*Ginger and Preston Madson*

MAKE AHEAD The biscuits can be made up to 1 day ahead and kept in an airtight container before proceeding with Step 4.

● HEALTHY ● MAKE AHEAD ◐ VEGETARIAN ● STAFF FAVORITE

breakfast biscuit sandwich

Bacon-Scallion Biscuits with Sorghum Butter

ACTIVE: 30 MIN; TOTAL: 1 HR
MAKES ABOUT 18 BISCUITS ●

"The perfect biscuit dough just barely comes together," says Hugh Acheson, an F&W Best New Chef 2002 and the chef-owner of Empire State South in Atlanta and Five & Ten in Athens, Georgia. "After it's lightly rolled out, the biscuits puff up when you bake them." He tops these flavorful bacon-and-scallion ones with butter that's mixed with sorghum syrup, a traditional Southern sweetener. People who don't eat meat can simply omit the bacon.

BISCUITS

½   pound sliced bacon
4½ cups all-purpose flour, plus more for dusting
2   tablespoons baking powder
2   tablespoons sugar
1   tablespoon kosher salt
1   teaspoon baking soda
2   sticks cold unsalted butter, cut into small pieces
1½ cups buttermilk
2   scallions, thinly sliced

SORGHUM BUTTER

1   stick unsalted butter, at room temperature
2   tablespoons sorghum syrup (see Note) or pure maple syrup
Salt

1. PREPARE THE BISCUITS Preheat the oven to 425°. Line a large baking sheet with parchment paper. In a large skillet, cook the sliced bacon over moderate heat until crisp, about 7 minutes. Drain the bacon on paper towels, then finely chop.

2. In a large bowl, whisk the 4½ cups of flour with the baking powder, sugar, kosher salt and baking soda. Using a pastry blender or 2 knives, cut in the cold butter until it is the size of small peas. Stir in the buttermilk, scallions and chopped bacon just until incorporated. Scrape the dough out onto a floured work surface and knead it gently just until it comes together.

3. Using a floured rolling pin, roll the biscuit dough out to a ½-inch thickness. Using a 3-inch round biscuit cutter, stamp out 16 rounds of dough. Gently gather the scraps to form 2 or 3 more biscuits. Place the bacon-scallion biscuits on the baking sheet and bake for about 25 minutes, until they are well risen and golden brown; turn the baking sheet once halfway through baking.

4. MEANWHILE, MAKE THE SORGHUM BUTTER In a small bowl, thoroughly blend the room-temperature butter with the sorghum syrup and season with salt.

5. Serve the bacon-scallion biscuits warm with the sorghum butter. —*Hugh Acheson*

NOTE Sorghum syrup, sometimes referred to as sorghum molasses, is available online at *zingermans.com.*

MAKE AHEAD The sorghum butter can be refrigerated for up to 2 days.

Chocolate Brioche with Sichuan Peppercorns

ACTIVE: 30 MIN; TOTAL: 4 HR
MAKES TWO 9-INCH LOAVES ● ●

Gontran Cherrier, who has an eponymous bakery in Paris's 18th arrondisement, spent several years in the pastry kitchen at elite Paris restaurants like L'Arpège and Lucas Carton. So when he creates a bread, he often thinks about pairing it with a dish. He made this light chocolate brioche with foie gras terrine in mind; the Sichuan peppercorns add a spicy, aromatic kick that's good with rich foods. It's also delicious with strawberry jam or quince paste.

¼   cup plus 1 tablespoon milk, warmed
¼   cup sugar
1   package active dry yeast
4½ cups all-purpose flour
¼   cup unsweetened cocoa powder, sifted
2   teaspoons salt
1   teaspoon finely ground Sichuan peppercorns (see Note)
½   cup semisweet chocolate chips
7   large eggs
2   sticks unsalted butter, at room temperature

1. In a small bowl, combine the warmed milk and 1 teaspoon of the sugar. Sprinkle the yeast over the milk and stir lightly. Let stand until foamy, about 5 minutes.

2. In the bowl of a standing mixer fitted with the paddle attachment, combine the flour, cocoa powder, salt, ground Sichuan peppercorns, chocolate chips and the remaining 3 tablespoons plus 2 teaspoons of sugar and mix well. With the machine at medium-low speed, beat in the yeast mixture. Add 6 of the eggs, 1 at a time, scraping down the side of the bowl as necessary. Reduce the speed to low and beat in the butter, 1 tablespoon at a time, until thoroughly incorporated, scraping down the side of the bowl a few times. The dough should be soft, smooth and slightly sticky.

3. Transfer the dough to a floured bowl, cover with plastic wrap and let stand in warm place until risen and puffy, about 1 hour.

4. On a floured work surface, pat down the dough. Gather it into a ball. Flour the bowl and return the dough to it. Cover and let stand again until risen, about 45 minutes.

5. Generously butter two 9-by-4½-inch loaf pans. Turn the dough out onto a floured work surface and cut it in half. Pat each half into a 9-by-8-inch rectangular loaf, roll it up to form a 9-by-4½-inch loaf and transfer to a prepared loaf pan, seam side down; neatly fold in the ends. Loosely cover with plastic wrap and let stand until the dough fills the pans, about 1 hour.

6. Preheat the oven to 350°. Beat the remaining egg and brush some over the tops of the loaves. Using a sharp knife, make a lengthwise slice in the center of each loaf. Bake for 35 minutes, rotating the loaves halfway through baking, until they sound hollow when tapped. Transfer the pans to a rack to cool slightly, then run a knife around the edges and turn the loaves out onto the rack. Serve the brioche warm or at room temperature. —*Gontran Cherrier*

NOTE Fragrant, mouth-numbing Sichuan peppercorns from China are available at most Asian markets and *thespicehouse.com.*

MAKE AHEAD The loaves can be wrapped well and frozen for up to 1 month.

● HEALTHY ● MAKE AHEAD ● VEGETARIAN ● STAFF FAVORITE

Brioche French Toast Stuffed with Apple, Raisins and Pecans

TOTAL: 45 MIN • 6 SERVINGS

"Breakfast is huge in the Midwest," says Megan Garrelts, co-owner and pastry chef at Bluestem restaurant in Kansas City, Missouri. At the restaurant, Garrelts stuffs her incredible French toast with more than 10 ingredients. This streamlined version of her recipe has just pecans, applesauce and golden raisins in the filling.

½ cup pecans
1 cup applesauce
½ cup golden raisins
Pinch of cinnamon
One 12-ounce loaf of brioche—
    cut into 12 slices, heels discarded
4 large eggs, beaten
½ cup heavy cream
2 tablespoons sugar
1 teaspoon pure vanilla extract
3 tablespoons unsalted butter
3 tablespoons canola oil
Confectioners' sugar, for dusting
Sweetened whipped cream,
    for serving

1. Preheat the oven to 350° and spread the pecans in a pie plate, then toast them for 8 minutes, until fragrant. Let cool, then finely chop the pecans and transfer to a bowl. Add the applesauce, raisins and cinnamon.
2. Spread the applesauce-pecan filling on 6 of the bread slices, top with the remaining bread slices and close.
3. In the pie plate, beat the eggs with the heavy cream, sugar and vanilla. Dip the sandwiches in the eggs and then transfer them to a baking sheet.
4. In each of 2 large nonstick skillets, melt half of the butter in the oil. Add the French toast and cook over moderate heat, turning once, until browned and cooked through, about 5 minutes. Dust the French toast with confectioners' sugar and serve with sweetened whipped cream. —*Megan Garrelts*
MAKE AHEAD The applesauce-pecan filling can be refrigerated overnight. Bring to room temperature before proceeding.

Lemon Challah Soufflé

ACTIVE: 45 MIN; TOTAL: 1 HR 45 MIN
12 SERVINGS ● ●

This isn't the kind of stressful soufflé you have to prepare at the last minute and serve immediately. Instead, it's more like bread pudding that can be made ahead of time and served hot or warm.

¾ cup all-purpose flour
¼ cup cornstarch
4 large egg yolks
1 large egg
2 cups whole milk
¾ cup plus 1½ teaspoons
    granulated sugar, plus more
    for dusting
2 tablespoons unsalted butter,
    softened
½ cup fresh lemon juice
1 teaspoon finely grated lemon zest
4 cups ½-inch-cubed challah
    (½ pound)
6 large egg whites
¼ teaspoon cream of tartar
Confectioners' sugar, for dusting

1. In a small bowl, whisk the flour and cornstarch. In a large heatproof bowl, whisk the egg yolks and whole egg with ¾ cup of the milk and three-fourths of the flour-cornstarch mixture until smooth. Gradually whisk in the remaining flour mixture until smooth.
2. In a medium saucepan, combine the remaining 1¼ cups of milk with 1½ teaspoons of the granulated sugar and bring to a boil, whisking. Slowly pour the hot milk into the egg mixture and whisk constantly until smooth. Whisk in the butter until melted. Add the lemon juice and zest and fold in the challah. Refrigerate until cooled.
3. Preheat the oven to 375° and butter a 9-by-13-inch baking dish. Dust with granulated sugar, tapping out the excess. In the bowl of a standing mixer fitted with a whisk, beat the egg whites with the cream of tartar until soft peaks form. Gradually add the remaining ¾ cup of granulated sugar in a steady stream and beat at high speed until the whites are firm and glossy. Fold the

meringue into the challah custard until no streaks of white remain. Transfer the mixture to the prepared baking dish.
4. Bake in the center of the oven until risen and golden, 45 minutes. Let rest for 10 to 30 minutes. Dust with confectioners' sugar and serve. —*Michael Symon*
MAKE AHEAD The Lemon Challah Soufflé can be prepared up to 2 hours before baking; let stand at room temperature.
WINE Effervescent, lightly sweet Moscato d'Asti: 2010 Umberto Fiore.

Chamomile Toast Crunch

TOTAL: 25 MIN • MAKES 4 SLICES

This riff on Cinnamon Toast Crunch breakfast cereal—a thick slice of brûléed bread, sitting in a pool of sweetened milk—combines the simple joy of buttered toast, the sugary crackle of crème brûlée and the indulgent moistness of *tres leches* cake.

1 cup half-and-half
¼ ounce dried chamomile
1 can sweetened condensed milk
1 stick unsalted butter, softened
4 thick slices of bakery white bread
Sugar

1. In a small saucepan, warm the half-and-half over moderately low heat almost to a simmer. Turn off the heat and add the chamomile. Steep, covered, for 10 minutes, then strain. Sweeten with condensed milk to taste.
2. Spread 2 tablespoons of butter on each slice of bread. Toast or bake the buttered bread until the edges are lightly browned.
3. Dip each piece of toast in sugar, then sprinkle on a bit more to coat evenly.
4. Torch the sugared toast on a metal rack set over a pan. Keep the torch nozzle 2 to 3 inches from the toast, and move it across the surface of the bread. Tip your pan to coax melted sugar toward unmelted sugar. Avoid torching the edges, because unsugared bread can ignite. If you're torchless or timid, use the broiler instead of a torch.
5. Serve the brûléed toast in a hefty puddle of sweet chamomile milk.
—*Anthony Myint*

Liège Waffles

ACTIVE: 35 MIN; TOTAL: 2 HR 35 MIN

MAKES ABOUT 16 WAFFLES ● ○ ○

Belgian pearl sugar is the key ingredient in these Liège-style waffles: The smooth balls of sugar add pops of sweetness and caramelize for a crispy exterior.

1½ tablespoons light brown sugar
1¾ teaspoons active dry yeast
⅓ cup lukewarm water
2 cups all-purpose flour
½ teaspoon salt
3 large eggs
1 teaspoon pure vanilla extract
2 sticks unsalted butter, melted (about 1 cup), plus more for brushing
1 cup Belgian pearl sugar (see Note)

1. In a small bowl, whisk the brown sugar and yeast into the lukewarm water and let stand until foamy, about 5 minutes. In the bowl of a standing mixer fitted with the paddle, mix the flour with the salt. Make a well in the center of the bowl and pour in the yeast mixture. Mix at medium speed until shaggy, about 1 minute. Add the eggs 1 at a time, mixing for 20 seconds between each. Whisk the vanilla with the 1 cup of melted butter. With the mixer at medium-low, gradually mix in the butter until smooth; the batter will be thick and very sticky. Cover the bowl with plastic wrap and let the batter rise in a warm place until doubled in size, about 1 hour and 45 minutes.
2. Stir the pearl sugar into the risen batter. Cover again and let rest for 15 minutes.
3. Preheat the oven to 250°. Preheat a Belgian waffle iron and brush it with melted butter. Gently stir the batter to deflate. Using about 2 tablespoons of batter for each, cook the waffles according to the manufacturer's directions until they are golden and crisp; brush the waffle iron with melted butter as needed. Transfer the waffles to plates or keep them warm in the oven, then serve. —*Malin Elmlid*

NOTE Belgian pearl sugar is available at specialty shops and *amazon.com*.

MAKE AHEAD The batter can be prepared through Step 1 and refrigerated overnight.

Yeasty Waffles

ACTIVE: 30 MIN; TOTAL: 2 HR 30 MIN

4 SERVINGS ○ ○

In *Cooking for Geeks*, a book that blends science with recipes, Jeff Potter offers a waffle recipe made with yeast instead of baking powder. A yeast enzyme called zymase helps make the waffles rich and sweet.

1¾ cups whole milk, at room temperature
½ cup unsalted butter, melted, plus more melted butter for the waffle iron
2½ cups sifted all-purpose flour
1 tablespoon active dry yeast (from 2 envelopes)
2 large eggs, at room temperature
2 teaspoons agave nectar or honey
1 teaspoon salt
Syrup, fresh fruit and softened butter, for serving

1. In a large bowl, combine the milk, ½ cup melted butter, flour, yeast, eggs, agave nectar and salt and whisk until smooth. Cover with plastic wrap and let stand until the batter is very puffy, about 2 hours at room temperature (or refrigerate overnight).
2. Preheat the oven to 250°. Preheat a waffle iron and brush it with melted butter. Gently stir the batter to deflate it. For each batch, fill the waffle iron about two-thirds full (the batter will spread and rise); brush the waffle iron with melted butter as needed.
3. Cook the waffles until golden and crisp. Transfer immediately from the iron to plates, or keep warm in the oven. Serve with syrup, fresh fruit and softened butter. —*Jeff Potter*

Strawberry-Almond Scones

ACTIVE: 30 MIN; TOTAL: 1 HR 45 MIN

MAKES 16 SCONES ● ○ ○

When baking these scones from pastry chef Breanne Varela of L.A.'s Tavern and the Larder at Tavern, be sure to use whole wheat pastry flour, which is less dense than whole wheat flour. Mixing in some all-purpose white flour also lightens the texture of the scones, so they're more delicate and tender.

SCONES

1½ cups all-purpose flour
1½ cups whole wheat pastry flour
¼ cup plus 2 tablespoons granulated sugar
1 tablespoon baking powder
½ teaspoon baking soda
½ teaspoon salt
1 stick cold unsalted butter, cubed
1¼ cups buttermilk, plus more for brushing
1½ cups sliced strawberries
2 tablespoons turbinado sugar (also called Sugar in the Raw)

TOPPING

½ cup sliced almonds
2 cups confectioners' sugar
3 tablespoons buttermilk
½ teaspoon pure almond extract
Pinch of salt

1. MAKE THE SCONES Preheat the oven to 400° and line 2 baking sheets with parchment paper. In a large bowl, combine the all-purpose and whole wheat pastry flours with the granulated sugar, baking powder, baking soda and salt. Using a pastry blender or 2 knives, cut in the butter until the mixture resembles coarse meal. Stir in the 1¼ cups of buttermilk and carefully fold in the sliced strawberries.
2. Scoop the dough into 16 mounds on the prepared baking sheets. Brush the scones with buttermilk and sprinkle with the turbinado sugar. Bake in the upper and lower thirds of the oven for 30 to 35 minutes, until the scones are golden and cooked through; shift the pans from front to back and top to bottom halfway through baking. Let the scones cool on a rack for 30 minutes.
3. MAKE THE TOPPING Lower the oven temperature to 350°. Spread the almonds in a pie plate and toast for about 8 minutes, until golden. Meanwhile, in a small bowl, whisk the confectioners' sugar with the buttermilk, almond extract and salt. Cover and let stand at room temperature.
4. Drizzle the scones with the glaze; top with the almonds, pressing so they adhere. Let dry for 10 minutes; serve. —*Breanne Varela*

● HEALTHY ● MAKE AHEAD ○ VEGETARIAN ● STAFF FAVORITE

strawberry-almond scones

breakfast and brunch

Apple Crumb Coffee Cakes

ACTIVE: 20 MIN; TOTAL: 1 HR
MAKES 18 MUFFINS ● ○ ○

STREUSEL

- 1 cup all-purpose flour
- ½ cup light brown sugar
- ½ teaspoon salt
- 5 tablespoons cold unsalted butter, cut into small pieces

CRUMB CAKES

- 1½ cups all-purpose flour
- 1 cup granulated sugar
- 1 teaspoon salt
- 1½ teaspoons baking powder
- ½ teaspoon baking soda
- ½ teaspoon cinnamon
- 1 stick cold unsalted butter, cut into small pieces
- ¾ cup sour cream
- 1 large egg, beaten
- 1 large Granny Smith apple, peeled and finely diced

1. MAKE THE STREUSEL Preheat the oven to 350°. In the bowl of a standing mixer fitted with the paddle, combine the flour with the brown sugar and salt. Add the butter and mix at medium-low speed until the mixture resembles coarse meal; continue mixing until very small clumps form. Transfer the streusel to a large plate and refrigerate until well chilled, about 10 minutes.

2. MAKE THE CRUMB CAKES Line 18 standard muffin cups with paper liners. Spray the liners with vegetable oil cooking spray. In the mixer bowl, combine the flour, granulated sugar, salt, baking powder, baking soda and cinnamon. Add the butter and beat at low speed until the mixture resembles coarse meal. Add the sour cream and egg; beat until the batter is smooth. Add the apple; beat just until incorporated.

3. Fill the muffin cups halfway with the batter. Press the streusel into clumps and sprinkle on top. Bake the cakes in the center of the oven for 30 minutes, until risen, golden and springy to the touch. Rotate the pans halfway through baking. Let the cakes cool slightly before serving. —*Spike Gjerde*

MAKE AHEAD The crumb cakes can be made 1 day ahead and kept in an airtight container. Rewarm before serving.

Glazed Cinnamon Rolls with Pecan Swirls

ACTIVE: 1 HR; TOTAL: 10 HR 30 MIN
MAKES 2 DOZEN ROLLS ● ○ ○

Baking these cinnamon rolls in big batches makes the effort worth it—they take time to prepare but are so satisfying.

DOUGH

- 2¼ teaspoons instant dry yeast
- 2 tablespoons warm water
- ¼ cup plus 1 teaspoon sugar
- 6 large eggs
- 4½ cups sifted all-purpose flour (1¼ pounds), plus more for rolling
- 1½ teaspoons salt
- 3 sticks unsalted butter, cut into ½-inch cubes and chilled

FILLING

- 4 ounces pecans (1 cup)
- 1½ cups light brown sugar
- 1 tablespoon cinnamon
- 1 cup sour cream
- 2 large eggs beaten with ¼ cup of water

SUGAR GLAZE

- 1½ cups confectioners' sugar
- 4 tablespoons unsalted butter, softened
- ¼ cup heavy cream
- 1 teaspoon pure vanilla extract

1. MAKE THE DOUGH In a medium bowl, combine the yeast with the warm water and 1 teaspoon of the sugar and let stand until foamy, about 5 minutes. Whisk in the 6 eggs. In the bowl of a standing mixer fitted with the dough hook, mix the 4½ cups of sifted flour with the salt and the remaining ¼ cup of sugar. Add the egg mixture and beat at medium speed until the dough is just moistened and very stiff. Add the butter a few cubes at a time, waiting until it is partially kneaded into the dough before adding more. Continue kneading until the butter is fully incorporated and the dough is silky, 8 to 10

minutes. Transfer the dough to an oiled bowl, cover with plastic wrap and refrigerate until chilled and slightly risen, at least 2 hours or overnight.

2. MAKE THE FILLING Preheat the oven to 350°. Spread the pecans in a pie plate and toast for about 8 minutes, until fragrant and browned. Let cool, then finely chop the pecans. Transfer to a medium bowl and stir in the brown sugar and cinnamon.

3. Line 2 baking sheets with parchment paper. On a floured surface, cut the dough into 2 pieces. Working with one piece at a time (while keeping the other refrigerated), roll the dough out to a 12-by-16-inch rectangle. Transfer the dough to a baking sheet and refrigerate until chilled. Repeat with the remaining dough.

4. Spread half of the sour cream over one sheet of dough, leaving a ½-inch border all around. Sprinkle with half of the pecan filling. Brush the long sides with some of the egg wash. Roll up the dough from a long side into a tight cylinder and pinch the ends to seal. Freeze the dough log until it is chilled, about 2 hours. Repeat with the remaining dough and filling. Cover and refrigerate the remaining egg wash.

5. Transfer the logs to a work surface and cut each one into 12 even slices. Set the slices on the baking sheet, cut side up. Cover with plastic wrap and freeze until firm, at least 3 hours and preferably overnight.

6. Unwrap the rolls and let stand at room temperature for 1 hour.

7. Preheat the oven to 350°. Brush the tops and sides of the rolls with the egg wash and bake in the center of the oven for 35 to 40 minutes, until golden and risen.

8. MEANWHILE, MAKE THE SUGAR GLAZE In a medium bowl, using an electric mixer, beat the confectioners' sugar with the butter, heavy cream and vanilla extract until thick and smooth. Spread the sugar glaze on the hot cinnamon rolls and let cool for about 20 minutes before serving.
—*Megan Garrelts*

MAKE AHEAD The unbaked cinnamon rolls and sugar glaze can be frozen separately for up to 1 month.

● HEALTHY ● MAKE AHEAD ○ VEGETARIAN ○ STAFF FAVORITE

apple crumb coffee cake

Raspberry-Swirl Sweet Rolls

ACTIVE: 30 MIN; TOTAL: 4 HR 30 MIN
MAKES 16 ROLLS ● ○ ○

DOUGH

1 cup milk
⅔ cup sugar
1½ tablespoons active dry yeast
1 stick unsalted butter, softened
2 large eggs
1 teaspoon finely grated lemon zest
½ teaspoon fine sea salt
4¼ cups all-purpose flour, plus more
   for dusting

FILLING

One 10-ounce package IQF
   (Individually Quick Frozen)
   raspberries (not thawed)
¼ cup plus 2 tablespoons sugar
1 teaspoon cornstarch

GLAZE

¾ cup confectioners' sugar
3 tablespoons unsalted butter, melted
1½ tablespoons heavy cream

1. MAKE THE DOUGH In a small saucepan, warm the milk over moderately low heat until it's 95°. Pour the warm milk into the bowl of a standing mixer fitted with the dough hook and stir in the sugar and yeast. Let stand until the yeast is foamy, 5 minutes. Add the softened butter, eggs, grated lemon zest and sea salt. Add the 4½ cups of flour and beat at medium speed until a soft dough forms, about 3 minutes. Increase the speed to medium-high and beat until the dough is soft and supple, about 10 minutes.

2. Scrape the dough out onto a lightly floured surface and knead it with your hands 2 or 3 times. Form the dough into a ball and transfer it to a lightly buttered bowl. Cover the dough with plastic wrap and let stand in a warm place until doubled in bulk, 1 to 2 hours.

3. Line the bottom of a 9-by-13-inch baking pan with parchment paper, allowing the paper to extend up the short sides. Butter the paper and sides of the pan. Turn the dough out onto a lightly floured work surface and, using a rolling pin, roll it into a 10-by-24-inch rectangle.

4. MAKE THE FILLING In a medium bowl, toss the frozen raspberries with the sugar and cornstarch. Spread the raspberry filling evenly over the dough. Tightly roll up the dough to form a 24-inch-long log. Working quickly, cut the log into quarters. Cut each quarter into 4 slices and arrange them in the baking pan, cut side up. Scrape any berries and juice from the work surface into the baking pan between the rolls. Cover the rolls and let them rise in a warm place until they are puffy and have filled the baking pan, about 2 hours.

5. Preheat the oven to 425°. Bake the rolls for about 25 minutes, until they are golden and the berries are bubbling. Transfer the pan to a rack to cool for 30 minutes.

6. MEANWHILE, MAKE THE GLAZE In a small bowl, whisk the confectioners' sugar with the butter and heavy cream until the glaze is thick and spreadable.

7. Invert the rolls onto the rack and peel off the parchment paper. Invert the rolls onto a platter. Dollop glaze over each roll and spread with an offset spatula. Serve warm or at room temperature.
—*Grace Parisi*

Sweet Potato Doughnuts

ACTIVE: 45 MIN; TOTAL: 3 HR 30 MIN
MAKES 2 DOZEN DOUGHNUTS ●

DOUGHNUTS

One 12-ounce sweet potato
3 tablespoons unsalted butter
½ cup whole milk
1 envelope instant dry yeast
½ cup granulated sugar
½ cup light brown sugar
1¼ teaspoons kosher salt
½ vanilla bean, seeds scraped
¼ teaspoon freshly ground nutmeg
1 tablespoon dark rum
1 large egg
2 large egg yolks
3¼ cups bread flour, plus more for rolling

TOPPING

1 cup granulated sugar
1 teaspoon cinnamon
4 tablespoons unsalted butter, melted

1. MAKE THE DOUGHNUTS Prick the sweet potato all over with a fork and cook it in a microwave at high power for 10 minutes, until tender. Let the sweet potato cool, then peel and puree; you should have about 1 cup.

2. In a small skillet, cook the butter over moderate heat until nutty and lightly browned, about 4 minutes. Scrape the browned butter and solids into a small bowl and let cool.

3. In the same skillet, heat the milk until just warm, about 105°. Pour the warm milk into the bowl of a standing mixer fitted with the dough hook. Add the yeast and let stand for 5 minutes. Gently mix in the granulated sugar, light brown sugar, salt, vanilla seeds, nutmeg and rum. Add the sweet potato puree, browned butter and solids, egg and egg yolks and beat until combined. Add the 3¼ cups of bread flour and beat at medium speed until the dough is evenly moistened, about 2 minutes. Increase the speed to moderately high and beat until a soft dough forms, about 5 minutes. Gather the dough into a ball and transfer to a buttered bowl. Cover and let the dough rise in a draft-free place for 1 hour.

4. Punch down the dough and let stand for 5 minutes. On a lightly floured surface, roll out the dough ½ inch thick. Using a 2¾-inch round cutter, stamp out as many rounds as possible. Using a smaller round cutter (1 inch), stamp out the centers. Transfer the doughnuts and holes to 2 parchment paper–lined baking sheets. Cover loosely with plastic wrap and let the doughnuts and holes rise in a warm place for 1 hour.

5. Preheat the oven to 400° and position racks in the upper and lower thirds. Bake the holes for 10 minutes and the doughnuts for about 20 minutes, until risen and golden.

6. MEANWHILE, MAKE THE TOPPING In a small bowl, combine the sugar and cinnamon. Put half of the hot doughnuts in a large bowl and drizzle with some of the melted butter; toss and turn to coat. Sprinkle with some of the cinnamon sugar and toss and turn until evenly coated. Repeat with the remaining doughnuts, butter and cinnamon sugar. Transfer the doughnuts to a platter; serve. —*Breanne Varela*

● HEALTHY   ● MAKE AHEAD   ○ VEGETARIAN   ● STAFF FAVORITE

raspberry-swirl sweet rolls

do-it-yourself doughnuts

Seattle's **Top Pot Doughnuts** has a cult following. Here, owners Mark and Michael Klebeck share their master recipe, along with three glazes and sugars.

make the doughnuts *According to writer Jess Thomson, who collaborated with the Seattle bakers on their book,* Top Pot Hand-Forged Doughnuts, *it's best to weigh flour on a kitchen scale instead of using measuring cups. "When we tested the recipes, that seemed to make a big difference."*

Vanilla Raised Doughnuts

ACTIVE: 1 HR; TOTAL: 3 HR 30 MIN
MAKES ABOUT 16 DOUGHNUTS OR
4 DOZEN DOUGHNUT HOLES ● ● ○

- 1 cup skim milk
- 1½ vanilla beans, split and seeds scraped
- ½ cup plus 1 tablespoon sugar
- Four ¼-ounce packages active dry yeast
- ¼ cup solid vegetable shortening
- 3 large egg yolks
- 2 teaspoons table salt
- ½ teaspoon baking powder
- ½ teaspoon ground mace
- 500 grams bread flour, sifted (3⅔ cups)
- Boiling water
- Vegetable oil, for frying

1. In a small saucepan, warm the milk, vanilla seeds and 1 tablespoon of the sugar over moderate heat until the temperature registers 105° on a candy thermometer. Transfer to the bowl of a standing electric mixer fitted with the dough hook. Add the yeast and let stand until foamy, about 5 minutes. Add the shortening, egg yolks and remaining ½ cup of sugar and beat at medium speed just until the shortening is broken up. Beat in the salt, baking powder and mace. At low speed, add the flour, 1 cup at a time, until the dough is firm but still tacky (you may need to add more or less flour to achieve the desired consistency).

2. Transfer the dough to a lightly floured work surface and knead a few times; pat it into a disk and transfer to a floured baking sheet. Dust with flour and cover with a towel. Place the baking sheet in the center of a turned-off oven. Set a large roasting pan on the bottom rack and fill it halfway with boiling water. Close the oven door and let the dough stand until doubled in bulk, about 1 hour.

3. Line 2 baking sheets with wax paper and dust with flour. Turn the dough out onto a floured work surface and roll out to a 12-inch round, ½ inch thick. For doughnuts, use a floured 2¾-inch doughnut cutter (or 2¾-inch and 1¼-inch cookie cutters) and stamp them out as close together as possible; alternatively, for doughnut holes, use a 1-inch cookie cutter. Transfer the doughnuts and/or holes to the baking sheets and return to the oven. Refill the roasting pan with boiling water and close the oven door. Let stand until the dough has doubled in bulk, 45 minutes.

4. Set a rack on a baking sheet and cover with paper towels. In a large saucepan, heat 2 inches of oil to 365°. Add 3 or 4 doughnuts at a time; adjust the heat to keep the oil between 350° and 360°. Fry the doughnuts until golden brown, 1 minute per side. If frying doughnut holes, cook them in batches of 12. Using a slotted spoon, transfer the doughnuts to the paper towels.

frying tip
Never drop the doughnuts flat into hot oil. "Insert them along their sides, like a coin into a slot, so that they don't splash," suggests Thomson.

for glazed doughnuts *Top Pot's bakers keep their extra-thick glazes just hot and thick enough to properly coat their doughnuts with one dip. The thinner home version at room temperature requires two dips. Each recipe makes enough for 16 doughnuts or 4 dozen doughnut holes.*

Rich Five-Spice Glaze
⏱ TOTAL: 5 MIN • MAKES 1½ CUPS ● ○

3½ cups confectioners' sugar
⅓ cup heavy cream
1½ teaspoons light corn syrup
¾ teaspoon Chinese five-spice powder
½ teaspoon pure vanilla extract
¼ teaspoon table salt
2 to 3 tablespoons hot water

In a medium bowl, mix all of the ingredients except the hot water. Using a handheld electric mixer, beat at low speed until smooth; add the hot water 1 tablespoon at a time until the glaze is thin enough for dipping. Use right away, or cover with plastic wrap and refrigerate for up to 1 week.

Kaffir Lime–Coconut Glaze
⏱ TOTAL: 20 MIN • MAKES 1½ CUPS ● ○

½ cup plus 2 tablespoons coconut milk
4 fresh kaffir lime leaves, twisted
3½ cups confectioners' sugar
1½ teaspoons light corn syrup
½ teaspoon pure vanilla extract
¼ teaspoon table salt

In a small saucepan, simmer the coconut milk and lime leaves for 2 minutes. Let cool slightly, then transfer the mixture to a bowl. Discard the lime leaves. Add the confectioners' sugar, corn syrup, vanilla and salt and beat at medium speed until smooth. Use the glaze right away or cover with plastic wrap and refrigerate for up to 1 week.

Tart Cranberry Glaze
⏱ TOTAL: 20 MIN • MAKES 1½ CUPS ● ○

1 cup fresh or frozen cranberries
2 tablespoons granulated sugar
¼ cup water
3½ cups confectioners' sugar
1½ teaspoons light corn syrup
½ teaspoon pure vanilla extract
¼ teaspoon table salt

In a small saucepan, combine the cranberries, granulated sugar and water and simmer, crushing the berries, until jammy, 8 minutes. Let cool slightly. Transfer to a bowl and add the confectioners' sugar, corn syrup, vanilla and salt. Using a handheld electric mixer, beat at medium speed until smooth. Use the glaze right away, or cover with plastic wrap and refrigerate for up to 1 week.

first dip While still warm, dip the doughnuts in the glaze to coat the tops; invert on a rack. Let stand.

second dip When the first coat is slightly hardened, dip doughnuts a second time; let glaze set again.

for sugared doughnuts *Flavored sugars are easy to make by blending herbs, dried fruits or spices with granulated sugar. Press doughnuts or roll doughnut holes in one of the flavored sugars below until they are coated.*

1. CRANBERRY SUGAR In a mini food processor, combine ¼ cup dried cranberries with ½ cup sugar and pulse until the sugar is pink and the cranberries are minced. Add another ½ cup sugar and pulse to combine.

2. MINT SUGAR In a mini food processor, pulse ½ cup tightly packed fresh mint leaves with ½ cup sugar until the sugar is bright green. Add another ½ cup sugar and, if desired, a few drops of peppermint oil and pulse to combine. Spread the sugar on a large plate and let dry at room temperature for 2 hours, stirring occasionally. Return the sugar to the food processor and pulse 2 or 3 times before using.

3. VANILLA SUGAR In a mini food processor, pulse 1 cup sugar with the seeds from ½ vanilla bean, just until the vanilla is evenly dispersed.

Sweet Breakfast Quinoa

🕐 **TOTAL: 25 MIN • 4 SERVINGS** ● ● ●

"This breakfast will make your day so productive," says Jill Donenfeld, founder of The Culinistas, a bicoastal private-chef service.

- 1 cup red quinoa, rinsed
- 2 cups water
- 1 tablespoon extra-virgin olive oil
- ¼ cup slivered almonds
- ½ cup dried apricots, cut into ½-inch pieces
- 2 tablespoons pure maple syrup
- ½ teaspoon finely grated orange zest
- ½ teaspoon cinnamon
- ¼ cup fresh ricotta cheese

1. In a small saucepan, cover the quinoa with the water and bring to a boil. Cover and cook over low heat until the water has been absorbed and the quinoa is tender, about 15 minutes. Lightly fluff the quinoa with a fork and cover it again.

2. In a medium skillet, heat the oil. Add the almonds and cook over moderate heat, stirring a few times, until golden brown, about 2 minutes. Add the apricots, maple syrup, orange zest and cinnamon and stir well until heated through.

3. Add the quinoa to the skillet and stir gently to incorporate the almonds and apricots. Transfer to bowls, top each portion with a tablespoon of ricotta and serve.
—*Jill Donenfeld*

MAKE AHEAD The breakfast quinoa can be made through Step 1 and refrigerated for up to 5 days. Reheat as needed or serve cold.

equipment tip

mini scoop A tablespoon-size scoop makes quick work of mini sundaes or small sweets like Elizabeth Falkner's Moroccan-Date Bonbons, at far right.

Incan Super-Power Bars

🕐 **TOTAL: 1 HR • MAKES 2 DOZEN 3½-BY-1-INCH BARS** ● ● ●

Most of the ingredients in these sticky, chewy, sweet-tart bars can be purchased in health-food stores (see also the online sources in the Super-Food Lexicon on page 330).

- 2 cups quinoa flakes (7 ounces)
- 1 cup sliced blanched almonds
- ½ cup salted roasted sunflower seeds (2½ ounces)
- ½ cup toasted wheat germ (2 ounces)
- 2 tablespoons chia seeds
- ¾ cup Incan berries, also known as golden berries and dried cape gooseberries (4 ounces), coarsely chopped
- ¾ cup tart dried cherries (4 ounces), coarsely chopped
- 4 tablespoons unsalted butter, plus more for greasing
- ½ cup plus 2 tablespoons light brown sugar
- ½ cup plus 2 tablespoons agave nectar
- 1½ teaspoons pure vanilla extract
- Scant ½ teaspoon salt

1. Preheat the oven to 350°. On a sturdy rimmed baking sheet, toss the quinoa with the almonds and toast for 20 minutes, until golden and fragrant. Transfer to a large bowl and stir in the sunflower seeds, wheat germ, chia seeds, Incan berries and cherries.

2. In a medium saucepan, combine the 4 tablespoons of butter with the brown sugar and agave nectar and bring to a boil. Cook over moderate heat, stirring, until the sugar is just dissolved, about 2 minutes. Stir in the vanilla and salt. Pour the mixture into the large bowl and stir until the dry ingredients are evenly coated.

3. Line the baking sheet with parchment paper and lightly butter the paper. Scrape the mixture onto the baking sheet and form into a 7-by-12-inch rectangle, pressing lightly to compact it; use a straight edge to evenly press the sides. Bake the bar for 10 minutes, until very lightly browned. Let cool slightly, then refrigerate until firm, 20 minutes.

4. Carefully invert the bar onto a work surface and peel off the paper. Cut the bar into twelve 1-inch-wide strips, then cut each strip in half to form twenty-four 3½-by-1-inch bars.
—*Grace Parisi*

Moroccan-Date Bonbons

🕐 **TOTAL: 30 MIN**

MAKES 30 BONBONS ● ● ● ●

San Francisco chef Elizabeth Falkner loves eating these energy-boosting, cardamom-spiced date bites made with almonds, walnuts and pistachios. "Eat two of these as a snack or with some juice for breakfast, and you're satisfied," she says.

- 2½ ounces sliced almonds (½ cup plus 2 tablespoons)
- ½ cup shelled pistachios (2 ounces)
- ¾ cup chopped walnuts (3 ounces)
- 1 pound moist pitted dates, chopped
- 4 pitted kalamata or dry-cured Moroccan olives, chopped
- ½ tablespoon finely grated fresh ginger
- ½ tablespoon honey
- ½ teaspoon finely grated orange zest
- ¼ teaspoon cinnamon
- ⅛ teaspoon ground cardamom
- ⅛ teaspoon orange flower water
- ⅛ teaspoon salt

1. Preheat the oven to 350° and spread the sliced almonds on a baking sheet, then toast for about 4 minutes, until golden. Let the almonds cool completely.

2. In a food processor, grind the pistachios to a coarse powder. Transfer to a plate. Add the toasted almonds to the processor and grind to a coarse powder. Add the walnuts, dates, olives, ginger, honey, orange zest, cinnamon, cardamom, orange flower water and salt and process to a paste.

3. Scoop up scant tablespoons of the date mixture and roll into balls. Roll the balls in the pistachio powder to coat them completely and serve. —*Elizabeth Falkner*

MAKE AHEAD The bonbons can be stored in an airtight container for up to 2 weeks.

● HEALTHY ● MAKE AHEAD ● VEGETARIAN ● STAFF FAVORITE

sweet breakfast quinoa

Apple Muesli with Goji Berries

TOTAL: 15 MIN PLUS OVERNIGHT CHILLING • MAKES 4 CUPS ● ● ○

"You can make this with any grain or fruit that goes with yogurt," says Malin Elmlid, a a Berlin-based baker who trades her home-made bread for artisanal ingredients. For her version of this cold cereal, she uses plain rolled grains, like oats or spelt, moistened with apples, coconut water and Greek yogurt. When a friend brought her a goji-berry tree to barter for bread, she added a few berries right from the branch.

  2 large apples, such as Granny Smith
  1 cup rolled oats, kamut or spelt
  3 tablespoons flax seeds
1¼ cups coconut water
1¼ cups plain 2 percent Greek yogurt
  ½ cup dried goji berries
  2 tablespoons fresh mint leaves, coarsely chopped
  3 tablespoons honey
Pinch of salt
Fresh berries, granola and chopped nuts, for garnish (optional)

1. Using a box grater set over a bowl, coarsely grate the apples; stop when you reach the core. Add the oats, flax seeds, coconut water, yogurt, goji berries and mint and stir until combined. Cover and refrigerate overnight.

super-food lexicon

açai This nutritious Amazonian berry is great pureed, as in the açai smoothie at right. *sambazon.com.*

chia seeds Ultra-marathoners swear by this omega 3–dense desert plant seed. *livingfuel.com.*

incan berries Packed with vitamins A and C and iron, this sweet-tart Andean fruit gives the Incan Super-Power Bars (page 328) a nice raisiny texture. *sunfood.com.*

2. Mix the honey and salt into the muesli and spoon into bowls. Garnish with berries, granola and nuts and serve. —*Malin Elmlid*

Steel-Cut Oatmeal with Soy Milk

ACTIVE: 5 MIN; TOTAL: 40 MIN
4 SERVINGS ● ● ●

Art Smith of Art and Soul in Washington, DC, swears by steel-cut oatmeal, which has an appealing chewy texture.

  2 cups water
  2 cups soy milk or skim milk
  1 cup steel-cut oats
  1 cup fresh berries
  1 cup plain fat-free Greek yogurt
  ¼ cup sliced raw almonds

In a medium saucepan, bring the water and soy milk to a boil. Add the oats, cover and simmer over low heat for about 30 minutes, until the oats are tender. Uncover and cook over moderate heat, stirring, until the oatmeal is creamy, about 3 minutes. Spoon the oatmeal into bowls and top with the berries, yogurt and almonds. —*Art Smith*

MAKE AHEAD The oatmeal can be refrigerated for up to 5 days. Reheat gently.

Açai Super Smoothie

TOTAL: 5 MIN
MAKES 2 LARGE DRINKS ● ○

Brazilian surfers first popularized açai, a freakishly nutritious berry. Now it has gone mainstream. This smoothie boosts açai's healthfulness with pomegranate juice.

One 3.5-ounce package frozen unsweetened açai puree
  2 bananas
  1 cup frozen raspberries
  1 cup pomegranate juice
  1 tablespoon agave nectar

In a blender, combine the frozen açai puree with the bananas, frozen raspberries, pomegranate juice and agave nectar and blend at high speed until smooth. Serve right away. —*Grace Parisi*

Three-Grain Cereal with Dates and Cinnamon

ACTIVE: 15 MIN; TOTAL: 40 MIN
4 SERVINGS ● ●

Quinn Hatfield, a competitive cyclist and the chef at Hatfield's in Los Angeles, takes a make-ahead approach when it comes to fueling his workouts. He cooks big batches of pearled barley and quinoa to keep in his refrigerator for this hot cereal, which comes together in minutes. The mixture of cinnamon and chopped dates makes this breakfast nicely sweet—no extra sugar needed.

  ⅓ cup pearled barley
  ¼ cup quinoa
Kosher salt
  6 ounces Medjool dates (about 8 dates with pits)
  1 cup quick-cooking rolled oats
Pinch of cinnamon

1. In a medium saucepan of boiling salted water, cook the pearled barley over moderate heat for about 30 minutes, until tender. Drain the barley in a colander and shake off all of the excess water.

2. Meanwhile, in a small saucepan, combine the quinoa, ½ cup of water and a pinch of salt and bring to a boil. Cover and simmer over low heat until the water is absorbed, about 15 minutes.

3. In a small, heatproof bowl, cover the dates with boiling water and let stand for 1 minute. Drain the dates in a colander and let them cool. Peel and pit the dates and chop them into ½-inch pieces.

4. In another medium saucepan, bring 2 cups of water to a boil. Add the oats and a pinch of salt and cook over moderate heat for 4 minutes, stirring constantly. Add the cooked barley and quinoa, cinnamon and half of the chopped dates and cook, stirring, until thickened, about 3 minutes. Spoon the cereal into bowls, sprinkle with the remaining dates and serve. —*Quinn Hatfield*

SERVE WITH Blueberries or walnuts.

MAKE AHEAD The cooked barley and cooked quinoa can be refrigerated in separate containers for up to 5 days.

● HEALTHY ● MAKE AHEAD ○ VEGETARIAN ● STAFF FAVORITE

apple muesli with goji berries

A Thanksgiving meal hosted by chef Michael Symon ends with a light, not-too-sweet apple brown Betty baked with brioche crumbs, OPPOSITE; *recipe, page 336.*

tarts, pies and fruit desserts

Country Apple Galette

ACTIVE: 30 MIN; TOTAL: 1 HR 30 MIN
PLUS COOLING • 8 SERVINGS ● ● ●

Master chef Jacques Pépin loves to serve this delicate apple tart as a buffet dessert because it's beautiful, easy to slice and simple to eat, pizza-style, while standing. The miraculously fast and versatile pastry dough comes together in a food processor in less than 20 seconds and can be filled with all sorts of fruits or vegetables. Because the tart is free-form, the pastry can be rolled into either a round or a rectangle.

PASTRY

1½ cups all-purpose flour
1½ teaspoons sugar
¼ teaspoon salt
1 stick plus 2 tablespoons
   cold unsalted butter,
   cut into small pieces
⅓ cup ice water

TOPPING

4 Golden Delicious apples
2 tablespoons sugar
½ teaspoon cinnamon
1 tablespoon honey,
   preferably wildflower
1 tablespoon unsalted butter,
   cut into small pieces

1. MAKE THE PASTRY In a food processor, combine the flour with the sugar, salt and butter and process for about 5 seconds. Sprinkle the ice water over the flour mixture and process until the pastry just begins to come together, about 10 seconds; you should still be able to see small pieces of butter in it. Transfer the pastry to a work surface, gather it together and pat into a disk. Wrap the pastry in plastic or wax paper and refrigerate until chilled. (You can also roll out the pastry and use it right away.)

2. MAKE THE TOPPING Peel, halve and core the apples and slice them crosswise ¼ inch thick. Set aside the larger center slices and coarsely chop the end slices and any broken ones; about half of the slices should be chopped. In a small bowl, combine the sugar with the cinnamon.

3. Preheat the oven to 400°. On a lightly floured work surface, roll out the pastry to a 12-by-14-inch rectangle and transfer to a large rimmed baking sheet. Spread the chopped apples over the pastry to within 1 inch of the edge. Drizzle the honey over the chopped apples. Decoratively arrange the apple slices on top in concentric circles or in slightly overlapping rows. Sprinkle the cinnamon sugar over the apples and dot with the pieces of butter. Fold the pastry edge up and over the apples to create a 1-inch border.
4. Bake the galette for about 1 hour, until the pastry is nicely browned and crisp and all of the apples are tender. Transfer the pan to a rack and let the galette cool. Serve warm or at room temperature. —*Jacques Pépin*
MAKE AHEAD The buttery pastry can be refrigerated overnight.

Old-Fashioned Apple Pie

ACTIVE: 1 HR; TOTAL: 2 HR 30 MIN PLUS
2 HR COOLING • 8 SERVINGS ● ●

AJ Perry, the owner and baker at Sassafras Bakery in Columbus, Ohio, uses a combination of sweet and tart apples for this double-crust pie. Perry starts the pie at a high oven temperature so the pastry sets before the filling softens, creating a gorgeous domed and lightly browned crust. This is a purist's pie that tastes of nothing but apples, with just a hint of spice and butter.

CRUST

2½ cups all-purpose flour,
   plus more for rolling
1 teaspoon salt
2 sticks unsalted butter, cut into
   ½-inch dice and chilled
¼ cup ice water

FILLING

3 pounds apples, such as Pink
   Lady, Golden Delicious, Cortland
   or Jonathan—peeled, cored and
   sliced ¼ inch thick
1 cup granulated sugar
⅓ cup all-purpose flour
½ teaspoon cinnamon
¼ teaspoon freshly grated nutmeg

2 tablespoons fresh lemon juice
2 tablespoons unsalted butter,
   cut into small dice
1 large egg, beaten
2 tablespoons turbinado sugar,
   for sprinkling

1. MAKE THE CRUST In a food processor, combine the 2½ cups of flour and the salt. Add the butter and pulse in 1-second bursts until the mixture resembles coarse meal. Drizzle the ice water over the dough and pulse in 1-second bursts until it just comes together. Turn the dough out onto a work surface, gather any crumbs and pat it into 2 disks. Wrap the disks in plastic and refrigerate until chilled, about 30 minutes.
2. Preheat the oven to 425°. On a floured work surface, roll out 1 disk of the dough to a 12-inch round, a scant ¼ inch thick. Gently ease the dough into a 9- to 10-inch deep-dish glass pie plate. Roll out the second disk of dough to a 12-inch round. Transfer to a wax paper–lined baking sheet and refrigerate.
3. MAKE THE FILLING In a bowl, combine the apples with the granulated sugar, flour, cinnamon, nutmeg and salt. Add the lemon juice and toss well. Let stand for 10 minutes, until the sugar dissolves slightly.
4. Scrape the apple filling and any juices into the pie plate and dot with the butter. Cover with the top crust and gently press the edges together. Trim the overhanging dough to about 1 inch and pinch to seal. Fold the dough rim under itself and crimp it decoratively. Brush the pie with the beaten egg and sprinkle with the turbinado sugar. Cut 3 small gashes in the top of the pie to vent the steam.
5. Bake the pie on the lowest shelf of the oven for 30 minutes. Lower the oven temperature to 365° and bake the pie for 45 to 50 minutes longer, until the fruit juices are bubbling through the steam vents and the crust is deeply golden on the top and bottom; cover the pie loosely with foil halfway through baking to keep it from getting too dark. Transfer the pie to a rack and let cool for at least 2 hours before serving. —*AJ Perry*
MAKE AHEAD The cooled pie can be refriger-

Apple Pie Sundaes with Cheddar Crust Shards

ACTIVE: 50 MIN; TOTAL: 2 HR
8 SERVINGS ● ● ●

Using a slightly tart apple, like a Pink Lady or Granny Smith, is key to this apple pie–frozen yogurt sundae from pastry chef Breanne Varela of L.A.'s Tavern and the Larder at Tavern; sautéing the apples brings out their sweetness. The crispy, salty cheddar crisps that accompany the sundaes are as good with cocktails as they are with desserts.

CHEDDAR SHARDS
¾ cup all-purpose flour
Kosher salt
4 tablespoons cold unsalted butter
½ cup shredded sharp cheddar cheese
2½ tablespoons cold water
¼ teaspoon cider vinegar
SUNDAE
6 tablespoons unsalted butter
6 large apples, such as Pink Lady or Granny Smith—cored, peeled and thinly sliced
¼ cup plus 2 tablespoons granulated sugar
¼ cup plus 2 tablespoons light brown sugar
½ teaspoon cinnamon
⅛ teaspoon freshly grated nutmeg
Kosher salt
2 pints vanilla frozen yogurt

ingredient tip

cinnamon Often used in baked goods like these apple desserts, it can also be blended with cumin and coriander to make an exotic spice rub for meats.

1. MAKE THE CHEDDAR SHARDS Preheat the oven to 350°. In a food processor, combine the flour with ¼ teaspoon of kosher salt. Coarsely grate the butter into the food processor. Pulse until the mixture resembles coarse meal. Add the shredded cheddar cheese and pulse twice. Add the cold water and cider vinegar and pulse just until the dough is evenly moistened. Turn the dough out onto a work surface and knead until it just comes together. Wrap the dough in plastic and keep in the refrigerator for at least 20 minutes or until chilled.

2. Line a baking sheet with parchment paper. On a lightly floured surface, roll out the chilled dough to a 9-inch square and transfer to the prepared baking sheet. Bake for about 40 minutes, until golden. Let the cheddar crust cool.

3. MEANWHILE, PREPARE THE SUNDAE In a large skillet, melt the butter. Add the apples and toss to coat. Add the granulated sugar, light brown sugar, cinnamon and nutmeg and season lightly with salt. Cook the apples over moderately high heat, stirring them frequently, until they are tender and translucent, about 15 minutes.

4. Add ½ cup of water to the skillet and bring to a boil. Remove from the heat. Transfer half of the apples to a blender or food processor and puree until smooth. Scrape the puree into a bowl and freeze until it is cold, about 30 minutes.

5. Soften the frozen yogurt slightly and transfer it to a large bowl. Fold in the cold apple puree and freeze until the frozen yogurt is firm, about 30 minutes.

6. Scoop the frozen yogurt into 8 serving bowls and top with the sautéed apples. Break the cheddar crust into large shards and serve with the sundaes.
—Breanne Varela

MAKE AHEAD The vanilla-apple yogurt from Step 5 can be frozen for up to 3 days. The sautéed apples can be refrigerated for up to 3 days; bring the fruit to room temperature before assembling the sundaes. The cheddar crust can be stored in an airtight container for up to 3 days. Recrisp in a warm oven before proceeding with Step 6.

Apple Brown Betty
📷 PAGE 333

ACTIVE: 30 MIN; TOTAL: 1 HR 30 MIN
PLUS COOLING • 10 SERVINGS ● ● ●

Chef Michael Symon's version of this classic dessert is great after a big meal because it isn't too sweet or too heavy.

6 cups cubed brioche or challah bread
1½ cups sugar
½ teaspoon freshly grated nutmeg
½ teaspoon cinnamon
1 teaspoon finely grated lemon zest
1 teaspoon finely grated orange zest
Pinch of salt
4 pounds Granny Smith apples, peeled, cored and thinly sliced
½ cup apple cider
2 tablespoons fresh lemon juice
2 tablespoons fresh orange juice
3 tablespoons cold unsalted butter
Vanilla ice cream or whipped cream, for serving

1. Preheat the oven to 350°. Spread the brioche on a baking sheet and toast until dry, about 8 minutes. Let cool, then pulse the bread into coarse crumbs in a food processor. Spread one-third of the crumbs in a buttered 9-by-13-inch baking dish in an even layer.

2. In a small bowl, combine the sugar with the nutmeg, cinnamon, lemon zest, orange zest and salt. Spread half of the apples over the crumbs in the baking dish and top with half of the sugar mixture. In another bowl, mix the cider with the lemon and orange juices; drizzle over the apples. Cover with another third of the crumbs and the remaining apples and sugar mixture. Cover with the remaining crumbs. Using a sharp knife, shave the butter as thinly as possible; dot it all over the top.

3. Bake the apple Betty in the center of the oven for about 1 hour, until the apples are tender and the juices are bubbling; cover the baking dish during the last 15 minutes to prevent the crumbs from getting too dark. Let cool for 30 minutes; serve with ice cream or whipped cream. *—Michael Symon*

MAKE AHEAD The dessert can be kept at room temperature overnight and reheated.

● HEALTHY ● MAKE AHEAD ● VEGETARIAN ● STAFF FAVORITE

apple pie sundae with cheddar crust shard

Apple Cider Cream Pie

ACTIVE: 45 MIN; TOTAL: 2 HR 15 MIN
PLUS COOLING • 8 SERVINGS ● ● ●

In 2009, Allison Kave and her boyfriend, Jay Horton, were winners in Brooklyn, New York's Pie Bake-Off with this clever pie. The challenge was to use a local ingredient, so they chose apple cider and developed this delicious combination of cream pie and apple pie. Winning the contest was the impetus for Kave to open First Prize Pies in Brooklyn.

CRUST

- 1 cup all-purpose flour, plus more for dusting
- 1 tablespoon cornstarch
- 1 tablespoon sugar
- 1 teaspoon kosher salt
- 1 stick unsalted butter, cut into ½-inch dice and chilled
- 3 tablespoons cold milk
- 1 teaspoon apple cider vinegar

FILLING AND TOPPING

- 2 cups apple cider
- 1 cup sugar
- ½ cup sour cream
- ¼ teaspoon salt
- 4 large eggs
- 1 cup heavy cream
- ½ teaspoon cinnamon

equipment tip

mixing bowls Trudeau's sturdy melamine mixing bowls have pour spouts and no-slip bottoms. They're perfect for whisking, whipping and pouring fillings like the custard in Allison Kave's prize-winning Apple Cider Cream Pie, above. *$17; cheftools.com.*

1. MAKE THE CRUST In a food processor, combine the 1 cup of flour with the cornstarch, sugar and salt. Add the butter and pulse in 1-second bursts until the mixture resembles coarse meal. Combine the milk and apple cider vinegar and drizzle it on top. Pulse in 1-second bursts until the dough just comes together. Turn the dough out onto a work surface, gather up any crumbs and pat into a disk. Wrap the dough in plastic and refrigerate until chilled, about 30 minutes.
2. On a floured work surface, roll out the dough to an 11-inch round, a scant ¼ inch thick; ease the dough into a 9-inch glass or ceramic pie plate. Trim the overhanging dough to 1 inch and fold it under itself. Crimp decoratively and refrigerate the crust until firm, about 15 minutes.
3. Preheat the oven to 425°. Line the crust with parchment paper and fill with pie weights or dried beans. Bake in the lower third of the oven for about 15 minutes, until the crust is barely set. Remove the parchment and pie weights. Cover the edge of the crust with strips of foil and bake for about 15 minutes longer, until the crust is just set but not browned. Press the bottom of the crust lightly to deflate it as it puffs; let cool. Lower the oven temperature to 350°.
4. MEANWHILE, MAKE THE FILLING AND TOPPING In a medium saucepan, boil the cider until it's reduced to ½ cup, about 10 minutes. Transfer to a bowl and let cool. Whisk in ¾ cup of the sugar, the sour cream and salt, then whisk in the eggs.
5. Pour the custard into the pie shell without removing the foil strips. Bake the pie in the lower third of the oven for 35 to 40 minutes, until the custard is set around the edge but the center is slightly jiggly. Let the pie cool completely.
6. In a medium bowl, using an electric mixer, beat the heavy cream with the remaining ¼ cup of sugar and the cinnamon until firmly whipped. Mound the whipped cream on the pie, cut into wedges and serve.
—*Allison Kave*

SERVE WITH Baked apple slices.

MAKE AHEAD The recipe can be prepared through Step 5 and refrigerated for 2 days.

Toasts with Ricotta and Warm Balsamic-Caramel Apples

TOTAL: 30 MIN • 6 SERVINGS ●

Chef April Bloomfield, of The Breslin, the Spotted Pig and John Dory restaurants in New York City, loves to combine hot and cold ingredients, as in her chilled ricotta served over warm apples. F&W's Grace Parisi created this amazingly fast version based on Bloomfield's dessert.

- Six ¾-inch-thick slices of white bakery bread or *pain de mie*
- 4 tablespoons unsalted butter, softened
- 1½ pounds Granny Smith apples (3 large)—peeled, cored and cut into thin wedges
- ¾ cup sugar
- 2 tablespoons balsamic vinegar
- ¼ cup plus 2 tablespoons water
- ¾ cup chilled ricotta cheese
- 2 tablespoons chopped marcona almonds

1. Preheat the broiler. Brush the bread with 1½ tablespoons of the softened butter. Broil the bread 4 inches from the heat for about 1 minute, turning once, until browned. Transfer the toasts to plates.
2. In a large skillet, melt the remaining 2½ tablespoons of butter. Add the apple wedges and cook over moderately high heat, stirring occasionally, until they are browned in spots, about 5 minutes. Add the sugar and cook the apples over moderate heat, stirring occasionally, until caramelized, 2 to 3 minutes. Add the balsamic vinegar and water and bring to a boil. Simmer over low heat until the apples are tender and the sauce is syrupy, about 4 minutes longer.
3. Using a slotted spoon, spoon the apples over the toasts and dollop the ricotta cheese on top. Drizzle with the balsamic-caramel syrup and sprinkle with the almonds. Cut each toast in half and serve right away.
—*Grace Parisi*

MAKE AHEAD The caramelized apples can be refrigerated overnight. Reheat gently, adding a tablespoon of water if necessary.

● HEALTHY ● MAKE AHEAD ● VEGETARIAN ● STAFF FAVORITE

apple cider cream pie

Apple Crisp with Dried Cranberries

ACTIVE: 30 MIN; TOTAL: 1 HR 25 MIN
PLUS COOLING • 10 SERVINGS ● ●

For this rustic dessert, chef Lee Woolver of the American Hotel in Sharon Springs, New York, recommends a tart apple, like the Northern Spy. To make the recipe more decadent, he often adds chocolate chips.

TOPPING

- 1 cup all-purpose flour
- 1 teaspoon cinnamon
- 1½ sticks unsalted butter, cut into small pieces
- 1 cup rolled oats
- ¼ cup packed light brown sugar
- 2 tablespoons granulated sugar
- ½ teaspoon salt

FILLING

- 8 medium Northern Spy or Granny Smith apples—peeled, cored and cut into ½-inch wedges
- ¼ cup sugar
- 2 tablespoons fresh lemon juice
- 1 cup dried cranberries
- ½ cup unsweetened apple juice
- 4 tablespoons unsalted butter, melted

1. MAKE THE TOPPING Preheat the oven to 350°. In a medium bowl, whisk the flour with the cinnamon. Cut in the butter with a pastry blender or your fingers until the mixture resembles coarse meal. Stir in the oats, brown and granulated sugars and salt.

2. MAKE THE FILLING In a large bowl, toss the apples with the sugar and lemon juice. Add the dried cranberries, apple juice and melted butter and toss again. Spread the filling in a 9-by-13-inch baking dish.

3. Sprinkle the topping evenly over the apples. Bake in the upper third of the oven until the topping is golden brown and the filling is bubbling, about 55 minutes. Let the crisp cool slightly and serve. —*Lee Woolver*

SERVE WITH Unsweetened whipped cream or vanilla ice cream.

MAKE AHEAD The crisp can stand at room temperature for several hours. Serve at room temperature or rewarm in a 350° oven.

Skillet-Baked Pear and Apple Crisp

ACTIVE: 30 MIN; TOTAL: 1 HR 30 MIN
PLUS COOLING • 6 TO 8 SERVINGS ● ●

In the fall, James Boyce, the chef at Cotton Row in Huntsville, Alabama, picks the apples and pears for this cinnamon-spiced crisp from trees right behind the restaurant. With Kentucky bourbon country only five hours north, he occasionally swaps out the Cognac in the filling here for bourbon.

TOPPING

- 1 cup light brown sugar
- 1 cup all-purpose flour
- ¼ cup pecans
- 2 teaspoons cinnamon
- 1 stick unsalted butter, cut into cubes

FILLING

- 1½ pounds Granny Smith apples— peeled, cored and thinly sliced
- 1½ pounds firm Bartlett pears— peeled, cored and thinly sliced
- ¾ cup dried currants
- ¼ cup light brown sugar
- 2 teaspoons cinnamon
- ¼ teaspoon ground cardamom
- ¼ cup honey
- 2 tablespoons Cognac

Vanilla ice cream, for serving

1. Preheat the oven to 350° and butter a 12-inch cast-iron skillet.

2. MAKE THE TOPPING In a food processor, combine the light brown sugar with the flour, pecans and cinnamon. Add the cubes of butter and pulse until the mixture is fine. Transfer the cinnamon-pecan topping to a bowl and press into clumps.

3. MAKE THE FILLING In a large bowl, combine the apples and pears with the currants, sugar, cinnamon, cardamom, honey and Cognac and stir until the sugar is dissolved. Spread the fruit in the skillet and scatter the topping over the fruit.

4. Bake the crisp in the center of the oven for about 1 hour, until the fruit is bubbling and the topping is browned. Let cool for 20 minutes before serving with ice cream. —*James Boyce*

Pear and Fig Pie-in-a-Jar

ACTIVE: 1 HR; TOTAL: 3 HR
MAKES 8 PIES ● ● ●

Three Babes Bakeshop in San Francisco offers this fun, portable pie: The pastry is baked in a half-pint jar, then filled with fig-and-pear syrup, honey-maple mascarpone cream, fruit and toasted walnuts.

PASTRY

- 2 cups all-purpose flour, plus more for dusting
- 2 teaspoons sugar
- ½ teaspoon salt
- 2 sticks unsalted butter, cut into ½-inch dice and chilled
- ¼ cup plus 3 tablespoons ice water
- 1 tablespoon apple cider vinegar

FILLING

- 1 cup dried Black Mission figs, stemmed and quartered
- 1 pound Bosc pears—peeled, cored and cut into ½-inch dice (2 cups), plus 8 pear slices for garnish
- 2½ cups apple cider
- 1 cup pear eau-de-vie
- ¼ cup honey

Two 1-inch-wide strips of lemon zest
- ¼ cup fresh lemon juice
- ¼ teaspoon cinnamon
- ⅛ teaspoon ground cloves
- ⅛ teaspoon ground allspice

Pinch of salt
- ½ cup walnuts

MASCARPONE CREAM

- 1 cup mascarpone
- ½ cup crème fraîche
- 2½ tablespoons honey
- 2½ tablespoons maple syrup
- 3 tablespoons fresh lemon juice
- 2 teaspoons pure vanilla extract

Pinch of salt

1. MAKE THE PASTRY In a food processor, combine the 2½ cups of flour with the sugar and salt. Add the diced butter and pulse in 1-second bursts until the mixture resembles coarse meal. Combine the ice water and apple cider vinegar and drizzle it on top.

● HEALTHY ● MAKE AHEAD ● VEGETARIAN ● STAFF FAVORITE

Pulse in 1-second bursts until the dough just comes together. Turn the dough out onto a work surface, gather up any crumbs and pat into 2 disks. Wrap the dough in plastic and refrigerate until chilled, about 30 minutes.

2. On a floured work surface, roll out 1 disk of the dough to a 12-inch square. Cut the square into quarters and gently ease each piece of dough into a wide-mouth ½-pint jar. Repeat with the remaining dough. Refrigerate until chilled, about 15 minutes.

3. Preheat the oven to 350°. Set the jars on a sturdy baking sheet and line each crust with foil, pressing it to the edges. Fill with pie weights or dried beans and bake for 20 minutes. Remove the foil and weights. Press out any bubbles and bake the crusts for about 30 minutes longer, until golden brown and cooked through. Let cool.

4. MEANWHILE, MAKE THE FILLING In a large saucepan, combine the quartered figs, diced pears, apple cider, eau-de-vie, honey, lemon zest, lemon juice, cinnamon, cloves, allspice and salt and bring to a boil. Simmer over moderately low heat until the figs are plumped and the pears are tender, about 20 minutes. Strain the poaching liquid into a heatproof bowl. Discard the lemon zest. Set the fruit aside. Return the liquid to the saucepan and boil until it is reduced to a thick syrup, about 12 minutes.

5. Spread the walnuts in a pie plate and toast for about 7 minutes, until fragrant. Let cool, then coarsely chop the nuts.

6. MAKE THE MASCARPONE CREAM In a bowl, whisk the mascarpone with the crème fraîche, honey, maple syrup, lemon juice, vanilla and salt.

7. ASSEMBLE THE PIES Drizzle half of the pear-fig syrup into the pie crusts. Top with half of the mascarpone cream followed by all of the fruit and the remaining cream. Garnish the pie with the pear slices, walnuts and the remaining syrup and serve. —*Anna Derivi-Castellanos*

MAKE AHEAD The pie crusts, fruit filling, fig-and-pear syrup and mascarpone cream can be refrigerated in separate airtight containers for up to 2 days. Recrisp the crusts before assembling the pies (Step 7).

Kaiserschmarrn with Peaches

⏲ **TOTAL: 30 MIN • 6 SERVINGS** ● ●

Kaiserschmarrn, a light Austrian pancake, can be eaten for dessert or breakfast.

- 4 tablespoons unsalted butter
- 3 firm, ripe medium peaches—peeled, quartered and sliced ¼ inch thick
- ¼ cup granulated sugar
- 1 tablespoon fresh lemon juice
- 1 cup all-purpose flour
- 1 cup milk
- 4 large eggs, separated
- 1 teaspoon finely grated lemon zest
- Pinch of salt
- ⅓ cup confectioners' sugar, plus more for dusting
- 1 pint blackberries

1. In a 12-inch nonstick skillet, melt ½ tablespoon of the butter. Add the peaches, 1 tablespoon of the granulated sugar and the lemon juice and cook over high heat, stirring occasionally, until the peaches are tender and lightly browned, about 5 minutes. Transfer the peaches to a plate and clean the skillet.

2. In a large bowl, whisk the flour, milk, egg yolks, zest and 2 tablespoons of the granulated sugar until smooth. In another bowl, beat the egg whites and salt with an electric mixer until soft peaks form. Beat in the remaining 1 tablespoon of granulated sugar until the whites are glossy. Fold the whites into the batter until no streaks remain.

3. In the skillet, melt 1 tablespoon of the butter. Add the batter, cover and cook over low heat until the bottom is golden and the top begins to set, 4 to 5 minutes. Slide onto a large plate. Carefully invert the skillet over the pancake. Using oven mitts, flip the skillet and the plate to return the pancake to the pan. Cook until the underside of the pancake is set and lightly browned, about 2 minutes.

4. Using a wooden or heatproof plastic spatula, cut the pancake in the skillet into 2-inch squares. Dot with the remaining 2½ tablespoons of butter, sprinkle with the ⅓ cup of confectioners' sugar and top with the peaches. Cook, tossing, until the pancake is caramelized, 5 minutes. Add the berries and toss until heated through, 1 minute. Transfer to a platter, sprinkle with confectioners' sugar and serve. —*Grace Parisi*

Peach Streusel Cake

ACTIVE: 20 MIN; TOTAL: 2 HR PLUS COOLING • 10 SERVINGS ● ●

STREUSEL
- ½ cup all-purpose flour
- ¼ cup packed light brown sugar
- ¼ teaspoon salt
- 3 tablespoons unsalted butter, softened
- 1 cup chopped toasted pecans

BATTER
- 2 cups all-purpose flour
- 1 teaspoon baking powder
- 1 teaspoon baking soda
- ½ teaspoon salt
- 1 stick unsalted butter, softened
- 1 cup sugar
- 2 large eggs
- 1 cup sour cream
- 2 teaspoons vanilla extract
- One 10-ounce bag frozen peaches, coarsely chopped

1. Preheat the oven to 325° and butter and flour a 9-inch springform pan.

2. MAKE THE STREUSEL In a bowl, using your fingers, combine the flour, brown sugar and salt. Add the butter and mix until smooth. Add the pecans; press the mixture into clumps.

3. MAKE THE BATTER In a bowl, whisk the flour, baking powder, baking soda and salt. In a large bowl, beat the butter and sugar at medium-high speed until light, 3 minutes. Beat in the eggs 1 at a time; beat in the sour cream and vanilla. Add the dry ingredients and beat at low speed until incorporated.

4. Spread two-thirds of the batter in the pan. Fold the peaches into the remaining batter; spoon into the pan. Scatter the streusel on top. Bake for 1 hour and 30 minutes, or until a toothpick inserted in the center comes out clean; loosely cover with foil for the last 15 minutes of baking. Transfer to a rack, cool for 30 minutes, then remove the ring and let cool completely before serving. —*Grace Parisi*

Raspberry-Glazed Peaches with Mascarpone

TOTAL: 40 MIN • 6 SERVINGS ● ●

These peaches are not only a great dessert, but also a delicious breakfast when served with yogurt and granola.

- 6 firm, ripe medium peaches, peeled and halved
- 2 tablespoons unsalted butter, melted
- 2 tablespoons sugar
- 1 pint raspberries
- ¼ cup raspberry preserves

Mascarpone and crushed amaretti, for serving

1. Preheat the oven to 425°. Butter a large glass or ceramic baking dish. In a bowl, toss the peaches with the butter and sugar, then arrange in the dish cut side down. Bake in the upper third of the oven for about 15 minutes, turning once, until just tender.
2. Meanwhile, in a saucepan, bring the raspberries, preserves and 2 tablespoons of water to a boil. Strain the glaze into a small bowl.
3. Spoon the glaze over the peaches and bake for 15 minutes longer, turning once and basting, until tender; transfer to bowls and top with a dollop of mascarpone. Spoon the juices on top, garnish with amaretti and serve. —*Grace Parisi*

Creamy Peach Tart with Smoky Almond Crust

ACTIVE: 20 MIN; TOTAL: 1 HR
8 SERVINGS ● ●

An almost-instant crust, made with vanilla wafer cookies and smoked almonds, is the secret to this simple and unusual tart.

- 2 cups vanilla wafer cookies, such as Nilla Wafers (5 ounces)
- ½ cup smoked almonds
- ¼ cup plus 2 tablespoons sugar
- 4 tablespoons unsalted butter, melted
- 8 ounces cream cheese, softened
- ¼ cup sour cream
- 1 egg
- 2 firm, ripe medium peaches, peeled and cut into thin wedges

1. Preheat the oven to 350°. In a food processor, combine the vanilla wafers with the almonds and 2 tablespoons of the sugar and process until fine. Add the melted butter and pulse until the crumbs are evenly moistened. Press the crumbs into the bottom and ½ inch up the side of a 9-inch springform pan. Bake for 10 minutes, until the crust is set.
2. Meanwhile, wipe out the food processor bowl. Add the cream cheese, sour cream, egg and 2 tablespoons of the sugar and process until smooth. Pour the custard into the crust and bake for 15 minutes, until set. Let the tart cool slightly and transfer to the freezer to chill, about 15 minutes.
3. In a bowl, toss the peaches with the remaining 2 tablespoons of sugar. Arrange the peaches in 2 concentric circles over the custard. Remove the ring, cut the tart into wedges and serve. —*Grace Parisi*

Honey-Roasted Apricots with Amaretti Cookies

ACTIVE: 10 MIN; TOTAL: 40 MIN
4 SERVINGS ● ●

Cookbook author and nutritionist Jessica Theroux drizzles apricots with honey before roasting (plums and peaches work well, too) and makes a crispy topping with crumbles of store-bought amaretti, Italian cookies made with egg whites and almond flour.

- 1 pound apricots, halved and pitted
- 1 tablespoon honey, heated
- ¼ teaspoon sugar

Pinch of ground cardamom
- ½ cup crushed amaretti cookies
- 2 tablespoons chilled heavy cream

1. Preheat the oven to 350°. Line a rimmed baking sheet with parchment paper. Arrange the apricots on the baking sheet, cut side up. Drizzle the honey on top and sprinkle with the sugar, cardamom and crushed cookies. Bake for 30 minutes, until softened and lightly browned.
2. In a bowl, whisk the cream until soft peaks barely form. Transfer the apricots to plates, spoon the cream on top and serve. —*Jessica Theroux*

Nectarine-Buttermilk Pops

ACTIVE: 45 MIN; TOTAL: 3 HR PLUS
4 HR FREEZING • MAKES 8 POPS ● ● ● ●

This sophisticated revamp of the Creamsicle, a childhood favorite, layers fresh nectarine puree with icy buttermilk. The little bit of ginger liqueur in the nectarine puree adds a pleasant zing while also giving the pops a softer, smoother texture.

- 2 pounds nectarines, thinly sliced
- 1 cup sugar
- 2½ tablespoons fresh lemon juice
- 3 tablespoons ginger liqueur, such as Domaine de Canton
- ¾ cup cold buttermilk
- ½ teaspoon finely grated lemon zest

1. In a medium saucepan, toss the sliced nectarines with ¾ cup of the sugar and 2 tablespoons of the lemon juice and let stand until juicy, about 20 minutes. Bring the nectarines to a boil and simmer over low heat, mashing lightly, just until softened, about 8 minutes. Let cool.
2. Transfer the nectarines to the bowl of a food processor and pulse to a coarse puree. Strain the puree, pressing hard on the skins to extract as much juice as possible. Add 2 tablespoons of the ginger liqueur and ½ cup of water to the puree; you should have about 3 cups of loose puree. Fill eight 6-ounce popsicle molds with half of the nectarine puree and freeze until firm but not solid, about 1 hour.
3. Meanwhile, in a bowl, combine the buttermilk with the remaining ¼ cup of sugar, ½ tablespoon of lemon juice, 1 tablespoon of ginger liqueur and the lemon zest. Whisk until the sugar is dissolved, then refrigerate.
4. Pour the buttermilk mixture into the popsicle molds and freeze for about 1 hour, until firm but not solid. Pour the remaining nectarine puree into the molds and add the sticks, pushing them nearly through the popsicles. Freeze until firm, at least 4 hours and preferably overnight.
5. Dip the molds in hot water for a few seconds, then unmold the popsicles and serve right away. —*Grace Parisi*

● HEALTHY ● MAKE AHEAD ● VEGETARIAN ● STAFF FAVORITE

nectarine-buttermilk pops

Free-Form Blueberry Tart

ACTIVE: 30 MIN; TOTAL: 3 HR 30 MIN
8 SERVINGS ● ●

PASTRY

- 1½ cups all-purpose flour, plus more for dusting
- 1 tablespoon minced candied ginger
- ¼ teaspoon salt
- 1½ sticks cold unsalted butter, cut into small pieces
- ¼ cup plus 1 tablespoon ice water

FILLING

- ¼ cup sugar, plus more for sprinkling
- 2 teaspoons finely grated lemon zest
- ¼ cup all-purpose flour
- 4 cups blueberries
- 2 tablespoons fresh lemon juice
- 1 egg white, beaten

1. MAKE THE PASTRY In a food processor, combine the 1½ cups of flour with the candied ginger and salt and pulse to mix. Add the butter and pulse until it is the size of small peas. Sprinkle on the ice water and pulse just until the pastry starts to come together. Turn the pastry out onto a lightly floured work surface and pat it into a disk. Wrap in plastic and refrigerate for 2 hours, or until firm.

2. Line a large baking sheet with parchment paper. On a lightly floured work surface, roll out the pastry to a 14-inch round about ⅛ inch thick. Fold the pastry in half and transfer it to the prepared baking sheet. Unfold the pastry and refrigerate for 15 minutes.

3. MAKE THE FILLING Preheat the oven to 375°. In a bowl, mix the ¼ cup of sugar, lemon zest and flour. Fold in the blueberries and lemon juice; let stand for 15 minutes.

4. Spoon the blueberries in the center of the pastry, leaving a 1½-inch border all around. Fold the pastry border up and over the blueberries, pleating it as necessary. Brush the egg white on the pastry and sprinkle with sugar. Bake for about 55 minutes, until the pastry is golden brown and the filling starts to bubble. Transfer the baking sheet to a rack and let the tart cool to warm. Cut into wedges and serve warm or at room temperature.
—*Jeremy Sewall*

Berry Ice Cream Pie

TOTAL: 45 MIN PLUS FREEZING
8 SERVINGS ● ●

Douglas Quint and Bryan Petroff of New York City's Big Gay Ice Cream Truck use store-bought ice cream to create inventive desserts, like this strawberry ice cream pie with a fresh blueberry sauce.

- 1¼ cups graham cracker crumbs (from 12 whole graham crackers)
- ⅓ cup light brown sugar
- ⅓ cup unsalted butter, melted
- 3 pints strawberry ice cream, softened slightly
- 1 cup white balsamic vinegar
- 2 pints blueberries, plus more for serving

1. Preheat the oven to 350°. In a bowl, stir the cracker crumbs, brown sugar and butter until evenly moistened. Press the crumbs into a 9-inch glass pie plate and bake for 10 minutes, until lightly browned. Let cool completely.

2. Meanwhile, line another 9-inch pie plate with plastic wrap and spread with 1 pint of the ice cream. Top with plastic wrap and freeze until firm, about 10 minutes. Spread another pint of ice cream on top of the plastic, cover with plastic wrap and freeze. Repeat with a final layer of ice cream and freeze until firm.

3. Meanwhile, in a medium saucepan, boil the balsamic vinegar over moderate heat until reduced to ⅓ cup, about 15 minutes. Add the 2 pints of blueberries and bring to a boil. Simmer over moderately low heat, crushing the berries, until thick and jammy, 8 to 10 minutes. Transfer the mixture to a bowl and freeze until chilled.

4. Transfer the top layer of flattened ice cream to the crust, spreading it to the edges. Top with half of the blueberry mixture. Repeat with the middle layer of ice cream and the remaining blueberry mixture and top with the final layer of ice cream. Freeze until firm, about 30 minutes. Cut the pie into wedges and serve with fresh blueberries.
—*Bryan Petroff and Douglas Quint*

MAKE AHEAD The pie can be wrapped in plastic and frozen for up to 1 week.

Hibiscus-Berry Gelatins

TOTAL: 30 MIN PLUS 5 HR SETTING
8 SERVINGS ● ●

A lovely way to serve raspberries, blackberries and blueberries: suspended in a rosy pink gelatin scented with hibiscus.

- 1 tablespoon dried hibiscus flowers (see Note)
- Three 1-inch strips of lemon zest
- 1 thyme sprig
- Boiling water
- 1 tablespoon unflavored powdered gelatin
- ½ cup sugar
- 1 tablespoon fresh lemon juice
- 2 cups mixed raspberries, blackberries and blueberries, plus more for garnish

1. In a large heatproof bowl, combine the dried hibiscus flowers, lemon zest and thyme sprig. Add 4 cups of boiling water and let stand for 15 minutes, stirring occasionally, until the liquid is rosy pink.

2. Strain the liquid into a microwave-safe pitcher, stopping when you reach the grit at the bottom. Measure out 3 cups. Pour 1 cup into a small bowl and sprinkle the gelatin over it. Let stand until softened, about 5 minutes. Scrape the softened gelatin into the pitcher and stir in the sugar and lemon juice. Microwave the mixture for 10 to 15 seconds, until the gelatin is melted and the sugar is dissolved. Refrigerate until chilled but not set, about 30 minutes.

3. Pour the mixture into eight ½-cup molds and refrigerate until partially set, about 30 minutes. Poke the 2 cups of berries into the gelatin and refrigerate until completely firm, at least 4 hours and preferably overnight.

4. Dip one mold at a time in a pan of hot water for about 5 seconds. Invert a plate over the mold and invert the mold and plate. Lift the mold off the gelatin, garnish with berries and serve. —*Grace Parisi*

NOTE Dried hibiscus flowers are available at health-food stores and tea shops.

MAKE AHEAD The molds can be refrigerated for up to 4 days.

● HEALTHY ● MAKE AHEAD ● VEGETARIAN ● STAFF FAVORITE

free-form blueberry tart

Strawberry and Wild Fennel Compote with Pound Cake

ACTIVE: 45 MIN; TOTAL: 3 HR
8 SERVINGS ● ○ ○

Pastry chef Bill Corbett of Absinthe Brasserie & Bar in San Francisco harvests his own fennel pollen for this dessert by hanging wild fennel flowers upside down; as they dry, the pollen falls into a container below. Wild fennel pollen can also be purchased online at *chefshop.com*.

POUND CAKE

2 sticks unsalted butter, softened, plus more for the pan
1¾ cups all-purpose flour, plus more for the pan
½ teaspoon salt
½ vanilla bean, split and seeds scraped
Finely grated zest of 2 oranges
4 large egg yolks
3 large eggs
1¼ cups sugar

COMPOTE

2 small, young wild fennel bulbs (or 1 small cultivated fennel bulb)—halved, cored and diced
½ vanilla bean—split, seeds scraped and bean reserved
Salt
1 pound small strawberries, diced
¼ cup plus 2 tablespoons sugar
2 tablespoons fresh lemon juice
Wild fennel pollen, for sprinkling

1. **MAKE THE POUND CAKE** Preheat the oven to 350°. Butter and flour a 9-by-4½-by-3-inch metal loaf pan. In the bowl of a standing electric mixer fitted with the paddle attachment, beat the 2 sticks of butter with the 1¾ cups of flour and the salt, vanilla seeds and orange zest until creamy. Scrape the mixture into a bowl. Add the egg yolks, whole eggs and sugar to the mixer bowl and beat at medium-high speed with the whisk attachment until pale and thick, about 4 minutes. Stir half of the whipped eggs into the flour paste, then fold in the rest.
2. Scrape the batter into the loaf pan and bake in the center of the oven for 1½ hours, until the cake is risen and a skewer inserted in the center comes out clean. Let the pound cake cool in the pan for 30 minutes, then turn out onto a wire rack to cool completely.
3. **MAKE THE COMPOTE** In a 9-by-13-inch nonreactive baking dish, combine the fennel, vanilla bean, a pinch of salt and 2 tablespoons of water. Cover with foil and roast until the fennel is tender, 30 minutes. Meanwhile, in a medium bowl, toss the strawberries with the sugar, lemon juice, vanilla seeds and a pinch of salt and let stand until juicy, 30 minutes.
4. Add the strawberries and their juices to the fennel, cover and roast for 30 minutes. Discard the vanilla bean and transfer the compote to a bowl. Slice the cake and set a slice on each plate. Top with the compote, sprinkle with fennel pollen and serve.
—*Bill Corbett*

Free-Form Pineapple, Mango and Berry Tarts

ACTIVE: 45 MIN; TOTAL: 3 HR
8 SERVINGS ● ●

"Río Negro is like the Garden of Eden, with fruit trees everywhere," Piero Incisa della Rocchetta says about the region in Patagonia where he makes wine. Local chef Mauricio Couly created these tarts filled with some of those fruits, like pineapple, mango and blueberries. The filling can, of course, vary depending on the season.

PASTRY

2 cups all-purpose flour
½ teaspoon salt
1½ sticks cold unsalted butter, cut into small pieces
½ cup ice water

FILLING

¼ pineapple—peeled, halved lengthwise and sliced crosswise 1/16 inch thick
½ mango, halved lengthwise and sliced crosswise 1/16 inch thick
1 small banana, sliced
8 medium strawberries, finely chopped
24 blueberries
2 tablespoons unsalted butter, melted
Sugar, for sprinkling

1. **MAKE THE PASTRY** In a food processor, pulse the flour and salt. Add the butter and pulse until it is the size of small peas. Sprinkle the ice water over the mixture and pulse until the pastry starts to come together. Transfer the pastry to a work surface and knead gently a few times until thoroughly blended. Divide the pastry in half and flatten into disks. Wrap the pastry in plastic and refrigerate until chilled, about 1 hour.
2. Preheat the oven to 400° and line a large baking sheet with parchment paper. On a lightly floured work surface, roll out 1 of the pastry disks ⅛ inch thick. Using a 5-inch plate as a guide, cut out 4 rounds and transfer to the prepared baking sheet. Repeat with the second pastry disk. Refrigerate the rounds until firm, about 10 minutes.
3. **MAKE THE FILLING** Arrange the pineapple, mango and banana slices on the pastry rounds and scatter the strawberries and blueberries on top. Bring the pastry edges up and around the fruit, pinching firmly to form a pleated rim on each tart. Refrigerate the tarts until firm, 10 minutes.
4. Brush the tarts with the melted butter and sprinkle with sugar. Bake for 35 minutes, until the pastry is browned and the fruit is bubbling. Let the tarts cool on a rack. Serve warm or at room temperature. —*Mauricio Couly*
SERVE WITH Crème fraîche or vanilla ice cream.
MAKE AHEAD The pastry dough can be refrigerated overnight.

Strawberries in Prosecco with Vanilla Ice Cream

⏱ TOTAL: 45 MIN • 8 SERVINGS ○

2½ pounds strawberries, sliced
¼ cup sugar
One 750-milliliter bottle chilled Prosecco
2 pints vanilla ice cream

In a bowl, toss the strawberries with the sugar and let stand until the sugar is dissolved, about 30 minutes. Spoon the berries and any syrup into glasses and top with the Prosecco and a scoop of ice cream. Serve right away. —*Ethan Stowell*

● HEALTHY   ● MAKE AHEAD   ○ VEGETARIAN   ○ STAFF FAVORITE

strawberry and wild fennel compote with pound cake

Mango-Basil Vacherin

ACTIVE: 45 MIN; TOTAL: 4 HR
8 SERVINGS ● ○ ○

Top Chef: Just Desserts Season 1 winner Yigit Pura perfected this crisp-creamy French dessert while at Daniel in New York. His variation here combines little lime meringue kisses, basil ice cream and mango sorbet.

  2 **pints mango sorbet**
BASIL ICE CREAM
  ¼ **cup sugar**
  ¼ **cup water**
  ¼ **cup packed basil leaves**
  2 **pints vanilla ice cream, softened**
LIME MERINGUE KISSES
  4 **large egg whites**
1½ **cups confectioners' sugar**
Finely grated zest of 2 limes
LIME WHIPPED CREAM
  1 **cup heavy cream**
  1 **tablespoon sugar**
Finely grated zest of 1 lime
Diced mango and basil leaves, for garnish

1. Using scissors, cut the cartons from the mango sorbet. Lay the sorbet on its side and cut each pint into 4 rounds. Arrange the sorbet slices on a plate lined with plastic wrap and freeze until firm.

2. MAKE THE BASIL ICE CREAM In a small saucepan, combine the sugar and water and bring the mixture to a boil. Add the basil leaves and blanch just until wilted, about 30 seconds. Let cool slightly, then transfer the mixture to a blender and puree until smooth. Let the puree cool. In a medium bowl, stir the basil puree into the vanilla ice cream; leave visible streaks in the ice cream. Freeze the basil ice cream until firm.

3. MAKE THE LIME MERINGUE KISSES Preheat the oven to 225°. Arrange racks in the top, middle and bottom of the oven and line 3 large baking sheets with parchment paper. In a medium bowl, whisk the egg whites and confectioners' sugar until smooth. Set the bowl over a pot of simmering water and whisk until warm, about 5 minutes. Remove from the heat and beat at high speed until soft peaks form. Beat in the lime zest.

4. Spoon the lime meringue into a pastry bag fitted with a ½-inch round tip and pipe ½-inch kisses onto the prepared baking sheets, about ½ inch apart. Bake for about 1¼ hours, until the lime meringues are firm and dry; shift the pans among the racks 3 times for even baking. Turn off the oven, prop the door open and let the meringues cool completely, about 1 hour.

5. MAKE THE LIME WHIPPED CREAM In a medium bowl, beat the heavy cream with the sugar until soft peaks form. Beat the grated lime zest into the whipped cream.

6. Arrange the frozen mango sorbet slices in the bottoms of shallow bowls or on dessert plates. Top with scoops of the basil ice cream. Top with some of the lime meringue kisses and dollops of the lime whipped cream. Garnish with diced mango, basil leaves and more lime meringue kisses. Serve the vacherin right away. —*Yigit Pura*

Pavlovas with Passion Fruit Curd

ACTIVE: 30 MIN; TOTAL: 2 HR 30 MIN
6 SERVINGS ○

  3 **large eggs, separated**
Pinch of salt
1¼ **cups superfine sugar**
2½ **tablespoons fresh lemon juice**
1½ **teaspoons cornstarch**
  ½ **vanilla bean, seeds scraped**
  ¼ **cup passion fruit puree or nectar**
  1 **stick cold unsalted butter, cubed**

1. Preheat the oven to 325° and line a large baking sheet with parchment paper. In the bowl of a standing electric mixer fitted with the whisk, beat the egg whites with the salt at medium-high speed until soft peaks form. At high speed, beat in ¾ cup of the sugar, a few tablespoons at a time, until the egg whites are stiff and glossy. Beat in ½ tablespoon of the lemon juice along with the cornstarch and vanilla seeds. Transfer the meringue to a pastry bag fitted with a 1-inch plain tip and pipe out six 4-inch rounds, about 1 inch thick. Using the back of a spoon, make a 1½-inch well in the center of each

meringue. Bake the meringues in the lower third of the oven for 5 minutes. Immediately lower the oven temperature to 225° and bake for 1 hour longer. Turn the oven off, prop the door open and let the meringues cool completely; they should be hard on the outside and soft on the inside.

2. Meanwhile, in a saucepan, combine the yolks with the passion fruit puree and the remaining ½ cup of sugar and 2 tablespoons of lemon juice. Cook over low heat, whisking, until the sugar dissolves. Add the butter and cook, whisking, until thickened, about 8 minutes. Immediately strain the curd into a bowl. Press a sheet of plastic wrap onto the surface of the curd and refrigerate until chilled.

3. Set the meringues on plates and fill the centers with passion fruit curd. Serve right away, passing extra curd at the table. —*Grace Parisi*

Honey-Roasted Pineapple

ACTIVE: 25 MIN; TOTAL: 1 HR
8 SERVINGS ● ● ○

  2 **ripe golden pineapples**
  1 **cup fresh orange juice**
  ½ **cup honey**

1. Using a serrated knife, peel the pineapples. Quarter them lengthwise, then remove the cores. Cut each quarter into 3 long, thin wedges and transfer to a large bowl. In a microwave-safe cup, combine the orange juice with ¼ cup of the honey and heat at high power until warm, about 15 seconds. Pour the juice over the pineapple and let stand for 30 minutes, stirring occasionally.

2. Preheat the oven to 450° and line 2 rimmed baking sheets with parchment paper. Drain the pineapple wedges and arrange them in a single layer on the baking sheets. (Reserve the juices for another use.)

3. Roast the pineapple wedges for about 10 minutes, until they are tender, shifting the pans from top to bottom and front to back halfway through. Arrange the pineapple on a large platter and drizzle with the remaining ¼ cup of honey. Serve warm. —*Jenn Louis*

● HEALTHY ● MAKE AHEAD ○ VEGETARIAN ○ STAFF FAVORITE

Minny's Chocolate Pie

ACTIVE: 20 MIN; TOTAL: 1 HR 30 MIN
PLUS COOLING
MAKES ONE 9-INCH PIE ● ● ●

Most of the food in the 2011 movie *The Help* was made by real Southern cooks. Newspaper columnist Lee Ann Flemming, one of the best bakers in Greenwood, Mississippi, made 53 chocolate pies during filming, preparing 12 vegan and gluten-free versions in just one day for actress Bryce Dallas Howard. Her fudgy version here—the character Minny's famous chocolate pie—is neither vegan nor gluten-free: It's as classic as they come. You can make your own crust, but Flemming uses packaged.

- 1 packaged pie dough crust, such as Pillsbury
- 1½ cups sugar
- 3 tablespoons unsweetened cocoa powder
- 4 tablespoons unsalted butter, melted
- 2 large eggs, beaten
- ¾ cup evaporated milk
- 1 teaspoon pure vanilla extract
- ¼ teaspoon salt
- Whipped cream, for serving

1. Preheat the oven to 350°. Ease the pie crust into a 9-inch pie plate and crimp the edges decoratively. Prick the crust lightly with a fork. Line the crust with foil or parchment paper and fill with pie weights or dried beans. Bake for 15 minutes, or until set. Remove the foil and weights and bake for about 5 minutes longer, just until the crust is dry but not browned.

2. Meanwhile, in a bowl, whisk the sugar with the cocoa powder, butter, eggs, evaporated milk, vanilla and salt until smooth.

3. Pour the filling into the pie shell and bake for about 45 minutes, until the filling is set around the edges but a little jiggly in the center. Cover the crust with strips of foil halfway through baking. Transfer the pie to a rack and let cool completely before cutting into wedges. Serve with whipped cream.
—*Lee Ann Flemming*

Cranberry-Glazed Pumpkin Pie

ACTIVE: 30 MIN; TOTAL: 1 HR 15 MIN
PLUS COOLING • 8 SERVINGS ● ● ●

CRUST
- 8 ounces gingersnaps, crushed (1½ cups)
- ½ cup walnuts
- 4 tablespoons unsalted butter, melted

FILLING AND TOPPING
- 1 cup canned pumpkin
- ⅓ cup light brown sugar
- 1 tablespoon honey
- ¾ teaspoon ground ginger
- ¾ teaspoon cinnamon
- ¼ teaspoon salt
- Pinch of ground cloves
- 2 large eggs
- ¾ cup heavy cream
- ¼ cup fresh orange juice
- ¼ cup water
- ½ cup granulated sugar
- 1 tablespoon all-purpose flour
- 2 cups fresh or frozen cranberries (8 ounces)
- ½ cup walnuts

1. MAKE THE CRUST Preheat the oven to 350°. In a food processor, pulse the gingersnaps with the walnuts until finely ground. Add the melted butter and pulse until the crumbs are moistened. Press the crumbs evenly into the bottom and up the side of a 9-inch glass or ceramic pie plate.

2. MAKE THE FILLING AND TOPPING In a medium bowl, whisk the pumpkin with the brown sugar, honey, ground ginger, cinnamon, salt, ground cloves, eggs and heavy cream. Pour the pie filling into the crust. Bake for 35 to 40 minutes, until the crust is deep brown and the filling is just set around the edge but still slightly jiggly in the center; cover the edge of the crust with strips of foil halfway through baking to prevent burning. Transfer the pie to a wire rack to cool.

3. Meanwhile, in a medium saucepan, combine the orange juice with the water, granulated sugar and flour and whisk until smooth. Add the cranberries and cook over moderate heat, stirring, until the liquid is thickened and glossy and the cranberries just begin to burst, 5 minutes. Carefully pour the hot glaze over the pie and refrigerate until chilled. Sprinkle the nuts on top of the pie just before serving. —*Deborah Callia*

MAKE AHEAD The pie can be refrigerated for up to 3 days.

Cherry Lambic Crisps

ACTIVE: 30 MIN; TOTAL: 1 HR 15 MIN
6 SERVINGS ● ● ●

New York City chef Phillip Kirschen-Clark uses Kriek, a Belgian lambic beer fermented with cherries, to intensify the fruit flavors in these excellent crisps.

- 1½ pounds dark cherries, pitted
- 1½ cups dried sour cherries
- ½ cup Kriek lambic beer
- 2 tablespoons honey
- 1 vanilla bean, split and seeds scraped
- Kosher salt and freshly ground pepper
- 4 tablespoons unsalted butter, melted and cooled slightly, plus more for greasing the ramekins
- ¼ cup granulated sugar
- ½ cup all-purpose flour
- ¼ cup almonds, coarsely chopped (about 1 ounce)
- 2 tablespoons dark brown sugar
- ¼ teaspoon cinnamon
- 1 teaspoon finely grated orange zest
- Pinch each of nutmeg and ground cardamom

1. In a bowl, mix the pitted and dried cherries, beer, honey, vanilla and a pinch each of salt and pepper. Let stand for 30 minutes.

2. Meanwhile, preheat the oven to 375°. Butter six 8-ounce ramekins and set them on a rimmed baking sheet.

3. In a medium bowl, combine the sugar, flour, almonds, brown sugar, cinnamon, orange zest, nutmeg and cardamom. Stir in the melted butter. Press the topping into clumps.

4. Spoon the cherry filling into the ramekins and sprinkle with the topping. Bake for about 30 minutes, until browned and bubbling. Serve warm or at room temperature.
—*Phillip Kirschen-Clark*

Salted Caramel Pie

ACTIVE: 30 MIN; TOTAL: 2 HR 30 MIN
PLUS 4 HR CHILLING • 8 TO 10 SERVINGS
● ● ○

The filling in this supereasy caramel lover's dream pie is sweetened condensed milk sprinkled lightly with sea salt and baked until thick and gooey.

1¼   cups graham cracker crumbs
        (about 5 ounces)
   4   tablespoons unsalted butter, melted
   ¼   cup light brown sugar
Two 14-ounce cans sweetened
        condensed milk
Fleur de sel
   2   cups heavy cream
   2   tablespoons confectioners' sugar

1. Preheat the oven to 350°. In a food processor, pulse the graham cracker crumbs with the melted butter and light brown sugar until the crumbs are moistened. Press the crumbs evenly into a 9-inch glass or metal pie plate. Bake for about 10 minutes, just until lightly browned. Let cool. Increase the oven temperature to 425°.
2. Scrape the condensed milk into a 9-by-13-inch glass baking dish and sprinkle with a scant ½ teaspoon of fleur de sel. Cover the dish with foil and place it in a roasting pan. Add enough hot water to the pan to reach one-third of the way up the side of the baking dish. Bake, lifting the foil to stir 2 or 3 times, until the condensed milk is golden and thickened, about 2 hours; add more water to the roasting pan as necessary. The consistency of the caramel should be like dulce de leche. Don't worry if it is lumpy; it will smooth out as it chills.
3. Scrape the caramel filling into the pie crust, smoothing the top. Spray a sheet of plastic wrap with vegetable oil spray and cover the pie. Refrigerate until the filling is chilled and set, at least 4 hours.
4. In a bowl, beat the cream and confectioners' sugar with an electric mixer until firm. Remove the plastic. Mound the whipped cream on the pie, sprinkle with fleur de sel, cut into wedges and serve. —*Carrie Cusack*

MAKE AHEAD The recipe can be prepared through Step 2 up to 5 days ahead. Refrigerate the crust and filling separately.

Caramel-Pecan Hand Pies

ACTIVE: 1 HR; TOTAL: 4 HR 30 MIN
MAKES 12 HAND PIES ● ○
At Seattle's High 5 Pie, owner Dani Cone has responded to popular demand by making these adorable, portable pies (she calls them "flipsides") available not just in the fall but year-round. When she tries to take them out of the rotation, customers get angry; one time, she says, a woman even cried.

PASTRY
   4   cups all-purpose flour
   4   teaspoons salt
   2   teaspoons sugar
   4   sticks unsalted butter (1 pound),
        cut into ½-inch dice and chilled
   ¾   cup ice water
FILLING AND TOPPING
1½   cups pecans (6 ounces)
   2   cups granulated sugar
   6   tablespoons unsalted butter
   ½   cup heavy cream
   2   teaspoons pure vanilla extract
Salt
   1   cup corn syrup
   5   large eggs, 1 egg beaten
   ¼   cup turbinado sugar, for sprinkling

1. MAKE THE PASTRY In a large (preferably 12-cup) food processor, combine the flour with the salt and sugar. Add the butter pieces and pulse in 1-second bursts until the mixture resembles coarse meal. Drizzle the ice water over the dough and pulse in 1-second bursts until it just comes together. Turn the dough out onto a work surface, gather up any crumbs and pat into 2 disks. Wrap the disks in plastic and refrigerate them until chilled, about 1 hour.
2. On a floured work surface, roll out 1 disk of the dough to a 16-inch square, a scant ¼ inch thick. Using a small pot lid or plate (5½ to 6 inches) as a template, cut out as many dough rounds as possible. Repeat with the second disk of dough. Reroll the

scraps, chilling if necessary, for a total of 12 dough rounds. Transfer the pastry rounds to parchment paper–lined baking sheets and refrigerate until chilled, about 20 minutes.
3. MEANWHILE, MAKE THE FILLING AND TOPPING Preheat the oven to 375°. Spread the pecans on a baking sheet and toast for about 8 minutes, until browned and fragrant. Let cool, then coarsely chop the nuts.
4. In a medium saucepan, combine 1 cup of the granulated sugar with ½ cup of water. Cook over moderate heat, swirling the pan gently once the caramel begins to form, until the caramel is medium-amber, about 9 minutes. Remove from the heat and whisk in the butter, cream, 1 teaspoon of the vanilla extract and a pinch of salt. Transfer 1 cup of the caramel to a large bowl and let cool slightly. (Save any remaining caramel for later use.) Whisk the remaining 1 cup of sugar and 1 teaspoon of vanilla extract and the corn syrup into the caramel in the bowl. Whisk in the 4 unbeaten eggs until smooth. Add the pecans and a generous pinch of salt.
5. Spray a 9-by-13-inch baking pan with vegetable oil spray. Pour the pecan filling into the pan and bake for about 30 minutes, until set. Let cool slightly, then scrape the pecan filling into a bowl and gently stir to recombine. Refrigerate until chilled, about 1 hour.
6. Working with one baking sheet at a time, brush the pastry surfaces lightly with some of the beaten egg, then scoop a scant ¼ cup of the pecan filling onto each round and fold the pastry over to make a turnover. Press the edges to seal and crimp with the tines of a floured fork. Refrigerate the hand pies while you prepare the rest.
7. Brush the tops of the pies with the beaten egg and sprinkle with the turbinado sugar. Using a sharp knife, make a small slit in the top of each pie. Bake the pies in the middle and lower thirds of the oven for 40 minutes, until the pastry is golden brown; shift the pans halfway through baking. Let the pies cool on the baking sheets before serving.
—*Dani Cone*
MAKE AHEAD The hand pies can be refrigerated for up to 4 days. Rewarm in the oven before serving.

● HEALTHY ● MAKE AHEAD ● VEGETARIAN ○ STAFF FAVORITE

salted caramel pie

Black-Bottom Banana Cream Pie

ACTIVE: 45 MIN; TOTAL: 1 HR 30 MIN PLUS 6 HR CHILLING • 8 SERVINGS ● ●● ●

Valeri Lucks, the co-owner and self-titled chief people wrangler and pie master at Milwaukee's Honeypie Cafe, says this pie marries two of her best-selling pies: chocolate cream and banana cream.

CRUST

1½ cups fine graham cracker crumbs (about 7 ounces)
½ cup sugar
½ teaspoon cinnamon
½ teaspoon salt
6 tablespoons unsalted butter, melted

FILLING AND TOPPING

½ cup granulated sugar
¼ cup cornstarch
4 large egg yolks
2½ cups milk
2 tablespoons unsalted butter
1 tablespoon pure vanilla extract
3½ ounces bittersweet chocolate, chopped
3 medium bananas, sliced ½ inch thick
1½ cups heavy cream
2 tablespoons confectioners' sugar
Chocolate shavings, for garnish

1. MAKE THE CRUST Preheat the oven to 350°. In a food processor, combine the graham cracker crumbs with the sugar, cinnamon, salt and melted butter and pulse until the crumbs are moistened. Press the crumbs evenly into a 9- to 10-inch deep-dish glass or ceramic pie plate. Bake for about 8 minutes, until the crust is lightly browned and set. Let cool completely.

2. MEANWHILE, MAKE THE FILLING AND TOPPING In a large saucepan (preferably with a rounded bottom), combine the granulated sugar with the cornstarch, egg yolks and ½ cup of the milk and whisk until smooth. Whisk in the remaining 2 cups of milk and cook over moderate heat, whisking constantly, until the custard is very thick, about 5 minutes. Remove from the heat and whisk in the butter and vanilla extract until the butter is melted. Pour half of the vanilla custard into a medium bowl.

3. Whisk the chopped chocolate into the custard in the saucepan until it is melted. Spread the chocolate custard evenly in the pie crust and top with the sliced bananas. Carefully spread the vanilla custard over the bananas. Refrigerate the banana cream pie until it is well chilled, at least 6 hours and preferably overnight.

4. In a medium bowl, using an electric mixer, beat the heavy cream with the confectioners' sugar until it is softly whipped. Mound the whipped cream on top of the pie. Garnish the banana cream pie with chocolate shavings and serve. —*Valeri Lucks*

MAKE AHEAD The pie can be made through Step 3 and refrigerated for up to 3 days. The crust can be frozen for up to 2 weeks.

Impossible Pie

ACTIVE: 20 MIN; TOTAL: 1 HR 30 MIN PLUS COOLING • MAKES TWO 9-INCH PIES ● ●

This riff on chess pie, a Southern classic, is from country singer Jennifer Nettles's great-grandmother Mildred. It's called impossible because it seems to miraculously form its own crust while baking.

1 stick unsalted butter, melted, plus more for greasing the pie plates
1¾ cups sugar
4 large eggs
½ cup self-rising flour
2 cups sweetened shredded coconut
2 cups milk

1. Preheat the oven to 350° and butter two 9-inch glass pie plates.

2. In a large bowl, whisk the melted butter with the sugar. Add the eggs and beat until smooth. Stir in the flour, coconut and milk. Divide the mixture between the pie plates and bake in the lower third of the oven for about 1 hour, until the pies are firm to the touch and golden. Transfer the pies to a rack and let cool completely before serving. —*Jennifer Nettles*

MAKE AHEAD The pies can be refrigerated overnight. Return them to room temperature before serving.

Brandy-Mascarpone Semifreddo

TOTAL: 1 HR PLUS 24 HR FREEZING 14 TO 16 SERVINGS ● ●

3 cups heavy cream
2 teaspoons powdered gelatin
Ice water
12 large egg yolks, at room temperature
1⅔ cups sugar
1½ tablespoons pure vanilla extract
1⅔ cups mascarpone (14 ounces)
½ cup brandy, such as Cognac or Armagnac
Stewed Winter Fruits in Spiced Wine Syrup (recipe follows), for serving

1. In a small saucepan, combine 1 cup of the heavy cream with the gelatin over low heat, stirring constantly, until the gelatin dissolves. Let cool completely.

2. Fill a large bowl with ice water and set aside. In a medium stainless steel bowl, whisk the egg yolks with 1 cup of the sugar and the vanilla extract. Set the bowl over a pan filled with 1 inch of simmering water and cook over moderately low heat, whisking constantly, until the mixture is pale and thick and registers 160° on an instant-read thermometer, about 10 minutes. Set the bowl in the ice water and let the egg-yolk mixture cool, stirring occasionally.

3. In the bowl of a standing mixer fitted with the whisk attachment, beat the remaining 2 cups of heavy cream with the mascarpone and the remaining ⅔ cup of sugar at medium-high speed until soft peaks begin to form. Gradually add the cream-gelatin mixture and brandy and beat until firm peaks form. Using a rubber spatula, fold one-fourth of the whipped cream mixture into the cooled egg-yolk mixture, then fold it into the remaining whipped cream until no streaks remain. Scrape the semifreddo mixture into a 10-cup silicone kugelhopf mold

● HEALTHY ● MAKE AHEAD ● VEGETARIAN ● STAFF FAVORITE

or another 8- to 10-cup mold, spreading it in an even layer. Press plastic wrap directly onto the surface of the semifreddo and freeze for at least 24 hours, until very firm.
4. Carefully peel the mold from the semi-freddo, shaking gently onto a platter. Cut into wedges; serve with the Stewed Winter Fruits in Spiced Wine Syrup. —*Valerie Gordon*

STEWED WINTER FRUITS IN SPICED WINE SYRUP
TOTAL: 1 HR PLUS COOLING
MAKES 8 CUPS ● ● ●

- 2 cups dry red wine
- 1 cup ruby port
- 1½ cups water
- ¾ cup sugar
- 1 vanilla bean, split lengthwise
- 20 black peppercorns tied in cheesecloth
- 1 cinnamon stick
- 3 quince—peeled, cored and cut into eighths
- 4 slices of candied orange or ¼ cup candied orange rind
- 8 plump dried pear halves (6 ounces)
- 10 plump dried Black Mission figs, stemmed
- ½ cup plump dried apricots (3 ounces)
- ½ cup plump pitted prunes (3 ounces)

1. In a large saucepan, combine the wine and port and bring to a boil. Add the water, sugar, vanilla bean, peppercorns and cinnamon stick and bring to a boil again. Add the quince and candied orange and simmer over moderately low heat until the quince are just tender, about 45 minutes.
2. Meanwhile, in a large microwave-safe bowl, cover the pears and figs with 1 inch of water. Microwave in 5-minute increments at high power until the fruit is plump but not mushy, 15 minutes; drain. Add the pears, figs, apricots and prunes to the wine syrup and simmer until all of the fruit is plump and very tender and the liquid is thick and syrupy, 15 minutes. Discard the cinnamon stick, vanilla bean and peppercorns and let cool. Serve the stewed fruit warm or chilled. —*VG*

Lemon-Fennel Compote
⏱ **TOTAL: 30 MIN • MAKES ABOUT 1 CUP**
● ● ● ●

- 1 fennel bulb—halved, cored and very thinly sliced on a mandoline
- ½ cup water
- ¼ cup honey
- 1 teaspoon finely grated lemon zest
- 1 tablespoon fresh lemon juice
- Salt
- 2 Medjool dates, pitted and thinly sliced lengthwise
- Fennel seeds, for garnish

1. In a saucepan, bring the fennel, water and honey to a boil. Cover and cook over high heat, stirring a few times, until the fennel is crisp-tender, about 2 minutes. With tongs, transfer the fennel to a bowl. Add the lemon zest and juice to the saucepan and boil until syrupy, about 2 minutes. Pour the syrup over the fennel and toss. Let the compote cool. Season lightly with salt.
2. Before serving, fold in the dates. Sprinkle with a few fennel seeds and serve. —*Marcia Kiesel*
SERVE WITH Assorted cheeses.

Pickled Grapes with Walnuts
⏱ **ACTIVE: 10 MIN; TOTAL: 45 MIN**
MAKES ABOUT 1 CUP ● ● ●

- 1 cup seedless red grapes, halved
- 1 tablespoon white balsamic vinegar
- ½ cup walnuts
- 2 tablespoons sugar

1. Preheat the oven to 350°. In a bowl, toss the grapes and vinegar. Let stand 15 minutes.
2. Meanwhile, put the walnuts in a pie plate and bake for about 6 minutes, until lightly browned. Let cool, then coarsely chop.
3. Drain the vinegar from the grapes into a small saucepan. Add the sugar and cook over moderate heat until syrupy, 2 minutes. Pour the syrup over the grapes, toss and let cool. Fold in the walnuts just before serving. —*Marcia Kiesel*
SERVE WITH Assorted cheeses.

the perfect cheese plate

Liz Thorpe of NYC's Murray's Cheese (murrayscheese.com) *recommends the three varieties below. For a stellar cheese plate, pair each with homemade condiments such as Lemon-Fennel Compote (left) and Pickled Grapes with Walnuts (below left).*

pecorino ginepro From Italy's Lazio region, this sheep-milk cheese is soaked in balsamic and juniper, then aged for four months.

consider bardwell dorset This funky cow-milk cheese from Vermont is washed in a dark Belgian-style ale, giving it a slight fruity flavor.

la tur This dense, creamy cheese from Piedmont is a blend of cow, goat and sheep milk. It's tangy and rich, with a moist, cakey center and oozy edges.

Chef Tory Miller and the staff at Madison, Wisconsin's L'Etoile play broom hockey, then gather inside to eat. For dessert: buttermilk cake with Riesling-poached pears, OPPOSITE; *recipe, page 356.*

cakes, cookies and more

cakes, cookies and more

Almond, Elderflower and Lime Travel Cakes

ACTIVE: 30 MIN; TOTAL: 1 HR 15 MIN

MAKES 2 DOZEN MINI CAKES ● ● ●

These miniature desserts were inspired by *cakes sucrés,* small French cakes meant for bringing to parties, picnics and other events.

CAKES

10 ounces almond paste, broken into 1-inch pieces (1 cup)

3 large eggs

2½ tablespoons cornstarch

Pinch of salt

4½ tablespoons unsalted butter, melted and cooled

1 tablespoon St-Germain or other elderflower liqueur

ICING

2 cups confectioners' sugar

2½ tablespoons heavy cream

2½ tablespoons St-Germain or other elderflower liqueur

1½ teaspoons fresh lime juice

½ teaspoon finely grated lime zest, plus zest strips for decorating

1. MAKE THE CAKES Preheat the oven to 350° and spray 2 mini-muffin pans with vegetable oil spray. In a food processor, pulse the almond paste several times until broken into small pieces; don't overprocess or the paste will become oily. Add the eggs and pulse until smooth. Add the cornstarch and salt and pulse until smooth. Add the butter and St-Germain and pulse until incorporated.

2. Scrape the batter into a small pitcher and pour it into the muffin cups, filling them about two-thirds full. Bake for about 22 minutes, until the cakes are golden, puffed and firm to the touch. Transfer the pans to a rack and cool for 20 minutes, then invert the cakes onto the rack to cool completely.

3. MAKE THE ICING In a bowl, mix the sugar, cream, St-Germain and lime juice. Using a handheld mixer, beat at low speed until smooth. Beat in the ½ teaspoon of grated lime zest. Spoon the icing over the cakes, allowing it to drip down the sides. Garnish with zest before serving. —*William Werner*

Buttermilk Cake with Riesling-Poached Pears

📷 PAGE 355

ACTIVE: 40 MIN; TOTAL: 1 HR 40 MIN

10 SERVINGS ● ● ●

"We get these crazy organic pears that are ugly as sin," says Tory Miller, the chef at L'Etoile in Madison, Wisconsin, of the Moonglow variety he uses throughout the cold winter months. Peeling them, though, reveals a fruit so beautiful and juicy that he prefers a minimalist approach, either serving them raw or poaching them in wine, such as the Riesling he uses here.

CAKE

2 cups cake flour

1 tablespoon baking powder

½ teaspoon salt

1 stick unsalted butter, softened, plus more for greasing

½ cup granulated sugar

½ cup light brown sugar

4 large egg yolks

Finely grated zest of 1 lemon

1½ teaspoons pure vanilla extract

⅔ cup buttermilk

PEARS

5 Bartlett pears

One 750-milliliter bottle Riesling

1 cup water

1 cup sugar

½ vanilla bean, split and seeds scraped

One 3-inch-long strip of orange zest

3 star anise pods

VANILLA CRÈME FRAÎCHE

1 cup crème fraîche

1 teaspoon pure vanilla extract

½ vanilla bean, split and seeds scraped

¼ cup confectioners' sugar

1. MAKE THE CAKE Preheat the oven to 350°. Butter a 9-inch cake pan and line it with a 9-inch round of parchment paper. Butter the parchment paper.

2. In a large bowl, sift together the cake flour, baking powder and salt. In another large bowl, using a handheld electric mixer, beat the stick of softened butter with the granulated sugar and light brown sugar at medium-high speed until light and fluffy. Add the egg yolks, one at a time, beating well between additions. Beat in the grated lemon zest and vanilla extract. At low speed, alternately beat in the flour mixture and the buttermilk until the mixture is almost blended. With a rubber spatula, carefully finish folding the mixture together just until smooth. Scrape the batter into the prepared cake pan and bake the buttermilk cake for about 35 minutes, until a cake tester inserted in the center comes out clean. Transfer the cake to a rack and let it cool completely.

3. POACH THE PEARS Peel and halve the pears. With a spoon, scoop out the cores and discard them. In a large saucepan, combine the Riesling, water, sugar, vanilla bean and seeds, orange zest strip and star anise pods. Bring the mixture to a boil, stirring to dissolve the sugar. Add the pear halves and simmer over moderate heat, turning once, until the pears are tender, about 5 minutes. Transfer the pears to a large plate. Discard the star anise pods, vanilla bean and orange zest strip. Boil the Riesling poaching liquid over high heat until it is reduced to 1 cup and syrupy, about 15 minutes. When the poached pears have cooled, cut them lengthwise into ⅓-inch-thick slices.

4. MAKE THE VANILLA CRÈME FRAÎCHE In a small bowl, combine the crème fraîche with the vanilla extract, vanilla seeds and confectioners' sugar.

5. Unmold the cake onto a plate and peel off the paper. Cut the cake into 10 wedges and transfer to plates. Place a sliced pear half alongside each cake slice. Spoon some of the Riesling syrup over the cake, top with some vanilla crème fraîche and serve. —*Tory Miller*

MAKE AHEAD The cake can be kept in an airtight container overnight at room temperature. The pears, Riesling syrup and vanilla crème fraîche can be refrigerated in separate containers overnight.

WINE Sweet honeyed Riesling from Canada's Niagara Peninsula region: 2007 Inniskillin Riesling Icewine.

● HEALTHY ● MAKE AHEAD ○ VEGETARIAN ● STAFF FAVORITE

almond, elderflower and lime tracel cakes

cakes, cookies and more

Vanilla Bean Cake with Salted Caramel Sauce

ACTIVE: 30 MIN; TOTAL: 2 HR
MAKES ONE 9-INCH CAKE ● ● ●

"I tried making this as an upside-down cake, which was a disaster, but then I realized I could just pour the caramel on top," says Valerie Gordon of Valerie Confections in Los Angeles.

2½ cups all-purpose flour
1 teaspoon baking powder
1 teaspoon salt
2 sticks unsalted butter, softened
1 cup granulated sugar
½ cup brown sugar
4 large eggs
¼ cup crème fraîche or sour cream
3 tablespoons vanilla paste (see Note) or 1 vanilla bean, seeds scraped
1 cup Salted Caramel Sauce (recipe follows)

1. Preheat the oven to 350° and butter and flour a 9-inch round cake pan. In a medium bowl, whisk the flour with the baking powder and salt. In a large bowl, using a handheld electric mixer, beat the butter at medium speed until creamy. Add both sugars and beat until fluffy. Add the eggs one at a time, beating well between additions, then add the crème fraîche and vanilla. At medium-low speed, beat in the dry ingredients until smooth and evenly combined.

2. Scrape the batter into the prepared cake pan and smooth the surface. Bake in the center of the oven for about 1 hour, until the cake is golden and springy and a toothpick inserted into the center comes out with a few moist crumbs attached to it. Let the cake cool in the pan for 20 minutes. Turn the cake onto a plate, then invert onto a rack and let cool completely.

3. Poke the top of the cake all over with a skewer and pour the caramel sauce over the cake, allowing it to seep in and drip down the side. Cut into wedges and serve.
—Valerie Gordon

NOTE Vanilla paste is available at select specialty food shops.

SALTED CARAMEL SAUCE
TOTAL: 15 MIN • MAKES 2 CUPS ● ●

¾ cup heavy cream
¼ cup light corn syrup
1¼ cups sugar
4 tablespoons unsalted butter
½ teaspoon sea salt

In a microwave-safe cup, combine the cream and corn syrup. In a medium, wide saucepan, spread the sugar in an even layer. Cook over moderate heat, without stirring, until it begins to caramelize. Swirl the pan and stir to incorporate the caramelized sugar, then microwave the cream mixture at high power for 2 minutes. Continue cooking the sugar until a medium-amber caramel forms, about 4 minutes. Remove from the heat; carefully add the hot cream, stirring with a long-handled spoon. Return the caramel to low heat; add the butter and salt, stirring until any hardened caramel is melted. Transfer the caramel to a heatproof glass jar; let cool. —VG

MAKE AHEAD The sauce can be refrigerated for up to 1 month. Rewarm before serving.

Tres Leches Cake with Strawberries

ACTIVE: 35 MIN; TOTAL: 5 HR 45 MIN
12 SERVINGS ● ●

This luscious dessert, made by soaking sponge cake in condensed milk, evaporated milk and cream, has just a hint of cinnamon.

CAKE
1½ cups all-purpose flour
2 teaspoons baking powder
½ teaspoon salt
3 large eggs, at room temperature
1 cup sugar
2 teaspoons pure vanilla extract
½ cup whole milk, at room temperature
1½ cups heavy cream
One 12-ounce can evaporated milk
1 medium cinnamon stick
2 whole cloves
One 14-ounce can sweetened condensed milk
½ teaspoon ground cinnamon

TOPPINGS
1 pint strawberries, thinly sliced
¼ cup sugar
Sweetened whipped cream and thinly sliced mint leaves, for serving

1. MAKE THE CAKE Preheat the oven to 350°. Lightly butter a 9-by-13-inch glass or ceramic baking dish. In a medium bowl, whisk the flour with the baking powder and salt. In the bowl of a standing mixer fitted with the paddle, beat the eggs with the sugar and 1 teaspoon of the vanilla at medium-high speed until very light and fluffy, about 10 minutes. Add half of the flour mixture and mix at low speed until just incorporated. Gradually add the whole milk, then mix in the remaining flour mixture.

2. Pour the batter into the prepared baking dish and bake for 25 minutes, or until the center of the cake springs back to the touch. Transfer the baking dish to a rack and let the cake cool for at least 30 minutes.

3. Meanwhile, in a medium saucepan, whisk the cream with the evaporated milk, cinnamon stick and cloves and bring to a boil over moderately high heat. Reduce the heat and simmer for 3 minutes. Remove from the heat, cover and let steep for 10 minutes.

4. In a heatproof bowl, combine the sweetened condensed milk with the remaining 1 teaspoon of vanilla and the ground cinnamon. Strain the steeped cream mixture into the condensed milk and stir to combine. Let cool for 20 minutes.

5. Using a fork, poke holes all over the cooled cake. Gradually pour the milk mixture over the entire cake. Cover with plastic wrap and refrigerate for at least 4 hours or overnight.

6. PREPARE THE TOPPINGS In a bowl, gently toss the strawberries with the sugar. Let stand at room temperature for 20 minutes, stirring occasionally to dissolve the sugar.

7. Cut the cake and serve with the strawberries, whipped cream and mint.
—Soledad Correa

MAKE AHEAD The tres leches cake can be made through Step 5 up to 2 days ahead. Prepare the strawberries, whipped cream and mint leaves just before serving.

358

● HEALTHY ● MAKE AHEAD ○ VEGETARIAN ● STAFF FAVORITE

Lemon-Glazed Citrus-Yogurt Pound Cake

ACTIVE: 20 MIN; TOTAL: 2 HR

MAKES 1 LOAF ● ●

Grapefruit juice in the cake and lemon juice in the glaze give this sweet, tender pound cake an especially citrusy taste. Be sure to use cake flour rather than the self-rising kind to ensure a lovely, feather-light texture.

CAKE

- 2 cups cake flour
- 1 teaspoon baking powder
- ¾ teaspoon baking soda
- ½ teaspoon salt
- ¼ cup grapefruit juice
- ½ cup full-fat plain yogurt
- 1 stick unsalted butter, softened
- 1 cup granulated sugar
- 2 large eggs
- 1 teaspoon finely grated lemon zest

GLAZE

- 3 tablespoons freshly squeezed lemon juice
- 3 tablespoons granulated sugar
- ½ cup confectioners' sugar
- 2 tablespoons unsalted butter, softened

1. MAKE THE CAKE Preheat the oven to 350°. Butter and flour a 9½-by-5-inch glass loaf pan. In a medium bowl, whisk the flour, baking powder, baking soda and salt. In a small bowl, whisk the grapefruit juice with the yogurt. In a medium bowl, using an electric mixer, beat the butter with the sugar at medium-high speed until fluffy. Beat in the eggs and lemon zest. Beat in the dry and wet ingredients in 3 alternating additions; scrape down the bowl as necessary.

2. Scrape the batter into the prepared loaf pan and bake for about 50 minutes, until the top is golden and lightly cracked and a toothpick inserted in the center comes out with moist crumbs attached. Loosely tent the cake with aluminum foil halfway through baking to slow the browning. Transfer the cake to a rack to cool for 20 minutes, then unmold and let cool.

3. MEANWHILE, MAKE THE GLAZE In a small microwave-safe bowl, microwave the lemon juice and granulated sugar at high power for about 20 seconds, until the sugar is dissolved. Transfer 2 tablespoons of the lemon syrup to a medium bowl and whisk in the confectioners' sugar and butter until smooth. Using a pastry brush, brush the lemon syrup all over the cake. Let stand for 10 minutes to allow the syrup to seep in. Spread the sugar glaze over the cake and let stand until completely dry, 30 minutes.

—Grace Parisi

MAKE AHEAD The glazed pound cake can be kept at room temperature in an airtight container for up to 4 days.

German Chocolate Cake

ACTIVE: 45 MIN; TOTAL: 3 HR

10 TO 12 SERVINGS ● ● ●

Sam German created the mild, dark baking chocolate called Baker's German's Sweet Chocolate in 1852; in the late 1950s, a Dallas newspaper published a recipe for German's Chocolate Cake. The dessert took the South by storm and has been a staple ever since.

CAKE

- 2½ cups cake flour
- ⅛ teaspoon cinnamon
- ⅛ teaspoon freshly grated nutmeg
- ¼ teaspoon salt
- 1 cup buttermilk
- 1 teaspoon pure vanilla extract
- 1 teaspoon baking soda
- 2 sticks unsalted butter, softened
- 2 cups sugar
- 4 large eggs, separated
- 6 ounces semisweet chocolate, melted and cooled

FROSTING

- 1¼ cup pecans
- 1 stick unsalted butter, softened
- 1 pound confectioners' sugar
- 1½ tablespoons unsweetened cocoa powder
- 1 teaspoon pure vanilla extract
- ¼ cup hot coffee
- ½ cup packed sweetened shredded coconut, plus more for garnish

1. MAKE THE CAKE Preheat the oven to 325°. Butter two 9-inch round cake pans. Line the bottoms with parchment paper, then butter and flour the paper.

2. In a small bowl, whisk the cake flour with the cinnamon, nutmeg and salt. In a measuring cup, stir the buttermilk with the vanilla extract and baking soda until combined. In the bowl of a standing electric mixer fitted with the paddle, beat the softened butter with the sugar until fluffy. Add the egg yolks and beat until they are incorporated, then beat in the melted chocolate, scraping down the side and bottom of the bowl as necessary. Beat in the dry and wet ingredients in 3 alternating batches, scraping down the side of the bowl occasionally.

3. Transfer the cake batter to a large bowl and wash out the mixing bowl. Add the egg whites to the mixing bowl and beat with the whisk until soft peaks form. Fold the beaten egg whites into the chocolate batter until no streaks remain.

4. Divide the batter evenly between the prepared pans and bake the cakes for about 45 to 50 minutes, until a toothpick inserted in the center comes out with just a few moist crumbs attached. Let the cakes cool slightly on a wire rack, then invert the cakes and peel off the parchment paper. Let the cakes cool completely.

5. MEANWHILE, MAKE THE FROSTING Spread the pecans in a pie plate and toast for about 12 minutes, until they are fragrant. Let cool, then coarsely chop 1 cup of the nuts, leaving the rest whole. In the bowl of a standing mixer fitted with the whisk (or using a handheld electric mixer), beat the softened butter with the confectioners' sugar and cocoa powder until combined. Add the vanilla extract and hot coffee and beat the frosting until fluffy. Fold in the ½ cup of shredded coconut and the chopped toasted pecans.

6. Place a cake layer on a plate and spread half of the frosting on top. Cover with the second cake layer and spread the remaining frosting on the top. Garnish the cake with shredded coconut and the whole toasted pecans. Cut the cake into wedges and serve.

—Martha Hall Foose

Take 5 Carrot Cupcakes

ACTIVE: 30 MIN; TOTAL: 1 HR
MAKES 14 CUPCAKES ● ○ ○

"No nuts, no fruit," is how chef Bryan Viet-meier describes the terrifically moist and carroty cupcakes he makes at Take 5 Urban Market in Seattle. He suggests freezing the cupcakes before frosting to firm them up, preventing crumbs.

  1 cup all-purpose flour
1½ teaspoons cinnamon
  1 teaspoon baking soda
  ½ teaspoon salt
  2 large eggs
  ¾ cup canola oil
  1 cup sugar
  1 teaspoon pure vanilla extract
1½ cups finely shredded carrots
     (from about 6 medium carrots)
Cream Cheese Frosting (recipe follows)

1. Preheat the oven to 350° and line 14 muffin cups with paper liners. Spray the liners with vegetable oil spray.
2. In a medium bowl, whisk the flour with the cinnamon, baking soda and salt. In a large bowl, using an electric mixer, beat the eggs with the canola oil. Gradually beat in the sugar at medium-high speed and beat until thick, about 3 minutes. Beat in the vanilla extract. Carefully fold in the dry ingredients with a rubber spatula, then fold in the shredded carrots.

super-simple icing

royal icing In a large bowl, beat 1 large egg white at medium speed until foamy. Beat in ½ pound confectioners' sugar, 1 cup at a time, until incorporated. Add ½ tablespoon fresh lemon juice and beat at high speed until the icing holds its shape, about 5 minutes. Thin with water as needed. —*Margaret Braun*

3. Spoon the batter into the prepared muffin cups and bake for about 25 to 30 minutes, until a toothpick inserted in the center of the cupcakes comes out clean. Let the cupcakes cool slightly in the pan, then transfer them to the freezer to chill.
4. Fill a pastry bag fitted with a ½-inch plain tip with the Cream Cheese Frosting. Pipe the frosting onto the carrot cupcakes and serve. Alternatively, use a knife to spread the frosting on the cupcakes and serve.
—*Bryan Vietmeier*

MAKE AHEAD The frosted cupcakes can be refrigerated for up to 3 days.

CREAM CHEESE FROSTING
TOTAL: 15 MIN • MAKES 1½ CUPS ● ○

  4 tablespoons unsalted butter, softened
  4 ounces cream cheese, softened
  ½ teaspoon pure vanilla extract
1¾ cups confectioners' sugar
     (8 ounces)

In a medium bowl, using an electric mixer, beat the butter with the cream cheese until the mixture is smooth. Beat in the vanilla extract and confectioners' sugar, then continue to beat the ingredients at high speed until the frosting is light and fluffy. —*BV*

Cocoa-Carrot Cake with Cocoa Crumble

ACTIVE: 40 MIN; TOTAL: 3 HR 30 MIN
MAKES 2 LOAVES ● ○ ○

San Francisco pastry chef William Werner likes carrot cake but was curious to experiment with the classic. So he added cocoa to the batter, resulting in this moist loaf with a chocolaty crumb topping.

CRUMBLE

  1 cup plus 2 tablespoons all-purpose flour
  ½ cup sugar
  ¾ cup almond flour (3 ounces)
  ¼ cup unsweetened cocoa powder
  ¼ teaspoon salt
  1 stick unsalted butter, softened

CAKE

  3 cups all-purpose flour
  ¼ cup unsweetened cocoa powder
  2 teaspoons baking powder
  1 teaspoon baking soda
  1 teaspoon salt
  ¾ teaspoon cinnamon
  2 cups sugar
  3 large eggs
1½ cups canola oil
  ⅓ cup crème fraîche or sour cream
  1 tablespoon finely grated ginger
  ½ vanilla bean, seeds scraped
  2 cups shredded carrots

1. MAKE THE CRUMBLE Preheat the oven to 350° and line a baking sheet with parchment paper. In the bowl of a standing mixer fitted with the paddle, combine the flour, sugar, almond flour, cocoa powder and salt. Add the butter and beat at medium-low speed until the dry ingredients are evenly moistened. Press the mixture into ½-inch clumps; refrigerate until firm, about 15 minutes. Spread the clumps on the baking sheet and bake for about 15 minutes, until fragrant and firm. Let cool. Wipe out the mixer bowl.
2. MAKE THE CAKE Butter and flour two 9-by-5-inch loaf pans. In a medium bowl, whisk the flour, cocoa powder, baking powder, baking soda, salt and cinnamon. In the mixer bowl, combine the sugar with the eggs, oil, crème fraîche, ginger and vanilla seeds and beat at medium speed until smooth. Gradually beat in the dry ingredients at low speed, scraping down the side of the bowl occasionally. Beat in the carrots.
3. Scrape the batter into the pans and top with the crumble. Bake in the center of the oven for 1 hour and 30 minutes, until a toothpick inserted in the center of the cakes comes out clean; cover the cakes loosely with foil during the last 30 minutes of baking. Transfer the pans to a rack and cool for 1 hour.
4. Lightly wrap the top of each cake in a sheet of foil to prevent the crumble from dislodging. Top with a rack and invert the cakes; remove the pans. Turn the cakes right side up and let cool completely before serving.
—*William Werner*

● HEALTHY ● MAKE AHEAD ○ VEGETARIAN ○ STAFF FAVORITE

take 5 carrot cupcakes

Amaro-Spiked Amaretti Cookies

ACTIVE: 30 MIN; TOTAL: 1 HR 10 MIN

MAKES ABOUT 3½ DOZEN COOKIES ● ● ●

While the names for amaretti cookies and *amaro* digestif both derive from the Italian word for bitter, amaretti are traditionally made with bitter almonds, while *amaro* gets its edge from roots, barks and other aromatics. Here, F&W's Grace Parisi marries the two in a deliciously chewy cookie.

One 7-ounce package pure
    almond paste, broken up
 1 cup sugar
Pinch of salt
 2 tablespoons *amaro* digestif,
    such as Amaro Lucano
 2 large egg whites
Pearl sugar, for decorating
    (see Note)

1. Preheat the oven to 375° and position the racks in the upper and lower thirds of the oven. Line 2 baking sheets with parchment paper. In a food processor, combine the almond paste, sugar and salt and process until very finely chopped. Add the *amaro* digestif and egg whites and process until smooth. Transfer the batter to a pastry bag fitted with a ½-inch plain tip and pipe scant 1-inch mounds of batter onto the prepared baking sheets, 2 inches apart. Sprinkle generously with pearl sugar.

2. Bake the cookies for about 15 minutes, until risen and lightly cracked; shift the pans from top to bottom and front to back halfway through baking. Let the cookies cool completely on the paper (the cookies will stick to the paper). Invert the paper onto a work surface and carefully peel it off the backs of the cookies. Repeat with the remaining batter, then serve. —*Grace Parisi*

SERVE WITH After-dinner drinks, espresso or fresh fruit.

NOTE Pearl sugar, a coarse-grain sugar, is available online at *kingarthurflour.com.*

MAKE AHEAD The amaretti cookies can be stored in an airtight container at room temperature for up to 3 days.

Buttery Hazelnut-Fig Biscotti

ACTIVE: 30 MIN; TOTAL: 2 HR

MAKES ABOUT 6 DOZEN BISCOTTI ● ● ●

2½ cups hazelnuts (10 ounces)
 14 ounces dried Calimyrna figs
1½ sticks cold unsalted butter, cubed
1¾ cups sugar
 3 large eggs
3½ cups all-purpose flour
 1 tablespoon baking powder
1½ teaspoons salt

1. Preheat the oven to 325° and position racks in the upper and lower thirds of the oven. Spread the hazelnuts on a baking sheet and toast for 12 to 14 minutes, until the skins blister. Let cool, then transfer the nuts to a kitchen towel and rub off as much of the skins as possible. Transfer the nuts to a cutting board and coarsely chop.

2. Meanwhile, in a microwave-safe bowl, cover the figs with water and microwave at high power for 1 minute, just until the figs are plump. Drain well. Trim off the stem ends and slice the figs ⅛ inch thick.

3. In the bowl of a standing mixer fitted with the paddle, beat the butter with the sugar at medium speed until smooth. Beat in the eggs. In a small bowl, whisk the flour with the baking powder and salt. Add the dry ingredients to the butter mixture and beat at low speed until combined. Add the nuts and figs and beat until combined.

4. Line 2 large baking sheets with parchment paper. Transfer the dough to a work surface and roll into six 10-by-1½-inch logs. Arrange the logs on the baking sheets and bake for 30 minutes, or until golden and firm. Let the logs cool for 15 minutes.

5. On a work surface, using a serrated knife, slice the logs on the diagonal ⅔ inch thick. Arrange the biscotti cut side up on the baking sheets and bake for about 18 minutes, until lightly browned. Let the biscotti cool, then serve or store in an airtight container. —*Julianne Jones*

MAKE AHEAD The biscotti can be stored in an airtight container at room temperature for up to 2 weeks.

Almond Crisps with Dried Cherries, Anise and Chocolate

ACTIVE: 30 MIN; TOTAL: 5 HR

MAKES 32 COOKIES ● ● ●

 ½ cup plus 2 tablespoons
    granulated sugar
 1 teaspoon anise seeds, crushed
 3 ounces sliced almonds (¾ cup)
1¼ cups all-purpose flour
 ¼ teaspoon salt
 ½ cup bittersweet chocolate chips
 ⅓ cup dried sour cherries
 6 tablespoons unsalted butter,
    cubed and chilled
 2 tablespoons ice water
 1 teaspoon pure vanilla extract
 1 tablespoon heavy cream
 2 tablespoons turbinado sugar

1. In a food processor, combine the granulated sugar and anise seeds and pulse once or twice. Add the almonds, flour and salt and pulse until the almonds are coarsely chopped. Add the chocolate chips and dried cherries and pulse until they are coarsely chopped. Add the butter and pulse until the mixture resembles coarse meal. Sprinkle on the ice water and vanilla extract and pulse until the dough is moistened.

2. Turn the dough out onto a sheet of plastic wrap and press to compact it. Using a straight edge, press the dough into a 4-by-10-inch rectangle and wrap it in plastic. Refrigerate until firm, at least 4 hours or overnight.

3. Preheat the oven to 350° and line 2 baking sheets with parchment paper. Brush the dough with the cream; sprinkle with the turbinado sugar. Pass a rolling pin over the top to help the sugar adhere. On a work surface, cut the dough in half to form two 5-by-4-inch rectangles. Cut each rectangle into sixteen 5-by-¼-inch slices. Lay the slices on the baking sheets and bake in the upper and lower thirds of the oven for about 30 minutes, until golden; shift the sheets from top to bottom and front to back halfway through baking. Transfer the baking sheets to racks and let the cookies cool completely.
—*Malika Ameen*

Dried Cranberry and Chocolate Cookies

◔ **ACTIVE: 15 MIN; TOTAL: 30 MIN**
MAKES 3 TO 4 DOZEN COOKIES ● ○

Cookbook author Sally Sampson adds dried cranberries and rolled oats to buttery chocolate chip cookie dough to make the cookies crunchier and more substantial. Her recipe is in the *Best Bake Sale Cookbook* by Gretchen Holt-Witt, whose proceeds benefit pediatric-cancer research.

- 2 cups all-purpose flour
- 1 cup quick-cooking or old-fashioned rolled oats
- 1 teaspoon baking powder
- 1 teaspoon baking soda
- 1 teaspoon kosher salt
- 2½ sticks unsalted butter (10 ounces), at room temperature
- 1 cup light brown sugar
- ½ cup granulated sugar
- 1 large egg, at room temperature
- 1 large egg yolk, at room temperature
- 1 tablespoon pure vanilla extract
- 1½ cups semisweet or white chocolate chips
- 1½ cups dried cranberries

1. Preheat the oven to 325°. Line 2 baking sheets with parchment paper.
2. In a medium bowl, mix the flour with the oats, baking powder, baking soda and salt. In a standing mixer fitted with the paddle, beat the butter and both sugars at medium speed until creamy. Add the egg followed by the egg yolk and vanilla, beating well between additions and scraping down the side of the bowl as necessary. Beat in the dry ingredients, then add the chocolate chips and cranberries and beat until incorporated.
3. Spoon heaping teaspoons of the dough onto the baking sheets, 2 inches apart. Bake for 12 to 15 minutes, until the cookies begin to brown at the edges. Let the cookies cool on the baking sheets, then transfer them to a rack to cool completely. —*Sally Sampson*

MAKE AHEAD The cookies can be stored in an airtight container for up to 4 days.

Chocolate Wafers with Ginger, Fennel and Sea Salt

◔ **TOTAL: 30 MIN • MAKES 16 WAFERS**
● ● ○ ○

Dark chocolate with a high cacao content is lower in sugar and higher in antioxidants than milk chocolate. For this ingenious snack, wafer-thin crispbreads are coated in dark chocolate so that they resemble candy bars studded with flaky Maldon sea salt, crystallized ginger and candied fennel seeds.

- 1½ teaspoons fennel seeds
- ¼ teaspoon sugar
- 7 ounces bittersweet chocolate (70 to 75 percent cacao), chopped
- 16 wafer-thin crispbreads, such as Finn Crisp (1½ by 3 inches)
- 2 tablespoons minced crystallized ginger

Maldon sea salt

1. Line a baking sheet with parchment paper and set aside. In a small skillet, toast the fennel seeds over moderate heat until fragrant, about 2 minutes. Add the sugar and cook, stirring frequently, until the sugar is melted and coats the seeds, about 15 seconds. Scrape the candied fennel seeds onto a plate and let cool. Crumble any clumps to separate the seeds.
2. Put the chocolate into a microwave-safe bowl and microwave in 30-second bursts until almost melted. Stir the chocolate until completely melted and an instant-read thermometer inserted in it registers 90°.
3. Working very quickly, dip a crispbread in the chocolate and use an offset spatula to spread the chocolate in a very thin layer so it completely coats the crispbread. Transfer to the prepared baking sheet and sprinkle with some of the fennel seeds, ginger and sea salt. Repeat with the remaining crispbreads, chocolate and toppings. Refrigerate the chocolate-covered crispbreads until just set, about 5 minutes, then serve.
—*Grace Parisi*

MAKE AHEAD The chocolate-covered crispbreads can be stored in an airtight container at room temperature for up to 5 days.

Chocolate Snickerdoodles

◔ **ACTIVE: 15 MIN; TOTAL: 30 MIN**
MAKES 3 DOZEN COOKIES ● ○

- 1¾ cups all-purpose flour
- 1 teaspoon baking soda
- ½ teaspoon baking powder
- Pinch of salt
- 1 stick unsalted butter, softened
- 1½ cups sugar
- 2 ounces unsweetened chocolate, melted and cooled
- 1 large egg
- 1 teaspoon cinnamon

1. Preheat the oven to 400°. In a medium bowl, sift the flour with the baking soda, baking powder and salt. In a large bowl, using an electric mixer, beat the butter with 1 cup of the sugar until creamy. Add the chocolate and the egg and beat until smooth. Beat in the dry ingredients until incorporated.
2. In a shallow bowl, mix the remaining ½ cup of sugar with the cinnamon. Roll the dough into 1-inch balls and roll in the cinnamon sugar. Transfer to 3 parchment paper–lined baking sheets and flatten to 2-inch rounds. Bake for 12 to 14 minutes, until the cookies are puffed and cracked. Transfer to racks and let cool. —*Grace Parisi*

easy ice cream sandwiches

To make ice cream sandwiches, layer one of the following between two cookies and freeze until firm.

dulce de leche ice cream with Chocolate Snickerdoodles, above.

pistachio ice cream with Dried Cranberry and Chocolate Cookies, at far left.

lemon sherbet with gingersnaps.

coconut sorbet with oatmeal-raisin cookies.

Baby Bûche de Noël Cookies

ACTIVE: 45 MIN; TOTAL: 3 HR 30 MIN
MAKES 16 COOKIES ● ●

Jessie Oleson, the Seattle pastry chef behind the blog Cakespy, cuts ropes of chocolate cookie dough into mini logs to resemble the classic French *bûche de Noël* cake.

COOKIES

- 6 tablespoons unsalted butter, softened
- 2 tablespoons granulated sugar
- 2 tablespoons light brown sugar
- ¼ teaspoon salt
- ½ teaspoon pure vanilla extract
- ¾ cup all-purpose flour
- ⅓ cup unsweetened cocoa powder
- 2 tablespoons heavy cream

FROSTING

- 2 ounces cream cheese, softened
- 1 cup confectioners' sugar, sifted
- ½ teaspoon unsweetened cocoa powder
- 1½ teaspoons heavy cream
- ½ ounce unsweetened chocolate, melted

1. MAKE THE COOKIES In a medium bowl, using an electric mixer at medium speed, beat the butter with the granulated sugar, brown sugar, salt and vanilla until smooth. Add the flour and cocoa and beat at low speed just until incorporated, then beat in the cream until smooth. Turn the dough out onto a work surface and roll it into two 16-inch-long ropes. Wrap the dough in plastic and refrigerate until firm, about 20 minutes.
2. Preheat the oven to 400° and line a baking sheet with parchment paper. Cut the cookie dough into 2-inch logs and arrange them on the baking sheet. Bake for 20 minutes, until the tops crack lightly and the cookies are firm to the touch. Transfer the baking sheet to a rack and let the cookies cool completely.
3. MEANWHILE, MAKE THE FROSTING In a medium bowl, using an electric mixer at medium speed, beat the cream cheese with the confectioners' sugar, cocoa and cream until smooth. Beat in the melted chocolate.

4. Spread the frosting on each of the cookies in lengthwise strips to resemble the bark of a tree. Return the cookies to the baking sheet and let stand at room temperature until the frosting firms up, about 2 hours. —*Jessie Oleson*

MAKE AHEAD The cookies can be stored in an airtight container for up to 3 days.

Semolina-Corn Sablés

ACTIVE: 30 MIN; TOTAL: 1 HR 30 MIN
PLUS COOLING • MAKES 30 COOKIES ● ● ●

Sablés are crisp French butter cookies. Instead of baking them—as in this version—San Francisco pastry chef William Werner typically dehydrates them. He also likes to combine sweet and savory flavors; here, he mixes crushed corn nuts into the buttery dough, which gives the cookies extra crunch.

- 1¼ cups almond flour (4½ ounces), see Note
- ⅓ cup confectioners' sugar
- 3½ tablespoons semolina
- 2 tablespoons cornstarch

Pinch of salt

- 4 tablespoons unsalted butter, softened
- 1 large egg white
- 1 tablespoon finely crushed corn nuts

1. In the bowl of a food processor, pulse the almond flour, confectioners' sugar, semolina, cornstarch and salt. Add the softened butter and pulse until smooth. Add the egg white and pulse until incorporated. Add the crushed corn nuts and pulse just until blended. Scrape the dough (it will be very soft) onto a sheet of plastic wrap and top with another sheet. Pat the dough into a rough 10-by-8-inch rectangle and transfer to a baking sheet. Freeze the dough until it is very firm, about 30 minutes.
2. Preheat the oven to 325° and line a baking sheet with parchment paper. On a floured surface, unwrap the dough and trim it to an even 10-by-8-inch rectangle. Cut lengthwise into 3 strips and then crosswise into 1-inch-wide rectangles. Arrange on the baking sheet, about ½ inch apart.

3. Bake the cookies for 30 minutes, until they are golden; transfer to a rack to cool. Serve. —*William Werner*

NOTE Look for almond flour, made from whole blanched almonds, at *kingarthurflour.com.*

Green Tea Sablés

ACTIVE: 30 MIN; TOTAL: 1 HR 30 MIN
MAKES ABOUT 2 DOZEN COOKIES ● ●

Ginkgo trees in San Francisco's Museum of Modern Art sculpture garden inspired these leaf cookies by in-house pastry chef Caitlin Williams Freeman.

- 1½ cups all-purpose flour
- ½ teaspoon baking soda
- ½ teaspoon fine sea salt
- 1 teaspoon matcha powder (see Note)
- 1 stick plus 3 tablespoons unsalted butter, softened
- ¾ cup sugar

1. Preheat the oven to 325°. In a small bowl, whisk the flour with the baking soda, salt and matcha powder.
2. In a large bowl, beat the softened butter until creamy. Beat in the sugar until light and fluffy, then beat in the flour mixture. Pat the dough into a 6-inch disk. Wrap in plastic and refrigerate until chilled.
3. On a lightly floured work surface, roll out the dough a scant ⅜ inch thick. Using a floured 2½-inch cookie cutter, stamp out as many cookies as possible. Carefully transfer the cookies to parchment paper–lined baking sheets, leaving 1 inch of space between them. Reroll the scraps, chill and stamp out more cookies. Bake the cookies one sheet at a time until they are lightly browned around the edges, about 16 minutes. Let cool slightly, then transfer the cookies to a rack to cool. —*Caitlin Williams Freeman*

SAFFRON SABLÉS Omit the matcha powder. Crumble ¼ teaspoon of saffron threads into ½ teaspoon of pure vanilla extract and add it to the butter in Step 2.

NOTE Matcha, a finely milled green tea, is available at Asian markets and *amazon.com.*

● HEALTHY ● MAKE AHEAD ● VEGETARIAN ● STAFF FAVORITE

baby bûche de noël cookies

cakes, cookies and more

Eggnog-Stuffed Cookies

ACTIVE: 35 MIN; TOTAL: 2 HR 30 MIN
MAKES 2 DOZEN COOKIES ● ○

The holiday-inspired filling for these tender ginger cookies combines cream cheese with store-bought eggnog, sugar and spices.

FILLING

- 4 ounces cream cheese, softened
- 1¼ cups confectioners' sugar
- 1½ tablespoons prepared eggnog
- ⅛ teaspoon freshly grated nutmeg
- ⅛ teaspoon cinnamon

COOKIES

- 1½ cups all-purpose flour
- ½ cup cornstarch
- 1 teaspoon ground ginger
- ½ teaspoon baking powder
- ¼ teaspoon salt
- 1 teaspoon cinnamon
- 2½ sticks unsalted butter, softened
- ⅓ cup packed dark brown sugar
- 3 large egg yolks
- 2 teaspoons dark molasses

Confectioners' sugar, for dusting

1. MAKE THE FILLING In a medium bowl, using an electric mixer at low speed, beat the softened cream cheese with the confectioners' sugar, eggnog, grated nutmeg and cinnamon. Freeze the filling until firm, about 30 minutes.

2. MEANWHILE, MAKE THE COOKIES Line 2 baking sheets with parchment paper. In a medium bowl, whisk the flour with the cornstarch, ground ginger, baking powder, salt and cinnamon. In a large bowl, using an electric mixer, beat the softened butter with the brown sugar at medium speed until fluffy. Beat in the egg yolks and molasses. Add the dry ingredients and beat at low speed until they are incorporated. Using a 2-tablespoon-size scoop, scoop 24 mounds of the dough onto the baking sheets and refrigerate until the dough is slightly firm, about 30 minutes.

3. Preheat the oven to 325°. Working with one baking sheet at a time, using floured hands, press a deep hollow in the center of each mound of dough and spoon in a level teaspoon of the cream cheese filling. Pinch the tops closed, creating a "kiss"; be sure to seal any cracks or holes. Repeat with the remaining dough and filling. Refrigerate until the cookies are firm, about 15 minutes.

4. Bake the cookies in the upper and lower thirds of the oven for about 30 minutes, until they are golden and the tops are lightly cracked; shift the sheets from top to bottom and front to back halfway through baking. Transfer the baking sheets to racks and let the cookies cool completely. Dust the tops of the cookies with confectioners' sugar before serving. —*Jessie Oleson*

MAKE AHEAD The cookies can be refrigerated for up to 4 days

Shortbread with Marmalade and Vanilla Ice Cream

ACTIVE: 1 HR; TOTAL: 2 HR 30 MIN
8 SERVINGS ● ○ ○

When making these buttery shortbread bars, "the key is to work the dough by hand," says Kenny Rochford, the general manager at Sonoma's Medlock Ames Winery. "No modern mixers here!"

- 3½ cups all-purpose flour
- ¾ cup sugar
- 3 sticks unsalted butter, at room temperature, plus more for greasing
- ½ cup Hand-Cut Orange-and-Lemon Marmalade (recipe follows), for serving

Vanilla ice cream and mint leaves, for serving

1. Preheat the oven to 300°. In a large bowl, mix the flour and sugar. Add the 3 sticks of butter and gently work it into the flour with your fingers until a dough forms.

2. Line a 10-by-15-inch rimmed baking sheet with parchment paper; butter the paper. Press the dough evenly into the prepared pan, about ⅓ inch thick. With a knife, score the dough into 2½-by-2-inch bars. Bake the shortbread for about 50 minutes, until pale golden and set. While the shortbread is still hot, cut it into bars. Transfer the baking sheet to a rack and let cool.

3. Set 1 shortbread bar on each plate and spoon about 1 tablespoon of the marmalade on each one. Top each shortbread with ice cream, garnish with mint and serve. —*Kenny Rochford*

MAKE AHEAD The shortbread can be kept in an airtight container for up to 3 days or frozen for up to 1 month.

HAND-CUT ORANGE-AND-LEMON MARMALADE

ACTIVE: 40 MIN; TOTAL: 2 HR 30 MIN
MAKES 6 CUPS ● ○ ○

Kenny Rochford's mother made a lot of marmalade when he was growing up. "I've got the bug myself now," he says. The best results, he advises, come from patiently waiting for the marmalade to set up on its own rather than adding pectin.

- 4 pounds oranges, scrubbed
- 4 lemons, scrubbed
- 5 cups sugar

1. Fill a large pot with water and add the oranges and lemons. Bring to a boil, cover and simmer over moderate heat for 1 hour, turning the fruit a few times. Set a colander over a bowl and gently drain the fruit.

2. When the fruit is cool enough to handle, halve the oranges and lemons and scrape the insides onto a large piece of dampened cheesecloth. Tie the cloth into a bundle. Cut the peels into very thin strips.

3. In a wide, heavy pot, combine the citrus peels with the sugar and 7 cups of water and bring to a boil, stirring to dissolve the sugar. Add the cheesecloth bundle and boil over moderately high heat for about 20 minutes, stirring occasionally. Using tongs or a slotted spoon, transfer the cheesecloth bundle to a bowl; when cool enough to handle, squeeze out as much liquid as possible. Add the liquid to the pot and discard the bundle. Continue cooking the marmalade until the syrup is very thick and glossy and the temperature registers 220° on a candy thermometer, about 20 minutes longer. Pour the marmalade into sterile jars, let cool and refrigerate. —*KR*

● HEALTHY ● MAKE AHEAD ○ VEGETARIAN ● STAFF FAVORITE

Coconut Macaroons

ACTIVE: 30 MIN; TOTAL: 1 HR
MAKES ABOUT 40 MACAROONS ● ● ●

"Before I married the macaroon, my maiden name was Cohen," says the man everyone calls Danny Macaroons. He launched a business selling the amazing coconut cookies he liked to bake on Passover. Now, they have a cult following and their own website, *dannymacaroons.com*. His sweet and chewy two-bite macaroons here have only five ingredients (not including the delicious bittersweet-chocolate drizzle). Cohen doesn't think all macaroons have to be round. "Make whatever shape you want," he says. "There are no rules."

One 14-ounce bag sweetened
    shredded coconut
One 14-ounce can sweetened
    condensed milk
1 teaspoon pure vanilla extract
2 large egg whites
¼ teaspoon salt
4 ounces bittersweet chocolate,
    melted

1. Preheat the oven to 350° and line 2 baking sheets with parchment paper. In a medium bowl, combine the coconut with the sweetened condensed milk and vanilla. In another bowl, using an electric mixer, beat the egg whites with the salt until firm peaks form. Fold the beaten whites into the coconut mixture.
2. Scoop tablespoon-size mounds of the mixture onto the baking sheets, about 1 inch apart. Bake in the upper and middle thirds of the oven for about 25 minutes, until golden; shift the sheets from top to bottom and front to back halfway through baking. Transfer the baking sheets to racks and let the cookies cool completely.
3. Dip the bottoms of the macaroons into the melted chocolate, letting any excess drip back into the bowl. Return the cookies to the lined baking sheets. Drizzle any remaining chocolate on top and refrigerate for about 5 minutes, until set. —*Danny Cohen*
MAKE AHEAD The macaroons can be refrigerated for up to 2 weeks.

Chocolate-Hazelnut Clouds with Cocoa Nibs

ACTIVE: 20 MIN; TOTAL: 1 HR
MAKES 16 COOKIES ● ● ●

"Spices in dessert are completely underrated," says Chicago pastry chef Malika Ameen. She adds a bit of cardamom along with crunchy cocoa nibs to these light and puffy chocolate meringues.

¼ cup hazelnuts
1 tablespoon unsweetened
    cocoa powder
2 teaspoons cornstarch
1½ teaspoons cocoa nibs
2 ounces bittersweet chocolate,
    finely chopped
⅛ to ¼ teaspoon ground cardamom
3 large egg whites
⅛ teaspoon cream of tartar
Pinch of salt
¾ cup sugar
½ teaspoon pure vanilla extract

1. Preheat the oven to 350° and line 2 baking sheets with parchment paper. Spread the hazelnuts in a pie plate and toast for 14 minutes, until the skins blister. Transfer the nuts to a kitchen towel and rub together to remove the skins. Coarsely chop the nuts and transfer them to a bowl. Add the cocoa powder, cornstarch, cocoa nibs, chocolate and cardamom. Lower the oven to 300°.
2. In a medium bowl, using an electric mixer, beat the egg whites with the cream of tartar and salt until soft peaks form. Add the sugar in a thin stream and beat until the whites are stiff and glossy. Beat in the vanilla. Fold in the dry ingredients, leaving some streaks.
3. Scoop 8 level tablespoon-size mounds of the meringue onto each baking sheet. Scoop the remaining meringue directly on top of the existing mounds, as if forming little snowmen.
4. Bake the cookies in the upper and lower thirds of the oven for about 30 minutes, until firm when tapped; shift the sheets halfway through baking. Transfer the sheets to racks and let the cookies cool before serving.
—*Malika Ameen*

Crisp Butter Cookies

ACTIVE: 30 MIN; TOTAL: 1 HR 40 MIN
MAKES ABOUT 2½ DOZEN COOKIES ● ●

1 cup all-purpose flour
¼ teaspoon salt
⅔ cup unsalted butter, softened
½ cup plus 1½ tablespoons sugar
1 large egg
1 teaspoon pure vanilla extract

1. In a small bowl, whisk the flour with the salt. In a medium bowl, using an electric mixer, beat the butter with the sugar at medium speed until creamy, about 3 minutes. Beat in the egg and vanilla. Add the flour and beat at medium-low speed until a very soft dough forms. Divide the dough in half, flatten into disks and wrap in plastic. Refrigerate the dough until firm, about 30 minutes.
2. Line 2 large baking sheets with parchment paper. On a well-floured surface, roll out one disk of dough ⅜ inch thick. Using a 2¼-inch round cutter, stamp out as many cookies as possible; transfer to the baking sheets. Repeat with the second disk of dough. Gather, chill and reroll the scraps, cutting out more cookies. Refrigerate for 15 minutes, until firm.
3. Preheat the oven to 350°. Bake the cookies for about 18 minutes, until golden, shifting the pans halfway through baking. Let the cookies cool for 5 minutes, then transfer to racks to cool completely. —*Ethan Stowell*

ingredient tip

chocolate Bars, not chips, melt best for shiny glazes like the dip and drizzle used for Danny Cohen's Coconut Macaroons, at far left.

Bacon-Bourbon Brownies with Pecans

ACTIVE: 30 MIN; TOTAL: 1 HR 40 MIN

MAKES 2 DOZEN BROWNIES ●

Kat Kinsman, the managing editor of the Eatocracy blog on *cnn.com,* tops her rich brownies with bacon and pecans. To enhance the smoky flavor, she mixes some of the bacon fat into the batter.

- ½ cup pecans
- ½ pound sliced bacon
- 8 ounces bittersweet chocolate, chopped
- 2 ounces unsweetened chocolate, chopped
- 1 stick plus 2 tablespoons unsalted butter
- 1 cup granulated sugar
- ½ cup packed light brown sugar
- 3 tablespoons bourbon
- 4 large eggs
- 1 teaspoon salt
- ¼ cup unsweetened cocoa powder
- 1½ cups all-purpose flour

1. Preheat the oven to 350°. Line a 9-inch square baking pan with parchment paper, allowing 2 inches of overhang on 2 opposite sides. Spray the paper with vegetable oil spray. Spread the pecans in a pie plate and toast for about 8 minutes, until fragrant. Let cool, then coarsely chop the nuts.

2. In a skillet, cook the sliced bacon over moderate heat, turning once, until crisp, about 6 minutes. Drain on paper towels and let cool; reserve 3 tablespoons of the bacon fat. Finely chop the bacon.

3. In a saucepan, combine both chocolates with the butter and stir over very low heat until melted; scrape into a large bowl. Using a handheld electric mixer, beat in the granulated sugar and light brown sugar with the reserved 3 tablespoons of bacon fat. Beat in the bourbon. Add the eggs and salt and beat until smooth. Sift the cocoa and flour into the bowl and beat until blended.

4. Scrape the batter into the prepared baking pan and sprinkle the bacon bits and toasted pecans on top.

5. Bake until the brownies are set around the edges but slightly wobbly in the center, about 50 minutes; a toothpick inserted into the center should have some batter clinging to it. Transfer the pan to a rack and let the brownies cool completely. Lift the brownies out of the pan using the parchment paper. Cut into squares or rectangles and serve.
—*Kat Kinsman*

Gooey Chocolate Chip Sandwich Bars

ACTIVE: 25 MIN; TOTAL: 1 HR 15 MIN

MAKES 32 BARS ● ○ ○

For these super-simple, indulgent bars, two layers of chocolate chip cookie dough are sandwiched with a fudgy, three-ingredient filling and baked.

- 2 cups semisweet chocolate chips
- One 14-ounce can sweetened condensed milk
- 2 teaspoons pure vanilla extract
- Dried Cranberry and Chocolate Cookie dough (page 363)

1. Preheat the oven to 350°. Lightly butter a 9-by-13-inch baking dish. Line the dish with parchment paper, leaving 1 inch of overhang on the long sides.

2. In a small saucepan, melt the chocolate chips in the sweetened condensed milk over low heat, stirring constantly, until smooth and thickened, 3 to 5 minutes. Remove from the heat. Stir in the vanilla and let cool to room temperature.

3. Press half of the cookie dough into the prepared baking dish. Pour the cooled chocolate mixture over the dough and spread evenly. Top with small dollops of the remaining cookie dough; don't worry if the dollops don't completely cover the chocolate mixture. Bake for 20 to 25 minutes, until the top is lightly browned. Let cool completely before cutting into bars.
—*Sally Sampson*

NOTE The cranberries can be omitted from the cookie dough if desired.

MAKE AHEAD The bars can be stored in an airtight container for up to 4 days.

Chocolate-Chip-Pecan Cookie Bars

ACTIVE: 20 MIN; TOTAL: 1 HR

MAKES 32 BARS ● ○ ○

Breanne Varela's chocolate chip cookies are hugely popular at Tavern in Los Angeles. Her chocolate chip bars here are easier to prepare than the cookies. Using whole wheat pastry flour instead of white makes the bars a bit healthier. Feel free to swap walnuts or almonds for the pecans, or use half nuts and half dried cranberries for tart, chewy bars.

- 1 cup pecans
- 4 tablespoons unsalted butter, softened
- 2 tablespoons canola oil
- ¼ cup plus 2 tablespoons granulated sugar
- ¼ cup plus 2 tablespoons light brown sugar
- 1 large egg
- 1 teaspoon pure vanilla extract
- 1½ cups whole wheat pastry flour
- ½ teaspoon baking soda
- ½ teaspoon kosher salt
- 1 cup semisweet chocolate chips

1. Preheat the oven to 350° and line the bottom of a 9-by-13-inch baking pan with parchment paper. Spread the pecans in a pie plate and toast for about 8 minutes, until golden. Chop the pecans and let cool.

2. In the bowl of a standing electric mixer, beat the butter and oil with the granulated sugar and brown sugar until creamy. Beat in the egg and vanilla until smooth. In a small bowl, whisk the flour with the baking soda and salt; beat the dry ingredients into the mixer at low speed. Add the chocolate chips and pecans; beat just until incorporated.

3. Transfer the dough to the prepared pan and press into an even layer. Bake for 20 minutes, until lightly browned and nearly set in the center. Let cool completely, then run a knife around the edges and invert the rectangle. Peel off the paper, invert onto a cutting board, then cut and serve. —*Breanne Varela*

MAKE AHEAD The cookie bars can be stored in an airtight container for up to 5 days.

● HEALTHY ● MAKE AHEAD ○ VEGETARIAN ● STAFF FAVORITE

bacon-bourbon brownies with pecans

Crêpes Suzette

🕐 TOTAL: 45 MIN • 6 SERVINGS ● ●

While restaurants traditionally make the buttery, orange-flavored sauce for this famous dessert tableside, master chef Jacques Pépin finds it easier to prepare largely in advance when entertaining. He does, however, flambé the liquor in front of his dinner guests and pours it over the platter of crêpes while it's still flaming.

CRÊPES

- 2 large eggs
- ¾ cup all-purpose flour
- ½ cup milk
- ⅛ teaspoon salt
- ½ teaspoon sugar
- ⅓ cup cold water
- 1 tablespoon canola oil
- 1 tablespoon unsalted butter, melted, plus more butter for the skillet

ORANGE BUTTER

- 6 tablespoons unsalted butter, softened, plus more for buttering
- ¼ cup plus 2 tablespoons sugar, plus more for sprinkling
- 1 tablespoon finely grated orange zest
- ⅓ cup fresh orange juice
- ¼ cup Grand Marnier
- 2 tablespoons Cognac

1. MAKE THE CRÊPES In a medium bowl, whisk together the eggs, flour, milk, salt and sugar until smooth; the batter will be thick. Whisk in the water, canola oil and 1 tablespoon of melted butter.

2. Heat a 6-inch crêpe pan or nonstick skillet and rub with a little butter. Add 2 tablespoons of the batter and tilt the skillet to distribute the batter evenly, pouring any excess batter back into the bowl. Cook over moderately high heat until the edge of the crêpe curls up and starts to brown, 45 seconds. Flip the crêpe and cook for 10 seconds longer, until a few brown spots appear on the bottom. Tap the crêpe out onto a baking sheet. Repeat with the remaining batter to make 12 crêpes, buttering the skillet a few times as necessary.

3. MAKE THE ORANGE BUTTER In a mini food processor, blend the 6 tablespoons of butter with ¼ cup of the sugar and the orange zest. With the machine on, gradually add the orange juice until incorporated.

4. Preheat the broiler. Butter a large rimmed baking sheet and sprinkle lightly with sugar. Place 2 rounded teaspoons of the orange butter in the center of each crêpe. Fold the crêpes in half and in half again to form triangles; arrange on the prepared baking sheet, pointing them in the same direction and overlapping slightly. Sprinkle with the remaining 2 tablespoons of sugar and broil on the middle shelf of the oven until they begin to caramelize, about 2 minutes. Using a long spatula, transfer the crêpes to a heatproof platter.

5. Meanwhile, in a small saucepan, heat the Grand Marnier and Cognac. Ignite the alcohol carefully with a long-handled match and pour the flaming mixture over the crêpes. Tilt the platter and, with a spoon, very carefully baste the crêpes until the flames subside. Serve them right away.

—*Jacques Pépin*

WINE Sauternes: 2009 Château Grillon.

Ricotta Blintzes with Lingonberry Syrup

ACTIVE: 45 MIN; TOTAL: 2 HR

10 SERVINGS ●

Tory Miller, the chef at L'Etoile in Madison, Wisconsin, uses a blast freezer to preserve local produce in the summer and fall. The device rapidly freezes foods before large ice crystals form, minimizing damage to fresh fruits and vegetables, including the lingonberries he simmers in maple syrup for these blintzes. Lingonberry jam makes a fine and much easier-to-find substitute.

BATTER

- ½ cup all-purpose flour
- ½ teaspoon baking powder
- Salt
- 4 large eggs
- ½ cup milk
- 1 tablespoon sugar
- 1 tablespoon unsalted butter, melted

FILLING

- 3 cups fresh ricotta cheese (24 ounces)
- ¼ cup sugar
- ¾ teaspoon cinnamon

SYRUP

- One 10-ounce jar lingonberry jam (see Note)
- 1 cup pure maple syrup
- Confectioners' sugar, for dusting

1. MAKE THE BATTER In a medium bowl, whisk the flour with the baking powder and a pinch of salt. In another medium bowl, whisk the eggs with the milk and sugar. Whisk the flour and egg mixtures together, then whisk in the butter. Cover and let the batter stand for 1 hour.

2. MAKE THE FILLING In a large bowl, mix together the ricotta, sugar and cinnamon.

3. PREPARE THE SYRUP In a medium saucepan, combine the lingonberry jam and maple syrup and simmer over moderate heat until slightly reduced, about 5 minutes.

4. Heat two 8-inch nonstick skillets. Spray with vegetable oil spray and add 2 tablespoons of batter to each. Swirl the skillets to distribute the batter and cook over moderate heat until golden brown on the bottom, 1 minute. Flip the crêpes and cook until brown spots appear on the bottom. Transfer the crêpes to a cookie sheet. Repeat with the remaining batter to make 20 crêpes.

5. Preheat the oven to 350°. Line another cookie sheet with parchment. On a work surface, spread 2 rounded tablespoons of the filling in the center of each crêpe. Fold each to form a rectangular packet. Arrange the blintzes on the cookie sheet, seams down. Bake until hot, about 15 minutes.

6. Rewarm the lingonberry syrup. Place 2 blintzes on each plate. Dust with confectioners' sugar, pour the warm syrup over the blintzes and serve right away. —*Tory Miller*

NOTE Lingonberry jam is available at Ikea or online at *lingonberryjam.com*.

MAKE AHEAD Unfilled, stacked crêpes can be refrigerated for up to 4 days.

WINE Frothy, lightly sweet Moscato d'Asti: 2010 Vietti Cascinetta.

● HEALTHY ● MAKE AHEAD ● VEGETARIAN ● STAFF FAVORITE

crêpes suzette

Coconut Crème Caramel

ACTIVE: 25 MIN; TOTAL: 1 HR 45 MIN
PLUS OVERNIGHT CHILLING
8 TO 10 SERVINGS ● ●

Malaysia-born fashion designer and dinner-party host extraordinaire Zang Toi stirs coconut milk into a lush custard to boost its flavor and richness. For a more Malaysian touch, Toi likes to use fragrant *pandan* juice (from the palm-like *pandan* tree). Vanilla extract is a good substitute.

- 1 cup granulated sugar
- ¼ cup water
- 10 large egg yolks
- ¾ cup light brown sugar
- 2 cups heavy cream
- One 13-ounce can unsweetened coconut milk
- 1½ teaspoons pure vanilla extract
- Pinch of salt
- ½ cup sweetened shredded coconut, toasted

1. Preheat the oven to 350°. In a medium saucepan, cook the granulated sugar with the water over moderate heat, brushing down the side of the pan with a wet brush, until a rich amber caramel forms, about 15 minutes. Quickly pour the caramel into a 9-inch square glass or ceramic baking dish to coat the bottom.

2. In a large bowl, beat the egg yolks and brown sugar until very thick, 2 minutes. Beat in the heavy cream, coconut milk, vanilla extract and salt and pour into the baking dish. Set the dish in a roasting pan. Pour hot water in the pan to come halfway up the dish's side. Bake for 1 hour, until the custard is just set but still jiggly in the center. Refrigerate the custard in the dish overnight.

3. Run a knife around the edge of the custard. Set the dish in a pan of hot water for 10 seconds. Invert a flat platter over the dish, then turn the custard and caramel onto the platter. Top with the toasted coconut and serve. —*Zang Toi*

MAKE AHEAD The crème caramel can be refrigerated in its dish, wrapped, for up to 2 days. Proceed with Step 3 before serving.

Butterscotch Pots de Crème with Caramel Sauce

ACTIVE: 30 MIN; TOTAL: 1 HR 30 MIN
PLUS 4 HR COOLING • 8 SERVINGS ● ● ●

"I have a lot of guys from Oaxaca in my kitchen, and they put salt on everything," says chef Travis Lett of Gjelina in Los Angeles. "One day, when we were developing this dessert, I saw one of them add salt and I thought, Hey, that's a great idea." After topping the pots de crème with caramel sauce and whipped crème fraîche, Lett sprinkles on crunchy flakes of Maldon sea salt.

POTS DE CRÈME
- 1½ sticks unsalted butter
- 1 cup dark brown sugar
- 5 cups heavy cream
- 1 scant tablespoon fine sea salt
- 1 vanilla bean, seeds scraped
- 6 large egg yolks
- Boiling water

CARAMEL SAUCE
- 1 cup sugar
- 1 teaspoon pure vanilla extract
- Whipped crème fraîche and Maldon sea salt, for serving

1. MAKE THE POTS DE CRÈME Preheat the oven to 325°. In a large saucepan, melt the butter. Add the dark brown sugar and cook over moderately high heat, whisking constantly, until the mixture is smooth and bubbling, about 5 minutes. Gradually whisk in the heavy cream. Return the mixture to a boil, whisking constantly. Add the fine sea salt and vanilla seeds.

2. In a large heatproof bowl, whisk the egg yolks. Gradually whisk in the hot cream mixture. Pour the custard through a fine-mesh strainer into eight 6-ounce ramekins. Set the ramekins in a small roasting pan and place the pan in the middle of the oven. Fill the roasting pan with enough boiling water to reach halfway up the sides of the ramekins. Cover the roasting pan with foil and bake for about 1 hour, until the custards are set but still slightly wobbly in the center. Transfer the ramekins to a baking sheet and refrigerate until chilled, about 4 hours.

3. MAKE THE CARAMEL SAUCE In a medium saucepan, mix the sugar with 2 tablespoons of water and cook undisturbed over high heat until a deep amber caramel forms, 6 minutes. Using a moistened pastry brush, wash down any crystals from the side of the saucepan from time to time. Remove from the heat. Add ⅔ cup of water and stir until smooth. Let the caramel sauce cool, then stir in the vanilla extract.

4. Top the pots de crème with the caramel sauce and whipped crème fraîche, sprinkle with Maldon sea salt and serve. —*Travis Lett*

MAKE AHEAD The pots de crème can be refrigerated in their ramekins, covered, for up to 2 days. Proceed with Step 3.

Petits Pots à l'Absinthe

TOTAL: 20 MIN PLUS 6 HR CHILLING
6 SERVINGS ●

"People always think [my husband] Didier is a bit of an outlaw because he is obsessed with absinthe," says Julianne Jones of Vergennes Laundry, a bakery in northwestern Vermont. She adds the spirit to these creamy puddings, giving them a subtle anise flavor, then serves them with fresh berries.

- 1 cup heavy cream
- ⅔ cup whole milk
- 2½ tablespoons sugar
- 1 teaspoon unflavored powdered gelatin dissolved in 2 tablespoons of water
- 1½ tablespoons absinthe
- Fresh berries, for serving

1. In a medium saucepan, combine the heavy cream, whole milk and sugar and bring to a simmer. Off the heat, whisk in the powdered gelatin and absinthe.

2. Strain the mixture into a pitcher and pour into six 4-ounce ramekins or bowls. Press a piece of plastic wrap directly onto the surface of the puddings and refrigerate until set, at least 6 hours. Serve with fresh berries. —*Julianne Jones*

MAKE AHEAD The pots à l'absinthe can be refrigerated in their ramekins, covered with plastic wrap, for up to 3 days.

● HEALTHY ● MAKE AHEAD ◔ VEGETARIAN ◔ STAFF FAVORITE

butterscotch pot de crème with caramel sauce

Chocolate Panna Cotta with Spiced Pepita Brittle

ACTIVE: 30 MIN; TOTAL: 2 HR 30 MIN
6 SERVINGS ● ●

This light, silky panna cotta tastes a lot like hot cocoa in custard form. The brittle is easy to make; heat sugar and water on the stove, swirl in butter and spiced *pepitas* (shelled pumpkin seeds), then let cool.

- 2 teaspoons unflavored powdered gelatin
- 2¾ cups whole milk
- ¾ cup plus 2 tablespoons sugar
- ¼ teaspoon salt
- 6 ounces bittersweet chocolate, chopped
- Vegetable oil
- ¾ cup salted roasted *pepitas*
- ½ teaspoon cinnamon
- ⅛ teaspoon freshly ground nutmeg
- ½ tablespoon unsalted butter

1. In a small bowl, sprinkle the powdered gelatin over ¼ cup of the milk and let stand until the gelatin is softened, about 5 minutes. In a medium saucepan, combine the remaining 2½ cups of milk with 2 tablespoons of the sugar and the salt and bring just to a simmer over moderate heat. Remove the milk from the heat and whisk in the softened gelatin until dissolved.

2. In a large microwave-safe bowl, melt the chopped chocolate at high power in 10-second intervals. Gradually whisk in the hot milk mixture until creamy. Strain the panna cotta mixture through a fine sieve into a large measuring cup.

3. Lightly brush six ½-cup ramekins with oil and set them on a baking sheet. Carefully fill the ramekins with the panna cotta mixture and refrigerate them for about 2 hours, until the panna cottas are firm.

4. Meanwhile, line a baking sheet with a silicone mat or lightly oiled parchment paper. In a bowl, toss the *pepitas* with the cinnamon and nutmeg. In a medium saucepan, combine the remaining ¾ cup of sugar with ⅓ cup of water and cook over high heat, swirling the pan gently, until a medium-amber

caramel forms, about 6 minutes. Remove from the heat and swirl in the butter and spiced *pepitas*. Pour the brittle onto the prepared baking sheet and spread it in a very thin layer. Let cool completely, about 20 minutes, then crack it into shards.

5. Run a knife around the panna cottas and invert onto plates. Garnish with the *pepita* shards and serve. —*Breanne Varela*

MAKE AHEAD The panna cottas can be refrigerated for up to 4 days. The *pepita* brittle can be stored in an airtight container at room temperature for up to 5 days.

Dark-Chocolate Pudding with Candied Ginger

TOTAL: 15 MIN PLUS 1 HR CHILLING
8 SERVINGS ● ●

"For me, ginger should be everywhere," says superchef Jean-Georges Vongerichten. "It's as good in marinades and vinaigrettes as it is in dessert." Here, candied ginger garnishes dark-chocolate pudding.

- ½ cup plus 1 tablespoon sugar
- ½ cup unsweetened cocoa powder
- 5½ tablespoons cornstarch
- ¼ teaspoon salt
- 1 quart half-and-half
- One 3.5-ounce bar bittersweet chocolate, chopped
- 1 teaspoon pure vanilla extract
- Lightly sweetened whipped cream and sliced candied ginger, for serving

In a medium bowl, sift together the sugar, cocoa powder, cornstarch and salt. In a large saucepan, add the half-and-half and whisk in the cocoa-powder mixture. Cook over moderate heat, whisking, until the pudding starts to bubble and thicken, about 4 minutes. Remove from the heat and stir in the bittersweet chocolate and vanilla. Pour the pudding into 6-ounce ramekins and let cool, then cover and refrigerate until chilled, about 1 hour. Top each pudding with whipped cream and candied ginger and serve.
—*Jean-Georges Vongerichten*

MAKE AHEAD The puddings can be refrigerated for up to 2 days.

Pumpkin Pie–Croissant Pudding

ACTIVE: 15 MIN; TOTAL: 1 HR
6 SERVINGS ●

Bakers make traditional diplomat pudding with soaked ladyfingers or cake baked with fruit and custard. In this unorthodox take, Frédéric Morin, co-chef at Joe Beef in Montreal, likes using the leftover croissants from Niemand Bakery in Kamouraska, Quebec. Morin says he always buys too much of everything ("Ask my wife," he says. "I even buy too many T-shirts"), so he created this simple recipe for using up his leftovers.

- ⅔ cup dark raisins
- ¼ cup rye whiskey
- 6 large croissants (about 1 pound), cut into 2-inch pieces
- Butter, for the dish
- 1 cup pumpkin pie filling
- 2 cups heavy cream
- 1 cup milk
- 7 eggs
- 1 cup sugar
- Pinch of salt
- Vanilla ice cream, for serving

1. Preheat the oven to 425°. Put the raisins in a small bowl and cover with the rye whiskey. Spread the croissant pieces on a baking sheet and toast in the oven for about 10 minutes, stirring once, until they are golden brown. Let the croissants cool.

2. Lower the oven temperature to 350°. Butter a 9-by-13-inch baking dish. In a large bowl, whisk the pumpkin pie filling with the heavy cream, milk, eggs, sugar and salt. In the prepared baking dish, toss the croissants with the raisins and whiskey. Pour the pumpkin mixture on top, pressing with the back of a spoon until most of the toasted croissants are moistened.

3. Bake for about 40 minutes, until the center is just set; tent with foil if the top starts to brown too quickly. Let cool to warm and serve with vanilla ice cream.
—*David McMillan and Frédéric Morin*

MAKE AHEAD The pudding can be refrigerated overnight. Reheat before serving.

● HEALTHY ● MAKE AHEAD ● VEGETARIAN ● STAFF FAVORITE

Rice Pudding with Butternut Squash and Sweet Milk Tea

ACTIVE: 45 MIN; TOTAL: 2 HR 30 MIN
8 SERVINGS ● ●

- 1 quart whole milk, plus more for thinning
- 3½ cups water
- 1 cup rice grits (see Note) or long-grain rice coarsely ground in a blender
- Salt
- ½ cup plus 1 tablespoon granulated sugar
- 1 cup strong-brewed black tea
- One 3-inch cinnamon stick, broken
- 4 cardamom pods, crushed
- ½ cup pecans
- 2 tablespoons unsalted butter
- 1 cup peeled and ½-inch-diced butternut squash
- 1 Granny Smith apple—peeled, cored and cut into 1-inch dice

1. In a medium saucepan, combine 3 cups of the whole milk with the water and bring to a boil. Stir in the rice grits and a pinch of salt and simmer over low heat, stirring often, until the rice is tender and pudding-like, about 1½ hours. Stir in ¼ cup of the granulated sugar, then cover the saucepan and remove from the heat.

2. Preheat the oven to 350°. Meanwhile, in a medium skillet, combine the black tea, cinnamon stick pieces, crushed cardamom and the remaining ¼ cup plus 1 tablespoon of granulated sugar and bring to a boil. Cook over moderate heat until the mixture is syrupy, about 10 minutes. Add the remaining 1 cup of milk and simmer 5 minutes longer. Strain the sweet milk tea.

3. Put the pecans in a pie plate and bake for about 8 minutes, until toasted. Let the nuts cool, then coarsely chop them.

4. In a large nonstick skillet, melt the butter. Add the diced squash and cook over moderate heat until browned on the bottom, about 3 minutes. Stir in the diced apple and cook, stirring occasionally, until the squash and apple are just tender, about 3 minutes longer.

5. Reheat the rice pudding until it is very warm. If it is too thick, thin it with whole milk, about ¼ cup at a time. Spoon the rice pudding into small bowls and pour the sweet milk tea on top. Spoon the squash, apples and pecans onto the pudding and serve.
—*Hugh Acheson*

NOTE Rice grits are available at specialty food stores or *ansonmills.com.*

MAKE AHEAD The rice pudding, sweet milk tea, cooked squash and apple can be refrigerated separately overnight. Store the toasted pecans at room temperature. Reheat the rice pudding gently, adding more milk as necessary before assembling.

Butterscotch Rice Pudding

⏱ TOTAL: 30 MIN • 4 SERVINGS ● ●
A quick thyme-scented butterscotch sauce made with butter, brown sugar and Scotch adds terrific flavor to rice pudding.

- 4 tablespoons unsalted butter
- 2 large thyme sprigs, plus thyme leaves for garnish
- 1 cup packed light brown sugar
- ⅓ cup Scotch
- ⅓ cup heavy cream
- Maldon sea salt
- 1 pound prepared rice pudding
- ½ cup roasted almonds, coarsely chopped
- ½ cup dried cranberries

1. In a medium saucepan, melt the butter with the thyme sprigs. Add the brown sugar and cook over moderately low heat, stirring occasionally, until melted and glossy, about 6 minutes. Remove from the heat and whisk in the Scotch. Cook over low heat until any hardened caramel is dissolved. Add the cream and whisk until the butterscotch is smooth and glossy. Discard the thyme sprigs and season the sauce with salt.

2. In a bowl, mix the rice pudding with the almonds and cranberries. Fold in ¼ cup of the butterscotch sauce and spoon into bowls. Drizzle with the remaining butterscotch sauce, garnish with thyme leaves and serve right away. —*Adam Erace*

Roman's Dairy-Free Chocolate-Coconut Ice Cream

TOTAL: 30 MIN PLUS 5 HR CHILLING AND FREEZING • MAKES 1½ QUARTS ● ●
Rori Trovato of Rori's Artisanal Creamery in Santa Barbara, California, creates all kinds of ice creams. Ironically, her son, Roman, has become lactose-intolerant. "Poor guy," Trovato says. "His mom opens an ice cream shop and he can't have any!" That's why she created this dairy-free flavor.

- 3 cups unsweetened coconut milk
- 3 tablespoons agave nectar
- 1¼ cups sugar
- ⅔ cup unsweetened cocoa powder
- 3 large egg yolks
- 1 tablespoon pure vanilla extract
- ½ cup unsweetened coconut flakes

1. Set a fine-mesh sieve in a large bowl set over a bowl of ice water.

2. In a large saucepan, whisk the coconut milk and agave nectar over moderately low heat until warm. In a medium heatproof bowl, whisk the sugar and cocoa powder. Gradually whisk in 1 cup of the warm coconut milk until smooth, then whisk in the egg yolks. Scrape the cocoa paste into the saucepan and whisk until blended. Cook the custard over moderate heat, whisking constantly, for about 6 minutes, until very hot and slightly thickened; do not let it boil. Immediately strain the custard into the prepared bowl and stir in the vanilla. Stir the custard until chilled.

3. Freeze the custard in an ice cream maker according to the manufacturer's directions. Transfer the ice cream to a large plastic container and freeze until firm, at least 4 hours.

4. In a small skillet, toast the coconut flakes over low heat until lightly browned, 4 minutes. Transfer to a plate and let cool. Serve the ice cream topped with toasted coconut.
—*Rori Trovato*

MAKE AHEAD The chocolate-coconut ice cream can be kept in the freezer for up to 2 weeks. The cooled toasted coconut flakes can be kept at room temperature in an airtight container for up to 3 days.

Ice Cream Bonbons

TOTAL: 30 MIN PLUS FREEZING
MAKES ABOUT 18 BONBONS ● ● ○

- 10 ounces extra-dark chocolate, finely chopped
- 2 ounces good-quality white chocolate from a bar, chopped
- 1 cup finely crushed chocolate wafer cookies
- 1 pint caramel, strawberry, chocolate, vanilla or coffee ice cream

Flaky sea salt, for sprinkling

1. In a medium heatproof bowl set over a pan of simmering water, melt the dark and white chocolates together. Scrape into a smaller bowl and let cool slightly.

2. Put the crushed chocolate wafer cookies on a small plate. Line 2 baking sheets with wax paper and place one in the freezer. Fill a cup with ice water.

3. Working very quickly, scoop a 1-tablespoon-size scoop of ice cream, packing it tightly. Transfer it to the melted chocolate. Using a skewer, poke the rounded top of the ice cream and coat the ball in the chocolate. Lift the bonbon, allowing the excess chocolate to drip into the bowl. Dip the bottom of the bonbon in the cookie crumbs and set on the baking sheet. Sprinkle salt on top. Let stand for 10 seconds, then transfer the bonbon to the baking sheet in the freezer. Repeat to form the remaining bonbons; dip the ice cream scoop in the ice water between scoops. Freeze the bonbons until firm, 30 minutes, then serve. —*Kendra Baker*

Apple-Butter Ice Cream with Ginger-Chocolate Ganache

⏱ **TOTAL: 45 MIN • 4 SERVINGS** ● ○

- 1 pint vanilla ice cream
- ⅓ cup apple butter
- 4 ounces bittersweet chocolate, chopped
- ⅓ cup heavy cream
- 2 tablespoons finely grated fresh ginger

Gingersnaps, for serving

1. Soften the vanilla ice cream in the microwave at high power for 10 seconds. Transfer the softened ice cream to a medium bowl and flatten it with a rubber spatula. Spread the apple butter on top and fold the vanilla ice cream over the apple butter 2 or 3 times. Freeze the apple-butter ice cream until it is firm, about 40 minutes.

2. Meanwhile, in a microwave-safe bowl, melt the chopped chocolate at high power in 10-second bursts. Whisk the heavy cream into the chocolate. Put the grated ginger in a fine strainer set over the chocolate ganache and press to extract as much of the ginger juice as possible. Whisk the ginger juice into the chocolate ganache.

3. Scoop the apple-butter ice cream into bowls, drizzle with the ginger-chocolate ganache and serve with gingersnaps. —*Adam Erace*

Ice Cream, Sorbet and Froyo Terrine

TOTAL: 20 MIN PLUS FREEZING
8 SERVINGS ● ● ○

- 1 pint pistachio ice cream
- 1 pint black currant or cherry sorbet
- 1 pint lemon frozen yogurt or ice cream

Chopped salted roasted pistachios, for serving

1. Line a 9-by-5-inch loaf pan with plastic wrap, leaving a few inches of overhang all around. Using scissors, cut the carton away from the pistachio ice cream and slice the ice cream into ½-inch-thick slabs. Pack the slabs into the loaf pan, pressing to fill any gaps. Freeze until firm, about 10 minutes. Repeat with the sorbet for the middle layer and then the frozen yogurt for the top layer, freezing the terrine for 10 minutes between layers. Press a sheet of plastic wrap on top of the terrine, fold the overhanging wrap over and freeze until firm, about 1 hour.

2. Unmold the terrine and transfer to a platter. Serve the terrine in slices and sprinkle with the chopped pistachios. —*Jeni Britton Bauer*

Hazelnut, Nutella and Caramel Ice Cream Sandwiches

ACTIVE: 30 MIN; TOTAL: 6 HR
MAKES 18 ICE CREAM SANDWICHES ● ● ○

At Las Vegas's Mix, Alain Ducasse created the Candy Bar, a four-layered pastry-cream dessert that's a two-day project. This streamlined recipe takes a fraction of the time.

- 1 cup hazelnuts (4 ounces)
- 1 cup confectioners' sugar
- 2 tablespoons all-purpose flour
- 4 large egg whites

Pinch of salt

- ¼ cup granulated sugar
- 4 ounces white chocolate, chopped
- 1 cup Nutella
- 6 sugar ice cream cones, crushed
- 1 pint caramel ice cream, softened

1. Preheat the oven to 375° and line a baking sheet with parchment. Spread the hazelnuts in a pie plate and toast until the skins split, about 12 minutes. Transfer the hazelnuts to a clean kitchen towel and let cool. Rub them together to remove the skins and transfer the nuts to a food processor. Add the confectioners' sugar and flour, then process until the nuts are finely ground.

2. In a large bowl, using an electric mixer, beat the egg whites with the salt at high speed until soft peaks form. Beat in the granulated sugar, 1 tablespoon at a time, until the whites are stiff. Using a rubber spatula, fold in the ground nuts. Spread the batter on the parchment in a 9-by-12-inch rectangle. Bake for 20 minutes, until golden. Prop the oven door open and let the dacquoise sit for 1 hour.

3. Meanwhile, in a microwave-safe bowl, melt the white chocolate in the microwave at high power in 1-minute intervals. Stir in the Nutella and crushed ice cream cones.

4. Invert the dacquoise onto a surface and peel off the paper. Spread evenly with the Nutella filling. Cut the dacquoise in half to make two 9-by-6-inch rectangles. Freeze until the filling is set. Spread the ice cream over one half. Close the sandwich and freeze until firm, at least 4 hours. Slice and serve. —*Alain Ducasse*

● HEALTHY ● MAKE AHEAD ○ VEGETARIAN ○ STAFF FAVORITE

ice cream bonbons

Rhubarb-Cheese Strudel with Vanilla Sauce

ACTIVE: 45 MIN; TOTAL: 2 HR
8 TO 10 SERVINGS ● ●

Strudel is a classic Austrian pastry made by wrapping layers of paper-thin dough around a variety of fillings. This simplified version, made with store-bought phyllo dough, features a cheesecake-like mixture and tangy rhubarb compote. A crème anglaise served alongside makes it extra-decadent.

RHUBARB COMPOTE

- 2 cups water
- 1 cup sugar
- 12 ounces rhubarb, cut into ½-inch pieces

STRUDEL

- ½ pound farmer cheese
- 1 stick unsalted butter—
  4 tablespoons softened,
  4 tablespoons melted
- ¼ cup confectioners' sugar
- ¼ cup cake flour
- 3 large eggs, separated
- 1 teaspoon finely grated lemon zest
- 1 vanilla bean, seeds scraped
- 2 tablespoons sour cream
- ¼ cup granulated sugar
- 10 sheets phyllo dough (from 1 package)

VANILLA CRÈME ANGLAISE

- 1 cup milk
- ¼ cup sugar
- 1 vanilla bean, split
- 2 large egg yolks
- 1 teaspoon cornstarch

1. MAKE THE COMPOTE In a large saucepan, bring the water to a boil. Add the sugar and stir to dissolve it. Add the rhubarb pieces and cook over low heat until softened but not falling apart, about 5 minutes. Using a slotted spoon, transfer ½ cup of the rhubarb to a small bowl and reserve for the filling.

2. MAKE THE STRUDEL Preheat the oven to 400° and line a large baking sheet with parchment paper. In a food processor, combine the farmer cheese with the 4 table-spoons of softened butter, the confectioners' sugar, cake flour, egg yolks, lemon zest and vanilla seeds and puree. Add the sour cream and process until creamy. Scrape the mixture into a large bowl.

3. In another bowl, using a handheld electric mixer, beat the egg whites at high speed until soft peaks form. Gradually add the granulated sugar and beat until the whites are stiff and glossy. Fold the beaten egg whites into the cheese filling.

4. Brush 5 sheets of phyllo with some of the melted butter, stacking them. With a long side of the phyllo facing you, spread half of the cheese filling along the bottom edge. Spoon ¼ cup of the reserved rhubarb over the cheese filling. Carefully roll up the strudel, tucking in the sides as you go. Using spatulas, gently transfer the strudel to the prepared baking sheet. Repeat with the remaining phyllo, cheese filling and ¼ cup of reserved rhubarb, and some of the melted butter. Transfer to the baking sheet, leaving a few inches between the strudels.

5. Brush the strudels with the remaining melted butter and bake them in the center of the oven for 45 minutes, turning the baking sheet once halfway through, until deeply golden (some of the filling may leak out). Let the strudels cool for 30 minutes.

6. MEANWHILE, MAKE THE CRÈME ANGLAISE In a medium saucepan, combine the milk with the sugar and vanilla bean and bring to a simmer. In a small bowl, whisk the egg yolks with the cornstarch. In a thin stream, whisk the egg yolks into the hot milk and simmer until the sauce is thickened and bubbling, about 3 minutes. Strain the crème anglaise into a heatproof bowl. Cover with plastic wrap and refrigerate.

7. Slide the strudels onto a work surface and slice each one into 4 or 5 pieces. Serve the strudel with the vanilla crème anglaise and the remaining rhubarb compote.
—*Wolfgang Ban and Eduard Frauneder*

MAKE AHEAD The vanilla crème anglaise and rhubarb compote can be refrigerated separately for up to 2 days. The strudel can be made earlier in the day and recrisped in the oven before slicing.

Mini Spiced Pumpkins

ACTIVE: 30 MIN; TOTAL: 1 HR 15 MIN
MAKES 1 DOZEN CAKES ● ● ●

These adorable spice cakes look like tiny pumpkins when they're covered with orange glaze and topped with a piece of dark licorice, twisted to resemble a stem.

MINI PUMPKINS

- 1 cup all-purpose flour
- 1½ teaspoons pumpkin pie spice
- ½ teaspoon baking powder
- ¼ teaspoon baking soda
- ¼ teaspoon salt
- ⅓ cup unsalted butter
- ½ cup granulated sugar
- 1 large egg
- 1 teaspoon pure vanilla extract
- ½ cup sour cream

GLAZE

- 1½ cups confectioners' sugar
- 2 tablespoons unsalted butter, melted
- 2 tablespoons water

Orange food coloring
Twelve 3-inch pieces of brown or black licorice twists, twisted

1. MAKE THE MINI PUMPKINS Preheat the oven to 350°. Coat a 12-cup mini Bundt cake pan with vegetable oil cooking spray. In a small bowl, whisk the flour with the pumpkin pie spice, baking powder, baking soda and salt. In a large bowl, using a handheld mixer, beat the butter with the granulated sugar at medium speed until fluffy. Beat in the egg and vanilla. Add the dry ingredients and the sour cream in 2 alternating batches, scraping down the bowl occasionally. Spoon the batter into the prepared Bundt cups. Bake in the center of the oven for 25 minutes, until the cakes are risen. Let cool slightly, then invert onto a rack to cool completely.

2. MAKE THE GLAZE In a bowl, whisk the confectioners' sugar, melted butter and water. Stir in the orange food coloring until it's a pumpkin shade. Pour the glaze over the pumpkins, spreading it gently to cover them completely; let dry. Stick a licorice piece on top of each cake to make a stem.
—*Grace Parisi*

● HEALTHY   ● MAKE AHEAD   ● VEGETARIAN   ● STAFF FAVORITE

mini spiced pumpkins

Ruby Grapefruit and Campari Ice Pops

TOTAL: 10 MIN PLUS OVERNIGHT FREEZING • MAKES 6 POPS ● ●

Using fresh-squeezed Ruby Red grapefruit juice instead of store-bought makes all the difference in these sweet-and-tart ice pops.

- ½ cup water
- ¼ cup plus 2 tablespoons sugar
- 1 teaspoon finely grated grapefruit zest
- 2½ cups fresh red grapefruit juice
- 4½ tablespoons Campari

1. In a small saucepan, combine the water, sugar and zest and bring to a simmer, stirring to dissolve the sugar. Pour the syrup into a bowl and add the grapefruit juice and Campari. Refrigerate until chilled.
2. Pour the mixture into six ½-cup ice-pop molds and freeze overnight. —*Nadia Roden*

MAKE AHEAD The grapefruit-Campari ice pops can be frozen for up to 3 weeks.

supereasy fruit ice pops

Almost any juice can be frozen in a pop mold, but here are some fun combinations to try. Zoku's Quick Pop Maker can freeze ice pops in as little as seven minutes. $50; williams-sonoma.com.

mango-lime Squeeze fresh limes into bottled mango juice.

pomegranate-elderflower Add St-Germain elderflower liqueur to pomegranate juice.

cranberry-lychee Add lychee juice or syrup from canned lychees to cranberry juice.

pineapple-coconut Stir coconut milk into fresh pineapple juice.

Ghostly Lemon Cake Pops

ACTIVE: 30 MIN; TOTAL: 1 HR MAKES 18 POPS ● ●

These Halloween-themed cake pops from F&W's Grace Parisi are easy to make: Crumble store-bought pound cake; mix with lemon juice, sugar and butter; then shape into mounds. When they're covered with white chocolate, the cakes look like ghosts. Make their faces with an edible decorating pen or dots of black frosting.

One 11- to 12-ounce plain store-bought pound cake
- 4 tablespoons unsalted butter, softened
- 1 teaspoon finely grated lemon zest
- 1 tablespoon fresh lemon juice
- ½ cup confectioners' sugar
- 18 popsicle sticks (see Note)
- ½ pound white chocolate, chopped
Edible decorating pens, for decorating (see Note)

1. Crumble the pound cake into the bowl of a food processor. Add the butter, lemon zest, lemon juice and confectioners' sugar and pulse to combine the ingredients. Transfer the mixture to a large bowl and shape into 18 mounds. Gently press the mounds into ghost shapes and ease each one onto a popsicle stick. Stand the pops upright in a large piece of Styrofoam.
2. In a large microwave-safe bowl, heat the white chocolate at high power until three-quarters melted. Stir until completely melted and cooled to 88° on an instant-read thermometer. Working quickly, dip the cake pops into the white chocolate, letting any excess drip back into the bowl. Stand the pops upright in the Styrofoam and let the chocolate set. Use the edible decorating pen to draw faces on the ghosts and serve. —*Grace Parisi*

NOTE Popsicle sticks and edible decorating pens are available at baking supply stores or online at *amazon.com*.

MAKE AHEAD The cake pops can be stored overnight in an airtight container.

Chocolate Mice

ACTIVE: 1 HR; TOTAL: 2 HR MAKES 3 DOZEN CHOCOLATE MICE ● ● ●

Three kinds of chocolate go into these icky-cute Halloween mice: semisweet chocolate in the creamy, cakey center and white and bittersweet in the crisp shell.

- 3 ounces cream cheese, softened
- 2 tablespoons unsalted butter, softened
- 1 cup confectioners' sugar
- 3½ ounces semisweet chocolate, melted and cooled
Two 9-inch round baked chocolate cake layers, warmed
- 4 ounces white chocolate, chopped
- 7 ounces extra-bittersweet chocolate, chopped
- ½ cup toasted pumpkin seeds
About 1 dozen black licorice whips, cut into 3-inch lengths

1. In a large bowl, beat the cream cheese with the butter, ½ cup of the confectioners' sugar and the melted chocolate. Crumble 1½ of the warm cake layers into the bowl and beat at low speed until incorporated. Roll level tablespoons of the mixture into 3 dozen ovals, tapering one end to shape the nose. Arrange the mice on a wax paper–lined baking sheet; press a toothpick into the tail end of each. Refrigerate until firm, 30 minutes.
2. Meanwhile, preheat the oven to 275°. Crumble the remaining ½ cake layer and spread on a rimmed baking sheet. Bake for 30 minutes, stirring frequently, until almost dry. Very finely crush the crumbs.
3. In a microwave-safe bowl, heat the white and extra-bittersweet chocolate together on high power until three-quarters melted. Stir the chocolates until completely melted and cooled to 90° on an instant-read thermometer. Working quickly, and using the toothpick as a handle, dip the mice into the chocolate to coat; let any excess chocolate drip back into the bowl. Roll the mice in the cake crumbs and press 2 pumpkin seeds into the heads of each mouse to make ears. Refrigerate until firm, about 20 minutes.

● HEALTHY ● MAKE AHEAD ● VEGETARIAN ● STAFF FAVORITE

4. In a bowl, combine the remaining ½ cup of confectioners' sugar with 1 to 2 teaspoons of water to make a stiff glaze. Transfer to a small plastic bag and snip off a tiny corner from one end. Pipe eyes on the mice. Remove the toothpicks and insert a licorice whip into each indentation for the tails. —*Grace Parisi*
MAKE AHEAD The chocolate mice can be refrigerated for 4 days.

Candy Corn and Chocolate Chip Cookies
ACTIVE: 45 MIN; TOTAL: 4 HR 45 MIN
MAKES 18 COOKIES ● ○

Christina Tosi, the pastry chef at New York's Momofuku, transforms her trick-or-treat haul into these irresistible Halloween treats.

- 1½ cups all-purpose flour
- ½ teaspoon baking powder
- ¼ teaspoon baking soda
- 1¼ teaspoons kosher salt
- 1½ sticks unsalted butter, softened
- 1¼ cups granulated sugar
- ½ cup light brown sugar
- 1 large egg
- ½ teaspoon pure vanilla extract
- Cornflake Crunch (recipe follows)
- ⅔ cup mini chocolate chips
- 1 cup candy corn (about 7 ounces)

1. In a small bowl, whisk the flour, baking powder, baking soda and salt. In the bowl of a standing mixer fitted with the paddle, beat the butter and sugars at medium-high speed until light and fluffy, 4 minutes. Beat in the egg and vanilla. At low speed, beat in the dry ingredients, then beat in the Cornflake Crunch, chocolate chips and candy corn. Mound ¼-cup scoops of dough 4 inches apart on 4 parchment-lined baking sheets. Flatten the cookies slightly and refrigerate until firm, about 3 hours.
2. Preheat the oven to 375° and position a rack in the center. Bake the cookies, one sheet at a time, for about 15 minutes, until they are browned around the edges but still a bit pale in the center. Let the cookies cool completely on the tray, then serve.
—*Christina Tosi*

CORNFLAKE CRUNCH
ACTIVE: 10 MIN; TOTAL: 45 MIN
MAKES ABOUT 3 CUPS ● ○

- 4 cups cornflakes (5 ounces), lightly crushed
- ½ cup dry milk powder
- 3 tablespoons sugar
- 1 teaspoon salt
- 10 tablespoons unsalted butter, melted

Preheat the oven to 275° and line a baking sheet with parchment. In a large bowl, toss the cornflakes with the milk powder, sugar, salt and melted butter until coated. Spread the mixture on a baking sheet and bake until golden and fragrant, about 20 minutes. Let the crunch cool completely. —*CT*

Maple Pecans
ACTIVE: 15 MIN; TOTAL: 50 MIN
MAKES 4 CUPS ● ○

- 4 cups pecans
- ½ cup pure maple syrup
- 2 tablespoons unsalted butter, melted
- ½ teaspoon kosher salt
- ½ teaspoon cayenne pepper
- ¼ teaspoon freshly ground black pepper
- 1 large egg white, at room temperature

1. Preheat the oven to 350° and spread the pecans on a large rimmed baking sheet; toast until they are fragrant, about 10 minutes. Let the pecans cool and lower the oven temperature to 250°.
2. Line 2 baking sheets with parchment paper. In a large bowl, toss the pecans with the maple syrup, butter, salt, cayenne and black pepper. In a medium bowl, whisk the egg white until frothy. Add the egg white to the pecans and toss well.
3. Spread the pecans on the lined baking sheets in a single layer. Bake for 40 minutes, until the nuts are golden brown. Immediately loosen the pecans from the paper with a spatula. Let cool completely on the baking sheets before serving. —*Sally Sampson*

Sesame-Chile Kettle Corn
TOTAL: 15 MIN • 6 SERVINGS ● ● ○

- 2 tablespoons canola oil
- 2 teaspoons toasted sesame oil
- ¼ cup plus 2 tablespoons popcorn kernels
- 8 dried *chiles de árbol*
- 2 tablespoons sugar
- 1 tablespoon black sesame seeds
- Salt

1. In a large nonstick saucepan, heat the canola oil, sesame oil, popcorn kernels and chiles over high heat until sizzling. Reduce the heat to moderate, add the sugar and cover. Cook, shaking the pan constantly, until half of the kernels are popped, about 4 minutes. Carefully remove the lid and add the sesame seeds, stirring once or twice. Cover the pan and cook, shaking, until the popping nearly stops.
2. Pour the kettle corn onto a baking sheet and sprinkle lightly with salt, tossing with your hands. Transfer the kettle corn to a serving bowl or an airtight container, discarding any unpopped kernels. —*Grace Parisi*

Snack Mix
ACTIVE: 5 MIN; TOTAL: 45 MIN
MAKES ABOUT 8 CUPS ● ● ○

- 2 cups coarsely broken mini pretzels
- ¼ cup light brown sugar
- 2 tablespoons granulated sugar
- ⅓ cup dry milk powder
- 6 tablespoons unsalted butter, melted
- 12 ounces mini chocolate candy bars, such as Reese's, chopped into ½-inch pieces

Preheat the oven to 275°. In a bowl, combine the pretzels with the sugars, milk powder and butter. Spread the mixture on a parchment paper–lined baking sheet and bake for about 20 minutes, until fragrant and lightly browned. Let cool completely. Transfer to a bowl and mix with the chopped candy bars. —*Christina Tosi*

Almond-Pistachio Nougat

TOTAL: 1 HR PLUS COOLING
MAKES ABOUT 2 POUNDS ● ●

For best results, keep the mixer with the egg whites close to the stove so you can work quickly when making this soft, chewy candy.

- 3   cups roasted almonds
- ¾   cup unsalted shelled pistachios
- ¼   cup cornstarch
- ¼   cup confectioners' sugar
- 1⅔ cups plus 1 tablespoon granulated sugar
- ¾   cup light honey
- 1¾ cups water
- 2   large egg whites, at room temperature
- Pinch of salt

1. Preheat the oven to 200° and spread the almonds and pistachios on a large baking sheet; keep warm in the oven. Line an 8-inch square baking pan with parchment paper, allowing the paper to hang over on two opposite sides. Lightly spray the paper with vegetable oil spray. In a bowl, combine the cornstarch and confectioners' sugar and dust the pan with half of the mixture.

2. In a medium saucepan, combine the 1⅔ cups of granulated sugar with ¼ cup of the honey and the water and bring to a boil. When the temperature of the syrup reaches 245° on a candy thermometer, after 20 to 30 minutes, bring the remaining ½ cup honey to a boil in a small saucepan. Continue cooking the sugar syrup.

3. Meanwhile, in the bowl of a standing mixer fitted with the whisk, beat the egg whites with the salt until firm peaks form. Add the remaining 1 tablespoon of granulated sugar and beat until combined.

4. When the pure honey reaches 265° on a candy thermometer, after about 5 to 8 minutes, add it in a fast, steady stream to the egg whites with the mixer at medium-high speed. When the syrup reaches 305°, add it to the egg whites in a fast, steady stream; beat at high speed until pale, 3 to 5 minutes. Using an oiled wooden spoon, immediately stir in the hot nuts (the nougat will be a bit stiff).

5. Scrape the nougat into the prepared pan, and, using oiled hands, press it into an even layer. Dust the remaining cornstarch mixture on top, cover and let cool.

6. Lift the nougat from the pan and brush off the excess cornstarch powder. Using a serrated knife, cut the nougat into ¾-inch slices. Cut the slices in pieces and serve.
—*Didier Murat*

MAKE AHEAD The nougat can be wrapped in wax paper and stored in an airtight container for up to 2 weeks.

Dark-Chocolate Bark with Roasted Almonds and Seeds

⋮ᗡ **ACTIVE: 20 MIN; TOTAL: 30 MIN**
MAKES 25 PIECES ● ● ●

- 1   pound dark chocolate (60 to 70 percent cacao)
- 1¼ cups roasted whole almonds
- ¾   cup salted roasted pumpkin seeds and sunflower seeds

1. Line a baking sheet with parchment paper. Using a sharp knife, finely chop the chocolate. In a bowl set over a saucepan of gently simmering water, heat the chopped chocolate, stirring occasionally, until it is about two-thirds melted; do not let the bowl touch the water. Remove the bowl from the saucepan and stir the chocolate until it is completely melted and the temperature registers 90° on a candy thermometer. If the chocolate has not melted completely and is still too cool, set it over the saucepan for about 1 or 2 minutes longer, stirring constantly; do not overheat.

2. Stir the almonds and seeds into the chocolate and spread onto the prepared baking sheet in a ½-inch-thick layer, making sure the nuts and seeds are completely covered in chocolate. Refrigerate the bark for about 10 minutes, until hardened. Invert the bark onto a work surface. Remove the parchment paper, break into 25 pieces and store or serve.
—*Jacques Torres*

MAKE AHEAD The broken bark can be stored in an airtight bag or container at cool room temperature for up to 10 days.

Chocolate-Espresso Snowballs

ACTIVE: 30 MIN; TOTAL: 2 HR
MAKES ABOUT 3 DOZEN COOKIES ● ● ●

The chocolaty cookies here are just sweet enough to balance the cocoa and coffee flavors without being overly sugary.

- 2   sticks softened unsalted butter, plus more for the cookie sheets
- ½   cup granulated sugar
- 2   teaspoons pure vanilla extract
- 1¾ cups all-purpose flour
- ¼   cup unsweetened cocoa powder
- 2   teaspoons instant espresso powder
- ½   teaspoon salt
- 2   cups finely chopped pecans
- Confectioners' sugar, for coating

1. In a large bowl, mix the 2 sticks of butter with the granulated sugar and vanilla until smooth. Stir in the flour, cocoa, espresso powder and salt until thoroughly blended. Stir in the pecans. Cover the dough and refrigerate for 1 hour.

2. Preheat the oven to 325°. Lightly butter 2 cookie sheets. Working in batches, roll the dough into tablespoon-size balls and place about 2 inches apart on the prepared cookie sheets. Bake in the upper and lower thirds of the oven for 15 minutes, until the tops are dry and the cookies are slightly firm to the touch. Let the cookies cool on the sheets for 10 minutes, then transfer to a rack to cool completely. Roll the cookies in confectioners' sugar to coat, then serve.
—*Linda Meyers*

Snickers Ice Cream Milk

⋮ᗡ **TOTAL: 15 MIN • 4 SERVINGS** ●

These fun candy bar–flavored shakes need just three ingredients and a blender.

- 2½ ounces Snickers bars, chopped
- 2   cups whole milk
- 1   pint vanilla ice cream

In a blender, combine the Snickers with the milk and puree until smooth. Add the ice cream, blend until smooth and serve.
—*Christina Tosi*

● HEALTHY ● MAKE AHEAD ● VEGETARIAN ● STAFF FAVORITE

chocolate-espresso snowballs

Home baker Malin Elmlid prepares for a brunch at her Berlin apartment, where she serves eye-opening mocktails called coffee-ginger shakeratos, OPPOSITE; *recipe, page 390.*

drinks

Tea Thyme

TOTAL: 5 MIN PLUS 2 HR STEEPING
MAKES 1 DRINK ●

Seattle mixologist and cocktail consultant Kathy Casey steeps vodka in English Breakfast tea for this drink. To sweeten it, she uses a local fig-flavored honey—"a great way to customize your cocktails," she says.

TEA VODKA

12 ounces vodka
 1 English Breakfast tea bag

COCKTAIL

 2 thyme sprigs

Ice

1½ ounces Tea Vodka
 ¾ ounce freshly squeezed
     lemon juice
 2 teaspoons honey mixed with
     2 teaspoons of warm water

vodka infusions

These infused vodkas are great served the Russian way, as an ice-cold shot after a toast.

Start with 2 cups vodka and add one of the following flavorings:

blueberry-bay leaf 12 ounces crushed blueberries; 5 bay leaves.

coffee-cocoa ¼ cup espresso beans, coarsely crushed; 2 tablespoons cocoa nibs, crushed.

raspberry 12 ounces crushed raspberries.

make the infusion In a large jar, combine the vodka with the flavorings. Cover the jar with its lid and let the mixture stand at room temperature for 2 weeks. Strain the vodka and discard the solids. Strain the infused vodka through a coffee filter into a clean jar and refrigerate for up to 3 months. —*Marcia Kiesel*

1. MAKE THE TEA VODKA In a jar, combine the vodka with the tea bag. Let stand at room temperature for 2 hours, then discard the tea bag. (Makes about 12 ounces. The infused vodka can be kept covered at room temperature for up to 1 month.)
2. MAKE THE COCKTAIL In a cocktail shaker, lightly muddle 1 of the thyme sprigs. Add ice and the 1½ ounces of Tea Vodka, the lemon juice and the honey syrup and shake well. Strain into a chilled martini glass or coupe and garnish with the remaining thyme sprig. —*Kathy Casey*

Cucumber Cocktail with Chamomile Tonic

TOTAL: 20 MIN PLUS 3 WEEKS TO MAKE THE TONIC • MAKES 1 DRINK ● ●

"Having a bitter drink before or after a meal is a way to slow down, which is always great for digestion," says Jovial King, the Vermont-based founder of Urban Moonshine, a line of artisanal bitters and tonics. King's Bitter Chamomile Tonic (recipe follows), vodka infused with dandelion greens, is delicious in this refreshing, unsweetened cocktail created by F&W's Marcia Kiesel.

 4 ounces seedless cucumber,
     unpeeled, coarsely chopped (1 cup)
 ½ cup small ice cubes
1½ ounces Bitter Chamomile Tonic
     (recipe follows)
 1 tablespoon chopped mint plus
     1 mint sprig for garnish
 1 tablespoon fresh lime juice

Pinch of salt

In a blender, combine the cucumber, ice, Bitter Chamomile Tonic, chopped mint, lime juice and salt and puree. Pour into a tumbler, garnish with the mint sprig and serve. —*Marcia Kiesel*

BITTER CHAMOMILE TONIC

TOTAL: 10 MIN PLUS 3 WEEKS STEEPING
MAKES ABOUT 1 QUART ● ● ●

Use this vodka infusion to prepare Marcia Kiesel's Cucumber Cocktail with Chamomile Tonic, above.

10 ounces dandelion greens,
     large stems discarded and greens
     finely chopped
 2 cups finely chopped fresh lemon
     balm or dried lemon verbena leaves
 1 cup dried chamomile flowers
 1 cup finely chopped fresh mint
1½ quarts vodka

Combine the greens and herbs with the vodka in a glass jar or container. Let stand in a cool, dark place for 3 to 4 weeks. Strain into a clean bottle and refrigerate for up to 3 months. —*Jovial King*

Dark and Stormy Death Punch

TOTAL: 30 MIN PLUS 4 HR FREEZING
8 SERVINGS ●

This Halloween-inspired take on the Dark and Stormy, a classic rum and ginger beer drink, features "eyeballs"—round ice cubes made with lychee syrup and lychees stuffed with cherries—floating in the punch bowl.

One 20-ounce can lychees in heavy syrup
 ¼ cup thinly sliced peeled fresh ginger
16 brandied cherries
 ¼ cup superfine sugar
 ½ cup fresh lime juice
12 ounces dark rum
Three 12-ounce bottles ginger beer
Ice

1. In a small saucepan, bring the lychee syrup and ginger to a boil. Remove from the heat, cover and let steep for 30 minutes.
2. Meanwhile, stuff 16 lychees with brandied cherries. Set each lychee in the cup of a mini muffin pan or in an ice cube tray. Strain the lychee-ginger syrup and pour it over the lychees. Freeze until firm, at least 4 hours.
3. Meanwhile, in a pitcher, stir the sugar into the lime juice until dissolved. Add the rum and refrigerate until chilled, about 1 hour.
4. Unmold the lychee ice cubes into a small punch bowl. Pour in the lime-rum mixture. Add the ginger beer, stir gently and serve in ice-filled glasses. —*Grace Parisi*
MAKE AHEAD The lychee ice cubes can be frozen for up to 1 week.

● HEALTHY ● MAKE AHEAD ● VEGETARIAN ● STAFF FAVORITE

Verdant Virtue/Vice Cocktail

🕑 **TOTAL: 10 MIN • MAKES 1 DRINK** ●

This intriguing cocktail gets its grassy hue from mint, basil and green Chartreuse, a spicy French herbal liqueur.

- 3 mint leaves, plus 1 mint sprig for garnish
- 3 basil leaves
- ½ ounce Simple Syrup (recipe below right)

Ice

- 1 ounce gin
- ½ ounce green Chartreuse

Juice of 1 lime

- 2 cucumber slices, 1 rosemary sprig and lime slices, for garnish

In a tall glass, muddle the mint and basil leaves with the Simple Syrup. Fill the glass with ice. Stir in the gin, Chartreuse and lime juice. Garnish with the cucumber slices, the rosemary and mint sprigs and a few lime slices. —*Kenny Rochford*

Silver Monk

🕑 **TOTAL: 5 MIN • MAKES 1 DRINK** ●

Big grains of salt rim many a margarita glass. But as this cocktail from New York mixologist Philip Ward proves, a pinch of salt can add complexity to bittersweet drinks.

- 2 cucumber slices, plus 1 cucumber spear for garnish
- 8 mint leaves

Pinch of salt

- ½ ounce Simple Syrup (recipe far right)

Ice

- 2 ounces blanco tequila
- ¾ ounce yellow Chartreuse
- 1 ounce fresh lime juice

In a cocktail shaker, muddle the cucumber slices with 7 of the mint leaves, the salt and the Simple Syrup. Add ice and the tequila, Chartreuse and lime juice and shake well. Double strain (through a cocktail strainer and a fine strainer) into a chilled coupe and garnish with the cucumber spear and remaining mint leaf. —*Philip Ward*

Tangerine Margaritas

🕑 **TOTAL: 15 MIN • MAKES 8 DRINKS** ●

Chef Jenn Louis's husband and business partner, David Welch, created these drinks for their latest restaurant, Sunshine Tavern, in Portland, Oregon. Instead of sugar, this drink is sweetened with fresh tangerine juice.

- 2 lime wedges

Kosher salt

- 9 ounces silver tequila
- 6 tablespoons fresh lime juice
- 6 tablespoons fresh tangerine juice
- 3 ounces orange liqueur

Ice

Rub the rims of 8 small margarita glasses with the lime wedges. Spread salt in a saucer and dip the rims of the glasses in the salt. In a cocktail shaker, mix half of the tequila, juices and orange liqueur. Add ice and shake vigorously. Strain into 4 glasses. Make the remaining drinks. —*David Welch*

Porch Crawler

🕑 **TOTAL: 5 MIN • MAKES 1 DRINK** ●

Chefs Frank Falcinelli and Frank Castronovo of Frankies Spuntino in Brooklyn, New York, helped devise this cooling drink using ingredients from Falcinelli's rooftop garden.

- 5 cherries, pitted, plus 1 cherry for garnish
- 3 mint leaves, plus 1 mint sprig for garnish
- 1 hot chile, such as serrano, halved and seeded

Ice

- 2 ounces white rum
- 1 ounce fresh lemon juice
- 1 ounce Simple Syrup (recipe at right)
- 2 ounces chilled club soda

In a cocktail shaker, muddle the 5 pitted cherries with the mint leaves and chile. Add ice and the rum, lemon juice and Simple Syrup; shake well. Strain into an ice-filled collins glass, stir in the club soda and garnish with a cherry and a mint sprig. —*Frank Castronovo and Frank Falcinelli*

Duls Cocktail

🕑 **TOTAL: 5 MIN**

MAKES 8 TO 10 DRINKS ● ●

A specialty of the Duls gelateria in Milan, the Prosecco-based cocktail adapted here is lightly sweet and surprisingly refreshing.

- 1 pound strawberries, chopped
- ¼ cup dark brown sugar

One 750-milliliter bottle chilled ruby port
One 750-milliliter bottle chilled Prosecco

- 2 tablespoons balsamic vinegar

Crushed ice

In a bowl, toss the strawberries with the sugar. In a pitcher, mix the port and Prosecco with the vinegar. Fill tall glasses with crushed ice and 2 tablespoons each of the strawberries. Top with the punch. —*Marcia Kiesel*

White Port and Tonic

🕑 **TOTAL: 5 MIN**

MAKES 14 TO 16 DRINKS ●

One 750-milliliter bottle chilled white port

- 1½ liters chilled tonic water

Ice

Mint leaves and lemon slices, for garnish

In a pitcher, mix the white port with the tonic water. Pour into ice-filled highball glasses and garnish each drink with a mint leaf and lemon slice. —*Marcia Kiesel*

simple syrup

A quick combination of sugar and water, this clear syrup is used to sweeten countless cocktails.

In a small saucepan, bring 1 cup water and 1 cup sugar to a boil over moderately high heat, stirring to dissolve the sugar; let cool. Use or refrigerate, covered, for up to 1 month. Makes about 12 ounces. —*F&W Test Kitchen*

drinks

The Savoy Daisy

⏱ **TOTAL: 5 MIN • MAKES 1 DRINK** ●

Erik Lorincz, head bartender at The Savoy hotel in London, updates the classic Daisy cocktail. Instead of using white sugar as a sweetener, he opts for muscovado, an unrefined brown sugar with a very moist texture and a strong molasses flavor.

Ice
- 2 ounces ruby port
- ¼ ounce Bacardi 8-year aged rum
- 1 ounce Diplomatico Reserva Exclusiva rum
- 2 tablespoons freshly squeezed lemon juice
- ½ teaspoon muscovado sugar
- ½ tablespoon grenadine
- 1 orange twist, for garnish

Fill a cocktail shaker with ice. Add all of the ingredients except the orange twist and shake vigorously. Strain into a chilled martini glass and garnish with the twist.
—*Erik Lorincz*

Cranberry-Spice Cocktail

⏱ **TOTAL: 5 MIN • MAKES 1 DRINK** ● ●

- 1 orange wedge
- 13 cranberries
- Three 1-inch pieces crystallized ginger—2 minced and 1 whole for garnish
- 2 ounces Aperol
- 1 ounce Lillet blanc
- 4 dashes Cranberry-Anise Bitters (page 391) or Peychaud's bitters

Ice
- 4 ounces hard cider

In a cocktail shaker, muddle the orange wedge with 10 of the cranberries and the minced ginger. Add the Aperol, Lillet blanc, bitters and ice. Shake well. Double strain the drink (through a cocktail strainer and a fine strainer) into an ice-filled collins glass and top with the hard cider. Garnish with the 3 remaining cranberries and the slice of crystallized ginger skewered on a toothpick.
—*Brad Thomas Parsons*

Aperol Spritz

⏱ **TOTAL: 5 MIN**
MAKES 14 TO 16 DRINKS ●

One 750-milliliter bottle chilled Aperol
One 750-milliliter bottle chilled Prosecco
¾ liter chilled seltzer
Ice
Orange slices, for garnish

In a pitcher, combine the Aperol, Prosecco and seltzer. Pour into ice-filled wineglasses and garnish each drink with an orange slice.
—*Marcia Kiesel*

The Big Texan Bourbon and Grapefruit Cocktail

⏱ **TOTAL: 5 MIN • MAKES 1 DRINK** ●

James Holmes, the chef at Austin's Olivia, serves these tangy-sweet bourbon drinks with appetizers when entertaining.

- 2 tablespoons fresh grapefruit juice
- 1½ ounces bourbon
- ½ tablespoon Simple Syrup (page 387)
- 2 basil leaves

Ice
- 1 grapefruit slice and 1 preserved cherry, for garnish

In a cocktail shaker, combine the grapefruit juice, bourbon, Simple Syrup and basil. Fill a chilled rocks glass with ice. Add 5 ice cubes to the shaker and shake well. Strain the drink into the ice-filled rocks glass. Garnish with the grapefruit slice and cherry. —*James Holmes*

Darjeeling Unlimited

⏱ **TOTAL: 5 MIN • MAKES 1 DRINK** ●

This refreshing tea-and-bourbon cocktail is a perfect summertime cooler. The pinch of salt helps enhance the tea's savory flavors.

Ice
- ½ cup cold brewed Darjeeling tea
- 3 ounces bourbon
- ¾ ounce Simple Syrup (page 387)
- ½ ounce fresh lemon juice
Pinch of salt
Lemon twist, for garnish

In an ice-filled cocktail shaker, combine the tea, bourbon, Simple Syrup, lemon juice and salt. Shake well. Strain the cocktail into a rocks glass, garnish with the lemon twist and serve. —*Dave Arnold and Emeric Harney*

Figgy-Orange Cocktail

⏱ **TOTAL: 5 MIN • MAKES 1 DRINK** ●

Ice
- 2 ounces bourbon
- ½ ounce Punt e Mes
- 1 tablespoon fresh orange juice
- ½ tablespoon Simple Syrup (page 387)
- 4 dashes Figgy-Orange Bitters (page 391) or Regans' Orange Bitters No. 6
Freshly grated nutmeg, for garnish

In an ice-filled cocktail shaker, combine the bourbon, Punt e Mes, orange juice, Simple Syrup and bitters. Shake well. Strain the drink into a chilled coupe. Garnish with freshly grated nutmeg. —*Brad Thomas Parsons*

Harvest Cocktail

⏱ **TOTAL: 10 MIN • MAKES 1 DRINK** ●

- ½ cup water
- ½ cup sugar
- 2 cinnamon sticks
Ice
- 2 ounces Laird's Apple Brandy
- ½ ounce Snap liqueur
- 4 dashes Woodland Bitters (page 391) or Angostura bitters
- 1 thin apple slice, for garnish

1. In a medium saucepan, combine the water, sugar and cinnamon sticks. Boil over moderately high heat, stirring occasionally, until the sugar is dissolved, about 5 minutes. Let the syrup cool. Discard the cinnamon sticks. **2.** In an ice-filled cocktail shaker, combine ½ tablespoon of the cinnamon syrup with the apple brandy, Snap liqueur and bitters. Stir well. Strain the drink into an ice-filled rocks glass and garnish with the apple slice. —*Brad Thomas Parsons*

● HEALTHY ● MAKE AHEAD ● VEGETARIAN ● STAFF FAVORITE

Coffee-Ginger Shakerato

📷 PAGE 385

⏱ TOTAL: 5 MIN • MAKES 1 DRINK ●

This clever coffee mocktail is sweetened with ginger syrup and orange marmalade. Marmalade made with Seville oranges is best here because it has a pleasing bitter edge.

Ice

¼ cup freshly brewed espresso
1 tablespoon Ginger Syrup (recipe follows)
1 teaspoon Seville orange marmalade
1 orange twist, for garnish

Fill a shaker with ice, then add the espresso, Ginger Syrup and orange marmalade; shake well. Double strain the drink (through a cocktail strainer and a fine strainer) into a coupe; garnish with the orange twist.
—*John Benjamin Savary*

equipment tip

mini food processor The mini processor component (below) of the Ninja Master Prep Pro is great for chopping small quantities of herbs. Its multiple blades working at once can crush solid ice cubes until perfectly fluffy for drinks like the Duls Cocktail on page 387. *$90; tryninja.com.*

GINGER SYRUP

⏱ ACTIVE: 5 MIN; TOTAL: 30 MIN
MAKES ¾ CUP ● ●

1 ounce peeled fresh ginger, peeled and thinly sliced
½ cup water
½ cup sugar

In a small saucepan, combine the fresh ginger, water and sugar and simmer until the sugar has dissolved. Cover and steep for about 20 minutes. Strain the syrup into a jar and let cool. —*JBS*

MAKE AHEAD The Ginger Syrup can be kept in the refrigerator for up to 1 month.

Ginger-Bay Syrup

⏱ ACTIVE: 10 MIN; TOTAL: 40 MIN
MAKES 2½ CUPS ● ●

The delicate fragrance of bay leaves is lovely with ginger. "I add this syrup to a cup of English Breakfast tea," F&W's Grace Parisi says. Also delicious with club soda or in hot toddies, this easy-to-prepare syrup makes a fabulous hostess gift.

¾ cup thinly sliced peeled fresh ginger (from one 4-inch piece)
2 cups sugar
2 cups water
1 fresh bay leaf
4 tablespoons freshly squeezed lemon juice
4 slices of candied ginger

In a food processor, chop the fresh ginger and sugar; transfer to a small saucepan. Add the water and bring to boil, stirring to dissolve the sugar. Add the bay leaf and simmer over moderate heat until slightly thickened and reduced to about 2½ cups, about 20 minutes. Add the lemon juice and simmer for about 1 minute. Let cool, then strain into a small pitcher, pressing on the solids. Pour the syrup into small bottles and add the candied ginger. Seal the bottles.
—*Grace Parisi*

MAKE AHEAD The syrup with candied ginger can be refrigerated for up to 4 months.

Ginger-Lemongrass Soda

ACTIVE: 10 MIN; TOTAL: 3 HR
MAKES 6 CUPS ● ●

Mixologists and chefs were the first picky drinkers to make their own sodas. Now more and more DIY-ers want to do it at home. F&W's Grace Parisi makes this soda with iSi's new Twist 'n Sparkle soda maker, which can carbonate beverages in less than 30 seconds (*$50; williams-sonoma.com*).

½ cup thinly sliced peeled fresh ginger
4 plump stalks of fresh lemongrass, cut into 2-inch lengths and smashed, plus stalks for garnish
6 cups water
1 cup sugar
3 tablespoons freshly squeezed lemon juice

Ice
Lemon wheels, for garnish

1. In a medium saucepan, combine the sliced ginger with the smashed lemongrass and 4 cups of the water and bring to a boil over high heat. Stir in the sugar. Cover and let the ginger-lemongrass syrup steep off the heat until cool, about 2 hours.

2. Strain the syrup through a fine-mesh sieve. Discard the ginger and lemongrass. Stir in the lemon juice and the remaining 2 cups of water. Refrigerate until chilled.

3. Make the soda according to the manufacturer's directions. Serve the soda in tall glasses over ice, garnished with lemon wheels and lemongrass stalks.
—*Grace Parisi*

BASIL-MINT SODA In a medium saucepan, simmer 1 cup water with 1 cup sugar until the sugar is dissolved. Add 1 cup each of basil and mint leaves and let steep for 1 hour. Strain the syrup and discard the herbs. Let the syrup cool completely. Stir 4 cups cold water and ½ cup fresh lime juice into the syrup. Make the soda according to the manufacturer's directions.

MAKE AHEAD The recipe can be prepared through Step 2 and refrigerated in an airtight container for up to 5 days.

● HEALTHY ● MAKE AHEAD ○ VEGETARIAN ● STAFF FAVORITE

do-it-yourself bitters

Infused with herbs and roots, bitters add depth and balance to cocktails. Here, three recipes from craft-cocktail enthusiast **Brad Thomas Parsons,** author of *Bitters*.

sarsaparilla
a vine with the flavor of root beer.

cassia chips
cinnamon-flavored bark from Asia.

devil's club root
has a deeply woodsy scent.

black walnut leaf
a tannic, mildly bitter ingredient.

gentian root
from a mountain plant; very bitter.

wild cherry bark
has a slight cherry-fruit aroma.

cinchona bark
the natural source of anti-malarial quinine.

All of the herbs and roots above are sold at dandelionbotanical.com.

Woodland Bitters

TOTAL: 20 MIN PLUS ABOUT 3 WEEKS
STEEPING • MAKES 14 OUNCES ● ○

- 2 cups overproof bourbon (such as Wild Turkey 101)
- 1 cup pecans, toasted
- 1 cup walnuts, toasted
- 4 cloves
- Two 3-inch cinnamon sticks
- 1 whole nutmeg, cracked
- 1 vanilla bean, split
- 2 tablespoons devil's club root
- 1 tablespoon cinchona bark
- 1 tablespoon chopped black walnut leaf
- 1 tablespoon wild cherry bark
- ½ teaspoon cassia chips
- ½ teaspoon gentian root
- ½ teaspoon sarsaparilla root
- 3 tablespoons pure maple syrup

Cranberry-Anise Bitters

TOTAL: 20 MIN PLUS ABOUT 3 WEEKS
STEEPING • MAKES 14 OUNCES ● ○

- 2 cups high-proof vodka (like Stolichnaya Blue 100 Proof)
- 1½ cups fresh or thawed frozen cranberries, each one pierced with a toothpick
- 1 cup dried cranberries
- 2 tablespoons chopped crystallized ginger
- 2 star anise pods
- One 3-inch cinnamon stick
- One 1-inch piece of fresh ginger, peeled and sliced ¼ inch thick
- 1 teaspoon gentian root
- ½ teaspoon white peppercorns
- 2 tablespoons Simple Syrup (page 387)

Figgy-Orange Bitters

TOTAL: 20 MIN PLUS ABOUT 3 WEEKS
STEEPING • MAKES 14 OUNCES ● ○

- 2 cups overproof bourbon (such as Wild Turkey 101)
- 1 cup dried figs (about 6 ounces), halved
- 8 green cardamom pods, crushed
- 4 cloves
- 2 fresh figs, halved
- Strips of zest from 3 oranges
- 1 tablespoon cinchona bark
- ½ teaspoon gentian root
- ¼ cup dried orange peel
- One 3-inch cinnamon stick
- 1 vanilla bean, split
- 2 tablespoons Rich Syrup (see Note)

---

1. In a 1-quart glass jar, combine all of the ingredients except the syrup. Cover and shake well. Let stand in a cool, dark place for 2 weeks, shaking the jar daily.

2. Strain the infused alcohol into a clean 1-quart glass jar through a cheesecloth-lined funnel. Squeeze any infused alcohol from the cheesecloth into the jar; reserve the solids. Strain the infused alcohol again through new cheesecloth into another clean jar to remove any remaining sediment. Cover the jar and set aside for 1 week.

3. Meanwhile, transfer the solids to a saucepan. Add 1 cup of water; bring to a boil. Cover and simmer over low heat for 10 minutes; let cool. Pour the liquid and solids into a clean 1-quart glass jar. Cover; let stand at room temperature for 1 week; shake the jar once daily.

4. Strain the water mixture through a cheesecloth-lined funnel set over a clean 1-quart glass jar; discard the solids. If necessary, strain the mixture again to remove any remaining sediment. Add the infused alcohol and the syrup. Cover and let stand at room temperature for 3 days. Pour the bitters through a cheesecloth-lined funnel or strainer and transfer to clean glass dasher bottles. Cover the bottles and keep the bitters in a cool, dark place.

NOTE To make Rich Syrup, in a small saucepan, dissolve 2 cups of demerara or turbinado sugar in 1 cup of water over moderate heat. Let cool before using, and reserve the rest for another use.

MAKE AHEAD The bitters can be stored at room temperature indefinitely. For best flavor, use within 1 year.

Sunset Punch

⏱ TOTAL: 10 MIN • 8 SERVINGS ●

8 ounces bourbon
8 ounces white vermouth
½ cup fresh lemon juice, plus
  lemon slices for garnish
¼ cup Simple Syrup (page 387)
12 ounces chilled ginger beer
Ice

In a punch bowl, combine the bourbon, vermouth, lemon juice and syrup. Add the ginger beer and lemon slices and serve over ice.
—*Ethan Stowell*

Almond-Fennel Cooler

⏱ ACTIVE: 10 MIN; TOTAL: 35 MIN
MAKES 1 DRINK ●

¾ ounce orgeat
  (almond-flavored syrup)
¾ ounce Fennel Syrup (recipe follows)
½ ounce fresh lemon juice
Ice
6 ounces chilled club soda
1 fennel frond, for garnish (optional)

In a collins glass, combine the orgeat, Fennel Syrup and lemon juice and stir well. Add ice, stir in the club soda and garnish with the fennel frond. —*Jennifer Colliau*

FENNEL SYRUP
⏱ TOTAL: 25 MIN
MAKES ABOUT 12 OUNCES ● ●

1 tablespoon fennel seeds
1 cup water
1 cup sugar

In a spice grinder, coarsely grind the fennel seeds. In a small saucepan, combine the ground fennel seeds with the water and bring to a boil. Remove from the heat, cover and let stand for 20 minutes. Pour the fennel liquid into a jar through a fine strainer. Add the sugar, cover and shake gently until the sugar is completely dissolved. Refrigerate for up to 1 month. —*JC*

Lemon-Rosemary Sun Tea

TOTAL: 10 MIN PLUS 4 HR STEEPING
MAKES 1½ QUARTS ● ● ●

Willi Galloway, author of the online gardening and cooking journal DigginFood, steeps lemon and rosemary for this iced tea. "Herbs are great for balcony gardens," she says.

¼ cup rosemary leaves
¼ large lemon, thinly sliced
1½ quarts cold water
Ice

In a large jar, bruise the rosemary leaves with a wooden spoon. Add the lemon and water, cover and let stand for 4 hours. Strain and serve in tall glasses over ice.
—*Willi Galloway*

MAKE AHEAD The strained tea can be refrigerated overnight.

Tomato Lemonade

⏱ TOTAL: 25 MIN • MAKES 10 DRINKS
● ● ● ●

Kat Kinsman, managing editor of CNN's Eatocracy food blog, is known for clever drinks like this lemonade. It's perfect on its own as a mocktail, but Kinsman recommends adding a shot or two of rye whiskey to make the tomatoey drink "reminiscent of a wonderfully tipsy deli sandwich." Gin or vodka would be a great addition as well.

¼ cup sugar
¼ cup water plus 3 cups ice water
2 pounds tomatoes, preferably yellow
  or orange, cored and chopped
½ cup fresh lemon juice
Ice
Lemon wedges and herb sprigs,
  for garnish

1. In a small saucepan, combine the sugar and ¼ cup of water and bring to a simmer over moderate heat, stirring to dissolve the sugar. Let the syrup cool.
2. In a food processor, puree the tomatoes and strain the puree through a sieve into a pitcher; discard the solids. Add the syrup, lemon juice and ice water and stir.

3. Fill 10 tall glasses with ice cubes. Pour the Tomato Lemonade into each glass, garnish with lemon wedges and herb sprigs and serve.
—*Kat Kinsman*

Pomegranate Cocktail Syrup

⏱ TOTAL: 30 MIN PLUS COOLING
MAKES 1 CUP ● ● ●

While she was pregnant, Valerie Gordon of Valerie Confections in L.A. made this syrup to add to sparkling water as a mocktail. But the syrup is equally good with sparkling wine.

1 cup sugar
⅔ cup hot water
2 cups pomegranate juice

In a saucepan, combine the sugar and hot water. Add the pomegranate juice and bring to a boil. Simmer over moderate heat until reduced to 1 cup, 20 minutes; let cool.
—*Valerie Gordon*

SERVE WITH Chilled sparkling wine or water.
MAKE AHEAD The syrup can be refrigerated for up to 1 month.

White Magic Espresso

⏱ TOTAL: 15 MIN • 10 SERVINGS ●

A cup of steaming white-chocolate milk with espresso is the ideal drink for a bitterly cold day. An added nip of brandy would make the drink even more warming.

1½ cups ground espresso beans
6 cups boiling water
5 cups milk
15 ounces white chocolate, chopped
Unsweetened cocoa powder, for dusting

1. Set a drip-coffee cone with a filter over a large heatproof glass measuring cup or pitcher and add the ground espresso to the filter. Slowly pour in the boiling water until you have 5 cups of coffee.
2. In a medium saucepan, scald the milk. Whisk until frothy. Whisk in the white chocolate. Pour the coffee into 10 warm mugs. Pour the milk over the coffee. Dust each serving with cocoa powder and serve.
—*Tory Miller*

● HEALTHY ● MAKE AHEAD ● VEGETARIAN ● STAFF FAVORITE

tomato lemonade

*shiitake and swiss chard soup
with hand-cut noodles,* PAGE 394

recipe index

recipe index

PAGE NUMBERS IN **BOLD** INDICATE PHOTOGRAPHS

recipe index

PAGE NUMBERS IN **BOLD** INDICATE PHOTOGRAPHS

recipe index

PAGE NUMBERS IN **BOLD** INDICATE PHOTOGRAPHS

recipe index

PAGE NUMBERS IN **BOLD** INDICATE PHOTOGRAPHS

recipe index

PAGE NUMBERS IN **BOLD** INDICATE PHOTOGRAPHS

recipe index

PAGE NUMBERS IN **BOLD** INDICATE PHOTOGRAPHS

recipe index

PAGE NUMBERS IN **BOLD** INDICATE PHOTOGRAPHS

recipe index

PAGE NUMBERS IN **BOLD** INDICATE PHOTOGRAPHS

recipe index

PAGE NUMBERS IN **BOLD** INDICATE PHOTOGRAPHS

contributors

recipes

hugh acheson, an F&W Best New Chef 2002, is the chef and co-owner of The National and Five & Ten in Athens, Georgia, and Empire State South in Atlanta. He is the author of *A New Turn in the South*.

omri aflalo is the chef at Michael Mina's Bourbon Steak in San Francisco.

jason alley is the chef and co-owner of Comfort restaurant in Richmond, Virginia.

billy allin is the chef and co-owner of Cakes & Ale restaurant and bakery in Decatur, Georgia.

malika ameen is the owner and pastry chef of By M Desserts.

erik anderson is a co-chef at the Catbird Seat in Nashville, Tennessee.

katherine anderson owns Marigold and Mint, a flower and herb shop in Seattle's Melrose Market.

josé andrés is the chef and co-owner of several restaurants in Washington, DC, Beverly Hills and Las Vegas. He is also the culinary director and partner of SLS Hotel and the author of *Tapas* and *Made in Spain*.

cathal armstrong, an F&W Best New Chef 2006, is the chef and co-owner of Restaurant Eve, The Majestic and Eamonn's a Dublin Chipper and co-owner of Virtue Feed & Grain, PX and Society Fair, all in Alexandria, Virginia.

dave arnold is the director of culinary technology at the French Culinary Institute in New York City.

kendra baker is the chef and co-owner of the Penny Ice Creamery in Santa Cruz, California.

sean baker is the chef and co-owner of Gather in Berkeley, California.

wolfgang ban is a co-chef and co-owner of Seäsonal Restaurant & Weinbar and Edi & the Wolf, both in New York City.

jimmy bannos, jr., is the chef and co-owner of the Purple Pig in Chicago.

mario batali is the chef and co-owner of over a dozen restaurants in New York, Las Vegas, L.A. and Singapore. He is also a co-owner of Eataly, a market and restaurant complex in New York. He has authored several cookbooks, including *Molto Batali,* and co-hosts ABC's *The Chew.*

rick bayless, an F&W Best New Chef 1988, is the chef and owner of Frontera Grill and Topolobampo, both in Chicago. Winner of Bravo's *Top Chef Masters* Season 1, he also hosts the PBS series *Mexico—One Plate at a Time* and has written numerous cookbooks, most recently *Fiesta at Rick's.*

skip bennett is the founder of Island Creek Oysters in Duxbury Bay, Massachusetts, and a co-owner of Boston's Island Creek Oyster Bar.

noah bernamoff is the chef and owner of Mile End in Brooklyn, New York.

john besh, an F&W Best New Chef 1999, is the chef and owner of August, Besh Steak, Lüke, American Sector and Domenica in New Orleans; La Provence in Lacombe, Louisiana; and Lüke in San Antonio. He is the author of *My New Orleans* and, most recently, *My Family Table.*

urs bieri is the chef at Abadía Retuerta winery's restaurant, Le Domaine, in Valladolid, Spain.

maxime bilet is the head chef for recipe research and development at the Cooking Lab in Bellevue, Washington, and a co-author with Nathan Myhrvold of the six-volume *Modernist Cuisine: The Art and Science of Cooking.*

richard blais, winner of *Top Chef: All-Stars* and host of Science Channel's *Blaise Off,* is the chef and owner of Flip Burger Boutique restaurants in Atlanta and Birmingham, Alabama, and co-owner of HD-1 in Atlanta.

april bloomfield, an F&W Best New Chef 2007, is the chef and co-owner of the Spotted Pig, The Breslin and the John Dory Oyster Bar, all in New York City.

mb boissonnault is a visual artist and a regular guest chef at the pop-up restaurant hosted by Dig Gardens in Santa Cruz, California.

david bouley, an F&W Best New Chef 1989, is the chef and owner of Bouley and Brushstroke, both in New York City. He is also a co-author of *East of Paris.*

graham elliot bowles, an F&W Best New Chef 2004, is the chef and owner of Graham Elliot and Grahamwich restaurants in Chicago.

james boyce is the chef and co-owner of Cotton Row, Pane e Vino and Commerce, all in Huntsville, Alabama.

margaret braun is a cake designer, sugar artist and the author of *Cakewalk.*

jeni britton bauer is the owner and creator of Jeni's Splendid Ice Creams shops in Ohio and Tennessee and the author of *Jeni's Splendid Ice Creams at Home.*

bowman brown, an F&W Best New Chef 2011, is a co-chef and co-owner of Forage in Salt Lake City.

tyler brown is the chef at the Hermitage Hotel's Capitol Grille in Nashville.

deborah callia is a chef at PieLab, a café, community space and culinary-arts classroom in Greensboro, Alabama.

marco canora is the chef and co-owner of Hearth restaurant and Terroir wine bars in New York City and the author of *Salt to Taste.*

mario carbone is a co-chef and co-owner of Torrisi Italian Specialties and Parm, both in New York City.

floyd cardoz, winner of *Top Chef Masters* Season 3, heads the kitchen at Danny Meyer's latest New York City restaurant, North End Grill.

kathy casey, a chef and mixologist, owns Kathy Casey Food Studios—Liquid Kitchen and Dish D'Lish "Food t' Go-Go." Her most recent cookbook is *Sips & Apps.*

frank castronovo is a co-chef and co-owner of three Frankies Spuntino restaurants, Prime Meats and Cafe Pedlar, all in New York City. He also co-authored *The Frankies Spuntino Kitchen Companion & Cooking Manual.*

jeff cerciello is the chef and owner of Farmshop in Santa Monica, California.

david chang, an F&W Best New Chef 2006, is the chef and owner of the Momofuku restaurant group, with restaurants in New York City, Sydney and Toronto. He is a co-editor of *Lucky Peach* food journal and a co-author of *Momofuku.*

gontran cherrier is the chef and owner of an eponymous bakery in Paris.

melissa clark is a food writer and columnist for the *New York Times* as well as a contributing editor for the online food site Gilt Taste. Her most recent cookbook is *Cook This Now.*

preston clark is the chef at El Paseo restaurant in Mill Valley, California.

amanda cohen is the chef and owner of Dirt Candy in New York City.

danny cohen is the baker and founder of Danny Macaroons in New York City.

contributors

jennifer colliau is a mixologist at the Slanted Door in San Francisco and owner of Small Hand Foods, an online shop for cocktail ingredients.

dani cone is the baker and owner of High 5 Pie in Seattle, Washington.

bill corbett is the pastry chef at Absinthe Brasserie & Bar in San Francisco.

soledad correa is the chef at Casa Silva Hotel & Winery in San Fernando, Chile.

chris cosentino is the chef at Incanto in San Francisco and Pigg in L.A. He is the author of the website OffalGood.com and co-creator of Boccolone, an online artisanal salumeria.

mauricio couly is the chef and co-owner of La Toscana Restaurante and Olivetto Restaurante in Patagonia, Argentina.

andrew curren is the chef and co-owner of 24 Diner in Austin.

carrie cusack is the chef at Simplethings Sandwich & Pie Shop in Los Angeles.

mathilde dalle owns Château de Campuget winery and inn in Costières de Nîmes, France.

jeremy daniels is a co-chef and co-owner of the Viking Soul Food truck in Portland, Oregon.

anna derivi-castellanos is a co-chef and co-owner of Three Babes Bakeshop, a pop-up pie shop in San Francisco.

traci des jardins, an F&W Best New Chef 1995, is the chef and co-owner of Jardinière, Mijita and Public House in San Francisco and Manzanita in Truckee, California.

harold dieterle, winner of *Top Chef* Season 1, is the chef and co-owner of Perilla, Kin Shop and Marrow in New York City.

matthew dillon, an F&W Best New Chef 2007, is the chef and owner of Sitka & Spruce, the Corson Building, Ferdinand the Bar and Joe Bar, all in Seattle.

rocco dispirito is an F&W Best New Chef 1999. His latest cookbook is *Now Eat This!*

jill donenfeld is the founder of The Culinistas, a private chef service in New York, Los Angeles, Malibu and Chicago.

kristin donnelly is a senior food editor at F&W.

vinny dotolo, an F&W Best New Chef 2009, is a co-chef and co-owner of Animal and Son of a Gun in Los Angeles.

david duband is an organic winemaker in the Côte de Nuits region in Burgundy, France.

alain ducasse is the chef and owner of 25 restaurants around the world, including the Plaza Athénée in Paris, Adour in New York and Washington, DC, and Mix in Las Vegas. The owner of École de Cuisine Alain Ducasse, he is also the co-author of *Ducasse Nature*.

hugue dufour is the former chef and co-owner of M. Wells in Long Island City, New York.

malin elmlid is a home baker in Berlin and founder of the Bread Exchange barter system.

adam erace is a co-founder of Green Aisle Grocery in Philadelphia and the restaurant critic for the *Philadelphia City Paper*.

jonathon erdeljac is the chef and owner of Jonathon's Oak Cliff in Dallas.

fabienne escoffier owns Ma Cuisine restaurant in Beaune, France.

pete evans is a chef, restaurateur and TV host in his native Australia. His latest cookbook is *Pizza*.

frank falcinelli is a co-chef and co-owner of three Frankies Spuntino restaurants, Prime Meats and Cafe Pedlar, all in New York City. He also co-authored *The Frankies Spuntino Kitchen Companion & Cooking Manual*.

elizabeth falkner is a chef and co-owner of Citizen Cake and Orson in San Francisco. Her book *Cooking Off the Clock* is forthcoming.

susan feniger is a chef, restaurateur and co-author of several books on Mexican cooking. She owns Street in Los Angeles and co-owns Border Grill in L.A., Santa Monica and Las Vegas.

adam fleischman is the chef and owner of the Umami Burger restaurant chain in L.A. and San Francisco and co-owner of Umamicatessen food hall, Red Medicine and 800°, all in L.A.

lee ann flemming writes a column for the *Greenwood Commonwealth* and is the author of the cookbook *Recipes and Remembrances*.

russell flint owns Rain Shadow Meats butcher shop in Seattle's Melrose Market.

jay foster is the chef and co-owner of Farmerbrown and Farmerbrown's Little Skillet, both in San Francisco.

jeremy fox is an F&W Best New Chef 2008.

mindy fox is the food editor of *La Cucina Italiana* magazine. Her most recent cookbook is *A Bird in the Oven and Then Some*.

jason franey, an F&W Best New Chef 2011, is the chef at Canlis in Seattle.

eduard frauneder is a co-chef and co-owner of Seäsonal Restaurant & Weinbar and Edi & the Wolf, both in New York City.

willi galloway is a journalist and author of the gardening and cooking blog DigginFood.

colby garrelts, an F&W Best New Chef 2005, is the chef and co-owner of Bluestem in Kansas City, Missouri, and a co-author of *Bluestem*.

megan garrelts is the pastry chef and co-owner of Bluestem in Kansas City, Missouri, and a co-author of *Bluestem*.

emilee gettle and her husband, **jeremiath gettle,** run the Baker Creek Heirloom Seed Company as well as Comstock, Ferré & Co. seed company. They also publish *The Heirloom Gardener* magazine.

jill giacomini basch co-owns Point Reyes Farmstead Cheese Company and its cooking school, The Fork, in Point Reyes Station, California.

antonio gianola is the regional manager of the Houston Mosaic Wine Group in Texas.

bryce gilmore, an F&W Best New Chef 2011, is the chef and owner of Odd Duck Farm to Trailer and Barley Swine, both in Austin.

spike gjerde is the chef and co-owner of Woodberry Kitchen in Baltimore.

marcy goldman created the online baking and lifestyle magazine BetterBaking.com. Her latest cookbook is *The Baker's Four Seasons*.

valerie gordon is the pastry chef and co-owner of Valerie Confections in Los Angeles.

dorie greenspan, the author of *Around My French Table*, runs CookieBar, a pop-up cookie shop and national delivery service.

alexandra guarnaschelli is the chef at Butter and The Darby in New York and host of *Alex's Day Off* on the Food Network.

kurt gutenbrunner is the chef and co-owner of Wallsé, Café Sabarsky, Blaue Gans, the Upholstery Store and Cafe Kristall, all in New York City. He also co-authored *Neue Cuisine*.

trina hahnemann, a chef and caterer in Denmark, is the author of *The Scandinavian Cookbook* and *The Nordic Diet*.

carla hall is the chef and owner of Alchemy, an online cookie company. She also co-hosts ABC's *The Chew*.

martha hall foose is a cookbook author whose works include *A Southerly Course*.

emeric harney is a tea blender for Harney & Sons tea company and general manager of the company's SoHo Tea House in New York City.

quinn hatfield is the chef and co-owner of Hatfield's in Los Angeles.

kerry heffernan is the chef at South Gate restaurant in New York City.

claus henriksen is the chef at Dragsholm Slot in Hørve, Denmark.

nikole herriott is the photographer and writer for the blog Forty-Sixth at Grace.

rory herrmann is the chef de cuisine at Bouchon in Beverly Hills.

james holmes is the chef and owner of Olivia restaurant in Austin, Texas.

mary hoover ran a soul food restaurant in Greenwood, Mississippi, for 30 years.

alex hozven owns the Cultured Pickle Shop in Berkeley, California.

piero incisa della rocchetta is a winemaker for Tenuta San Guido, his family's Sassicaia winery in Tuscany, and Bodega Chacra winery in Patagonia, Argentina.

stephanie izard, an F&W Best New Chef 2011, is the chef and co-owner of Girl & the Goat and Little Goat in Chicago. She won *Top Chef* Season 4 and co-authored *Girl in the Kitchen.*

nicolas jammet co-founded Sweetgreen, a salad and frozen yogurt chain, in Washington, DC, Maryland, Virginia and Pennsylvania.

emma jessen krut is a home cook who participates in Malin Elmlid's Bread Exchange.

signe johansen, author of the cookbook *Secrets of Scandinavian Cooking...Scandilicious,* writes a food blog called Scandilicious.

julianne jones is the baker and co-owner of Vergennes Laundry in Vergennes, Vermont.

paul kahan, an F&W Best New Chef 1999, is a co-chef and co-owner of Blackbird, Avec, The Publican and Big Star, all in Chicago.

aki kamozawa is a co-author of *Ideas in Food* and a blog of the same name.

sanjeev kapoor is an international celebrity chef based in India, where he has a daily cooking show. He has more than 20 restaurants and 140 cookbooks to his name. His most recent cookbook is *How to Cook Indian.*

kevin kathman is the chef at Barbette restaurant in Minneapolis.

allison kave founded First Prize Pies in Brooklyn, New York.

douglas keane, an F&W Best New Chef 2006, is the chef and owner of Cyrus in Sonoma.

hubert keller, an F&W Best New Chef 1988 and cookbook author, is the chef and owner of Fleur de Lys in San Francisco, Fleur in Las Vegas and Burger Bar in San Francisco, Las Vegas and St. Louis. He is also a judge on Bravo's *Top Chef: Just Desserts.*

marcia kiesel is the F&W Test Kitchen supervisor and co-author of *The Simple Art of Vietnamese Cooking.*

ronnie killen is the chef and owner of Killen's Steakhouse in Pearland, Texas.

josh kilmer-purcell co-owns Beekman Farm in Sharon Springs, New York. He is a co-star of *The Fabulous Beekman Boys* and co-author of *The Beekman 1802 Heirloom Cookbook.*

bill kim is the chef and owner of Urbanbelly and Belly Shack, both in Chicago.

jovial king is the founder and formulator of Urban Moonshine in Burlington, Vermont.

kat kinsman is the managing editor of CNN's food blog, Eatocracy.

phillip kirschen-clark was the opening chef of Vandaag in New York City.

gabriel kreuther, an F&W Best New Chef 2003, is the chef at The Modern in New York.

dennis lee is the chef and a co-owner of Namu restaurant in San Francisco.

ludo lefebvre is the chef and owner of LudoBites and LudoTruck, both in L.A., and a co-author of *Crave: The Feast of the Five Senses.*

dmitry leonov is the chef at Khachapuri restaurant in Moscow.

benjamin leroux is a biodynamically minded winemaker with a domaine in Beaune, France.

chantal leroux, mother of winemaker Benjamin Leroux, is a home cook in Burgundy, France.

travis lett is the chef and co-owner of Gjelina and Gjelina Take Away in Venice, California.

james lewis, an F&W Best New Chef 2011, is the chef-owner of Bettola in Birmingham, Alabama.

louis-michel liger-belair owns Domaine du Comte Liger-Belair in Burgundy, France.

chris lilly is the chef and co-owner of Big Bob Gibson Bar-B-Q in Decatur, Alabama, and Monroe, North Carolina. He is also the author of *Big Bob Gibson's BBQ Book.*

kacie loparto harvests seaweed in Maine and sells it on her website, *shesellsseaweed.com.*

erik lorincz is the head bartender of the American Bar at The Savoy hotel in London.

bruno loubet is the chef and owner of Bistrot Bruno Loubet at the Zetter Hotel in London.

jenn louis is the chef and co-owner of Lincoln restaurant, Sunshine Tavern and Culinary Artistry catering company in Portland, Oregon.

valeri lucks is the baker and co-owner of Honeypie Cafe in Milwaukee and Northdown Cafe and Taproom in Chicago.

lachlan mackinnon-patterson, an F&W Best New Chef 2005, is the chef and co-owner of Frasca Food and Wine in Boulder, Colorado.

ginger madson and her husband, **preston madson,** are co-chefs at Freemans and Peels, both in New York City.

santos majano is the chef at Soif Wine Bar in Santa Cruz, California.

tony mantuano, an F&W Best New Chef 1986, is the chef and co-owner of Spiaggia and Terzo Piano in Chicago and Mangia Trattoria in Kenosha, Wisconsin. He also co-authored *The Spiaggia Cookbook* and *Wine Bar Food.*

jennifer mclagan is the author of several cookbooks, including *Bones* and *Fat.*

david mcmillan is a co-chef and co-owner of Joe Beef and Liverpool House in Montreal and co-author of *The Art of Living According to Joe Beef: A Cookbook of Sorts.*

george mendes, an F&W Best New Chef 2011, is the chef and owner of Aldea restaurant in New York City.

linda meyers, a designer and home cook, sells decorative items on her website, *warymeyers.com.* She is also a co-author of *Wary Meyers' Tossed & Found.*

tory miller is the chef and co-owner of L'Etoile in Madison, Wisconsin.

rob milliron is the chef at Homegrown in Seattle's Melrose Market.

carlo mirarchi, an F&W Best New Chef 2011, is the chef and co-owner of Roberta's restaurant in Brooklyn, New York.

robert moore is a co-owner of the Little Flower Candy Company and the chef and owner of Moore's Delicatessen in Burbank, California.

masaharu morimoto is the chef and owner of numerous restaurants, including Morimoto in Philadelphia, New York and Waikiki as well as Wasabi in Mumbai and New Delhi and XEX in Tokyo. He is a star on *Iron Chef America* and the author of *The New Art of Japanese Cooking.*

frédéric morin is a co-chef and co-owner of Joe Beef and Liverpool House in Montreal. He also co-authored *The Art of Living According to Joe Beef: A Cookbook of Sorts.*

didier murat co-owns Vergennes Laundry, a bakery in Vergennes, Vermont.

david myers, an F&W Best New Chef 2003, is the chef and restaurateur at Comme Ça in L.A. and Las Vegas, Sola and David Myers Café in Tokyo and Pizzeria Ortica in Costa Mesa, California.

nathan myhrvold founded the Cooking Lab, a state-of-the-art culinary lab in Bellevue, Washington. He is a co-author of the six-volume *Modernist Cuisine: The Art and Science of Cooking.*

anthony myint is the chef and co-owner of Mission Chinese Food, Commonwealth Restaurant and Mission Bowling Club, all in San Francisco. He is also a co-author of *Mission Street Food.*

andré natera is the chef at the Fairmont Hotel's Pyramid Restaurant & Bar in Dallas.

jennifer nettles is the lead singer of the country-music band Sugarland.

jeremy nolen is the chef at Brauhaus Schmitz, a German beer hall and restaurant in Philadelphia.

jessie oleson, a writer and illustrator, is the owner of CakeSpy Shop in Seattle, creator of the blog CakeSpy and a co-author of *CakeSpy Presents Sweet Treats for a Sugar-Filled Life.*

contributors

jamie oliver is a food writer, cookbook author and host of ABC's *Jamie Oliver's Food Revolution*. The chef and owner of Jamie's Italian restaurants in the U.K., Dubai and Sydney and co-owner of Barbecoa in London, he also oversees the social enterprise Fifteen Foundation. His most recent cookbook is *Jamie Oliver's Meals in Minutes*.

dj olsen is the chef at Lou restaurant in L.A.

yotam ottolenghi is a co-owner of Nopi and the Ottolenghi chain of prepared-foods shops in London. He writes for the *Guardian* and has co-authored two books, *Ottolenghi* and *Plenty*.

gwyneth paltrow is an Academy Award–winning actress, author of the cookbook *My Father's Daughter* and founder of the online lifestyle newsletter Goop.

chris pandel is the chef and co-owner of The Bristol and Balena restaurants, both in Chicago.

grace parisi is F&W's Test Kitchen senior recipe developer and writes the magazine's Fast column. She is also the author of *Get Saucy*.

charlie parker is the chef at Plum restaurant in Oakland, California.

brad thomas parsons writes about food and cocktails. He is the author of *Bitters: A Spirited History of a Classic Cure-All*.

dave pasternack is the chef at Esca and Il Pesce, both in New York City.

sean paxton founded *homebrewchef.com*, a website about cooking with beer.

veronica pedraza is the creamery manager at Jasper Hill Farm in Greensboro, Vermont.

zakary pelaccio is the chef and owner of the Fatty Crab, Fatty 'Cue and Fatty Snack restaurants in New York City and the US Virgin Islands and founder of Suka restaurant in London. He is also the founder and creative director of the Cooking Room, a food literacy program for elementary school students.

béatrice peltre writes the online food journal La Tartine Gourmande.

jacques pépin is an F&W contributing editor, master chef, TV personality and the dean of special programs at the French Culinary Institute in New York. He is the author of several cookbooks, most recently *Essential Pépin*.

mathieu perez is the chef at Aux Deux Amis restaurant in Paris.

aj perry is the baker and owner of Sassafras Bakery in Columbus, Ohio.

bryan petroff is a co-founder of the Big Gay Ice Cream Truck and shop in New York City.

viet pham, an F&W Best New Chef 2011, is a co-chef and co-owner of Forage in Salt Lake City.

ryan poli is the chef at Tavernita in Chicago.

alfred portale is the chef and co-owner of Gotham Bar and Grill in New York and Gotham Steak in Miami. His most recent cookbook is *Alfred Portale Simple Pleasures*.

jeff potter is the author of *Cooking for Geeks: Real Science, Great Hacks, and Good Food*.

michael psilakis, an F&W Best New Chef 2008, is the chef and owner of Kefi and Fishtag in New York. He is the author of *How to Roast a Lamb*.

yigit pura, winner of *Top Chef: Just Desserts* Season 1, is the pastry chef at Taste Catering and Event Planning in San Francisco.

douglas quint is a co-founder of the Big Gay Ice Cream Truck and shop in New York City.

kent rathbun is the chef and owner of seven restaurants in Texas, including Abacus in Dallas.

brent ridge co-owns Beekman Farm in Sharon Springs, New York. He is a co-star of *The Fabulous Beekman Boys* and co-author of *The Beekman 1802 Heirloom Cookbook*.

joël robuchon is the chef and owner of restaurants around the world, including L'Atelier in New York City and Paris. His most recent cookbook is *The Complete Robuchon*.

kenny rochford is the general manager of Medlock Ames Winery in Healdsburg, California.

hans röckenwagner is the chef and owner of 3 Square Café + Bakery and Röckenwagner Bakery in Los Angeles.

nadia roden is the chef and owner of Lily Lolly's Ice Kitchen and the author of *Granita Magic*.

sebastien rubis is the chef at The 3 Nagas Hotel in Luang Prabang, Laos.

gabriel rucker, an F&W Best New Chef 2007, is the chef and owner of Le Pigeon and Little Bird in Portland, Oregon.

sally sampson is a cookbook author and the founder and president of *ChopChop*. Her most recent book is *The 100-Calorie Snack Cookbook*.

steven satterfield is the chef and co-owner of Miller Union in Atlanta.

john benjamin savary is a participant in Malin Elmlid's Bread Exchange.

jonathon sawyer, an F&W Best New Chef 2010, is the chef and owner of the Greenhouse Tavern and Noodlecat in Cleveland.

pedro miguel schiaffino is the chef and owner of Malabar restaurant in Lima, Peru, and the chef for Aqua Expeditions cruise line.

michael schwartz is the chef and owner of Michael's Genuine Food & Drink in Miami and Grand Cayman and Harry's Pizzeria in Miami.

jeremy sewall is the chef and co-owner of Island Creek Oyster Bar in Boston and Lineage restaurant in Brookline, Massachusetts.

jeremy seysses is a winemaker at Domaine Dujac in Morey St-Denis, France.

debra shaw is the cafeteria manager at the Golden Age Nursing Home in Greenwood, Mississippi.

jon shook, an F&W Best New Chef 2009, is a co-chef and co-owner of Animal and Son of a Gun in Los Angeles.

steve sicinski is the chef at Topnotch Resort and Spa in Stowe, Vermont, and a co-author of *Journey of Taste*.

jane sigal, a contributing editor at F&W, is a journalist and food writer. She recently co-authored *Neue Cuisine*.

nancy silverton, an F&W Best New Chef 1990, is the founder of La Brea Bakery and Short Order burger bar in L.A. as well as the Pizzeria Mozza restaurants in L.A., Singapore and Newport Beach, California. She is the author of several cookbooks, most recently *The Mozza Cookbook*.

joshua skenes, an F&W Best New Chef 2011, is the chef and owner of Saison in San Francisco.

eric skokan is the chef and owner of the Black Cat in Boulder, Colorado.

art smith is the chef and co-owner of Table Fifty-Two in Chicago and Art and Soul in Washington, DC.

andré soltner, dean of classic studies at the French Culinary Institute in New York City, was the chef and owner of New York's Lutèce for more than 30 years. He is the co-author of *The Lutèce Cookbook*.

bob spiegel is the chef and co-owner of Pinch Food Designs, a catering company in New York.

larry stone is the president and sommelier of Evening Land Vineyards in California, Oregon and Burgundy.

ethan stowell, an F&W Best New Chef 2008, is the chef and co-owner of four Seattle restaurants, including Tavolata. He is also the author of *Ethan Stowell's New Italian Kitchen*.

alex stupak is the chef and owner of Empellón Taqueria and the forthcoming Empellón Cocina, both in New York City.

doug svec is the chef at Social Restaurant + Wine Bar in Charleston, South Carolina.

heidi swanson is the creator of the online recipe journal 101 Cookbooks. Her most recent cookbook is *Super Natural Every Day*.

michael symon, an F&W Best New Chef 1998, is the chef and owner of Lola, Lolita and B Spot, all in Cleveland, and Roast in Detroit. He is a co-host of ABC's *The Chew* and co-author of *Michael Symon's Live to Cook*.

h. alexander talbot is a co-author of *Ideas in Food* and a blog of the same name.

giuseppe tentori, an F&W Best New Chef 2008, is the chef at Boka Restaurant and GT Fish & Oyster in Chicago.

jessica theroux runs a holistic nutrition consulting practice in Berkeley, California, and is the author of *Cooking with Italian Grandmothers.*

patrick thibaud is the chef at Château de Campuget in Costières de Nîmes, France.

jess thomson co-authored the forthcoming *Top Pot Hand-Forged Doughnuts.*

zang toi, an avid cook and dinner-party host, is the owner and designer of the House of Toi.

jacques torres is the dean of pastry arts at the French Culinary Institute in New York City, the owner of Jacques Torres Chocolate in New York and New Jersey and the author of several cookbooks, including *A Year in Chocolate.*

rich torrisi is a co-chef and co-owner of Torrisi Italian Specialties and Parm, both in New York City.

christina tosi is the pastry chef and co-owner of the Momofuku Milk Bars in New York City and the author of *Momofuku Milk Bar.*

james tracey is the chef de cuisine at Craft in New York City.

rori trovato is the chef and owner of Rori's Artisanal Creamery in Santa Barbara, California.

marcie turney is the chef and co-owner of Lolita, Barbuzzo and Bindi; Grocery, a prepared-foods and catering market; and Verde, a chocolate and flower shop, all in Philadelphia.

chris ubick is a film property master who prepared food for the 2011 movie *The Help.*

tina ujlaki is the executive food editor at F&W.

breanne varela is the pastry chef at Tavern and the Larder at Tavern in Los Angeles.

marc vetri, an F&W Best New Chef 1999, is the chef and owner of Vetri, Osteria, Amis and the forthcoming Alla Spina, all in Philadelphia. He is a co-author of *Rustic Italian Food.*

bryan vietmeier is the chef at Take 5 Urban Market in Seattle.

michael voltaggio, winner of *Top Chef* Season 6, is the chef and owner of Ink. restaurant and Ink.Sak sandwich shop, both in Los Angeles.

jean-georges vongerichten, an F&W contributing editor, is the chef and co-owner of more than a dozen restaurants around the world, including Jean Georges in New York City and Shanghai. He is the author of five cookbooks; his most recent is *Home Cooking with Jean-Georges.*

marja vongerichten, host of PBS's *The Kimchi Chronicles,* co-authored *The Kimchi Chronicles: Korean Cooking for an American Kitchen.*

megan walhood is a co-chef and co-owner of the Viking Soul Food truck in Portland, Oregon.

robb walsh is a co-owner of El Real Tex-Mex Café in Houston. His latest cookbook, *Texas Eats,* will be published in spring 2012.

philip ward is the mixologist at Mayahuel in New York City.

jonathan waxman is the chef and owner of Barbuto in New York City. His most recent cookbook is *Italian, My Way.*

david welch is the beverage director and co-owner of Lincoln restaurant and Sunshine Tavern in Portland, Oregon.

patricia wells, former restaurant critic for the *International Herald Tribune* and *L'Express,* is a cooking teacher, cookbook author and journalist. Her most recent book is *Simply Truffles.*

laura werlin has written five books about cheese. Her latest is *Grilled Cheese, Please!*

william werner is a pastry chef in San Francisco.

tre wilcox, who competed on *Top Chef* Season 3, is the chef and owner of Marquee Grill in Dallas.

caitlin williams freeman is the in-house pastry chef for the San Francisco Museum of Modern Art and the pastry chef at the Blue Bottle Coffee Company, also in San Francisco.

kevin willmann, an F&W Best New Chef 2011, is the chef and owner of Farmhaus in St. Louis.

paula wolfert, an F&W contributing editor, is the author of several cookbooks, most recently *The Food of Morocco,* an update of her classic *Couscous and Other Good Food from Morocco.*

joe wolfson is the chef at Ham and High in Montgomery, Alabama.

tim wood is the chef at Carmel Valley Ranch in Carmel, California.

lee woolver is the chef at the American Hotel in Sharon Springs, New York.

ayako yoshikawa gordon founded Pure Concepts, which makes and sells jam and other prepared foods.

hiroki yoshitake is the chef and co-owner of Sola restaurant in Paris.

ricardo zarate, an F&W Best New Chef 2011, is the chef and co-owner of Mo-Chica and Picca restaurants in Los Angeles.

hoss zaré is the chef and owner of Zaré at Flytrap restaurant in San Francisco.

andrew zimmern, an F&W contributing editor, writes the weekly Kitchen Adventures column on *foodandwine.com.* He is also the host and co-creator of the Travel Channel's *Bizarre Foods with Andrew Zimmern* and author of *The Bizarre Truth.*

photographs

antonis achilleos 41, 145, 163, 221, 265, 288, 289, 297, 301, 303

cedric angeles 175, back cover (ribs)

quentin bacon 13, 23, 51, 97, 101, 135, 141, 149, 197, 259, 267, 291, 317, 325, 361, 389

dana gallagher 339, 351

ethan hill 104

raymond hom 180, 181

jody horton 11

ingalls photography 6, 142, 143

p-a jorgensen 159

john kernick 4, 30, 31, 33, 43, 59, 69, 81, 95, 119, 125, 192, 193, 268, 269

dave lauridsen 45, 373

ailine liefeld 331, 384, 385

david malosh front cover, 67, 77, 79, 85, 185, 223, 239, 326, 327, 365, 379

kate mathis 21, 65, 102, 103, 140, 147, 161, 162, 198, 205, 206, 283, 347, 357, back cover (cakes)

martin morrell 234, 235

marcus nilsson 123, 152, 153, 173

kana okada 27, 273

con poulos 17, 35, 73, 91, 93, 105, 107, 113, 117, 137, 189, 199, 209, 211, 229, 231, 241, 245, 247, 253, 257, 263, 271, 275, 281, 287, 295, 299, 315, 321, 323, 332, 333, 335, 337, 343, 353, 371, 394

david prince 194, 255

tina rupp 157, 179, 233, 329, 377

seth smoot 227

fredrika stjärne 38, 39, 55, 62, 63, 86, 87, 201, 284, 285, 305, 309, 369, 383, 393

petrina tinslay 111, 133, 277, 306, 307

michael turek 8, 9, 53, 183, 214, 215, 249, 345, 354, 355, back cover (salad)

jonny valiant 47, 49, 129, 167, 170, 171, 217, 311, 391

anna williams 83, 187

product images Calphalon (99), Fagor (68), Istock (155), Le Creuset (139), Lindt (367), Ninja Master (390), Huy Fong Foods (146), Trudeau (338), Williams-Sonoma (328)

measurement guide

basic measurements

gallon	quart	pint	cup	ounce	tbsp	tsp	drops
1 gal	4 qt	8 pt	16 c	128 fl oz			
½ gal	2 qt	4 pt	8 c	64 fl oz			
¼ gal	1 qt	2 pt	4 c	32 fl oz			
	½ qt	1 pt	2 c	16 fl oz			
	¼ qt	½ pt	1 c	8 fl oz	16 tbsp		
			⅞ c	7 fl oz	14 tbsp		
			¾ c	6 fl oz	12 tbsp		
			⅔ c	5⅓ fl oz	10⅔ tbsp		
			⅝ c	5 fl oz	10 tbsp		
			½ c	4 fl oz	8 tbsp		
			⅜ c	3 fl oz	6 tbsp		
			⅓ c	2⅔ fl oz	5⅓ tbsp	16 tsp	
			¼ c	2 fl oz	4 tbsp	12 tsp	
			⅛ c	1 fl oz	2 tbsp	6 tsp	
				½ fl oz	1 tbsp	3 tsp	
					½ tbsp	1½ tsp	
						1 tsp	60 drops
						½ tsp	30 drops

u.s. to metric conversions

The conversions shown here are approximations. For more precise conversions, use the formulas to the right.

volume		weight		temperature		conversion formulas
1 tsp	= 5 mL	1 oz	= 28 g	475°F	= 246°C	tsp × 4.929 = mL
1 tbsp	= 15 mL	¼ lb (4 oz)	= 113 g	450°F	= 232°C	tbsp × 14.787 = mL
1 fl oz	= 30 mL	½ lb (8 oz)	= 227 g	425°F	= 218°C	fl oz × 29.574 = mL
¼ c	= 59 mL	¾ lb (12 oz)	= 340 g	400°F	= 204°C	c × 236.588 = mL
½ c	= 118 mL	1 lb (16 oz)	= ½ kg	375°F	= 191°C	pt × 0.473 = L
¾ c	= 177 mL			350°F	= 177°C	qt × 0.946 = L
1 c	= 237 mL	**length**		325°F	= 163°C	oz × 28.35 = g
1 pt	= ½ L	1 in	= 2.5 cm	300°F	= 149°C	lb × 0.453 = kg
1 qt	= 1 L	5 in	= 12.7 cm	275°F	= 135°C	in × 2.54 = cm
1 gal	= 4.4 L	9 in	= 23 cm	250°F	= 121°C	(°F – 32) × 0.556 = °C